JOURNALISM, GENDER AND POWER

Journalism, Gender and Power revisits the key themes explored in the 1998 edited collection *News, Gender and Power*. It takes stock of progress made to date, and also breaks ground in advancing critical understandings of how and why gender matters for journalism and current democratic cultures.

This new volume develops research insights into issues such as the influence of media ownership and control on sexism, women's employment and "macho" news cultures, the gendering of objectivity and impartiality, tensions around the professional identities of journalists, news coverage of violence against women, the sexualization of women in the news, the everyday experience of normative hierarchies and biases in newswork, and the gendering of news audience expectations, amongst other issues.

These issues prompt vital questions for feminist and gender-centred explorations concerned with reimagining journalism in the public interest. Contributors to this volume challenge familiar perspectives, and in so doing, extend current parameters of dialogue and debate in fresh directions relevant to the increasingly digitalized, interactive intersections of journalism with gender and power around the globe.

Journalism, Gender and Power will inspire readers to rethink conventional assumptions around gender in news reporting—conceptual, professional, and strategic—with an eye to forging alternative, progressive ways forward.

Cynthia Carter is Reader in the School of Journalism, Media and Culture, Cardiff University, UK. She has published widely on children, news, and citizenship; feminist news and journalism studies; and media violence. Her recent books include *Current Perspectives in Feminist Media Studies* (2013) and the *Routledge Companion to Media and Gender* (2014). She is a founding Co-Editor of *Feminist Media Studies* and serves on the editorial board of numerous media and communication studies journals.

Linda Steiner is Professor in the College of Journalism, University of Maryland, USA, and Editor of *Journalism & Communication Monographs*. Recent co-authored or co-edited books include: *Key Concepts in Critical-Cultural Studies* (2010), *Routledge Companion to Media and Gender* (2013), *The Handbook of Gender and War* (2016), and *Race, News, and the City: Uncovering Baltimore* (2017). She has published over 100 book chapters and refereed journal articles.

Stuart Allan is Professor and Head of the School of Journalism, Media and Culture at Cardiff University, UK. His publications include *Citizen Witnessing: Revisioning Journalism in Times of Crisis* (2013) and the edited collections, *The Routledge Companion to News and Journalism* (revised edition, 2012) and *Photojournalism and Citizen Journalism: Co-operation, Collaboration and Connectivity* (2017). He is currently researching the visual cultures of news imagery in war, conflict, and crisis reporting, amongst other projects.

JOURNALISM, GENDER AND POWER

Edited by Cynthia Carter, Linda Steiner and Stuart Allan

Routledge
Taylor & Francis Group

LONDON AND NEW YORK

First published 2019
by Routledge
2 Park Square, Milton Park, Abingdon, Oxon OX14 4RN

and by Routledge
52 Vanderbilt Avenue, New York, NY 10017

Routledge is an imprint of the Taylor & Francis Group, an informa business

British Library Cataloguing-in-Publication Data
A catalogue record for this book is available from the British Library

Library of Congress Cataloging-in-Publication Data
Names: Carter, Cynthia, 1959– editor. | Steiner, Linda, editor. | Allan, Stuart, 1962– editor.
Title: Journalism, gender and power / edited by Cynthia Carter, Linda Steiner and Stuart Allan.
Description: London ; New York : Routledge, 2019. | Includes bibliographical references and index.
Identifiers: LCCN 2018048103 | ISBN 9781138895324 (hardback : alk. paper) | ISBN 9781138895362 (pbk. : alk. paper) | ISBN 9781315179520 (ebook)
Subjects: LCSH: Women in journalism. | Women in the mass media industry. | Women and journalism. | Women—Press coverage.
Classification: LCC PN4784.W7 J68 2019 | DDC 070.4082—dc23
LC record available at https://lccn.loc.gov/2018048103

ISBN: 978-1-138-89532-4 (hbk)
ISBN: 978-1-138-89536-2 (pbk)
ISBN: 978-1-315-17952-0 (ebk)

Typeset in Bembo
by Apex CoVantage, LLC

CONTENTS

FIGURES

TABLES

CONTRIBUTORS

Stuart Allan is Professor and Head of the School of Journalism, Media and Culture at Cardiff University, UK. His publications include *Citizen Witnessing: Revisioning Journalism in Times of Crisis* (2013) and the edited collections, *The Routledge Companion to News and Journalism* (revised edition, 2012) and *Photojournalism and Citizen Journalism: Co-operation, Collaboration and Connectivity* (2017). He is currently researching the visual cultures of news imagery in war, conflict, and crisis reporting, amongst other projects.

Helen Baker is Research Fellow at the ESRC Centre for Corpus Approaches to Social Science (CASS) at Lancaster University, UK. She has published research on tsarist Russia and, more recently, has focused on the benefits of using large corpora in the study of the past, particularly in order to explore the ways in which marginalized people were perceived in early modern public discourse.

Paul Baker is Professor of English Language, Lancaster University, UK. His research involves applying corpus linguistic methods to carry out discourse analysis and examine linguistic representations of identities. His books include *Polari: The Lost Language of Gay Men* (2002), *Public Discourses of Gay Men* (2005), *Using Corpora in Discourse Analysis* (2006), *Sexed Texts: Language, Gender and Sexuality* (2008), and *Using Corpora to Analyse Gender* (2014).

Carolyn M. Byerly is Professor and Chair of the Department of Communication, Culture, and Media Studies at Howard University, USA. Her work situates race and gender in the political economy of news, media policies, media ownership, and media employment, both within the United States and internationally. Her research has appeared in three books, which she co-authored or edited, as well as dozens of book chapters and academic journals.

Jamie C. Capuzza chairs the Department of Communication at the University of Mount Union, USA. Her work appears in *Communication Quarterly*, *International Journal of Transgenderism*, *Newspaper Research Journal*, and *Communication Education*. Her book, co-edited with Leland Spencer, *Transgender Communication Studies: Histories, Trends, and Trajectories* (2015), won awards from the National Communication Association and the Organization for the Study of Communication, Language. Capuzza was named Gender Scholar of the Year (2018) by the Southern States Communication Association.

Cynthia Carter is Reader in the School of Journalism, Media and Culture, Cardiff University, UK. She has published widely on children, news, and citizenship; feminist news and journalism studies; and media violence. Her recent books include *Current Perspectives in Feminist Media Studies* (2013) and the *Routledge Companion to Media and Gender* (2014). She is a founding Co-Editor of *Feminist Media Studies* and serves on the editorial board of numerous media and communication studies journals.

Erika Falk is Program Director of the Israel Institute, Washington, DC, USA. She is the author of *Women for President: Media Bias in Nine Campaigns* (2010) and has published extensively on women and politics. She is also author of *Becoming a New Instructor: A Guide for College Adjuncts and Graduate Students* (2012). She trains instructors in the United States and abroad on how to have greater impact in the classroom.

Nicky Falkof is Associate Professor in Media Studies at the University of the Witwatersrand, Johannesburg, South Africa. Her current research interests center on gender, race, and anxiety in the urban global south. She also writes on popular culture, with publications on subjects as diverse as South African romantic comedies, Teenage Mutant Ninja Turtles, and Mad Men. She is the author of *Satanism and Family Murder in Late Apartheid South Africa* (2015).

Suzanne Franks is Professor and Head of the Journalism Department at City University, London, UK and former BBC broadcaster. She has published widely on international news and women in the media. Her books include *Women and Journalism* (2013), for the Reuters Institute for the Study of Journalism, where she was a visiting fellow, *Reporting Disasters: Famine, Politics, Aid and the Media* (2013), and *Having None of It: Women, Men and the Future of Work* (2000).

Barbara Friedman is Associate Professor in the School of Media and Journalism and adjunct faculty in the Department of Women's and Gender Studies at the University of North Carolina at Chapel Hill, USA. Her research focuses on gender and race in contemporary and historical media. She co-directs The Irina Project (TIP), which analyzes media representations of sex trafficking and provides resources for accurate, responsible reporting of the issue. She is former editor of *American Journalism*.

Rosalind Gill is Professor of Social and Cultural Analysis at City University, London, UK and Professorial Fellow at the University of Newcastle, Australia. She is author of several books including *Gender and the Media* (2007) and *Mediated Intimacy: Sex Advice in Media Culture* (with M. Barker and L. Harvey, 2018). She is currently co-writing a book with Shani Orgad on the "cult(ure) of confidence," to be published in 2019.

Patricia Holland is a researcher, writer, and lecturer, specializing in various aspects of media—particularly television, journalism, and issues around feminism and childhood. She has published widely in these fields. Her most recent book is *The New Television Handbook* (2017). Currently, she lectures part-time at Bournemouth University, UK and has previously worked as an independent filmmaker, a television editor, and a freelance journalist.

Lis Howell is Emeritus Professor at City University, London, UK, where she had previously taught practice-based journalism. She was a broadcast journalist at the BBC and Sky, the first woman Head of News at ITV and special advisor to the House of Lords Communication Select Committee reporting on *Women in News and Current Affairs Broadcasting* (2012). Howell launched the "Expert Women" project at City University in 2012, publishing some of its findings in *Journalism Practice* (with J. Singer, 2016).

Anne Johnston is the Parker Distinguished Professor in the School of Media and Journalism and adjunct faculty in the Women's and Gender Studies department at the University of North Carolina at Chapel Hill, USA. Her research focuses on gender and media, gendered violence, and news coverage of sex trafficking. She is co-director of The Irina Project, a research and training program and web-based resource focused on the ethical and accurate portrayal of sex trafficking.

Sahar Khamis is Associate Professor of Communication and Affiliate Professor of Women's Studies at the University of Maryland, College Park, USA. She researches Arab and Muslim media, focusing on cyberactivism and gender activism. Her latest co-edited book is *Arab Women's Activism and Socio-Political Transformation: Unfinished Gendered Revolutions* (2018). She is also the co-author of *Islam Dot Com: Contemporary Islamic Discourses in Cyberspace* (2009) and *Egyptian Revolution 2.0: Political Blogging, Civic Engagement and Citizen Journalism* (2013).

Catharine Lumby is Professor of Media at Macquarie University, Australia, and the author and co-author of six books. She was the foundation Chair of the Media and Communications Department at the University of Sydney and the Director of the Journalism and Media Research Centre at UNSW. Lumby worked as a print and television journalist at the Sydney Morning Herald and the ABC prior to joining academia. She has been awarded 10 Australian Research Council grants.

Sarah Mallat teaches communication arts and media studies at the Lebanese American University and American University of Beirut, Lebanon. She specializes in digital and media literacy, with particular research interests in gendered stereotypes in Arab media, media and body image, toxic masculinity, and media's effects on children. She has participated in the Media and Digital Literacy Academy of Beirut, an initiative of the Institute of Media Research and Training, since its founding in 2013.

Jad Melki is Associate Professor of Journalism and Media Studies, Chairperson of the Communication Arts Department, and Director of the Institute of Media Research and Training at the Lebanese American University, Lebanon. Melki's research focuses on media literacy, conflict journalism, media and war, and gender studies in the Arab region. He won the 2015 UNESCO-UNAoC International Media and Information Literacy Award for advancing Arab media literacy through the Media and Digital Literacy Academy of Beirut.

Noha Mellor is Professor of Media at the University of Bedfordshire, UK and Adjunct Professor of Middle Eastern Studies at Stockholm University, Sweden. She has published widely on topics related to Arab journalism, pan-Arab media, Arab women journalists, political Islam, and media. Her most recent publications include *Political Islam and Global Media* (2016), *The Egyptian Dream—Egyptian Identity and Uprisings* (2015), and *Voice of the Muslim Brotherhood* (2017).

Isabel Molina-Guzmán is Professor of Latina/Latino Studies and Media & Cinema Studies at the University of Illinois Urbana-Champaign, USA. She is author of *Dangerous Curves: Latina Bodies in the Media* (2010) and *Latinas/Latinos on TV: Colorblind Comedy on the Postracial Network Era* (2017). Among other edited collections and academic journals, her work has appeared in *Latino Studies* and *Journalism*. She is Co-Editor of *Feminist Media Studies*.

April Newton is a PhD candidate at University of Maryland's Phillip Merrill College of Journalism, USA, and a faculty member at Loyola University of Maryland, USA. She is researching the experiences of women as journalists, mass media ethics, and the digital transformation of journalism, as well as the relationship between those topics.

Claudia Padovani is Associate Professor of Political Science and International Relations, University of Padova, Italy. She is chair of the Working Group on Global Media Policy (IAMCR) and on the steering committee of Mapping Global Media Policy. She researches the transformation of global political processes; gender, media, and policy developments; and transnational mobilizations around media and communication rights. She recently co-edited *Gender Equality and the Media: A Challenge for Europe* (with K. Ross, Routledge/ECREA, 2016).

Allissa V. Richardson is Assistant Professor, Annenberg School for Communication and Journalism, University of Southern California, Los Angeles, USA. She has published in *The Black Scholar, Digital Journalism, Journalism and Mass Communication Educator, Journalism Studies*, and *Teaching Media Quarterly*. Her forthcoming book is *Bearing Witness While Black: African Americans, Smartphones and the New Protest #Journalism* (2019). She is a Nieman Foundation Visiting Journalism Fellow at Harvard University, an Apple Distinguished Educator, and 2012 Journalism Educator of the Year for the National Association of Black Journalists.

Karen Ross is Professor of Gender and Media, Newcastle University, UK. Her teaching and research are focused on the various inter-relationships between gender, news, and politics. She has published numerous papers and books on these topics including *Gender, Politics and News* (2017) and *Gender Equality and the Media: A Challenge for Europe* (with C. Padovani, Routledge/ECREA, 2016). She is currently principal investigator on an EU-funded project on *Advancing Gender Equality in the Media* (2017–2019).

David Rowe is Emeritus Professor of Cultural Research, Institute for Culture and Society, Western Sydney University, Australia; Honorary Professor, Faculty of Humanities and Social Sciences, University of Bath, UK; and Research Associate, Centre for International Studies and Diplomacy, SOAS University of London, UK. His current areas of research include sport, journalism, art, and urban leisure. His most recent book is the co-edited *Making Culture: Commercialization, Transnationalism, and the State of "Nationing" in Contemporary Australia* (2018).

Sharifa Simon-Roberts is a PhD student in the Communication, Culture and Media Studies program at Howard University, USA. Her research examines issues related to television, especially in the age of new communication technologies. She has also collaborated on research concerned with women and journalism labor unions. Her work has been presented at numerous academic conferences.

Linda Steiner is Professor in the College of Journalism, University of Maryland, USA, and Editor of *Journalism & Communication Monographs*. Recent co-authored or co-edited books include: *Key Concepts in Critical-Cultural Studies* (2010), *Routledge Companion to Media and Gender* (2013), *The Handbook of Gender and War* (2016), and *Race, News, and the City: Uncovering Baltimore* (2017). She has published over 100 book chapters and refereed journal articles.

Katie Toms is a PhD candidate at City University, London, UK. Her research examines findings from the UK's Leveson Inquiry, a judicial public investigation into the culture, practices, and ethics of the British press. She focuses on evidence given by women's organizations regarding sexualized images of women in the tabloid press, exploring how the Inquiry facilitated establishment of a wider and deeper understanding of the problematic nature of women's representation in contemporary news and popular culture.

Sahana Udupa is Professor of Media Anthropology at the Ludwig Maximilian University Munich, Germany, where she leads a five-year European Research Council Starting Grant project on digital politics (fordigitaldignity.com). She researches and teaches digital politics, journalism cultures, online nationalism, and extreme speech. She is the author of *Making News in Global India: Media, Publics, Politics* (2015) and co-editor of *Media as Politics in South Asia* (with S. McDowell, 2016).

Nikki Usher is Associate Professor at the George Washington University, USA and Visiting Associate Professor at the University of Illinois Urbana-Champaign, USA. Her research focuses on how journalism is changing in the digital and platform eras, publishing widely on news production processes, business models, innovation, and journalism and political communication. She is the author of *Making News at The New York Times* (2014) and *Interactive Journalism: Hackers, Data, and Code* (2016).

Haiyan Wang is Associate Professor at the School of Communication and Design in Sen Yat-sen University, China. Her work covers a wide range of topics in Chinese media, critical journalism, and women in media. She is the author of *The Transformation of Investigative Journalists in China: From Journalism to Activism* (2016) and over 30 research articles, appearing in *Media, Culture and Society, Journalism, International Journal of Communication* and other leading journals.

Beverly M. Weber is Associate Professor of German Studies and Jewish Studies at the University of Colorado Boulder, USA. She is the author of *Violence and Gender in the "New" Europe: Islam in German Culture* (Palgrave, 2013) and numerous articles on race, gender, and Islam in Germany. Current book projects include *Decolonizing Hospitality and Refugee Migration in Contemporary Germany*, and the co-authored *Precarious Intimacies: The Politics of Touch in Contemporary European Cinema* (with M. Stehle).

INTRODUCTION TO *JOURNALISM, GENDER AND POWER*

Cynthia Carter, Linda Steiner, and Stuart Allan

Academic research exploring the complex, uneven ways in which gender relations shape journalism's institutional forms, practices, and epistemologies has evolved quite dramatically since the publication of *News, Gender and Power* (Carter, Branston, & Allan, 1998). To an encouraging extent, this is a good news story. The past two decades have witnessed significant advances in women's day-to-day experience of news reporting around the world, with many enjoying fulfilling, rewarding careers that are difficult to envisage when coping with the "macho cultures" of the newsworld in the last century. Certainly, the number of women choosing to be a journalist has never been higher; many of them determined to overcome whatever institutionalized sexism—and racism—puts in their path. Nevertheless, the concerted push for progress remains a test of resilience, with much work to do. Relatively few news organizations ensure women are on equal footing with their male counterparts in senior, decision-making editorial roles, for example, where there should be scope to make a real difference in rethinking more traditional approaches to news gathering, presentation, and interpretation. Similarly, all too often equal pay for equal work remains an elusive ambition, with persistent patterns of sexist discrimination proving disappointingly impervious to change (Byerly, 2013b; Franks, 2013; Rodny-Gumede, 2015).

Turning to news coverage of gender-related issues, it is readily apparent many of the topics recurrently ignored, trivialized, or marginalized in the late 1990s now routinely feature on a regular basis across the mediascape. As we will see in the pages to follow in this volume, serious problems continue to constrain much of this reporting, but this is not to deny the significance of journalistic attention directed toward global concerns. Examples include gender-based violence, forced marriage, female genital mutilation, girls' access to education, employment opportunities and wages, reproductive rights, and maternal health, amongst others (Global Citizen, 2015). Moreover, feminist and gender-sensitive challenges to the sexual objectification of women and girls, essentialist conceptions of femininity or masculinity projected onto sexual difference, or the naturalization of heteronormative hierarchies have become much more "mainstream" topics than may have seemed possible two decades ago. Delving into the production factors underpinning this coverage, researchers have highlighted important improvements while, at the same time, recognizing how gendered power dynamics shape newsroom culture, often via tacit, ostensibly "commonsensical" norms, values, and beliefs. Even those journalists quick to alert their readers, listeners, or viewers to instances of sexism in public life sometimes seem reluctant to extend this type of critique to their own news organizations.

A central aim of *Journalism, Gender and Power* is to revisit for purposes of further elaboration and investigation several themes set out in *News, Gender and Power*. In the course of taking stock of progress made to date, however, it strives to break new ground in advancing critical understandings of how and why gender matters for journalism's democratic cultures. Key research problematics analyzed in the first volume two decades ago included issues of ownership and control for the "malestream" news media, women's employment and discriminatory news cultures, the gendering of objectivity and impartiality, tensions around the professional identities of journalists, news reporting of sexual violence, the sexualization of women within news representations, the everyday experience of gendered biases or prejudices in newswork, and the gendering of news audience expectations, amongst other issues. Viewed from the vantage point of today, each of these issues looks very different, yet remains a compelling point of departure for explorations concerned with reimagining journalism in the public interest. Our contributors are committed to interrogating familiar perspectives, and in so doing pursue searching questions promising to extend current parameters of dialogue and debate in fresh directions.

New challenges

The extent to which women's voices are included in the news as reporters and presenters as well as news actors and sources has been a central point of concern in journalism over the past 20 years. Nonetheless, improvements have materialized only very slowly. Developments have been somewhat uneven across national contexts and, rather surprisingly, on some news platforms in certain countries women journalists have lost previously gained ground and their numbers have fallen (Macharia, 2015). Also remaining are exigent challenges in areas such as the treatment of women journalists by their sources, as well as within their own news organizations as measured by, for instance, hiring practices, the allocation of assignments, promotion, and pay (Byerly, 2013a; Franks, 2013). Advancement on these fronts, some commentators fear, has begun to level off in many parts of the world.

With regard to pay, for example, *Financial Times* journalists in the UK threatened to strike in 2017 after discovering a near-13 percent gender pay gap between men and women at the newspaper. A union representative claimed there was a growing sense managers "have not been taking this matter seriously enough," adding the apparent lack of transparency about executive pay at the FT "does not inspire confidence" (cited in Ruddick, 2017; Zillman, 2017). Also attracting headlines was a case involving four foreign editors at the BBC, where it was alleged the two women employed in this role earned about half as much as their male counterparts. According to Carrie Gracie, who resigned as China Editor, this amounted to evidence of the BBC perpetuating a "secretive and illegal" pay culture (Collins, 2018). "When my case became news, women wrote to me from all over the country to recount horror stories about unequal pay and the difficulties they faced in trying to put it right," she stated at the time. "My own experience has taught me how lonely and challenging this can be" (cited in Tobitt, 2018). Turning to the US, research by the *Los Angeles Times* Guild, an organization seeking to unionize the newspaper, reported that women and journalists of color are underpaid by thousands of dollars each year. Additionally, their pay data for about 320 full-time unionized journalists found that women of color earned "less than 70 cents for every dollar earned by a white man." This gap is partly due to the fact that for historical reasons the paper's most senior journalists are white men. However, it is also true that "individual women and journalists of color, on average, make thousands of dollars less than white and male coworkers of similar ages and job titles" (LA Guild, 2018).

Looking at the gendered character of story allocation, the Women's Media Center (2017) in the US provided evidence from a broad-scale survey that men get 62.3 percent and women 37.5 percent of the bylines at the top 20 news organizations in the country. The figure for women had only marginally improved from their research the previous year when it was 37.3 percent. With regard to broadcasting, in a comparison between 2015 and 2016, WMC found that reports by women anchors, field reporters, and correspondents actually declined, falling to 25.2 percent in 2016 from 32 percent when the WMC published its 2015 "Divided" report (see also Kitch, 2015). Reporting on a newsroom-wide meeting in 2017 on digital innovation at *The New York Times*, Public Editor Liz Spayd recalled an "all male cast at the podium, the chief architects behind the most important strategic document since the celebrated innovation report in 2014. Was this a portrait of a newsroom's future or of the gender that will remain in charge of it?," she asked. For Spayd, this event highlighted a "piercing problem" at the paper where women had "skidded down the power structure" since the dismissal of Executive Editor Jill Abramson in 2014. Since then, fewer women have been heads of important departments and fewer women are coming up through the top job pipeline. As a result, "fewer women decide what big stories are assigned, what broad coverage priorities are set, and what a re-envisioned *Times* should look like" (Spayd, 2017).

Globally, women journalists are more likely to be part of the precarious freelance journalism marketplace that has resulted from "market fragmentation, consolidation, and the participatory media culture" (Antunovic, Grzeslo, & Hoag, 2017; see also Smith, 2015). Reasons given for this vary, but seem to be particularly related to the "cultural norms, labor practices and gender role expectations" that more often for women than men tend to lead to them leaving full-time journalism (often for the reason of raising children or sexism, which is rife in the newsroom) or leave journalism completely (Massey & Elmore, 2011; Örnebring & Möller, 2018).

Data gathered from 114 countries for the 2015 Global Media Monitoring Project (GMMP) report, "Who Makes the News?" (Macharia, 2015), confirms that while the gender gap in terms of both the percentages of women reporting the news and amount of news media content about women narrowed between 1995 and 2005, progress has stalled since (see also Ross, Boyle, Carter, & Ging, 2016). By 2015, women reported just 37 percent of the stories and were 25 percent of the people seen, heard, or read about in the news around the world. The proportion of stories that clearly problematize gender stereotypes has likewise not changed much since 2005, still hovering between 3 percent and 4 percent. The 2015 report also, sadly, confirmed that digital news platforms cannot be said, at least not yet, to sustain greater degrees of plurality around gender representation than legacy media.

No wonder, then, that with a sense of urgency around these findings, the World Association for Christian Communication (WACC), GMMP's sponsor, organized a 2017 symposium to support the gender and communication projects of civil society organizations from around the world. The symposium report, *The New York Declaration*, offered a feminist vision for the media and a call to action. It expresses concerns about how "tabloidization and relativization" of social and political issues, condemns much of the world's news media as overly obsessed with the trivial and lacking in depth and seriousness, as well as offering a warning around issues related to free expression, including censorship, self-censorship, religious fundamentalism, terrorism, and extreme political movements.

Later in 2017, every edge of this multifaceted relationship articulating journalism, gender, and power was sharply exposed with the bombshell—and Pulitzer Prize-winning—news reports about rape, sexual molestation, and harassment allegedly perpetrated by Hollywood producer Harvey Weinstein (Ryan, 2018). What came next was a flood of allegations about men in other professions and industries, including journalism. "It's top down, this culture of older men who have all this power and you are nothing," one unnamed veteran news producer said of the culture at CBS (Farrow, 2018). Furthermore, during a speech accepting an award for her reporting of alleged sexual misconduct by former news anchor Charlie Rose of CBS News, *Washington Post* journalist Irin Carmon warned that stories of abuse in the news industry were still being suppressed and that the problem is a system privileged men use to "kill" stories (Farrow, 2018). Shortly after this event came the explosive revelations of women around the globe publicly voicing often hitherto hidden experiences of sexual violence as part of the social media #MeToo campaign that has been widely, and largely empathetically, covered by the world's news media.

These recent events mark a potential turning point in journalism's coverage of sexual violence globally and discussion around gender equality in society more widely. That said, it is obviously difficult to judge the extent to which they might positively affect issues of workplace harassment for women journalists around the world (Dries, 2013; Edwards, 2018; Kong, 2018; Krasilnikov, 2018; Lai, 2017; Monnerat, 2018; Neason, Daton, & Ho, 2018; North, 2016; Osakwe, 2017; Petersen, 2018; Wearmouth, 2017) or indeed disrupt longstanding journalism-gender-power dynamics in the newsroom in general (Chambers, Steiner, & Fleming, 2004; Djerf-Pierre, 2007; Kitch, 2015; North, 2009; Ross & Carter, 2011; Steiner, 1998, 2014). Such events also provide a powerful impetus for the research-led interventions presented in the chapters to follow.

We hope readers of this volume will discover engaging insights and challenging perspectives on its pages while, at the same time, finding inspiration to rethink conventional assumptions—conceptual, professional, and strategic—with an eye to forging alternative, progressive ways forward.

References

Antunovic, D., Grzeslo, J., & Hoag, A. M. (2017). Ice cream is worse, and joblessness is not an option. *Journalism Practice*. doi:10.1080/17512786.2017.1410069

Byerly, C. (2013a). *Global report on the status of women in the news media*. Washington, DC: International Women's Foundation.

Byerly, C. (Ed.). (2013b). *The Palgrave international handbook of women and journalism*. London: Palgrave Macmillan.

Carter, C., Branston, G., & Allan, S. (Eds.). (1998). *News, gender and power*. London: Routledge.

Chambers, D., Steiner, L., & Fleming, C. (2004). *Women and journalism*. London: Routledge.

Collins, L. (2018, July 23). How the BBC women are working toward equal pay. *The New Yorker*. Retrieved from www.newyorker.com/magazine/2018/07/23/how-the-bbc-women-are-working-toward-equal-pay

Djerf-Pierre, M. (2007). The gender of journalism: The structure and logic of the field in the twentieth century. *Nordicom Review*, Jubilee Issue, 81–104.

Dries, K. (2013, February 12). Female journalists harassed at offices all around the damn globe. *Jezebel*. Retrieved from https://jezebel.com/female-journalists-harassed-at-offices-all-around-the-d-1475118268

Edwards, C. (2018, February 5). Italian journalists denounce sexual harassment in open letter. *The Local*. Retrieved from www.thelocal.it/20180205/italian-journalists-denounce-sexual-harassment-in-open-letter

Farrow, R. (2018, July 28). Les Moonves and CBS face allegations of sexual misconduct. *The New Yorker*. Retrieved from www.newyorker.com/magazine/2018/08/06/les-moonves-and-cbs-face-allegations-of-sexual-misconduct

Franks, S. (2013). *Women and journalism*. London: I.B. Taurus.

Global Citizen (Hans Glick). (2015). 9 key issues affecting girls and women around the world. Retrieved from https://www.globalcitizen.org/en/content/9-key-issues-affecting-girls-and-women-around-the/

Kitch, C. (2015). Women in the newsroom: Status and stasis. *Journalism & Mass Communication Quarterly*, *92*(1), 35–38. doi.org/10.1177/1077699014563523

Kong, L. L. (2018, January 15). Female journalists, male politicians and the epidemic of sexual harassment in Asean. *Asian Correspondent*. Retrieved from https://asiancorrespondent.com/2018/01/journalists-sexual-harassment-asean/#vAdqlDQ58acEfCwi.97

Krasilnikov, S. (2018, February 28). Fourth journalist accuses Russian deputy Slutsky of sexual harassment. *The Moscow Times*. Retrieved from https://themoscowtimes.com/news/fourth-journalist-accuses-russian-deputy-slutsky-sexual-harassment-60649

LA Guild. (2018, April 11). *It's in the data: Tronc underpays women and people of color at the LA Times*. Retrieved from https://latguild.com/news/2018/4/11/its-in-the-data-tronc-underpays-women-and-people-of-color-at-the-la-times

Lai, C. (2017, December 5). No #MeToo in China? Female journalists face sexual harassment, but remain silent. *Hong Kong Free Press*. Retrieved from www.hongkongfp.com/2017/12/05/no-metoo-china-female-journalists-face-sexual-harassment-remain-silent/

Macharia, S. (2015). *Who makes the news?* Global Media Monitoring Project 2015. Toronto: WACC. Retrieved from http://cdn.agilitycms.com/who-makes-the-news/Imported/reports_2015/global/gmmp_global_report_en.pdf

Massey, B. L., & Elmore, C. L. (2011). Happier working for themselves? *Journalism Practice, 5*(6), 672–686. doi:10.1080/17512786.2011.579780

Monnerat, A. (2018, December 5). *Brazilian journalists report daily sexual harassment and gender discrimination in newsrooms.* Retrieved from https://knightcenter.utexas.edu/blog/00-19064-brazilian-journalists-report-daily-sexual-harassment-and-gender-discrimination-newsroo

Neason, A., Dalton, M., & Ho, K. K. (2018, January 31). Sexual harassment in the newsroom: An oral history. *Columbia Journalism Review.* Retrieved from www.cjr.org/special_report/sexual-harassment-newsroom-survey-me-too.php

North, L. (2009). *The gendered newsroom.* Creskill: Hampton.

North, L. (2016). Damaging and daunting: Female journalists experiences of sexual harassment in the newsroom. *Feminist Media Studies, 16*(1), 495–510. doi.org/10.1080/14680777.2015.1105275

Örnebring, H., & Möller, C. (2018). In the margins of journalism: Gender and livelihood among local (ex-)journalists. *Journalism Practice, 12*(8), 1051–1060. doi: 10.1080/17512786.2018.1497455.

Osakwe, F. (2017, November 20). #GIJN: Female investigative journalists admit facing sexual harassment. *The Guardian.* Retrieved from https://guardian.ng/features/gijn-female-investigative-journalists-admit-facing-sexual-harassment/

Petersen, A. H. (2018, Winter). The cost of reporting while female. *Columbia Journalism Review.* Retrieved from www.cjr.org/special_report/reporting-female-harassment-journalism.php

Rodny-Gumede, Y. (2015). Male and female journalists' perceptions of their power to influence news agendas and public discourses. *Communicicatio, 41*(2), 206–219. doi:10.1080/02500167.2015.1066409

Ross, K., Boyle, K., Carter, C., & Ging, D. (2016). Women, men and news: It's life, Jim, but not as we know it. *Journalism Studies, 19*(6), 824–845. doi.org/10.1080/1461670X.2016.1222884

Ross, K., & Carter, C. (2011). Women and news: A long and winding road. *Media, Culture and Society, 33*(8), 1148–1165. https://doi.org/10.1177/0163443711418272

Ruddick, G. (2017, July 31). FT journalists threaten to strike over gender pay gap. *The Guardian.* Retrieved from www.theguardian.com/media/2017/jul/31/ft-journalists-threaten-to-strike-over-gender-pay-gap

Ryan, L. (2018). *The reporters who uncovered Harvey Weinstein sexual abuse just won the Pulitzer Prize.* Retrieved from www.thecut.com/2018/04/pulitzer-prize-2018-weinstein-investigation-reporters.html

Smith, V. (2015). *Outsiders still: Why women journalists love—and leave—their newspaper careers.* Toronto: University of Toronto Press.

Spayd, L. (2017, March 4). The declining fortunes of women at *The Times. The New York Times.* Retrieved from www.nytimes.com/2017/03/04/public-editor/the-declining-fortunes-of-women-at-the-times.html

Steiner, L. (1998). Newsroom accounts of power at work. In C. Carter, G. Branston, & S. Allan (Eds.), *News, gender and power* (pp. 145–159). London: Routledge.

Steiner, L. (2014). Glassy architectures in journalism. In C. Carter, L. Steiner, & L. McLaughlin (Eds.), *The Routledge companion to media and gender* (pp. 620–631). London: Routledge.

Tobitt, C. (2018, June 29). BBC apologises to Carrie Gracie and admits ex-China editor was underpaid. *Press Gazette.* Retrieved from www.pressgazette.co.uk/bbc-apologises-to-carrie-gracie-and-admits-ex-china-editor-was-underpaid/

WACC. (2017, March 11). *The New York Declaration*. Retrieved from http://sindikat-novi narjev.si/wp-content/uploads/The-New-York-Declaration-on-Gender-and-Media.pdf

Wearmouth, R. (2017, November 2). Female journalists unite to shine light on sexual harassment in the media. *Huffington Post*. Retrieved from www.huffingtonpost.co.uk/entry/second-source-harassment_uk_59fba27de4b01b4740495b5a

Women's Media Center. (2017). *The status of women in the U.S. media 2017*. Retrieved from www.womensmediacenter.com/reports/the-status-of-women-in-u.s.-media-2017

Zillman, C. (2017, July 31). FT journalists threaten to strike as Britain's gender pay gap debate rages on. *Fortune*. Retrieved from fortune.com/2017/07/31/gender-pay-gap-ft-bbc/

PART I

The gendered politics of news production

1

GETTING TO THE TOP

Women and decision-making in European news media industries

Karen Ross and Claudia Padovani

Introduction

When women become editors-in-chief at a major media house, it makes front-page news, usually because they are the first woman at the helm, astonishing as that might be in the second decade of the twenty-first century. For example, when Jill Abramson became the first woman editor at *The New York Times* in 2011, she broke a run of 160 years of men editors. When Katherine Viner did the same thing at the *Guardian* in 2015, 195 years of male editing privilege came to an end. Women are rarely CEOs of major media concerns and the BBC has never had a woman Director-General since it began life under John Reith in 1922. While the BBC's strapline has always been to inform, educate, and entertain the public, it does not seem to have a similar interest to *represent* it. At a time when women dominate journalism classrooms around the world—a trend seen across the globe for the past two decades—one might ask why so few women manage to reach the top jobs. Why do men stay in the profession longer and move upwards more quickly and much further. What solutions could be imagined for what clearly is a problem?

Here, we draw on the findings of a major study of gender and decision making across major European media organizations. We first sketch out the key relevant literature and discuss the provenance of this research and the primary findings of the research undertaken between 2011 and 2012 regarding women occupying senior roles in news media; the policies in place for women's career advancement amongst our sampled media organizations; and the experiences of senior women who participated in the study. Reflecting on those findings six years on, we argue that until the problems of gender-based discrimination are acknowledged and strategies put in place to support an equality culture in the workplace, media organizations will continue to squander and marginalize the talents of their women staff. This is bad for business and bad for society.

A short skirt through the literature

The relationship of women to news has been the subject of much research over the past 50 years, as indicated elsewhere in this collection. One of the first efforts to document and analyze the women and decision-making specifically was commissioned by UNESCO and reported on as *Women and Media Decision-making: The Invisible Barriers* (1987). In her introduction to the book, Margaret Gallagher (1987, p. 14) commented that "men's attitudes, beliefs and even organizational procedures [showed a] surprising degree of consistency across the studies." As we discuss below, inequalities are both structural and attitudinal and can slyly discriminate against women despite equality legislation. In 1995, Gallagher led a 43-nation study of employment patterns in the media, again finding that women struggled to achieve advancement. Ten years later, Robinson (2005) suggested that despite the numbers of women entering broadcast journalism, they advanced unevenly into decision-making roles, doing best in larger organizations, but mostly stuck in the lower ranks.

Scholarship undertaken in the past few years shows depressingly similar results. The largest global study of women's employment in news companies to date (International Women's Media Foundation (2011) collected data from 522 companies in 59 nations studied and showed that overall, men held three-quarters of both top management and board positions: women's presence was strongest in routine news gathering roles and weakest in technical roles (e.g. camera work, creative direction). This study also found significant national differences, with regional patterns looking very similar to our own. The strength of these studies is their comparative focus, regardless, to some extent, of the number of or which countries have been sampled, because they indicate very similar patterns in women's employment which seem to be stable over time and space, suggesting structural rather than situational reasons for women's thwarted career ambitions. While some studies have provided slightly more optimistic findings, the general trend shows little significant progress. Melki and Mallat (2016, p. 57) point to a constellation of factors that systematically "discourage and block women's entry into the news field, push those who made it out of the profession, and keep those who have endured down and siloed in specific roles away from decision-making and policy-setting positions." Those factors included gender discrimination, sexual harassment, and the lack of a legally and socially enabling environment, precisely the same factors reported elsewhere.

This returns us to the importance of workplace culture and normative frameworks (see also Löfgren Nilsson & Örnebring, 2016; North, 2016a). Even where improvements have been noted, they have tended to be tied to shifts in the practices of particular media organizations rather than signaling a wider trend. For example, Djerf-Pierre (2007) suggests that women tend to fare better in jobs at public service broadcasters and the more popular press than elsewhere in journalism. Nevertheless, glass ceiling and indeed glass walls barriers to lateral movement within an organization, often due to sexism and/or prejudice still constitute a significant barrier to women's advancement: not only do women struggle to achieve promotion (vertical segregation), but they are also "encouraged" into areas of the media work that are less prestigious and less likely to lead to career opportunities (horizontal segregation).

Interestingly, sometimes both men and women deny the impact of gender on either their professional practice or their working environment. That said, a comment made by one interviewee in a study of Portuguese journalists betrays a clearly gendered understanding of so-called gender-neutral norms: "in journalism, we are all men" (quoted in Lobo, Silveirinha, Torres da Silva, & Subtil, 2017, p. 1148). In direct contradiction to the imagined gender-neutrality of contemporary journalism practice in Europe, a survey of 390 Spanish journalists conducted as part of the global *Worlds of Journalism* study found that women had higher levels of education and earned less than men but men hold three-quarters of the posts with managerial responsibility and make two-thirds of the decisions related to content (De-Miguel, Hanitzsch, Parratt, & Berganza, 2017). In other words, women are better qualified than men colleagues, but were not being promoted at the same rate or paid the same salary as their men colleagues. Nor have women made more progress in digital media although these organizations often have flatter structures and little history of an old boys' network. Edstrom and Facht's 2018 study of the top 100 media firms across the world again shows a significant lack of women among the leadership of such corporations, including major digital companies like Alphabet, Facebook, Apple, and Amazon: 80 percent of boards of directors are men, 17 percent of the management are women and only six women are CEOs in the entire top 100 list.[1] It's hard to make sense of these trends without concluding that somewhere along the line, sex-based discrimination is taking place, unconsciously or otherwise.

Other actors on the media stage are also interested to learn why women face such challenges in achieving positions of authority in the media. Professional bodies such as the International (and European) Federation of Journalists, the UK's *Women in Journalism* group, any number of NGOs such as the European Women's Lobby, and the various Working Groups of the European Commission and the Council of Europe, have either undertaken or commissioned studies over the past few years (see, for example, European Commission, 2010; EWL, 2010). Women also struggle to get a seat at the boardroom table, both in terms of media organizations themselves, but also in relation to media regulators. In October 2012, European Commissioner Viviane Reding formally proposed that the European Parliament should enact legislation to accelerate the number of women in the boardrooms of public companies. The proposal aimed to achieve a 40 percent presence of the underrepresented sex among non-executive directors of the top 5000 publicly listed companies by 2020, and by 2018 for publicly funded organizations. Her proposal was derailed by her colleagues' insistence that the imposition of quotas was illegal under the Commission's own regulations. The much more flimsy "objective" of gender equality was agreed upon; but achieving this is unlikely, given the historic failure of voluntary codes of conduct to deliver for women.[2]

Indeed, very few studies have focused specifically on existing policy strategies and regulatory interventions to clarify if and to what extent they support women in progressing their media careers and reduce unequal power relations in media environments more broadly (Chaher, 2014; Gallagher, 2008, 2011; Nenadic & Ostling, 2017; Padovani, 2014; Sarikakis & Nguyen, 2009). This marginal attention to policy becomes even more problematic if we consider that the Beijing Platform for Action (BPfA)—a milestone document adopted by the United Nations in 1995 indicating "women and media" as a critical area of intervention for the international community—clearly called on governments and other actors to promote media policies that highlight a gender and to support research on media policies. One major section of the Beijing document also encouraged "the participation of women in the development of professional guidelines and codes of conduct or other appropriate self-regulatory mechanisms to promote a balanced and non-stereotypical portrayals of women by the media" (par. 241.d) while calling for media organizations themselves to "elaborate and strengthen self-regulatory mechanisms and codes of conduct" to comply with these objectives. Yet, all these policy aspects have been widely ignored. This makes inclusion of a focus on the policy provisions adopted by media companies in comparative international studies like the one discussed here all the more important.[3] What we make clear is that developing gender equality policies and support mechanisms is *not* widespread in the media sector; adoption of such policies varies widely both within regions and across regions; and internal policies are important but not sufficient to produce effective, gender-sensitive media in terms of content, access, and participation or in decision-making. More research is needed to fully grasp the challenges that characterize media policies in their relation to gender equality principles and the lived realities of inequality.

Rationale for the study

In 2011, the European Union set aside funding, to be managed through the European Institute for Gender Equality,[4] to support research on the extent to which the ambitions of Area J of the BPfA had been achieved. Area J has two aspects, one relating to the participation and access of women to expression and decision-making in and through media and new communication technologies, and the other to promote a balanced and non-stereotyped portrayal of women in the media. The co-authors of this chapter were commissioned by EIGE to form a team to conduct the research; we draw on the findings from that project below, focusing on the gendered decision-making aspect.[5]

Research design and methods

The EIGE-commissioned research aimed to explore: the extent to which women occupy decision-making positions in large-scale media organizations across Europe, including on management boards; how senior women actually experience their media workplace; and the existence (or otherwise) of gender-equality and/or women-focused policies that have been initiated by the media organizations in our sample. Because the study was funded by the EU via EIGE, a clear imperative was to produce useable findings at the policy level, so a crucial outcome was the development of a set of indicators which could be adopted by the European Council and thereafter used by member countries and media industries alike, against which individual media outlets, both public and private, could benchmark themselves and drive forward an agenda for change. A total of 99 organizations were sampled across the (then) 27 EU Member States and Croatia, comprising 39 public sector organizations,[6] 56 privately funded companies and 4 companies with mixed funding: we also interviewed 65 senior women media professionals from across the European media sector. As Croatia has since joined the EU, we will henceforth describe the participating countries as EU-28. Our sample of media organizations included a range of TV, radio and print media outlets, including 30 newspaper titles. Although we do not disaggregate our findings by media type in our discussion, our preliminary analysis suggests newspapers are similar to other commercial media. Moreover, most of the women media professionals we interviewed worked (or had worked) in fact-based news media as journalists, editors, or managers.

Project findings

Women and the top jobs

The most striking if not entirely unexpected finding, given previous research, as illustrated in Figure 1.1 below, is the low number of women who occupy senior decision-making positions or have seats on boards: only 30 percent of the positions were held by women, including 26 percent of "ordinary" board seats and 22 percent deputy seats.

Around one-third of all positions we counted in public service broadcasting organizations and around one-quarter of positions in the private sector are occupied by women. Public service broadcasting and organizations with mixed funding were much more likely to appoint women into senior roles (59%) than private organizations (41%). While Figure 1.1 aggregates all the data for all the countries, drilling down to the individual country levels shows that in some countries,

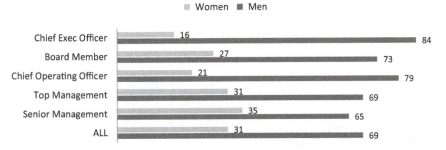
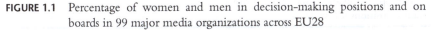

FIGURE 1.1   Percentage of women and men in decision-making positions and on boards in 99 major media organizations across EU28

women are present in relatively high numbers at both strategic and operational levels in relation to the EU-28 average, with Eastern Europe and the Scandinavian countries showing positive outcomes for women. On the face of it, this appears somewhat contradictory, given the very different socio-cultural contexts of those regions in terms of gender equality. In parts of Eastern Europe, historical "accident" accounts for this positive finding: women have been working in the media for a long time as no prestige was associated with the profession and State censorship restricted power and autonomy. The subsequent political and economic shifts across Eastern Europe have resulted in many men quitting the media for more prestigious and well-paid professions, leaving women, with their more limited mobility and job opportunities, well placed to take on senior positions. However, a number of women we interviewed said that while many senior women are on the editorial staffs, the responsibility for making the most significant decisions remained with men. The strong showing for women in Scandinavian countries is less unexpected given a relationship between national policies and a positive culture relating to gender equality and the presence of women in senior roles (Ross & Padovani, 2016).

Policy support for gender equality

Table 1.1 shows that among the 99 media organizations we sampled, just under half reported the existence of some equality policy which at least mentioned gender. Less than one in five organizations have a policy explicitly focused on gender. In terms

TABLE 1.1 Take up policies, monitoring, and practical measures (%)

Policies	Public/Mixed	Private	Total
Equality opportunities/diversity policy	9	10	19
Gender Equality policy/code of conduct	10	4	14
Code Of conduct (mentions gender)	6	5	11
External code of conduct (general)	3	2	5
Implementation and monitoring mechanisms			
Committee responsible for (monitoring) equality policy	9	6	15
Equality/Diversity Officer	9	4	13
Equality/Diversity Department	6	6	9
Practical measures			
Policy on sexual harassment	12	11	23
Dignity at work policy	10	9	19
Policy on maternity leave	10	7	17
Policy on paternity leave	9	6	15
Harassment Advisors	3	2	5
Policy on parental leave	1	0	1
Equality awareness training for staff	6	3	9
Leadership/management training for women	4	2	6
Trainee positions for women	3	0	3

Source: All data were collected from the EU Member States and Croatia during July–November 2012.[7]

of formal policies, these included gender equality plans, diversity policies, and equality and diversity codes. A similar number of (but often different) organizations had established formal mechanisms to monitor their gender and/or equality strategies and nine organizations had an Equality or Diversity Department. In terms of support measures, the most frequently cited intervention related to sexual harassment, although even fewer than 25 percent of organizations mentioned this, followed by a dignity at work policy (19%) and a maternity leave policy (17%). These policies tended to be *in addition to* whatever structures organizations were required by national laws. Moreover, only six organizations supported structured training programs for women, although slightly more (9%) provided equality awareness training for staff.

Public companies were more likely than private ones to have policies: 38 percent of public media organizations operated a gender-equality policy or had a code of conduct in place; only 17 percent of private companies had adopted such measures. A similar trend could be observed in relation to support and implementation mechanisms: a diversity department could be found in 14 percent of public but only in 6 percent of private companies. While 21 percent public media had an equality/diversity officer, only 7 percent in the private sector did. This situation is not surprising, given that national legislation generally regulates the working practices of PSBs. What is perhaps surprising is that any private companies have taken steps to establish policies that go beyond the minimum legally required.

Our analysis did not provide clear evidence that broad policy frameworks, such as gender equality policies or codes of conduct, make a difference in reducing unequal power relations across the media organization. However, the findings nevertheless suggest that more specific support and practical measures in promoting women in decision-making positions—such as maternity leave or equality training activities—can play a significant role. We also noted the opportunity for women to occupy strategic positions was almost twice as high when such measures were in place.[8] Interestingly, some of the organizations participating in the study told members of the research team they had no need to develop gender-specific policies as they had never had any complaints. Such complacency in the face of ongoing and well-documented gender discrimination is hard to understand, but without a clear commitment to equality (in all its forms) from senior management, also formalized in (self)regulatory provisions, then staff will always be vulnerable to discriminatory practices, both explicit and unintentional. Power is wielded in different ways and women need to be careful about how they confront misogynistic and unfair treatment. That said, unions and equality-based NGOs have played a useful part in supporting women in making judicial challenges against their media employer on grounds of both sex and age discrimination. Nevertheless, we found some organizations have taken a very proactive approach to gender equality, not only by developing policies and codes, but also through monitoring and review initiatives.[9]

> Men previously got employed based on references or by being 'helped' into organizations much more. Now there is more of an open process which may help women to perform better.
>
> *(Sondra, PSB)*

Women talk out their experience

Unsurprisingly, the women[10] we interviewed had a range of perspectives about how they had crafted their own careers. They suggested that the combination of work-place culture and attitudes of senior managers had been highly influential in helping or hindering their career aspirations. A macho workplace, unsupportive managers, ineffective (or non-existent) equality policies, and low-level harassment were all mentioned as markers of a woman-unfriendly working environment. Problems in relation to structural, environmental, and policy issues were exacerbated by the prevalence of "informal" processes where male managers boosted and advocated for their male subordinates when promotion opportunities arose. Women were much less likely to have such sponsors working behind the scenes for them and were generally not part of informal workplace networks, which are consolidated and nurtured through shared cultural practices such as after-hours drinking and sports. It would seem that the "old boys' network" is alive and well.

Women offered mixed views of women-only activities, programs, and training courses as strategies to help develop women's careers. Some said programs and train-ing specifically targeted at women are effective. One Swedish woman who had par-ticipated in a management course for women journalists, said: "We learnt about the kind of problems women can meet. It also got social networks. I think these kinds of courses are important." (Julia, PRN, North) Susanne (PSB, South) also valued pro-grams such as mentoring, networking, and confidence-building training for women but did not see a need to improve on women's professional skills; she argued that young women who wish to pursue a career in journalism are *already* better qualified and more committed than men of the same age. Several women described a demon-strable need for "safe spaces" where women can develop their skills in a supportive environment where they do not have to compete with men to make their voices heard. One of the key issues around women's ascent into management positions was having the *confidence* to go for the promotion. "I have found one thing, common to many women in management positions, not just in the media. They all seem to ask, 'Why me? Do I really deserve to be here? Can I really do this job?' Training would be great, to combat this. I would encourage a lot of employees to follow such train-ing, because there is leadership at so many levels in this job" (Clare, PRM, South).

However, some women did not believe women-only training was either necessary or even helpful, for a variety of reasons. "I have never received any management train-ing designed specifically for women. Management training is always very useful. I think women are more accurate and more careful. Men tend to think in more general terms than women. Can you influence that with training?" (Tarja, PSB, North). Lydia (PTV, South) said that she doesn't believe in women-only training and would not attend management training specifically for women; men and women are equal, she asserted, so special training for women is unnecessary. Carmen suggested that even if the con-tents of such courses were useful, "If society does not change, no matter how many courses there are for women, the glass ceiling still won't break" (Carmen, PRM, South). Jenni argued that the problem with programs and training aimed solely at women is that it suggests, in some way, women are deficient and in need of something special to help them achieve parity. Despite these very different views on the value of programs and activities focused solely on women, all the women who *had* undertaken them found them to be extremely beneficial. Additionally, some of the reasons for doubting their helpfulness turned on how they could be perceived rather than the intrinsic value for the intended target group. Many of the interviewees also mentioned the importance of mentors and having good role models as they progressed through their careers, "I had a female boss very early on in my career who taught me what it could be like to be up there and still be me." (Katharina, PRN, North)

Our findings echo those of other studies, both contemporary and historic. They show that despite the proportion of women in any given workforce, their numbers on entering journalism at the ground are very different to those we observe in management. One reason is that a certain percentage of women leave to have families. Despite the so-called postfeminist age, women are still the primary carers for children (and indeed older family members), and either never return to paid employment or pay a heavy price for their career break. Or, some women are not ambitious and have no wish to get their feet under the executive table. But given the high numbers of women who do enter the news profession, we have to assume that some of them do indeed aspire to the top job, stay in the profession, accumulate significant expertise and experience and put themselves forward for promotion. However, most are unsuccessful, demonstrated by the low number of women who currently occupy top team positions. The experience of *those* women is troubling because women themselves say the culture of the working environment stymies their prospects and ambitions, not their own weaknesses. We found overall though, just less than a third of all senior positions were held by women, they tended to occupy the lowest tier of management (just 16% were CEOs) and were often based in support departments such as HR or Legal Services, rather than in the more prestigious areas such as commissioning or editorial. This suggests both vertical and horizontal segregation are in play, with particular paths mapped out for women and men based on their sex rather than their aptitude (see also North, 2016b).

Fostering gender equality in the media: three indicators

Despite any number of recommendations and guidelines from many different actors which evidence a continuing awareness of gender inequalities at the level of policymaking and governance, gender equality remains a fond wish, not a reality. Equality principles have not being implemented in relation to traditional media or to the digital landscape, as part of a gender mainstreaming approach. It was against this background of rhetorical commitment, but with little significant change in women's experiences, that three indicators to measure the progress of media industries in achieving the goal of gender equality were proposed as drivers for change. On the face of it, they are not extraordinarily innovative, but they do present a set of benchmarks for measuring change in a very clear way and that could be associated with targets and timescales with which to achieve change, if consistently applied.

The Council of the European Union officially approved three indicators in 2013.[11] Indicator 1 tracks the proportion of women and men in executive decision-making posts across a range of management and operational functions, including: Chief Executive Officer, Chief Operating Officer (e.g. Director-General, Editor-in-Chief, Top and Senior Level operational management). Indicator 2 provides information on the proportion of women and men on the important decision-making boards which govern media organizations, including the most senior external oversight committees (either of the organization or its parent company), responsible for the strategic direction of each media organization, for example the Board of Governors or the Board of Trustees. Indicator 3 is concerned with the existence of policies, including those relating to: gender equality, equal opportunities/diversity; sexual harassment or dignity at work; parental leave; mechanisms for implementing and monitoring gender equality such as committees and officers; and practical measures aimed at supporting women's career development such as leadership/management training for women; equality awareness training for staff; flexible working arrangements.

Of course, these indicators (not the only ones relating to gender and equality) are useful only if applied to data at a certain point and then reapplied some time later to see whether change occurred, demonstrating progress towards gender equality. EU Member States were not mandated to apply these indicators in any way. Without the force of law, these will be used only by those media organizations committed to the equality agenda. The news media's track record on this is not inspiring.

Conclusion

The findings provide little in the way of optimism for either the career aspirations of women or the likely achievement of the BPfA goals or equality goals such as the Sustainable Development Goals (SDGs). The timeline for achieving the SDGs is 2030, but without an action plan, they are as likely to fall short of success as all the other goals that have gone before them.

Our study had a regional focus on only 99 organizations across 28 countries. Nonetheless, it comprises *all* the public service broadcasters (39 separate organizations) in the European Union; and the 56 private organizations constitute some of the major European media corporations, most of which have international parent companies and operate across Europe and beyond, if not functionally then in terms of reach: the four organizations with mixed funding (public and private) are also major media players. Obviously, the sample size prevents making grand claims about the media landscape. But we would certainly argue that the findings are typical of large media organizations and provide a snapshot, at the very least, of the European media landscape. Moreover, although the findings are now several years old, given the current state of play in relation to the number of women CEOs of major media houses in Europe, we suspect that very little has changed in the intervening years.

Women continue to be underrepresented (i.e., relative to their numbers in the media workforce more generally) in the decision-making structures of major media organizations, both at operational levels as senior managers and at strategic levels, as CEOs and board members. We suggest that historical gender inequalities reflect heavily entrenched patriarchal norms and perpetuate women's unequal access to power and decision making.

Our data also show there is no automatic cause-effect relationship between the promotion of a gender equality culture and significant numbers of women in decision-making positions: sometimes the two things went together and sometimes not. More research is needed to clarify, for example, the links between the adoption of gender equality measures, the overall socio-cultural and economic context within which the media operate and women's access to power structures. Based on our findings, there may be different reasons that explain the different situations found in Eastern Europe, the Scandinavian countries, and other regions. Either way, the existence of gender equality policies is not enough to enable change: without detailed planning, shared commitment, and support mechanisms such as monitoring and training opportunities, even the best framed policy measures are only so many words on a page. What our interviewees made clear and as so many other studies have found, workplace cultures—with their micro-harassments, sexist norms, and private nepotisms—thwart women's ambitions and waste their potential.

The testimonies of many of the senior women we interviewed also made clear the crucial role of senior managers in recognizing and valuing difference and in acknowledging the needs of working parents (i.e., "mothers") and those with caring responsibilities (again, read "women"). However, the clearest evidence of an organization's commitment to gender equality is the construction of a formal, publicly promoted and integrated equality strategy and policy framework that includes mechanisms for evaluation and action, supported by human and other resources. This is important in structural terms, so that an equality ethos is firmly embedded in the organization rather than championed by one or two people as a hobby. It also provides a clear signal to *all* employees that equality issues are taken seriously and that behavioral change must follow policy change. Furthermore, policy provisions not only state the principles according to which change is to be pursued, they are also crucial in guaranteeing sustainability after inequalities *have* been addressed and power-sharing structures established.

Any number of external interventions have been made over the past years in an effort to effect changes in the media. Professional media associations have been active in developing practical strategies to support such change.[12] The IFJ/EFJ handbook, *Getting the Balance Right: Gender Equality in Journalism* (2009) urged women to audit their organizations to identify the roles and posts held by women and men and to campaign for equal pay and more supportive conditions for working parents. The strengths of that publication included its insider perspective and knowledge, but also the provision of practical ways in which individuals and groups could advocate on their own behalf, constituting an important tool for empowerment. Two years later, the Council of Europe's Steering Committee for Equality between Women and Men published its report, *Women and Journalists First*, originally conceived as a document with "a strong plea to re-think current habits and procedures in making quality news [in order to realize] democracy in practice, quality in journalism and an end to gender stereotyping" (CDGE, 2011, p. 2). In late 2012, the IFJ and the World Association for Christian Communication (WACC) published a resource kit for gender-ethical journalism and media house policy (WACC/IFJ, 2012). In other words, a lot has been going on in terms of guidance to improve the situation for women within media industries. Yet inequalities persist.

What needs to be kept in mind is the interplay between multiple forms of inequality that still characterize media operations and structures, so that women's access to decision-making and power-sharing positions is addressed through a proactive engagement with "media gender equality regimes," understood here as "interrelated practices, meanings and processes, including normative developments, aimed at transforming systematic gender disparities that characterize the media sector" (Padovani & Pavan, 2017). Only by tackling the interplay of different forms of inequality—representation, participation, access to resources, working conditions, education and training—will women and men come to share power in ways that benefit all. Whilst it is impossible to say with any certainty that more women working in the media decision-making posts will affect media content and overall output, the simple act of having a greater diversity of people making key decisions about media content *would*, we argue, make a difference. Promoting more women into decision-making positions is not about lowering the competency threshold or making special provision for less talented women as some managers fear, but rather about giving excellent women the opportunity to succeed. In the end, encouraging colleagues to take gender equality seriously is good for all staff and, as recent studies on boardroom performance show, good for business (McKinsey & Co., 2012).

The Council of the European Union formally adopted the three indicators we developed, but how they will be used at a practical level remains unclear. One of the key issues, as the research team pointed out at the time, is that someone must pay for monitoring, either media organizations themselves or via some other form of external funding. Someone must pay for, and devote human and time resources to, the collection of data, its analysis and reporting. Will this be done at the national or the regional level? What are the incentives for organizational compliance? Could sanctions be applied by national governments on publicly funded organizations if they fail to set or monitor targets? No one has answers to these questions. What *is* clear, however, is that a range of gender-focused targets, goals, and deadlines have been developed for both media organizations and society more generally over the past few decades, none of which have been met. Perhaps they are still perceived as simply "reminders" to keep equality issues on the socio-political agenda. In reality, however, as long as gender equality remains an aspiration rather than a legal requirement, change will be a very long time coming.

Notes

1 The list of top 100 media corporations for the study comes from the Media Data Base, Institute of Media and Communication Policy (December 2017) and is available at nordicom.gu.se/en/statistics-facts
2 http://ec.europa.eu/justice/newsroom/gender-equality/news/121114_en.htm#Press.
3 See also Byerly, 2013.
4 The European Institute for Gender Equality (EIGE) is an EU-funded but autonomous body, to which the EU delegates its gender equality work.
5 Karen Ross, Claudia Padovani, Erzebet Barat, and Monia Azzalini comprised the core team and they were joined by researchers working in all 27 EU Member States and Croatia, together with Elena Pavan who worked as the statistical data consultant to the project. The data and information used/presented were collected in 2012/2013 as part of the *Study on Area J of the Beijing Platform for Action: Women and the Media in the European Union* carried out for the European Institute for Gender Equality under contract EIGE/2012/OPER/07. The views presented here are those of the authors and they do not necessarily reflect the opinion or position of the European Institute for Gender Equality.
6 Because several countries split PSB into separate entities for TV and radio, 39 public sector organizations were included; in some multilingual countries, e.g. Luxembourg and Austria, different PSBs serve different language communities.
7 Out of 99 organizations in the survey, only those which include any of the above codes and policies have been included, whilst some of the other organizations in the sample may have some or all of these policies, the research team were unable to find any evidence during the conduct of the project.
8 For detailed discussion and visual syntheses on these points, see EIGE Report (2013, 40 sg).
9 Some of these positive examples are currently being collected in a Resources Bank of good practices in the context of a European-funded project aimed at "Advancing Gender Equality in Media Industries" (AGEMI) to be completed by 2019.
10 We used the following "codes" to provide some basic demographic detail about each of the interviewees quoted in this chapter: PSB (public service broadcaster), PTV (private TV station), PRN (private newspaper), and PRM (private media organization). We changed all names and indicated where they work in Europe as Central, North, or South. All data were collected October to November 2012.
11 www.consilium.europa.eu/uedocs/cms_data/docs/pressdata/en/lsa/137546.pdf
12 EFJ/IFJ, *A handbook on gender equality good practices in European journalists' unions*, Brussels, I/EFJ, 2012.

Bibliography

Byerly, C. M. (Ed.). (2013). *The Palgrave handbook of women and journalism*. New York, NY: Palgrave Macmillan.

Chaher, S. (Ed.). (2014). *Public policies on communication and gender in Latin America: The path ahead of us.* Buenos Aires: Asociación Civil Comunicación para la Igualdad (English text: pp. 98–192).

Council of Europe, Steering Committee CDEG. (2011). *Women and journalist first: A challenge to media professionals to realise democracy in practice, quality in journalism and an end to gender stereotyping.* Retrieved from www.coe.int/t/dghl/standardsetting/equality/03themes/women-media/CDEG_2011_15_en_handbook.pdf

De-Miguel, R., Hanitzsch, T., Parratt, S., & Berganza, R. (2017). Women journalists in Spain: An analysis of the sociodemographic features of the gender gap. *El profesional de la información, 26*(3), 497–506. https://doi.org/10.3145/epi.2017.may.16

Djerf-Pierre, M. (2007, Jubilee). The gender of journalism: The structure and logic of the field in the twentieth century. *Nordicom Review*, 81–104.

European Commission. (2010). *More women in senior positions—Key to economic stability and growth.* Luxembourg, EU.

European Commission Advisory Committee on Equal Opportunities for Women and Men. (2010). *Opinion on "Breaking gender stereotypes in the media."* Brussels: European Commission.

European Women's Lobby. (2010). *From Beijing to Brussels: An unfinished story.* Retrieved from www.womenlobby.org/spip.php?article124&lang=en

Gallagher, M. (1987). Introduction. In *Women in media decision-making: The invisible barriers.* Paris: UNESCO.

Gallagher, M. (1995). *An unfinished story: Gender patterns in media employment.* Paris: UNESCO.

Gallagher, M. (2008). Feminist issues in the global media system. In L. Shade & K. Sarikakis (Eds.), *Feminist interventions in international communication: Minding the gap.* Lanham, MD: Rowman & Littlefield.

Gallagher, M. (2011). Gender and communication policy: Struggling for space. In R. Mansell & M. Raboy (Eds.), *The handbook of global media and communication policy* (pp. 451–466). Oxford: Wiley-Blackwell.

International Federation of Journalists. (2009). *Getting the balance right: Gender equality in journalism.* Brussels: IFJ.

International Women's Media Foundation. (2011). *Global report on the status of women in the news media.* Washington, DC. International Women's Media Foundation. Retrieved from www.iwmf.org/our-research/iwmf-global-report/

Lobo, P., Silveirinha, M. J., Torres da Silva, M., & Subtil, F. (2017). In journalism, we are all men. *Journalism Studies, 18*(9), 1148–1166.

Löfgren Nilsson, M., & Örnebring, H. (2016). Journalism under threat. *Journalism Practice, 10*(7), 880–890.

McKinsey & Company. (2012). *Women matter 2012: Making the breakthrough.* McKinsey & Co. Retrieved from www.mckinsey.com/client_service/organization/latest_thinking/women_matter

Melki, J. P., & Mallat, S. E. (2016). Block her entry, keep her down and push her out. *Journalism Studies, 17*(1), 57–79.

North, L. (2016a). Damaging and daunting: Female journalists' experiences of sexual harassment in the newsroom. *Feminist Media Studies, 16*(3), 495–510.

North, L. (2016b). The gender of "soft" and "hard" news. *Journalism Studies, 17*(3), 356–373.

Nenadic, I., & Ostling, A.(2017, March). Public service media in Europe: Gender equality policies and the representation of women in decision-making roles. *Comunicazione Politica, 2,* 209–232.

Padovani, C. (2014). Gaps in media and communication governance: Towards a gender-aware research and advocacy agenda. In A. V. Montiel (Ed.), *Media and gender: A scholarly agenda for the global alliance on media and gender.* Paris: UNESCO.

Padovani, C., & Pavan, E. (2017, March). The politics of media gender equality: Lessons learned and struggles for change twenty years after the Beijing Fourth World Conference on Women. Introduction to *ComPol.*

Robinson, G. J. (2005). *Gender, journalism and equity: Canadian, US and European perspectives.* Cresskill, NJ: Hampton Press.

Ross, K., & Padovani, C. (Eds.). (2016). *Gender equality and the media: A challenge for Europe.* London and New York, NY: Routledge, ECREA.

Sarikakis, K., & Nguyen, E. T. (2009). The trouble with gender: Media policy and gender mainstreaming in the European Union. *Journal of European Integration*, *31*(2), 201–216.

World Association for Christian Communication/IFJ. (2012). *Learning resource kit for gender-ethical journalism and media house policy*. Toronto: WACC. Retrieved from http://whomakes thenews.org/articles/learning-resource-kit-for-gender-ethical-journalism#english

2

WOMEN AND TECHNOLOGY IN THE NEWSROOM

Vision or reality from data journalism to the news startup era

Nikki Usher

In 2011, in trying to imagine a future for journalism that would take better advantage of programming and programmers, the Knight Foundation created a slide to present about the "The Hacker Journalist." One side of the slide was a man dressed in a V-neck sweater wearing glasses. He was the reporter, described using keywords like "wordsmith," "big picture thinker," "contrarian," and "investigator." The other side of the slide also showed a man, wearing a t-shirt with html code on it, "chill clothes," and headphones. This man, a programmer, was described as "independent," a "problem solver," "process oriented," and a "builder." The fusion of this programmer and this reporter was the hacker journalist, what Knight dubbed "Journalist 2.0." This bearded man carried a tablet and was wearing a flannel shirt and New Balance-type sneakers. Words attached included "translator," "impactor," "info distiller," "pragmatic," and "data visualizer." The slide itself was loosely based on an actual programmer, Brian Boyer, who had won a Knight-funded scholarship for journalism graduate school at Northwestern, then went on to run programming and data journalism teams at *The Chicago Tribune* and NPR, now working for a news startup.

The Knight Foundation's vision for the future of journalism has one glaring problem: the hacker journalist of the future was assumed to be white and male. Even the programmer's beard itself is more symbolic than the Knight slide-maker perhaps knew: male programmers are known for their beards. Moreover, researchers suggest that these beards are a performative aspect that asserts programmers' masculinity and rugged individualism (Ensmenger, 2015). When shown this image in reviewing a part of my then-forthcoming book on journalists who code (Usher, 2016), a female programmer journalist muttered to me the bearded programmer trope was a bit overdone and annoying, because women code in journalism, too, and in fact are a critical part of hacker journalism.

Women have been coding, doing data visualization and data analysis, and working more generally in journalism technology just as long as men, albeit in smaller numbers. But technology brings with it a toxic culture that has long marginalized women. As journalism is becoming more technologically oriented and sophisticated, questions about the future interplay between gender, technology, and journalism become increasingly important. Women who code are and will be part of the future of journalism, so critical inquiry into the gendered dimensions of this subfield of journalism is warranted. Here, therefore, I look specifically at the case of US journalism, although the fusion of programming with journalism has exploded across the globe, as evidenced by the creation of a chapter of the group Hacks/ Hackers, which brings together hacks (journalists) with hackers (journalists) on every continent except Antarctica (Lewis & Usher, 2014). A broad overview of the state of women in journalism technology and/or women in STEM-style journalism is difficult, in part because it's problematic to delineate what and whom journalism technology includes (Coddington, 2015). As a result, this chapter intends to inspire future research rather than provide a definitive accounting.

Certainly, around the world, women from all sectors are calling out past abuses by more powerful men. In the US and elsewhere, women journalists have come forward to name men journalists guilty of abuses ranging from sexual harassment to sexual assault. Women are demanding respect and jobs. As the editors of this book have chronicled, gender inequality can be seen across journalism in news production and news content. But, journalism's gender problems seem fewer compared to the tech industry, which has become almost synonymous with gender discrimination and harassment. In 2015, Ellen Pao, who later became CEO of Reddit, brought a gender discrimination and harassment lawsuit against the venture capital firm she worked for. In 2017, abuses across the tech industry attracted new scrutiny, particularly after a woman recalled rampant abuses while working as an engineer at Uber (Fowler, 2017). Her revelations, along with reports from other women, led to pressure that caused Uber's CEO to take a leave of absence. At Google, a male developer authored a 10-page memo arguing against gender diversity in tech and that "biological causes" made women less good at programming than men (Hicks, 2017). The gross male startup culture these women in tech raged against reared its ugly head at Vice (Steel, 2017), a journalism venture that had refashioned itself as a startup thanks to an infusion of private equity funding, replete with the hard charging startup mythos (Carlson & Usher, 2016); unfortunately, this startup energy was accompanied by a hyper-masculine culture abhorrent to women who worked there.

The fusion of an industry with existing gender problems with another industry where gender problems are even worse means that scholars, journalists, and future journalists need to think critically how to address existing problems and those on the horizon. Nonetheless, the news industry is perhaps one of the more welcoming places for women to do more technically oriented and STEM-situated work, and journalism schools are well-positioned to overcome traditional hurdles facing women in technology. This exploratory chapter reviews some of the tensions, past and present, facing women working in journalism technology. I provide historical perspective and contemporary analysis, using empirical data based on interviews with key informants who have exerted significant influence in the field. Some of them requested to see the article prior to publication, enabling an informal "member checking" of my analysis. After drawing attention to areas of particular concern, I conclude by suggesting a path forward as journalism becomes increasingly technologically oriented.

Issues tech brings to journalism

In general, women in the US are severely underrepresented when it comes to computer science: they comprise only 18 percent of undergraduate majors and 20.4 percent of PhDs (NSF, 2017). In math and statistics, ratios are a bit better, with women making up 43 percent of these majors. It is noteworthy that historically, coding was once a woman's job. Women worked as "human computers," even in the early days of computing doing repetitive math tasks, when computers were more like calculators (Grier, 2013). And, as depicted in the movie and Margot Lee Shetterly's book *Hidden Figures*, African American women worked as the coders and mathematicians who helped launch the US's first person (John Glenn) into space. Like many other fields that have become lucrative, when "pink labor" shifted to become men's work, prestige and pay grew (Duffy, 2017).

Today, women face distinct difficulties in the tech workforce. Across the globe women are less likely to enter STEM fields and more likely to leave them, with a key reason being the hostility they face in the workplace. As an *Atlantic* article called "Why is Silicon Valley So Awful to Women in Tech," (Mundy, 2017) explained: "Workplace conditions, a lack of access to key creative roles, and a sense of feeling stalled in one's career" are the main reasons women leave. "Undermining behavior from managers" is a major factor.

Women make up a tiny percentage of developers at places like Google and Facebook; Google's 2016 diversity numbers revealed a 70/30 split across the company, with women holding only 19 percent of technical roles (Eadicicco, 2016). This is the tech culture staring down journalism; the pipeline problems and diversity issues found in tech today could well become significant problems facing journalism.

Journalism has become increasingly technical. In addition to the data journalists who are the heirs of the legacy of computer-assisted reporting, journalism has come to embrace a subfield of journalists who program. Their work uses programming to code projects that might include interactive displays or animation, where the coding languages they use are primarily intended for web and mobile content creation. When these journalists are looking for new jobs, they include on their resumes the "stack" of programming languages that they know. These might include Ruby, Python, JavaScript (in particular facility with D3), CSS, HTML, or PHP, just for starters. Many programmer journalists are also doing data journalism, and may also build tools to enable other journalists to more easily create interactives or do data analysis (Usher, 2016). This work is the kind of programming one might find in the tech industry. Some of these programmer journalists might be working on machine learning, predictive analytics, or engage in algorithmic accountability journalism that seeks to investigate the black box algorithms that are used not just on social media but across e-commerce, by governments, and beyond (Personal communication, Meredith Broussard, December 20, 2018). Increasingly, some journalists at both legacy and digital-first news organizations are doing tech work of the sort found deep in the bowels of a tech company, from research and development to data science to product management and software creation. Journalism has become part and parcel a STEM field. No longer, at least supposedly, can journalists be English majors or creative types frightened of math. But structural disadvantages that women face in technology and STEM loom large as a potential limiting factor for a tech-driven future of journalism that is gender inclusive.

How journalism became a STEM industry

While immersive long-form journalism and responsive mobile and web data interactives have become increasingly part of day-to-day editorial content creation, the history of journalism's fusion with computation in editorial work goes back to the dawn of modern computing. As Cox's (2000) history of computer-assisted reporting outlines, the first major use of computers for reporting was to predict the outcome of the 1952 presidential election, which correctly predicted Eisenhower's win.

We might think of women in journalism technology as reflecting three distinct eras of tech innovation in digital journalism—and the memories, recollections, and assessment of the state of women in this area of journalism reflect this historical trajectory. The first era encompasses the rise of computation in journalism; the second of programming and interactives in journalism, currently ongoing; and the third of tech as product and strategy in journalism, which is emerging on the horizon (Usher, 2017; Royal, 2017). This categorization helps bring into view some of the trends in women doing journalism technology work.

The first era: CAR and data journalism

In the US, this first era started when investigative journalism began to include more distinct data components. This commenced in the 1970s with Philip Meyer, but became institutionalized in the early 1990s with the formation of the Missouri Institute for Computer Assisted Reporting, which later became the National Institute for Computer-Assisted Reporting. Meyer also mentored and trained the first generation of computer-assisted journalists. Many of his mentees, including a few women, became important voices in the development of CAR and data journalism, including working as journalism educators. The heirs to these CAR journalists are today's data journalists, who might be thought of as working with updated versions of the spreadsheets used long ago, and who may be using programming to find insights within the data they are trying to investigate. Some of these journalists may then engage in sophisticated statistical analysis. Still others might combine these skills to build a database or visualize the data for news consumers to see online or on mobile, working with graphic design programs.

The women who were part of this early era of data journalism recall distinctly how few women there were. Cheryl Phillips, formerly of *The Seattle Times* and now a professor at Stanford, recounts that at the 1995 conference of the National Institute for Computer-Assisted Reporting (NICAR) she attended "there were so few women there" (personal communication, January 2, 2018). In 1998, she helped launch a "Women of CAR" dinner, as only eight or nine women attended a conference of 300 or 400 people, with the majority being white men. Mindy McAdams, now at the University of Florida and formerly of the *Washington Post*, remembers a similar scene. For McAdams, the combination of age and gender worked together to make her feel "like an inconsequential human," or at least she felt that older white men looked at her this way, though McAdams notes that this was more a confidence issue than a reality. She also describes these eight or nine women in a sea of white older men wearing "drip dry shirts" (personal communication, January 15, 2018). This reflects a particular generational moment in journalism, but these proportions are a reality still in technology today. At these first NICARs, Phillips recalls, "I didn't feel like they were trying to exclude women; it is just the way it was back then." McAdams recalls a slightly less inviting experience, noting: "These guys knew cool things but didn't know very well how to communicate about it . . . they weren't welcoming but they weren't reluctant or off-putting or pushing you away."

Phillips is perhaps emblematic of a first generation of female CAR journalists now working in data journalism. She said she began looking at CAR in part to distinguish herself as a journalist, recalling: "I started in the 1980s in newsrooms, and like every woman journalist of that era, I have lots of stories of just being talked over and not listened to and all the good assignments went to men." CAR gave her the comeback, a special skill that no one else had. As a young journalist, she did a short stint at *USA Today* while on loan from a small Gannett newspaper in Montana. The opportunity gave her the chance to work with data editors including Philip Meyer, which she described as "life changing." Both Phillips and McAdams, who began coding to generate their own insights and tools, credit strong mentorship—by men and women mentors—with the growth of the field. Twenty years later, so many women attend NICAR that finding an appropriate venue to book the "Women in CAR" dinner has become difficult; no longer can these women sit together at one table.

The second era: programmers in journalism (today)

The second era, which took hold in the mid-2000s, might be thought of as the programmer era of computation in journalism. This is not to say that CAR didn't involve programming, or that today's data journalists don't also program. The point is that coding, as designated for digital editorial projects, became increasingly part of daily newswork. The arrival of this programming moment in journalism and the invention of the "hacker journalist" as myth and reality were anchored by key moments such as Adrian Holovaty's Google Maps mashup of crime in Chicago in 2005 and the start in 2007 of Northwestern's Medill School scholarship to bring programmers into the newsroom. Unfortunately, this might be considered the moment when the "programmer" became common parlance, what the OED defines as "a male computer programmer who engages in stereotypically male-oriented activities and macho behavior." The arrival of the bro programmer, empowered as cool with desirable skills having been relegated to nerd-dom for much of his earlier life (Reagle, 2017), reflects a tech culture that usually looks the other way when startups bring "booth babes" to conferences to hawk their wares and when implicit bias marginalizes women to less prestigious technical roles. The more toxic frustrations have been addressed by recent testimony from Silicon Valley. Mostly, programmers are part of newsrooms today, integrated into newsroom workflows as another subfield of journalism (Fink & Anderson, 2015), albeit one with great prominence and influence in journalism.

Women working at the intersection of programming and journalism tend to feel positively about journalism compared to other types of tech work. Nonetheless, Meredith Broussard, a former features editor at the *Philadelphia Inquirer* who also worked as a software developer at AT&T Bell Labs and the MIT Media Lab and now a programmer journalist teaching at NYU, argues that "journalism technology has basically inherited all of the practices and biases of the larger tech community. . . . [I]n the tech world, the people with the real power are the engineers and developers" (personal communication, December 20, 2017). Broussard left a career in tech for journalism, and has found the journalism world more hospitable because it is a more gender balanced field as a whole.

However, women remain the minority in programming journalism. McAdams, who moved from CAR reporting into more programming focused work, sees this new generation of male programmer journalists as more hospitable to women than the previous one. She notes that many of them went to college in the 1990s and 2000s, tend to be younger, and tend not to focus on gender: these men are not, she said, going to ask women to go get the coffee. Moreover, she noted that women have more opportunities to gain respect: "Now particularly in NICAR and particularly in coding circles within journalism, women wear their capabilities in a more visible way, you've got a GitHub account and before someone has met you face to face they have seen your code." My interviewees suggest that despite evidence that today's brogrammers as a whole have been accused of gender bias and even outright harassment, men programmer journalists arguably are at least more aware of these issues than their tech company counterparts.

Michelle Minkoff, a programmer journalist, says that over the seven years she's spent in the field, she's encountered very few incidents of sexism. Nonetheless, she did point out that in the early 2010s, it was helpful to be different (e.g. not male) because it made her more of a familiar face. She credits some of her most important mentors as male programmer journalists, noting, "It's always been about the work" (personal communication, December 26, 2017). Over time, she has also gravitated online and offline to more women-specific tech groups, who have given both career and coding advice. Nonetheless, she notes, she would rather not stand out because of gender.

Men programmer journalists tend to agree that journalism is more welcoming to female programmers than is the tech industry. As Derek Willis, a longtime news apps developer and data journalist who has worked at *The New York Times* and *Pro-Publica*, and a well-regarded mentor (including to Minkoff), "I do think journalism often is a more welcoming profession for women than many software industry jobs, but that's a low bar, and journalism has its own systemic issues." Moreover, he sees openness as critical to the development of the field. "Most of us working in this part of journalism are inventing our jobs as we go," he said. "So being open to the voices of others is not only helpful but often essential" (personal communication, December 16, 2017).

Journalism education offers a tremendous opportunity for journalism to avoid the pipeline problem that the tech industry is facing. Women comprise the majority of journalism and mass communication students, so these programs can create coding classes that may be more inclusive than traditional computer science classes. McAdams has noted that the gender dynamics of her coding for journalism classes are favorable to this dynamic. Women tend to code collaboratively more often than male students, and a female-dominant classroom creates a comfortable environment for women to ask questions, a significant difference from more traditional coding instruction environments. "They are not the only woman in the room, they are not 10 percent or 20 percent in computer engineering or CS classes, they are in there [her classes] used to being the majority and are the majority."

Cindy Royal, a professor at Texas State University, has written and commented extensively about the opportunities for tech-inspired journalism education (see Royal, 2017). Royal told me:

> In my experience, women are most successful learning programming in a curriculum that provides context and support. . . . Mass communication programs have a responsibility to their students . . . because journalism as a whole has tremendous potential for interactive storytelling, data analysis and product management.
>
> *(personal communication, December 30, 2017)*

Programming (and programmatic thinking) is relevant across a broad swath of disciplines. Royal's argument is that more coding instruction across the university will help eliminate some of these pipeline problems. "The result will be that more people from a range of diverse backgrounds can code and influence the direction of technology," she notes. Some 51 percent of the students in Royal's Digital Media Innovation program at Texas State University are women; 16 percent of the students enrolled in computer science at the university are women.

That said, women programmer journalists do face challenges. While journalism might be more open to women who code, representation remains an issue. In 2016, two-thirds of presenters at the NICAR conference were men; that proportion reached near parity in 2018. Implicit bias plagues male-dominant teams. For instance, Minkoff has received some emails that began with "hey gents" and promotional material for various events that use pictures or cartoons exclusively of male developers. Open source projects created by men have been nicknamed after female stereotypes. Spending too much time thinking about these instances of implicit bias is distracting, she says, but these sorts of unintended slights are a reality. Until these assumptions are challenged, the status quo will continue.

Other female programmers have been discouraged by the general gender discrimination they see in newsrooms overall as well as on teams with programmer journalists. Heather Bryant, now a fellow at Stanford, explained why she left newsrooms (personal communication, December 19, 2017):

> Part of that is frustration with legacy processes that I watch my network of amazing badass women colleagues have to fight every single day to make progress on either their work or in improving the nature of the newsrooms they're in.

Bryant relays that when she tells men about her projects, their reaction can be described as a Venn diagram: men are almost generally always concerned about "all the things that will be hard, all the challenges to look out for, all the things I need to keep in mind, all the ways what I'm doing could fail." Although these comments are sometimes helpful, others offer "obstacles and usually little else." Her engagement with women about her projects has been decidedly different, and these interactions tend to be more collaborative, with women facilitating introductions, asking engaging questions, and creatively brainstorming about how to move her work forward.

Broussard likewise expressed caution: while teams may seem more inclusive, women may be getting shifted to less influential roles in the journalism technology arena. She sees more women working in user experience and product management roles than lead developer roles. This trend concerns her because developers have more job security and more prestige, and while women are in technical roles, they may be pushed into less significant or valued ones. While the outlook for journalism is rosier than the tech industry as a whole, Willis' points out that's not exactly an accomplishment for the profession, given that the tech industry offers such a low bar for comparison. In journalism, the representation of women in STEM-related work is a problem and sets in motion other reasons to be concerned.

The third wave of tech in journalism

Journalism has become increasingly technical, not only in terms of the skills required to produce editorial content, but also in terms of its environment, as startup thinking and culture invades the newsroom. This startup energy infusion and culture influence can be traced to a few key moments in the past half-dozen years. In 2013, venture capital investors began pouring money into original content-producing news startups in addition to news aggregators and platforms with a strong interest in journalism (e.g. Medium)—to the point that Pando Daily, the niche tech news site, referred to the trend as "content's holy shit moment" (McKenzie & Lacey, 2013). In 2013, approximately $300 million dollars got invested, with money coming from traditional venture backers as well as venture funds for large media organizations. The sector hit a fever pitch over the next three years with some tremendous deals; in 2014, Buzzfeed gained legitimacy in the tech sector with a $50 million investment by Andreessen Horowitz, one of the premier Silicon Valley venture capital firms. Business Insider was bought by Axel Springer, an enormous European digital publishing house with numerous newspapers, magazines, and multimedia news brands, for $442 million in 2015. Even legacy media got a burst of the venture world, when former Facebook executive Chris Hughes purchased the *New Republic*, a weekly political news magazine.

Some of this energy has cooled for a variety of concerns about return on investment; but this is not unique to news startups, as venture investment has cooled industry-wide (Martin, 2017). Nonetheless, this energy not only provided the potential for new tech-minded digital news organizations to launch and grow, but also signaled the importance of having a technical side to the news product. The Knight Foundation moved away from funding content-focused startups to prototypes, and helped back a media-focused VC incubator, Matter VC. *The New York Times* also launched a short-lived experiment to incubate startups with an initiative called TimesSpace.

This cultural shift to innovation in journalism is tied to Silicon Valley's entrepreneurial culture. Thinking about this wave of tech into journalism requires thinking past the role of programmers in the newsroom and about the culture of startups more generally—from funding to product. Even if women are not doing technical work themselves, they may be working, leading or even starting a news outlet branding itself as startup (or one that actually is a startup). Technical work in journalism often moves beyond just programming to include the kind of technological problem solving and entrepreneurial thinking found at a tech company.

Since the arrival of web content management systems in many news organizations, the teams charged with making sure they work are often located in IT divisions associated with the newsroom. Now, these teams are increasingly important in helping reduce load time and facilitating speedy posting on the Web (Benton, 2017). Some large legacy newsrooms have R&D labs, while many large chains and premiere news organizations have internal intraprenurship efforts (the embedding of startups within the newsrooms) to build products and software for editorial and business purposes (Boyles, 2016). They might be building prototypes for all sorts of software and hardware or doing sophisticated network analysis such as *The New York Times'* Cascade Project, which mapped influencers on social media for *Times* stories.

Certainly, the further we move from editorial content to the business side of journalism, whether we call product designers and UX (user-experience) specialists "journalists" becomes a boundary issue worthy of close scrutiny. Regardless of what these newsroom employees are called and where they sit in the news organization's org chart, the kind of people who have the technical expertise found in startups or technology companies will also need to be part of the future of journalism. The importance of the role of technical staff in news organizations will continue to grow.

At news startups, the common assumption was that these companies were half-media company and half-tech company, a necessity for securing funding from venture backers (Usher, 2017). As my research found, these startups described themselves as seeing product development and technical expertise, business concerns, and editorial development on equal setting. Making clear a "Chinese wall"—an information barrier to prevent exchanges or communications that could lead to conflicts of interest—was of less concern. Moreover, these startups talked about both their engagement with developing algorithms with predictive capacities and their investment in building software platforms. Data science has become a critical aspect of the future of the news business as news organizations try to chart analytics, build digital retention strategies, and understand the social spread of news.

White men headed many of the buzzy startups from Buzzfeed (although Buzzfeed is notable in data science, with its success strategy highlighting a woman as team leader) to FiveThirtyEight to Bleacher Report. During the wave of startup energy in 2013 and 2014, Emily Bell, a journalism prognosticator and innovator herself, expressed concern over women's future in this news startup world. Her *Guardian* piece "Journalism startups aren't a revolution if they're filled with all these white men" reflected this concern. Her point was well-taken regarding the marginalization of women in the news startup scene even when they were involved in starting companies. Ezra Klein is often credited as the founder of Vox, but one of his two co-founders was a woman. Melissa Bell, the technical brains behind the launching of the new site, served as *The Post*'s platform director before moving to Vox (Moses, 2015), but the pre-launch coverage featured Klein, not Bell (see Coscarelli, 2014).

Women entrepreneurs aiming to garner funding for their news startups face significant barriers. In tech generally, women founders receive about 2 percent of all venture funding, and the trendline is getting worse, not better (Zaraya, 2017). The news tech sector is no exception. In 2014, I interviewed Lara Setrakian, CEO of News Deeply, a long-form site. She explained that her experiences trying to raise VC money were tinged with both implicit and overt sexism. She described sexual passes that male VCs made at her to the diminishment of her enterprise. She was repeatedly told to look for funders who fund women entrepreneurs. Nonetheless, she was steadfast in her efforts to create a successful for-profit company. Setrakian (2017) later wrote about her sexual assault at the hands of a prominent ABC producer.

This development in journalism and the fetishization over the "startup" may prove more challenging for women than the integration of programming into editorial. As Elite Truong of Vox, product manager for audience experience, explained:

> I wrote a piece on what people in hybrid roles in the newsroom are up against: innovator imposter syndrome coupled with all the inherent institutional and personal biases of partners and collaborators and stakeholders who may or may not regard you as an equal because you may be a woman, or identify as non-binary, or parent, or LGTBQ, or have a different professional background, or belong to any other minority. You have to represent being a woman and all those other identifiers that are underrepresented in tech and journalism, and that is often harder than the work itself at hand.
>
> (personal communication, December 22, 2017)

In addition, she was tired of having to keep educating colleagues about the importance of diversity. It was a constant effort to figure out which battles were most important to fight when trying to overcome the "default white male perspective" at work. One of these challenges included "educating people on how to write in a considerate way on women engineers' pull requests"—essentially meaning that she needed to train colleagues how to respectfully respond to requests from women for coding collaboration on open source platforms.

Women working at the intersection of tech strategy and tech development in news organizations today deal with these sorts of sexist comments that, while not intentionally rude or anti-women, are nonetheless frustrating over time. For example, Alexis Lloyd played a pivotal role as the creative director of The New York Times' R&D lab until she left to become chief design officer at the news startup, Axios. Lloyd, who "designs and builds compelling user experiences that demonstrate innovative ways of engaging with information and with the world around us," tweets regularly about these issues. One particularly trenchant tweet was a reminder of the prominence of women in technical fields—as well as the type of implicit bias prevalent in product development: "Let's please stop using 'your/my mom' as a proxy for the technologically illiterate. Half the moms I know are designing apps and shipping code" (Lloyd, 2017).

This isn't on the order of the sexist passes Setrakian had to deal with. Nonetheless, these comments, like the "hey gents" emails Minkoff described, are the tiresome reminders that men are indeed in charge. They create a difficult choice. Calling out these issues requires expenditure of what Trong referred as a "use of social capital" and what Minkoff described as drawing attention to difference. On the other hand, this type of language merits critique because it perpetuates an assumed position of male dominance in these fields. Going forward, as this startup culture continues to grow in journalism, women in both legacy and non-legacy newsrooms will face an incursion of a tech culture that has been hostile and unwelcoming to women. If the future of journalism involves this kind of wholesale cultural infusion that moves beyond editorial product to company culture, we all have reason to be concerned.

Future outlook

The overall portrait of the future of women in journalism technology tells a mixed story of inclusion and exclusion. The historical trajectory appears encouraging, with the first generation of women data journalists receiving significant respect and having achieved notable success. And women do report feeling welcome, although still outnumbered, as programmer journalism has become normalized into the newsroom. More concerning is the infusion of startup culture throughout journalism. This goes beyond new skills and reflects an orientation and approach that celebrates an organizational culture that has been notoriously hostile to women.

There are also consequences for academics hoping to study the fusion of technology and journalism. In *Interactive Journalism* (2016), I wrote a methods section that ended on a note about gender—an issue that I had not explicitly dealt with, despite the potential relevance to a research question, which looked at the rise of programming in journalism. What I had experienced in my research, particularly early on, was a combination of ego and dismissiveness; many of my male interviewees mocked me for not knowing tech terminology, an attitude present in both in-person interviews and on Twitter. This was at least anecdotally different from how a male collaborator was received. Together with Seth C. Lewis, I wrote three papers (see Lewis & Usher, 2014). and a couple of blog posts about the intersection of technology and journalism on Nieman Journalism Lab. In an effort to promote our work, we tweeted similar content about our efforts. The online responses I received were far more aggressive and critical than Lewis' engagement, with my detractors pointing out my ignorance, rather than offering a useful recommendation or insight. Moreover, the dismissiveness I encountered during in-person interviews with subjects was not a sentiment Lewis encountered talking to some of the same research subjects.

Another cautionary tale emerged when I sent an early set of proofs to a major person in the field. This man found few faults with the analysis in the main text, and saved his critique for the methods section and in particular, the small section in which I addressed gender dynamics. My comment that my sample was more gender balanced than the field as a whole drew a sharp rebuke. I was reminded that women were in charge of both *The New York Times* and *The Washington Post*'s graphics desks (which blend programming and data visualization). It is important not to let the success of a few women at the highest level stand as evidence of overall equal opportunities for women in the field; yet this newsroom leader was quick to defend a critique of gender imbalance with anecdotal evidence of the success of a few stars.

Moreover, women may be more prone to newsroom economic pressures, which work in subtle ways to discriminate against their equal earning power. Derek Willis pointed out that newsrooms simply can't pay the same salaries as a big tech company. If newsrooms are more hospitable to women, that's progress. On the other hand, these newsrooms are also in some way getting a bargain on important skills as a result of this tolerance. Moreover, pressure to produce open source code may have unintended consequences as a whole. Putting code on the GitHub repository is a way for programmers to show skill at coding—and for women, it's a way to challenge any gender-based assumptions that they don't know what they're doing. However, open source labor is generally free, particularly for adaptations and forking off main code. This disadvantages women who are already working during the day and who, at home, disproportionately take on emotional labor. For a woman, working on open source code "for free" means doing additional unpaid labor coding to prove their chops when they are already crunched for time. To encourage women to do this outside of paid employment is exploiting that flexible labor potential and earning power. Moreover, open source communities can be extremely hostile to women (Ford, Smith, Guo, & Parnin, 2016).

Other issues may build over time for scholars pursuing this line of research that may have an impact on women's recognition in the field. Journalism studies often offers opportunities to speak to blended audiences of practitioners and scholars, particularly in Europe, where the regard for the role of research in newsroom innovation can be greater than in the US. Although I was the first scholar to complete and publish a book on this subject, men are invited to give talks on forthcoming books years out from development. Sometimes these colleagues even confide to me they thought I should have been invited, if not instead of them, then along with them; and some of them have responded to invitations by pushing my name forward. This is personal experience of scholarly reception, but there is evidence that women get invited to fewer talks than men. A study across top 50 US universities of invited talks of a cross-discipline sample revealed that men gave twice as many talks as women, even controlling for departmental gender representation (Nittrouer et al., 2018). If male tech-minded journalists are leading newsroom teams or professional associations, or even if men dominate selection committees, women academics may well face even greater challenges to receiving speaking invitations, which may ultimately harm their academic success.

We can all take comfort in the demographic changes within journalism schools that may favor more women entering the STEM side of news. The conversations around gender inequity in the tech industry and in creative industries such as entertainment and journalism have taken on new resonance. Yet journalism has made notably less progress in diversity and representation than it should have. It may now be even getting worse. Between 2009 and 2015, newsrooms saw statistically significant drops in the number of black women, Latinas, and Asian American women (Williams, 2015). Add into this mix a growing recognition that technical skills are important to the future of journalism and a fetishization for the big money startups and their presumably innovative and flexible culture, and the likely trajectory is for women to be marginalized. There is a need to be vigilant, ensuring that questions about the interplay between gender, tech, and the future of journalism receive attention, and when necessary, constructive action.

References

Bell, E. (2014, March 12). Journalism startups aren't a revolution if they're filled with all these white men. *The Guardian*. Retrieved from www.theguardian.com/commentisfree/2014/mar/12/journalism-startups-diversity-ezra-klein-nate-silver

Benton, J. (2017, January 17). This is *The New York Times'* digital path forward. *Nieman Lab.* Retrieved from www.niemanlab.org/2017/01/this-is-the-new-york-times-digital-path-forward/

Boyles, J. L. (2016). The isolation of innovation: Restructuring the digital newsroom through intrapreneurship. *Digital Journalism, 4*(2), 229–246.

Carlson, M., & Usher, N. (2016). News startups as agents of innovation: For-profit digital news startup manifestos as metajournalistic discourse. *Digital Journalism, 4*(5), 563–581.

Coddington, M. (2015). Clarifying journalism's quantitative turn: A typology for evaluating data journalism, computational journalism, and computer-assisted reporting. *Digital Journalism, 3*(3), 331–348.

Coscarelli, J. (2014, April 11). Ezra Klein on Vox's launch, media condescension, and competing with Wikipedia. *New York Magazine.* Retrieved from http://nymag.com/daily/intelligencer/2014/04/ezra-klein-interview-vox-launch.html

Cox, M. (2000). *The development of computer-assisted reporting.* Presentation at the Association for Education in Journalism and Mass Communication.

Duffy, B. E. (2017). *(Not) getting paid to do what you love: Gender, social media, and aspirational work.* New Haven: Yale University Press.

Eadicicco, L. (2016, July 1). Google's diversity efforts still have a long way to go. *Time.* Retrieved from http://time.com/4391031/google-diversity-statistics-2016/

Ensmenger, N. (2015). "Beards, sandals, and other signs of rugged individualism": Masculine culture within the computing professions. *Osiris, 30*(1), 38–65.

Fink, K., & Anderson, C. W. (2015). Data journalism in the United States: Beyond the "usual suspects." *Journalism Studies, 16*(4), 467–481.

Ford, D., Smith, J., Guo, P. J., & Parnin, C. (2016). *Paradise unplugged: Identifying barriers for female participation on stack overflow.* Proceedings of the 2016 24th ACM SIGSOFT International Symposium on Foundations of Software Engineering, ACM, pp. 846–857.

Fowler, S. (2017, February 19). *Reflecting on one very, very strange year at Uber.* Retrieved from www.susanjfowler.com/blog/2017/2/19/reflecting-on-one-very-strange-year-at-uber

Grier, D. A. (2013). *When computers were human.* Princeton: Princeton University Press.

The Hacker Journalist (2011). *Knight news challenge: Interim review—The early winners, 2007–2008.* Miami: The Knight Foundation. Retrieved from http://redubllc.com/knight-news-challenge-interim-review/

Hicks, M. (2017, August 10). What the Google gender "manifesto" really says about Silicon Valley. *The Conversation.* Retrieved from http://theconversation.com/what-the-google-gender-manifesto-really-says-about-silicon-valley-82236

Lewis, S. C., & Usher, N. (2014). Code, collaboration, and the future of journalism: A case study of the hacks/hackers global network. *Digital Journalism, 2*(3), 383–393.

Lloyd, A. (2017, November 8, 9:42 AM). Twitter post. Retrieved from https://twitter.com/alexislloyd/status/928256424047730688

Martin, S. (2017, January 13). Startup funding frenzy cools. *The Wall Street Journal.* Retrieved from www.wsj.com/articles/startup-funding-frenzy-cools-1484310605

McKenzie, H., & Lacy, S. (2013, October 15). Vox's new mega-round puts a bow on content's "Holy Shit" moment. *Pando Daily.* Retrieved from https://pando.com/2013/10/15/voxs-new-mega-round-puts-a-bow-on-contents-holy-shit-moment/

Moses, L. (2015, July 6). The rapid rise of vox media's Melissa Bell: An explainer. *Digiday.* Retrieved from https://digiday.com/media/unusual-talents-vox-medias-melissa-bell

Mundy, L. (2017, April). Why is Silicon Valley so awful to women? *The Atlantic.* Retrieved from www.theatlantic.com/magazine/archive/2017/04/why-is-silicon-valley-so-awful-to-women/517788/

National Science Foundation. *"Field degree: Women—Computer Science." Women, minorities and disabilities in science and engineering.* Retrieved www.nsf.gov/statistics/2017/nsf17310/digest/fod-women/computer-sciences.cfm

Nittrouer, C. L., Hebl, M. R., Ashburn-Nardo, L., Trump-Steele, R. C. E., Lane, D. M., & Valian, V. (2018). Gender disparities in colloquium speakers at top universities. *Proceedings of the National Academy of Sciences, 115*(1), 104–108.

Personal communication, Cheryl Phillips. (2018, January 2).

Personal communication, Meredith Broussard. (2017, December 20).

Personal communication, Mindy McAdams. (2018, January 15).

Personal communication via email, Cindy Royal. (2017, December 30).

Personal communication via email, Elite Truong. (2017, December 22).

Personal communication via email, Derek Willis. (2017, December 16).

Personal communication via email, Heather Bryant. (2017, December 19).

Personal communication via email, Michelle Minkoff. (2017, December 26).

Reagle, J. (2017). Nerd vs. bro: Geek privilege, idiosyncrasy, and triumphalism. *First Monday, 23*(1).

Setrakian, L. (2017, October 27). I'm one of Mark Halperin's accusers: He's part of a bigger problem we need to fix. *The Washington Post.* Retrieved from www.washingtonpost.com/opinions/im-one-of-mark-halperins-accusers-hes-part-of-a-bigger-problem-we-need-to-fix/2017/10/27/a304f5e0-ba65–11e7-be94-fabb0f1e9ffb_story.html?utm_term=.e448088a680f

Steel, E. (2017, December 23). At Vice, cutting-edge media and allegations of old-school sexual harassment. *The New York Times.* Retrieved from www.nytimes.com/2017/12/23/business/media/vice-sexual-harassment.html

Usher, N. (2016). *Interactive journalism: Hackers, data, and code.* Urbana, IL: University of Illinois Press.

Usher, N. (2017). Venture-backed news startups and the field of journalism: Challenges, changes, and consistencies. *Digital Journalism,* 1–18.

Williams, A. T. (2015, July 22). Why aren't there more minority journalists? *Columbia Journalism Review.* Retrieved from www.cjr.org/analysis/minority_journalists_newsrooms.php

Zaraya, V. (2017, March 13). Venture capital's funding gender gap is actually getting worse. *Fortune.* Retrieved from http://fortune.com/2017/03/13/female-founders-venture-capital/

3

WHEN ARAB WOMEN (AND MEN) SPEAK

Struggles of women journalists in a gendered news industry

Jad Melki and Sarah Mallat

Having already documented the continued marginalization of women journalists in Arab countries in our previous research (Melki & Mallat, 2013), this chapter investigates the specific challenges Lebanese journalists face in climbing the corporate ladder. We examine the role of institutionalized prejudice and implicit bias against women leaders in perpetuating a masculine newsroom culture that reinforces a glass ceiling. Lebanese newsrooms are a "boyzone" with a "bloke's club" mentality—a men-centric workplace culture that prioritizes men's values, preferences, and management styles over women's (North, 2014; Ross, 2005). This affects the implementation of official policies on such things as parental leave and childcare assistance, which disproportionately impact on women journalists. We also highlight women's attempts to navigate between the socially divergent roles of professional versus wife/mother and to overcome a double-bind situation. They compete in an androcentric industry while simultaneously confronting patriarchal norms (Walby, 1990) that trivialize women's extradomestic work and tether them disproportionately to household duties (Hitti & Moreno-Walton, 2017).

We build on several years of data collection, including three separate surveys, focus groups and qualitative interviews with Arab journalists and news managers across the news media landscape (Melki & Mallat, 2013, 2014; Palmer & Melki, 2018). The latest study, conducted in 2016–2017 provides the main data for this chapter. We surveyed 308 journalists and undertook in-depth interviews with 25 news managers from major broadcast, print, and online news operations in Lebanon. The survey used a random stratified sampling technique that ensured representation of participants from various levels of the news institutions' hierarchies. It gauged different perceptions and attitudes about career trajectory, workplace practices, newsroom culture, and the challenges of balancing work and personal/familial responsibilities. The qualitative interviews sought news managers' accounts about the circumstances, reactions, and repercussions of professional advancement in the news industry and how this differs between men and women.

Although the empirical data focuses on Lebanon, many findings apply more generally to the Arab region, especially since many participants work at multiple Arab news outlets. Lebanon differs significantly from most Arab countries, particularly in its free press, pluralistic political culture, and liberal employment regulations. Nevertheless, the country's diverse socioeconomic, demographic, and cultural mix intersects with most Arab societies. In addition, Lebanon offers a best-case scenario for women journalists in the Arab news industry given its comparatively advanced state of social and political liberties and civil rights. The chapter concludes with a discussion of the theories used in our research. Although they are grounded Western concepts, we find them to be largely applicable to Lebanon and some Arab societies, albeit differing in degree from one Arab state to another.

Journalism, gender, and glass ceilings

Lebanon's media landscape remains the most open, free, and diverse in the Arab region, with a wide variety of local, regional, and international news outlets and journalists (Al-Najjar, 2011; Global Media Monitoring Project, 2015; Salloukh, Barakat, Al-Habbal, Khattab, & Mikaelian, 2015). It is a complex, pluralistic society and, uniquely in the region, it has no official religion. Instead, it has 18 officially recognized religious sects (known as "confessions"), each of which has corresponding ethno-sectarian political representatives in Parliament who govern the country and control affiliated and mostly partisan media outlets (El-Richani, 2016). Gendered social norms and employment opportunities are also liberal relative to the rest of the region; women's workforce participation is higher than most neighboring Arab countries, except oil-rich Gulf states, where the higher percentage comes mainly from women who are migrants (World Bank, 2017; Young, 2016). In addition, Lebanon's robust women's rights movement has achieved significant gains in the past two decades, especially in the area of domestic and gender-based violence (Salameh, 2014). Nevertheless, deep-seated patriarchal attitudes impede women from reaching high-level posts, and men outnumber women by a three-to-one ratio in the labor force (World Economic Forum, 2015). Women's political representation has consistently remained low despite the enfranchisement of women in 1953. Women represent 9 percent of legislators and senior officials in government. They occupy 3.2 percent of Parliament (the legislative branch) and 4.5 percent of the cabinet of ministers (executive branch) ("Patriarchy and Sectarianism," 2017). No legal framework or professional code of conduct exists that addresses gendered practices in the workplace (Khalaf, 2010).

Within this paradoxical environment women journalists struggle against a 2:1 gender gap, pay inequity, and other discriminatory practices in the workplace—including rampant sexual harassment and gender discrimination—that prove hostile to their professional advancement (Melki & Mallat, 2014). Yet, since women are largely excluded from the highest positions within the media, they have little influence on policymaking that could lead to greater gender equality. Lebanese media continue to echo "patriarchal discourse" (Civil Society Knowledge Center,

2017, para. 38), reflecting the global status quo. The agenda-setting influence of news media created by men, for men, further exacerbates the situation; the persistent privileging of men's voices over women's contributes to the ongoing secondary status of women as citizens (Ross & Carter, 2011, p. 1148). Around the world, women lack proportional representation in the majority of newsrooms and are severely underrepresented at the levels of senior management and ownership (Byerly, 2011; Lennon, 2013). Based on research in 114 countries, including Lebanon, the Global Media Monitoring Project's most recent report (2015) concluded that progress towards gender equality in the news media has effectively ground to a halt worldwide.

The Lebanese news media landscape is no exception. While women comprise more than three-quarters of journalism students in the country, they account for less than one-third of the workforce, with the greatest disparity at top-level management (Byerly, 2011; Melki, 2009). A vast majority of women experience gender discrimination and sexual harassment at some point in their journalism careers; one in ten have considered quitting their jobs due to gender discrimination or sexual harassment (Melki & Mallat, 2014). Such conditions persist now, particularly given that newsroom's gender policies do not show support for gender equality and few organizations have policies on sexual harassment. There are no explicit stipulations on gender equality in the Lebanese Press Syndicate's code of professional conduct nor in Lebanese labor laws and the constitution (Gatten, 2012). These deficiencies compound the overall neglect of the journalism industry in fostering gender-neutral newsrooms and empowering women to climb the corporate ladder.

The stubborn persistence of the glass ceiling across various industries in the corporate world defies country borders, political systems, and cultural contexts. Particularly salient in the news industry, it segregates women into low-paying, entry level jobs and discourages them from advancing up the corporate hierarchy (Byerly, 2011; Steiner, 2014). With a few exceptions, women remain confined to low-level positions, trapped by "sticky floors beneath glass ceilings that bar their access to higher status and higher paying positions" (Bruckmüller, Ryan, Haslam, & Peters, 2013; Cohen, 2001, p. 278). Across all levels of the corporate news hierarchy they have not achieved pay parity and are more likely to leave journalism to pursue other careers or to become primary caregivers.

Promotions and pay and family connections

Given the legally disenabling climate, laissez-faire corporate culture, rampant gender discrimination and sexual harassment, and stubbornly patriarchal social norms, it is not surprising that women journalists in Lebanon experience these obstacles on a more magnified scale. Our 2016–2017 survey confirmed this notion: 95 percent of women occupied low to middle-range ranks in the corporate news hierarchy compared to 88 percent of men, while men (12%) significantly outpaced women (5%) at the higher ranks. Similarly, men were more likely to manage other journalists: 22 percent of men and 12 percent of women managed between one and five employees, and 24 percent of men and 15 percent of women managed six or more employees. A parallel gap in income emerged: 32 percent of men and 48 percent of women made $1,000 or less per month, while 56 percent of men and 47 percent of women made $1,001 to $3,000 per month, and 12 percent of men compared to 6 percent of women made more than $3,000 per month.

Moreover, on every level, men's income correlated more strongly than women's with other variables, including age, education, experience, seniority, and number of employees managed. In other words, women do not experience equal benefits as men in proportion to their professional investment. Correlation tests between these variables and the seniority variable also reveal the same trend. These results point to two mechanisms working in tandem. On one hand, despite having higher qualifications, educational attainment, and managerial experience, a significant number of women are denied the seniority and pay levels they deserve. On the other hand, this also implies that women who occupy senior positions with high incomes may have achieved such status through nepotism and *wasta* (Arabic for connections). Interviews corroborate our previous finding that the few women in the highest echelons of corporate news are there due to familial relationship with men owners (Melki & Mallat, p. 2014); their positions ultimately uphold the industry's patriarchal interests, rather than challenging them.

Describing the start of her career trajectory in the early 1990s, the head of operations at a major Lebanese TV station laments: "Knowing Lebanon, you know that you have to know someone to support you to get into the journalism business." Many women journalists we interviewed matter-of-factly echoed this view, categorizing nepotism and *wasta* as quintessential characteristics of the Lebanese news industry. Referring more specifically to the gendered aspect of promotion, an editor-in-chief of an online news outlet emphasizes: "I don't know any woman who got a managerial or chief position in the media in Lebanon without a family connection." According to her, part of the problem lies with persistent implicit gender biases: "Being a woman is always stigmatized. You have to prove yourself, make double or triple the effort to show your higher ups that you have the same capabilities or deserve the same salaries [as men]." She describes how being both a woman and Lebanese (as opposed to a foreigner) adds another layer to the underestimation of her capabilities:

> The managers back then [in 2008] didn't take me seriously; the fact that I had more experience [than the foreign reporters] or could speak Arabic didn't really matter to them. I had to fight to get political stories. The 20-year-old American [guy] who had no experience in journalism or the Middle East would get the more complicated political stories solely because of his white male privilege. It took them two years to notice that I was actually qualified to do more.

The glass ceiling for Lebanese women journalists rests at the senior professional level (e.g., senior writers, directors, producers), where women occupy approximately

43 percent of positions (Byerly, 2011). A token number of women occupy senior management, governance, or ownership positions, but even those are largely nepotistic appointments based on family ties (Melki & Mallat, 2014). Many appointments are used to circumvent Lebanese media laws, which prevent one individual from owning more than 10 percent of any television or radio station. Prominent men politicians cum media owners allocate company stocks to their women relatives, effectively maintaining majority control of the company.

This situation makes it more challenging for young women to climb journalism's career ladder, particularly in the face of a macho newsroom culture and aggressive competition, compounded by the uncertainty and fluctuation in the mainstream news industry. One woman, who had worked at several regional news outlets since 2006, describes her experience as the head online editor of a Lebanese television station: management did not give her adequate support; her supervisors and editorial team constantly dismissed her as being too outspoken and pushy. She attributes this treatment to being both a woman and young. She was eventually let go, allegedly because of political pressure in response to her investigative reporting on the country's garbage crisis in mid-2015. She feels that her "ruffling of political feathers was a convenient scapegoat" and it was merely a matter of time before her employer found an excuse to dismiss her. Her executive producer and head of operations, a woman, did little to help her case. In her opinion, this was due to the *Queen Bee* effect. That is, women in positions of authority treat women subordinates more critically, and prevent senior women from supporting other women (Ellemers, 2014). The roots of this effect stem from discriminatory experiences that successful women encounter on their way to the top. In a separate interview, the same executive producer whom the junior journalist accuses of harsh and unfair treatment reports facing sexual harassment and gender discrimination during her own career. This may point to an unconscious attitude among senior women journalists along the lines of: *if I had to struggle to get here, so should you.*

Another interviewee's experiences with multiple women managers at various Arab news outlets corroborates this Queen Bee phenomenon:

> When I started at *The Daily Star*, we had a [woman] editor that we used to call 'flavor of the week.' [We would ask each other]: who is she going to make cry this week? And it was only the girls she would pick on. We were much younger [than her]. [Then, at] Dubai TV, the reason I resigned was a woman who would insist on calling me on [my day off]. At al-Arabiya TV, I also left the news and moved to current affairs [because of] a woman. After that, she became a sweetheart! It was a personal thing; she just didn't want me in the news.

This vicious cycle of women holding other women back is another effect of patriarchal work cultures. According to Ellemers (2014, p. 50), "Queen Bee responses emerge as a strategy to cope with gender bias in organizations." Such unsupportive attitudes are not unique to women, but pervade the competitive corporate environment, especially when jobs are scarce and senior positions are limited.

Nevertheless, as the experiences of these women illustrate, the demographic dis-parities in the Lebanese news industry point to a local manifestation of both sticky floors (Booth, Francesconi, & Frank, 2003) and glass ceilings.

Many organizational decision-makers, particularly older men, cling to the view that women are unsuited for leadership and do not make good managers. Our survey shows that although the vast majority of men and women (71% versus 76%) believe both genders are equally effective decision-makers, significantly more men than women (26% versus 14%) believe men are more effective decision-makers. Additionally, more women than men (49% versus 35%) believe men can advance into positions of authority more easily; 60 percent of men versus 47 percent of women believe both genders have equal opportunity to advance into such posi-tions. Very few men (5%) and women (4%) believe it is easier for women to do this. Similar trends emerge in relation to promotion and pay raise.

The woman directing Lebanon's National News Agency (NNA) explained that when her appointment as director was announced, "one very senior male colleague expressed his disagreement . . . [because] 'this position needs a man.'" The Minister of Information defended his decision, replying that he was informing, not asking for permission. The NNA director scoffs that such attitudes remain prevalent and counters that "women actually make better managers than men, because they are used to juggling multiple tasks, switching gears at a moment's notice, and managing crises big and small." A man manager at another news station agrees that women "are easier to work with. They are more diplomatic and not so quick to get angry or frustrated." Yet, he would prefer more men in the newsroom because he feels they can handle more pressure: "They can travel at any moment and don't have the demands of home to keep up with."

Leaky pipelines

Such contradictory attitudes hint at another prevalent trend: Women are often pushed out of the news industry via *leaky pipelines* (Henningsen & Højgaard, 2006), particularly if they decide to marry and have children—the paramount goal for many women in the Middle East (Karam & Afiouni, 2016). Although these atti-tudes stem from deeply engrained socio-cultural norms, they are exacerbated by organizational structures that do not support or encourage women who attempt to engage simultaneously in professional advancement and marriage/motherhood.

Many Lebanese women journalists leave the profession early or opt for career tracks that effectively remove them from the competition and preclude them from advancing into higher managerial positions. Most women journalists are pre-dominantly young, unmarried, and childless; the majority have worked for less than a decade as journalists (Melki & Mallat, 2014). In contrast, men, particularly at the managerial level, are older, more likely to be married with children, and report greater career longevity. Our recent survey shows that 65 percent of women compared to 52 percent of men have never been married. In addition, more men (39%) than women (32%) have children. The gap widens further up the managerial hierarchy, and this data does not account for the increased likelihood of married women to drop out of the news industry when they have children.

Because men have historically dominated the journalism industry, the global newsroom culture can be disproportionately hostile to women with family responsibilities (Ross, 2001). Media scholars also argue that journalistic values coincide with and derive from masculine values, and women are socialized into accepting these values (Beam & Di Cicco, 2010). The ideal journalist "is always available" (Robinson, 2005, p. 102). Such dedication, particularly the irregular hours and always being on-call, fundamentally contradicts the idea of work-life balance.

What's more, women entering the news industry are often prevented from advancement from the start, as superiors assume they will scale back their ambitions or quit once they get married and have children. Many journalists note the anxiety surrounding this issue (Melki & Mallat, 2014), especially considering that the current 70-day maternity leave stipulated by Lebanese labor law falls short of the 14-week international standard (Alabaster, 2012). Questions also arise about how many women utilize available maternity leave out of concern that they will be "mommy tracked" (Williams, 2004).

Domestic tethers

Research on *domestic tethers* (Hitti & Moreno-Walton, 2017) highlights the impact of unequal domestic gendered division of labor in perpetuating inequality at work. Women worldwide continue to shoulder the majority of unpaid domestic work, with the Middle East having the highest gender disparity (Gates, 2016). Because work-life balance generally comes at the expense of career advancement, a significant proportion of women opt for part-time employment, reduced work schedules, or extended leave from work. Even women who work full-time, however, feel the impact of domestic tethers on career advancement (Hitti & Moreno-Walton, 2017). When men's and women's home responsibilities compete with their work responsibilities, it is invariably the women's work duties that suffer. They are more likely to sacrifice work and advancement opportunities in favor of household duties. When conflict emerges between spouses due to domestic pressures, women typically prioritize home over work. Men do the opposite, disproportionately advancing men's career advancement.

Our survey corroborates these domestic tethers to extreme extents. Overwhelmingly more women say they are primarily responsible for housework and childcare, while more men relegate such duties to their spouses: 47 percent of women compared to 7 percent of men say they are the primary childcare giver; 40 percent of men compared to 6 percent of women say their spouse is primarily responsible for childcare; 39 percent of women compared to 2 percent of men say they are primarily responsible for housework; and while 43 percent of men say their spouse primarily takes care of household chores, no woman said this.

A few men (9%) and almost one-third of women (31%) say they outsource household duties. This means a significant proportion of women rely on themselves or outside help for housework, while almost all men delegate this work—and the *organization* of outsourcing it—to their spouses. Globally, organizing household management remains overwhelmingly women's purview (Schulte, 2014) and requires significant time and mental energy, regardless of whether the male spouse ends up implementing these chores. These demands distract from other professional and personal tasks and create "mental clutter" (Schulte, 2014), the invisible yet mentally taxing domestic work that women continue to handle alone, even in households where men shoulder significant domestic duties.

Motherhood penalty and fatherhood bonus

Marriage and children have a detrimental effect on women's careers and significantly contribute to the wage gap. In contrast to this *motherhood penalty*, marriage and children have a positive impact on men's careers and income. Our survey confirms this *fatherhood bonus*: married men journalists are more likely than those who are unmarried to be in the higher income brackets. More importantly, married men (45%) are five times more likely than unmarried men (9%) to be in the highest income category; married women (25%) are only 2.5 times more likely than unmarried women (10%) to be so. The opposite is also true: unmarried men (45%) are 2.8 times more likely to be in the lowest income category than married men (16%), while unmarried women (53%) are only 1.4 times more likely than married women (37%) to be so. Although married men and women are more likely than those who are unmarried to occupy senior positions, this is only statistically significant for men ($p = 0.01$), not for women ($p = 0.35$).

Again, these numbers should take into consideration higher attrition by women, especially for married journalists with children. Our interviews included questions about the pressures of domestic life. In comparison to men, more unmarried women in managerial or senior positions say that journalism's career demands prohibit marriage and having a family. One woman who worked at multiple Arab news outlets before becoming the director of Orbit TV, a regional Arab television network, stated:

> I am not married because no man would accept my work[ing]. Maybe I should have gotten married. Maybe I will regret it in the future, but not now. I am free and happy and able to fully focus on my career. My personality is too strong, and Lebanese men are too weak mentally to accept ambitious and opinionated women.

Another single woman who recently retired elaborates on her 30-year career:

> There was no time for a personal life. Very few men put up with my career. I had to choose between job security or being under someone else's thumb. I had men walk out on me because I was getting too much attention

professionally, or because I needed to work. [In the 1980s], men weren't in the habit of being subservient to women. So, it was a combination of that mentality, and also the fact that I simply didn't have time for relationships.

The married women journalists we interviewed also pointed to the lack of corporate policies and progressive thinking supporting working mothers as a way of prohibiting women journalists from having a work-life balance. In particular, married women in upper-management positions feel greater pressure than men to juggle professional duties and family commitments. The majority of surveyed men and women agree it is easier for men to return to work after the birth of a child and to balance family life and work. Furthermore, the majority of men and most women (52% versus 47%) believe it is easier for men to have a family and climb the corporate ladder. While a significant proportion of men and women (44% vs 41%) feel it is equally easy for both men and women to do so, only 12 percent of women and 4 percent of men believe it is easier for women. The editor-in-chief of a leading French-language business magazine refers to this discrepancy as the "culpabilization of the working mother":

> When you have to think about your children, you can't be fully dedicated to your job, and vice versa. I constantly have to restrain myself because I could work non-stop, but then I would get negative backlash about how I'm neglecting my children and my family.

Another veteran journalist with over 20 years of experience at local and regional print, television, and online news outlets highlights the gendered divide in relation to work-life balance, one that men do not necessarily have to grapple with on a daily basis:

> The phrase: 'the problem is that you're a mom' has been repeated to me so many times, and it wasn't fair. A few years later, one of the guys who told me this was telling me how he couldn't show up to the office for weeks because his mother was sick. And I told him: you know the beauty of it, nobody tells you the problem is that you're a son. You're made to feel that it's a problem to have children, and it shouldn't be. But for men, it's: oh, he's so supportive of his wife, he takes care of his family.

Rather than seeing marriage and childrearing as obstacles to professional development, men news managers emphasize the positive and supportive role of their spouses as domestic caretakers and primary caregivers. They acknowledge this traditionally gendered division of roles gives them greater leeway to focus on their careers. However, many men news managers concomitantly admit their commitment to their careers took a toll on their personal lives. Several lament they are not as present in their children's lives as they would like to be. Others allude to marital tension as a result of working weekends and odd hours. The general manager of a local news radio station explains:

> It made a huge difference that my wife is a teacher because her work hours meant that she was able to take care of the kids. I wasn't able to spend enough time with them when they were growing up, not nearly as much as I wanted.

The CEO of Lebanon's public television station agrees:

> My career success kept me away from my daughters. The feeling of guilt at being away so often, missing out on so much of my daughters' childhoods, is so strong that I [compensate by giving] them whatever they need or want [financially].

Echoing similar sentiments, the director of news and political programming at a competing, private television station admits that he feels guilty for missing out so much of his kids' childhood: "My wife raised our daughter mostly on her own. I'm trying to make up for it now, but I didn't really have any other choice at the time. I had to support my family." Likewise, the regional photography manager for the leading French newswire in the region and a veteran conflict photojournalist, recounts how the demands of journalism—particularly magnified for war reporters—have taken their toll on his personal life:

> My first marriage didn't affect my career choices or development; on the contrary, my career choices affected the marriage. [My ex-wife] wanted to [expand] her career in Cyprus, but she couldn't, and that affected the whole relationship because my career was overshadowing hers. My work also affected my daughter. My absence [in her life] was mainly due to the divorce, but my work did affect her. Once she told me: 'I don't want you to go there. I don't want you to get killed.' She was nine. . . . It was like a huge slap in the face.

Even married men news managers who do not have any children feel the strain of trying to maintain work-life balance. The managing editor of one of the leading Lebanese dailies notes:

> [My wife and I] don't spend much time together. I leave for work early in the morning and by the time I get home she is already asleep. I only take Saturdays off but even then, I find myself working when I should be spending downtime with her. . . . My life now is totally dedicated to my work. We don't have kids yet. We don't have time.

Clearly, Lebanese journalists of both genders recognize that the inherent demands of the industry lead to discord between their professional and personal lives. While the effects are more significant for women's careers, men's testimonies also highlight how hyper-masculine newsroom norms resulting from internalized patriarchal structures negatively affect men and women. Contrary to assumptions that men-dominated newsrooms benefit men by prioritizing men's needs (Stelter, 2002), recent studies suggest that men increasingly value greater work-life balance, particularly in collectivist Arab cultures that place a high value on the family. According to a recent survey, the overwhelming majority of Lebanese men (83%) and women (84%) support parental leave for fathers (El Feki, Heilman, & Barker, 2017). This points to a growing societal shift in perceptions: work-life balance continues to evolve from solely a women's issue into an increasingly broader corporate and social issue relevant to all. Perhaps it could be in Lebanese and Arab news outlets' best interest to adopt a more "feminized" organizational culture, one that places increased value on teamwork, collaboration, and work-life balance (Everbach, 2006). Admittedly, such realizations, even by upper management, may not necessarily translate into greater pay parity or equitable career mobility for women without broader legal reform.

The literature on work-life balance and family-friendly workplace policies suggests that as long as women are the only ones taking parental leave, both job discrimination and pressure on women to opt out of careers will only increase (Bewley, Ebel, & Forth, 2016). While seemingly contrary to corporate interests, policies that promote parental leave for all employees may actually help companies' bottom lines by preventing attrition and lowering turnover rates. Replacing an employee costs up to 20 percent more than instituting flexible and family-friendly workplace policies (Boushey & Glynn, 2012). This is especially true for the news industry, which increasingly requires advanced degrees and specialized training.

Varying impact of cultural norms on women journalists in Lebanese, Arab, and Western newsrooms

Our study draws on gender theories rooted in Western societies—such as the glass ceiling, leaky pipelines, sticky floors, and the Queen Bee. In our view, they are useful for examining the largely Lebanese news industry, albeit with varying degrees of significance. Lebanese women journalists echo the experiences of their Western counterparts, despite differences in political, economic, legal, and particularly cultural contexts. Partial explanation for these similarities lies in the parallel structures of modern corporate news institutions and standard processes and demands of the news industry worldwide. Such consistencies also stem from certain shared characteristics among professional journalists regardless of nationality: they are ambitious, passionate, idealistic, and dedicated to the profession's underlying ethos. Similarly, research on the dynamics of business entrepreneurship, which attracts comparably ambitious personalities, confirms the notion that women entrepreneurs in Western societies and the Arab region share many traits and face similar obstacles (Schroeder, 2013). Yet it is imperative to consider the degrees to which socio-cultural obstacles differ across nations and social milieus.

Our interviews confirm that Lebanese women journalists are fiercely passionate about their profession and ready to make personal sacrifices to advance their careers. However, such attitudes represent both defiance and a culture clash that many bulwarks of the rigid Arab patriarchy are not ready to reckon with and even consider a threat to the moral (i.e., highly gender normative) fabric of society. Even in 2018, social norms dictate that if a Lebanese woman *must* work outside of the home, she should opt for flexible and less demanding employment that will not distract from her primary domestic roles. As such, many segments of society do not consider journalism a suitable or appropriate profession for women. Reflecting this reality, many women studying journalism repeatedly struggle against their parents' strong objections to this college major. What sets the journalism profession in Lebanon apart from its Western counterparts is that it tends to disproportionately attract empowered, independent women with strong career ambitions whom have already overcome many cultural obstacles and defied traditional gender roles and restrictions.

As such, the main differences between what Western and Lebanese women journalists face lies squarely in the cultural sphere, particularly around issues of domestic tethers and patriarchal newsroom culture. Many Western societies have made major progress toward closing the gender gap in the workplace, but have failed at balancing unpaid domestic work, which continues to disproportionately fall on women. This remains an even more daunting problem in Lebanon. Although the majority of Lebanese society assumes that women share the burden of breadwinning and have a professional career of their own, significant conservative sectors continue to frown upon women entering historically men-dominant professions—journalism being one of them. This discourages many women from entering the profession, curtails ambitions of career development, and limits access to particularly challenging journalistic specialties or advancement into demanding managerial positions. More importantly, most Lebanese men continue to see themselves as the main financial providers in the family. A woman's potential to professionally outperform her spouse, either financially or in terms of success, is considered a sign of emasculation and remains a potent stigma in most conservative (and even some liberal) families. While the idea of men as primary caregivers has become increasingly popular in some Western cultures, it remains alien to Lebanon. This reflects the persistent view of women as primary—if not sole—caregivers and consequently works against the idea of the equal division of domestic burdens.

When comparing Lebanon to the Arab region, we should read these concepts within the context of shifting social norms and ideologies that continue to ebb and flow. We cannot overgeneralize our conclusions. Moreover, to offer solutions requires conducting more localized research that accounts for variations in Arab media systems and national specificities, as well as high unemployment rates, fragile economies, unstable politics, rise of fundamentalist groups, and widespread corruption and nepotism that plague the region. What we *can* argue is that our findings apply to many parts of the Arab region, but with varying degrees.

Certain structural factors make Lebanon different from many Arab countries, including its democratic system, pluralistic political culture, liberal employment regulations, free press, and comparatively advanced state of political liberties and civil rights. These cultural factors have even greater impacts in other Arab countries, with nation-specific structural factors offering localized explanations for differences. The patriarchal norms, family pressures, and domestic tethers, for instance, might play a more significant role in conservative Arab societies, while presenting less of a challenge for Arab women working outside their countries, especially in the UAE, Qatar, and Bahrain, where expatriates enjoy more personal freedoms and operate far away from the peering eyes of their families and societies (Mellor, 2013). The masculine newsroom culture and rampant gender discrimination, we suspect, would have greater significance in many Arab outlets compared to Lebanese newsrooms. For example, Saudi Arabia's ultra-conservative employment policies forbid women from most occupations and impose a strict gender segregation system; these eliminate any chance for women journalists to compete with men (Kurdi, 2014). Nonetheless, women working in pan-Arab newsrooms, particularly satellite TV news, may find relative advantages over men in certain on-camera roles, especially given the high demand for "pretty" women reporters and anchors (Mellor, 2013).

This does not transfer to other news specialisms, such as war correspondents, where the patriarchal mentality demands that institutions protect their seemingly vulnerable women journalists (Palmer & Melki, 2018). Editors often reject women journalists' requests to cover conflict, claiming they do not want to bear responsibility if something happens to them. Simultaneously, many women journalists who cover conflict counter such restrictions with other advantages over men, including their ability to enter conservative homes, interview women, and access powerful men who may perceive a woman journalist as less threatening (Palmer & Melki, 2018). In a sense, the war and conflict plaguing the Arab region has offered some advancement opportunities for ambitious Arab women journalists, but also many problems and obstacles. Women's rights suffer dramatically during wars and political instability, where central governments collapse or weaken, and tribal subcultures fill the political vacuum, such as in Iraq, Syria, Yemen, and Libya, but also in other countries that experienced the "Arab Spring." Moreover, violence against women—not only in war zones but generally in public spaces and popular protests—brings increased risks for women journalists in many Arab countries. Rampant sexual harassment in countries such as Egypt, Iraq, and Jordan likely plays a bigger role than in Lebanon (Rezaian, 2017). Moreover, Arab women journalists covering controversial political issues are more vulnerable than men to campaigns of shame, especially in cultures that attach a high value to women's honor and morality. "Accusations of sexual misconduct, designed to humiliate, are often a tool of repression used [sic] to silence critical journalists. They are not limited to women, but such allegations can be dangerous and socially detrimental for a woman living in a conservative Muslim society" (Rezaian, 2017, p. 6).

Lebanese media are more commercial and driven by advertising than most local news operations in the Arab region, which tend to be government-owned or subsidized. Nepotism and corruption play a bigger role than merit in the latter institutions. While men and women can benefit from such practices, corruption invariably serves men in conservative patriarchal societies. Finally, many Arab countries offer much narrower press freedoms than Lebanon. This may also impact Arab women journalists disproportionately, at least in their ability to report on gender discrimination and women's rights issues in their countries. Such structural factors exacerbate the effects of the glass ceiling, leaky pipelines, and sticky floors and create intensely magnified gendered environments promoting further queen bee behaviors by the few women journalists in positions of power, rather than providing loci for empowering other women journalists. The situation renders discriminatory practices throughout each country invisible to society and outside of political discourse, since the news media get blocked from seriously discussing them.

Middle Eastern news media occupy a privileged position for discussion, negotiation, and challenging of patriarchal gender norms that ultimately harm everyone. The Lebanese news industry could lead by example in addressing gender inequity in the private and public spheres, by promoting increased dialogue on gender roles, enacting internal corporate policies discouraging sexism and leveling the playing field, and supporting legislative reforms recognizing women's basic human rights as equal workers and citizens. Such a shift would likewise necessitate a parallel industry-wide reckoning with gender inequity and imbalance *within* the profession. This is long overdue and would have positive effects for both journalists and the news media.

References

Alabaster, O. (2012, May 1). 10-week maternity leave too short: Mothers. *The Daily Star*. Retrieved from www.dailystar.com.lb/News/Local-News/2012/May-01/171995-10-week-maternity-leave-too-short-mothers.ashx

Al-Najjar, A. (2011). Contesting patriotism and global journalism ethics in Arab journalism. *Journalism Studies, 12*(6), 747–756.

Beam, R. A., & Di Cicco, D. T. (2010). When women run the newsroom: Management change, gender, and the news. *Journalism and Mass Communication Quarterly, 87*(2), 393–411.

Bewley, H., Ebel, M., & Forth, J. (2016). *Estimating the financial costs of pregnancy and maternity-related discrimination and disadvantage*. Manchester: Equality and Human Rights Commission.

Booth, A. L., Francesconi, M., & Frank, J. (2003). A sticky floors model of promotion, pay, and gender. *European Economic Review, 47*(2), 295–322.

Boushey, H., & Glynn, S. J. (2012). There are significant business costs to replacing employees. *Center for American Progress, 16*.

Bruckmüller, S., Ryan, M. K., Haslam, A., & Peters, K. (2013). Ceilings, cliffs, and labyrinths: Exploring metaphors for workplace gender discrimination. In M. K. Ryan & N. R. Branscombe (Eds.), *The SAGE handbook of gender and psychology* (pp. 450–463). London: Sage Publications.

Byerly, C. (Ed.). (2011). *The global report on the status of women in news media*. Washington, DC: International Women's Media Foundation. Retrieved from www.iwmf.org/our-research/global-report/

Civil Society Knowledge Center. (2017). *Women's achievements in Lebanon: A historical overview of women's achievements in Lebanon*. Beirut, Lebanon: Lebanon Support. Retrieved from http://civilsociety-centre.org/gen/women-movements-timeline/4939

Cohen, T. F. (2001). *Men and masculinity: A text reader.* New York, NY: Brooks, Cole.

El Feki, S., Heilman, B., & Barker, G. (Eds.). (2017). *Understanding masculinities: Results from the international men and gender equality survey.* Cairo and Washington, DC: UN Women and Promundo-US.

Ellemers, N. (2014). Women at work: How organizational features impact career development. *Policy Insights from the Behavioral and Brain Sciences, 1*(1), 46–54.

El-Richani, S. (2016). *The Lebanese media: Anatomy of a system in perpetual crisis.* Oxford: Palgrave Macmillan.

Everbach, T. (2006). The culture of a women-led newspaper: An ethnographic study of the *Sarasota Herald-Tribune. Journalism and Mass Communication Quarterly, 83*(3), 477–493.

Gates, M. (2016). *More time.* Gatesnotes 2016 Annual Newsletter. Retrieved from www.gatesnotes.com/2016-Annual-Letter#ALChapter3/

Gatten, E. (2012, May 8). Sexual harassment rife in workplaces. *The Daily Star.* Retrieved from www.dailystar.com.lb/News/Local-News/2012/May-08/172647-sexual-harassment-rife-in-workplaces.ashx#axzz1vbx5Bk7z/

Global Media Monitoring Project. (2015). *Who makes the news?* World Association for Christian Communication. Retrieved from http://cdn.agilitycms.com/who-makes-the-news/Imported/reports_2015/global/gmmp_global_report_en.pdf/

Henningsen, I., & Højgaard, L. (2006). The leaking pipeline [øjebliksbilleder af kønnede in-og eksklusionsprocesser i Akademia]. *Dansk Sociologi, 13*(2), 25–49.

Hitti, E., & Moreno-Walton, L. (2017). The gender gap in medical leadership: Glass ceiling, domestic tethers, or both? *Common Sense, 24*(3), 26–27. Retrieved from www.aaem.org/publications/common-sense/

Karam, C. M., & Afiouni, F. (2016). Institutional logics of patriarchy and the legitimacy of women not engaging in paid work. *Academy of Management Proceedings, 1,* 12500.

Khalaf, M. C. (2010). Lebanon. In S. Kelly & J. Breslin (Eds.), *Women's rights in the Middle East and North Africa: Progress amid resistance* (pp. 249–282). New York, NY: Freedom House.

Kurdi, E. (2014). *Women in the Saudi press* (Doctoral Dissertation), Cardiff University.

Lennon, T. (2013). *Benchmarking women's leadership in the United States.* Denver, CO: University of Denver Women's College.

Melki, J. (2009). Journalism and media studies in Lebanon. *Journalism Studies, 10*(5), 672–690.

Melki, J., & Mallat, S. (2013). Lebanon: Women struggle for gender equality and harassment-free newsrooms. In C. Byerly (Ed.), *Palgrave international handbook on women and journalism* (pp. 432–450). New York, NY: Palgrave Macmillan.

Melki, J., & Mallat, S. (2014). Block her entry, keep her down, and push her out: Gender discrimination and women journalists in the Arab world. *Journalism Studies, 17*(1), 57–79.

Mellor, N. (2013). Gender boundaries inside pan-Arab newsrooms. *Journal of Gender Studies, 22*(1), 79–91.

North, L. (2014). Still a bloke's club: The motherhood dilemma in journalism. *Journalism, 17*(3), 315–330.

Palmer, L., & Melki, J. (2018). Shape shifting in the conflict zone: The strategic performance of gender in war reporting. *Journalism Studies, 19*(1), 126–142.

Patriarchy and sectarianism: A gendered trap: Baseline of women in politics: The case of Lebanon. (2017). *Hivos.* Retrieved from https://mena.hivos.org/news/baseline-study-women-lebanese-politics/

Rezaian, Y. (2017). How women journalists are silenced in a man's world: The double-edged sword of reporting from Muslim countries. *Shorenstein Center on Media, Politics and Public Policy.* Retrieved from https://shorensteincenter.org/women-journalists-muslim-countries-yeganeh-rezaian/

Robinson, G. J. (2005). *Gender, journalism and equity: Canadian, U.S., and European perspectives.* Cresskill, NJ: Hampton Press.

Ross, K. (2001). Women at work: Journalism as en-gendered practice. *Journalism Studies, 2*(4), 531–544.

Ross, K. (2005). Women in the boyzone. In S. Allan (Ed.), *Journalism: Critical issues* (pp. 287–298). Maidenhead: Open University Press.

Ross, K., & Carter, C. (2011). Women and news: A long and winding road. *Media, Culture and Society, 33*(8), 1148–1165.

Salameh, R. (2014). *Gender politics in Lebanon and the limits of legal reformation.* Civil Society Knowledge Center, Lebanon Report. Retrieved from http://cskc.daleel-madani.org/paper/gender-politics-lebanon-and-limits-legal-reformism-en-ar/

Salloukh, B., Barakat, R., Al-Habbal, J. S., Khattab, L. W., & Mikaelian, S. (2015). *Politics of sectarianism in postwar Lebanon.* Chicago, IL: Pluto Press.

Schulte, B. (2014). *Overwhelmed: Work, love, and play when no one has the time* (Kindle ed.). New York, NY: Sarah Crichton Books.

Schroeder, C. M. (2013). *Startup rising* (Kindle ed.). New York, NY: Palgrave Macmillan.

Steiner, L. (2014). Feminist media theory. In R. S. Fortner & P. Mark Fackler (Eds.), *The handbook of media and mass communication theory* (pp. 359–379). Malden, MA: Wiley-Blackwell.

Stelter, N. Z. (2002). Gender differences in leadership: Current social issues and future organizational implications. *The Journal of Leadership Studies, 8*(4), 88–99.

Walby, S. (1990). *Theorizing patriarchy.* Oxford: Basil Blackwell.

Williams, J. C. (2004). The maternal wall. *Harvard Business Review.* Retrieved from https://hbr.org/2004/10/the-maternal-wall/

World Bank. (2017). *Labor force participation rate, female (% of female population ages 15+) (modeled ILO estimate).* Retrieved from https://data.worldbank.org/indicator/SL.TLF.CACT.FE.ZS/

World Economic Forum. (2015). Global gender gap report. *World Economic Forum.* Retrieved from http://reports.weforum.org/global-gender-gap-report-2015/economies/#economy=LB/

Young, K. E. (2016). *Women's labor force participation across the GCC.* The Arab Gulf States Institute in Washington. Retrieved from www.agsiw.org/wp-content/uploads/2016/12/Young_Womens-Labor_ONLINE-2.pdf/

4

SEEKING WOMEN'S EXPERTISE IN THE UK BROADCAST NEWS MEDIA

Suzanne Franks and Lis Howell

The status of women in UK broadcasting, as well as in many other countries, raises many important questions about gender-based discrimination in the news (Ross & Carter, 2011). This chapter looks at the disproportionate use of male over female experts in flagship news programs. Surveys administered by postgraduate students from the journalism department at City University, London, show that in 2013 male experts used as interviewees on flagship news programs outnumbered women experts by 4.4 to 1. By 2016 that ratio had narrowed to 3 to 1. Statistics show, however, that the overall ratio of UK experts at that time was 2.5 men to women, at senior levels in law, academia, politics, and as expert court witnesses (Howell & Singer, 2016). So how is it that broadcasters discriminate against women in this way when seeking expert contributors?

Feminist news research shows that one of the ways in which such discrimination is manifest is related to the limited presence and visibility of women in senior positions, both on and off air. In the early years of broadcasting in the UK, women were barely visible in any prominent role. They were neither seen nor heard in senior roles on and off screen, and were largely limited to cosmetic and supporting roles to men. Notably, also, not until the 1970s were "women's voices" deemed "acceptable" to read and present mainstream television news bulletins (Franks, 2011; Beard, 2017). A global process of gradual change occurred in subsequent years, whereby more women were able to rise into editorial and management positions in news organizations (IWMF, 2015).

A similar and contentious debate concerns onscreen ageism. Why are male presenters able to age gracefully, whereas women after a certain age disappear completely? (Moran, 2012). In 2007, Women in Journalism, a networking and campaigning organization for women journalists in the UK, published a report "The Lady Vanishes at 45" (Campbell, 2007), which addresses this question and calls for an end to such age discrimination. Additionally, a number of high-profile women over the years have used their experience to challenge this stereotype and argued for the need for women on screen to represent the wider age profile of the population (Craft, 1988; Revoir, 2012; Plunkett, 2011; BBC, 2011). The preference for younger women on screen particularly affects women experts, as expertise, authority, and seniority are usually associated with age.

A related field of feminist journalism research has focused on both women's presence as reporters in relation to the representation of women in the news and use of women as expert sources. For instance, the most comprehensive, longitudinal analysis of the gender balance of news reporting is the Global Media Monitoring Project (GMMP), which originated with the 1995 UN Conference on Women held in Beijing (*WACC*). This survey is hosted by the portal "Who Makes the News," an education and campaigning resource that focuses upon the gender composition of the news media from across the world. Every five years the GMMP analyzes select indicators of gender in the news media, including the gender of those involved in the content and production of news stories, including newsreaders, presenters, and journalists; the most recent survey in 2015 offered comparisons from 114 countries on who featured in radio, television, newspaper, and online news. What is striking is the slow rate of change over the years of the project. In 2000 the GMMP found that only 21 percent of news subjects—those who are interviewed and whom the news is about—were women. (*Global Media Monitoring Project*, 2000) The GMMP 2015 report noted that that women make up only 24 percent of the persons heard, read about, or seen in newspaper, television, and radio news, exactly the same percentage as in 2010. Women are about twice as likely, however, to be featured as victims in news stories and they are more likely to be shown in a newspaper photograph. When they do feature in the news they are more likely to be identified by their family status.

The gender gap also varies depending on the topic of the news: "The gender gap is narrowest in stories on science and health, the major topic of lowest importance on the news agenda occupying only 8 percent of the overall news space; women make up 35 percent of the people in news under this topic, in contrast to only 16 percent in political news stories. The gap is widest in news about politics and government in which women are only 16 percent of the people in the stories." The report noted that women were three percentage points less visible in political news than they had been five years earlier in 2010.

Additionally, the 2015 report confirms not only that more men than women feature in the news, but also that they are featured in different ways (Blumell, 2017): women are more likely to be present in news stories as victims, celebrities, or silent fashion icons. Men are more likely to feature as actors and agents in news stories. The significance of this disparity is that women are frequently shown as case studies or victims rather than experts. To some extent this is a function of wider matters of societal roles, which is well beyond the scope of individual reporters who produce news stories. Given current definitions of newsworthiness, if men are doing more newsworthy things and occupying a greater proportion of newsworthy roles then they are likely to feature more prominently in news reports. However, the role of expertise and punditry in news stories is far more dependent, we argue, upon the often deliberate choices exercised by production teams, where producers make conscious choices about whom to invite as experts. So, whilst the Pope or President or prominent CEO might be a man—and the news story will have to incorporate this—reporters make choices about which individuals to interview for comments on what is going on. This disparity in who features in the news is the key issue behind these studies about the use of female expertise. The crucial point is that the choice of who should *comment* on the news and offer background expertise to the viewers is very much within the control and ambit of news producers.

The particular focus of this chapter is the extent to which women are being selected and invited to speak and to contribute expertise on air within broadcast news items. This issue is important because, as this research demonstrates, more women are available and able to be used as experts on flagship news programs than journalists choose to use. To support this claim, we draw upon data from a series of quantitative analyses we carried out with student researchers in the Department of Journalism, City University, London over several years that examined gender balance in UK broadcast news, focusing on who is commenting and contributing expertise in news and current affairs.

Hearing the disparities

A key moment in the trajectory of concern about gender balance regarding the use of news experts in the UK was the high-profile BBC Radio 4 morning radio show the *Today* program. Scholars typically see this as *the* agenda setting national news program of record (Donovan, 2013); it is required listening of the political elites in the UK. In October 2012, for a segment on breast cancer, the presenter John Humphreys interviewed two male scientists but *no* women. Humphreys even asked one of the men what he would do, were he a woman offered breast screening. At that time, all but one of the program's presenters were men. In the same week a male presenter had discussed teenage pregnancy with exclusively male interviewees (Franks, 2013).

Two years previously, in an item that aired on the *Today* program, Professor Lis Howell had publicly criticized the lack of women interviewed during the 2010 general election. Her remarks were published in *Broadcast Magazine*, a UK trade magazine aimed at industry workers (The Airwaves are not Fair Waves 2010). The radio item that she was criticizing featured a lengthy profile of a marginal electoral constituency, where every representative person interviewed was male. This article piqued the attention of *Broadcast Magazine*'s editor, Lisa Campbell, who asked Howell to continue to look at the ratio of men to women interviewed on the *Today* program, and also other news programs, on the basis of some surveys already done by postgraduate journalism students.

This grew into a monthly opinion piece by Howell in *Broadcast Magazine*, backed up by more survey material collected by students in the Department of Journalism, City University, London. They counted the numbers of women experts used on a variety of UK news programs. This formed the basis of the "Expert Women" campaign initiated by Campbell in *Broadcast Magazine* (Campbell, 2012). The students surveyed five editions of a variety of given news programs in one week in a month—the same week in the same month for all the monitored programs. They counted the number of "experts" interviewed on these programs and logged them by gender. For the survey, the classification of experts included unique achievers in a particular field; people holding important roles in business, government, or society; and commentators used to verify or endorse a story. Broadly, experts were defined as all the people able to speak with authority on a topic, based on more than simply their personal experience. The student monitors also recorded case studies (for example, people used as an example of a particular medical condition or in a particular situation, but not authority figures); they logged the gender of participants in "vox pops"; people who were witnesses; and ordinary people caught up in news events. In addition, the gender of reporters, presenters, and correspondents was also noted.

The study showed, from the frequency with which some experts were used, that as well as having expertise and knowledge, an expert also needed to be someone whom journalists considered interesting or engaging. A study of the use of one bioethicist as a US media source suggested he was called on so often because he "understands news routines, provides pithy quotes, and supports public engagement" (Kruvand, 2012). This tallied with Howell's "Expert Women" survey results, where some experts (predominantly but not exclusively male) were called on repeatedly by broadcasters.

At the time of the 2012 controversial male-only interviews on the *Today* episode about teenage pregnancy and breast cancer, many listeners, including feminist campaigner Caroline Criado Perez, complained to BBC Radio Four's "Feedback" program about the absence of expert women's voices. The City University data provided empirical evidence that women were underrepresented as experts on the *Today* program and other programs in the UK.

The period from March 2012 to October 2013, across the wide variety of programs surveyed, had enough data from four flagship news programs to provide a viable sample. Table 4.1 covers this period expressed as a ratio of male to female experts.

This was an average of 4.4 to 1 men to women appearing as experts in these four mainstream broadcast programs. However the ratio of female expertise in society as demonstrated by the number of senior women in academia, law, politics, or on the lists of expert witnesses used in courts, runs at a rate of 2.5 men to every

TABLE 4.1 Male and female experts on air 2012/13

Program	No. of male experts compared to female
BBC News at 10	3.7–1
ITV News	5–1
Today	3.9–1
Sky News	5–1

TABLE 4.2 Gender of experts on ITV by subject categories July 2013

Subject	No. of male experts compared to female
British politics	10–1
Sport	6–1
International politics	6–1
Foreign news	5–1
Home news	5–1
Entertainment	4–1
Health	2–1

woman (Howell & Singer, 2016) not 4.4 to 1. So by comparison it appeared that broadcasters were underrepresenting the number of women experts in society.

As a subsidiary study, students who were monitoring news output took a measurement of expert sources for three weeks in July 2013 on ITV News only, which was divided not only by gender but also by subject. Table 4.2 reveals some interesting disparities on the presence of women. The most significant gender gap was in the area of domestic UK politics. When the survey was done in 2013, ten times as many British men were interviewed about politics as women. At this time the Cabinet of the UK Government had a ratio of 2.5 men to one woman and the Shadow Cabinet (the opposition) had a ratio of 1 man to 1 woman. So the disparity between women actually involved at a high level in politics, and the women shown on the news as authority figures in politics, was striking. The extent to which politics is a male dominated subject is something that has been explored elsewhere (Ross & Carter, 2011; Ross, Boyle, Carter, & Ging, 2016).

Widening the questions

Alongside this survey, in Fall 2013 Howell conducted 25 in-depth interviews with male and female journalists not taking gender into account—including producers, editors, and reporters—on site at the three news organizations whose content was monitored for this study: BBC News (which produces both the BBC News at Ten and the *Today* radio program), ITN News (which produces the ITV News at 10), and Sky News. Rather than being asked set questions, interviewees were invited to discuss their attitudes about expert interviewees, their approach to selecting experts for on-air appearances, their awareness of any gender disparities, the guidance they received from higher-level staff or managers, and other issues. The aim of these interviews was to try and ascertain why journalists invited a disproportionate number of men to be authoritative commentators on these programs. The journalists were aware of the disparity. These are examples of some of their responses:

Sky News female journalist: 'Our guests reflect male-dominated public life.'
BBC 'News at Ten' journalist: 'It's our job to hold authority figures to account, and they are usually men.'

ITN journalist: 'I don't think the quest for a female voice should override the quest for the person who can make the best contribution to the programme.'

BBC News journalist: 'Journalism needs to reflect society, not manufacture a false view of society.'

These journalists did not recognize that the view of society that their news programs presented was an inaccurate reflection of the level of female expertise available in society. They believed that the true ratio of male expertise to female expertise was exactly as presented on their programs and that there was no way in which they could increase the number of women experts on air.

In addition 32 women responded to a questionnaire sent to participants in the BBC "Expert Women" training days—a BBC initiative which was a direct result of the *Broadcast Magazine* articles in 2013 (see below). The questionnaire included three open-ended questions asking for respondents' opinions about factors influencing women's decisions whether or not to agree to be interviewed on air. Interestingly the most quoted reason for declining to appear (other than logistical reasons) was the fear of seeming "pushy" or self-important (Howell & Singer, 2016).

"(There's) the fear of appearing too 'pushy' or overconfident by thinking you can do it. To me it often looked like the realm of a few 'famous' people (mainly men) and I had 'no right' to be there, even though I knew I had a lot to say on issues of my expertise," said one academic.

"I didn't want to be seen as uppity . . . having taken a lot of criticism," said a female scientist.

"I thought it would be seen as pushy or arrogant by mainly male colleagues," said another academic.

In October 2013, the editorship of the magazine changed, and the *Broadcast Magazine* campaign ceased. But Howell's students continued to survey five "flagship" news programs: Sky News; BBC News at Ten, ITV News at Ten; BBC Radio 4 *Today*; and Channel Four News. The student monitors surveyed five editions of each program every month. The surveys took place across a working week. All five editions of each program were surveyed in the same week in order to make comparisons.

The first tranche of new figures, covering October 2013 to March 2014 were announced at the first City University, London "Women on Air" conference in April 2014. (*Women on Air*, 2014) Statistical analysis of the data (Table 4.3) showed

TABLE 4.3 Ratio of expert men to women October 2013 to March 2014 (*Women on Air*, March 2014)

Program	No. of male experts compared to female
Sky News	4.7–1
ITV News at Ten	4–1
BBC News at Ten	4–1
BBC Radio 4 *Today*	3.6–1 (a slight improvement on 2013)
Channel 4 News	4–1

that, despite the "Expert Women" campaign that had been promoted widely in *Broadcast Magazine*, the ratio of male to female experts was still 4 men to 1 woman.

Missing opinions

The research—embracing quantitative surveys of experts on air; interviews with production teams; and the questionnaires sent to women who considered themselves as experts who might make themselves available to journalists—raised two issues. First, far fewer women were being invited to appear as expert commentators than were able and available. Second, women appeared more hesitant to contribute even when they were asked. Journalists who were interviewed said that producers did identify women experts but found them reluctant to appear on air. "I can persuade most people to participate, but women often tell me they're not the best person," an experienced female producer said (Howell & Singer, 2016).

Many journalists agreed that women are more likely than men to protest that they are not the best or the right person. Often, the journalists reported, these experts suggested a man instead. Another journalist agreed: "Women are harder to book. There are fewer of them, and you have to seek them out and build up a relationship." A senior female producer remarked:

> You get 'I'm not really sure I'm the right person.' And you say 'Why not? Because the sort of things you'll be asked on air are the sort of things we've just been talking about.' Then you get 'Oh, I'm very nervous.'. . . You often get 'Oh well, I should probably clear that with my boss,' and the boss is invariably a man. . . . They don't quite say 'I don't really want to put myself forward' but that's the message they're kind of giving.
>
> *(Howell & Singer, 2016)*

Journalists expressed frustration that in a busy news schedule a producer would spend a long time trying to persuade a woman to appear on air, only to be told that she did not feel sufficiently qualified to appear and they should approach someone else. One male producer explained:

> Especially with the time constraints, you will stick to (who) you know will perform and will give you what you want, and that's totally natural.

Howell also sent an online questionnaire, which was answered by 40 junior broadcast journalists. Fifteen said that women took longer to agree to appear than men and exhibited more insecurity about their performance even when they were sure of their subject. One frustrated male BBC local radio producer commented:

> I have spent twenty minutes trying to persuade a woman to come on the programme, and then she goes and says 'no.'

The junior broadcast journalists who approached women to appear on news programs were usually tasked with "guest booking" for demanding senior producers or presenters. They had to deliver experts in a limited time frame. No leeway was given to take account of the fact that women experts would take more time to persuade because women experts had fewer role models; or were constrained by fear of seeming "pushy"; or were conscious that they were likely to be criticized (Watson & Hoffman, 2004). Interestingly, few women experts or journalists who contributed to either the questionnaires or face-to-face interviews mentioned pressures of childcare or domestic commitments as usual reasons given for not being able to appear on air. The women experts who responded to the questionnaire were largely working women with successful careers who had already organized their domestic responsibilities, and who had put themselves forward for the BBC "Expert Women" confidence building program (see below).

This research demonstrating the paucity of female experts on broadcast news was consistent with other evidence about the role of women as commentators in the media. In her 2013 study Franks noted the dearth of female opinion writing: just a quarter of comment pieces were by women, surveyed in the Guardian Datablog; commissioning editors described difficulties in persuading women to contribute (Franks, 2013). Similarly, in the US, women were seen as reluctant to pontificate because they feared they were not sufficiently expert (Zofia Smardz, 2005). In 2012, the *Columbia Journalism Review* published an analysis entitled "It's 2012 Already: Why is Opinion Writing Still Mostly Male?" (Fry, 2012). In the US, this problem led to the formation of a website known as the Op-Ed project, which was predicated on research showing that women wrote only 20 percent of comment pieces in the US media. The Op-Ed project campaigned for a greater range of voices and tries to support and encourage women to pursue comment and opinion writing (*The OpEd Project*, 2012).

Once again, as with the female broadcast experts, it appeared that women were not being asked. When they were asked, women often seemed reluctant to participate or put themselves forward, which sometimes caused frustration on the part of the journalist. A further study by the European Journalism Observatory in 2017 substantiated these findings, that women were not well represented in opinion and commentary writing (Lees & Anson, 2017).

Both anecdotal and scholarly evidence link this disinclination to voice opinion, in part, to the hostility to female commentators expressed in social media. There are many examples that have highlighted the scale of abuse that women face when they put forward opinions on controversial matters. This is an international problem (Pew Centre, 2017) and the UK has seen many high profile examples. Online abuse has been targeted at broadcasters (e.g., Professor Mary Beard, the eminent classics scholar), feminist campaigners (e.g., Caroline Criado Perez, who argued for women to be represented on UK banknotes) and politicians on a wide range of matters (Moore, 2017). Some female journalists have felt so discouraged by the abuse they get when they voice opinions on matters of controversy that they feel disinclined to enter the fray and question whether they should "retreat" to safe and uncontroversial subject areas where women are "allowed" to voice views (Franks, 2013).

Watson and Hoffman's (2004) illuminating study asked mixed-gender groups of US management students to solve a fictitious workplace problem. In half of the 40 groups, a woman received a "hint" to the answer; in the other half, a man got the hint. The exercise found no gender differences in problem-solving success. Yet other group members rated the informed women as significantly less likable than the informed men. The participants, the researchers suggested, regarded women who seemed well informed to be misfits or even "black sheep" in the way they defied the prevailing norm. This supports the notion that trolling and other forms of abuse would indicate; women are much more likely to be disliked than men, when they appear as authority figures.

Changing voices

Another initiative involved the setting up in 2013 of an expert women database, The Women's Room http://thewomensroom.org.uk/index.php, an initiative established by Caroline Criado Perez (The Women's Room, 2013). The database rapidly attracted hundreds and then thousands of women experts to submit their details and thereby make themselves available to broadcast requests. The site also encouraged women to break down the notion of "expert" to get away from the idea that an expert needed formal education in a particular area. This redefinition of "expert" would, it was hoped, broaden the notion of expertise to include many more women with expertise gained from everyday experiences such as parenting; gardening; crafts; etc. (Steiner, 2009). The breadth of expertise was very varied— from physical sciences, engineering, medicine, economics, local government, arts, media, and many more areas.

A second major impact was the establishment of "Expert Women" days in 2013, focusing on confidence building, by the BBC Academy in order to support and encourage female experts and to allay their fears of being seen as "pushy." These days also aimed to clarify for the participants the process by which experts were booked and used. Thirty places were offered to women who considered themselves experts and who wanted to appear on TV and radio, but had never had the chance. Some 2000 women applied, a response that staggered the organizers. In response to the demand the BBC academy eventually rolled out the scheme to four regional centers and ultimately coached 164 women in a year. The BBC monitored the outcome of its training days and by December 2013, of the 164 women it trained, 66 had made 244 appearances. This meant that a fifth of the women who participated in the scheme appeared on air for the first time within six months of attending the sessions. (The BBC rested the scheme from 2013 to 2016 when leadership changed at the BBC Academy, but the program was resumed in 2017.) Although the "Expert Women" training days might be seen as patronizing to women and unnecessary in an ideal world, they at least showed that the BBC acknowledged the paucity of women experts on the news and was applying some pressure to producers to use more women.

In 2014 the House of Lords launched an enquiry into women in news and current affairs broadcasting, reporting in January 2015. With Howell as special advisor, and witnesses from the regulators, the broadcasting industry and academia, the House of Lords Communications Select Committee addressing this issue recalled two long-standing concerns about women's involvement:

> The first [issue] is the representation of women who work within the broadcasting industry on news and current affairs—either on air (as presenters or reporters) or behind the scenes (in newsgathering production or corporate affairs). The second issue is the representation of women as experts on news and current affairs programmes.
>
> *(House of Lords, 2015)*

Nevertheless, the House of Lords argued against mandatory quotas:

> Given the dangers quotas could pose to editorial content, we do not recommend the use of mandatory quotas for female experts in broadcast news and current affairs at this time. If no progress is made in this regard the issue of quotas should be revisited. Broadcasters should create internal databases to ensure they have enough female experts represented in news and current affairs programmes. Where internal databases prove inadequate, they should be supplemented by external databases.
>
> *(House of Lords, 2015, para 169)*

More encouraging figures were presented by City University, London, derived from the surveying between May 2014 and September 2015 (Table 4.4).

BBC News at Ten was in the same place as in 2012 with at least 3.9 male experts to each woman. ITV News at Ten had gone backwards with a ratio of 4.9 male experts to each female expert. This meant that Sky News improved by 34 percent; Channel Four News improved by 37 percent; the *Today* program improved by 19 percent; but BBC News at Ten remained much on par—a 2 percent improvement. ITV News was 22 percent worse.

The change in the use of women experts was further confirmed in 2016 at the second City University, London "Women on Air" conference. The results of the

TABLE 4.4 Expert men and women on air May 2014 to September 2015

Program	No. of male experts compared to female
Sky News	3–1
Channel Four News	2.6–1
BBC Radio 4's *Today*	2.9–1
BBC News at Ten	3.9–1
ITV News	4.9–1

TABLE 4.5 Change in proportions of female to male experts appearing on TV—by program

Program	Increase ratio of women experts
Sky News	2.8 men—1 woman—a 10% improvement since May 2014/ September 2015
ITV News at Ten	3.6 men—1 woman—a 3% improvement since May 2014/ September 2015
BBC Radio *Today*	2.8 men—1 woman—a 3% improvement since May 2014/ September 2015
BBC News at Ten	3.8 men—1 woman—a 3% improvement since May 2014/ September 2015

monitoring survey showed that between October 2015 and March 2016, the ratio of expert women to expert men had improved (Table 4.5). Channel Four's figures were 2.2 men to 1 woman, a 15 percent improvement since the previous period.

Conclusion

The House of Lords report was explicit in calling for better representation of women throughout news and current affairs broadcasting. However, it left the implementation to the broadcasters. This "soft touch" approach means that independent surveys and evidence that can be used to apply pressure to broadcasters are more needed than ever. Broadcasters also need to address the constraints that affect women experts if they are to give an accurate and fair view of our society. Some evidence suggests that attitudes toward female authority might change if more women are seen in positions of authority (Eagly, Gartzia & Carli, 2014). In any case, public service broadcasters have an obligation to represent women more fairly, even if it takes time and effort on the part of journalists.

The level of publicity that the House of Lords report attracted has gradually led to shifts in practices. The inauguration of the database for expert women was a demonstrable innovation, as were the "Expert Women" days established by the BBC Academy to assist and give confidence to potential female expert interviewees. Nevertheless, the expert women monitoring project at City University is ongoing and remains limited to a simple proposition—that more women experts are able and available to participate in news programs on TV and radio in the UK than are used at present. In the period over which it has been running so far there has been an observable shift in the ratio of male to female experts on mainstream broadcast news output. There are now at least 25 percent more women experts on air on flagship news programs than there were in 2013. This is the result of many factors, but the publicizing of the survey study at City University has played a part in this change.

However, this project will not have achieved its aims until the ratio of men to women experts is at least under 2.5 to 1 across all flagship programs—reflecting the ratio of male to female expertise in society generally (Howell & Singer, 2016). The challenge remains to increase the broadcasters' awareness that much is still to be done, even in this straightforward, limited and focused area, and to keep the pressure on them to do it.

References

Barnett, E. (2013). *BBC launches expert women database and YouTube channel*. Retrieved from www.telegraph.co.uk/women/womens-business/9940426/BBC-launches-expert-women-database-and-YouTube-channel.html

BBC News. (2011). *Miriam O'Reilly wins Countryfile ageism claim—BBC News*. Retrieved from www.bbc.co.uk/news/entertainment-arts-12161045

Beard, M. (2017). *Women & power: A manifesto*. London: Profile Books.

Blumell, L. (2017). She persisted . . . and so did he: Gendered source use during the Trump access Hollywood scandal. *Journalism Studies*, online. https://doi.org/10.1080/14616 70X.2017.1360150

Campbell, A. (2007). *The lady vanishes at 45*. Retrieved August 22, 2017, from http://women injournalism.co.uk/the-lady-vanishes-at-45/

Campbell, L. (2012). *Broadcast launches "Expert Women" campaign*. Retrieved from www.broad castnow.co.uk/news/people/broadcast-launches-expert-women-campaign/5037709. article

City University. (2016). *Research reveals proportion of women in flagship broadcast news shows*. Retrieved from www.city.ac.uk/news/2016/may/new-research-reveals-proportion-of-women-experts,-reporters-and-presenters-in-the-news

Craft, C. (1988). *Too old, too ugly, and not deferential to men: An anchorwoman's courageous battle against sex discrimination*. Rocklin, CA: Prima Pub. and Communications.

Donovan, P. (2013). All our todays: Forty years of Radio 4's "Today" programme. *Arrow*.

Eagly, A. H., Gartzia, L., & Carli, L. L. (2014). Female advantage: Revisited. In S. Kumra, R. Simpson, & R. J. Burke (Eds.), *The Oxford handbook of gender in organizations*. Oxford: Oxford University Press.

Franks, S. (2011). Attitudes to women in the BBC in the 1970s: Not so much a glass ceiling as one of reinforced concrete. *Westminster Papers in Culture and Communication, 8*(3), 123–142.

Franks, S. (2013). *Women and journalism*. London: I.B. Tauris & Co. Ltd in association with the Reuters Institute for the Study of Journalism, University of Oxford.

Fry, E. (2012). *It's 2012 already: Why is opinion writing still mostly male?* Retrieved from www. cjr.org/behind_the_news/its_2012_already_why_is_opinio.php

Global Media Monitoring Project. (2000). Retrieved from http://whomakesthenews.org/articles/global-media-monitoring-project-200

Global Media Monitoring Project. (2015). Retrieved from http://whomakesthenews.org/gmmp/gmmp-reports/gmmp-2015-reports

House of Lords. (2015). *Women in news and current affairs broadcasting*. London.

Howell, L., & Singer, J. B. (2016). Pushy or a princess? Women experts and British broadcast news. *Journalism Practice*, 1–17. doi:10.1080/17512786.2016.1232173

IWMF. (2015). *IWMF global report | International Women's Media Foundation (IWMF)*. Retrieved from www.iwmf.org/our-research/iwmf-global-report/

Kruvand, M. (2012). Dr. Soundbite: The making of an expert source in science and medical stories. *Science Communication, 34*(5), 566–591. doi:10.1177/1075547011434991

Lees, C., & Anson, H. (2017). *Where are all the women journalists in UK newspapers?* Retrieved from http://en.ejo.ch/ethics-quality/where-are-all-the-women-journalists-in-uk-newspapers

Moore, S. (2017). Why is drowning in vitriol the price women pay for being in politics? *The Guardian*. Retrieved from www.theguardian.com/commentisfree/2017/jul/10/drowning-vitriol-price-women-pay-politics-online-abuse-yvette-cooper

Moran, C. (2012). *How to be a woman*. London: Ebury Press.

The OpEd Project. (2012). Retrieved from www.theopedproject.org/

Pew Centre. (2017). *Online harassment 2017*. Retrieved from www.pewinternet.org/2017/07/11/online-harassment-2017/

Plunkett, J. (2011). Countryfile's Miriam O'Reilly wins BBC ageism claim. *The Guardian*. Retrieved from www.theguardian.com/media/2011/jan/11/countryfile-miriam-oreilly-tribunal

Revoir, P. (2012). *I got it wrong on older women: BBC boss admits there ARE too few on TV | Daily Mail Online*. Retrieved from www.dailymail.co.uk/news/article-2098498/I-got-wrong-older-women-BBC-boss-admits-ARE-TV.html

Ross, K., Boyle, K., Carter, C., & Ging, D. (2016). Women, men and news: It's life Jim, but not as we know it. *Journalism Studies*, 1–22. doi:10.1080/1461670X.2016.1222884

Ross, K., & Carter, C. (2011). Women and news: A long and winding road. *Media, Culture & Society*, *33*(8), 1148–1165. doi:10.1177/0163443711418272

Smardz, Z. (2005). Just give it a shot, girls. *The Washington Post*. Retrieved from www.washingtonpost.com/wp-dyn/articles/A2538-2005Mar26.html??noredirect=on

Steiner, L. (2009). Gender in the newsroom. In K. Wahl-Jorgensen & T. Hanitzsch (Eds.), *The handbook of journalism studies*. New York, NY and London: Routledge.

Watson, C., & Hoffman, L. R. (2004). The role of task-related behavior in the emergence of leaders: The dilemma of the informed woman. *Group & Organization Management*, *29*(6), 659–685. doi:10.1177/1059601103254263

Women on Air. (2014). Retrieved from www.city.ac.uk/centre-for-law-justice-and-journalism/projects/women-on-air

The Women's Room—Find an Expert (2013). Retrieved from http://thewomensroom.org.uk/findanexpert

5

PRETTY IN PINK

The ongoing importance of appearance in broadcast news

April Newton and Linda Steiner

Introduction

In the 1970s and 1980s in the United States, women anchors and reporters were encouraged to adopt an androgynous presence, with blazers, medium length blond hair, and tasteful jewelry. Apparently assuming that an overtly sexy look would distract or alienate viewers (Rouvalis, 2006), television executives left little room for deviation from the norm. When Diane Allen was hired to replace Jessica Savitch, a very popular Philadelphia anchor who was going national, Allen was told to dye her hair the same shade of blonde as Savitch. After 20 years on television, Allen was demoted because she had gained weight (personal communication, 2005). Allen filed three complaints with the Equal Employment Opportunity Commission charging the CBS affiliate in Philadelphia with sexism and ageism. Ultimately, she settled her complaints and quit on-air reporting.

In a dress code change that occurred swiftly across network and cable television, women now show off bold jewelry and bare arms. As the *Washington Post* put it (Boyle, 2012): "They now flank themselves in bright sleeveless sheath dresses and stiletto heels, renouncing the once hard-and-fast edicts of television news: no bare legs, no long hair, no feminine distractions from the news." But if appearance rules for women and men have changed over time, what has not changed is a practice by both station management and viewers of closely monitoring women's appearance for adherence to current rules. Moreover, however they change, the standards are far more demanding and narrowly defined for women than for men.

Clothes, cosmetics, hair, and jewelry are the most visible apparatus for performing gender, as well as for resisting conventional requirements of gender identity. This chapter, focusing on the US context, investigates the experiences of on-air news anchors regarding their appearance. News reports offer anecdotal evidence of women broadcasters complaining about what they regard as unfair, excessive, and/or sexist (and sometimes racist) criticism of their physical appearance. This chapter investigates whether occasional anecdotes are illustrative of more widely experienced norms. Specifically, we studied what kinds of comments—approving or disapproving—broadcast anchors have received from audience members, colleagues, or bosses; whether and how anchors respond to these comments; and how the experiences of men and women differ.

We first summarize the history of compliance and resistance to the surveillance of women in television broadcasting, the enforcement of these appearance codes, and responses to it. Some women confronted their critics; others sued for discrimination after being fired or demoted because of appearance. Then we discuss how often, and in what contexts, contemporary women broadcasters draw criticism of their appearance, and whether men have similar experiences of surveillance, critique, or criticism.

History of compliance and resistance

Some of the appearance strictures and standards can be very specific and narrowly defined, especially when these come from station management, officially or unofficially. Among the many shows to issue guidelines, CBS This Morning insists that women hosts cannot repeat an outfit within 30 days (Brannigan, 2015). Others hire fashion consultants who come to the studio or the anchor's home. The president of a market research firm that consults with news networks claims women now enjoy "far more liberty to be feminine." But lower necklines and higher hemlines may also be encouraged to boost ratings. Complaining about the "short, skimpy, tight" clothes that MSNBC asked her to wear when "Morning Joe" started, co-host Mika Brzezinski described herself as "a hostage to fashion by network executives and stylists" (Boyle, 2012).

Kiran Chetry (Irby, 2016), a former CNN and Fox News anchor, listed even more rules she had followed: "Dye your hair blonde, wear your skirts shorter, wear your skirts longer, don't wear pantsuits. They said get Botox, because when you report and the sun is on you, you look angry, and nobody likes angry women on television." Chetry recalled several viewer complaints about her appearance, with viewers insisting she needed a wig because her hair was too thin.

Christine Craft was one of the first women to sue for sex discrimination after being demoted from her co-anchor position at KMBC-TV in Kansas City.[1] Craft insisted that she had obeyed all orders: she changed her hair, bought the required jewelry, and followed the consultant's schedule for clothes with the "proper" colors and necklines. Nonetheless, Craft claimed, her supervisor deemed her "too old, unattractive and not deferential enough to men" (Craft, 1986). Many other US women subsequently filed suit on similar grounds. Janet Peckinpaugh, 48, was awarded $3.79 million in 1999 when her Hartford, CT, station demoted her as anchor. She knew her "shelf-life" was expiring when the station complained about her glasses and her bangs (Allen, 1999). The Weather Channel settled a 2003 sex discrimination suit after firing a 41-year-old woman, apparently, following advice from image consultants, wanting younger women with a "sexier look" with "top buttons open." In 2011, a Fox political reporter settled a discrimination (and retaliation) suit claiming that to boost ratings, her Hartford television station encouraged women anchors to wear tight tops on Fridays, nicknamed Big Boob Fridays (Buhl, 2011).

The problem is particularly acute for women of color. The Euro-American beauty standard with which US mass media bombard audiences has devastating effects on African American women, and other women of color, who try to adhere to these standards, but are simultaneously excluded from and pitted against that dominant beauty standard (Patton, 2006). As Patton and others acknowledge, sometimes women creatively use their appearance to survive a workplace while remaining true to self. Patton mentions a variety of hairstyles as ways to mark beauty, boldness, rebellion, and self-confidence. These challenges to white standards, however, do not always succeed. WABC told Melba Tolliver to straighten her Afro before covering Tricia Nixon's 1971 wedding. In 1981, a San Francisco co-anchor was suspended for wearing her hair in cornrows. Julie Chen, a news anchor of Chinese heritage, said a boss once warned her that her career would be limited due to her "Asian eyes" (CBS News, 2013). Chen tearfully admitted on the television show *The Talk* that she had plastic surgery after an agent made this a condition of representing her.

Nor is the issue exclusive to the US. Recent narratives from women journalists around the world (Japan, Malaysia, the UK, Australia, India, China, Slovenia, Russia) about sexual harassment and comments on their bodies and appearance suggest that our findings apply well beyond the US. In Australia, for example, Sky news anchor Tracey Spicer (2014) complained of having become "a painted doll who spent an hour a day and close to $200 a week putting on a mask." She decided to reduce her required beauty routine, which included applications of 16 cosmetics, and stopped wearing heels that caused bunions and osteoarthritis. Spicer said her confidence was eroded by criticism. One viewer suggested she get rid of "the scarecrow hair." Shortly after she gave birth, her boss said, "You're porking up a bit."

At a widely quoted public lecture, Australian Channel Nine *Today* host Lisa Wilkinson (2013) listed several problems causing her despair, including journalists who simultaneously decried and engaged in sexism and misogyny with "*uncaring ease*":

> I despair that every time a female journalist is profiled in the press, her age is usually mentioned by the second paragraph, as if it is a measure of her sexual currency and just how long it will be, before it expires.

Wilkinson mentioned a retired male journalist who said he could no longer watch the news because young female journalists "*are apparently TOO attractive for him to concentrate.*" That said, she emphasized that among viewers, her harshest critics are women. Similarly, a viewer emailed Annabel Crabb, of ABC's 7.30, to complain: "*Whoever did your make-up last night obviously doesn't like you. . . . You looked like a two-bit hooker . . .*" (Mann, 2013).

Several UK women likewise were allegedly fired when they no longer had a young woman's glamorous looks. Miriam O'Reilly (who won an age discrimination case against the BBC), declared: "How a woman looks and whether that appeals to whoever is hiring and firing, can determine the length and success of a career, not her ability to do the job." According to *Good Morning Britain* host Anne Diamond (2016), "the supposedly PC BBC is often the worst offender" for treatment of "screen wives." When presenter Susanna Reid apparently needed "fixing" to appear less harsh and increase viewership, *Good Morning Britain* urged her to lighten her hair, wear brighter colors, consider her skirt length, and look "sympathetic" towards interviewees by nodding a lot (Yaqoob, 2014).

Theories of gender display

Scholars have long studied how gender is "done" both in daily encounters and in various workplaces, and how sexism simultaneously over-determines the performance of gender and undermines the status of women. The sociologist Erving Goffman noted that, at least for jobs in public view, women are chosen on the basis of appearance, i.e., because they are "young and attractive beyond what random selection ought to allow" (Goffman, 1977, p. 318). But the point is that what Goffman called *gender displays*—highly scripted strategic behavior—nearly always disadvantage women. Economic approaches to the issue seem resigned to audience or customer tastes and preferences being used to justify employers' gendered appearance requirements; employers have long assumed substantial prerogatives with respect to the dress and appearance of their employees (Bartlett, 1994).

Adding to Bourdieu's categorization of forms of capital, Catherine Hakim (2010), a sociologist, says women invest in the right makeup, clothes and hairstyle, and other forms of stylistic presentation to raise their workplace's "erotic capital." Recalling how desirability relative to scarcity, supply, and demand determine market value, she argues that women generally have more erotic capital than men because women work harder at it and are well placed to exploit their erotic capital. Describing the beauty premium and the ugliness penalty, Daniel Hamermesh, an economist, calls this link between looks and success "pulchronomics" (2013, p. 39); he offers evidence that better-looking people earn significantly more than do their "homely" counterparts.

Feminist legal theorist Katharine Bartlett (1994) challenges feminists' assumption that evaluating dress and appearance rules without regard to community norms and expectations is possible or even desirable. Moreover, she notes that legal strategies to eliminate mandatory codes fail to address the disadvantage to women, nor are codes always disadvantageous. Nonetheless, she agrees that workplace dress codes that insist on stereotypically feminine dress may promote the subordination of women:

> It is a sign of the pervasiveness of gender coding in the symbolic system of dress and appearance that few female-associated dress or appearance conventions exist that are not linked with stereotypes about women that emerged

from or have been interwoven with their historically inferior status. Courts should find all such conventions discriminatory 'on the basis of sex,' unless narrowly tailored to sex differences in ways that do not perpetuate this historically inferior status.

(p. 2570)

Audiences consistently attend far more to the physical appearance of women broadcast news professionals than of men's. A British study found that women viewers placed nearly equal importance on the appearance of male and female anchors but men put somewhat higher emphasis on the necessity of attractive female anchors (Mitra, Webb, & Wolfe, 2014). Men who perceived women broadcasters as more sexually appealing also believed those anchors to be more professional generally, although they perceived less sexually attractive women as more competent to address typically masculine subjects such as war and politics; women viewers were less likely to differentiate in this way (Grabe & Samson, 2011). Another study that garnered enormous news media publicity showed a robust and positive effect of increased beauty on perceptions of women's social power/competence (Etcoff et al., 2011).[2] The researchers found that people perceived women wearing makeup as more likable, competent, and trustworthy.

The sexualization of news anchors as a promotional tool and device for attracting certain kinds of audiences puts the burden on women to be sexually attractive, while maintaining journalistic credibility (Chambers, Steiner, & Fleming, 2004). Meltzer likewise clearly stated the problem for women journalists who gain attention and notoriety through network promotion:

> [I]t causes these women to become known for the wrong reasons. Appearance is a 'catch 22'; journalists are not supposed to become known for their looks, but their success with audiences is partly based on their appearance, so their news organizations exploit it.

(Meltzer, 2010, p. 60)

Online lists and rankings of "beautiful" (aka "hot" and "sexy") women journalists abound. This causes a profound, abiding sense of professional insecurity among women. They hear accusations that they got hired only because of their gender and looks, not their abilities. Michael Buerk, a UK journalist, made this assumption explicitly: Women get jobs as newsreaders and television presenters "mainly because (they) look nice," he said; this justified firing women when they age, "much as you would prune the raspberries to make way for new growth" (O'Reilly, 2014). They are as visible as their male counterparts, but not necessarily seen as equally serious. Nor are their long-term job prospects the same as those of male counterparts. Former ABC correspondent Judy Muller underwent plastic surgery given her understanding of the continuing relevance of an old slogan: "Men can still get bald and portly. Women cannot turn grey and wrinkled" (Marlane, 1999). A survey of women and men news anchors found that women ranked the emphasis on their physical appearance as their primary career barrier, while men ranked the same concern at 27th out of 34 items (Engstrom & Ferri, 2000). Once proud of her unkempt appearance, Greta Van Susteren grew so bothered by public criticism that she got plastic surgery (Meltzer, 2010).

Networks vary in both their aesthetic and the level of pressure on women to comply. Fox's national anchors probably represent the extreme in glamor: their "uniform" includes body-hugging dresses and false lashes. Even guests get "made up." One of the several explanations Mundy (2012) offers for the network's preference for "Fox glam" is that women in Fox's largely conservative audience are less squeamish than progressive ones about exploiting their looks. The long-standing interest in the appearance of now-former Fox News Chairman Roger Ailes has also been used to explain this; although anchors at the one Fox affiliate we interviewed did not describe a more egregious attitude (the news director at the other Fox affiliate did not allow interviews).

Thus, we ask: *How do men and women news broadcasters experience criticism and/ or support for their physical appearance on-air?* Given both anecdotal and survey data, what can we find out at a granular level about *how broadcasters feel about criticism and make sense of it?*

Method

The first author conducted semi-structured, in-depth interviews with 10 news anchors and two meteorologists from the Baltimore and Washington, DC, television markets. According to Nielsen data from 2016, Baltimore is the 26th largest television market in the United States; Washington, DC is the seventh largest television market with almost 2.5 million homes. Anchors worked at the four main network affiliates, ABC, CBS, Fox, and NBC in both markets.[3] After Institutional Review Board approval, we recruited participants by email after identifying them from station websites as news or sports anchors or meteorologists. One interview was conducted in a university seminar room; the rest were conducted in coffee shops or at the broadcasters' workplace. All interviews were digitally recorded, with the participants' informed consent (their names are changed here).

Baltimore and Washington, DC are both racially diverse and the television stations' on-air broadcasters are likewise racially diverse. Because no official demographic statistics are available, the race of those listed as news or sports anchors or meteorologists on their station websites, as of 2016, was determined using the anchors' station biographies, professional memberships, Wikipedia entries, news articles, etc. Broad race categories were used to categorize interview subjects as white, black (or biracial), Asian (or biracial), or Hispanic/Latinx (or biracial) based on the categorization the individuals themselves preferred. In both markets, a nearly even number of men and women work as news or sports anchors or meteorologists. Significantly, more anchors, overall, work in Washington, DC, partly because one of the stations runs two news operations, including a local 24-hour broadcast. In both markets, the number of anchors who identify as black (or biracial) is identical for men and women. For this research, six men and six women were interviewed; of these, four were black and one was Asian American.

Participants discussed:

1   their career in television, what they do on-air, and how they came to be at the current station;
2   how they prepare for the workday and for going on-air, including their routine in terms of appearance; and the "look," if any, they try to project on air;
3   whether they talk with coworkers about appearance and the effort needed to maintain appearance; and management input regarding on-air appearance;
4   how viewers respond to their appearance, how they feel about those comments; and
5   whether they observed gendered differences in the frequency and types of appearance-related comments the on-air talent gets.

Each interview was transcribed, coded, and entered into NVivo, a qualitative and mixed methods coding software program, where it was re-coded in order to determine recurring and substantial themes.

Notably, the interviews included in this chapter were conducted during the Fall and winter of 2015 and 2016, before the explosion of the so-called #MeToo movement, the hashtag used by women around the world to share their stories of sexual harassment and assault, in workplaces and private spaces, including in newsrooms. In the wake of the sexual harassment, rape, and assault allegations against movie mogul Harvey Weinstein, which became open and public in October, 2017, the conversation is changing about power, sex, and gender. Some of the responses the interviewees gave us might have been different, had the interviews instead occurred in this transformed context.

Findings

Both men and women working in the Baltimore and Washington, DC, television markets say their appearance is an ongoing topic of open discussion for viewers and their station management. Moreover, frustration over the importance of appearance was common. Hannah, a white news anchor, said that in her three decades on the air, discussion of her appearance has consumed more time than actually tending to her appearance:

> I was just telling somebody this last week who's a professional hair person [that] ... my appearance, what I wear, how my hair looks, my makeup, takes up about an hour of my day. I work 9 hours days. . . . Only about an hour of it is spent . . . in front of the mirror. But unfortunately, it is the thing that I get the most feedback on, and that I get the most criticism on, and that people talk about the most.

Howard, a black anchor who has spent two decades at the news desk, said he sometimes feared viewers were less interested in the content of his broadcasts than in his ties:

I just told you about an MX missile that was heading toward your house: all you can focus on is the tie? I just told you about a guy, a rapist that ran through the hallway of your kid's junior high school, and all you cared about was my tie? Come on, man.

So, while both women and men often expressed irritation, women perceived a distinctly stronger sense of criticism about their appearance than men do. Men participants recalled mostly hear positive and supportive comments from others about their appearance. A white news anchor in his mid-sixties, for example, could recall perhaps a couple of news directors in the last five years who had seemed to look at him while he was on-air but he was confident that their gaze was not at all disapproving. Other men had similar trouble recalling, or were unable to recall, any instances of criticism:

> James, Black news anchor, in his mid-thirties: *I don't get a whole lot of feedback about my appearance because . . . I think because I have a pretty, um, clean cut, classic look. I don't really do wild things on air.*
> Ken, Black news anchor, in his mid-sixties: *You know, I'd be stunned if I got a call from somebody that was incredibly critical, you know what I mean? Not even on social media do they get personal about your look.*
> Ian, white meteorologist, probably in his mid-fifties: *You know, I don't think I've ever really had a comment that's criticized my physical appearance.*

Notably, race does not seem to make a difference to the men participants regarding this particular theme: Neither white nor black men participants mentioned feeling the sting of criticism with respect to their appearance. Indeed, a search on Google, Google News, and LexisNexis turned up no stories of men complaining about surveillance of their on-camera appearance. To the contrary: one Australian morning news anchor wore the same suit, every day for a year, to test public reaction. Apparently, he received no notice or comment from viewers (Olheiser, 2014).

Women told us that the bulk of comments about their appearance was positive and supportive, but every woman interviewed could recall at least one critical comment from a viewer or station management. Sometimes the criticism seemed reasonable. For example, advising broadcasters against wearing certain jewelry, colors, patterns, or styles of clothing on television was fair when, prior to the switch to high-definition broadcasting, small, tight patterns would not come through well, appearing to move (often described as "swimming" or "merengue-ing") on their own. Our participants say the switch to high-definition broadcasting ended most concerns about tight patterns but raised new concerns about makeup and jewelry. Ivy, a black news anchor in her early forties, said she has received comments—she did not describe these as criticisms—from coworkers regarding clothing and jewelry. People told her, she said, that the pattern of her dress was merengue-ing, and thus distracting. Likewise, she recalled a producer telling her that her necklace was "doing this real flash effect" and advised against her wear it on camera.

Other broadcasters said their managers, occasionally at the behest of image consultants hired by the station, issued general edicts against certain colors or styles of dress, in pursuit of a professional look. Hannah said at one point her manager required very subdued, traditionally masculine colors of all the women broadcasters. Similar to Christine Craft decades ago, Hannah explained that years back, "we were given a mandate: no bright patterns, no bright colors. He wanted blacks and grays, he wanted us to look serious." Clarifying that the mandate applied only to women, Hannah added:

> He was emphasizing, like, credibility, serious news, blah, blah, blah. Then, after a while, he totally relaxed on that, and changed, and said he wanted things to be lighter and so all of the sudden we could.

In neither of these cases was the criticism regarded as personal. Ivy recounted her story to illustrate that she heard no criticisms of her level of taste. Hannah recounted her story to indicate both the mercurial qualities of her manager, whom she describes as having double standards regarding men's and women's appearances, but also the general, rather than personal, nature of some of his criticisms.

At other times, women we interviewed described criticism that seemed very specific and personal, although the weight of the criticism varied. Managers' comments are sometimes personally insulting, as was the case for Lisa, whose news director spoke to her after she wore a dress on-air that he apparently thought looked like a prairie skirt:

> So he goes, 'Never wear that again. . . . You're dressing too old for your age. You need to dress more trendy, more fashionable.'

Lisa said the news director's embarrassing instructions made her question her style sense:

> I was like, 'Oh, my God, okay, wow, what . . . ?' I don't think my clothes are, like, frumpy or bad. . . . There was one thing he didn't like and decided to make a bigger deal out of it. But then again, maybe I do dress, like, really frumpy.

Karen recalled a hurtful experience when, not wanting her loose shirt to wrinkle before her broadcast, she had not yet put on a belt over the shirt. Her assistant news director called Karen into her office and said people had been asking if Karen was pregnant. When Karen assured her she was not, the woman apparently said: "Thank God, because [the general manager] would be so upset if you were." Karen told us she was very slim, so the comment felt especially egregious and even threatening: The woman might have been issuing a veiled, and potentially illegal, warning.

Hannah described feeling similarly knocked off balance by a woman news director. Hannah had replaced a well-respected, older white man as anchor. Apparently concerned that some viewers would have difficulty adjusting to a woman anchor, the news director gave Hannah frank, explicit direction regarding her appearance. Hannah regarded the strong criticism as having a purpose. This made it easier to swallow, as did the fact that it came from a woman:

I remember it, so clearly it had an effect on me. I was sort of like, 'oooh, ouch.' But she was doing it to help me and I knew that.

Melissa, an Asian American woman in her late twenties, said she, too, understood criticism that seemed intended to promote her individual appearance rather than simply to constrain it. She described what happened after, two days in a row, she styled her hair like reality star and fashionista Kim Kardashian's hair.

> They said, 'We don't want you doing that anymore.' They were like, 'You looked good before, just go back to that. That was consistent. Just stick to the side part.'

Melissa was essentially told that she needed permission to change her hair. None of the men reported ever having been told they could not alter their hair without permission. In fact, one of the men discussed his own attempts, or coworkers', to grow facial hair as not only acceptable but something that draws no attention.

For Melissa, understanding the need for a consistent appearance made the criticism of her temporary hairstyle seem more fair, more tolerable. Jennifer, a white news anchor in her mid-forties, said she has grown to understand that consistency is very important to station executives. Still, she said, her bosses often "nitpick." Eventually she felt compelled to take a stand and she asked her union officials to come in and help.

> He basically said to them, 'Unless you're paying for anything, you cannot keep calling her in.' And they've since left me alone . . .

Ivy likewise said that certain requirements on the part of television station management are simply part of the job. According to Ivy, when her first news director hired her:

> They'd done some focus group, and the consensus was my hair was too long and I looked too sexy. So they asked me to cut it, and I did. I just felt like it was part of the job, right? When you embark on this career, there are some things that you accept and some of the things that you accept are that you won't have quite as much control over your destiny as you might like. . . . That becomes the unwritten statement that you co-sign. You agreed to this. So, you can't complain about it because you knew that going in. This is the gig; this is how it works. And somebody may say to you, 'I think you should wear something different.'

On the other hand, managing interactions with critical viewers can be very difficult, particularly when the criticism is crass or crudely delivered. Ivy expressed frustration when people approach her in public and say:

> 'Oooh, girl, I'm so glad you colored your hair, I don't know what was going on with your hair.' Meanwhile, you know, they look like they have a rat on top of their head but, of course, I can never say that to them, right?

Lisa, the meteorologist, mentioned men who write from prison to tell her, "Your ass is really big." In light of the #MeToo movement, we revisited the interview transcripts and noted that Lisa described herself as, luckily in her opinion, unlikely to be the recipient of so-called dick pics, the colloquial term for images received via text or email of male genitalia. She explained that she knew at least one coworker, also an anchor, who received such photos from viewers. Interviewees recounted sexually charged statements and actions with giggles, eye-rolls, or minimizing statements such as, "It's part of the job." Again, we doubt whether the anchors would recount such stories with the same patience now that the #MeToo movement has opened a conversation about the limits of what women should have to endure in the workplace (Gilbert, 2017).

The need to manage interactions gracefully, when viewers feel free to criticize or insult, or to make sexually aggressive statements to an anchor, can change women's way of living. Because of viewer commentary, particularly face-to-face, Karen said she always wears some makeup.

> I never got out of the house without makeup on because it's the one day that you leave and someone is like, 'Oh, she looks totally different.' I hear that all the time. I'll got to yoga class and hear, 'You look so different,' and it's like, no shit. Sorry. . . . I'm in a hot yoga class, I'm not going to be wearing fake eyelashes. . . . It's constant.

Lisa, a white meteorologist in her twenties, noted that the intense focus on her appearance often makes her long to switch to radio:

> A lot of times . . . I would prefer if I could do radio . . . because I could still do it (meteorology). . . . The days that maybe I wouldn't be on air . . . were my most favorite days because I could just go in, be a little bit more casual, didn't have to have all the makeup on.

Does the platform make a difference?

Nearly 90 percent of US television broadcasters recently surveyed believe social media has increased the amount of criticism that broadcast journalists receive about their appearance; nearly 100 percent agreed women get more criticism from viewers than do men (Finneman & Yakabe, 2016). Our participants agree. They all reported getting comments and criticism from viewers via in-person contact, email, phone, and, increasingly, social media. When discussing their experiences of comment and criticism, ten of the participants first mentioned email or social media (they seemed to use those terms interchangeably). Only two emphasized in-person contact.

A few of them acknowledged that the anonymity provided by some of social media platforms makes it different, i.e., uglier. No wonder Hannah plans to deactivate all her social media accounts once she quits television work. Hannah suggested that anonymous comments are often "meaner" than those with names attached:

That's something somebody should do a PhD study on, how the world of social media has brought out the ugly in people, not the pretty. Anonymity does not provoke the best in human beings. I think it provokes the worst.

Ken, on the other hand, enjoys social media and describes himself as a "heavy" user, maintaining an active presence on different platforms. Yet he too mentioned the darker side of social media engagement:

> A lot of men think they're entitled to say whatever they want to women because, number one, the women are on-air, and because they (the men) are anonymous for the most part. Though some men will sign their names and stuff but a lot of these comments are comments they would never make in person. So they're lowlifes. . . .

The other participants described viewers' comments and criticisms as being similar across Twitter, Facebook, or email. The men received few comments or criticism, regardless of which platform commenters used. Women likewise received criticism in apparently similar quantity and quality regardless of the digital platform.[4] Lisa mentioned, again with relief, that she never receives the racier or more egregiously insulting messages that some of her colleagues do, no matter how viewers communicate.

In part, the women may be protected by their companies' use of filters, at least through their work email accounts. Many local television stations, including those for which our participants work, filter emails sent to the general newsroom account. As a result, the anchors and reporters often do not see abusive or highly critical emails. A couple of women, for example, acknowledged managers occasionally share positive comments but, they suspected, may not share some negative comments.

Karen takes care to separate her work and personal social media because of the ease with which viewers can find her online and she doesn't want people to see pictures of her son:

> Usually, if they have a question about something I'm wearing, they'll email our newsroom and then somebody will forward it to me. If it's a negative comment, I would assume it goes that way as well.

The one story of explicit criticism that any of the men participants told began with an in-person encounter. Louis, who is in his early thirties, now works for a Washington, DC, news bureau but previously worked as a Florida television anchor. He recalled one woman who came up to him in a café, and, after telling him that she had watched him every morning for a long time, added:

> She said, 'I've always wanted to tell you I hate your hair . . . specifically, this part, right here, on your head.' And I said, 'Okay.'

Louis said the incident prompted him to mention her the next morning during his broadcast, figuring that it took a lot of "chutzpah" for her to come up and tell him how she felt. The woman continues to this day to send him messages.

All the men we interviewed agreed that the women with whom they work face different challenges regarding appearance. All of them mentioned the fact that women receive much greater scrutiny and criticism. James recalled pregnant cow-orkers who were told, "It's time to go on leave to have your baby" or "Don't turn that way." James said: "I can only imagine how that would impact somebody to get those sorts of reactions from people regularly and it's completely unnecessary."

Howard agreed that the pressures about appearance are unending for women. Like James, Howard assumed the criticism must have an impact:

> I can go a month and never hear a single comment about what I wear. And then I can go 6 months and hear a hundred comments; 99 percent of them are all positive. But a woman's hair is different one day, colored different one way or another, it's one strand or a clump is hanging a little bit out of balance, the dress fits her a way that just happens to tick off, or just get under the skin of, a viewer, one way or another, either it's too loose or too frumpy, it's too tight. You know, there's no winning for a woman pretty much.

Ian, the meteorologist, expressed relief that he did not need to deal with, or man-age, similar criticism. Indeed, explaining why he is happy to be a man rather than a woman, he described his pity for women who work the early morning shows:

> They get here at, like, 2:30, to go on air at 4:30. And half an hour or 45 min-utes of that is getting ready. That's built into my day. I get here when I have to get here in order to complete the show. So I, I feel sorry for them (chuckles), I mean, that would be horrible, you know? I mean, that would not be any fun.

Discussion

As with women nationally and perhaps even globally, women news anchors in Washington, DC and Baltimore endure a great deal more criticism for their appearance than men. Both women and men claimed during interviews that the bulk of their interactions with their station management and with their viewers is positive and supportive. Women, however, pinpoint specific instances of criticism from which men are immune. Indeed, men are also aware that women face more criticisms than men. What's more, even comments that appear at first glance to be supportive, such as management requests that a woman maintain a specific look because it is "working" for her, are often criticisms of her attempt to assert control over her appearance. Consistent with the experiences of women in a variety of domains, even when their bodies are not so literally on visible display, clothing, hair, physique are an ongoing project, demanding enormous attention and care, time and financial outlay as well as costs to their physical health. Again, women generally understand the standard, although they work to greater and lesser degrees to meet—or resist—it. Moreover, the standard of the time, although it changes, creates a particularly narrow tightrope for women who also want to be taken seriously and whose work depends on being taken seriously. These women journalists, who have spent years learning their profession, mastering skills, are unsurprisingly uneasy with the knowledge that their job is always in jeopardy if they do not invest extraordinary effort into their appearance.

Our research confirms previous studies indicating that for women, the overemphasis they perceive others place on their physical appearance is a primary career concern. Some women easily manage the resulting insecurity. For others it's a source of great consternation. Meanwhile, calls for media organizations to be (more) sensitive to social media issues and to do more to shield their employees from bullying and gratuitous critiques of appearance may be irrelevant if, whether in the name of audience engagement or for the sake of attracting audiences, broadcast management itself engages in this policing of women.

Black anchors, both women and men, spoke of feeling responsibility for representing their community positively. Further study of women of color could offer insights into the specific implications of on-air broadcasters' race. The way in which people of color perceive themselves as serving as representatives and ambassadors for their race highlights the importance of maintaining a particularly high degree of professionalism and of avoiding racial stereotypes in their appearance and it deserves investigation.

These respondents often referred to "double standards." But they seemed to avoid calling the problem "sexism." Although sexism seemingly has been erased from feminist theoretical vocabularies, perhaps because complaints seemed unduly negative and/or uncreative (Ahmed, 2015), sexism is also a distinct possibility as explanation and problem. Ahmed's (2015) point is that in the twenty-first century, complaints about sexism seem like old-fashioned whining. Contemporary women do not want to present themselves as victimized nor do they want to seem to fall into a pattern—again one that to them seems outmoded and unfair—of monolithically, as women, accusing all men of sexism.

Since October, 2017, journalists in broadcast, print, and digital newsrooms have described their own experiences with sexual harassment and gender bias. They concede they did not always recognize these for what they were. Some ignored harassment and bias in order to pursue careers they loved; others left journalism because of harassment, bias, or worse (Pasha, 2017; Goldstein, 2017). Feeling able to challenge sexism, to assert principle on one's own behalf and on behalf of others is a matter of power. It will be important to learn how to empower women, going forward, to resist sexually aggressive comments and criticism of their bodies, in light of growing awareness that no one should be forced to work in environments where these behaviors are tolerated, however grudgingly. Both the bystander intervention that the #MeToo movement proposes, and the fact that men understood the unfairness of the obsession with their colleague's appearance, suggests the possibility that men might also intervene with "lookism" and sexism. Indeed, it suggests an opportunity to shift the burden of changing the workplace's double standard from women to men, and from individuals to management. Certainly publicly confronting sexism (or racism, or sexism as interstructured with racism) is required in any effort to resolve it.

Notes

1 Craft also sued for age discrimination. The case went back and forth in court in the early 1980s; ultimately, Craft lost.
2 Procter & Gamble, which sells two cosmetic lines, subsidized the study, which involved showing adults photographs of white, African American, and Hispanic women wearing different levels of makeup.
3 The one exception was that personnel at the affiliate where the first author's spouse is an anchor were not interviewed.
4 Analyses of the target and content of 70 million readers comments on the *Guardian* online news site showed that although the majority of their regular opinion writers are white men, of the 10 writers who received the most abuse and dismissive trolling, eight were women (four white and four non-white) and two black men (Gardiner et al., 2016). Two of the women and one of the men were gay. Notably, the appearance of some *Guardian* women staffers, i.e., non-broadcast, also drew criticism.

References

Ahmed, S. (2015). Sexism—A problem with a name. *New Formations: A Journal of Culture/Theory/Politics, 86*, 5–13.

Allen, M. (1999, January 24). *Hartford lawsuit recounts the brief shelf life of a TV anchorwoman.* Retrieved from www.nytimes.com/1999/01/24/nyregion/hartford-lawsuit-recounts-the-brief-shelf-life-of-a-tv-anchorwoman.html

Bartlett, K. T. (1994). Only girls wear barrettes: Dress and appearance standards, community norms, and workplace equality. *Michigan Law Review, 92*, 2541–2582.

Boyle, K. (2012, November 26). The colorful evolution of newswomen's attire. *The Washington Post.*

Brannigan, M. (2015, November 23). *How America's top morning tv anchors get dressed.* Retrieved from https://fashionista.com/2015/11/morning-tv-anchors-style

Buhl, T. (2011, January 6). *Former Fox 61 reporter Sindland settles discrimination case against courant publisher.* Retrieved from http://ctwatchdog.com/business/former-fox-61-reporter-sindland-settles-discrimination-case-against-courant-publisher

CBS News Staff. (2013, September 12). Julie Chen reveals she had plastic surgery to make eyes look bigger. *CBS News.* Retrieved from www.cbsnews.com/news/julie-chen-reveals-she-had-plastic-surgery-to-make-eyes-look-bigger/

Chambers, D., Steiner, L., & Fleming, C. (2004). *Women and journalism.* New York, NY: Routledge.

Craft, C. (1986). *Christine Craft: An anchorwoman's story.* Santa Barbara, CA: Capra Press.

Diamond, A. (2016, March 16). *Having to sit on the right of male presenters? That's just the start of TV sexism!* Retrieved from www.dailymail.co.uk/femail/article-3496029/Having-sit-right-male-presenters-s-just-start-TV-sexism-woman-says-s-30-years.html

Engstrom, E., & Ferri, A. J. (2000). Looking through a gendered lens: Local U.S. television news anchors' perceived career barriers. *Journal of Broadcasting & Electronic Media, 44*(4), 614–634. doi:10.1207/s15506878jobem4404_6

Etcoff, N. L., Stock, S., Haley, L. E., Vickery, S. A., & House, D. M. (2011). Cosmetics as a feature of the extended human phenotype: Modulation of the perception of biologically important facial signals. *PloS One, 6*(10), e25656.

Finneman, T., & Yakabe, S. (2016, April 26). *Social media bullying affects journalists.* Retrieved from www.rtdna.org/article/social_media_bullying_affects_journalists

Gardiner, B., Mansfield, M., Anderson, I., Holder, J., Louterand, D., & Ulmanu, M. (2016, April 12). *The dark side of comments.* Retrieved from www.theguardian.com/technology/2016/apr/12/the-dark-side-of-guardian-comments

Gilbert, S. (2017, October 16). The movement of #MeToo. *The Atlantic.* Retrieved from www.theatlantic.com/entertainment/archive/2017/10/the-movement-of-metoo/542979/

Goffman, E. (1977). The arrangement between the sexes. *Theory and Society, 4*(3), 301–331.

Goldstein, K. (2017, November 13). The news industry has a sexual harassment problem. #NowWhat? *Nieman Reports.* Retrieved from http://niemanreports.org/articles/the-news-industry-has-a-sexual-harassment-problem/

Grabe, M., & Samson, L. (2011). Sexual cues emanating from the anchorette chair: Implications for perceived professionalism, fitness for beat, and memory for news. *Communication Research, 38*(4), 471–496.

Hakim, C. (2010). Erotic capital. *European Sociological Review, 26*(5), 499–518. doi:10.1093/esr/jcq014. Retrieved from www.esr.oxfordjournals.org

Hamermesh, D. S. (2013). *Beauty pays: Why attractive people are more successful.* Princeton, NJ: Princeton University Press.

Irby, K. (2016, May 16). *Female anchors face a laundry list of wardrobe requirements.* Retrieved from www.charlotteobserver.com/entertainment/tv/article77852062.html

Mann, E. (2013). *Lisa Wilkinson and Annabel Crabb lament viewer obsession with female TV journalists' appearance.* Retrieved from www.dailylife.com.au.proxy-um.researchport.umd.edu/news-and-views/lisa-wilkinson-and-annabel-crabb-lament-viewer-obsession-with-female-tv-journalists-appearance-20131028-2wbge.html

Marlane, J. (1999). *Women in television news revisited: Into the twenty-first century* (1st ed.). Austin: University of Texas Press. Retrieved from http://catdir.loc.gov/catdir/enhancements/fy0609/98048678-t.html

Meltzer, K. (2010). *TV news anchors and journalistic tradition: How journalists adapt to technology.* New York, NY: Peter Lang.

Mitra, B., Webb, M., & Wolfe, C. (2014, November). Audience responses to the physical appearance of television newsreaders. *Participations, 11*(2).

Mundy, L. (2012, September). Foxy ladies. *The Atlantic.* Retrieved from www.theatlantic.com/magazine/archive/2012/09/foxy-ladies/309054/

Olheiser, A. (2014, November 17). A man wears the same suit on TV almost every day for a year: Nobody cared. *The Washington Post.*

O'Reilly, M. (2014). *Michael Buerk's comments show sexism still exists in the TV industry.* Retrieved from www.theguardian.com/commentisfree/2014/apr/08/michael-buerk-women-sexist-tv-industry

Pasha, S. (2017, October 20). As a woman in media, sexual harassment was the norm: I was told to keep it to myself. *Public Radio International.* Retrieved from www.pri.org/stories/2017-10-20/female-journalist-sexual-harassment-was-norm-i-was-told-keep-it-myself

Patton, T. O. (2006). Hey girl, am I more than my hair? African American women and their struggles with beauty, body image, and hair. *NWSA (National Women's Studies Assn.) Journal, 18*(2), 24–51.

Rouvalis, C. (2006, September 5). Judged by their looks? Female broadcasters criticize news industry's double standard. *Pittsburgh Post-Gazette.* Retrieved from March 30, 2016.

Spicer, T. (2014, November 16). Tracey Spicer: This is what I look like without make-up. Retrieved from www.dailylife.com.au/dl-beauty/tracey-spicer-this-is-what-i-look-like-without-makeup-20141115-3kfbl.html

Wilkinson, L. (2013, October 28). The incredible speech by Lisa Wilkinson everyone is talking about today. Retrieved from www.mamamia.com.au/lisa-wilkinsons-andrew-olle-media-lecture/

Yaqoob, J. (2014, July 5). ITV bosses worried about Susanna Reid's image after seeing *Good Morning Britain* viewing figures plummet. Retrieved from www.mirror.co.uk/tv/tv-news/itv-bosses-worried-susanna-reids-3816952#ixzz36mfnoeey

6

WOMEN, JOURNALISM, AND LABOR UNIONS

Carolyn M. Byerly and Sharifa Simon-Roberts

The need for research

In 2015, CBS journalist Aimee Picchi (2015) reported a new and surprising trend: rising numbers of women joining labor unions across occupations. Although membership was generally dropping off, the percentage of women had increased to 45 percent of all US union members. By the year 2025, Picchi said, women could be a majority of union members in the United States, something that would help them advance occupationally and economically. Picchi's news report cited research by the Institute for Women's Policy Research (IWPR, 2015) that documented both women's expanding membership in unions and the ways that unions had helped them to close the wage gap, minimize pay secrecy, and solve other historic problems for women and racial minorities.

A decade earlier, feminist scholar Jeannie Rea (2005) observed a similar trend in Australia. She noted that women's union membership was on the rise globally. Unions had become a force for change, she said, because feminists had organized within them, pushing pro-woman agendas beginning in the 1970s. Since then, Rea said, unions have been critical to women in reforming, among other areas, "government policy and practice on women and gender equality from industrial and workplace issues to the broader issues of law reform, access to education, health improvement, media behavior" (p. 53).

Some studies have shown that the rise in women's membership in trade unions across occupations in many nations in the 1970s and 1980s occurred not just because more women were entering the labor force but also because unions were adopting specific strategies to attract women members (ILO, 1999; IWPR, 2015; McCreadie & Nightingale, 1994). The increases in membership among women, however, did not mean women took on leadership roles within those unions (ILO, 1999; Mosco & McKercher, 2009). Because women constitute a small number of decision-makers, their ability to raise the topics that specifically affect women is limited.

Schmitt and Woo (2013) found a substantial boost in pay and benefits for unionized women workers relative to their non-union counterparts in the US. The Institute for Women's Policy Research (IWPR) found that women who belonged to unions across occupations in the United States had a wage advantage over non-union women workers, with those wages up to 30 percent higher than their non-union sisters in some cases. Union women were also more likely to have a pension plan than those not belonging. While union membership in the US has generally declined over the last decades, the IWPR also found that the number of women in unions had increased. Even so, women have not attained leadership positions in the US unions (IWPR, 2015).

Bednarczyk (2013) noted that women belonging to trade unions in Europe have reached a reached a critical mass of 40 percent and had been able to challenge the system of workplace oppression. She also observed that neoliberal (i.e., pro-free-market, pro-corporation) reforms have led to a loosening of regulations in favor of corporate control, however; as a result, the state has weakened and this has hurt women in the paid workforce. Women who have taken on senior roles, however, have used their positions to shape their activism; they emphasized making sure unions served the needs of working women (Kirton, 1999). This was crucial because even when women were welcomed into trade unions, they frequently faced opposition from men; moreover, political strategies marginalized "women's interest as irrelevant to the central men's business of trade unionism" (Franzway, 2000, p. 31).

Despite women's greater numbers and involvement in labor (or trade) unions since the mobilization of women's liberation movements four decades ago, academic research on women in journalism (and other media and information) trade-specific unions, is still limited. This dearth of scholarship on what Mosco and McKercher (2009) called female knowledge workers also makes difficult assessing the actual impacts of union membership on women's occupational status in journalism. Indeed, journalism scholars in general have shown limited interest in labor unions, although labor unions are important to communication studies given the growth of employment in the communications industries (McKercher & Mosco, 2006, p. 493). To sketch an exploratory picture of women's participation in journalism trade unions, in relation to their status in news organizations, this chapter compares existing data available from national, regional, and global-level sources. We define a journalist as someone employed for reporting, editing, or news production in an established news organization. Because our investigation focuses on the newspapers, and radio and television stations surveyed for *Global Report on the Status of Women in News Media* (Byerly, 2011), the picture drawn here is thus partial. But it lays a foundation for future studies.

Women's right to communicate

Underlying the present study is the premise that women's participation and occupational standing in the journalism profession is connected to women's freedom of speech, i.e., women's right to communicate. The feminist logic is that more women reporters, editors, and producers will expand the ability for women on the inside to speak for themselves, and, through that eventual hoped-for critical mass, be able to also speak for women in the broader society. Critical mass theory in relation to women's ability to influence outcomes within organizations dates to Rosabeth Kanter's (1977) work on corporations but has found broad application over the years (Childs & Krook, 2008; Dahlerup, 1988). This premise of critical mass was enshrined in two sections of the 1995 UN Fourth World Conference for Women, in Beijing, whose Platform for Action included two key and oft-cited items on women and media equality. Part J1 advocates increasing the participation and access of women to expression and decision-making in and through the media and new technologies of communication; part J2 promotes a balanced and non-stereotyped portrayal of women in the media (Section J, 1995). Feminists attending the Beijing conference pushed for this language to emphasize the ways in which media enabled women's freedom of speech, something they believed to be basic to women's full participation in their societies. They also wanted to illuminate their intent to address the longstanding problem of women's marginalization within and by news and other media industries.

In fact, Section J has inspired a number of national-level policy initiatives aimed at furthering gender equality. For example, following the Beijing conference, the Korean Women's Development Institute, a research body established by the government, organized a meeting, one outcome of which was the adoption of Ten Policy Priorities for Women. Its document called for increasing women's participation in media decision-making to 30 percent by 2005, the development of standards for assessing gender discrimination in the media, and the development and distribution of public service ads on women's issues (Gallagher, 2001, p. 41). Later research showed that the adoption of such goals has been hard to achieve: by 2011 in South Korea, women made up only 25 percent of the journalistic workforce in the eight companies surveyed, with nearly all of those at junior reporting levels and only around 6 percent in management (Byerly, 2011, p. 259). This finding does not negate the premise that more women in journalism fields (particularly at the top) may be able to amplify women's voices, or that women in decision-making roles within journalism unions may be able to strengthen women's influence in newsrooms.

Other scholars have connected women's participation in media decision-making with women's right to communicate, something embodied in Article 19 of the Universal Declaration of Human Rights, adopted by the United Nations General Assembly already in 1948. In Mexico, Vega Montiel (2012) worked actively with feminist journalists, human rights lawyers and other advocates to move Section J principles into a legal framework for gender equality in telecommunications policy. Their lobbying was effective, and in 2014, Mexican legislators approved an overhaul of telecommunications statutes that included nine provisions aimed at eradicating sexist stereotypes, promoting access to resources so women and youth might develop their own programming, and assuring balanced perspectives in content along gender lines, among other things (Chaher, 2016, pp. 138–142). However, the impact of these events on women's standing within the journalism profession per se, or socially and politically, remains to be seen (Gurría, 2017).

Most of the research on the connections between the status of women in journalism and women's free speech or right to communicate consists of small-scale national and regional studies. Most notable is Vega Montiel's (2012) edited volume *Communication and Human Rights*, whose contributing authors make a clear case for research that examines structural and other elements of why and how women as well as those of diverse backgrounds do or do not have access to the means to communicate. Gallagher's (2012) chapter charts the numerous ways that women's silence has obscured the real conditions of their lives—death from childbirth, lower wages, domestic and sexual violence. Gallagher emphasizes that women's lives change once they have the means to communicate and can begin to pose these conditions as problems to be addressed. Byerly and Ross (2006) interviewed 38 women journalists from 11 different nations, who explained how they had worked within their newspapers, radio, and television stations to cover issues and events relevant to women, to interview more women, and to push for expanded gender equality in coverage. This shows that even women employed in traditional newsrooms work to exercise their right to communicate and thereby participate in public life.

Women and journalism trade unions

Feminist scholarship on women's membership and involvement in journalism or other communication unions forms a small but important literature. Chambers, Steiner, and Fleming (2004) took note of women journalists' difficulties getting male-dominated unions to address discrimination, observing that it was not until the 1970s that the American Newspaper Guild finally addressed sex discrimination in journalism (pp. 90–91). In that same time period, they said, women in Britain's National Union of Journalism Training Scheme faced "a de facto quota of 25 per cent places for women" (p. 134). Even after one UK union, the National Union of Journalists, established an equality council in the mid-1990s, the group was unable to show any evidence of women's prospects for promotion (p. 137).

Peters (2001) observed that an increase in the number of women members in journalists' unions mirrored the growth of women in journalism. In such unions across North America and Latin America, women outnumber men. And, while globally the number of women who were part of union decision-making bodies was higher than the number of women in management positions in the media, the pattern has been underrepresentation in key leadership roles. In 2010, the International Federation of Journalists acknowledged the problem by undertaking a region-by-region campaign to try to launch a "global sea change in attitudes towards women that is seen both within and increasingly reflected by the media" (Mahmoudi, 2010, preface).

Unions have been important in shaping journalism and other media industries. For example, communication-related unions in the United States advocated heavily for radio reform in the years after the Second World War (Fones-Wolf, 2006). Canadian labor unions were similarly important in broadcast media policymaking

(Coles, 2006). Unionism having helped to foster collective identity for Québec's journalists in the 1900s, the "configuration of Québec journalism that emerged in the 20th century was characterized by the development of professional journalists as a self-organized group, resting mainly on the social mechanism of unionism" (Demers & Le Cam, 2006, p. 659).

The International Federation of Journalists (IFJ) and European Federation of Journalists (EFJ) together surveyed women in European journalism trade unions in 2001, 2006, and 2012. According to its website the IFJ, which represents about 600,000 members in 140 countries, holds as one of its key tenets the objection to all types of discrimination. The group's 2006 survey of women found that the profession of journalism was becoming feminized, as women approached equal numbers with men in both freelance and regular employment; however, women's membership in unions began to decline slightly between 2001 and 2006 (IFJ/EFJ, 2012). That IFJ/EFJ report said that an overall decline in union membership throughout Europe in these same years coincided with an economic slump across Europe. IFJ/EFJ's most recent survey (2012) found women's membership to be bouncing back (as had the economy regionally). Women have also begun to attain leadership positions within journalism unions in many of the nations surveyed (IFJ/EFJ, 2012, p. 8) and in other regions of the world, such as Australia (Rea 2005).

Women's status in news and media professions

Byerly (2011) and Ross and Padovani (2013) document the glass ceiling for women in journalism and other media professions at senior decision-making levels. In 2008–2009, when Byerly's team collected global data, women accounted for 36 percent of reporters, but they occupied only around a fourth of the positions in top management and on boards of directors (Byerly, 2011). Newsroom glass ceilings in middle and senior management levels tend to prevent women from advancing to higher positions in their field or to roles that would enable them to contribute significantly to the decision-making processes, which affect such things as equality policies in employment, hiring and firing, and content decisions. Regions such as Nordic Europe and Eastern Europe had higher proportions of women in governance and top management—36 percent and 37 percent, respectively, and in South Africa, where women were around 80 percent of those in senior management (p. 9). Although the majority of Finnish journalists are women, and women are 70 percent of Finland's Union of Journalists' nearly 16,000 members, men still dominate the more senior management and governance roles of news organizations (Savolainen & Zillacus-Tikkanen, 2013, pp. 51–55). At the other end of the spectrum were Asia and Oceanic nations, where women journalists were barely 13 percent of those in senior management roles (p. 9).

Ross and Padovani (2013) similarly found women underrepresented in decision-making roles of the 100 media companies they surveyed in 28 European nations, even though women comprised 68 percent of the graduates of university journalism programs and had entered the field in greater and greater numbers in recent years in Europe. Both hierarchical segregation and glass ceiling in media workplaces mean that women are steered into certain kinds of reporting or media formats (e.g., magazines) that had less chance of advancement (Ross & Padovani, 2013, p. 18).

Ross and Padovani (2013) note that gendered values that lead to persistent discrimination are passed along from generation to generation (p. 19), and are also evident in news content. Macharia's (2015) report, *Who Makes the News*, the latest product of the 20-year longitudinal research conducted by the World Association of Christian Communication (WACC), notes that women reported only 37 percent of stories in newspapers, television, and radio newscasts in the 104 nations examined (p. 9). What is alarming is that it has remained constant over the last 10 years (Macharia, 2015). Since 2000, the dominance of men news presenters in broadcast has decreased in Latin America by 14 percent, in Africa by 11 percent, and in other parts of the world by single digits (Macharia, 2015). Not surprisingly, women are also seriously marginalized in news content, accounting for only 24 percent of news subjects globally, with only 10 percent of articles including women as their central focus (Macharia, 2015).

Other regional studies bear out these global-level findings. Ross and Carter (2011) found that while women had become more involved in the British and Irish news media and presented a wider range of topics, their "voices, experiences and expertise [continued] to be regarded by news industries as less important than those of men" (p. 1148). Exceptions in a couple of nations in the Global South (e.g., Uganda and South Africa) and Eastern and Nordic nations, merit further scrutiny as to how and why such variation occurs in women's standing. Notwithstanding progress in the Nordic region, where the emphasis on gender equality is strong, women continue to be underrepresented in news media; unfortunately, the trend appears to be repeating itself in digital media (Mannila, 2017).

Methodology

Our current study sought to learn more about women in journalism and communication labor unions generally, as well as whether women's status in news organizations appears to be related to their union membership. Our research was challenged by several things, including the difficulty of obtaining a breakdown by gender in many unions and by the fact that journalism and communication workers are organized by specific occupations differently from nation to nation. Labor unions in many nations do not reveal members' gender or occupation; very few make data bases containing such data available to the public. When we contacted two large communication unions in the USA for breakdowns of their memberships by gender, our phone calls and email messages were not returned. [1] Using a modest data set, we sought to answer three questions:

1   What is known about women's status in journalism, within and across nations?
2   What is known about women's status in journalism and other media-related labor (trade) unions, within and across nations?
3   Does there appear to be a relationship between women's leadership in journalism unions and their status in newsrooms?

We got raw data for comparable years (2008–2010), for 13 different nations. We also, with permission, performed secondary analyses on data from the following studies: Byerly's (2011) *Global Report on the Status of Women*, which surveyed 522 news companies in 59 nations; International Federation of Journalists/European Federation of Journalists' (2012) *Survey Report on Women in Journalists' Unions in Europe*, which surveyed 21 unions and associations in 20 countries; and the International Federation of Journalists' (2010) *Women Journalists: Partners in Trade Union Leadership*, which surveyed 18 unions in 16 countries.

The linear regression analysis employed a standard statistical software to arrive at descriptive statistics and to perform simple correlation analysis (Pearson's r) to establish the level of significance in associations between variables, where possible. Because of the limited amount of data (only 13 nations), however, findings will be suggestive rather than definitive, and will be most useful in identifying areas for further investigation.

Findings

Overview of findings

The figures in Table 6.1 dramatically illustrate the great dearth of available data on women in journalism unions, with union data found for only 13 of the original

TABLE 6.1 Women in journalism organizations' decision-making positions in relation to journalism union involvement

Countries (from global report)	Women in governance: (%)	Women in top-level management (%)	Women's membership in journalism unions (%)	Women's leadership in journalism unions (%)
*Bulgaria	39.3	53.5	58.0	65.0
Egypt	12.5	20.0	34.3	8.3
Estonia	16.7	57.1	55.0	66.0
Finland	37.0	34.7	57.0	46.2
France	16.7	33.3	36.0	33.3
Germany	23.7	20.5	34.5	24.6
Jordan	11.9	12.0	19.1	9.0
Lithuania	30.8	28.6	58.0	71.0
Morocco	16.7	27.8	26.2	26.3
Norway	37.5	33.3	43.2	46.0
Spain	17.6	20.0	48.4	46.2
Sweden	34.1	39.8	51.7	50.0
United Kingdom	36.5	30.2	39.2	27.6

Source: The *Global Report on the Status of Women in the News Media* (Byerly, 2011), IFJ/EFJ reports (2012), and IFJ (2010). Table 6.1 only includes the 13 nations from the *Global Report* for which we were able to get union membership data for a comparable time frame.

NOTES:

* Bold facing denotes nations with higher representation of women in decision roles, both in *Global Report* findings and in journalism labor unions.

59 nations of the *Global Report*, as listed in Table 6.1. We note that the IFJ/EFJ (2012) included two Journalists' labor unions in Germany in their report. The data for the two trade unions were analyzed separately. Some of the figures in Table 6.1 show women's membership in journalism unions for the nations to be low. For example, women represent only 19 percent and 26.2 percent of the membership in the Jordan Press Association (JPA) and the National Union of the Moroccan Press—Syndicat National de la Presse Marocaine (SNPM)—respectively, even though women have expanded their participation in the profession of those nations in recent decades. This lack of involvement among women in trade unions and "status of women across the region [remain] linked to social conservative practices and to the enforcement of Personal Status Codes," according to the IFJ (IFJ, 2010, p. 1). However, the low percentages of women journalists joining journalism unions suggests they are not benefitting from the potential benefits that union membership can bring in terms of better pay and working conditions.

The statistics for membership and leadership in journalism trade unions appear to go nearly hand in hand in some nations. Women's union leadership is highest in Lithuania, Estonia, and Bulgaria at 71 percent, 66 percent, and 65 percent respectively. These countries also have some of the highest percentages of women in decision-making roles in news organizations, as found in the *Global Report* study, and also shown here. Table 6.1 also suggests a relationship between women's higher level of representation in decision-making roles of their news organizations, and their percentages of membership and leadership in journalism unions. Bold facing shows this relationship in Bulgaria, Finland, and Sweden. However, no similar correlation exists in Lithuania and Spain, where women have both high representation and leadership positions in journalism unions, but are low in the decision-making ranks of top management and governance in the news organizations. To explain this anomaly requires further research.

In Egypt and Jordan, fewer than 10 percent of union leaders are women. The IFJ (2010) found that in the Middle East and Arab World, women "remain poorly represented in their executive boards where men maintain an overwhelming majority" (p. 1). To combat this problem, "some unions in the region have adopted policies that promote women journalists in the union, including through increased participation in thematic committees or a quota for women on the board as is the case in Morocco" (IFJ, 2010, p. 1). In 2008, the Syndicat National de la Presse Marocaine (SNPM) declared a 25 percent minimum female participation in the union's board, and in 2009, 26.3 percent of board members were shown to be women, indicating some success (IFJ, 2010).

In the United States, the Communication Workers of America (CWA), which includes the Newspaper Guild, says that it advances the cause of 700,000 workers in "telecommunications and information technology, the airline industry, news media, broadcast and cable television, education, healthcare and public service, law enforcement, manufacturing and other fields" (Communications Workers of America, 2017, para. 1). Although this union represents journalists and other media professionals, information on its membership (including gender and occupational breakdown) is not publicly available; union representatives did not respond to our repeated efforts to discuss access. We were similarly unsuccessful in obtaining a gender or occupational breakdown for the 160,000 members of the Screen Actors' Guild-American Federation of TV and Radio Artists (SAG-AFTRA), whose members include broadcast journalists.

The statistical findings presented in Figure 6.1 provide a more detailed view of the data in Table 6.1 and show the relationship between women journalists and the unions that exist to advance them within the profession. That correlation, as shown in Figure 6.1, is highly significant ($r^2 = 0.8085$, $r = 0.8991$, $p = 0.00003$, $N = 13$), showing a very strong linear relationship between the percentage of women who belong to journalism unions and the percentage of women who hold leadership positions in those unions of the nations examined.

Although the number of nations is small, the data are compelling and suggest the merit of the critical mass theory by suggesting that the greater the percentage of women within a union, the greater chance women will hold positions of leadership in those unions. Critical mass theory also predicts that holding leadership roles better enables women to influence the priorities of the organization, an empirical question for future pursuit.

We have aggregated data for 13 nations, with Bulgaria, Estonia, and Lithuania showing particularly strong relationships between women as members and unions

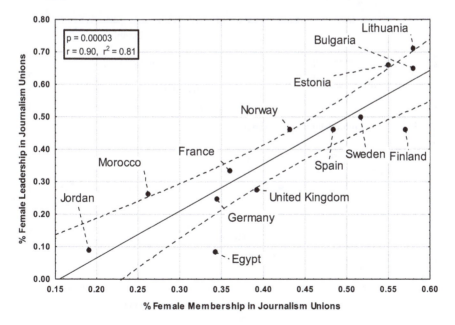

FIGURE 6.1 Relationship of percentage of female membership to percentage of female leadership in journalism unions

leadership, with the Nordic nations of Sweden and Finland also relatively strong. Both gender equality in the workplace and the history of labor unions are strong in these nations. Edstrom (2013) indicates that gender parity within journalism unions has also been a goal, and that the unions closely monitor equality in employment as well as in news content of the Swedish media.

Figure 6.2 compares women's leadership in journalism unions to women's positions in top management of news organizations for the 13 nations examined. These data indicate a highly significant relationship ($r^2 = 0.55$, $p = 0.004$, $r = 0.74$, $N = 13$) between the percentage of women holding leadership positions in journalism unions and the percentage of women in top-level management positions of news organizations surveyed in those same nations. We focused on women in top-level management in newsrooms because it is at this level where women are most likely able to influence organizational and journalistic decisions regarding hiring, promotion, and newsroom policies. As Figure 6.2 shows, Estonia, Bulgaria, and Sweden have both a high level of women holding leadership positions in their unions and women who have achieved positions in top-level management in their news organizations. The *Global Report* had found gender parity in Bulgarian and Estonian newsrooms to be particularly high at all levels of the news organization, except in governance, where women were only at 39 percent in the 10 news companies surveyed in Bulgaria, and 16.7 percent of the 10 companies surveyed in

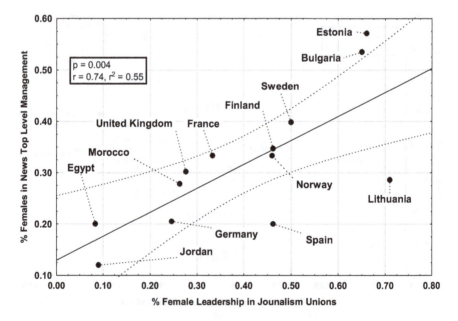

FIGURE 6.2 Relationship of percentage of female leadership in journalism unions to percentage of females in top-level management of news organizations

Estonia (Byerly, 2011). Nastasia and Nastasia (2013) explain women's high occupational standing in the news organizations of Bulgaria and other nations of the former Eastern Bloc as a holdover from the days of Soviet domination when the journalism profession became feminized and when women generally excelled in the labor market. They also emphasize that women journalists (and other professionals) experienced discrimination nonetheless in the form of lower pay, few benefits, and the expectation they would still meet all of the household roles at the end of the paid workday.

The Nordic nations of Sweden, and to a somewhat lesser extent, Finland and Norway, show very positive linear relationships between top-level management and women's leadership in journalism. Gender parity is relatively high in the Nordic nations, with women in the 30–40 percentiles in the senior and top management roles of newsrooms (Byerly, 2011). These nations have a long history of press freedom and gender equality. And, as noted earlier, the journalism union of Sweden has actively pursued gender equality within the profession. The situation is somewhat different in the neighboring Nordic nations. Savolainen and Zillacus-Tikkanen (2013) note that the majority of journalists in Finland are women, and that women have also avidly sought out union membership and leadership. Even so, the authors lament that women's representation in senior and top-level management of news companies does not reflect this feminization of the profession, nor are they as well paid as men. Figure 6.2 shows that in both Finland and Norway, women's leadership in journalism unions as well as their achievement of top positions in newsrooms is modest.

Discussion

Although data were limited, the 13 nations for which we obtained comparable data by year are diverse geographically, in terms of press/media systems, and in levels of democracy and freedom of expression. This diversity provides a level of confidence in indicating a strong relationship between women's membership in unions, their advancement to leadership within those unions, and the likelihood of advancement into decision-making levels of news companies where they are employed for the years examined. Yet numbers do not tell the whole story. The empirical question this raises is how such advancement has affected their lives materially and personally in years since.

Despite calls by scholars and practitioners for women to be better represented in journalism and media industries, and given their increasing participation in these industries since the 1970s, women have yet to reach parity at the higher levels of news organizations. Clearly more scholarship is needed regarding both individual nations and at the global level. The paucity of statistical data available on the membership and leadership of women in communication-related trade unions makes this a challenging task. Many—perhaps most—labor unions across the world are reluctant to make public their membership data in relation to gender and other demographics.

Ironically, the two examples of nations quoted at the beginning of this chapter, where women's union membership was said to be increasing, i.e., the United States and Australia, were nations where we could get no data at all on women in journalism unions. Louise North (personal communication, September 2017), an Australian journalist and media scholar, who studies women in news industries of that nation, said that the Media, Entertainment, and Arts Alliance (MEAA), Australia's largest communication union's annual report (MEAA, 2017) is the closest the union gets to providing rough numbers on its members. The union, she said, would not give her a gender breakdown. In fact, North said, the union had been critical of her research, which questioned why the union had published a report on gender and journalism in 1996 but had never addressed the disparities it brought to light or conducted a follow-up survey to determine whether changes had occurred. Qualitative research into the nexus between women, unions, and journalism is also needed to understand the human experiences behind the numbers. A particularly useful study to undertake would be to examine union commitments to gender equality, and to discern strategies that women have employed to push for such commitments and their implementation. Future studies might also incorporate analyses of whether and to what extend unions are addressing the recent gender politics associated with sexual harassment and exploitation, and how these problems affect women's status in journalism and in journalism unions. This particular line of investigation is suggested by issues raised by women employed in the industry who revealed their victimization through the #MeToo and #TimesUp movements—movements which have spread across the world.[2]

On a positive note, female members in journalism trade unions in some nations outnumber their male counterparts and women have assumed leadership positions. Moreover, some unions are making a greater effort to acknowledge the contribution of women to the industry and the labor movement as a result of women's activism within those unions. Many unions have started putting measures in place to sustain the growth of its female membership and also to ensure that the welfare of female members is better addressed. According to the IFJ/EFJ (2012), trade unions that represent journalists in Bulgaria (Union of Bulgarian Journalists) and Lithuania (Lithuanian Journalists' Union) have the highest percentage of female members at 58 percent. In Finland (Suomen Journalistiliitto—Union of Journalists in Finland), Estonia (Estonian Union of Journalists), and Sweden (Svenka Journalistforbundet—Swedish Union of Journalists), women also outnumber men with membership rates of 57 percent, 55 percent, and 51.7 percent, respectively. Based on these statistics, it appears that in countries in Eastern and Nordic Europe, women participate in trade unions at higher rates than elsewhere.

One conclusion that can be drawn from both our review of published research and our small-scale study here is that women's status in journalism and organized labor warrants more scholarly attention. Our recent study of 13 nations is a start but only that. This particular path of inquiry is wide open for further research.

Notes

1 Ross and Padovani (2013) also encountered this problem when trying to get gender-specific employment information from many individual companies.
2 In 2006 Tarana Burke coined the phrase MeToo to support women who had survived sexual assault. The phrase was adopted in 2017 by women who brought forth allegations of sexual harassment by prominent men in the entertainment and journalism industries. The #MeToo movement paved the way for #TimesUp, a legal defense fund and anti-sexual harassment initiative backed by prominent women in the entertainment industry.

References

Bednarczyk, A. (2013). *Gender and labor—Women can benefit from trade unions? Krytyka.org—Nauka, Polityka, Kultura, Społeczeństwo*. Retrieved from http://krytyka.org/gender-and-labor-women-can-benefit-from-trade-unions/

Byerly, C. M. (2011). *The global report on the status of women in news media*. Washington, DC: International Women's Media Foundation.

Byerly, C. M., & Ross, K. (2006). *Women and media: A critical introduction*. Malden, MA: Wiley-Blackwell.

Ceulemans, M., & Fauconnier, G. (1979). *Mass media: The image, role and social conditions of woman*. Paris, France: UNESCO.

Chaher, S. (2016). Politicas de género y comunicación en México a partir de la apbrobación de la Ley Federal de Telecomunicaciones y Radio Difusión en materia egualdad de género. In S. Chaher (Ed.), *Entre andares y retrocesos* (pp. 138–142). Buenos Aires, Argentina: Asociación Civil Comunicación para la igualdad y la Defensoría del Público de Servicios de Comunicación Audiovisual de Argentina.

Chambers, D., Steiner, L., & Fleming, C. (2004). *Women and journalism*. London: Routledge, Taylor & Francis.

Childs, S., & Krook, L. M. (2008). Critical mass theory and women's political representation. *Political Studies, 56*, 725–736. doi:10.1111/j.1467-9248.2007.00712.x

Coles, A. L. (2006). Acting in the name of culture? Organized labour campaigns for Canadian dramatic programming. *Canadian Journal of Communication, 31*(3), 519–539. doi:10.22230/cjc.2006v31n3a1765

Communications Workers of America. (2017). *About CWA*. Retrieved from www.cwa-union.org/about

Dahlerup, D. (1988). From a small to a large minority: Women in Scandinavian politics. *Scandinavian Political Studies, 11*(4), 275–297.

Demers, F., & Le Cam, F. (2006). The fundamental role played by unionism in the self-structuring of the professional journalists from Québec. *Canadian Journal of Communication, 31*(3), 659–674. doi:10.22230/cjc.2006v31n3a1839

Edstrom, M. (2013). Sweden: Women reach parity but gender troubles persist. In C. M. Byerly (Ed.), *The Palgrave international handbook of women and journalism* (pp. 39–50). Basingstoke: Palgrave Macmillan.

Fones-Wolf, E. A. (2006). Defending listeners' rights: Labor and media reform in post-war America. *Canadian Journal of Communication, 31*(3), 499–518. doi:10.22230/cjc.2006v31n3a1759

Franzway, S. (2000). Sisters and sisters? Labour movements and women's movements in (English) Canada and Australia. *Hecate, 26*(2), 31–46.

Gallagher, M. (2001). *Gender setting: New agendas for media monitoring and advocacy*. London: Zed Books.

Gallagher, M. (2012). Women's human and communication rights. In A. Vega Montiel (Ed.), *Communication and human rights* (pp. 87–94). Coyoacán, Mexico: Autonomous University of Mexico.

Gurría, A. (2017, January 10). *Presentation of the OECD review of gender policies in Mexico*. OECD website. Retrieved from www.oecd.org/mexico/presentation-of-the-oecd-review-of-gender-policies-in-mexico.htm

International Federation of Journalists. (2010). *Women journalists: Partners in trade union leadership*. Brussels, Belgium: IFJ.

International Federation of Journalists/European Federation of Journalists. (2012, November). *Survey report on women in journalists' unions in Europe*. IFJ/EFJ Conference on gender equality in journalists' unions: Confronting the financial crisis, empowering women, Athens, Greece. Retrieved from www.ifj.org/fileadmin/images/Gender/Gender_docu ments/IFJEFJ_Survey_Report_on_Women_in_Unions_in_Europe.pdf

International Labour Office. (1999). *Key indicators of the labour market 1999*. Geneva, Switzerland: ILO.

IWPR. (2015). *Union advantage for women, the*. Washington, DC: Institute for Women's Policy Research (IWPR). Retrieved from https://statusofwomendata.org/press-releases/unionized-women-earn-more-than-nonunionized-women-in-every-u-s-state/

Kanter, R. M. (1977). Some effects of proportions on group life. *American Journal of Sociology, 82*(5), 965–990.

Kirton, G. (1999). Sustaining and developing women's trade union activism: A gendered project? *Gender, Work and Organization, 6*(4), 213–223. doi:10.1111/1468-0432.00084

Macharia, S. (2015). *Who makes the news?* Global Media Monitoring Project. Toronto, Canada: World Association for Christian Communication.

Mahmoudi, S. E. (2010). Preface. In *Women journalists: Partners in trade union leadership*. Brussels, Belgium: IFJ. Retrieved from http://mmlr-files.s3.amazonaws.com/s3fs-public/library/material/women-partners-in-tu-leadership-gender-fact-shets-en.pdf

Mannila, S. (2017). *Women and men in the news: Report on gender representation in Nordic news content and the Nordic media industry*. Denmark: Rosendahls.

McCreadie, S., & Nightingale, M. (1994). Challenges for women trade unionists. *Social Alternatives, 12*(4), 39–42.

McKercher, C., & Mosco, V. (2006). The labouring of communication. *Canadian Journal of Communication, 31*(3), 493–497. doi:10.22230/cjc.2006v31n3a1841

MEAA. (2017). *Media Entertainment and Arts Alliance (MEAA) website*. Retrieved from www.meaa.org/

Mosco, V., & McKercher, C. (2009). *The laboring of communication: Will knowledge workers of the world unite?* Lanham, MD: Rowman & Littlefield.

Nastasia, S., & Nastasia Diana, Y. (2013). Bulgaria: Cinderella went to market, with consequences for women journalists. In C. M. Byerly (Ed.), *The Palgrave international handbook of women and journalism* (pp. 27–38). Basingstoke: Palgrave Macmillan.

Peters, B. (2001). *Equality and quality: Setting standards for women in journalism* (IFJ Survey on the status of women journalists). Brussels, Belgium: International Federation of Journalists. Retrieved from https://docuri.com/download/woman-in-journalism_59bf393ff58 1716e46c3d4cf_pdf

Picchi, A. (2015, September 9). Why women may be the new face of labor unions. *CBS News*. (online). Retrieved from www.cbsnews.com/news/why-women-may-be-the-new-face-of-labor-unions/

Rea, J. (2005). Women and trade unions: Do women need unions or unions need women? *Social Alternatives, 24*(2), 50–54.

Ross, K., & Carter, C. (2011). Women and news: A long and winding road. *Media, Culture & Society, 33*(8), 1148–1165. doi:10.1177/0163443711418272

Ross, K., & Padovani, C. (2013). *Review of the implementation of the Beijing platform for action in the EU member states: Advancing gender equality in decision-making in media organisations.* Luxembourg: European Institute for Gender Equality.

Savolainen, T., & Zillacus-Tikkanen, H. (2013). Finland: Women journalists, the unequal majority. In C. M. Byerly (Ed.), *The Palgrave international handbook of women and journalism* (pp. 51–65). Basingstoke: Palgrave Macmillan.

Schmitt, J., & Woo, N. (2013, December). *Women workers and unions.* (Report). Washington, DC: Center for Economic and Policy Research.

Section, J. (1995). *The United Nations fourth world conference on women platform for action.* Retrieved from www.un.org/womenwatch/daw/beijing/platform/media.htm

Vega Montiel, A. (2012). Prologue. In A. Vega Montiel (Ed.), *Communication and human rights* (pp. 15–17). Coyoacán, Mexico: Autonomous University of México.

PART II

News discourses, sexualization, and sexual violence

PART II

*News discourses,
sexualization, and
sexual violence*

7

TRENDING NOW

Feminism, postfeminism, sexism, and misogyny in British journalism

Rosalind Gill and Katie Toms

Introduction

In the last few years feminism has gained spectacular visibility across media and popular culture. As Sarah Banet-Weiser (2018b) observes, "everywhere you turn, there is an expression of feminism—on a T-shirt, in a movie, in the lyrics of a pop song, in an inspirational Instagram post, in an acceptance speech." The news media have been crucial to this, reporting on popular feminist campaigns and feminist demonstrations and women's marches, as well as centering feminism as an issue—whether substantively in terms of equal pay or sexual violence, or more broadly as something to be routinely explored by politicians, actors, and pop stars. "The new DO: Calling yourself a feminist" announced *Glamour* magazine in the US (Halpin, 2013), cementing a wider impression that no interview of a high-profile woman is complete without asking about her views of, or, identification with feminism.

For many—including us—this new and heightened visibility of feminism is cause for optimism, particularly after the 1990s and early 2000s, when feminist activists struggled hard to achieve *any* news coverage for their causes, and when feminism was widely repudiated (McRobbie, 2009), even by people who supported gender equality in principle (Scharff, 2012). However, while welcoming the new "luminosity of feminism" (Gill, 2016, p. 614) across the media, we must be cautious of the claim that this new mediated visibility means that journalism is somehow becoming feminist. We underscore the importance of thinking of any period, conjuncture, or moment—including our own—as structured by complexities and contradictions. So, new ideas, moods, or movements do not necessarily displace other trends, but co-exist with them.

We will argue that alongside the visibility of feminism in contemporary news media several other currents are equally prominent. First, we suggest that a set of circulating ideas, values and framings understood as a postfeminist or neoliberal sensibility still hold sway. These ideas have not been displaced by the new enthusiasm for feminism. Second, the news media remain highly sexist. On a daily basis, mainstream journalism still trivializes women and subjects women to offensive judgments about their appearance and competence. Third, misogyny has become a terrifying live force; "comments" and vicious trolling against women in the public eye represent chilling ripostes to the assumption that news media provide safe spaces for feminist ideas. Looking at empirical examples drawn from the UK news media, we show the contradictoriness of the current moment and advocate approaches that can theorize the coexistence of these different ideas/themes/motifs/ideologies.

Feminism

Feminism is undoubtedly "having a moment" (Valenti, 2014b). Reflecting the dramatic resurgence of interest in the term, the *Merriam-Webster Dictionary* made "feminism" its "word of the year" in 2017. During the 2000s, the word sexism seemed in danger of disappearing altogether from critical vocabularies (Gill, 2011; Williamson, 2003), and news editors deemed feminist campaigns about domestic violence, rape, or unequal pay "a yawn," too dull to make it onto the news agenda (Gill, 2016). But that sense of "gender fatigue" (Kelan, 2009) has given way to a moment of new energy, excitement, and interest. Feminism has become "sexy." "You've read the papers, you've seen the news: feminism is back," a British lifestyle site for women announced in 2015 (Moore, 2015). Glossy magazines launched "feminism" issues, and fashion companies rushed out t-shirts declaring "This is what a feminist looks like."

Accounts of this surge in interest in feminism typically identify several key events. Many regard Beyoncé's performance at the 2014 MTV Video Music Awards, when she performed her song "Flawless" in front of a huge sign emblazoned "FEMINIST," as a foundational moment in the rise of "popular feminism" (Banet-Weiser, 2018a; Keller & Ryan, 2018; Valenti, 2014a). The performance used sampled words from the TED talk (and later book) by Nigerian novelist Chimamanda Ngozi Adichie titled "We Should All Be Feminists." Emma Watson's, 2014 UN talk launching the HeForShe campaign, telling men "gender equality is your issue too" is also frequently referenced as a turning point (Watson, 2014). Watson became the "face" for *Elle*'s "feminism" issue after the magazine brought in high-profile advertising companies to help it "rebrand" feminism (Candy, 2014). Among mainstream media platforms, magazines have become a key site of this feminism (Favaro & Gill, 2018), as have popular TV shows such as *Girls* and *Orange Is the New Black*, comics such as Amy Schumer and Bridget Christie, and British columnist Caitlin Moran. In the same moment, "manifestoes" by high-profile women such as Facebook COO Sheryl Sandberg and New America CEO (and Director of Policy Planning under Secretary of State Hillary Clinton) Anne-Marie Slaughter helped to cement persistent gender inequality as a topic for discussion in quality news outlets.

Activist campaigns have been central to this too—both on the streets and in online spaces, often moving across and between sites. The now global SlutWalk movement was significant as an expression of anger against sexual violence and sexual double standards, raising the profile and visibility of popular feminism. In turn, the flourishing of feminist digital activism has been extraordinary (Banet-Weiser, 2018a; Keller & Ryan, 2018; Retallack, Ringrose, & Lawrence, 2016) with blogs and websites such as Everyday Sexism, The Vagenda, Black Girl Dangerous, Feministing, Crunk Feminist Collective and Jezebel, and a proliferation of social media campaigns from NastyWomen to NotOkay to SayHerName. Online platforms enable "doing feminism in the network" (Rentschler & Thrift, 2015, p. 331), facilitating the emergence of feminist communities of support (Keller & Ryan, 2018), "peer-to-peer witnessing" (Rentschler, 2014, p. 76), and "affective solidarities" (Keller, Mendes, & Ringrose, 2018) such as in relation to #BeenRapedNeverReported.

The immense pain and anger many felt after Donald Trump's presidential victory in 2016 was a further impetus to feminist action, leading to women's marches and the International Women's Strike involving women in 50 countries. Since Trump's inauguration in January 2017, and the exposure of Hollywood producer Harvey Weinstein's alleged sexual harassment, coercion and rape of numerous women, feminism has not left the news agenda in the US, the UK and in many other countries around the world. The energy and vitality of feminist organizing around the MeToo and TimesUp hashtags has provoked unprecedented levels of journalistic interest, underscored by creative and highly visual protests (e.g., women celebrities dressing in black for major awards ceremonies). This is feminism designed for a 24-hour news cycle and a culture dominated by images. It is also feminism that depends upon the logics of platform capitalism and its metrics of likes, shares, and followers. Contemporary mediated feminism circulates in what Banet-Weiser calls an "economy of visibility" that has kept feminism "trending" (Banet-Weiser, 2018a).

This account of the renewed visibility of feminism is, of course, partial. It is largely based on US events and movements, and risks becoming hegemonic, of taking on the status of a myth-like origin story. Greater geographical specificity helps to complicate and disrupt this narrative. Other Anglophone countries bring out different dimensions and textures. In Australia, anger and activism united in a key moment that led to the Destroy the Joint movement—after an outburst by radio presenter Alan Jones that Prime Minister Julia Gillard was "destroying the joint" by pledging AUD \$320m to support the advancement of women in the South Pacific. In New Zealand in 2013, a group of men deliberately intoxicated teenage girls, gang-raped them, and posted the images of this to social media. This provoked large demonstrations against rape culture, victim blaming, and the lack of support for women's organizations; these were widely reported and discussed in news media. The election in 2018 of Jacinda Ardern, while pregnant, as New Zealand's Prime Minister has generated national and international conversations about the perennial issue of combining work with parenting/caring for dependents.

In the UK, vibrant campaigns such as "No More Page 3," which challenged the daily appearance of topless models in the tabloid press, and "Lose the Lads' Mags," which addresses the sexism of men's magazines, drew significant media attention (García-Favaro & Gill, 2016). Indeed, even a single advert could become a focus point. For example, 70,000 people signed a petition against Protein World's now notorious billboard picturing a thin model in a bright yellow bikini with the slogan "Are you beach body ready?" This campaign also garnered enormous media critique; UK journalists focused on the issues raised by the advert, and diverse feminist responses to it, including a major demonstration in London in 2015.

By late 2017—and in the wake of #MeToo—feminist stories were central to the UK news agenda, regularly featuring on prime-time news bulletins. The BBC's gender-based pay discrimination became a huge news story, and the gender pay gap at news companies remains a prominent news topic, as UK companies and organizations with more than 250 employees are now required to audit and publish their gender pay differentials. In 2018, the Parole Board of England and Wales reported its intention to release early the notorious rapist John Worboys, whose conviction for drugging and raping 12 women in his cab, with over 100 victims suspected in total, had provoked widespread public revulsion. News of his impending release immediately generated protest against the criminal justice system's culture of disrespect and disregard towards rape victims. Stories about the protest were sympathetically reported across the news media, albeit perhaps because it resonated with an enduring focus on "law and order." After two victims managed to crowdfund a judicial review, the High Court overturned the Parole Board decision and Worboys will remain in prison indefinitely.

The concern remains, however, that feminist ideas, topics, and debates, will not last as a notable focus of news and that journalists will tire of stories about gender. As with other struggles, at any given moment the news agendas may shift: a backlash may emerge; the story may become "stale." Questions should also be asked about the extent to which inclusion of feminist issues primarily occurs in publications targeted at middle class, educated audiences. Discussion of #MeToo is extensive in *The Guardian*, the BBC's *Newsnight*, and on *Channel 4 News*. But to what degree is it reaching popular audiences and changing the conversation more generally?

Moreover, which *kinds* of feminism achieve visibility in news media? Who and what becomes feminism's public face, besides young, beautiful, film and music (eminently click-able) celebrities and heavyweight "power feminists" for "think pieces"? Clearly, feminist visibilities are profoundly shaped by class, race, and disability as well as sexuality and age. Reflecting the values of the mainstream news media more generally, white, middle, and upper-class, able-bodied feminists can command journalists' attention far more easily than can women who are working class, of color, or disabled. Despite vibrant feminist activism in the UK against austerity, racism, deportations of migrants, and benefits cuts that target disabled people, these protests have received relatively little attention—aside from "feminist spectaculars" by organizations like Sisters Uncut. Black feminist organizations routinely struggle to achieve news coverage for their campaigns (e.g., Southall Black Sisters or Women Against Fundamentalism), reflecting an ongoing racism and classism within reporting about feminism (Jonsson, 2014). Visibility is also related to the ideological complexion of the politics (Gill, 2016, p. 616) and a campaign's degree of challenge to the status quo (Rottenberg, 2014). Corporate-focused and neoliberal feminisms concerned with, say, small changes to the gender balance of corporate boards, are more news media-friendly than radical, anti-capitalist, or anti-colonial feminisms. A "feminism of the 99%" that highlights interlocking intersectional practices of oppression is necessary (Emejulu, 2017).

Sexism

The revitalized feminist landscape discussed above co-exists with enduring sexism. Indeed, it is striking how much of the current feminist activism focuses on "cultural sexism." This is epitomized by "the ugly wallpaper of women's lives [– such as] Page Three, lads' mags, music videos, the dearth of women in broadcasting, street harassment. In a world in which women have equality under the law, but not in reality, activists are tackling attitudes and influences" (Cochrane, 2013). Sexism manifests in the news media with "endless variety and tedious monotony" (Fraser & Nicholson, 2011, p. 234).

The sexual objectification of women is one key area where sexism in news media remains problematic. Feminists have achieved some success in dealing with the most notorious instances of this. For example, Page 3 of *The Sun* newspaper no longer shows a bare-breasted glamor model every day, and many of the lads' mags have closed down. Yet, the tabloid press relies on "sexualised" images of women across its pages, often with little or no relation to the story being reported. Some tabloid newspapers boast a "nipple count" in excess of 100 for each issue of the paper, and feature adverts for sexual services such as phone sex lines or escort agencies as well as editorial content. The problem is not limited to tabloid press. The organization Women in Journalism found that both *The Times* and *Daily Telegraph* frequently printed large images of semi-naked women and images of women celebrities in revealing outfits on their front pages, with little news-related reason or relevance (Carter, Turner, & Paton, 2012; Martinson, Bawdon, Ryan, Cochrane, & Corrigan, 2012). Such content confirms that women's value resides in their sexual attractiveness.

The obsession with women's appearance goes beyond images and text that represent women for their sexual value. Appraisals of women's appearance remain a common way for news reports to diminish or demean a woman. The clichéd descriptors "blonde," "brunette," and "redhead" show an obduracy despite being mocked—and are never applied to men. News media routinely comment upon and pick apart the appearance of women in the public eye; fat-shaming is particularly common (Gay, 2018; West, 2017). The bodies of women celebrities are subject to levels of surveillance that are increasingly forensic: no "flaw" is too trivial to be discussed, perhaps even magnified in photos taken with telescopic lenses. Even when ostensibly praising or celebrating the beauty and desirability of a woman, such discourse is sexist: it is all about the practice of gendered power. In 2013 a UK working group participating in the United Nations Commission on the Elimination of Discrimination Against Women (CEDAW) asserted:

> [a] persistent portrayal of women as sexualised objects in the print-based media is clearly discriminatory in nature, it is un-paralleled for men, and it

exists without context. . . . [L]ack of press regulation on the issue is inconsistent with other forms of media, and equality legislation, and it allows for the sexual objectification of women in mainstream media to continue unchecked.

(UK CEDAW Working Group, 2013)

Sexism directed at women politicians is also ubiquitous (Ross, 2003). This was well-documented in the reporting of Hillary Clinton's 2016 election campaign (Blumell, 2017; Vickery & Everbach, 2018; Wilz, 2016). It is also a feature of UK news, from former Prime Minister Tony Blair's "babes" in 1997 to former Prime Minister David Cameron's "cuties" in 2010. Current Prime Minister Theresa May's taste in shoes is a matter of commentary across the journalistic spectrum. In the run-up to the 2017 General Election in Britain, *The Sun* launched "the first of our Heel-ection Specials—girls in lingerie designs inspired by Theresa May's shoes. Kelly Hall pays homage to the PM's leopard-print heels and reckons the Tory leader will knock spots off her rivals." Stating "Mrs May is renowned for her fabulous footwear," the piece was accompanied by a close-up of May's feet and several images of her wearing leopard-print shoes. The lingerie designer was quoted as saying: "I also admire how she makes the tough decisions while dressing with style—as Marilyn Monroe said, 'Give a girl the right shoes, and she can conquer the world'" (Jehring, 2017). This coverage followed "trousergate" on May's sartorial choices; it preceded "Legs-It," where a *Daily Mail* front page image of Scottish first minister Nicola Sturgeon and Theresa May was headlined with the caption: "Never mind Brexit, who won Legs-it!" (*Daily Mail*, 2017). What is interesting is the knowingness of this sexism, its deliberate intention to provoke.

Other troublingly sexist features include news coverage of sexual assaults and rapes. These are still often treated in a salacious or titillating manner and are premised on several "rape myths" that uphold racist, classist, and sexist assumptions. Sexual double standards are pervasive in news about court cases; reporting tends to express empathy with the perpetrator and excessively discuss women's clothing, behavior, alcohol consumption, etc.

One of the challenges in dealing with sexism in news is the right-wing moral discourse embedded in UK regulation. This is constructed around issues of taste, decency, and the likelihood of content tending to "deprave" the audience—rather than a political discourse concerned with human rights and discrimination. The Editors' Code of Practice has no specific clause compelling journalists, editors, or proprietors not to be sexist or discriminatory against groups/categories/classes of people. Crucially, there is no recourse to complain about such material, unless an individual was the subject of the material themselves (IPSO, 2018). Additionally, UK laws on hate speech and hate crime make no reference to sex or gender as categories, making mounting a legal case difficult. The lack of a specific focus on discriminatory representation or depiction constitutes a major stumbling block in legal objections to sexist material.

One potentially important opportunity to intervene around this issue was the UK Government's Inquiry during 2011–2012 into journalists' illegal phone hacking of celebrities and others in the public eye, such as a missing schoolgirl Milly Dowler. Chaired by Lord Justice Brian Leveson, the Inquiry raised important questions about the conduct of the news media and was notable for taking evidence from feminist organizations regarding how reporting fed into a wider culture of sexism, sexual objectification, and misogyny. Leveson's 2012 report indicted the print media's "failure to treat women with dignity and respect" and called journalists' practice of "demeaning and degrading women" a serious concern (Leveson, 2012).

In taking evidence from many interested parties, including newspaper editors, the Leveson Inquiry was also instructive in highlighting the *kinds* of justifications that journalists use to defend themselves against accusations of sexism. Dominic Mohan, then editor of *The Sun*, for example, was notable in the sheer variety of the justifications he presented for the paper's continued presentation of semi-naked women on a daily basis.[1] He used 10 different arguments in addition to a generic one around "free speech."

1 **Heritage**—Portraying women this way has always happened. Therefore, it is harmless, "an innocuous British institution."
2 **Humor**—It's a bit of banter. "The Sun's humour and its light-hearted nature has really been the key to its success," but critics have no sense of humor.
3 **Female agency**—The models choose to pose and some "made quite a good living out of wearing not too many clothes."
4 **Women support it**—Therefore, it can't be sexist. For example, when asked about a piece testing a department store's shape-enhancing knickers by watching "men's reaction to a woman's bottom when she stands at the bar and bends down at work," Mohan stated that the fact that "a female" did the testing made the approach acceptable.
5 **Men are likewise objectified**—"We've carried photographs also" of David Beckham and Cristiano Ronaldo.
6 **Corporate social responsibility**—*The Sun* does a lot of work in support of women so looking "at Page 3 in isolation" is wrong.
7 **It's a celebration of women's bodies**—Unlike contrasting "unhealthy" images, these are "good role models."
8 **It's up to the reader/ audience responsibility**—No one is "compelled to buy the newspaper."
9 **It's all about context**—Any problematic images and stories "represent quite a small percentage" of *The Sun's* content.
10 **Other media are worse perpetrators**—"As a parent myself I'm more concerned about the images that my children might come across on the Internet" and on social media.

This analysis is important for feminists concerned with challenging media sexism because it illuminates the nature—and variety—of the argumentation used to justify sexist content. Many of these arguments would likely be recognizable across media, platforms and national contexts as justifications or defenses of sexist content.

Misogyny

Virulent misogyny is also a growing problem, both on news sites (via the comments sections) and when women who become subjects of news reporting are targeted for attack (García-Favaro & Gill, 2016). According to one Australian study, online misogyny is so widespread that it is "at risk of becoming an established norm" (Norton Symantec, 2016). The Women's Media Center (2015) identifies multiple different forms of online harassment targeted at girls and women: gender-based slurs and harassment, non-consensual photography, exploitation, doxing (i.e., publishing personal details), defamation, death or rape threats, mob attacks, hate speech, stalking, unsolicited pornography, online impersonation, spying and sexual surveillance, slut-shaming, swatting (e.g., filing false emergency service reports), and grief trolling. The goal is to "embarrass, humiliate, scare, threaten, silence, extort, or in some instances encourage mob attacks of malevolent engagements" (Women's Media Center (WMC), 2015). An important body of work in media studies attempts to categorize diverse forms of online misogyny, including "gendertrolling" (Mantilla, 2015), "online sexual harassment" (Megarry, 2014), "disciplinary rhetoric" (Cole, 2015), and "e-bile" (Jane, 2014b).

Emma Jane (2014a, p. 558) argues that "gendered vitriol" has become so ubiquitous online that "issuing graphic rape and death threats [against women] has become a standard discursive move . . . when Internet users wish to register their disagreement with and/or disapproval of women." Such threats often involve what she dubs "lascivious contempt" in which posts simultaneously threaten brutal forms of sexual assault and torture, and contemptuously denigrate the victim, as in, "She's so fugly, I wouldn't even bother raping her from behind with a box cutter" (Jane, 2014a, p. 562). Cole (2015) argues that such brutal and violent threats are often unexpectedly paired with humor; they are followed, for instance, by "LOL" or a laughing emoji. Online misogyny seeks to "discipline feminists into silence while simultaneously proclaiming that their version of rape is somehow funny. . . . The use of humour to qualify rape does not disarm the threat; rather it highlights the social acceptability of rape as a tool to discipline women" (Cole, 2015, p. 357).

Examples are—unfortunately—legion. In the US, well-known cases of Gamergate and The Fappening (leaking nude photographs and videos of celebrities) are extensively discussed examples of "toxic technocultures" (Massanari, 2017), the "networked misogyny" of men's rights organizations (Banet-Weiser, 2018a), and the alt right (Vickery & Everbach, 2018). Particular platforms are central to the abuse, especially Reddit and 4Chan. Twitter is also a forum for vicious attack. Milo Yiannopoulos was forced to leave Twitter in 2016 for online harassment of Ghostbusters actor Leslie Jones. His response was to assert: "I, Donald Trump and the rest of the alpha males will continue to dominate the Internet without feminist whining. It will be fun!" (cited in Vickery & Everbach, 2018).

The UK has seen several well-documented cases of harassment and abuse of feminists. Jessica Phillips, a Labour MP known for her progressive gender politics, spoke out after receiving 600 rape and death threats *in just one day* in 2017. Caroline

Criado-Perez successfully lobbied the Bank of England to put Jane Austen on the new £10 banknote rather than Winston Churchill; his inclusion would have meant that only men would appear on British currency. At the height of her campaign Criado-Perez was receiving 50 death and rape threats per hour on social media, often itemizing in cruel chilling detail the way these threats would be carried out. Academic classicist Mary Beard faced similar abuse after an appearance on the BBC's televised weekly political panel debate in 2013. The violent threats and comments about her appearance, age, genitals, and intelligence level coincided with her television and radio appearances—when she occupies traditionally masculine public space. Gina Miller, a private citizen who launched a campaign in 2009 to promote integrity and high standards in public life, came to fame in 2016 for her opposition to Brexit. Her personal safety and that of her children continue to be repeatedly threatened because she won a legal battle to require Parliamentary approval for any Brexit "deal." A man who used Facebook to promise money to anyone who would kill her was imprisoned for three months, and numerous "cease and desist" notices have been issued against others threatening her. She has shown extraordinary courage throughout this ordeal but has at times been reported as too fearful to leave her home given threats of acid attacks.

Attacks on Gina Miller, a British citizen of Indian and Guyanese heritage, highlight the racism as well as the misogyny that underpin these attacks. This was also clear in relation to Diane Abbott, the shadow Home Secretary. In 1987 Abbott was elected as Britain's first black woman MP. She receives, on a daily basis, vicious attacks that are both racist and sexist. Abbott detailed this shocking abuse in a piece for *The Guardian*, stating:

> suppose that someone had told me back then that 30 years on I would be receiving stuff like this: 'Pathetic useless fat black piece of shit Abbott. Just a piece of pig shit pond slime who should be fucking hung (if they could find a tree big enough to take the fat bitch's weight'). I think that even the young, fearless Diane Abbott might have paused for thought.
>
> *(Abbott, 2017)*

Abbott expressed concern about the message racist and sexist abuse online sends to women about being involved in politics and public life:

> Not only does it tend to marginalize the female 'offender,' but other women look at how those of us in the public space are treated and think twice about speaking up publicly, let alone getting involved in political activity. Who needs their intelligence, motivation, and personal appearance to be savaged in the tabloids and online? Better to stay silent or say whatever the men are saying.
>
> *(Abbott, 2017)*

The academic scholarship reflects how mediated forms of harassment are an extension of—not a departure from—cultural and historical roots of offline discrimination, sexism, racism, homophobia, and misogyny (Vickery & Everbach, 2018). Not all women experience misogyny and harassment in the same ways. Black women, women of color, lesbian women, Muslim women, and immigrant women are disproportionately targeted, experiencing harassment in different ways from white, heterosexual, non-disabled women, and other women from dominant cultural groups. Lucy Hackworth (2018) urges reframing scholarly discourse about harassment to avoid homogenizing it in ways that highlight only the experiences of white, heterosexual, middle-class, able-bodied women—including through notions that elevate gender above other aspects of identity. She argues that "just gender" usually means "just white women." The hashtag SolidarityIsForWhite-Women highlighted white feminists' contribution to, and complicity in, the silencing of black women online (Hackworth, 2018). To address the implicit exclusions of notions like gendertrolling, Moya Bailey coined the term misogynoir to describe anti-black misogyny maintaining that the concept was needed to "give intersectionality a break from doing a lot of the heavy lifting for black feminist thought" (Bailey, 2013, p. 341). This is vital, Hackworth claims:

> By not including discussions of race and other important identity categories, the terminology about online harassment itself currently implies that women are a homogenous group that experience gendered harassment homogenously. Even if we make a point to include harassment sent to people who embody other identities within our research of just gender, this still does not provide an accurate picture of the experiences of women online. This language [...] has the effect of othering women who don't fit the dominant and default notion of what a woman is. Identities cannot and should not have to be switched off or ignored. A woman of colour online cannot turn off her race, and nor can she avoid the fact that her harassment will be gendered, and racialized, and at times both.
>
> *(2018, pp. 8–9)*

Online misogyny is frequently studied, primarily on social media. However, the "comments" sections of newspapers and news broadcasters are also prime locations for hateful discourse. Analyzing 70 million comments posted to its website over ten years, *The Guardian* discovered that of the ten most abused writers, eight are women (four white, four black/minority ethnic), and the other two are black men (Gardiner et al., 2016). In our research analyzing more than five thousand comments posted to sites such as *BBC News* and the *Huffington Post* in response to news stories about "lads' mags," we found disturbing patterns of misogyny, homophobia, and Islamophobia (García-Favaro & Gill, 2016). This was even more striking given that these were *moderated* sites, and the data corpus thus excluded all comments moderators had deemed hate speech, offensive, or in other ways inappropriate. We noted escalating sexism and misogyny organized around claims that (i) gendered double standards disadvantage men; (ii) male (hetero)sexuality is under threat; (iii) women and wider society are at war with the "normal bloke"; and (iv) feminism is unconcerned with equality but rather "out to get men" and thus men are fighting for their very survival. The use of war metaphors to construct women as attackers and men as victims was striking.

Undoubtedly misogynistic and racist culture has been fuelled and exacerbated by the rise of the Right in the United States, Italy, the Netherlands, Germany, and the UK, among other countries. As Banet-Weiser argues:

> When US President Donald Trump can attack women in politics and in the press with misogynistic and racist insults as a matter of course, indeed can casually suggest grabbing women 'by the pussy' and just as casually dismiss it as 'locker room talk'; when many young women come to expect hateful and violent comments that shame and judge their bodies on the videos they post on social media; when rape culture has been named as a common feature of most college campuses in the US, misogyny has shifted from a set of questionable expressions and practices to structuring, often invisible context for our everyday lives and routine.
>
> *(Banet-Weiser, 2018a)*

Postfeminism

Since coming to prominence in the 1990s, the term postfeminism has been characterized in various ways: as a backlash against feminism; to refer to an historical shift, a time "after" (second wave) feminism; to capture a sense of an epistemological break within feminism, suggesting an alignment with other "post" movements (poststructuralism, postmodernism, and postcoloniality); and to propose connections to Third Wave feminism. In two influential formulations, postfeminism has been characterized as a "gender regime" (McRobbie, 2009) or "sensibility" (Gill, 2007) deeply enmeshed with neoliberalism. From this perspective, postfeminism is a critical analytical term that refers to empirical regularities or patterns in contemporary cultural life. These include the emphasis on individualism, choice, and agency as dominant modes of accounting; the disappearance—or at least muting—of vocabularies for talking about both structural inequalities and cultural influence; the "deterritorialization" of patriarchal power and its "reterritorialization" (McRobbie, 2009) in women's bodies and the beauty-industrial complex (Elias et al., 2017); the intensification and extensification of forms of surveillance, monitoring, and disciplining of women's bodies (Gill, 2007); and the influence of a "makeover paradigm" that extends beyond the body to constitute a remaking of subjectivity—what has been characterized the "psychic life of postfeminism" (Gill, 2017).

Highlighting the continued force of postfeminism may seem paradoxical at a moment characterized by the resurgence of feminism and its unprecedented visibility in the news. Nevertheless, our contention is that a postfeminist sensibility remains a powerful force, with key postfeminist themes and motifs animating both news reporting and features. Indeed, our analysis of a London *Evening Standard* (2015) magazine celebrating "New Gen Fem" notes that the warm embrace of feminism as an identity had not displaced the postfeminist sensibility (Gill, 2016). First, we highlighted the curiously *contentless* celebration of feminism, in which "journalists and the women they are interviewing seem not only uninterested in specifying what being a feminist means to them, but actively resistant" (Gill, 2016, p. 622). Instead, feminism was conveyed through a celebration of all things female and through a defiant pose that asserted "you go, girls!" and "I'm not afraid to call myself a feminist." Feminist symbols and icons have also been remade for a new moment—e.g., the feminist fist but with long varnished fingernails. Second, a lexicon of "struggles" and "battles" was used, yet the individuals highlighted as "gender warriors" turned out to be liberal politicians and celebrity journalists/ media moguls such as Tina Brown. Journalists focused on the worlds of corporate and celebrity culture—models, actresses, and high-level women in commercial corporations.

More generally, this celebration of feminism is suffused with individualistic discourses of meritocracy. A black model replays a familiar script of "rags to riches" so that the racism of the fashion industry is reframed in terms of a distinctly postfeminist aspiration: to be the first British Indian model to do a Victoria's Secrets show. At best, sexism is reversed rather than challenged—viz an article about "boyeurism" that celebrates how "forward thinking women are now indulging in objectification too." Meanwhile, journalists seize on rare examples of women earning more than men to suggest that obdurate problems like pay inequities are a thing of the past. "Choice" and "empowerment"—key parts of postfeminism's lexicon—are endlessly recycled and used to demand "rights" such as lipstick and high heels. Such discourses caused one feminist scholar to remark: "Of all the dangerous patterns . . . the one that seems most problematic and troubling . . . is the cultural tendency to twist and corrupt empowerment discourses so they become clichéd, commodified, detrimental and ultimately disempowering" (Fahs, 2011, p. 276). Rather than being positioned to challenge a sexist or misogynist culture, much of the *Evening Standard*'s New Gen Fem magazine copy seemed directed at older feminists—depicted as censorious and instilling what journalist Polly Vernon calls a "feminist fear of getting it wrong": FFGW. In fact, Vernon's (2015) book *Hot Feminist* is a prime example of postfeminist discourse. As do a myriad of magazines and newspaper columnists, she calls her feminism "rebranded": "What kind of feminist does that make me? The shavey-leggy, fashion-fixated, wrinkle averse, weight-conscious kind of feminist. The kind who likes hot pink and boys; oh, I like boys! I like boys so much . . ." (2015, p. 13). Vernon says her position on feminism means—conveniently—anything you want it to: it's "modern feminism with style, without judgement."

The themes brought out in this analysis are not typical of contemporary feminisms themselves. What we are interested in is how feminism materializes and is made visible and intelligible in the news. Postfeminist tropes and themes—such as the ones highlighted above—remain central to discussions of gender and feminism in news. They are evident even in liberal and intelligent news sites, for example, in endless pieces about whether you can be a feminist and get married/shave your legs/go on a diet. They are seen, too, in the reductive, individualistic framing of decision-making about work and parenting and in the ways that "feminist" issues are framed. Rather than displacing postfeminism, a resurgent feminism co-exists with a dominant postfeminist and neoliberal sensibility.

Conclusion

This chapter examined several different forces currently shaping contemporary news reporting of gender. We noted several critical questions about the diffusion of feminist ideas beyond an educated middle-class audience, asking about the kinds of feminism and feminists gaining the greatest visibility in the news. Alongside feminism, we pointed to several other notable—and troubling—trends, including the persistence of sexism as a force structuring news, and the rise of popular misogyny in news comments sections often in direct response to news stories. If feminism is trending, then so too are sexism and misogyny in all their class-based, racist, disablist, fat-shaming, and homophobic variants. Postfeminism remains a live force, a dominant sensibility that shapes news coverage, channeling it through individualist discourses and foci that downplay the need for social transformation.

Besides highlighting the variety of opposing forces that shape news about gender, we also want to draw attention to an important theoretical point about how feminist journalism scholars think about continuity and change. We argue for the importance of moving beyond a taken-for-granted and unquestioned assumption of displacement—the idea that new ideas or trends automatically displace older ones. The goal is a more complicated but realistic understanding of the ways that multiple and contradictory ideas can *co-exist* in the same moment, field, plane. A major challenge for feminist journalism studies is how to attend to the new, the seemingly novel, changed aspects of a situation—such as the sudden visibility of feminism as a topic of news—whilst not becoming mesmerized by them, and always holding on to a sense of continuities. Attention to the *contradictions* of news culture is an important part of being a feminist journalism scholar. Despite the contemporary "feminist zeitgeist," the tenacity of anti-feminist ideas remains striking, even in this new moment. Postfeminism, sexism, and misogyny are also trending now.

Note

1 Katie Toms's thesis deals with this, as does her article in progress.

References

Abbott, D. (2017, February 14). I fought racism and misogyny to become an MP: The fight is getting harder. *The Guardian*. Retrieved from www.theguardian.com/commentisfree/2017/feb/14/racism-misogyny-politics-online-abuse-minorities

Bailey, M. (2013). New terms of resistance: A response to Zenzele Isoke. *Souls*, *15*(4), 341–343. doi:10.1080/10999949.2014.884451

Banet-Weiser, S. (2018a). *Empowered: Popular feminism and popular misogyny*. Durham, NC: Duke University Press.

Banet-Weiser, S. (2018b). Popular feminism: #MeToo. *Los Angeles Review of Books*. Retrieved from https://lareviewofbooks.org/article/popular-feminism-metoo/#!

Blumell, L. E. (2017). She persisted . . . and so did he: Gendered source use during the Trump access hollywood scandal. *Journalism Studies*, 1–20.

Candy, L. (2014, December). Emma Watson: The fresh face of feminism. *Elle Magazine*.

Carter, M., Turner, M., & Paton, M. (2012). *Real women—The hidden sex: How national newspapers use photographic images of women in editorial*. London. Retrieved from http://womeninjournalism.co.uk/real-women-the-hidden-sex/

Cochrane, K. (2013). *All the rebel women: The rise of the fourth wave of feminism*. London: Guardian Books.

Cole, K. K. (2015). "It's like she's eager to be verbally abused": Twitter, trolls, and (en)gendering disciplinary rhetoric. *Feminist Media Studies*, *15*(2), 356–358.

The Daily Mail (2017, March). Never mind brexit, who won legs-it! *The Daily Mail*.

Elias, A., Gill, R., & Scharff, C. (2017). Aesthetic labour: Beauty politics in neoliberalism. In A. Elias, R. Gill, & C. Scharff (Eds.), *Aesthetic labour: Dynamics of virtual work* (pp. 3–49). London: Palgrave Macmillan.

Emejulu, A. (2017). Feminism for the 99%: Towards a populist feminism? Can feminism for the 99% succeed as a new kind of populism? *Soundings: A Journal of Politics and Culture*, *66*, 63–67.

Evening Standard. (2015, October). New gen fem issue. *Evening Standard Magazine*.

Fahs, B. (2011). *Performing sex: The making and unmaking of women's erotic lives*. Albany, NY: Suny Press.

Favaro, L., & Gill, R. (2018). Feminism rebranded: Women's magazines online and "the Return of the F-Word." *Revista Dígitos*, *4*, 37–66.

Fraser, N., & Nicholson, L. J. (2011). Social criticism without philosophy: An encounter between feminism and postmodernism. In M. Eagleton (Ed.), *Feminist literary theory: A reader* (3rd ed., pp. 234–235). Chichester: Wiley-Blackwell.

García-Favaro, L., & Gill, R. (2016). "Emasculation nation has arrived": Sexism rearticulated in online responses to lose the lads' mags campaign. *Feminist Media Studies*, *16*(3), 379–397. Routledge. doi:10.1080/14680777.2015.1105840

Gardiner, B., Mansfield, M., Anderson, I., Hoolder, J., Louter, D., & Ulumanu, M. (2016). The dark side of *Guardian* comments. *The Guardian*. Retrieved from www.theguardian.com/technology/2016/apr/12/the-dark-side-of-guardian-comments

Gay, R. (2018). *Hunger: A memoir of (My) body*. London: Corsair.

Gill, R. (2007). Postfeminist media culture: Elements of a sensibility. *European Journal of Cultural Studies*, *10*(2), 147–166.

Gill, R. (2011). Sexism reloaded, or, it's time to get angry again! *Feminist Media Studies*, *11*(1), 61–71.

Gill, R. (2016). Post-postfeminism? New feminist visibilities in postfeminist times. *Feminist Media Studies*, *16*(4), 610–630.

Gill, R. (2017). The affective, cultural and psychic life of postfeminism: A postfeminist sensibility 10 years on. *European Journal of Cultural Studies*, *20*(6), 606–626. doi:10.1177/1367549417733003

Hackworth, L. (2018). Limitations of "just gender": The need for an intersectional reframing of online harassment discourse and research. In J. R. Vickery & T. Everbach (Eds.), *Mediating misogyny: Gender, technology and harassment* (pp. 51–70). London: Palgrave Macmillan.

Halpin, M. (2013). The new do: Calling yourself a feminist. *Glamour Magazine*. Retrieved from www.glamour.com/story/the-new-do-calling-yourself-a-feminist

IPSO. (2018). The editors' code of practice. *IPSO*. Retrieved from www.ipso.co.uk/editors-code-of-practice/

Jane, E. A. (2014a). Back to the kitchen, cunt: Speaking the unspeakable about online misogyny. *Continuum, 28*(4), 558–570. Taylor & Francis. doi:10.1080/10304312.2014.924479

Jane, E. A. (2014b). "Your a ugly, whorish, slut" understanding e-bile. *Feminist Media Studies, 14*(4), 531–546.

Jehring, A. (2017, May 19). Heel-election special. *The Sun*. Retrieved from www.thesun. co.uk/news/3598102/kelly-pays-homage-to-pms-leopard-print-heels-and-reckons-theresa-may-will-be-a-shoe-in-on-jun-8/

Jonsson, T. (2014). White feminist stories: Locating race in representations of feminism in *The Guardian. Feminist Media Studies, 14*(6), 1012–1027.

Kelan, E. K. (2009). Gender fatigue: The ideological dilemma of gender neutrality and discrimination in organizations. *Canadian Journal of Administrative Sciences, 26*(3), 197–210.

Keller, J., Mendes, K., & Ringrose, J. (2018). Speaking "unspeakable things": Documenting digital feminist responses to rape culture. *Journal of Gender Studies, 27*(1), 22–36.

Keller, J., & Ryan, M. E. (2018). *Emergent feminisms: Complicating a postfeminist media culture.* Abingdon: Routledge.

Leveson, The Right Honourable Lord Justice. (2012). *An inquiry into the culture, practices and ethics of the press.* London. Retrieved from www.rte.ie/documents/news/leveson.pdf

Mantilla, K. (2015). *Gendertrolling: How misogyny went viral.* Santa Barbara and Denver: ABC-CLIO.

Martinson, J., Bawdon, F., Ryan, S., Cochrane, K., & Corrigan, T. (2012). *Seen but not heard: How women make front page news.* London. Retrieved from http://womeninjournalism. co.uk/wp-content/uploads/2012/10/Seen_but_not_heard.pdf

Massanari, A. (2017). #Gamergate and the fappening: How Reddit's algorithm, governance, and culture support toxic technocultures. *New Media & Society, 19*(3), 329–346.

McRobbie, A. (2009). *The aftermath of feminism: Gender, culture and social change.* London: Sage Publications.

Megarry, J. (2014). Online incivility or sexual harassment? Conceptualising women's experiences in the digital age. *Women's Studies International Forum, 47*(Part A), 46–55.

Moore, L. (2015). Feminism is back! *Female First.* Retrieved from www.femalefirst.co.uk/ books/radical-feminism-finn-mackay-587163.html

Norton Symantec. (2016). Norton study shows online harassment nears epidemic proportions for young Australian women. *Symantec Press Release.* Retrieved from www.syman tec.com/en/au/about/newsroom/press-releases/2016/symantec_0309_01

Rentschler, C. A. (2014). Rape culture and the feminist politics of social media. *Girlhood Studies, 7*(1), 65–82.

Rentschler, C. A., & Thrift, S. C. (2015). Doing feminism in the network: Networked laughter and the "Binders Full of Women" meme. *Feminist Theory, 16*(3), 329–359.

Retallack, H., Ringrose, J., & Lawrence, E. (2016). "Fuck your body image": Teen girls' Twitter and Instagram feminism in and around school. In J. Coffey, S. Budgeon, & H. Cahill (Eds.), *Learning bodies: Perspectives on children and young people* (pp. 85–103). Singapore: Springer.

Ross, K. (2003). Women politicians and malestream media: A game of two sides. *Centre for the Advancement of Women in Politics, Queens University Belfast, Occasional Paper, 1*, 1–13. Retrieved from www.qub.ac.uk/cawp/research/media.PDF

Rottenberg, C. (2014). The rise of neoliberal feminism. *Cultural Studies, 28*(3), 418–437.

Scharff, C. (2012). *Repudiating feminism: Young women in a neoliberal world.* Abingdon: Routledge.

UK CEDAW Working Group. (2013). *Women's equality in the UK—A health check.* London. Retrieved from http://thewomensresourcecentre.org.uk/wp-content/uploads/WRC-CEDAW-Booklet_final-links.pdf

Valenti, J. (2014a). Beyoncé's "Flawless" feminist act at the VMAs leads the way for other women. *The Guardian*. Retrieved from www.theguardian.com/commentisfree/2014/aug/25/beyonce-flawless-feminist-vmas

Valenti, J. (2014b). When everyone is a feminist, is anyone? *The Guardian*. Retrieved from www.theguardian.com/commentisfree/2014/nov/24/when-everyone-is-a-feminist

Vernon, P. (2015). *Hot feminist: Modern feminism with style without judgement.* London: Hachette.

Vickery, J. R., & Everbach, T. (2018). The persistence of misogyny: From the streets, to our screens, to the white house. In J. R. Vickery & T. Everbach (Eds.), *Mediating misogyny: Gender, technology, and harassment* (pp. 1–27). London: Palgrave Macmillan.

Watson, E. (2014). Emma Watson at the HeForShe campaign 2014—Official UN video. *United Nations.* New York, NY: United Nations. Retrieved from www.youtube.com/watch?v=gkjW9PZBRfk

West, L. (2017). *Shrill: Notes from a loud woman.* London: Quercus.

Williamson, J. (2003, May 31). Sexism with an alibi. *The Guardian*. Retrieved from www.theguardian.com/media/2003/may/31/advertising.comment

Wilz, K. (2016). Bernie bros and woman cards: Rhetorics of sexism, misogyny, and constructed masculinity in the 2016 election. *Women's Studies in Communication, 39*(4), 357–360.

Women's Media Center (WMC). (2015). The status of women in the U.S. media 2017. *Women's Media Center (WMC) report.* New York, NY. Retrieved from www.womensmediacenter.com/bsdimg/statusreport/2015/Status.of.Women.2015.pdf?p=page/-/statusreport/2015/Status.of.Women.2015.pdf

8

US NEWS COVERAGE OF TRANSGENDER LIVES

A historical and critical review

Jamie C. Capuzza

Media representations of social identities are not arbitrary or neutral; they reflect a dominant meaning system. News media play a critical role in establishing and modifying dominant social narratives about human identities and how news consumers make sense of them. Of importance here is the news media's role in the broader cultural discourse of what is to be gendered, and specifically, the power of news media to define, legitimate, and regulate the boundaries of gender identities, both cisgender and transgender.

"Transgender" is an umbrella term for persons whose gender identity, gender expression, or behavior does not conform to that typically associated with the sex to which they were assigned at birth. Transgender people use a wide range of terms to describe themselves including, but not limited to, "non-binary," "transsexual," "genderqueer," "gender non-conforming," "transman," or "transwoman." "Cisgender" is a term for a person whose gender identity and expression conform to that typically associated with the sex to which they were assigned at birth.

Social assumptions about the gender binary and about gender essentialism, sex/gender congruency, and gender stability play out in daily journalism in ways that often contribute to transphobia and reinforce cisnormativity. In this regard, media typically "reproduce rather than challenge dominant gender arrangements and ideologies, specifically the assumption that there are two and only two, obviously universal, natural, bipolar, mutually exclusive sexes that necessarily correspond to stable gender identity and gendered behavior" (Birrell & Cole, 1990, p. 3).

In many ways, representations and narrative forms typically deployed in US news coverage of transgender communities delegitimize gender variant identities and support cisnormativity. Until very recently, journalists constructed a dominant narrative about what it means to be transgender through content narrowly focused on bodily transformation structured on a before-and-after format, both of which assimilated transgender identities neatly into the gender binary. This persistent pattern of recognition, representation, and interpretation offered up a preferred reading of what it can mean to be transgender and influenced how news consumers made sense of transgender identities and expression. In many ways, news media delimited certain types of transgender voices and privileged those that are deemed more palatable for cisgender audiences (and to the audience trying to attract those audiences). In this regard, journalists gendered the news by reinforcing the ideological power that manifests social assumptions related to the gender binary and gender stability; they reinforced cisnormativity even in stories about transgender lives.

Transgender advocates, academics, media critics, and news professionals themselves have identified and criticized many of these journalistic practices as a type of gender policing. Transgender people and their advocates have worked to gain media attention and to challenge the news media's power to represent them narrowly. They thereby joined the ranks of other marginalized groups calling for a more multidimensional representation of their communities. This work was an important step toward obtaining political power for the transgender movement.

In addition to providing better understanding of gender diversity, opportunities for challenging gender assumptions, and giving voice and agency to transgender populations, improving news coverage is critical for both physical and psychological health of gender non-conforming people. Inconsistent and biased coverage has led to and reinforced stereotypes and prejudice potentially fueling discrimination and even violence. According to a UK study by Transmedia Watch (n.d.), most transgender respondents felt coverage was inaccurate and precipitated verbal and physical abuse. Rather than engage negative coverage, many transgender people do not use traditional media, instead focusing on social media such as YouTube for a safe space to negotiate their identities (Kosenko, Bond, & Hurley, 2016; Marciano, 2014; McInroy & Craig, 2015; O'Neill, 2014; Raun, 2010; Ringo, 2002). News outlets wishing to engage transgender audiences and their supporters, and those who want to create a trans-inclusive news culture and professional ethic, are beginning to recognize the negative consequences of their journalistic practices and have sought out ways to modify them.

This chapter examines the ideological gendering of news and specifically its role in both supporting *and* challenging cisnormativity, as well as the transgender people's responses to news coverage of their communities. I also discuss recent efforts to improve coverage of transgender people and issues that are results of internal changes within the news industry and those made as a result of transgender advocacy.

The current state of transgender new coverage

Invisibility

Historically, news coverage in the US rendered transgender lives invisible. Much the same as other stigmatized groups, transgender people were "symbolically annihilated" by both news and entertainment media (Gerbner & Gross, 1976; Tuchman,

1979). Underreporting and episodic news treatment of transgender people's lives long denied news consumers the opportunity to learn about the full spectrum of gender expression and, meanwhile, communicated to transgender people that neither they nor their issues were worthy of serious, sustained attention (Capuzza, 2015; Capuzza 2016). According to a study of news coverage produced between 2004–2013 by 13 newspapers, the amount of coverage increased over those 10 years, but most of the news was episodic (Billiard, 2016). Only *The New York Times* and the *Boston Globe* increased overall coverage in a statistically significant way. The amount of coverage provided by major news outlets did not increase significantly until after 2015, when a *Time* magazine cover story, headlined "The Transgender Tipping Point," featured Laverne Cox, a transgender actress highly popular for her role as an inmate in the television program "Orange Is the New Black." The story identified social and legal gains for transgender communities and quoted Cox declaring a new era of visibility.

However, not all types of transgender people were considered equally newsworthy. Exploring the ideological gendering of news with an intersectional approach offers evidence that transgender men and transgender women of color received far less media attention than white transgender women (Capuzza, 2015; Li, 2018). Moreover, US news media particularly delegitimize non-binary gender identities by rendering them invisible. Stories about people who identify as both masculine and feminine, as neither masculine nor feminine, or who alternate between the two seldom were the focus of major news outlets (Capuzza, 2015; Siebler, 2010; Skidmore, 2011; Squires & Brouwer, 2002; Willox, 2003). More recently, Li (2018) found that national news outlets that ran stories about transgender issues after Caitlyn Jenner's *20/20* interview were more likely to mention the non-binary gender identities.

Another way that reporters render transgender lives invisible is by underreporting their murders in crime news (MacKenzie & Marcel, 2009). Some 27 transgender people, most of whom were transgender women of color, died of fatal violence in 2016, the highest number reported in a single year (GLAAD, 2016). This number does not include transgender people whose deaths were incorrectly reported due to misgendering by police. The first time that violence against a transgender person was prosecuted under the US federal Hate Crimes Act, extended to cover sexuality and gender identity in 2009, occurred only in May 2017. While certain particularly brutal cases have received extensive news coverage, most have received scant attention. One study of crime news of US broadcast, cable and Spanish-language outlets for the first two months of 2015 found that journalists ignored an epidemic of violence against transgender people (Maza, Lopez, & Percelay, 2015). Maza, Lopez, and Percelay found that while MSNBC and CNN carried more substantial coverage of trans hate crimes than other US news outlets, but in general, this life-and-death issue received minimal media attention.

As time has passed, some news agencies are taking a more extensive and more inclusive approach to their coverage of transgender communities. An era of visibility has begun: transgender lives and issues are now deemed newsworthy with more regularity. The amount of news coverage increased dramatically in April 2015 when Caitlyn Jenner came out as transgender on ABC's *20/20*. This show was a unique opportunity to educate news consumers who normally would not watch a program about a transgender person, but did so because of Jenner's fame as an Olympian and as a reality show celebrity. *Vanity Fair's* 2015 cover story about Jenner broke single-day online traffic record of 9 million unique visitors (Morrison, 2016). Much the same as famed basketball player Magic Johnson's disclosure of his HIV-positive status provided an impetus for increased and more nuanced news coverage of AIDS, Jenner's coming out generated interest in and broadened the scope of the discussion of gender and expression. Consequently, transgender-related stories in national news outlets appearing after Jenner's *20/20* interview were more likely to mention racial, sexuality, class, and gender differences when discussing the complexity of transgender lives (Li, 2018).

Passing and deception

On the rare occasion transgender people or issues were deemed newsworthy, typically one of two narratives was constructed. First, the press often constructed a media frame around "passing," implying that transgender identities were inauthentic or deceptive and thus that transgender people deserve rejection, discrimination, and even violence for misrepresenting themselves to others. This form of journalistic delegitimization too often involved victim blaming, particularly in crime news. For example, transgender people have been frequently vilified in news accounts of their murders, blaming them for deceiving their killers and justifying a "transpanic" defense (Cram, 2012; Johnson, 2013; Schilt & Westbrook, 2009; Sloop, 2000; Squires & Brouwer, 2002; Willox, 2003). The National LGBT Bar Association, an affiliate of the American Bar Association, defines "transpanic" as a defense tactic in which the jury is asked to find a victim's gender identity to blame for the defendant's excessive violence. For example, Brandon Teena was a transgender man whose rape and murder in Nebraska in 1993 received extensive news attention; that coverage depicted Teena as someone whose deceptions justified his murder as retribution (Sloop, 2000; Willox, 2003). The murder of Teena also was depicted in the Academy Award–winning movie, *Boys Don't Cry* and in the documentary, *The Brandon Teena Story*. As a result, although more journalists are moving toward a hate crime frame than a deception frame, and victim blaming has decreased, transgender victims are still portrayed within the narrow confines of the gender binary and often misgendered (Billard, 2018). In short, while coverage of this type of crime has improved, more remains to be done.

Coming out narratives and wrong body discourse

Alternatively, the press constructed a uniform "coming out" narrative that typically featured wrong body discourse and reinforced a "pre-op or post-op" ideology (Morrison, 2016; Seibler, 2012). Most news stories discussed the transgender person's first feelings of being born in the "wrong body," described how that person came out to others, and then detailed information about medical transition. These stories tended to dwell on a person's pre-transition life with a primary focus on the body and on gender reassignment surgery (Bucar & Enke, 2011). News stories that focus on "pre-operative" or "post-operative" status inaccurately suggest that a person must have surgery in order to transition and tend to overemphasize personal information about genitals. Many transgender people choose not to or cannot medically transition. Constructing a dominant narrative such as this one reinforced the erroneous idea that transgender identity requires surgical transition, thereby confusing cisgender audiences and troubling transgender audiences.

This "wrong body" narrative dates back to 1952 with the media frenzy over Christine Jorgensen's transition. After serving in the US Army during World War II, Jorgensen traveled to Denmark to undergo gender reassignment surgery to become the first known American transgender woman. As Skidmore (2011) argued in her study of reporting about Jorgensen, news discourse successfully created a space for a "good transsexual," as compared to a "sexual deviant"; however, this discourse also legitimated a normative definition of transgender identity that highlighted a physical transition process at the expense of other types of gender variance.

A more recent case in point is that of Gwen Araujo, a transgender California teenager murdered in 2002 by four men. None of these defendants was convicted of hate crime. The defense attorneys employed a "trans panic defense" much the same as in the Brandon Teena case. News coverage of Araujo frequently depicted her as "born in the wrong body." Studying news coverage of this case, Barker-Plummer (2013) concluded that this story "represents a narrative of containment in which challenges raised by gender nonconformity were recuperated through the mobilization of "fixing" strategies and especially by the use of wrong body discourse" (p. 710). Framing transgender identity as a fixable biological problem delegitimizes transgender lives. Additionally, this type of coverage often devolves into sensationalism and fails to inform news consumers about wider issues faced by transgender communities.

Misnaming, misgendering, and the problems with pronouns

Writing about transgender subjects has proven difficult for reporters in a variety of ways including misnaming, misgendering, and pronouns. Writing about a population that is small in size, but yet so diverse has been challenging, especially when most news consumers are probably unfamiliar with terms such as "genderqueer" or "gender fluid" and when reporters write and speak in a language that is itself gendered. The linguistic choices of news professionals matter. Barker-Plummer (2013) emphasized: "As cultural mediators, journalists are on the front lines of this change for publics and the linguistic choices they make may have widespread regressive, or progressive, consequences." (p. 719).

Researchers have documented numerous incidences when news media misnamed or misgendered transgender people. Both of these practices constrain transgender agency and delegitimize transgender self-identification (Barker-Plummer, 2013; Billiard, 2016; Capuzza, 2015; Hale, 1998; Schilt & Westbrook, 2009; Siebler, 2010; Sloop, 2000; Squires & Brouwer, 2002; Willox, 2003). When journalists used terms such as "formerly a man," "gender-bender," or wrote preferred names in quotation marks, they called into question the authenticity of transgender identities; negatively influencing the self-perceptions of transgender people and limiting cisgender people's understanding of gender variance.

Before many news agencies updated their stylebooks, journalists often used a gendered pronoun that was in keeping with the sex the transgender person was assigned at birth or alternated between masculine and feminine pronouns as the story, invariably within a "before and after" frame, rather than using preferred pronouns. Writing about non-binary identities proved even more difficult as reporters and editors refused to acknowledge or employ gender-neutral pronouns thus rendering some transgender identities unspeakable.

An interesting case was that of Chelsea Manning, who received considerable media attention given her court-martial in 2013 for violating the Espionage Act by disclosing military documents to WikiLeaks. After she came out as a transgender woman, major news outlets initially referred to Manning using masculine pronouns and her birth name, Bradley; most resisted her request to be called Chelsea or to use feminine pronouns. Because journalists and news consumers were accustomed to seeing Manning presenting as a man, the initial coverage of her trial vigorously contested her identity. According to Hackl, Becker, and Todd (2016), journalists were confused about how best to refer to Manning at the time of her transition. In that two-week period, reporters used male gender pronouns 983 times and female gender pronouns only 145 times. A study of newspaper articles about Manning spanning her initial coming out, her sentencing, and her request for clemency found that eventually 70 percent of the articles used Manning's preferred name and pronoun (Capuzza, 2015). The number increased over time, indicating that journalists can improve their coverage of transgender lives if sufficient pressure comes from transgender advocates or news industry leaders to do so.

Sexualization

Journalists, like many others, also delegitimized transgender identities by conflating sexuality and gender failing to see important distinctions between the two. Just as cisgender people are found along the full spectrum of human sexualities, so are transgender people. Like others, reporters often use the "LBGTQIA" acronym with little regard for important differences among these populations, including both those of a personal nature as well as those related to political agendas. One all-encompassing acronym is confusing in that the letters combine sexualities and gender identities into one unwieldly combination that creates the impression there is social solidarity and a shared political agenda when that is not always the case. Furthermore, headlines often include the LBGTQIA acronym, but the copy is limited to sexual identities with little to no mention of gender diversity. More recently, however, transgender-related US national news stories appearing after Jenner's *20/20* interview were more likely to distinguish transgender issues from those of lesbians, gays, or bisexuals (Li, 2018). This indicates that reporters are developing a more accurate understanding of the distinction between sexual identities and gender identities.

Conflating sexuality and gender contributed to the sensationalizing of transgender people as hypersexual. Reporters historically have sexualized the transgender body, especially those of transgender women, primarily through a focus on genitals as the source of gender identity (MacKenzie & Marcel, 2009; Meyerowitz, 1998; Ryan, 2009; Schilt & Westbrook, 2009; Sloop, 2000; Squires & Brouwer, 2002). This sexualization dates back to the 1950s coverage of Christine Jorgensen, which focused on her gender reassignment surgery and her feminine grace to legitimize her as a woman (Arune, 2006; Meyerowitz, 1998). Sexualizing transgender people continues today as news coverage of Jenna Tacklova illustrates. Tacklova gained news attention in 2012 when she won a lawsuit allowing her to compete in the Miss Universe contest after initially being disqualified because she was a transgender woman. Tamlin, Quinlan, and Bates (2017) argued that Talackova challenged notions of who can compete as a "true" woman while simultaneously supporting cisnormative understandings of womanhood and sexuality. Granted, all beauty contestants are often subjected to objectification and sexualization, but in their framing of this story, news coverage Talackova's body differed and extended to her legal identity sex/gender identity. Talackova's word was not sufficient to prove she was a "real woman." Rather, reporters provided medical evidence of her genital status and emphasized her beauty and sexuality to "prove" her womanhood. The press's focus on genitalia and sexualization contributes to sensationalism.

Sourcing

One way journalists ascribe normative discourses is by their selection of who to use or not use as sources in their stories. Journalists' ability to choose who speaks (or does not speak) in news coverage enables them to frame news without appearing to do so (Schneider, 2012, p. 72). Sourcing is a means of establishing a hierarchy of credibility. In a study of *The Washington Post, The New York Times, USA Today,* and *Time,* Capuzza (2014) found that 58 percent of the stories sampled quoted a transgender person and 42 percent paraphrased a transgender person at least once. In the majority of cases, that source was a male-to-female person. Typically, only one transgender source was used per story and transgender sources were more likely to appear in hard rather than soft news. Thus, while transgender people were not absent in stories about them, sourcing was limited and showcased one transgender identity over others disproportionately. Providing voice for transgender citizens more consistently and more representatively could help dispel stereotypes and provide cisgender audiences with more nuanced and complete understanding of gender diversity.

Stylebooks

As the quantity of stories about transgender lives increased and as transgender advocates increased pressures for improved coverage increased, major news agencies began amending style guides. Style guides establish journalistic practices that directly affect how news stories are constructed and how reporters interact with sources. Up until 2006, the widely used Associated Press Stylebook's only guidance for journalists were entries entitled "sex changes" and "transsexual" that read "see sex changes." That year, a more specific "transgender" entry was added to refer to anyone whose gender identity differed from his or her "sex at birth," including individuals who have not had reconstructive surgery. The new entry also instructed journalists to refer to transgender people using their preferred pronouns.

While this entry was an important addition to the manual, it created the practical problem of birth sex verification necessitating overly personal questions about genitals. Essentially, a double standard was created requiring reporters to verify the sex and gender of transgender people, but not of cisgender people. The entry addressed gender expression, but it ignored internal gender identity leaving reporters to wonder which physical characteristics constitute transgender. This problem was not addressed in the 2013 edition of the stylebook which reworded the entry for "transgender" as follows:

> Use the pronoun preferred by the individuals who have acquired the physical characteristics of the opposite sex or present themselves in a way that does not correspond with their sex at birth. If that preference is not expressed, use the pronoun consistent with the way the individuals live publicly.

Moreover, the 2013 entry supported the gender binary using the term "opposite sex" and failed to acknowledge the existence of genderqueer identities located along a gender spectrum. Lastly, the revised manual did not adopt gender-neutral pronouns.

The year 2015 brought several more updates to stylebooks. For example, *The New York Times* used the honorific "Mx" instead of "Mr.," "Mrs.," or "Ms," in a 2015 story about Barnard College student Caleb LoSchiavo, who identifies as non-binary. The newspaper's management indicated this honorific would be used only on rare occasions and did not amend its style guide (Corbett, 2015). Second, the *Washington Post* permitted "they" and "theirs" to be used as singular pronouns. Third, the Associated Press Stylebook added an entry for "cross-dresser" which instructed journalists to use that term instead of "transvestite." The stylebook did not have an entry on "transvestite" until this point (Perlman, 2015).

Guidance for journalistic writing about transgender people continues to evolve. In March 2017, the entry, "gender," was revised in the Associated Press Stylebook to avoid language implying a gender binary and to account for cisgender, intersex, and transgender identities as follows:

> Not synonymous with sex. Gender refers to a person's social identity while sex refers to biological characteristics. Not all people fall under one of two

categories for sex or gender, according to leading media organizations, so avoid references to both, either or opposite sexes or genders as a way to encompass all people. When needed for clarity or in certain stories about scientific studies, alternatives include men and women, boys and girls, males and females.

(Shepard, 2017a)

Additionally, this stylebook indicated that "they" could be used as a singular pronoun, but advised to do so sparingly. Finally, the acronym "LGBTQ" was adopted to reference gay, lesbian, bisexual, transgender, and queer people with the caution that, "the word queer can be considered a slur in many contexts, so limit use of the word to quotes and names of organizations, following rules for obscenities, profanities, vulgarities as appropriate. Note that *sex, gender* and *sexual orientation* are not synonymous. See *gay* or *gender*." (Sopelsa, 2017).

Further revisions to the Associated Press Stylebook were made in October 2017 instructing journalists not to describe a transgender person as "born" a certain sex and to identify someone as transgender only if relevant to the story. Additionally, the agency warned against referring to people as "transgendered or transsexual," "a transgender," and only to use the term "trans" as a second reference or in headlines. Finally, the Associated Press specified, "For medical procedures often but not always used for a transition, say sex reassignment or gender confirmation" (Shepard, 2017b). The evolution of language used to write and speak about transgender people is important to document because language shapes perceptions. It also is important to note these changes did not come without controversy. The level of readiness and resistance to stylebook rule changes varied considerably both inside news agencies and among news consumers.

Reporter education

In addition to adhering to improved style guides, reporters are educating themselves on how to adequately cover transgender people. More and more journalists are interested in telling LBGTQIA stories and are motivated to tell those stories from an informed and inclusive standpoint. For example, *The New York Times* ran a series of editorials in 2015 entitled, "Transgender Today," with an initial staff of 20 people, all of whom focused on how to cover transgender communities with increased sensitivity. The newspaper's management invited transgender people to tell their own stories on *The New York Times* website, thus increasing the authenticity of the coverage and giving voice to this all-to-often silenced population. Additionally, more journalists are reaching out to Transgender Studies scholars to ensure their coverage is high quality. For example, according to the University of Arizona website, Susan Stryker, a professor of gender and women's studies and the author of several books on transgender identities, is regularly contacted as an authority by a range of media outlets such as NPR, *Time Magazine, The Advocate*, among others. More journalism educators also are incorporating this issue into their classrooms.

Furthermore, many news outlets are attempting to learn from their mistakes. Metareporting, or media self-criticism, enables journalists to acknowledge their mistakes and to show that they've learned from them. Headlines such as: NPR's ombudsman Elizabeth Jensen's "Lots of transgender stories; not as many transgender voices," journalist Christine Grimilda's *Columbia Journalism Review* essay, "I tripped up reporting about gender and sexuality. Here's what I learned," or ESPN'S Christina Kahrl's guest editorial critiquing writer Caleb Hannen's article outing an athlete who later committed suicide all illustrate a conscientious practice of professional self-reflection on the part of reporters. Academic and professional organizations such as The Poynter Institute and the National Gay and Lesbian Journalists Association also encourage an open debate among journalists on how best to report about transgender communities and support transgender news professionals.

Trans advocacy

Some efforts at improving news coverage are internally motivated such as reporter education while others are externally motivated. Considerable credit goes to transgender advocacy organizations that have pressured the news industry to address biased and inaccurate reporting. Over the years, the political acumen of these spokespersons has increased significantly. Organizations such as the National Center for Transgender Equality, Transgender Law Center, HRC (Human Rights Campaign), GLAAD, and Trans Media Watch carefully monitored news coverage of transgender communities. When coverage was problematic, advocates from organizations such as these contacted news agencies informing them of their concerns and offered advice about how best to address problems. Additionally, advocates wrote about problematic media coverage in their own media outlets including websites, blogs, and tweets. For example, both Katie Couric and Piers Morgan drew considerable criticism when they asked transgender guests—including model Carman Acarrera, writer and TV host Janet Mock, and actor Laverne Cox—about their genitals. Cox responded as follows:

> The preoccupation with transition and surgery objectifies trans people. And then we don't get to really deal with the real lived experiences. The reality of trans people's lives is that so often we are targets of violence. We experience discrimination disproportionately to the rest of the community. Our unemployment rate is twice the national average; if you are a trans person of color, that rate is four times the national average. The homicide rate is highest among trans women. If we focus on transition, we don't actually get to talk about those things.
>
> *(Cooper, 2014)*

Her response became a teaching moment and a catalyst for other transgender people to speak out about how best to conduct media interviews.

Advocacy organizations also supplied journalists with more extensive guidelines for covering transgender communities accurately than many industry style guides provided. For example, GLAAD provides several online resources such as its *Media Reference Guide: In Focus—Covering the Transgender Community*, among other sources on its website at GLAAD.org. NLGJA provides a list of dehumanizing terms to avoid in their website at nlgja.org including: "deceptive," "fooling," "pretending," "posing" or "masquerading," "she-male," "he-she," "it," "tranny," "shim," and "gender-bender." They suggest avoiding "sex change," "pre-operative," or "post-operative."

Staffing and newsroom culture

In 2008, Eden Lane, of Colorado Public Television, became the first transgender television journalist in the US. Some transgender journalists such as Meredith Talusan, a writer for BuzzFeed, Zoey Tur of *Inside Edition,* and journalist Danica Roem also are known publicly as transgender. Yet, the number of transgender journalists working in the US is difficult to specify because many may not feel comfortable coming out or they think it is a personal matter not necessary to self-disclose.

Newsroom diversity remains a challenge for the industry. Newsroom diversity leads to more expansive and less biased reporting that better reflects the diversity of audiences (Stewart, 2015). Creating support for transgender journalism students and newsroom cultures that are trans-supportive may improve coverage of these communities. For example, a study of Twitter user responses to Diane Sawyer's *20/20* interview with Caitlyn Jenner documented a positive reception led by celebrities such as Oprah Winfrey and Perez Hilton. Via Twitter, audience members indicated support for Jenner. Researchers identified themes developed by respondents such as bravery, support, and truth (Miller & Behm-Morawitz, 2016). Sawyer's careful preparation for this high-stakes interview provided a useful model that other reporters could follow.

The future directions for transgender news coverage

Acknowledging that neither the news industry nor transgender communities are monolithic or live in a vacuum, it is still possible to identify points of general consensus and existing differences of opinion among journalists and transgender advocates in terms of what improvements in news coverage have been successful and what work yet remains. News professionals and members of transgender communities alike clearly attest to the fact that the norms of journalism are beginning to change when it comes to coverage of transgender lives. Both constituencies agree that transgender lives finally are deemed newsworthy and journalists are treating transgender experiences as one of social and political importance. Additionally, consensus holds that what makes transgender lives newsworthy and how those stories are told reflect a higher degree of accuracy and sensitivity now than in the past. Stories sensationalizing gender reassignment surgeries, genitals, and personal appearance or misusing terms related to transgender identity and name-calling are decreasing in number, as are stories using the "before-and-after" format and wrong body discourse. Finally, many journalists respectfully use chosen names and pronouns more often and style guides continue to evolve.

On the other hand, some journalists and transgender advocates may disagree on what work remains or how best to capitalize on this momentum. Moreover, not all news professionals have reflected critically about coverage of transgender lives, and even among those who have, viewpoints differ in terms of the sufficiency of improvement made to date. As one example, debates over the necessity of gender-neutral pronouns (i.e., "xe," "ze") persist. Additionally, many transgender advocates and media critics bemoan the fact that the vast majority of news narratives, even those about transgender people, are grounded in the gender binary, sex/gender congruency, and gender stability. News stories of transgender lives tend to provide personal narratives rather than institutionalized discrimination or interrogations of cisnormativity. The fact that transgender people largely have been closeted and most cisgender people have had limited one-on-one interaction with a transgender person makes this dominant narrative all the more powerful in establishing interpretive frameworks used by news consumers to understand gender diversity.

Only time will tell if improvements made to date will become more far reaching in the future or how this dominant narrative will change over time. For example, will stories ever be written in a way in which being transgender is not the defining characteristic of that individual? Will news coverage directly confront deeply held social assumptions related to cisnormativity? Will news coverage become more inclusive, inviting the voices of gender fluid and genderqueer people to become part of this narrative?

Until recently, transgender lives and issues have not consistently been deemed newsworthy; several journalistic practices, such as those discussed in this chapter, delegitimized these citizens. Moreover, such coverage denied cisgender people the opportunity to learn about gender diversity or to question social assumptions about gender. A dominant narrative of what it *means* to be transgender within social, cultural, and political contexts was scripted and journalists played a significant role in writing that script. This script constructed a normative definition of "transgender," one that was largely assimilative in nature casting transgender people as either masculine or feminine at the expense of recognizing non-binary identities. Media are one site where hegemonic ideologies such as cisnormativity can be challenged. Many transgender advocates are doing exactly that, both in their own use of social media to create alternative spaces for gender expression and by monitoring, and when necessary, contesting news media industries. A true challenge to the role news media play in perpetuating cisnormativity is not a matter of simply "improving" images of transgender people or countering "stereotypes" of them in reporting, however. Contesting cisnormativity within press coverage will require a shift in the ideological gendering of news, one that reveals the often unspoken, contradictory, and ever-changing rules about the "normality" of gender and the consequences of those rules.

References

Arune, W. (2006). Transgender images in the media. In L. Castaneda & S. Campbell (Eds.), *News and sexuality: Media portraits of diversity* (pp. 111–133). Thousand Oaks, CA: Sage Publications.

Barker-Plummer, B. (2013). Fixing Gwen: News and the mediation of (trans)gender challenges. *Feminist Media Studies, 13*(4), 710–724.

Billard, T. J. (2016). Writing in the margins: Mainstream news media representations of transgenderism. *International Journal of Communication, 10*, 4193–4218.

Billard, T. J. (2018). TMS: A bibliography of transgender media studies. Retrieved March 2, 2018, from https://www.thomasjbillard.com/tms/

Birrell, S., & Cole, C. (1990). Double fault: Renee Richards and the construction and naturalization of difference. *Sociology of Sport Journal, 7*(1), 7–21.

Bucar, E., & Enke, A. (2011). Unlikely sex change capitals of the world: Trinidad, United States, and Tehran, Iran, as twin yardsticks of homonormativity. *Feminist Studies, 37*(2), 301–328.

Capuzza, J. C. (2014). Who defines gender diversity? Sourcing routines and representation in mainstream U.S. news stories about transgenderism. *International Journal of Transgenderism, 15*(3), 115–128.

Capuzza, J. C. (2015). What's in a name? Transgender identity, metareporting, and the misgendering of Chelsea manning. In L. G. Spencer & J. C. Capuzza (Eds.), *Transgender communication studies: Histories, trends, and trajectories* (pp. 93–110). Lanham, MD: Lexington Books.

Capuzza, J. C. (2016). Improvements still needed for transgender coverage. *Newspaper Research Journal, 37*(1), 82–94.

Cooper, T. (2014). What not to say to a transgender person. *CNN.* Retrieved October 10, 2017, from www.cnn.com/2014/01/15/living/transgender-identity/index.html

Corbett, P. (2015). Mx.? Did the times adopt a new, gender-neutral courtesy title? *The New York Times.* Retrieved October 13, 2017, from www.nytimes.com/2015/12/03/insider/mx-did-the-times-adopt-a-new-transgender-courtesy-title.html

Cram, E. (2012). Angie was our sister: Witnessing the trans-formation of disgust in the citizenry of photography. *The Quarterly Journal of Speech, 8*(4), 411–438.

Gerbner, G., & Gross, L. (1976). Living with television: The violence profile. *Journal of Communication, 26*, 172–199.

GLAAD. (2016). 2016 was the deadliest year on record for transgender people. *GLAAD.* Retrieved from August 19, 2017, www.glaad.org/blog/2016-was-deadliest-year-record-transgender-people

Hackl, A., Becker, A., & Todd, M. (2016). "I am Chelsea Manning": Comparison of gendered representation of private manning in U.S. and international news media. *Journal of Homosexuality, 63*(4), 467–486.

Hale, J. (1998). Consuming the living, dis(re)membering the dead in the butch/FTM borderlands. *GLQ, 4*(2), 311–348.

Johnson, J. (2013). Cisgender privilege, intersectionality, and the criminalization of CeCe McDonald: Why intercultural communication needs transgender studies. *Journal of International and Intercultural Communication, 6*(2), 135–144.

Kosenko, K. A., Bond, B., & Hurley, R. (2016). An exploration into the uses and gratifications of media for transgender individuals. *Psychology of Popular Media Culture*, 1–15.

Li, M. (2018). Intermedia attribute agenda setting in the context of issue-focused media events: Caitlyn Jenner and transgender reporting. *Journalism Practice, 12*(1), 56–75.

MacKenzie, G., & Marcel, M. (2009). Media coverage of the murder of U.S. transwomen of color. In L. M. Cuklanz & S. Moorti (Eds.), *Local violence, global media: Feminist analyses of gendered representations* (pp. 79–106). New York, NY: Peter Lang.

Marciano, A. (2014). Living the virtuReal: Negotiating transgender identities in cyberspace. *Journal of Computer-Mediated Communication*, *19*, 824–838. http://dx.doi.org/10.1111/jcc4.12081

Maza, C., Lopez, C., & Percelay, R. (2015). How national media outlets cover transgender stories. *Media Matters for America*. Retrieved September 23, 2015, from www.mediamatters.org/research/2015/04/08/report-how-national-media-outlets-cover-transge/203034

McInroy, L. B., & Craig, S. L. (2015). Transgender representation in offline and online media: LGBTQ youth perspectives. *Journal of Human Behavior in the Social Environment*, *25*, 606–617. doi.org/10.1080/10911359.2014.995392

Meyerowitz, J. (1998). Sex change and the popular press: Historical notes on transsexuality in the United States, 1930–1955. *GLQ*, *4*(2), 159–188.

Miller, B., & Behm-Morawitz, E. (2016). Exploring social television, opinion leaders, and Twitter audience reactions to Diane Sawyer's coming out interview with Caitlyn Jenner. *International Journal of Transgenderism*, *18*(20), 2–15. doi.org/10.1080/15532739.2016.1260513

Morrison, S. (2016). Covering the transgender community. *Neiman Reports*, 22–29.

National LGBT Bar Association. *Gay and transgender panic defense*. Retrieved September 8, 2017, from www.lgbtbar.org/what-we-do/programs/gay-and-trans-panic-defense/

O'Neill, M. G. (2014). Transgender youth and YouTube videos: Self-representation and five identifiable trans youth narratives. In C. Pullen (Ed.), *Queer youth and media cultures* (pp. 34–45). London: Palgrave Macmillan.

Perlman, M. (2015). Un-gendered. *Columbia Journalism Review*. Retrieved October 8, 2017, from www.cjr.org/language_corner/language_changes_were_fond_of.php

Raun, T. (2010). Screen-births: Exploring the trans- formative potential in trans video blogs on YouTube. *Graduate Journal of Social Science*, *7*, 113–130.

Ringo, P. (2002). Media roles in female-to-male transsexual and transgender identity development. *International Journal of Transgenderism*, *6*. Retrieved from September 23, 2015, from www.iiav.nl/ezines/web/ijt/97-03/numbers/symposion/ijtvo06no03_01.htm

Ryan, J. (2009). *Reel images: Examining the politics of trans images in film and media* (doctoral dissertation), Bowling Green, OH: Bowling Green State University.

Schilt, K., & Westbook, L. (2009). Doing gender, doing heteronormativity: "Gender normals," transgender people, and the social maintenance of heterosexuality. *Gender & Society*, *23*(4), 440–464.

Schneider, B. (2012). Sourcing homelessness: How journalists use sources to frame homelessness. *Journalism*, *13*(1), 71–86.

Seibler, K. (2012). Transgender transitions: Sex/gender binaries in the digital age. *Journal of Gay & Lesbian Mental Health*, *16*, 74–99.

Shepard, K. (2017a). Associated press issues new guidance on sex, gender: Avoid referring to "both" or "either" sexes. *The Washington Times*. Retrieved October 10, 2017, from www.washingtontimes.com/news/2017/oct/10/ap-stylebook-transgender-coverage-dont-say-trans-p/

Shepard, K. (2017b). AP stylebook on transgender coverage: Don't say trans person was "born a girl or boy." *The Washington Times*. Retrieved October 10, 2017, from www.washingtontimes.com/news/2017/oct/10/ap-stylebook-transgender-coverage-dont-say-trans-p/

Skidmore, E. (2011). Constructing the "good transsexual": Christine Jorgensen: Whiteness, and heteronormativity in the mid-twentieth-century press. *Feminist Studies*, *2*(37), 270–300.

Sloop, J. (2000). Disciplining the transgendered: Brandon Teena, public representation, and normativity. *Western Journal of Communication*, *64*(2), 165–189.

Sopelsa, B. (2017). AP stylebook embraces singular "they" as singular, gender-neutral pronoun. *NBC News*. Retrieved October 10, 2017, from www.nbcnews.com/feature/nbc-out/ap-stylebook-embraces-they-singular-gender-neutral-pronoun-n739076

Squires, C., & Brouwer, D. (2002). In/discernible bodies: The politics of passing in dominant and marginal media. *Critical Studies in Mass Communication, 19*(3), 283–310.

Stewart, A. (2015). Why newsroom diversity works. *Nieman Reports*. Retrieved October 17, 2017, from http://niemanreports.org/articles/why-newsroom-diversity-works/

Tamlin, E., Quinlan, M., & Benjamin, B. (2017). Accessing womanhood: Jenna Talackova and the marking of a beauty queen. *Sexuality & Culture, 21*(3), 703–718. doi:10.1007/s12119-017-9416-z

Trans Media Watch. (n.d.). *How transgender people experience media*. Retrieved September 20, 2015, from www.transmediawatch

Tuchman, G. (1979). Women's depiction in the mass media. *Signs, 4*, 528–542.

Willox, A. (2003). Branding Teena: (Mis)representations in the media. *Sexualities, 6*, 407–425.

9

GENDERED VIOLENCE IN, OF, AND BY SPORT NEWS

David Rowe

Introduction: modes of mediated sporting violence

The media—especially television—value violent moments in sport. These incidents can be endlessly replayed and dissected, offering spectacular moments that might involve deep ethical debate, but also present snippets of action, collisions, and confrontations that are the visual equivalent of fun fair thrill rides. These "showreels" can lay claim to involving journalism because they are both witness and record of actual events, however confected, accompanied by commentary of varying depth. Violent moments in the media have also come to define and celebrate a "hegemonic" form of masculinity. That is, men's propensity to excel at sporting violence can be voyeuristically enjoyed. Violence is a key feature of the appeal to sports audiences, and as such a pivotal means by which men's sport can be judged to be superior to women's sport. Women athletes either cluster in "decorous" sports that lack violent appeal, or, when they do enter the masculine domain of contact sport, can be dismissed as a pale imitation of the "real thing." The rise of women's sport in general, including contact forms, however, makes it important to examine how journalists respond to the phenomenon of legitimate and illegitimate sport violence.

Violence in the field of athletic play is not the only expression of violence in the sporting sphere. News media also cover off-field violence by sportsmen—often against women, including their spouses—males being, as in the wider society, the vast majority of perpetrators. Some have argued that sportsmen are over-represented in this regard (Benedict, 1997). Cases abound of leading sportsmen being convicted of spousal abuse, including Floyd Mayweather Jr., Dennis Rodman, and O.J. Simpson. In one notorious 2014 case, gridiron player Ray Rice was seen on a hotel camera dragging his then fiancée Janay Palmer out of an elevator after allegedly rendering her unconscious; the charges were dropped after the couple married and he undertook counseling under court supervision (Ranker, 2017). The prominence of such sportsmen generates full-blown media scandals that illuminate both the violent conduct and its attendant social norms, and the media's role in publicizing and interpreting them (Rowe, 1997). Violence by male sport fans during and following sport events, including domestic violence, has also been well documented (McKay, Messner, & Sabo, 2000). Extending the concept to incorporate other modes of gendered violence that are less literally about physical force but are more symbolic (though not necessarily less hurtful) in nature, are the intrusive sexualization of sportswomen, their "symbolic annihilation" through neglect and trivialization (Cooky, Messner, & Hextrum, 2013), sexist and homophobic vilification by means of gender-based insults (Rowe, 2014), and the sexually violent "trolling" in mainstream media comments and social media posts of women who comment critically on sexism in sports culture (Ford, 2014; Riley, 2016).

Editors, journalists, camera operators, and photographers may all be implicated in these modes of gendered violence through either action or inaction. The scale and complexity of these manifestations of gendered violence in the "media sports cultural complex" (Rowe, 2004) is considerable. Therefore, this chapter focuses principally on representations of gender and violence in contact sport by the news media, analyzing its role in countering and reinforcing modes of masculinity and femininity.

Violence, news, sport, and entertainment

As a key element of ethical conduct, news organizations and journalists are expected to take a serious and considered approach to reporting violence. Conventionally defined as the exertion of damaging physical force on people and/or objects (although, as discussed below, this may be intangible), violence is an integral aspect of news. It is inherently newsworthy, having a direct bearing on life and death matters that lend themselves to dramatic, disturbing news narratives (Wykes, 2001). The connection between violence and news values is evident in the selection, placement and ordering of news, use of language, and deployment of headlines, still photography and moving images. So, journalists must reflect deeply on their management of violence. For example, journalism ethics textbooks conventionally include sections on how to cover violent crime, war, and terrorism, the point being that these important issues should be handled in ways that are not misleading, voyeuristic or gratuitous. Yet, no such consideration is given regarding sport news.

Sports journalism often covers contact sport, especially that involving teams. Sports such as American (gridiron) and association football (soccer), the rugby "codes" (union and league), and ice hockey all routinely involve physical collisions that frequently lead, accidentally or by design, to injury. The norms that govern these sporting contests give considerable license to behavior that, in other contexts, would be condemned as unequivocally violent. Physical conduct in sport that would lead to apprehension by the police and sanction by the courts if occurring outside the stadium, is widely—and often wildly—celebrated within it. Much of the concern hinges on whether the rules of each sport have been transgressed.

Where officially unapproved actions occurred, the governing bodies of sport apply their various disciplinary codes. However, a rupture between formal control of violent athlete conduct, and informal responses to it, is frequently evident.

Spectators (depending on their athlete and team affiliation), "live" media commentators, and journalists cheer "big hits" and "strong tackles," with match officials required to make instant judgments about whether legitimate or illegitimate force has been exerted, or are called upon to assess whether an act causing injury was intentional or accidental. In the case of brawls and fights—also often relished by those watching—decisions are made about *provocateurs* and retaliators, often being cast as "villains" and "victims" in news narratives. Increasingly, additional referees and umpires who are in a studio and possess multi-angle and -speed visual technologies assist the on-field officials; subsequent tribunals also decide on guilt and innocence and then apply appropriate penalties. Sports journalists and media commentators are necessarily embroiled in these processes, framing their own judgments and evaluating the players' actions, the determinations of the officials, and the validity of the rules. In this sense, journalists act as popular arbiters of sporting violence to which, via media omnipresence, the bulk of the citizenry may become witness.

Elias and Dunning (1986) analyze these questions of violence and pleasure in sport; they use figurational sociology to posit a "civilising process" within which "sportisation" sees ready resort to ungoverned violence and violent pastimes gradually give way to forms of legitimized violence that operate under specific rules. These sporting contests developed into industries involving spectators watching professional practitioners engage in athletic displays of violence on their behalf. Feminist sociologists such as Jennifer Hargreaves (1994) have criticized the inadequacy of this theory's treatment of gender relations, and a broader tendency within sport to glorify a gladiatorial male image. The media, including journalists, are required, then, to address these questions of the ethics of mediated physical leisure. Meanwhile, sports journalists often seem predisposed to see sport as somehow exempt from rules of conduct that apply in other domains.

Kevin Young (2012) finds that most tabloid, broadsheet, and television sports journalists resist the idea of an association between the media's treatment of sport and its wider social consequences. With reference to professional ethics, he pressed his interviewees on their use of dramatic, often bloody photographs or multiple replays of violent sport incidents. He reports that sports journalists generally replied that these practices responded to audience expectations; therefore, they had little compunction in emphasizing violent acts in print, broadcast, and online news stories. For example, in the case of "hits" and fights in ice hockey, Young found that many journalists felt that they had scant choice but to cover them intensively given the development in the capabilities of media technology, the economics of the media, and the preferences of sport fans. According to sport psychologists, for some fans, enjoyment of a sporting contest is closely connected to vigorous physical clashes that damage the participants' bodies; fans may also relish ensuing confrontations that are not within the rules but enhance the dramatic spectacle (see, for example, Bryant, Comisky, & Zillmann, 1981; Gunter, 2006; Raney & Kinnally,

2009). As Wayne Wanta (2013) has observed, this body of research suggests that gender and sport fandom influence mood and enjoyment levels following exposure to violent sports programming. Women and non-sports fans, Wanta found, tended to react less favorably to this violent content, meaning that its primary "constituency" is men sport fans, among whom can be counted the majority of sports journalists.

Despite limited changes to the professional sports journalism workforce in some countries, most editors, columnists, and reporters are still men, even in the US, where the workforce gender balance might be expected to be more even (Morrison, 2014). Young (2012) points out that sports journalism remains dominated by a "masculinist occupational culture" that matches that of sport itself. Some journalists freely admitted to Young that they enjoyed being able to watch fighting in the National Hockey League, and regarded it as a legitimate part of the game (usually with the proviso that it did not cause serious injury). We must be wary of rigid gender stereotypes regarding attitudes surrounding contact sport and violence (as discussed below). Nonetheless, the institutional domination of both sport and media by men has enabled attitudes, values and practices to flourish that favor men over women.

Intermittent multi-sport events, like the Olympics and the Commonwealth Games, do have much more gender-equitable sporting coverage. For example, women athletes received a greater percentage of prime-time broadcast television coverage during the 2014 Sochi Winter Games than in the previous five Winter Olympics (Billings, Angelini, & MacArthur, 2017). NBC devoted 47.7 percent of its prime-time Olympic coverage to women in 2014, compared to 52.3 percent to men (excluding mixed pair events). This 4.6 percent gender gap was the smallest recorded for a Winter Olympiad since the longitudinal studies of Olympic media coverage by Billings and his colleague Susan Tyler Eastman began at the 1994 Lillehammer Olympics.

Individual sports that follow world circuits, such as tennis and golf, also provide prominent media coverage of women (although it remains less than that of men). But, men are typically at the center of major sports leagues enjoying saturation media attention. Not all of these sports involve contact (baseball and cricket, for example, forbid bodily contact between players) and equivalent leagues exist for women (such as the US's National Women's Soccer League and the Women's National Basketball Association), as well as women-dominated sports leagues (notably the new Suncorp Super Netball in Australia and the Vitality Netball Superleague in the UK). Still, men's contact team sport receives much more extensive media coverage and, of particular economic importance, broadcast rights revenue (Rowe, 2004).

The contact sports mentioned so far are not necessarily the most violent. Boxing and the Ultimate Fighting Championship (UFC) involve greater direct, confrontational violence between competitors that is an integral part of their rules and spectator appeal. Motor sports, such as the US's National Association for Stock Car Auto Racing (NASCAR) and Australia's V8 Supercars, also rely heavily on spectacular "showreels" involving high-speed collisions and crashes in their adver-tisements and news coverage. Nonetheless, the density, frequency, and popularity of team contact sports turn them into the stuff of everyday news, which is structured in highly predictable ways—the newspaper sports section, broadcast news sports segment, online news website sports link, and so on. Sport news derives its news-worthiness from narrative—what happened, why, who was responsible, etc.—and still photography and video action. News material is produced as being of primary interest to fans of the participating teams, followed by fans of the sport and of sport in general, and finally to the components of a general media audience that may have little interest in sport at all. Therefore, if sport news is to attract maximum attention, it is likely to emphasize the most striking and controversial aspects of sport contests. Eyes can be drawn to violent incidents, frequently replayed at vari-ous angles and at a range of speeds, in rendering these events as newsworthy both in and outside sports reports. As most of these actions are being performed by men, this news necessarily focuses on key issues concerning masculinity: are men acting violently towards other men in legitimate or illegitimate ways? Is this conduct a function of maleness/masculinity, such as in the familiar saying that "boys will be boys," and in laments by NFL fans such as then-US Presidential candidate Donald Trump (quoted in Boren, 2016), that "football has become soft like our country"? Has sport developed as a socially sanctioned way of expressing this masculinity and of cathartically discharging its violent impulses? Is exposure to violent behavior via sport socially detrimental, inducing imitative behavior among spectators, especially boys and other men?

Sport cannot entirely control the social and political discourse in which it is embedded. It may sometimes appear to be a hermetically sealed world—as another frequently circulated saying "what happens on the field stays on the field" indicates. But sport cannot be separated from the web of social relationships in which it oper-ates. It is constructed and enacted by people, and supported by a range of other social institutions, including families, schools, governments, bureaucracies, enterprises, and corporations. Crucially, its reliance on the news and entertainment media, and sub-sequent cultural visibility, even for those who do not follow it, means that sport business becomes in a sense everyone's business. So, when violent acts occur on the field of play, sport becomes a catalyst for debates about the state and trajectory of society—in this case sport and gender relations, and the articulation between sport, masculinities and femininities. News organizations play a major role in this domain because, as the principal communicative engines of sport (Wenner, 1998), they must take responsibility for how they represent it, and for the information, ideologies, and mythologies that they promote, repress, challenge, and reproduce.

Sport, news, and the spectacle of violent masculinity

Most sport in the media is male-centered, but not all sportsmen get equal cover-age. Calculations of newsworthiness are made according to sporting popularity, although the relationship between media visibility and popularity in sport has a certain circularity. Male contact team sports are featured routinely in news stories. Something can always be discussed—current performances, prospects, controversies, injuries, stadium facilities, fan perspectives, the exchange of sports labor between clubs, and so on. What is called sport news is, as in other beats, largely predictable and mainly of interest to dedicated sport followers. How can the media aggregate citizens and consumers who are committed, indifferent, and hostile to sport in the name of news? One key technique is to emphasize drama and to draw in audiences with action. Here media with sound and moving images have a clear advantage. Given intensified competition for attention and thus a relentless process of "fishing for eyeballs" (Hutchins & Rowe, 2012, p. 1), a spectacular try, touchdown, slam dunk, goal, and so on will attract many people's attention. But interpreting the action on screen beyond registering spectacular images demands some preexisting knowledge of sport. Sports fans will be able to decode what they are watching on the sports news readily in terms of the specific routines and rules of sport, but many others will not possess the same capacity to do so. There is, though, one form of action that can be easily, perhaps universally decoded—violence—especially when accompanied by forceful commentary.

Violence, then, is situated at the confluence of sport and news, especially when it is illegitimate. News footage of a violent act on the field of play can claim consequence beyond sport, invoking debates about inappropriate and even criminal behavior. The subject is also deeply gendered. Physical force, including its violent expression, is a domain where men are historically viewed to dominate women— literally. Men are widely held to be more competent than women in corporeal confrontation and violence—indeed, sports culture is predominantly framed on the basis that men's sport is superior to women's because it is usually "faster, higher, stronger" (the Olympic motto) and also more compelling because it is tougher and more aggressive. The "big hits" are more likely to be covered in television news bulletins, from which those deemed to be the most notable migrate to the internet, where they are compiled into highlights shows. They almost exclusively feature men.

For example, "Biggest Sporting Hits" (2014) is a 3.5-minute compilation, published on YouTube, of physical confrontations both within and outside the sporting rules, drawn exclusively from male team contact sports—rugby league, rugby union, American football, ice hockey, and Australian rules football. The compilation, which has no commentary and is accompanied only by percussive electronic music, shows a series of clashes between players: several are shown to be injured and to lose consciousness. It ends by showing an Australian rules footballer being knocked out; the final section focuses on the prone player and repeats the incident in slow motion. By December 2018 it had attracted 75,432 views and elicited 91 comments, including "lets wear pads like a bunch of bitchs [sic]" (pete a), "It was a nice way to finish off a good clip: a Carlton player being sent into a fucking coma!" (chronic pig), and "Not much soccer in there. Mostly Dominion sports: NFL, NHL, NRL, AFL, ARFU. Is this the legacy of the British Empire? Ultra-violent gladiator sports to thin out the herd and create a race of super warriors to perpetuate the dominance of the Anglo-Saxon/Norman/Briton race. Show me a ping-pong match that can rival this" (Todd Hill).

Such online material (some with a racial dimension) can be described as its own genre of male sport violence. A simple Google search for "sport big hits" produced 27,600,000 results and more videos with names including "BIGGEST Hits in Sports History!" and "Greatest Hits of All Time (in any sport)." The latter includes association football, baseball, and boxing, again exclusively involving men. There were also multiple links to newspaper and magazine articles, Facebook pages, sport TV videos, etc. Although some links involved spectacular sporting moments that were not violent or discussed sports play rather than just showing "hits," much of this material simply celebrated dangerous collisions. Copying and posting moving images of violent sporting incidents cannot be described as journalism in a conventional sense, but neither is this activity entirely disconnected from it. Viewers have already had access to them through the media, by means of sports programs or coverage in general or sport news bulletins and articles. These journalistic texts may either criticize or celebrate male sports violence; but irrespective of the attitude adopted, they rely heavily on the graphic, de-contextualized, rapid-fire visual representation of violence.

This constant representation of sportsmen and violence works to construct frames of sporting masculinity and to carry sport far beyond, amplifying it in the process. When interpreting the actions of sportsmen on the field, including but not limited to violent ones, journalists constantly refer to other roles, making frequent reference, for example, via connotation and metaphor, to the military world. Sportsmen are regularly presented as "warriors" engaged in "battles" and "wars." Heroism is contrasted with treachery and cowardice, and sacrifice in the service of a noble cause is glorified, while self-interest and even self-preservation are denigrated. Although comparing sports contests to wars is hyperbolic and insensitive (in suggesting, for example, that a team losing a sport contest or a player getting injured are remotely comparable to the tragedies of war), it is not surprising that sports journalists and commentators will reach for such everyday dramatic language in practising popular communication (Lopez-Gonzalez, Guerrero-Sole, & Haynes, 2014). Indeed, for all its exaggeration and tastelessness, soldiers and people engaged professionally in contact sports have something in common. Both operate in highly institutionalized, male-dominated worlds in which corporeal risk and potentially serious consequences for health are expected. Yet, until recently, sports journalists have tended to ignore, or at least underplay, the bodily implications of constant and sometimes traumatic contact between bodies and, in some cases, between inanimate sport equipment (which may include "protective" helmets, bats, balls etc.) and living athletes. Questions surrounding the duty of care of sports organizations have generally been put more forcefully by associations representing athletes, sport academics, and even insurance companies than by sports journalists.

The incidence of traumatic brain injury in sport, once focused mainly on boxing and wrestling, have now registered in sports including gridiron, rugby union, and association football (Lewis, 2014). While this issue is receiving belated attention, neither the general nor sports media were at the forefront of highlighting it in the public sphere through investigative, critical journalism. Instead, sports journalists and commentators have been largely complicit, along with many sport fans, in celebrating the form of masculinity that plays down the impact of injury on the field. Sports culture is replete with heroic tales of "playing hurt"—that is, continuing to perform despite injuries such as concussions and bone fractures, with the implicit and sometimes explicit suggestion that not to "carry on" in these circumstances is a dereliction of duty towards team, club, and even nation (Borden, 2013).

In this respect, the mediation of sport plays a part. Most of those who witness sporting encounters do so from afar and, despite increasingly intense audio-visual monitoring of violent incidents in sport, close-ups and replays may, paradoxically, maintain and even accentuate that distance. Such moving images can resemble those generated by video games—making appreciation of the flesh-and-blood dimensions of what is seen and heard difficult. We must be cautious about advancing a simple thesis about violent media causing desensitization (that is, that repeated exposure to mediated violence reduces its shock effect on the viewer, and may be transportable into the domain of everyday life). Yet, another classic media theory suggests that a process of "cultivation" can encourage the expectation of violence in mediated sport that may carry over into the home and the street (Ruddock, 2011). While this is a complex and controversial area for both the entertainment and news media, the ethical issues that it raises about the responsible representation of violence need serious consideration.

Moreover, the difference between relatively routine coverage of sporting violence and extraordinary cases of a fatality needs acknowledgment, as does the likelihood of a more serious treatment of the subject. For example, in 2014 the Australian cricketer Phillip Hughes died after being struck on the neck (beneath his protective helmet) while batting in a low-profile game. His death prompted global institutional media coverage and a massive social media response, including posting symbolic images of a leaning cricket bat (Samuels, 2014). This tragic event stimulated debates about both mitigating the dangers of sport and encouraging more civility within it, including by reducing the incidence of violent and abusive language (so-called sledging) against opponents. Here, two modes of sporting masculinity emerge: an evocation of the image of the honorable competitor who respects opponents and privileges the game over the result versus the ruthless, unprincipled partisan who pursues sporting victory by any means possible. Sports journalists tend to oscillate between favoring one or other end of this means–end schema, usually in relation to their own sporting affiliations (that is, like fans, being more tolerant of transgressions by sportsmen and teams that they support).

Sports like cricket, baseball, and rugby union, with their historical connections to male social elites and to "quality" sports journalism in broadsheet newspapers and public service and elite private broadcasters, are more orthodox and legitimate environments for these discussions of sporting ethics. Rather less comfortable sporting subjects are some ultra-violent sports that have developed as overtly *mediatized* (Frandsen, 2016). That is, instead of being established first and then getting media coverage, they were largely invented as creatures of the media. The media presentation of Mixed Martial Arts (MMA—popularly known as "cage fighting") is an increasingly conspicuous form of this version of violent sporting masculinity.

Gender, the cage, and the 'Violent Femme'

The most prominent manifestation of MMA is the Ultimate Fighting Championship (UFC). The spectrum of Mixed Martial Arts events ranges from regulated, professional and amateur contests with more or less media coverage to "underground" events with very few rules and a strong orientation to gambling, as is depicted in the 1999 film *Fight Club*. It also includes specific forms such as *Felony Fights*, which has a website and DVD collections showing fighters with criminal backgrounds in the US fighting each other, or against more "respectable" opponents such as police officers and war veterans. Michael Salter and Stephen Tomsen (2012, p. 311) graphically describe its website content:

> The violence of these clips and the social rebelliousness evident in raucous heavy metal and thrash music, obscene language and sexist imagery of semi-nude women could be intended to offend or reject middle-class sensibilities. . . . Within the clips, many combatants treat their own serious wounding as a mark of personal status. A sensual enjoyment of violence merges with the evident masculine status claim of most victors or even the amused glee expressed by the vanquished at the end of clips.

This is obviously not a mainstream sporting activity, but it resonates across a wider field of masculinity, media, and violence. As Salter and Tomsen (2012, p. 320) note:

> The depictions of white reflexive sadomasochism in *Fight Club* and less mainstream media such as *Felony Fights* resonate with viewers by drawing on these largely unconscious and unarticulated cultural logics of violence and the supposed burden and costs of masculine power.

The media, which are pivotal to the UFC's economic success, must manage their relationship to, and representation of, its violence. Like any sport event, it becomes "news" because it is watched—but its newsworthiness, in a familiar feedback loop, affects awareness and interest. This is less of a professional ethical dilemma in non-contact sports like tennis or even in rule-governed contact sports like gridiron. But in the case of what the late conservative US politician John McCain called "human cockfighting" (Mwangaguhunga, 2011), it is more difficult to manage ethically. Available across pay-per-view, subscription, mobile and network television, in DVD and as a video game, media reach was a key element in the US$4 billion acquisition in 2016 of UFC by the California-based talent agency WME-IMG (Merced, 2016). UFC's media profile gained additional impetus in 2017 when UFC Lightweight

Champion Conor McGregor participated in a boxing match against the (aforementioned) leading boxer Floyd Mayweather Jr, with an estimated legal pay per view audience of over four million (and an estimated three million illegally downloading it) (Dawson, 2017; Pugmire, 2017).

Longstanding anxiety about damaging social messages projected by televising boxing are now resonating through newspaper deliberations such as "MMA Sends Mixed Messages about Violence in Sport" (Mael, 2017). The sport-violence-masculinity nexus is a particular focus, but it becomes even more troubling to conventional discourse when the participants are women. Gender-based critiques of violent sport and media often hinge, as discussed above, on their connection to men and masculinity, and, especially, on whether men are biologically predisposed to be violent or socialized into being so in seeking to exercise domination over women and other men. The sociological evidence firmly rejects the biologically essentialist notion that men are inherently violent, emphasizing instead how social structures, relations and identities generate violence according to a range of forms of power, many of which are controlled or exercised by some men at the expense of other men, as well as of women and children (Connell, 2000; McKay et al., 2000). Such debates echo concerns about the "outsourcing" of violence as pleasure in sport and media and the normalizing of aggressive behavior (Sarre, 2015). But sport is not only a man's world. Indeed, it is complicated by the involvement of women as agents of legitimate and illegitimate violence in sport.

Given the historical dominance of sport by men, women's involvement as both athletes and spectators raises questions about whether they are emulating aspects of masculinity that ought to be condemned, or are simply exercising their right to enjoy sports that provide dangerous and violent experience and spectacle. Such matters of "gender appropriateness" become especially prominent in media discourse when a woman is a victim or perpetrator of sport violence. An especially prominent figure embodying this issue is UFC celebrity Ronda Rousey, who was knocked out by a high kick from Holly Holm in the much-publicized main event at UFC 193 in Melbourne in November 2015. The intense media coverage leading up to the bout had highlighted the politics of gender. Some of Rousey's previous public pronouncements—for example, describing some other women as "do-nothing bitches" (quoted in Convery, 2015) and as just trying "to be pretty and be taken care of by somebody else" (quoted in Valenti, 2015)—contributed to this news media discourse, which became even more intense after the dramatic (legal) violent end to the fight. A substantial backlash ensued against Rousey, especially in social media. Sarah Kurchak (2016) observed:

> Love her, hate her, or continue to struggle with a deep ambivalence about her that you can't completely articulate, you can't deny that Ronda Rousey is a trailblazer. She was the first female UFC champion, the face that helped bring women's mixed martial arts to the sport's biggest stage, and helped to keep it there. . . . Even in defeat, she managed to break new ground: she became the subject of the sport's first viciously major backlash. . . .

As suddenly and shockingly as she'd paved the way for other women in the sport, she'd also shown them how easily the public can turn on anyone— particularly a woman who never knew her place in what remains a male- dominated sport and industry.

This focus on "the public" renders problematic the efficacy of professional journalism in setting the agenda in news and commentary: the backlash emanates principally from networked social media rather than institutional media. In both domains, though, gender asymmetry lays down a familiar, delicate path to follow in the public sphere:

They must be confident, but not too confident, because public vulnerabil- ity and ego are almost equally perilous in their positions. They're aware of how precarious and short the life span of a favored female fighter can be and they're choosing their words as carefully as they'd plan their strikes or takedowns.

(Kurchak, 2016)

Such statements apply in varying ways to any sportswoman's dealings with contem- porary digitally networked media sport (Hutchins & Rowe, 2012)—and, indeed, in other public domains such as parliamentary politics. However, the presence of social media and their often uncivil, if not misogynistic treatment of women, does not absolve professional media workers, and the formal media environments in which they operate, from their responsibility of countering the ingrained gendered inequalities in their work routines. While the sexualization, marginalization and disparagement of sportswomen by the sports and wider media are well documented (Fink, 2015), the assertion of femininities that "break the mould" is discomfiting for many journalists and disruptive of their "set piece" routines. Andy Ruddock (2015), for example, noted that sexism figured prominently in Rousey's promotional press conference appearance in Melbourne prior to her fight with Holm:

Rousey knows her body is a challenge to the usual order of things in media culture. Hence the "do-nothing bitch" philosophy that has launched its own apparel range. In a post on the UFC videolog, Rousey says:

Listen, just because my body was developed for a purpose other than fucking millionaires doesn't mean it's masculine. I think it's femininely badass as fuck because there's not a single muscle on my body that isn't for a purpose, because I'm not a do-nothing bitch.

But let me ask you this: have you ever seen a [celebrity footballer] David Beckham presser [press conference] where journalists addressed the first three questions to someone else? Because that's what happened yesterday. Rousey, Holm and under card fighters Joanna Jedrzejczyk and Valerie Letourneau listened as Dana White was interrogated.

When attention finally turned to Rousey, the pressing question was how she felt about appearing in *Entourage* and being name-checked by Beyoncé.

Journalists' awkward handling of gender, especially with regard to femininity and feminism, reveals the extent to which sport remains a testing ground where familiarity with aggressive masculinity may meet an unaccustomed "badass" femininity. Likening women cage fighters to their counterparts in bodybuilding, Charlene Weaving (2014, p. 137) argues that the resultant pressures demand shifting between challenging passive female stereotypes and exhibiting at least some signs of conventional feminine sexual address:

> Women can achieve lived body experiences, and manipulate their bodies in non-feminine ways. However, outside the cage, they may be 'forced' by their medial [sic] profile to adopt a hyper-feminine persona.

Weaving notes that Rousey told a *USA Today* interviewer, in a reversal of the general wisdom applying to sportsmen (Rowe, 2010), and indicating a more aggressive response to sex than traditional notions of femininity, that she has as much sex as possible before a fight on the theory that it raises testosterone levels:

> There do not appear to be comparable interviews with male UFC fighters discussing their preferred timing of their sexual activity. By highlighting her sexual intercourse activities, Rousey helps to ensure she is portrayed in heterosexual, if not entirely feminine, manner.
>
> *(Weaving, p. 137)*

During the interview Rousey was eager to assert that the sex in question is heterosexual (avoiding the stereotype of the tough, lesbian sportswoman) and part of an ongoing relationship: "Rousey quickly clarified that her training regimen depends on whether she has a steady boyfriend or not. 'I don't put out Craigslist ads or anything,' she said" (Chase, 2012). Here, potentially gender-transgressive sexual assertiveness is mitigated by the rather curious linkage of Rousey's training method to her relationship status with an intimate male other in the context of a supermarket tabloid interview.

UFC may be an extreme case, but less explicitly violent sports can be readily framed in ways that present relatively unexceptional instances of violence enacted by sportsmen as particularly shocking when performed by sportswomen. Hence, in 2016 when Australia established a national AFL Women's (AFLW) league, considerable support emerged for the initiative. But, when participating sportswomen were injured on live, prime-time television, sometimes as a result of foul play, considerable disquiet was evident. For example, the Australian Broadcasting Corporation's (ABC's) (2017) *Offsiders* Sunday morning program, which reviews the preceding week's sport, gave considerable attention to the relatively novel prospect of a sportswoman facing a disciplinary tribunal after being reported by officials for a *prima facie* violent act.

When the Collingwood club's Sophie Casey knocked out Melbourne's Meg Downie (*Daily Mail Australia*, 2017), she was charged with engaging in "careless, rough conduct" (using unnecessary physical force) that resulted in "high impact to the head" and was suspended for two weeks. While an equivalent incident would certainly have gained considerable publicity in the professional men's game, it was even more newsworthy in the women's, with particular stress on the corporeal vulnerability arising, according to a leading male player, from their semi-professional status (Morris, 2017). The same article quoted a leading Australian cricketer, Alyssa Healy, saying that such conduct arose from seeking to emulate men's toughness:

> Most sport is very male dominated. . . . When you go out there you want to prove that you're just as good as the blokes. Footy is that you want to tackle hard and make that contest. Maybe the girls are going just a little bit too hard and maybe it will even itself out.
>
> *(Morris, 2017)*

This cautionary tale (multiply syndicated across News Corp Australia outlets) reveals that on-field violence by sportswomen, and the corresponding peril that it presents to other women participants, expresses a legitimate concern for their wellbeing. But it also illustrates that the media, especially male sports journalists and their mainly male sources, are still coming to terms with gendered expectations that violence on the field of play is a predominantly masculine practice, and that, when carried out by women, it constitutes a double transgression of the rules of the game and of traditional gender expectations.

Conclusion: violence and the sports journalist

Legitimate and illegitimate violence are integral elements of sports news. Sport organizations, editors and journalists must confront the ethics of its representation and interpretation. I have argued here that men's dominance of both sport and sports journalism, and the instantaneous news value that can be extracted from violence, favors a form of violent masculinity that renders sporting violence as entertainment. This is not to argue that all sport, even that of a contact nature, is inherently violent. But extensively covered violent incidents can be easily translated into sporting highlights. Sports media highly prize these dramatic moments because they attract viewers, listeners, and readers of varying orientations to sport; many sports journalists and fans experience "sportified" violence, especially by men, as mediated pleasure. The differential responses by journalists and the wider media to the violence of sportsmen and sportswomen on the field of play starkly reveals the gendered nature of this regime of pleasure. Tolerance and even encouragement of sportsmen to be violent in some circumstances in expressing their masculinity manifests as discomfort and disapprobation when conducted by women in repudiating historically inherited conceptions of femininity.

Journalists, willingly or otherwise, must operate within and against this structure of gender power in sport and media. They are both professionals who are expected to uphold their ethical code and, almost universally, are fans of athletes, clubs, and countries. Journalists are also themselves gendered and sexed subjects, of course. The politics of gender in sport and media may once have appeared quite simple—mainly white, assumed heterosexual men covering other mainly white, assumed heterosexual men. Violent expressions of masculinity could be quite easily accommodated within this largely self-enclosed world. But, as the boundaries of sport became more porous, and as women asserted their rights more vigorously and gendered identities have become more fluid, this masculine edifice has begun (despite considerable resistance) to crumble. Neither the physical toll of on-field physical trauma, nor the wider off-field consequences of homophobia and spousal abuse, can be ignored. In most countries, sports journalists have been slow to adjust to the changing gender order apparent in other social and occupational spheres (Horky & Nieland, 2013). Journalism's ethical compulsion to engage critically with the sport-masculinity-violence nexus, therefore, demands an auto-critique of its persistently masculinized professional *milieu*.

References

Australian Broadcasting Corporation. (2017, February 12). *Offsiders*. Retrieved from http://iview.abc.net.au/programs/offsiders/NC1714V006S00#playing

Benedict, J. (1997). *Public heroes, private felons: Athletes and crimes against women*. Boston, MA: Northeastern University Press.

Biggest Sporting Hits. (2014, May 9). *YouTube (JDWbuddy)*. Retrieved from www.youtube.com/watch?v=m0Kl1L2LUhk

Billings, A. C., Angelini, J. R., & MacArthur, P. J. (2017). *Olympic television: Broadcasting the biggest show on earth*. London and New York, NY: Routledge.

Borden, S. (2013, November 4). No heroism in playing after a head injury. *The New York Times*. Retrieved from www.nytimes.com/2013/11/05/sports/soccer/no-heroism-in-tottenham-goalies-playing-on-after-head-injury.html

Boren, S. (2016, January 10). Donald Trump: NFL "football has become soft like our country has become soft." *The Washington Post*. Retrieved from www.washingtonpost.com/news/early-lead/wp/2016/01/10/donald-trump-nfl-football-has-become-soft-like-our-country-has-become-soft/?utm_term=.936ef1d3f113

Bryant, J., Comisky, P., & Zillmann, D. (1981). The appeal of rough and tumble play in televised professional football. *Communication Quarterly, 29*, 256–262.

Chase, C. (2012, November 30). UFC's Ronda Rousey tries to "have as much sex as possible before I fight." *USA Today*. Retrieved from www.usatoday.com/story/gameon/2012/11/30/ronda-rousey-sex-before-fights/1737683/

Connell, R. W. (2000). *The men and the boys*. Berkeley, CA: University of California Press.

Convery, J. (2015, November 13). Ronda Rousey's uneasy relationship with feminism. *ABC—The Drum*. Retrieved from www.abc.net.au/news/2015-11-12/convery-ronda-rouseys-uneasy-relationship-with-feminism/6934290

Cooky, C., Messner, M. A., & Hextrum, R. H. (2013). Women play sport, but not on TV: A longitudinal study of televised news media. *Communication and Sport, 1*(3), 203–230.

Daily Mail Australia. (2017, February 12). Thought women's AFL was going to be soft? The bone-jarring moment Melbourne demon is knocked unconscious and has to be stretchered off the field. Retrieved from www.dailymail.co.uk/news/article-4214882/Meg-Downie-stretch ered-field-bump.html#ixzz4YR3eslZ4

Dawson, A. (2017, August 29). An estimated 3 million people illegally streamed Mayweather v McGregor. *Business Insider Australia*. Retrieved from www.businessinsider.com.au/ 3-million-people-watched-the-mayweather-v-mcgregor-fight-illegal-stream-box-office-ppv-records-2017–8?r=US&IR=T

Elias, N., & Dunning, E. (1986). *Quest for excitement: Sport and leisure in the civilising process.* Oxford: Basil Blackwell.

Fink, J. S. (2015). Female athletes, women's sport, and the sport media commercial complex: Have we really "come a long way, baby"? *Sport Management Review, 18*(3), 331–342.

Ford, C. (2014, September 29). Sports journalist Erin Riley trolled after commenting on AFL grand final. *Daily Life*. Retrieved from http://www.dailylife.com.au/news-and-views/dl-opinion/sports-journalist-erin-riley-trolled-after-commenting-on-afl-grand-final-20140929-3gvs0.html

Frandsen, K. (2016). Sports organizations in a new wave of mediatization. *Communication & Sport, 4*(4), 385–400.

Gunter, B. (2006). Sport, violence, and the media. In A. A. Raney & J. Bryant (Eds.), *Handbook of sport and media* (pp. 353–364). Hillsdale, NJ: Lawrence Erbaum.

Hargreaves, J. (1994). *Sporting females: Critical issues in the history and sociology of women's sports.* London: Routledge.

Horky, T., & Nieland, J-U. (Eds.). (2013). *Quality and quantity of sports reporting: An international comparative study of print media.* Hamburg: Horky Sport & Kommunikation.

Hutchins, B., & Rowe, D. (2012). *Sport beyond television: The internet, digital media and the rise of networked media sport.* New York, NY and Abingdon: Routledge.

Kurchak, S. (2016, January 12). How the Ronda Rousey backlash has changed the game for female fighters. *Vice Sports*. Retrieved from https://sports.vice.com/en_ca/article/3dgnnv/ how-the-ronda-rousey-backlash-has-changed-the-game-for-female-fighters

Lewis, J. G. (2014, October 1). Brain injury in sport is an unfolding tragedy—We're only now starting to count the cost. *The Conversation*. Retrieved from https://theconversation. com/columns/jordan-gaines-lewis-113643

Lopez-Gonzalez, H., Guerrero-Sole, F., & Haynes, R. (2014). Manufacturing conflict narratives in real Madrid versus Barcelona football matches. *International Review for the Sociology of Sport, 49*(6), 688–706.

Mael, J. (2017, February 26). MMA sends mixed messages about violence in sport. *The Boston Globe*. Retrieved from www.bostonglobe.com/ideas/2017/02/26/mixed-mar tial-arts-sends-mixed-messages-about-violence-sport/PYKySrcjKgCOMIm2axqpwK/ story.html

McKay, J., Messner, M., & Sabo, D. (Eds.). (2000). *Masculinities, gender relations, and sport.* Thousand Oaks, CA: Sage Publications.

Merced, M. J. (2016, July 11). U.F.C. sells itself for $4 billion. *The New York Times*. Retrieved from www.nytimes.com/2016/07/11/business/dealbook/ufc-sells-itself-for-4-billion.html

Morris, T. (2017, February 13). AFLW must clamp down on foul play after "Unacceptable" big hits says Tadhg Kennelly. *FOX Sports*. Retrieved from www.foxsports.com.au/afl/ aflw-must-clamp-down-on-foul-play-after-unacceptable-big-hits-says-tadhg-kennelly/ news-story/707d0e701a58e4aff7ed119ea001b2ff

Morrison, S. (2014, February 19). Media is "failing women"—Sports journalism particularly so. *Poynter*. Retrieved from www.poynter.org/news/media-failing-women-sports-journalism-particularly-so

Mwangaguhunga, R. (2011, August 23). *UFC: Human cockfighting or utterly captivating*. IFC. Retrieved from www.ifc.com/2011/08/ufc-human-cockfighting-or-utterly-captivating

Pugmire, L. (2017, September 1). As final numbers emerge, *Showtime* calls Mayweather-McGregor a "massive" pay-per-view success. *Los Angeles Times*. Retrieved from www.latimes.com/sports/boxing/la-sp-mayweather-mcgregor-ppv-20170901-story.html

Raney, A. A., & Kinnally, W. (2009). Examining perceived violence in and enjoyment of televised rivalry sports contests. *Mass Communication & Society, 12*, 311–331.

Ranker. (2017). *Athletes charged with domestic violence*. Retrieved from www.ranker.com/list/athletes-charged-with-domestic-violence/people-in-sports

Riley, E. (2016, June 25). This is what happens when you call out sexism in Australia. *The Guardian*. Retrieved from www.theguardian.com/commentisfree/2016/jun/25/this-is-what-happens-when-you-call-out-sexism-in-australia

Rowe, D. (1997). Apollo Undone: The sports scandal. In J. Lull & S. Hinerman (Eds.), *Media scandals: Morality and desire in the popular culture marketplace* (pp. 203–221). Cambridge: Polity Press and New York, NY: Columbia University Press.

Rowe, D. (2004). *Sport, culture and the media: The unruly trinity* (2nd ed.). Maidenhead and New York, NY: Open University Press, McGraw-Hill Education.

Rowe, D. (2010). Attention La Femme! Intimate relationships and male sports performance. In L. K. Fuller (Ed.), *Sexual sports rhetoric: Global and universal contexts* (pp. 69–81). New York, NY: Peter Lang.

Rowe, D. (2014). Sport, masculinisation and feminisation. In C. Carter, L. Steiner, & L. McLaughlin (Eds.), *Routledge companion to media and gender* (pp. 395–405). London: Routledge.

Ruddock, A. (2011). Cultivation analysis. In V. Nightingale (Ed.), *Handbook of media audiences* (pp. 340–359). Oxford: Wiley-Blackwell.

Ruddock, A. (2015, September 17). Ronda Rousey is ferocious in the cage, and in gender politics. *The Conversation*. Retrieved from https://theconversation.com/ronda-rousey-is-ferocious-in-the-cage-and-in-gender-politics-47648

Salter, M., & Tomsen, S. A. (2012). Violence and carceral masculinities in *Felony Fights*. *British Journal of Criminology, 52*(2), 309–323.

Samuels, J. (2014, November 28). Bat tribute to Phillip Hughes goes global. *YouTube*. Retrieved from www.youtube.com/watch?v=l8HVzPvbWbw

Sarre, R. (2015, March 27). Why boxing and cage fighting should be banned—But won't be. *The Conversation*. Retrieved from https://theconversation.com/why-boxing-and-cage-fighting-should-be-banned-but-wont-be-38901

Valenti, J. (2015, November 13). Rousey shows not every female champion needs to be a feminist icon. *The Guardian*. Retrieved from www.theguardian.com/sport/2015/nov/13/ronda-rousey-feminism-complex-imperfect-divides-womens-rights-activists-equal-pay-transgender-rights

Wanta, W. (2013). Reflections on communication and sport: On reporting and journalists. *Communication & Sport, 1*(1–2), 76–87.

Weaving, C. (2014). Cage fighting like a girl: Exploring gender constructions in the Ultimate Fighting Championship (UFC). *Journal of the Philosophy of Sport, 41*(1), 129–142.

Wenner, L. (Ed.). (1998). *MediaSport: Cultural sensibilities and sport in the media age*. New York, NY: Routledge.

Wykes, M. (2001). *News, crime and culture*. London and Sterling, VA: Pluto Press.

Young, K. (2012). *Sport, violence and society*. Abingdon, Oxon and New York, NY: Routledge.

10

IRRECONCILABLE DIFFERENCES? FRAMING DEMAND IN NEWS COVERAGE OF UK ANTI-TRAFFICKING LEGISLATION

Barbara Friedman and Anne Johnston

Introduction

News media and journalists' sources regularly invoke "modern-day slavery" to describe the brutality of human trafficking, which includes forced labor, domestic servitude, and commercial sexual exploitation. Certainly, the abuses endured by trafficked individuals—who may be regularly beaten, starved, drugged, raped and/or confined—summon to mind the viciousness of the transatlantic slave trade. "If you think slavery ended in 1865," began a Boston radio broadcast about trafficking in that US city, "think again" (Martin, 2013).

Yet, this narrative shorthand may be misleading, in part because it forces individuals into categories—*trafficked/not trafficked*—that "do not neatly fit the reality of their experiences" (Marschke & Vandergeest, 2016, p. 41; see also Brennan, 2014; Bales & Soodalter, 2010). Research on labor migration, for example, questions the assumption "that we can clearly distinguish between situations where workers are forced to accept restrictions on mobility, and situations where workers voluntarily agree to these restrictions in order to obtain employment" (Marschke & Vandergeest, 2016, p. 41).

Audiences may similarly be left confused by news coverage that equates sex trafficking with non-trafficked prostitution (Doezema, 2010; Kempadoo, 1998; Nguyen, Furman, & Ackerman, 2015). One *Irish Times* reader complained in a Letter to the Editor (November 12, 2014) "While all decent people will favour measures to protect exploited and abused women, the widely differing views being expressed on your pages on prostitution and the law certainly make it difficult for an ordinary layperson to make sense of the whole matter." In representing both as forms of sexual slavery, the news media appear to suggest that all prostitutes are "trafficked" and bereft of agency or self-direction (Abrams, 1995). Galusca (2012) attributes this treatment to the socio-political convergence of anti-prostitution feminism and anti-sex-trafficking activism, as well as twenty-first-century igno-rance of the complexities of women's migration and work. Sanghera (2012) like-wise attributes persistent myths about trafficking—for example, the belief that consent in prostitution is based on false consciousness—to "the ideological burdens of the prostitution and sex wars transmigrating into the anti-trafficking arena." Calls for "questioning, challenging, and complicating" understandings about trafficking are often "dismissed as a pro-prostitution position," a "dead-end scenario" (p. 4).

This chapter examines United Kingdom print and online news coverage of trafficking at the time of the Modern Slavery Bill, announced in 2013 by Prime Minister Theresa May and passed into law in 2015. Although the UK had laws already in place prohibiting sexual exploitation and violence, the Modern Slavery Bill endeavored to bring all legislation related to human trafficking under one Par-liamentary act. As the bill was debated in Parliament, some members wanted the legislation to also criminalize the purchase of sex. The targeting of demand for sex (i.e., as opposed to supply) was under consideration by legislative bodies through-out the UK, and foregrounded the schism between those who view all prostitu-tion as coercive, a form of sex slavery; and those who believe prostitution can be a legitimate form of labor, a facet of "sex work," whose practitioners have agency and deserve rights and protections from abuse (Farley, 2004). This study's focus is how 2013–2015 news coverage characterized prostitution as either "trafficking" or "not trafficking" in response to calls to criminalize the purchase of sex. We argue that the coverage of prostitution as it was raised during the debate over the Modern Slavery Bill framed it as a conflict between two sides over a single issue rather than two distinct issues. As a result, the coverage perpetuated "tired and unresolvable debates" (Kelly, 2003, p. 143) that pitted anti-prostitution feminists against pro-sex work advocates. This may have prevented audiences from understanding the com-plexities of the global sex trade and the impacts of anti-trafficking policy.

News coverage of the Modern Slavery Bill, we further argue, drew on a master narrative, "an overarching cultural narrative as well as a framework of knowledge and action" (Snajdr, 2013, p. 230). A master narrative becomes the "normal" view because it is standardized and repeated across discursive sites, including the news. In coverage of this debate, the master narrative represented all sex work or prostitution as trafficking and violence against women—a perspective that privileges Western views (Kempadoo, 1998) and may obscure and hinder women's autonomy, particu-larly regarding transnational migration for economic opportunities.

News media have been central to the discourse on sex trafficking (Johnston, Friedman, & Shafer, 2014; Johnston, Friedman, & Sobel, 2015; Sanford, Martinez, & Weitzer, 2016). In addition to raising awareness among the general public about the issue, journalistic accounts contribute toward a dominant discourse about traf-ficking from which interventions may emerge; that is, they are "recast back into the sphere of official government policy agendas" (Snajdr, 2013, p. 243). Thus, whether the audience, which includes policymakers, view individuals in the commercial sex industry as either victims in need of rescue or, conversely, as "active agents" seeking good working conditions (Marschke & Vandergeest, 2016, p. 45) may influence how needs are prioritized and how resources are allocated (Belanger, 2014). "News media can play a significant role in forging consensus in the policy process by how it frames its coverage of an issue" (Gulati, 2011, p. 367). If news framing of an issue such as trafficking or prostitution influences the laws that govern the issue, then scrutinizing the news coverage is important.

Background

In the UK 2013 was a banner year for anti-trafficking legislation: Theresa May, then Home Secretary, announced efforts to draft a Modern Slavery Bill to "abolish the evil in our midst" (May, 2013). May's initiative was preceded by unanimous support in the Northern Ireland Assembly for a bill to end human trafficking and related forms of exploitation[1] and followed by a similar bill in Scotland.[2] By 2015, parliaments or assemblies in each of the UK's three nations and regions had passed comprehensive anti-trafficking laws.[3]

Several amendments were proposed to the Modern Slavery Bill. For example, Labour Party MP Fiona Mactaggart proposed an official review of the links in England and Wales between prostitution, human trafficking, and sexual exploitation. In response to growing concern over the trafficking of individuals for exploitation, legislation passed in 2009 had made it illegal to purchase sex from "a prostitute subjected to force."[4] Mactaggart and her allies now sought to criminalize the purchase of sex in all circumstances. In targeting demand, they cited the 1999 Swedish law, which prohibits the purchase of sexual services and views all prostitution as a form of sexual violence. The argument undergirding the so-called Nordic model is that demand for commercial sex creates the conditions that allow for sex trafficking; criminalizing demand thus reduces the potential for sex trafficking (Ekberg, 2004; Hughes, 2000). "We should see prostitution as a problem not of badly behaved women but of men who pay to own those women's bodies," Mactaggart said in Parliamentary debate. "It is vile exploitation and a form of modern slavery that we should end."[5]

Mactaggart's views and policy objectives align with a "feminist abolitionist" position that views prostitution as an institution of male domination and a major component of sex trafficking (Levy & Jakobsson, 2013). Feminist abolitionists "recognize no distinction between "forced" and "free-choice" prostitution, and hold that in tolerating, regulating, or legalizing prostitution, states permit the repeated violation of human rights to dignity and sexual autonomy" (Anderson, 2013, p. 146). Speaking generally, this group views "all people who sell sex as victims" of a "patriarchal society that commodifies women's bodies" (Nichols, 2016, p. 63).

Still other constituencies assert that prostitution can be a consensual form of labor; this leads to the argument that policymakers and law enforcement use narratives of slavery, trafficking, and sexual violence to intrude on the rights of legal sex work and to regulate female sexuality (Adams, 2003). One way this perspective is expressed is through language choice. In contrast to "prostitution" the term "sex work" "is a political assertion that monetized sex is a kind of labor that—like other forms of labor—should be remunerated, safe, and legal. . . . It suggests an income-generating activity rather than a totalizing identity" (Wardlow, 2004, p. 1018). This perspective emerges from liberal feminism, in which women's control over their bodies is paramount, and sex work "may be a rational choice for survival or earning a living, or for sexual empowerment or autonomy" (Nichols, 2016, p. 63). Victimization is acknowledged, but attributed to "the illegality of sex work, not the sex work itself, which forces sex workers into unsafe working conditions and exposes them to further harm in arrest, fines, and jail time" (Nichols, 2016, p. 62). Intersectional and transnational feminists further locate the "problem of prostitution" in the conditions that limit individuals' choices, including the feminization of poverty, restrictive immigration policies, and the failure of development projects to prioritize gender equality (Kelly, 2003).

Leveraging contemporary concern over the issue of trafficking and historical awareness of the brutality of slavery, feminist abolitionists have been successful in forging influential coalitions with anti-abortion activists and conservative religious groups that otherwise might not support feminist causes (Doezema, 2006, p. 6). On the other hand, for Brennan, calling abuses regarding forced labor "modern-day slavery" is misleading and even sensational: although victims may be "not quite free," trafficking is not protected by a legal framework based on race, nor is anyone born into a race-based enslaved status (2014, p. 7). Regarding trafficking as "slavery," moreover, supports the media's "voyeuristic catalogue of abuse and dramatic stories of escape or rescue" (9).

These different ways of thinking about prostitution and sex trafficking—underpinned by notions of agency and victimhood—surface in news coverage of the issues. When stories lack context, audiences may find it difficult to weigh the ideologies or strategies that inform them. Thus, despite increased public awareness of human trafficking, an understanding of the distinctions between sex trafficking and prostitution, as they do or do not relate to modern-day slavery, has not necessarily followed.

News frames and their influences

As part of the news-production process, frames "enable journalists to process large amounts of information quickly and routinely [and to] package the information for efficient relay to their audiences" (Gitlin, 1980, p. 7). Frames "select some aspects of a perceived reality and make them more salient in a communicating text, in such a way as to promote a particular problem definition, causal interpretation, moral evaluation, and/or treatment recommendation for the item described" (Entman, 1993, p. 5). The selected elements "move from textual structures to mental structures" (Reese, 2010, p. 22) and become "important in influencing individuals' judgments or inference-making" (Pan & Kosicki, 1993, p. 57). Themes offer "an idea that connects different semantic elements of a story into a coherent whole . . . [and] make a frame communicable through the news media" (Pan & Kosicki, 1993, p. 59). Frames are influenced by factors internal and external to the media (Shoemaker & Reese, 2014), such as politics (Berns, 2004; Pew Research Center, 2011), regulatory requirements (Dekavalla, 2016), and owner interests (Manning, 2001), to name a few. Framing is closely associated with decisions made throughout the news gathering process, such as story selection, arrangement of information, and narrative style (Iyengar, 1991).

While journalists make decisions about what sources among many possible ones they consult and quote in a story, what those sources have to say about an issue can influence the frame (Dekavalla, 2016). Hall, Critcher, Jefferson, Clarke, and Richards (1978) argue that routinized sourcing of news stories enables powerful individuals and institutions to become the "primary definers" of issues, with journalists assuming "a crucial but secondary role in reproducing the definitions of those who have privileged access . . . to the media as 'accredited sources'" (p. 58). Similarly, Gulati (2011) has shown that "the news media mostly echo the narratives presented by major participants in the policy process and, thus, help support the dominant views" (p. 367). Thus, news frames, built by journalists and their sources, can "construct particular meanings and . . . advance specific ways of seeing issues" (Carragee & Roefs, 2004, p. 218).

Frames do not independently change audience opinion. Rather, as Gamson and Modigliano (1989) note, media discourse and public opinion operate as "parallel systems" (p. 2) that interact in the process of meaning-making. Still, the cultural "rootedness" (Reese, 2010, p. 22) of frames creates a framework for reasoning about an issue. And, when social issues are linked in media coverage through the use of familiar or master narratives, audiences may be conditioned to think about a problem and its solutions in a particular way (Berns, 2004). If sex trafficking and prostitution are repeatedly linked in news coverage, it may become difficult to know how to evaluate the problem of sex trafficking distinct from the labor needs and practices of sex workers. Indeed, audiences and policymakers may feel like the layperson writing to the *Irish Times* editor and find it "difficult . . . to make sense of the whole matter." In this analysis, we focus on how news media linked those issues as they covered the discussion and debate about human trafficking and modern-slavery legislation.

Method

We used Lexis-Nexis to collect articles as well as opinion matter from print and online UK news sources[6] between June 1, 2014, to March 31, 2015, that reported about efforts to pass anti-trafficking legislation in England and Wales, Scotland, and Ireland. Once duplicates were eliminated, 97 remaining items were analyzed for frames that linked or delinked prostitution to sex trafficking or modern-day slavery. The sample was made up of 19 "hard news" stories, 61 feature-news stories; this included coverage of events and passage and debate on bills, interviews with trafficking advocates and with sex workers, as well as side-by-side debates between these groups. The corpus also included five letters to the editor and 12 commentary/opinion pieces, including some written by advocates, by current or former sex workers, and by politicians/religious leaders.

We distinguish "hard news" as coverage that is "timely, important and consequential, such as politics, international affairs and business news" (Newman, Fletcher, Levy, & Nielsen, 2016, p. 97) and having a straightforward delivery. "Feature news" refers to stories that go beyond the basic who-what-where-when to look at an issue in-depth or to profile an individual, for example. Feature stories have less immediacy than hard news, although they may address similarly substantive topics. For the sake of clarity and efficiency, we refer to hard news stories as "news" and feature news as "features." "Commentaries" refer to opinion essays written by a staff or syndicated columnist, or contributed by a non-staff member—usually a subject matter expert—and in response to an issue currently in the news.

The analysis included examination of the sources making claims about the conditions of sex work and sex trafficking, but our interest is primarily with those whose interests are served by the frames and themes found in coverage. In addition, where we offer examples for support of our findings, we distinguish among the types of news coverage (i.e., news, features, and commentary), as some research indicates audiences assign more or less credibility to certain categories of news (Meyer, Marchionni, & Thorson, 2010).[7]

Findings

Collectively, the coverage we studied represented competing claims about what constituted trafficking and slavery. Two frames emerged, one linking prostitution to sex trafficking and slavery, and another that delinked them. As a key finding, the frames shared three dominant themes: violence, choice, and feminism.

Violence

Proponents of efforts to criminalize the purchase of commercial sex framed prostitution and trafficking as twin forms of violence inflicted on women by men; they made no distinction between forced prostitution and non-trafficked prostitution. For example, MP Fiona Mactaggart was quoted as collapsing all prostitution into "this grotesque form of exploitation" and reinforcing its link to violence. In announcing her plan to introduce several amendments to the Modern Slavery Bill, Mactaggart told a London *Times* reporter, "Prostitutes are far more likely than other women to be murdered, usually by their clients, and nearly three-quarters have experienced physical abuse" (Woolf, 2014). Another MP told a Sheffield *Star* reporter that prostitutes were "trafficked into the country to be repeatedly raped" ("MP Calls for Reform," 2014). The law-makers' narrative was that women in the commercial sex industry, whether forced or non-coerced, were endangered, necessitating laws for their protection. The origin of the threat was traffickers, certainly, but the laws must also target men's demand for sex. As a crime commissioner put it to the Newcastle *Evening Chronicle*, criminalizing demand would "ensure the protection and safety of women" who were subject, as prostitutes, to "[danger] . . . fear, and intimidation" (Thompson, 2014). This coverage brought in the voices of anti-prostitution activists, but primarily relied on governmental and other official sources.

In contrast, content that delinked prostitution with trafficking and slavery acknowledged violence as a potential sex-work hazard, a negotiated risk different from violence suffered by trafficking victims. Within this frame, violence was a result of existing policies that did not protect sex workers and something that would be made worse by anti-trafficking laws. For example, a sex worker told the *Derry Journal* that criminalizing demand would "push sex workers and their clients underground . . . [and] result in a rise of incidents of rape and other sex attacks on women." She added, "Instead of demonising us, why don't the government regulate and legalize what we do so more of us can pay our taxes and national insurance toward more important things like the NHS?" (Quinn, 2014).

Sex workers' allies, too, speculated about violence that could result from criminalizing demand. A representative of sex workers' rights organization SCOT-PEP told a Glasgow *Herald* reporter, for example, that "criminalizing those who pay for sex hampers sex workers' ability to screen clients for their own safety," because buyers would be more likely to withhold information or lie about their identity for fear of being arrested and charged (Christie, 2014). An unnamed spokesman for SCOT-PEP told a *Scottish Daily Mail* reporter: "If they think this law will reduce trafficking, they've been misinformed. The Swedish government cannot show a reduction in trafficking, but sex workers in Sweden are more vulnerable, isolated, and afraid" (Roden, 2015). Citing the arguments of a network of human rights-focused NGOs, an *Irish Times* columnist wrote that criminalizing the purchase of sex would "place sex workers at greater risk of violence and exploitation" (Meredith, 2014b).

Thus, sex workers and their allies acknowledged violence as a possibility, but as news sources they argued it would be exacerbated if prostitution was conflated with trafficking and subject to legislation that targeted demand. Their stated preference was that sex workers be allowed to participate in the legalized labor economy, part of a broader call for officials to view sex workers as individuals with agency rather than trafficked victims or sex slaves.

Choice

In coverage linking prostitution to sex trafficking, victims' experiences were used to explain trafficking. These experiences depicted victims held captive, their traffickers having imprisoned them in locked rooms and threatened them or their loved ones with harm if they tried to escape. In these scenarios, the victims were not free to leave, due to physical restraint or other means of control. Literal or figurative captivity was a motif that reappeared in coverage linking prostitution with trafficking and slavery, and it perpetuated the belief that prostitution could not be freely chosen. For example, in a *Belfast Telegraph* commentary, the director of a domestic violence center described women "trapped in prostitution," the same designation that appears in Northern Ireland's anti-trafficking bill (Campbell, 2014). A *Birmingham Mail* reporter concluded that prostitutes "live in fear of rape or other violent assaults" (Grierson, 2014). News coverage referred to captivity in explicit and implicit ways to equate the conditions of sex work and sex trafficking. Taken collectively, the coverage depicted individuals as victims unable to exit prostitution or escape traffickers on their own, and as dependent upon rescue by law enforcement and charity organizations (Cohen, 2014; Gibbons, 2014).

Yet the issue of choice also featured prominently in the frame to legitimate sex work and delink it from trafficking and slavery. Sex workers and their allies argued that individuals had the right to choose what they did with their bodies. "We have a right to profit from our sexual and emotional labour," wrote a sex worker in a jointly written *Guardian* commentary (Lee, Bindel, Corvid, & Gupta, 2015). To deny sex workers that choice, argued another, was a violation of the European social charter specifically, and of human rights generally (Kilpatrick, 2014). "The majority of sex workers like myself are independent, and 70 percent are single mothers trying to earn a living in these hard times," argued Laura Lee, who told a *Guardian* reporter she intended to use her law degree to fight anti-prostitution legislation. "No one has the right to take that option away from them" (McDonald, 2015). A Belfast sex worker told a reporter that she "cried and cried" when sex buying was criminalized there. "The city I love is taking away my means of earning. I don't want this. I have the abilities to work. Why are they taking my job away?" (Topping, 2014). Thus, the charge was that the government was wresting individuals' power to choose this particular form of labor.

Feminism

A third theme shared across news coverage involved feminism. In news coverage that framed prostitution as sex trafficking, sources made ideological connections between feminism and anti-trafficking efforts, as a way to legitimate a position and to reinforce the notion that this was about "women fighting for women." For example, "We speak on behalf of women who cannot speak for themselves" said the director of Women's Aid Federation Northern Ireland in a commentary, noting the agency's "proud feminist roots." Its position in favor of criminalizing sex buying was consistent with "all of the major international and local women's organisations," she wrote (Campbell, 2014). In a London *Guardian* commentary, writer Julie Bindel, in arguing that prostitution could never be made safe, identified with "feminists and human-rights defenders" fighting for the rights of women and girls to not be prostituted (Lee et al., 2015).

Although references to feminism came more often from abolitionist sources in the news that linked prostitution to trafficking, some sex workers used feminism to defend their choices and suggest their views put them on the right side of the issue. For example, a sex worker told a *Scottish Daily Mail* reporter: "I consider myself a feminist. Feminism is about supporting women and listening to our voices. As a female sex worker, my voice should count, too" (Roden, 2015).

But more typically within the frame that delinked prostitution and trafficking, references to feminism were a way to undermine professed enlightenment and the sincerity of the campaign to criminalize the purchase of sex. Women's groups that targeted sex buyers were discredited as "*so-called* feminist groups" (emphasis added) (Meredith, 2014a), for example. Sex workers charged feminists with restricting legal sex work by "getting into bed" with politicians (thus, the not-so-subtle suggestion that these anti-prostitution feminists were prostituting themselves). Sex workers questioned the alliance between some women's groups and evangelicals, arguing for example that it was "a smokescreen in a moral crusade to end prostitution" (Jacobs, 2014). Their allies in Parliament agreed: "We find ourselves in an interesting position, where those from a more evangelical persuasion, who possibly seek to ban prostitution for religious and moral reasons, find themselves in agreement with a more radical feminist perspective," said Anna Lo, a member of the Northern Ireland Assembly (Edwards, 2014). An *Irish Times* columnist remarked that "When radical feminists and religious fundamentalists join forces, facts tend to go out the window, often with dangerous consequences for those they seek to 'save'" (Meredith, 2014b).

The use of iconic victims to link trafficking and prostitution

The news coverage we studied shared the themes of violence, choice, and feminism. Those themes were marshaled in different ways, however, to frame arguments that either linked or delinked prostitution and trafficking. Additionally worth noting is that each of the two positions introduced unique themes in favor of their arguments. For example, the use of iconic victim narratives fulfilled a journalistic imperative to humanize stories by showing the personal impact of an issue, and strengthened the link between prostitution and trafficking. As Northern Ireland contemplated the criminalization of sex buying as a facet of anti-trafficking legislation, the harrowing experiences of one particular survivor-turned-advocate, "Anna," appeared repeatedly (Johnson, 2014a, 2014b; "Sex Trafficking Survivor," 2014; Srikantiah, 2007). A feature in the Northern Ireland edition of *The Sun* recounted "Brave Anna's" experience and included a not-so-subtle reference to the blockbuster movie franchise "Taken" and its sensationalized representation of sex trafficking: "Former model Anna was training to be a nurse in London when she was 'taken' by a Romanian gang" who beat her, locked her in a room naked, and threatened to murder her family if she tried to escape. Now that she was finally free, the journalist wrote, Anna's "one wish is for laws criminalising men who pay for sex" (Johnson, 2014a). The feature uses colorful language characteristic of *The Sun* and quotes the survivor at length. The only other source in the story is a representative of an anti-trafficking organization, who expresses support for proposed legislation in Ireland to criminalize the purchase of sex.

"Vanessa," another trafficking victim, was similarly "locked in a room and made to have sex with many men. . . . These men would demand I did what they wanted as they had paid money for me," according to a feature in the London *Times* for which she was a source (Gibbons, 2014). In the *Times* feature, the discursive arrangement of Vanessa's story obscures the trafficker and instead focuses attention on the men who "paid money for [her]" and the harm their demand inflicted, thus it serves arguments in favor of the criminalization of sex buying.

Iconic victim narratives tend to be narrowly constructed, notes Srikantiah, to emphasize the exploitation of women or girls (not men or boys) trafficked for sex (not labor), and to render the force, fraud, or coercion elements of trafficking so explicit as to be inarguable. In this way, they are especially persuasive in shaping and sustaining law enforcement priorities and regulatory policies related to trafficking (2007, p. 187). Anna's story, wrote one reporter, "has acted as a wake-up call to cops and politicians and been instrumental in dramatic law changes" (Johnson, 2014b). "Vanessa's" call for a law against the purchase of sex reproduced the end-demand platform of the charity group providing her assistance. Her plea, conveyed by the reporter, explicitly conflated sex trafficking and prostitution: "If I could say something that would stop trafficking for prostitution, it would be simple: Do not allow people to buy sex," she said. "If there was no prostitution, no woman would be trafficked for this purpose" (Gibbons, 2014).

Equivalence as a theme to delink prostitution and trafficking

In the coverage studied, sex workers and their allies delinked prostitution and trafficking by drawing parallels between sex work and other kinds of labor. For example, in a *Guardian* commentary, Margaret Corvid, a dominatrix, wrote, "We do sex work for the same reasons anyone works—to make a living" (Lee et al., 2015). In a feature for the *Irish Mirror*, a journalist referred to Josh Brandon (the only male sex worker quoted in this period of news coverage) as an "entrepreneur" that had "paved his own way to wealth." To the reporter, Brandon remarked, "It's a nine-to-five for me. It's no different from other people's work" (Kelly, 2014).

Whereas research has made clear that some individuals turn to sex work because their options are limited by factors such as poverty, addiction, or restrictive immigration policies (Nichols, 2016), equivalence with "nine-to-five" jobs was an important way for sex workers to express their agency to choose this form of labor rather than being forced into it. "Do people get involved out of desperation? We all work for money. Does that mean we are all desperate?" a sex worker rhetorically asked an *Irish Examiner* reporter. "This work suits me very, very well. It has low overheads and high profit margins. And I enjoy it really, really greatly" (Law Reform, 2014).

Discussion and conclusion

Frames can do many things, but two of the most important things they do is to define the problem and to suggest a solution or remedy to that problem (Entman, 2004). The frame that linked prostitution to trafficking defined the problem as one that victimized women and girls, enslaving them in a cycle of violence, robbing them of choice, and violating their basic human rights. Although a range of sources was represented in the news (government figures, feminist abolitionists, iconic victims, law enforcement), ultimately these individuals spoke with one voice. The narrative was cohesive and the message consistent: protect vulnerable women and girls from a life of sexual captivity and violence. And the solution to the problem of trafficking (which included prostitution) was presented and packaged in the Modern Slavery Bill.

In contrast, stories that framed sex work as a legitimate form of labor and delinked it from prostitution defined the problem in numerous ways: sex workers wanted the freedom to choose the profession that best suited them, even if the work risked violence; and they wanted the considerations, the rights, and protections afforded other workers. In comparison to those who spoke in favor of targeting demand on behalf of "vulnerable" others, many sex workers who were quoted in the news spoke in individualistic terms (i.e., "the work suits me," "It's a nine-to-five for me"). The themes within this particular frame complicated ideas about victimhood and agency in important and compelling ways. As a result, however, no single problem was defined; no single way was offered to think about this issue. Absent the clarion voice that characterized their opponents' position, the frame that delinked sex work from trafficking failed to offer a comparably neat solution.

In the news, sex trafficking and the purchase of sex became two sides of one issue, rather than two discrete issues. Although sex workers and their allies argued for these issues to be disconnected, the presence of a master narrative reinforced the "understanding" that prostitution is a form of trafficking, and trafficking involves prostitution. The strength of this link—which advantaged anti-prostitution feminists—was derived not from a universally agreed-upon definition of trafficking; indeed, the news coverage made clear there was disagreement. Rather, iconic victimization stories and other evidence marshaled in favor of the end-demand platform resonated with cultural myths that dictate gender-appropriate sexual behavior, and historical myths that exploit the belief that "all women are potential victims of sexual enslavement" (Doezema, 2010, p. 38) and invoke the UK's "unfinished" role in abolishing the slave trade (Pollitt, 2014). The connection between trafficking and prostitution may have gained additional strength in the hands of journalists who "prefer to see prostitutes as always already exploited and exploitable, always rescuable though never able to rescue themselves or others" (Galusca, 2012, p. 15).

A basic function of news is to monitor and report on activities of the halls of power. In doing so, journalism expresses its own form of power. As UK lawmakers formulated an official response to the problem of trafficking, journalists marshaled sources that helped frame for their audiences the boundaries of the debate, and, in so doing, began a process of legitimizing certain voices and marginalizing others. It can be argued the name of the legislation—the Modern Slavery Bill—presupposed that "trafficking" also constituted "slavery." Thus, in a debate that turned on the commodification of bodies for sexual labor, parties who sought to distinguish between forced prostitution and non-trafficked prostitution were already disadvantaged.

The purchase of sex was made illegal in Ireland in 2017. A similar prohibition remains under consideration by the Scottish government. The fact that it was ultimately not part of the 2015 Modern Slavery Act should not be viewed as a reversal of progress. Parliament agreed to official studies of the connection between prostitution and trafficking in England and Wales—as a result of the campaign targeting demand, prostitution has been enshrined and narratively framed within official debates about trafficking. End-demand proponents in the UK used news media to construct discursive boundaries in the debate over modern-day slavery by adopting a singular voice and consistent narrative about prostitution as trafficking. In the news, the issue of the criminalization of demand pitted the framing acumen of feminist abolitionists and trafficking survivors against sex workers and their allies, their differences seemingly irreconcilable. This left lawmakers to determine the disposition of women's laboring bodies, and left audiences to resolve for themselves the contradictions in coverage.

Notes

1 Northern Ireland Assembly, Criminal Law (Human Trafficking) (Amendment) Act 2013. Irish Statute Book. www.irishstatutebook.ie/eli/2013/act/24/enacted/en/print.
2 Scottish Parliament, Human Trafficking and Exploitation (Scotland) Act, www.legislation.gov.uk/asp/2015/12/contents.
3 The United Nations (2000) defines human trafficking as the recruitment, transportation, transfer, harboring, or receipt of persons by means of the threat or use of force or other forms of coercion, of abduction, of fraud, of deception, of the abuse of power or of a position of vulnerability or of the giving or receiving of payments or benefits to achieve the consent of a person having control over another person, for the purpose of exploitation. Exploitation shall include, at a minimum, the exploitation of the prostitution of others or other forms of sexual exploitation, forced labor or services, slavery or practices similar to slavery, servitude or the removal of organs. The UN Optional Protocol of Trafficking in Human Beings ("Palermo Protocol") classifies prostitution as an element of trafficking.
4 Although lawmakers have considered at various times the criminalization of prostitution, "the act of prostitution is not in itself illegal, but a string of laws criminalizes activities around it," such as operating a brothel or soliciting sex on the street (Casciani, 2008). The purchase of sex did become illegal in Northern Ireland in June 2015.
5 Parl. Deb., H.C. (November 4, 2014) 763. https://publications.parliament.uk/pa/cm201415/cmhansrd/cm141104/debtext/141104-0004.htm.
6 From England and Wales: *Evening Standard (London)*, *Times (London)*, *Independent (London)*, *Guardian*, *Manchester Evening News*, *Daily Telegraph (London)*, *Sun*, *Daily Record and Sunday Mail*, *Sunday Telegraph (London)*, *Northern Echo*, *Plymouth Herald*, *Yorkshire Post*, *Hull Daily Mail*, *Evening Chronicle*, *East Anglian Daily Times*, *Star (Sheffield)*, *Sheffield Telegraph*, *Daily Post (North Wales)*, *South Wales Argus*, *standard.co.uk*, *dailyrecord.co.uk*, *birminghammail. co.uk*; from Scotland: *Aberdeen Evening Express*, *Herald (Glasgow)*, *Scotsman*, *Scottish Star*, *Scottish Express*, *Scottish Daily Mail*, *National*, *Aberdeen Press and Journal*; and from Ireland and Northern Ireland: *Derry Journal*, *Irish Times*, *Irish Independent*, *Ulster Star*, *Belfast Telegraph Online*, *Belfast Telegraph*, *News Letter (Belfast)*, *Irish Daily Mirror*, *Irish Examiner*, *Metro Herald*, *Impartial Reporter*.
7 At least one study faults news organizations for failing to label different forms of content, and using inconsistent terminology when labels were used (Iannucci, 2017).

References

Abrams, K. (1995). From autonomy to agency: Feminist perspectives on self-direction. *William & Mary Law Review, 40*(3), 805–846.
Adams, N. (2003). Anti-trafficking legislation: Protection or deportation? *Feminist Review, 73*(1), 135–139. doi:10.1057/palgrave.fr.9400084

Anderson, B. (2013). *Us and them? The dangerous politics of immigration control*. New York, NY: Oxford University Press.

Bales, K., & Soodalter, R. (2010). *The slave next door: Human trafficking and slavery in America today*. Berkeley, CA: University of California Press.

Belanger, D. (2014). Labor migration among Vietnamese migrants in Asia. *Annals of the American Academy of Political and Social Science, 653*(1), 87–106.

Berns, N. S. (2004). *Framing the victim: Domestic violence, media, and social problems*. New York, NY: Routledge.

Brennan, D. (2014). *Life interrupted: Trafficking into forced labor in the United States*. Durham, NC: Duke University Press.

Campbell, A. (2014, October 20). My view: Bill is a victory for women. *Belfast Telegraph*.

Carragee, K. M., & Roefs, W. (2004). The neglect of power in recent framing research. *Journal of Communication, 54*(2), 214–233.

Casciani, D. (2008). Q&A: UK prostitution laws. *BBC News*. Retrieved from http://news.bbc.co.uk/2/hi/uk_news/7736436.stm

Christie, L. (2014, July 29). Group hits out over exclusion from talk on sex bill. *The Herald* (Glasgow).

Cohen, D. (2014, August 1). I was suicidal when I came here, says sex worker who leapt from abortion clinic window to flee trafficker. *Evening Standard* (London).

Dekavalla, M. (2016). Issue and game frames in the news: Frame-building factors in television coverage of the 2014 Scottish independence referendum. *Journalism, 19*(11), 1588–1607.

Doezema, J. (2006). Abolitionism. In M. H. Ditmore (Ed.), *Encyclopedia of prostitution and sex work* (Vol. 1 A-N, pp. 4–7). Westport, CT: Greenwood Press.

Doezema, J. (2010). *Sex slaves and discourse masters: The construction of trafficking*. London: Zed Books.

Edwards, R. D. (2014, November 17). Why I despair at new alliance of our moral zealots. *Belfast Telegraph*.

Ekberg, G. (2004). The Swedish law that prohibits the purchase of sexual services. *Violence Against Women, 10*(10), 1187–1218.

Entman, R. (1993). Framing: Toward clarification of a fractured paradigm. *Journal of Communication, 41*(4), 51–58.

Entman, R. (2004). *Projections of power: Framing news, public opinion, and US Foreign policy*. Chicago, IL: University of Chicago Press.

Farley, M. (2004). "Bad for the Body, Bad for the Heart": Prostitution harms even if legalized or decriminalized. *Violence Against Women, 10*(10), 1087–1125.

Galusca, R. (2012). Slave hunters, brothel busters, and feminist interventions: Investigative journalists as anti-sex-trafficking humanitarians. *Feminist Formations, 24*(2), 1–24. https://doi.org/10.1353/ff.2012.0018

Gamson, W. A., & Modigliani, A. (1989). Media discourse and public opinion on nuclear power: A constructionist approach. *American Journal of Sociology, 95*(1), 1–37.

Gibbons, K. (2014, October 11). Ministers urged to act against sex trafficking. *Times* (London).

Gitlin, T. (1980). *The whole world is watching*. Berkeley, CA: University of California Press.

Grierson, J. (2014, August 11). Sex workers living in fear of rape or other violent assaults. *Birmingham Mail*.

Gulati, G. J. (2011). News frames and story triggers in the media's coverage of human trafficking. *Human Rights Review, 12*(3), 363–379.

Hall, S., Critcher, C., Jefferson, T., Clarke, J., & Richards, B. (1978). *Policing the crisis: Mugging, the state, and law and order*. London: Palgrave Macmillan.

Hughes, D. (2000). Men create the demand, women are the supply. Lecture on Sexual Exploitation, Queen Sophia Center, Valencia, Spain. Retrieved from http://www.uri.edu/artsci/wms/hughes/demand.htm

Iannucci, R. (2017, August 16). News or opinion? online, it's hard to tell. *Poynter*. Retrieved from www.poynter.org/news/news-or-opinion-online-its-hard-tell

Iyengar, S. (1991). *Is anyone responsible? How television frames political issues*. Chicago, IL: University of Chicago Press.

Jacobs, R. (2014, October 22). Opinion: Ban on buying sex will put women in greater danger. *News Letter*.

Johnson, J. (2014a, October 25). I was raped for profit. *The Sun* (England).

Johnson, J. (2014b, October 11). Trafficked girl meets Robinson. *The Sun* (England).

Johnston, A., Friedman, B., & Shafer, A. (2014). Framing the problem of sex trafficking: Whose problem? What remedy? *Feminist Media Studies*, *14*(3), 419–436.

Johnston, A., Friedman, B., & Sobel, M. (2015). Framing an emerging issue: How US print and broadcast news media covered sex trafficking, 2008–2012. *Journal of Human Trafficking*, *1*(3), 235–254.

Kelly, L. (2003). The wrong debate: Reflections on why force is not the key issue with respect to trafficking in women for sexual exploitation. *Feminist Review*, *73*(1), 139–144.

Kelly, S. (2014, August 8). I'm Britain's highest paid sex worker: Gay escort claims he earns twice prime minister's salary. *Irish Daily Mirror*.

Kempadoo, K. (1998). Introduction: Globalizing sex workers' rights. In K. Kempadoo & J. Doezema (Eds.), *Global sex workers: Rights, resistance, and redefinition* (pp. 1–28). New York, NY: Routledge.

Kilpatrick, C. (2014, October 17). David Ford in bid to Scupper Bill making it illegal to pay for sex. *Belfast Telegraph* (Online).

Law Reform (2014, June 21). Law reform will make prostitution more dangerous. *Irish Examiner*.

Lee, L., Bindel, J., Corvid, M., & Gupta, R. (2015, March 24). Should it be illegal to pay for sex? *The Guardian*.

Levy, J., & Jakobsson, P. (2013). Abolitionist feminism as patriarchal control: Swedish understandings of prostitution and trafficking. *Dialectical Anthropology*, *37*, 333–340.

Manning, P. (2001). *News and news sources: A critical introduction*. London: Sage Publications.

Marschke, M., & Vandergeest, P. (2016). Slavery scandals: Unpacking labour challenges and policy responses within the off-shore fisheries sector. *Marine Policy*, *68*, 39–46.

Martin, P. (2013, January 29). Human trafficking: Modern-day slavery in America. *WGBH*. Retrieved from http://news.wgbh.org/post/human-trafficking-modern-day-slavery-america

May, T. (2013, October 14). The abhorrent evil of human trafficking taking place on London's streets. *Metro*. Retrieved from http://metro.co.uk/2013/10/14/theresa-may-the-evil- of-modern-day-slavery-taking-place-on-londons-streets-4144671

McDonald, H. (2015, March 22). Sex worker to launch legal challenge against NI prostitution ban. *The Guardian*.

Meredith, F. (2014a, December 12). Back-slapping will cost us dear. *Belfast Telegraph*.

Meredith, F. (2014b, October 29). Stormont law endangers NI sex workers. *Irish Times*.

Meyer, H. K., Marchionni, D., & Thorson, E. (2010). The journalist behind the news: Credibility of straight, collaborative, opinionated, and blogged "News." *American Behavioral Scientist*, *54*(2), 100–119.

MP calls for reform of the prostitution laws. (2014, June 16). *The Star* (Sheffield).

Newman, N., Fletcher, R., Levy, D. A. L., & Nielsen, R. K. (2016). *Reuters institute digital news report 2016*. Oxford: Reuters Institute for the Study of Journalism.

Nguyen, C., Furman, R., & Ackerman, A. R. (2015). Sex work and agency: Decriminalization of prostitution. In A. R. Ackerman & R. Furman (Eds.), *Sex crimes: Transnational problems and global perspectives* (pp. 113–125). New York, NY: Columbia University Press.

Nichols, A. J. (2016). *Sex trafficking in the United States: Theory, research, policy, and practice*. New York, NY: Columbia University Press.

Pan, Z., & Kosicki, G. M. (1993). Framing analysis: An approach to news discourse. *Political Communication, 10*(1), 55–75.

Pew Research Center/Internet and Technology. (2011). *The state of the news media, 2010*. Washington, DC: Pew Research Center. Retrieved from www.pewinternet.org/2010/03/15/state-of-the-news-media-2010/

Pollitt, M. (2014, October 16). Unfinished abolitionists: Britain returns to the frontline of the war on slavery. *New Statesman.*

Quinn, A. (2014, October 28). Derry sex worker says new law is a joke. *Derry Journal.*

Reese, S. (2010). Finding frames in a web of culture: The case of the war on terror. In P. D'Angelo & J. Kuypers (Eds.), *Doing news framing analysis: Empirical, theoretical, and normative perspectives* (pp. 17–42). New York, NY: Routledge.

Roden, A. (2015, February 6). Make buying sex on streets illegal, say Church leaders. *Scottish Daily Mail.*

Sanford, R., Martinez, D. E., & Weitzer, R. (2016). Framing human trafficking: A content analysis of recent US newspaper articles. *Journal of Human Trafficking, 2*(2), 139–155.

Sanghera, J. (2012). Unpacking the trafficking discourse. Chap. 1 in K. Kempadoo, J. Sanghera, & B. Pattanaik (Eds.), *Trafficking and prostitution reconsidered: New perspectives on migration, sex work, and human rights* (pp. 3–24). Boulder, CO: Paradigm.

Sex trafficking survivor tells why she supports DUP bill. (2014, October 19). *News Letter.*

Shoemaker, P. J., & Reese, S. D. (2014). *Mediating the message in the 21st century: A media sociology perspective*. New York, NY: Routledge.

Snajdr, E. (2013). Beneath the master narrative: Human trafficking, myths of sexual slavery, and ethnographic realities. *Dialectical Anthropology, 37*, 229–256. doi:10.1007/s10624-013-9292-3

Srikantiah, J. (2007). Perfect victims and real survivors: The iconic victim in domestic human trafficking law. *Boston University Law Review, 87*, 157–211.

Thompson, C. (2014, October 22). PCC backs plan to make sex for sale illegal. *Evening Chronicle.*

Topping, A. (2014, October 23). Northern Ireland prostitution ban divides opinion. *The Guardian.*

United Nations (2000, November 15). General Assembly Resolution 55/25, *United Nations convention against transnational organized crime*. Retrieved from https://www.unodc.org/pdf/crime/a_res_55/res5525e.pdf

Wardlow, H. (2004). Anger, economy, and female agency: Problematizing "prostitution" and "sex work" among the Huli of Papua New Guinea. *Signs, 29*(4), 1017–1040.

Woolf, M. (2014, November 2). MPs call for buying sex to be illegal. *Sunday Times* (London).

11

PATRIARCHY AND POWER IN THE SOUTH AFRICAN NEWS

Competing coverage of the murder of Anene Booysen[1]

Nicky Falkof

In the early hours of February 2, 2013, Anene Booysen left the pub where she had been drinking with friends in the working-class town of Bredasdorp, in South Africa's Western Cape province. Around 4am, a security guard patrolling a nearby building site heard a series of low screams. He called the police, who discovered the 17-year-old lying in the dirt, abandoned to an agonizing death. She had been violently raped, severely assaulted, mutilated, and disemboweled. Her intestines had been pulled out of her body and lay on the ground around her, covered in sand.

Booysen was rushed to a nearby hospital but died of her injuries soon after. Before her death she told police that one of her attackers had been a man named "Zwai." This information quickly led to the arrests of Jonathan Davids, 22, known as Zwai, and Johannes Kana, 21. Davids was eventually released because investigators could not find convincing forensic evidence linking him to the crime. Kana was convicted of rape and murder and given two consecutive life sentences. Although Booysen told police she had been assaulted by a group of men, no other arrests were made.

Booysen was young, "colored" (a contested but common South African term for mixed racial heritage), and poor. The astonishing brutality of her death, unusual even in a country with one of the highest rates of rape and sexual assault in the world (Anguita, 2012), garnered significant media and political attention. Public outrage around gender-based violence was exacerbated the following week, when model Reeva Steenkamp was murdered by her boyfriend, the athlete Oscar Pistorius.[2] A wave of collective outrage appeared in the wake of these murders, much as it did after earlier spectacular femicides like that of Afrikaans socialite Bubbles Schroeder in 1949 (Wade, 1993). But despite these moments of anger, little has changed for women—particularly poor women, queer women, and those of color—in South Africa.

This chapter is concerned with coverage that appeared in mainstream newspapers in the three months following Booysen's death. It isolates two competing discourses that characterized reporting on the murder. The first, with fewer column inches, featured activists, academics, health professionals, and NGO and civil society workers. I have called this a "feminist" discourse as the people cited here position themselves within an ideological frame related to feminism. These experts called Booysen's death a consequence of hegemonic patriarchy and a national culture that supported "toxic masculinities": "patriarchal constructions of a heteronormative masculinity that regards violence as both natural and integral" (Haider, 2016, p. 557). The second, which I have called a "political" discourse due to its proponents' involvement in formal political structures, featured politicians, union organizers, police, and other state and politically aligned actors. These experts decried the "scourge" of rape and sexual violence as an element of general South African lawlessness without associating it with masculinity or with men.

I argue that despite the presence of the first position, the supremacy of the second reveals how prevalent imaginings of rape and sexual violence in South Africa fixate on victims to the exclusion of perpetrators. In this way, dominant discourses disseminated through the media condemn gendered violence while concurrently evading critique of violent masculinities. Paradigmatic stories like Booysen's become symbolic of abstract ideas about crime and social decay, politicized to suit the agendas of various players on the public stage. Meanwhile the need to interrogate violent modes of masculinity within a highly patriarchal society is consistently deferred.

Analysis of news coverage of sexual violence in South Africa (as elsewhere) remains an important task for scholars. Although it is one of the least reported crimes, official rates of rape remain consistently high (Factsheet: South Africa's Crime Statistics, 2017). Intimate partner femicide, the killing of a woman by her romantic partner, is the leading cause of murder of women in South Africa (Mathews, Jewkes, & Abrahams, 2015).[3] At the time I was writing this chapter, South African social media were awash with the hashtag #menaretrash, a term that emerged in response to the April 2017 murder of 22-year-old Karabo Mokoena, whose charred body was found abandoned in a field outside Johannesburg. Mokoena's former boyfriend Sandile Kagiso Mantsoe was said to have confessed and was soon arrested (*Sowetan*, May 11, 2017). In May the body of Lerato Moloi, who lived openly as a lesbian in the township of Soweto, was found in a field near her home. Two men, both known to her, were arrested. Journalists speculated that Moloi was yet another victim of "corrective rape," in which rape is used as a "disciplinary mechanism for non-normative sexuality" (Morrissey, 2013, p. 74). In 2017 accusations of sexual assault were also made against a number of men who belong to organizations or groups that are known for their radical politics, such as the #FeesMustFall student movement and the far left Economic Freedom Fighters party. This tendency reveals how even within supposedly progressive spaces, violence against women is commonplace.

News media stories about acts of extreme gendered violence like those perpetrated on Booysen are important because they reveal some of the ways in which anti-rape statements can bolster the patriarchal structures that underpin a culture of masculine impunity. By repeating frightening narratives about an ever-present threat of violence, these representations can further limit women's everyday lives and behaviors. The visibility of the female victim coupled with the invisibility of the male perpetrator in South African news coverage of violence against women is part of a rhetorical structure that allows public discourse to avoid broadly discussing the social consequences of masculine violence. The ways in which Booysen's murder was represented have consequences for how South Africans think about their country's high rate of violence against women, as well as about gender more generally.

Sexual violence in the news

Various scholars have considered the ways in which sexual and gendered violence are constructed within the media. For instance, in the 1990s Lisa Cuklanz studied how rape was represented across a variety of US news and entertainment media, finding that feminist perspectives and victims' narratives began to appear more frequently in mainstream media (1996). Similarly, Shannon O'Hara analyzes the prevalence of myths about "virginal" victims and "monstrous" rapists in newspaper coverage in the US and UK (2012). More recently, Carrie Rentschler shows how young feminist activists in the US and Canada use social media to undermine and parody mainstream media's complicity in "rape culture" (2014, 2015).

Some apply an intersectional perspective to consider how class, race, and religion impact reporting about violence against women. Marian Meyers has shown how retrogressive attitudes to race influence unsympathetic coverage of violence against African American women in newspapers and on television in the US (2004). Barbara Baird analyzed Australian news coverage of three gang rape cases, showing how "a gendered project of white salvation" was discursively elaborated (2009, p. 386). Newspaper coverage of violence against Muslim women in Gulf states repeats traditional and patriarchal assumptions about the secondary status of women (Halim and Meyers, 2010). These and other scholars show that, in Europe and North America, news media reportage of crimes against women can normalize men's violence. Less has been written on representations of gendered violence in the global south.[4] An important contribution to scholarship in this area is Pumla Dineo Gqola's *Rape: A South African Nightmare* (2015), which dissects the "phenomenon" of rape in South Africa. Aside from this text, which includes a discussion of Anene Booysen, little research, to my knowledge, analyzes news coverage of rape of and violence against women in South Africa, particularly from a critical perspective.

Sources and methods

I begin my analysis by discussing news coverage of feminist commentators who regard Booysen's death as a consequence of violent hegemonic masculinity. Following Douglas Kellner's suggestions for developing critical-cultural studies,

I approach this first set of responses using an ideological textual analysis to show "how the cultural meanings encoded in a text's various "languages" convey ideological effects" (Kellner, 2011, p. 11). I thematically classify these texts into a set of interlinking ideas, given my primary interest in the shared ideological positions that underlie these texts. I then undertake a critical discourse analysis of a second set of articles; these feature rhetoric that, without considering the perpetrators of these acts, condemns the "crisis" of rape in South Africa. Hook writes that "discourse itself is both constituted by, and ensures the reproduction of, the social system, through forms of selection, exclusion and domination" (2007, p. 101). CDA is particularly useful here given its "overtly political stance" (Lazar, 2005, p. 2). CDA advances "a rich and nuanced understanding of the complex workings of power and ideology in discourse in sustaining a (hierarchically) gendered social order" (Lazar, 2005, p. 1). This approach requires close reading of selected texts.

This second, and more numerically prevalent, position contains a contradiction: while these statements echo the rights-based position that sexual violence must be ended, the disavowal of hegemonic masculinity as a component in South Africa's high rates of violence tacitly supports the conditions of sociality that fail to censure that violence. Feminist commentators talk about rape as a social problem that is explicitly related to masculinity and to men. Political commentators talk about rape without discussing the features and conditions of the perpetrators of violence; these experts thereby reproduce a social system that ignores and thus obliquely condones aggressive, hyper-masculine performances of gender even as they condemn the acts of violence that those performances can result in. In both instances my focus is less on the discourses used in the media texts themselves and more on those utilized by the various experts whose positions were repeated throughout the press coverage. Newspapers performed a mediating function, attempting to "make sense of the world for others" (Kress, 2009, p. 43) by selecting what material to publish and offering readers certain types of information or opinions.

South Africans have various ways of accessing news through the media. Broadcast media are prevalent and social media are steadily increasing in importance despite the digital divide that restricts access by income (Chiumbu & Ligaga, 2013). Nonetheless newspapers remain an influential source for information on current events (see, for example, Moyo & Moqasa, 2017). For this project I used SA Media, a comprehensive database of press clippings. My research assistant and I searched all newspapers indexed between February 3 and May 3, 2013, the three months after the murder, using the keywords "Anene" and "Booysen." Of the 368 articles this search produced, I analyzed those from the 10 news sources that carried the most coverage.[5] There was no discernible difference in how much the two discourses appeared in different newspapers. I included only articles from English-language newspapers; articles that were repeated verbatim in more than one newspaper were removed. Following these deletions, a corpus of 147 unique articles remained. All 147 were read, summarized, and classified according to which, if either, of the two discourses they contained. Notably, the vast majority of this corpus—122 articles—appeared during February 2013, in the weeks immediately following the murder. By March coverage had tailed off almost entirely despite the approach of the trial, as public interest in the case waned and the news cycle moved on.

Feminist reactions: masculinity and responsibility

Of the corpus of articles analyzed for this chapter, 46 included elements of what I refer to as "feminist" discourse. I discuss these thematically, drawing out notions that were repeated across the coverage.[6] Many of the feminist experts whom journalists used spent time debunking globally common rape myths, such as rape victims being either virginal paragons of purity or badly behaved women who were "asking for it" (O'Hara, 2012). Soon after reports of the murder began to emerge Albert Fritz, a member of the ruling African National Congress (ANC), told news sources that young people should "be more careful" to avoid this sort of violence. In response the NGO Sonke Gender Justice wrote in the *Cape Times* on February 8, 2013, "Anene knew at least one of her killers, just as most women who are victims or survivors of sexual violence do. Such comments perpetuate the false notion that victims are to be blamed." As well as pointing out the common trend of blaming women victims of sexual violence (Suarez & Gadalla, 2010), these responses make clear the gulf between beliefs about rape as the act of a violent stranger and the statistical realities of partners, friends, family members, and acquaintances as enactors of violence, discussed above with reference to intimate femicide. They show that violence is quotidian and everyday rather than exceptional and abnormal (Scheper-Hughes, 1992).

In a letter to the *Argus* on February 27, 2013, a male reader wrote,

> The recent spate of crimes against women suggests rape and murder have no class or race distinction, and abject poverty in townships or opulent wealth in plush suburbs are not distinguishing factors. We are living in a sick society and men must take responsibility.

This draws on the parallel deaths of Booysen and Reeva Steenkamp to undermine ideas about gendered violence being solely a consequence of poverty or race and to associate this problem with men in general.

Liz Cowan, an activist and counselor at the Rape Crisis Cape Town NGO, told *The Star* (February 28, 2013) that the root of the problem "lies in people's attitudes, across all cultures and classes, when they cling to outdated, harmful myths and stereotypes that perpetuate rape and violence." Among these harmful myths she listed beliefs that wives and sex workers are not rape-able; that only strangers rape; that women's clothing, behavior, and general demeanor explain rape; that men are incapable of "holding back" back once they become sexually aroused; and that most rape accusations are false. Citing Albert Fritz's comments as an example, she wrote, "All these myths blame the victim and exonerate 'normal' men in normal situations."

Sally Matthews, an academic and activist interviewed by the *Cape Times* (February 20, 2013), suggested that high rates of rape may in part be due to prevalent ideas about female passivity, delicacy, childlikeness, and unsuitability for anything but motherhood. Similarly, an 18-page supplement in the *Argus*, titled "Rape in SA: What you need to know," listed a series of myths including "women say no when they mean yes," "victims must have bruises," and "black men rape white women" (March 28, 2013). Articles like this attempted to dismantle common ideas about female culpability and male blamelessness in issues of sexual violence.

Some feminist commentators who were interviewed by journalists blamed socialization and poor parenting for South Africa's high rates of sexual violence and called for cultural change in gender relations. These claims suggested that part of the problem is that boys are raised within a hyper-masculine culture that supports violent behavior and male sexual entitlement. Rachel Jewkes, a researcher with the Medical Research Council, told the *Cape Times* that families need to change their approach so that boys learned not to think of women as possessions: "It is these ideas that underscore the idea of rape. We need to build a society where the worst thing that could happen to a family is that their son is a rapist" (February 8, 2013). Rape statistics, she told the same paper in a later interview, show that it is "terribly common" among men to have raped, meaning that "we do need to address childhood socialization" (*Cape Times*, February 11, 2013).[7]

An article titled "It starts with teaching our boys" quoted Liesl Gerntholtz, director of Women's Rights Division at Human Rights Watch, saying, "We need to think about how we educate our boys and young men, and not just in the classrooms. . . . This is not just a job for schools and universities, but for mothers and fathers, communities and the government" (*Star*, February 14, 2013). Similarly, Carol Bower, a consultant on children's rights, explained to the *Cape Times*,

> We need to raise children who do not see violent response as the first option in a disagreement. . . . We must teach our children [that] men are not intrinsically superior to women; that masculinity is about more than having multiple sexual partners . . . that women have roles other than mothering; that fathers can be nurturing and sensitive.
>
> *(February 18, 2013)*

Kelley Moult, an academic at the University of Cape Town, told the *Star*, "The real problem is that we have a particularly violent and hyper-masculine society. We teach our boys to take what they want" (February 12, 2013). Psychologist Devi Rajab told a journalist, "When I look around I see little collective shame or remorse . . . I see how we socialise our boys to be 'real' macho men" (*Star*, February 20, 2013). Chandre Gould, a researcher at the Institute for Security Studies, explained to an interviewer, "Changing the high rate of violence and rape starts with how we care for and protect children" (*Star*, February 21, 2013).

Reports like these gave space to experts who used Booysen's case to suggest that men who perpetrate violence against women were not just individually monstrous or pathological but were products of a structural system of relations that failed to instill empathy in boys as children. Families, schools, and other institutions were thus implicated in sexual violence, making it a social problem rather than a "women's problem."

Another theme that emerged within feminist responses centered on the failure of the state and the media to deal with the issue of sexual violence. Numerous experts interviewed in the press decried the fact that it took a murder as gruesome as Booysen's to compel the media to pay attention to gender-based harm when most killings of women went largely unnoticed (for example *Star*, February 11, 2013; *Star*, February 12, 2013; *New Age*, February 21, 2013). Others pointed out the lack of funding for organizations like Rape Crisis, which work on the front lines of sexual violence and are often survivors' only support (for example *Cape Times*, February 11, 2013; *Argus*, February 12, 2013; *Argus*, April 26, 2013). Synnov Skorge, director of a center that works with survivors of sexual and domestic abuse, told a *Cape Times* journalist that

> Anene's brutal rape and murder has highlighted the crisis we are in—the government has voiced its outrage but it must do so much more, starting with the actual implementation and resourcing of services and improving the justice system for survivors.
>
> *(February 12, 2013)*

Some suggested that the state, judicial system, and police force were failing in their duty of care. Survivors were not given appropriate resources and "compliance with the Domestic Violence Act [was] shockingly low" (*Cape Times*, February 28, 2013). Andisiwe Kawa, an activist and gang-rape survivor, wrote in an op-ed,

> We have a constitution that promises us the right to safety and security and justice, but in reality we don't have those. We have this nice, world-class leg-islation, but it's not implemented for the people on the ground who require it. It is useless legislation.
>
> *(Star, February 11, 2013)*

The *New Age* interviewed sociologist Shafinaaz Hassim, who explained, "That these incidents have been highlighted drags civil society out of its apolitical numb-ness and crass denialism and demands that we get involved in supporting women in every way that we can" (February 21, 2013). Journalist Christi van de Westhuizen accused the government of failing to meet its legal obligations as a member of the InterParliamentary Union (IPU). She wrote,

> Laws should be framed by the acknowledgement that violence against women is a form of gender-based discrimination. This point is of particular significance in South Africa, as some politicians persist with misattributing violence against women to generalised social challenges. Such a gender-blind

> approach makes it impossible to analyse and transform the unequal power relations that underpin this kind of violence.
>
> *(Star, March 12, 2013)*

While critiques of the state and the media did emerge within what I have classified as political discourses of gendered violence, they were generally restricted to attacks on rival parties or politicians. These feminist responses, on the other hand, took a much broader approach, showing the way in which the state *as an institution* as well as the ANC as a party were complicit in this ongoing crisis.

The final significant theme in this first mode of discourse turns on patriarchy, a "system of social structures and practices in which men dominate, oppress and exploit women" (Walby, 1989, p. 214). The term itself, unusually for mainstream media, appeared frequently in newspaper articles. For instance, the *Cape Times*, citing an activist from the South African NGO Coalition, reported that "until society did away with patriarchy the scourge of rape would continue" (February 18, 2013). According to Jewkes, "We're still dealing with a patriarchal society, where men see themselves as privileged and as doing anything they can get away with, and that includes raping" (*Star*, February 11, 2013). Elizabeth Petersen, of the South African Faith and Family Institute, asked in the *Cape Times*, "Where do we begin to address the multi-layered nature of sexual and gender-based violence? For centuries, the call to confront and dismantle oppressive systems like patriarchy has been met with silence from those who continue to benefit from it" (February 11, 2013). Citing Moult and Jewkes, the *Star* wrote that "the violent patriarchy prevalent in our society . . . most influences the likelihood of South African men becoming rapists" (February 12, 2013). The term also cropped up in letters to newspapers and even in statements made by politicians (see for example *Argus*, February 11, 2013 and February 13, 2013; *New Age*, March 8, 2013).

Other feminist commentators, without necessarily using the word itself, clearly laid blame for gendered violence squarely at the feet of male hegemony. According to Gerntholtz, "Violence against women will stop when men stop perpetrating it. We need to be clear about that. For as long as men rape, beat and kill women, the violence will not stop" (*Star*, February 14, 2013). Similarly, Matthews told the *Cape Times*,

> The men who rape and kill are not strange monsters. . . . There is no murder or rape gene which drives some to kill or rape while the rest of us look on in horror. Rather, the attitudes that help make such behaviors possible are present in many.
>
> *(February 20, 2013).*

Activist Gillian Schutte, writing in the *Star*, stated bluntly,

> In South Africa the war on women is nothing less than a national calamity as women and children have become victims of a crisis of masculinity. . . . In

Africa and other patriarchal societies, women are under siege as they fight to resist the energy of male hostility and control. . . . It is men who have declared war on women and it is women who spend an inordinate amount of their energy protecting themselves from this onslaught of male violence.

(February 26, 2013)

In sum, feminist-aligned experts quoted by the national press in the wake of Booysen's murder consistently debunked myths that blamed victims and/or assumed the naturalness of rape. They called for more appropriate socialization of children by schools and families. They pointed out the failings of the state, media, and other institutions; and they named violent masculinities and patriarchal hegemonies as causes for these crimes. Analysis of the statements of politicians and policymakers suggests, however, that, despite their consistent presence, feminists' arguments had little impact on how the state presented sexual violence.

Political reactions: denial, deferral, monstrosity

Of the articles analyzed for this chapter, 62 contain elements of what I classify as political discourse. Here, I discuss some of those texts to illustrate the way in which political responses to Booysen's murder failed to acknowledge the prevalence of the masculine perpetrator of gendered violence. Perhaps the most significant indicator is the series of statements made by former South African president Jacob Zuma, whose own attitude to women is notorious. In 2005, for example, before taking on the presidency, he was charged with the rape of a woman he had known since her childhood (he was controversially acquitted in 2006).[8] Gqola calls Zuma's behavior during the rape trial a "masculinist spectacle": a "hypervisible . . . performance of patriarchal masculinity in public spaces, where such performance hints at masculine violence or a contest between forms of manhood" (2009, p. 65).

In the wake of Booysen's murder Zuma released a statement calling for the harshest possible penalties for her attackers, saying,

> The whole nation is outraged at this extreme violation and destruction of a young human life. This act is shocking, cruel and most inhumane. It has no place in our country. We must never allow ourselves to get used to these acts of base criminality to our women and children.
>
> *(Star, February 8, 2013)*

Although Zuma demands penalties for the murderers, his phrasing implies a looking away from the realities of who undertakes these acts. The same article quotes him describing violence against women as a "scourge": this suggests a plague, a horrible inexplicable social condition. He states that "the whole nation" should be outraged about what is happening to "our" country and "our" women and children. Zuma repeats a familiar patronizing rhetoric that places women alongside children as objects of collective—for which read masculine—ownership, positioning them less as full participants in the socio-political sphere than as passive objects of its policies. He interpellates an imagined audience, and consequently an imagined community (Anderson, 2006), that is male, and that must act to protect women, who are external to the collective. Zuma never gestures to the complicity of patriarchal structures of dominance in these "acts of base criminality." Most importantly, he does not expect the reader to consider the culpability of "our" men.

Pressure on Zuma to respond to Booysen's death and to gender-based violence in general increased in the run-up to the State of the Nation address, when opposition figures and newspaper editorials repeatedly called on him to "deal with" these issues (for example *Star*, February 13, 2013; *Star*, February 14, 2013). However, Zuma's address took the same position, stating, "The brutal gang rape and murder of Anene Booysen and other women and girls in recent times has brought into sharp focus the need for unity in action to eradicate this scourge" (*Cape Times*, February 15, 2017). His calls for "unity" and "action" demand a coherent collective response to crime without acknowledging its perpetrators. The use of passive voice serves to associate only the victims with their own murders, which are classified as part of an abstract event that has no named cause or origin.

In early March 2013 Zuma launched a national campaign against rape at a school. He told the gathered schoolchildren:

> South Africa faces a problem of the ongoing abuse of women and children including violent attacks on defenceless women and girls. We have to build a more caring society in which the rights of all are respected, especially the rights of women and children. . . . No woman or child should be beaten, raped, stabbed, shot or attacked in any manner anywhere, whether by known or unknown attackers.
>
> (Cape Times, *March 1, 2013*)

Again in this statement Zuma elides women with children as people who are objects rather than subjects of the state: socially inferior, vulnerable and in need of special protections. Likewise, in stating that "we have come together to say that these horrendous attacks must stop" (*New Age*, March 1, 2013), Zuma failed to discuss who "we" are making this statement to, who might be responsible, and who needs to be stopped. This is particularly ironic given that Zuma himself, a few years earlier, would have been the object of these very protests. Perpetrators remain an abstract absence, subsumed beneath the narrative of violence as a collective social problem that "we" all need to deal with.

Responses from elsewhere within the political sphere took a similar tack. In a parliamentary debate a number of cross-party MPs called for "'concrete' action, rather than empty words, political grandstanding, or point-scoring" on what was referred to as "a war, an onslaught, barbarian, devastating and inhumane." Speakers said that "only communities acting together could start the process of decreasing crimes against women" and that "a decline in the 'moral fibre' of the nation had exacerbated violence" (*Argus*, February 27, 2013). While these calls for the state to do something were couched in dramatic language, they shied away from specifying anything about where this evil stemmed from. Vague invocations of rape as a consequence of moral decay echoed anxieties about more general social ills without acknowledging the gendered dimension of these acts. Opposition politicians used women's bodies as currency for their ongoing attacks on the ANC as the cause of South African criminality.

Along with other organizations (including the ANC), the Congress of South African Trade Unions (COSATU) organized a rally in Cape Town to protest rape and violence "against women and children." Provincial secretary Tony Ehrenreich stated, "This rally is about getting Cape Town to unite against rape and violence on women and children. This requires all of us to come together and fight this thing" (*Cape Times*, February 8, 2013). The "us" here is designed to exclude those who undertake these forms of violence, suggesting that perpetrators of rape are unusual and exceptional, in the face of evidence that suggests that an astonishingly high number of South African men admit to raping women.[9] A COSATU spokesperson compared Booysen's murder to that of Jyoti Singh, who died from her injuries after being assaulted and gang-raped on a bus in Delhi in 2012, saying,

> We must show the world that South Africans are no less angry [than Indians] at such crimes and make an equally loud statement of disgust, and protest in the streets. We need to unite as a nation to make criminals scared of society's outrage.
>
> (*Cape Times, February 8, 2013*)

Much like Zuma's statements, this suggests that violence is a national issue: it offers an opportunity for the nation to assert its moral rectitude, as India did in the wake of the Singh murder. Again, however, there is no sense here of who the suggested protests will be directed against. The perpetrators of these brutalities are called "criminals," tying them into an ongoing South African narrative about the persistence of crime. The gendered nature of this form of violence is ignored in favor of a larger framework of lawlessness and social problems.

A few weeks later COSATU organized another mass rally. This time Ehrenreich promised that the organization would support local gender advocacy groups, but added,

> We will do our best to bring an end to the abuse of women. We owe it to Anene and the many women raped on a daily basis. . . . The attack on the women and children of our nation is a threat to all of us.
>
> (*Star, February 15, 2013*)

While the policy aims being articulated are in line with calls from gender equity advocates, the discourse suggests a differentiation between the "we" of the nation and the women and children who suffer these attacks. Again, the victims of crime are highlighted while the perpetrators remain obscured. This statement contrasts "women and children" on one hand with "we" on the other. So, if this imagined we is masculine, then it excludes and makes invisible the men who are responsible for these crimes.

One statement within this second discourse does include mention of the problem of patriarchy. It appeared within an argument between the ANC's Basic Education Minister Angie Motshekga, also a high-ranking member of the ANC Women's League (ANCWL), and Helen Zille, then leader of the Democratic Alliance (DA), South Africa's official opposition. Launching an anti-rape project in schools, Motshekga told reporters,

> We will fight patriarchy by socialising our kids at home and the depiction of women [sic]. . . . To Zille we are saying we must fight patriarchy. The way we will fight patriarchy is the way we project women. . . . She is driving patriarchy. She is promoting the fact that we are nothing as women.

According to the *New Age*, Zille's spokesman, Zak Mbhele, said Motshekga's accusation connecting Zille to patriarchy was absurd, when the ANCWL had said the ANC was not ready to have a woman leader. Mbhele said the ANCWL had even supported sexist comments made by President Jacob Zuma (February 22, 2013).

In this exchange, ideas about patriarchy and gender become a means for women politicians to undermine each other rather than an explanation for violence and a possible way of moving beyond it. As well as turning Booysen's murder into a moment for political gain, these statements again ignore the protagonists of gender-based harm. Patriarchy is framed as a problem *between women*, with little reference to the violent masculinities that are forged by and that benefit from it. Perpetrators remain conveniently invisible even as politicians adopt the language of progressive feminism, mimicking the co-opting double-speak that Angela McRobbie discusses (2009) in the context of UK politics in the early 2000s.

Conclusion

Feminist discourses shaped at least some of the South African news coverage of the rape and murder of Anene Booysen. In quoting and interviewing feminist academics, NGO workers, mental health professionals and activists, journalists provided space for an acknowledgment that patriarchy and violent masculinity underpinned the epidemic of violence that South African women face; that boys need to be socialized differently; that cultural change is essential; and that state, media, and institutional failures play a part in endemic misogyny and its consequences. The second, dominant news discourse, citing politicians and people aligned with political bodies, described sexual violence in dramatic terms as a plague on society and insisted that something must be done to curb or to end it, but avoided any discussion of gender as a cause of these crimes while concurrently infantilizing women.

The second of these discourses was more numerically prevalent, taking a primary defining position in the news texts examined here. This on its own suggests its larger influence. It is clear that despite some degree of media coverage of feminist positions on the causes for and counters to sexual violence, the discourses emerging from politicians and policymakers and being disseminated by the news media, by and large, did not take these positions into account. Politicians consistently failed to acknowledge the gendered character of these types of crimes. While they were quick to speak about defending "women and children," men were largely absent from the narrative, except as an implied and central "we" to whom their statements of national responsibility were addressed. There was no sense of the very quotidian nature of violence against women and girls and the fact that the vast majority of it is relational, occurring between people already known to each other. The invis- ibility of both perpetrators and patriarchy led to a description of sexual and gender violence as an almost abstract crime, a "scourge" on the nation that emerges from unknown places and is thus impossible to counter except with empty words.

In a country where vicious killings of women are an everyday occurrence, the young men who killed Anene Booysen were not exceptional, and, other than its brutality, her death was not exceptional. Despite some coverage of feminist posi- tions that offer active ways to counter these manifestations of violence, dominant discursive responses to her murder that were reported in the South African news media failed to properly account for the relation between gender and violence, or to ask the simpler but more disturbing question of how and why it is that young South African men are capable of enacting such atrocities on the women in their communities. This failure reveals a dangerous limitation within political responses, as evinced in mainstream newspaper coverage, to the heart-breaking and ongoing crisis of violence against women and girls in South Africa.

Notes

1 The research was undertaken with the assistance of Ruth Glocer. It is part of an ongoing project on risk, anxiety, and moral panic in South Africa, funded by a Friedel Sellschop award from the University of the Witwatersrand and a Thuthuka Early Career Fellowship awarded by the National Research Foundation of South Africa.

2 The violent death of Steenkamp, who was wealthy and white, got very different press coverage. Booysen's death received a flurry of attention that soon died down. Steenkamp, on the other hand, was the subject of more media coverage during the crime year April 1, 2012 to March 31, 2013 than all other female South African murder victims combined (Brodie, 2018).

3 Matthews et al. (2015, p. 108) cite data showing that in 2013 intimate femicides comprised 30.8–45.3 percent of global female homicides, while the rate of these murders in South Africa was more than double that number.

4 Important exceptions include the chapters on China, Peru, Serbia, Rwanda, and Pakistan in Cuklanz and Moorti's edited collection *Local Violence, Global Media: Feminist Analyses of Gendered Representations* (2009).

5 Newspapers that appear in this analysis, in order of the amount of coverage they carried, are *The Star, Cape Times, Cape Argus, New Age, Citizen, Times, Daily Dispatch, City Press* and *Mail & Guardian*.

6 Notably, the majority of those interviewed by newspapers were white; this was consistent across all news outlets surveyed. Black or African feminist voices are barely heard in the coverage. This is also a valuable area for further research, as it suggests the way in which

performances of expertise in the South African media remain associated with retrogressive ideas about the authority of whiteness.

7 Jewkes and her collaborators have frequently made this argument in their peer-reviewed research (Jewkes et al., 2011; Matthews et al., 2004, 2015; Morrell et al., 2013).

8 After the trial Zuma's accuser, Fezekile Ntsukela Kuzwayo, sought political asylum in the Netherlands. She died in 2016, aged just 41. According to Ronnie Kasrils, South Africa's former Minister of Intelligence, "Her life was completely smashed in 2005 and 2006. She was abused, hounded and castigated. It broke her ... [She is a symbol] for all of us who are abused in this violent, disgusting and patriarchal way" (*Guardian*, October 10, 2016).

9 A cross-sectional study of 1686 South African men showed that 27.6 percent had raped a woman, 4.7 percent of those within the previous 12 months. Of those rapes, 75 percent were perpetrated before the rapist was 20 years old (Jewkes et al., 2011).

References

Africa Check. (2017). *Factsheet: South Africa's crime statistics for April to December 2016.* Retrieved July 27, 2017, from https://africacheck.org/factsheets/factsheet-south-africas-crime-statistics-april-december-2016/

Anderson, B. (2006). *Imagined communities: Reflections on the origin and spread of nationalism.* London: Verso.

Anguita, L. A. (2012). Tackling corrective rape in South Africa: The engagement between the LGBT CSOs and the NHRIs (CGE and SAHRC) and its role. *The International Journal of Human Rights, 16*(3), 489–516.

Baird, B. (2009). Morality and patriarchal white sovereignty. *International Feminist Journal of Politics, 11*(3), 372–391.

Brodie, N. (2018). *Suspicion and the home front: A framing analysis of the ideal victims and super predators in South African news media coverage of femicide.* Johannesburg: WISER, Wits University.

Chiumbu, S. H., & Ligaga, D. (2013). "Communities of strangerhoods?" Internet, mobile phones and the changing nature of radio cultures in South Africa. *Telematics and Informatics, 30*(3), 242–251.

Cuklanz, L. M. (1996). *Rape on trial: How the mass media construct legal reform and social change.* Philadelphia: University of Pennsylvania Press.

Cuklanz, L. M., & Sujata, M. (Eds.). (2009). *Local violence, global media: Feminist analyses of gendered representations.* New York, NY: Peter Lang.

Gqola, P. D. (2009). "The difficult task of normalising freedom": Spectacular masculinities, Ndebele's literary/cultural commentary and post-apartheid life. *English in Africa, 36*(1), 61–76.

Gqola, P. D. (2015). *Rape: A South African nightmare.* Johannesburg: MF Books.

Haider, S. (2016). The shooting in Orlando, terrorism or toxic masculinity (or both?). *Men and Masculinities, 19*(5), 555–565.

Halim, S., & Meyers, M. (2010). News coverage of violence against Muslim women: A view from the Arabian gulf. *Communication, Culture & Critique, 3*(1), 85–104.

Hook, D. (2007). *Foucault, psychology and the analytics of power.* Basingstoke: Palgrave Macmillan.

Jewkes, R., Sikweyiya, Y., Morrell, R., & Dunkle, K. (2011). Gender inequitable masculinity and sexual entitlement in rape perpetration South Africa: Findings of a cross-sectional study. *PLoS One, 6*(12), e29590.

Kellner, D. (2011). Cultural studies, multiculturalism, and media culture. In G. Dines & J. M. Humez (Eds.), *Gender, race, and class in media: A critical reader* (pp. 7–18). Thousand Oaks, CA and London: Sage Publications.

Kress, G. (2009). Linguistic processes and the mediation of "reality": The politics of newspaper language. *International Journal of the Sociology of Language, 1983*(40), 43.

Lazar, M. M. (2005). Politicising gender in discourse. In M. M. Lazar (Ed.), *Feminist critical discourse analysis: Gender, power, and ideology in discourse* (pp. 1–29). Houndmills, Basingstoke, Hampshire and New York, NY: Palgrave Macmillan.

Mathews, S., Jewkes, R., & Abrahams, N. (2015). "So now I'm the man": Intimate partner femicide and its interconnections with expressions of masculinities in South Africa. *The British Journal of Criminology, 55*(1), 107–124.

Matthews, S., Abrahams, N., Martin, L. J., Vetten, L., van der Merwe, L., & Jewke, R. (2004). *Every six hours a woman is killed by her intimate partner.* Policy Briefs. Cape Town: Medical Research Council.

McRobbie, A. (2009). *The aftermath of feminism: Gender, culture and social change.* London: Sage Publications.

Meyers, M. (2004). African American women and violence: Gender, race, and class in the news. *Critical Studies in Media Communication, 21*(2), 95–118.

Morrell, R., Jewkes, R., Lindegger, G., & Hamlall, V. (2013). Hegemonic masculinity: Reviewing the gendered analysis of men's power in South Africa. *South African Review of Sociology, 44*(1), 3–21.

Morrissey, M. E. (2013). Rape as a weapon of hate: Discursive constructions and material consequences of black lesbianism in South Africa. *Women's Studies in Communication, 36*(1), 72–91.

Moyo, L., & Moqasa, N. A. (2017). News coverage of HIV/AIDS in selected South African newspapers. *Journal of Communication, 8*(1), 28–43.

O'Hara, S. (2012). Monsters, playboys, virgins and whores: Rape myths in the news media's coverage of sexual violence. *Language and Literature, 21*(3), 247–259.

Rentschler, C. A. (2014). Rape culture and the feminist politics of social media. *Girlhood Studies, 7*(1), 65–82.

Rentschler, C. A. (2015). #Safetytipsforladies: Feminist Twitter takedowns of victim blaming. *Feminist Media Studies, 15*(2), 353–356.

Scheper-Hughes, N. (1992). *Death without weeping: The violence of everyday life in Brazil.* Thousand Oaks, CA: University of California Press.

Suarez, E., & Gadalla, T. M. (2010). Stop blaming the victim: A meta-analysis on rape myths. *Journal of Interpersonal Violence, 25*(11), 2010–2035.

Wade, M. (1993). *White on black in South Africa: A study of English-language inscriptions of skin colour.* Basingstoke: Palgrave Macmillan.

Walby, S. (1989). Theorising patriarchy. *Sociology, 23*(2), 213–234.

12

NO MORE PAGE 3? SEXUALIZATION, POLITICS, AND THE UK TABLOID PRESS

Patricia Holland

How to look at a Page 3 girl

"Hello boys. Look at your woman, now back to me. Now back to your woman, now back to me." The speaker in a *Sun* newspaper promotional video is an attractive young woman standing naked from the waist up in a bathroom. She has a towel around her waist, and her long wavy hair conceals her nipples but not her naked breasts. "Sadly, she isn't me, but that's OK, because if you keep reading Page Three every day I'll be in your hands smiling at you as if you were with me." And she catches a beach ball, thrown from who knows where, as the background magically changes to a tropical beach. Now she is wearing a bikini. "Anything is possible when you read Page Three and imagine that I'm your lady."[1]

The video, still available on YouTube, echoes the long running principle behind *The Sun* newspaper's notorious Page 3 models. The speaker is a scantily clad woman, the direct address is to a viewer, presumed to be a man. The invitation is to share sexual pleasure, even if only in fantasy. However, the video is dated June 2015, six months *after The Sun* had apparently dropped the controversial image of a flirtatious young woman with naked breasts, which had epitomized the paper since its first appearance in 1970.

On January 20, 2015 *The Sun* appeared without the notorious topless model, and let it be known that this was its new policy. "*The Sun* axes Page 3!" proclaimed the press. However, two days later, readers who opened the paper were faced by a young woman wearing nothing above the waist but a necklace and a knowing wink. "Further to reports in all other media outlets, we would like to clarify that this *is* Page 3 and this *is* a picture of Nicole, 22, from Bournemouth" read the caption (1.23.2015). But this was just *The Sun* playing a prank. Nicole was the last Page 3 to appear *completely* topless. But, just like the YouTube video, she carried a message. *The Sun* was making it clear that, although it may amend some images, it will not change its attitude. To emphasize the point, a few weeks later it announced a "cleavage week" and a "cracking cleavage competition" (3.25.2015). Topless models continue to pose on page three, with nipples disguised: covered by a scarf, a hand gesture or some other device. Meanwhile *completely* naked breasts may well appear on other pages, justified by a storyline. On June 28, 2017 *The Sun* found no fewer than four such justifications. Topless women appeared on pages 5, 11, 23, and 24, to say nothing of a suggestive image on the front page. To emphasize that the obsession with breasts had not abated, in May 2017 *The Sun* had announced the results of its "breast competition": "After 1,000 boobilicious entries . . . we're down to the last knockers. Our brilliant Bust in Britain contest drew an incredible 1,000 entries this year—and we've saved the breast for last" (5.15.2017). "Saucy" jokes, puns, and innuendo, together with an invitation to readers to participate, remain *The Sun's* currency, and a central feature of tabloid journalism.

Far from becoming more respectful of women, as the changes to Page 3 might indicate, the paper and its associated websites have become, if anything, more sexually explicit, to use Ariel Levy's (2005) terms, more "raunchy." The newspaper finds many reasons to put a skimpily dressed woman on its front page, and readers who turn the page will still meet the gaze of a near naked woman posing for their benefit. Her cleavage is usually prominent, while numerous devices are deployed to hide her nipples. The heading on May 12, 2017 jokes, "Stella's got it covered": "Supermodel Stella Maxwell dares to bare, yet still manages to protect her modesty in her latest magazine shoot." Wearing nothing but an elaborate necklace, Stella uses one hand to cover her crotch and the other, her breasts.

In recent years, the pictures on page three of *The Sun* have become less remarkable, not because they are more modest, but because their sexualized display and spectacular values can be found across the newspaper. Taking a random example: on the front page of June 21, 2017 the headline: "IT AIN'T HALF HOT BUM! Record UK heat wave fuels bare bot craze" is illustrated by a picture of "Miss Sun Bum Tori Ree" and captioned "Scores of cheeky folk are posing for more pictures with their behinds on show." And many additional pictures are spread across pages four and five, headed "SUN & MOON." In addition the paper invites readers to take part and "email us your peachy snaps." The opportunities for jokes, puns, and "nudge nudge, wink wink" double entendres are endless. *The Sun's* pages and websites continue to be dominated by what I have described elsewhere as the "Page 3 principle" (Holland, 1983, p. 99). This is a process by which the popular press, and *The Sun* in particular, have urged women not to be spoil sports, but to be active participants: to reveal all and join in the fun.

One characteristic of the early Page 3s was their direct address to their readers, inviting men to respond, and urging women to be proud of their bodies and their sexual appeal. To be a Page 3 was an expert performance, inviting a collaboration between readers and model. However, when David Dinsmore took over as editor in 2013, he ditched the speech bubble that, over the years, had given Page 3 girls a voice.[2] Although it could be argued that they were merely ventriloquizing the voice of *The Sun*, nevertheless in many ways the defiant self-assertion and jaunty presence of those early Page 3s, directly addressing women as well as men, was more of a positive presence, asserting themselves as active individuals. Eliminating the speech bubble may have been a more significant change than covering the nipples.

I have long argued that the overall tone and context of *The Sun's* presentations is more important than the image in isolation. This context has been changing. In the early days there was something almost innocent about Page 3s, reveling in their "naughtiness." They were an important part of *The Sun's* political address at a time when the women's liberation movement was campaigning for women's equality, and was also making common cause with gay rights, children's rights, trade unions, and oppositional movements. The introduction, in 1970, of a young woman posing topless on page three contributed to a deliberate redefinition of working class readers as consumers and pleasure seekers rather than as politically conscious workers and citizens. After all, "Life's more fun in your number one Sun!" (Holland, 1983, p. 85). Ironically, *The Sun* had originated as a makeover from the *Daily Herald*, a radical trade union publication (Engel, 1996, p. 250). Hence, I would argue that the issue is not nakedness in itself, but the constant reproduction and perpetuation of a hypersexualized gender difference, which has wider social and political implications.

Despite scandals and controversy, *The Sun* is still the best-selling newspaper in the UK.[3] It has long been entangled with UK politics, and, I would argue, has played a significant role in the late twentieth-century move to a political consensus strongly influenced by neoliberal attitudes. In this chapter I will focus on the ways in which the newspaper addresses its readers, both in its printed and online forms, and will consider the politics of gender in the light of a wider politics, as newer forms of feminism and postfeminism echo the Page 3 claims of empowerment and assertive sexuality.

The politics of *The Sun*

The Sun is a *cultural* phenomenon, with Page 3 at the heart of its image. Nevertheless, over its turbulent history the paper has claimed a great deal of direct influence on the political process: it was "*The Sun* wot won it," its front page asserted, after the 1992 Conservative victory (4.11.1992). Certainly its proprietor, Rupert Murdoch has long been close to the centers of power. He was, allegedly, Margaret Thatcher's favorite businessman, and, in the run up to the 1997 General Election, Labour leader Tony Blair thought it was worth flying to Australia to meet him. "The Sun Backs Blair" was the resulting headline, accompanied by a smiling picture of the politician (3.18.1997).

As well as being a powerful businessman, Murdoch is known as an interfering proprietor driven by a commitment to free market structures and the profit motive. He is vehemently opposed to public service and publicly funded organizations, especially the BBC (Evans, 1983; Chippendale & Horrie, 1999; McKnight, 2013). His political stance is reflected in *The Sun* as it addresses its working-class readers with an emphasis on consumerism and individualism. The paper was in tune with the rise of a neoliberal politics, which would have its heyday in the 1980s under

Margaret Thatcher. Throughout its pages, *The Sun*, as part of the Murdoch empire, would actively promote the values of self-interest and competition. In this respect, in asserting women's self-confidence through sexuality and pleasure seeking, Page 3 was able to ventriloquize the "voice of *The Sun*" as effectively as the news stories or features. There is a clear link between the invocation of self-interest and sexual pleasure epitomized by Page 3, and the politics of the paper.

The Sun makes its abhorrence of left-wing politics clear, with attacks on the Labour Party as "a dreary and embittered band." "Here's how Page 3 will look under Kinnock, fat chance of fun!" It headlined a picture of a fat woman in a bathing costume on election day 1992, while on the front page it placed Labour leader Neil Kinnock's head in a light bulb, headlined "If Kinnock wins today will the last person to leave Britain please turn out the lights" (4.9.1992). Following its brief support for Labour in the Blair years, the paper returned to its traditional allegiances in the 2010s. The June 2017 election was greeted with "Cor-Bin" (6.8.2017). This time the Labour leader, Jeremy Corbyn, was placed in a dustbin, even though the rest of the press had taken note of the surge in Labour support, which destroyed the Conservative Government's majority. *The Sun's* explicit aim, to transform working class consciousness, has long involved an open attack on working-class solidarities and trade unions in particular. No other newspaper has inspired such hatred amongst many who might be expected to be its natural supporters, giving rise to campaigns that have run for decades.

Thirty years after the Wapping dispute of 1986–1987, the campaign to boycott *The Sun* and to keep a memory of the events alive, is still active. In 1986, Murdoch sacked most of the unionized workforce and moved *The Sun* and *News of the World*, together with *The Times* and the *Sunday Times* away from their traditional base in Fleet Street to a secretly prepared base in Wapping, East London. The skilled printers and compositors were no longer needed and were replaced overnight by a workforce trained in new technologies. More than 5000 employees were sacked, including cleaners and canteen workers as well as printers. The move provoked a year-long picket and protest outside the Wapping works by print workers, trade unionists, and many journalists. It was later revealed that Murdoch had received advice from his lawyers that the cheapest way to dispose of a workforce with out-dated skills, would be to provoke a strike.[4] Page 3 girl Samantha Fox demonstrated her support of Murdoch's move by riding through the picket lines waving from the top of an armored car. "Sexy soldier, Sam Fox, inspects her loyal troops in the War of Wapping" was *The Sun's* front-page headline (2.4.1986). It "was one of the defining moments of the 1980s" wrote journalist Peter Martin (Martin, 1997). In later interviews, Samantha Fox identified herself as a working class East End girl who aimed to speak for people from her own background.[5] The Wapping dispute campaign continues, with a traveling exhibition and a lively website including an archive of relevant films, books, and photographs.[6]

The Sun's reporting of the disaster at the Hillsborough Football Stadium in Sheffield on April 15, 1989, likewise meant that many who might be expected to be natural *Sun* readers were outraged by the way the tragedy was reported in its pages. Ninety-six people were killed in a crush amongst Liverpool fans during the FA Cup semi-final between Liverpool and Nottingham Forest. Despite *The Sun's* reliance on many pages of football to attract its readers, Kelvin McKenzie, editor at the time, had taken up with enthusiasm the familiar narrative of unruly football supporters, which had been circulated by a police force anxious to deny responsibility. Under the headline "The Truth" the paper alleged that the crush was caused by drunken fans who had even urinated on the dead and injured. From that point on, *The Sun* faced a boycott in Liverpool. A major campaign was launched to win justice for those killed or maimed and to establish the facts (Scraton, 2009).[7] It took two major reports, two coroner's inquests, and more than two and a half decades of campaigning by relatives and supporters before it was finally confirmed, in 2016, that the police had, in fact, opened the gates to the already crowded enclosure, even though the area was penned in by wire fencing.[8] The police had then falsified their reports so that it appeared that the fans were to blame.

Now under editor Dominic Mohan, *The Sun* apologized for its reporting and its smearing of the Liverpool fans in an article headed "Hillsborough the real truth" (4.6.2016).[9] However, the anger has not abated. The campaign "Total Eclipse of the S★n," makes common cause with the Wapping campaign to urge a boycott of the paper.[10] In February 2017 Liverpool Football Club banned *Sun* reporters from Liverpool matches, and the campaign has been lobbying the other Liverpool based football club, Everton, to do the same.[11] On April 1, 2017 the *Spectator* reported that the campaign "has already pressured many cab drivers to refuse passengers carrying *The Sun*, and is forcing supermarkets as well as small newsagents to stop stocking it." *The Sun* responded in a conciliatory tone "A new generation of journalists on the paper congratulate the families on the hard fought victory they have achieved through the inquest."[12]

Parallel to these class-based campaigns, feminist campaigns against *The Sun* have been equally vocal. The role of Page 3 has not gone unchallenged.

No more Page 3?

Feminist opposition to Page 3 has a long history. In 1986 and again in 1988 Labour MP Clare Short put a Private Member's Bill to parliament, the Indecent Displays (Newspapers) Bill. This would make it an offense "to publish in newspapers pictures of naked or partially naked women in sexually provocative poses." Although it won a great deal of support in the House of Commons, Short was an opposition MP, and for procedural reasons the Bill was never put forward (Short, 1991).

Clare Short later explained that she had specified pictures in newspapers, with Page 3 in mind, because *The Sun* and other tabloids that had followed its lead, were part of mainstream media. Unlike "top shelf" publications, the tabloids were widely circulated and easily available to all, including children. In response to cries of "censorship" she distanced herself from the moral purity campaign run by Mary Whitehouse, and from the too-broad provisions of the controversial Obscene Publications Act (1959/1964). Short wrote, "We must always remember we are acting in the name of freedom and human dignity, and we must not support any proposal that would endanger precious freedoms in the name of our dignity" (Short, 1991, p. 25).

Her move was greeted with derision by *The Sun*. Although it approached its readers with an appeal to pleasure and fun, the newspaper attacked those whose views it did not share with unbridled virulence and mockery. It responded to Clare Short's Bill with headlines like "Fat, jealous Clare brands Page 3 porn." It superimposed her face on a topless model and invited male MPs who had voted against the Bill to pose on page three "with their favourite lovely." Four of them did (Short, 1991, p. 6). At the same time Clare Short received more than 5000 letters, the vast majority of them from women who supported her. Many of them described their feelings as victims of rape, including one whose rapist constantly repeated, "You ought to be on Page 3." Many began "I am not a feminist, but . . ." (pp. 5–6). Later a selection of the letters was published, together with Short's account of her campaign (Short, 1991). Many years later, when she left politics, she told a journalist that she was still opposed to Page 3. In response, "busloads of Page 3 girls parked outside my house all day in the hope of setting up embarrassing photos. . . . And there were mock-up pictures of me as a very fat Page 3 girl" (*Independent* 10.22.2004).

As time went on, an increasing number of feminist campaigns drew attention to the objectification of women, both on page three and throughout *The Sun* and other tabloids. The organization "Object," founded in 2003, working together with the long-standing "Fawcett Society" (named after the nineteenth-century suffragist Millicent Fawcett), managed to achieve a tightening of the law around lap dancing clubs.[13] Other campaigns included "End Violence Against Women," "Eaves Housing for Women," and "Turn your back on Page 3," which invited supporters to "Paint a t-shirt or any other item of clothing with the slogan written on the back! Feel free to get creative!"[14] And, in 2010 the demand for legislation once more reached parliament. MP Lynne Featherstone proposed a limit on children's ability to purchase newspapers containing topless women, while Labour's Harriet Harman argued for legislation to ban Page 3 and similar images. *The Sun* responded that the Featherstone was a "battleaxe" while Harman was a "harridan" and a "feminist fanatic" (Leveson, 2012, Vol 2, Ch 6, Section 8).

When actor and writer Lucy-Anne Holmes launched her innovative "No More Page 3" campaign in 2012, she made the most of available online opportunities.[15] At first she worked alone, "using all the free tools the internet provides,"[16] creating a website, social media sites, and an online petition. Later she gathered an active team around her. "Together we weathered the responses of 'you're frigid/ugly/jealous' or 'you're only doing this because you've got shit tits' and being wished dead," she wrote. "We just kept going with humour and kindness. We never really bashed *The Sun*, we kept going with warmth."

The petition began:

> A light hearted petition to the Editor of *The Sun*
> We are asking David Dinsmore to drop the bare boobs from *The Sun* newspaper.
> We are asking very nicely.
> Please, David.
> No More Page 3[17]

Tactics included initiating debates, selling t-shirts, organizing demonstrations, and creating a YouTube video called *The Experiment*. For this, the team cut out all the pictures of men and women in *The Sun* over a period of six months in 2014. The video shows them pasting them up in two sections on a wall, to compare how they were presented. "How many sports women?" asked a caption. "None." "What are the women doing? Posing." It concludes, "The two sides are utterly different. Men look like real life, the women look manufactured." And the video went viral.[18] They "got really cross with that," Holmes later told the *Huffington Post*.[19]

"No More Page 3" built up active regional groups and won support from MPs, trade unions, and other organizations campaigning around women's issues, including "Rape Crisis" and "Women's Aid." A letter to the editor was signed by 154 MPs, together with elected mayors and local councilors. Holmes also published a list of MPs "who haven't signed (yet)" on her website. And she interviewed men, picking out likely *Sun* readers, and asking if they would stop buying the paper if Page 3 were eliminated. None said they would, because they mainly bought it for sports.[20]

By 2014 Holmes increasingly felt the paper "hit back" against the campaign.

"We were getting bigger and louder, and we were quite relentless," she told the *Huffington Post*. "But it wasn't just us, there's a wider movement that wants to discuss issues of inequality. . . . When society is trying to evolve, *The Sun* can't pretend it's a modern paper with that 1970s clanger going on there." *The Sun's* proprietor Rupert Murdoch was bombarded online by supporters of the campaign in a "Tweet Murdoch Day." He responded, tweeting, "Page 3 so last century! You maybe right, don't know but considering."[21]

When Page 3 was finally modified on New Year's Day, 2015, Brendan O'Neill argued in the right-wing *Daily Telegraph* that this "'outdated institution' had only hung on because of 'feminist do-gooders,' and because of the 'elevation of Page 3 from a naughty page in a national newspaper into a boxing-ring of values that pitched the political class against a paper that perceives of itself as plucky, unapologetic, a tribune of the people."[22]

When the *Huffington Post UK* contacted *The Sun* for a comment about "No More Page 3," a spokesperson said:

> *The Sun* will always be written for its readers rather than the middle-class twitterati that don't actually buy the paper. *The Sun's* readers support our campaigns on domestic abuse, breast cancer and the armed forces that have made a real, appreciable difference, raising money, awareness and support for causes that really matter.[23]

Lucy-Ann Homes was convinced that the paper's management had wanted to change, but did not want her campaign to get the credit. But, as we have seen the change, when it came, made very little difference.

Murdoch and Leveson

The pressure from feminists regarding Page 3 had come at a difficult time for Rupert Murdoch. As proprietor of *News of the World*, *The Times*, and *Sunday Times*, as well as *The Sun*, and with a major share in Sky television, he was effectively the biggest media proprietor in the UK. In 2011 he was planning to expand his empire, and had put in a bid to buy the 61 percent of Sky he did not already own. The plan drew strong opposition because of the enormous media power this would give to a single proprietor. Nevertheless, the signs were that the Conservative government would allow the deal to go ahead, when a scandal broke. An investigation by the *Guardian* newspaper revealed that *The Sun's* sister paper, the *News of the World*, had been illegally hacking into the phones of celebrities and others in the news. In particular the mobile phone of a missing schoolgirl, Milly Dowler, who was later found murdered, had been interfered with. (Davies, 2014). The police launched an investigation into the accusations of phone hacking, and a public inquiry led by Lord Justice Brian Leveson, was set up to investigate the "Culture, Practices and Ethics of the British Press." Murdoch himself was called in front of a House of Commons select committee and declared himself deeply humbled.[24]

This was an opportunity for campaigners against Page 3 and the other "Page 3 tabloids," which published similar and often more extreme images of women. In a submission to the Inquiry on behalf of "Object," its CEO Anna Van Heeswijk, argued that there was "no marked difference between the content which exists in . . . classified pornographic materials and the contents within some of these mainstream Page 3 tabloids" (Leveson, 8.10). She added "Some Page 3 tabloids apply a demeaning and sexualising lens beyond those who choose to appear in their pages with breasts exposed: even the most accomplished and professional women are reduced to the sum of their body parts" (Leveson, 8.15).

Leveson's report, published in 2012, was unequivocal about the ethics of the press. Leveson agreed that "the Page 3 tabloid press often failed to show consistent respect for the dignity and equality of women generally, and that there was a tendency to sexualise and demean women" (8.18). But the findings which confirmed illegal conduct, including phone hacking, by the *News of the World*, and possibly other papers, were even more damning. The parallel police investigations led to the arrest of more than 50 journalists, most of them from the Murdoch owned *Sun* and *News of the World*.[25] Five *News of the World* journalists were convicted of illegal behavior.

Following the report, Murdoch put his bid to buy Sky television on hold, closed the *News of the World*, and set about re-organizing his companies, splitting his newspapers from his film and television interests. In addition, he launched *The Sun on Sunday* to fill the gap left by the *News of the World*. *The Sun* itself had had a narrow escape, and Murdoch was anxious to protect it from the ongoing scandals. It is possible to speculate that covering up Page 3 girls' nipples in 2015, was part of a move to greater respectability.

Feminisms and the sexualization of culture

Page 3 has been modified since 2015. However, not only has the tone of the newspaper not changed, but the Page 3 culture is even more pervasive. "Feminism," argued Suzanne Moore in *The Guardian*, "is no longer about power and the reality of women's lives. . . . A movement that once imagined new ways to live, has become a self-improvement course, with empowerment as a personal goal." Feminism has become "polite, unthreatening and marketable." She concludes "It is not enough to have more women in power if they are not challenging the system." (2.18.2017). In this cultural climate, "the Page 3 principle" has become mainstream, together with forms of feminism that reflect the changing political environment.

Feminist scholars, in particular Angela McRobbie and Rosalind Gill, have observed the ways in which new forms of feminism have developed in parallel with political change, moving towards an embrace of individualism and consumer choice. Writing at the time of Tony Blair's New Labour government (1997–2010) Angela McRobbie described what she saw as a new "sexual contract" offered to young women through women's magazines, advertisements, and other media (McRobbie, 2000). In tune with the "third way" politics of New Labour, the new feminisms of the twenty-first century no longer criticized capitalism, but focused on culture and lifestyle issues. In addition, the contract required "an abandonment of a critique of patriarchy" (McRobbie, 2009, p. 57). Third way politics, McRobbie argued, claimed that because "the political issues associated with feminism are now understood to be widely recognised and responded to," it was assumed that feminism was no longer needed. Instead, many young women had become part of what she described as a "post-feminist masquerade." This requires that they "should become actively engaged in the production of self," paying attention to appearance and self-monitoring. This fits well with the Page 3 assertion of pleasure and empowerment. Page 3 was postfeminist before its time. However, McRobbie noted that this situation also "permits the subtle renewal of gender injustices, while vengeful patriarchal norms are also re-instated" (2009, p. 55).

Nearly a decade later, we live in a highly sexualized media environment (Gill, 2016). This is reflected on television, in advertisements, magazines, and online, as well as in the popular press, where *The Sun* continues to make a significant contribution. Naked bodies are frequently on show. Sexual encounters—both hetero- and homo-sexual—are often represented in films and television programs. And the media feed each other. *The Sun* gives a great deal of space to programs like *Love Island* and *Big Brother*. On July 26, 2017, under the headline "SEX, SEX, SEX," it devoted its front page and a double page spread to "romps too raunchy to screen" on the Channel Four reality-cum-game-show *Love Island*. Then on September 21 it profiled the BBC serial *Doctor Foster*, with a front page and a double page spread given over to "Hate sex," featuring female commentators arguing the pros and cons of sex with "someone you hate." Of course, this too was an occasion for explicit pictures and a great deal of nudity.

Today's hyper-sexualization is documented in detail by Natasha Walter in her account of glamor modeling, the sex industry, and pornography through the eyes of young women who participate in these industries (Walter, 2010/2015). For many of the women she speaks to, overt sexuality is seen as a form of empowerment. "Women can say . . . I'm doing this for myself. It's something to be proud of" one young woman tells her (p. 28). She describes a "wider change in culture, in which images and attitudes of soft porn come flooding in at young women from every side of the media" (p. 26), and notes that "the rise of a culture in which it is taken for granted that women will be valued primarily for their attractiveness, has become inescapable for many young women" (p. 63). As I have argued, the tabloid press, and *The Sun* in particular, has played an important role in bringing about these changes. And I would point to the persistence of the Page 3 principle. Especially when they apparently spoke for themselves, Page 3s were anticipating the postfeminist move, described by Rosalind Gill as a change from sex object to desiring sexual subject (Gill, 2003). Having kept a close eye on the development of feminism within this changing climate, Gill has emphasized the contradictory position of women in this context, together with the "entanglement of feminist and anti-feminist ideas" (Gill & Scharf, 2011, p. 4).

Postfeminism

The concept of postfeminism, implying that feminism is no longer relevant, was noted by Susan Faludi as long ago as the late 1980s, when she documented a "backlash" against feminism and women's rights, accompanied by a re-assertion of masculine language (Faludi, 1991). But by 2010 "postfeminism" had lost its hyphen: Rosalind Gill points to the different ways in which the term is used. It does not necessarily suggest that feminism is over, but, by analogy with "postmodernism," it can imply a new type of feminism, partly growing out of, and partly rejecting the old (Gill, 2003). In a later article she discusses how the language and practice of feminism has been re-appropriated for this new context. In this "postfeminist" mood new forms of feminism, influenced by an individualistic, pleasure-seeking femininity, co-exist with a renewed misogyny (Gill, 2016, p. 612).

For Gill, postfeminism is "a distinctive, contradictory but patterned *sensibility* intimately connected to neoliberalism." She argues that

> a multiplicity of different feminisms [are] circulating in mainstream media culture, many of them in tension with each other. This distinctive, depoliticised sensibility characterises increasing numbers of films, television shows, advertisements and other media products, and is made up of a number of interrelated themes: the notion that femininity is a bodily property; the shift from objectification to subjectification; an emphasis upon self surveillance, monitoring and self-discipline; a focus on individualism, choice and empowerment; the dominance of a 'makeover' paradigm; and a resurgence of ideas about natural sexual difference.
>
> *(2007a, p. 3)*

Page 3 fits well into this description. In addition *The Sun* specializes in "irony and knowingness," described by Gill as "a way of establishing a safe distance between oneself and particular sentiments or beliefs, at a time when being passionate about anything or appearing to care too much seems to be 'uncool'" (2007a, p. 20). In postfeminist media culture, as in *The Sun*, irony has become a way of "having it both ways," of expressing sexist, homophobic or otherwise unpalatable sentiments in an ironized form, while claiming this was not actually "meant." Gill concludes, "It is precisely the knowingness of the 'transgression,' alongside the deliberate artic-ulation of feminist and anti-feminist ideas that signifies a postfeminist sensibility" (2007a, p. 7).

In many ways Page 3 prefigured postfeminism. It was partly a reaction against second wave feminism, and partly a transformation of it, with its appeal to women's sexualized self-assertion and confidence. And, as I have shown, it is "intimately con-nected to neoliberalism" with its stress on "freedom," individualism, and "choice." Within today's sexualized society we can see a widespread embrace of the Page 3 principle.

Newspapers: narrative, community, and context

To understand the continuing role and current political purchase of Page 3 and the Page 3 principle it is important to consider its position within the context of the daily news publication, both in its paper form and online, and the ways in which it addresses its readers. Like all newspapers that have survived into the twenty-first century, *The Sun*, with its red banner logo, its big block headlines, striking photo-graphs and scantily dressed pin-ups, has overflowed beyond the printed pages. For several years a great deal of *The Sun*'s online content, including Page 3, was only available to subscribers. But in October 2015 News UK's chief executive, Rebekah Brooks, announced that the paywall would be dropped. "Get 'em out for the . . . readers" headlined the online technology newsletter *The Register*. [26]

One of *The Sun*'s earliest slogans was "Life's more fun with your number one *Sun*." That intimate tone (it's *your Sun*) continues to be sustained throughout the paper and its various online formats, seeking to create a community of readers and *Sun*-lovers. Together with its puns, rhymes and "saucy" jokes, the emphasis on fun still marks the "voice of *The Sun*": the commentary that leads the reader through the pages. Expressed through the headlines and picture captions, with emphasis and heightened emotion, it is designed to provoke a reaction, whether laughter or out-rage. And *The Sun* is a *visual* paper. In the print version the front page remains all important, aiming to catch the eye on supermarket shelves where the paper com-petes with the other tabloids, including *The Star*, prominently labeled as "cheaper than *The Sun*." Led by the voice of *The Sun*, readers find their way through a pre-dictable structure, which develops a range of familiar narratives. The Page 3 prin-ciple dominates the pages, until the sports pages take over with their celebration of masculine bodies in motion. Favored back page pictures include mid-game action shots and the open-mouthed shout of triumph or anger.

Following *The Sun* online is a different experience, in which readers are invited to be more proactive. Although the online content overlaps with and has many similarities to the paper version, the carefully planned *structure* is different, and its content more personalized. Instead of following a predictable structure, from headlines through to sport, online readers are invited to create their own individual pathways. A visit to www.thesun.co.uk will call up the Home Page and the day's main story, usually illustrated by pictures or videos. From here on it is up to the reader. Headings offer football; sport (including more football—clearly the most interesting sport for *Sun* readers); TV and Showbiz; Fabulous; News; Money; Motors; and Travel. Each of these is subdivided yet again, and every page includes links and teasers, both in the margin and below the main text, offering more stories, more pictures and videos, with advertisements and sponsored content stirred into the mix.

Teasers in the margin of every page remind readers what else is on offer, and the Page 3 principle can be followed under many headings. But online, unlike the Page 3 girl's "double address" in the paper version (Holland, 1983, p. 88), there is a clearer distinction between material addressed to men (under "Sport" and "Motors"), and that to women ("Fabulous"). The Page 3 principle operates differently in the two cases. For example, on October 1, 2017, "Football" takes us, after many pictures of (male) players and reports of matches, to scantily clad "Girlfriends," an item on "The sexiest sports reporter" (a woman, previously a model), and a reminder of "6 UK dating sites you could try." Whereas under "Fabulous," we find stories addressed specifically to and about women. Almost all these presentations are obsessed by body image. They reflect the Page 3 principle as they prioritize appearance and sexuality, while featuring women of various shapes and ages. The first feature shows a fat model posing, and is headed "I learned to love my body." Below comes "Body revolution: Five women bare all and reveal how they learned to love their imperfections." The five naked women, who are posing together, each covering her crotch and nipples with her hands, are middle aged and older. "Even though I'll be 90 in a couple of years, I still shop at Fat Face and Dorothy Perkins—the same stores as my daughter Emma, 52, and granddaughter Susi, 20," says Annelisa Count.

Meanwhile, the Page 3 archive offers the familiar pictures of models, once more with covered or pixielated nipples, and, no doubt making a point, a campaigner wearing a "No More Page 3" t-shirt. It is clear that the Page 3 principle is thriving. Far from being abandoned following feminist campaigns, the principle has adjusted in various ways to the complex mood of the 20teens. However contentiously, it has in some ways been incorporated into feminism itself.

Final note: CoppaFeel and free the nipple

I will close with two campaigns that take up the Page 3 principle, and transform it with irony and humor. The breast cancer awareness campaign, CoppaFeel! was launched by Kristin Hallenga, in 2009, when she was diagnosed with breast cancer at the age of 23. She and her twin sister Maren contacted celebrities and media outlets to create a high-profile campaign, which included the use of giant inflatable "boob" costumes for "flash dances" and public stunts. In 2014 Kristin Hallenga began to work as a columnist for *The Sun*, writing about her experiences with cancer, and promoting a "Check 'Em Tuesday," campaign which features Page 3 models encouraging readers to check their breasts for signs of cancer every Tuesday. When the campaign was criticized by "No More Page 3," CoppaFeel! argued that an awareness of the early signs of the disease should be publicized as widely as possible.[27]

In contrast to the specific focus of CoppaFeel!, a recent campaign which began in the USA claims to be "a premiere voice for gender equality, utilizing all forms of modern media to raise awareness and effect change on various social issues and injustices," including "the areas of the inequality of men and women that are still being experienced in the world today." This is Free the Nipple, which, far from claiming that "you too can be a Page 3 girl," "seeks the equality, empowerment, and freedom of all human beings." Women and men campaigners take to the streets naked to the waist. "If men can show their nipples, why can't we?"[28]

However, as Angela McRobbie (2000) points out, addressing the manifestation without addressing the underlying politics does not remove basic "gender injustices." Nevertheless, humor and ironic reflection are valuable replacements for anger and confrontation, a lesson which, arguably, postfeminism has taken on board.

Notes

1 www.youtube.com/watch?v=Tm0X-yzOdos2 June 11, 2015. Accessed September 15, 2017.
2 www.theguardian.com/media/shortcuts/2013/jun/26/suns-page-3-models-get-dressed
3 www.pressgazette.co.uk/print-abc-metro-overtakes-sun-in-uk-weekday-distribution-but-murdoch-title-still-britains-best-selling-paper
4 www.wapping-dispute.org.uk/
5 www.youtube.com/watch?v=-BFJbn5sWDc
6 www.wapping-dispute.org.uk/
7 www.liverpoolfc.com/hillsborough/contact
8 https://en.wikipedia.org/wiki/Hillsborough_disaster
9 www.thesun.co.uk/archives/news/915727/hillsborough-the-real-truth/
10 www.facebook.com/groups/1576357575995356/?ref=group_header
11 www.huffingtonpost.co.uk/entry/the-sun-liverpool-fc-ban_uk_589ed2a5e4b03df370d6aeb8
12 www.guardian.com/football/2017/feb10/liverpool-ban-the-sun-newspaper-over-hillsborough-coverage
13 www.theguardian.com/world/2012/apr/15/anna-van-heeswijk-page-three-tabloid
14 https://turnyourbackonpage3.wordpress.com/2011/07/
15 https://nomorepage3.wordpress.com/faqs/
16 www.theguardian.com/commentisfree/2017/mar/08/feminist-battle-women-activists-campaigns
17 www.change.org/p/david-dinsmore-take-the-bare-boobs-out-of-the-sun-nomorepage3
18 www.youtube.com/watch?v=lNlKjUfmaUA
19 www.huffingtonpost.co.uk/2015/03/08/lucy-ann-holmes-no-more-page-3-the-sun_n_6826762.html
20 https://nomorepage3.wordpress.com/men-on-page-three/

21 http://metro.co.uk/2013/02/11/rupert-murdoch-hints-page-threes-days-are-num
    bered-3401985/
22 www.telegraph.co.uk/women/womens-politics/11357671/The-campaign-against-
    Page-3-kept-it-going-a-decade-longer.html
23 www.huffingtonpost.co.uk/2015/03/08/lucy-ann-holmes-no-more-page-3-the-
    sun_n_6826762.html
24 www.youtube.com/watch?v=YzRXLwEp9z0
25 www.pressgazette.co.uk/in-depth-the-63-uk-journalists-arrested-andor-charged-fol
    lowing-the-news-of-the-world-hacking-scandal/
26 www.theregister.co.uk/2015/10/30/the_sun_drops_paywall/
27 https://en.wikipedia.org/wiki/CoppaFeel!#cite_note-Daily_Mail.2C_One_hundred_
    jiggling_breasts.3F_Must_be_the_CoppaFeel_flashmob.21-5
28 http://freethenipple.com/ Thanks to Abigail Grant for alerting me to this campaign.

Bibliography

Chippindale, P., & Horrie, C. (1999/2005). *Stick it up your punter*. London: Pocket Books.

Davies, N. (2014). *Hack attack: How the truth caught up with Ruert Murdoch*. London: Chatto and Windus.

Engel, M. (1996). *Tickle the public: One hundred years of the popular press*. London: Victor Gollancz.

Evans, H. (1983). *Good times, bad times*. London: Weidenfeld and Nicolson.

Faludi, S. (1991/1992). *Backlash: The undeclared war against women*. London: Chatto and Windus.

Gill, R. (2003). From sexual objectification to sexual subjectification: The resexualisation of women's bodies in the media. *Feminist Media Studies, 3*(1), 99–106.

Gill, R. (2007a). Postfeminist media culture: Elements of a sensibility. *European Journal of Cultural Studies, 10*(2), 147–166.

Gill, R. (2007b). *Gender and the media*. Cambridge: Polity Press.

Gill, R. (2016). Post postfeminism? New feminist visibilities in postfeminist times. *Feminist Media Studies, 16*(4), 610–630.

Gill, R., & Scharf, C. (Eds.). (2011). *New femininities: Postfeminism, neoliberalism and subjectivity*. Basingstoke: Palgrave Macmillan.

Grose, R. (1989). *The Sun-sation*. London: Angus and Robertson.

Holland, P. (1983). "The page three girl speaks to women, too" in *Screen* 24 n3 May/June reprinted in Rosemary Betterton (ed) *Looking On* London: Pandora Press 1987 and P. Marris & S. Thornham (Eds.), *Media studies: A reader*. Edinburgh: Edinburgh University Press 1996.

Holland, P. (1998). The politics of the smile: "soft news" and the sexualisation of the popular press. In C. Carter, G. Branston, & S. Allan (Eds.), *News, gender and power*. London: Routledge.

Leveson, L. J. (2012). *An inquiry into the culture, practices and ethics of the press* (4 Vols.). Department for Digital, Culture, Media and Sport. Retrieved from www.gov.uk/government/uploads/system/uploads/attachment_data/file/270939/0780_i.pdf

Levy, A. (2005). *Female Chauvinist pigs: Women and the rise of raunch culture*. New York, NY: Free Press.

McKnight, D. (2013). *Murdoch's politics: How one man's thirst for wealth and power shapes our world*. London: Pluto Press.

McRobbie, A. (2000). Feminism and the third way. *Feminist Review, 64*(1), 97–112.

McRobbie, A. (2004). Post-feminism and popular culture. *Feminist Media Studies, 4*(3).

McRobbie, A. (2009). *The aftermath of feminism*. London: Sage Publications.
Martin, P. (1997, February 16). The sad tale of Mr Fox. *Observer Life*.
Scraton, P. (1999/2009). *Hillsborough: The truth*. Edinburgh: Mainstream Publishing.
Short, C. (1991). *Dear Clare: This is what women feel about page three*. London: Radius.
Walter, N. (2010/2015). *Living dolls: The return of sexism*. London: Virago.

13

PAGE 3 JOURNALISM

Gender and news cultures in post-reforms India

Sahana Udupa

Across a broad swath of countries in the global South that adopted the economic liberalization policies in the 1990s, a significant transformation of the media industries accompanied changes in the economic-political spheres. In these years, state-controlled media gave way to intensely competitive private news markets and radically pluralized fields of online media (Hasan, 2016; Rahman, 2016; Udupa, 2017). Commercial television news expanded at a blistering pace with a growing number of domestic players attached to varied businesses and an equally significant number of international news chains aiming for a global audience. Newspapers were not left behind. While print news media circulations continued to decline in the West, a 21 percent increase in the global circulation in the last five years was largely driven by strong print markets in India and other parts of Asia (World Association of Newspapers, 2017).[1] As television news and online media grew in reach and volume, print media likewise expanded and underwent major transformation in their operational scale, production logics, and conceptions of news. Mainstream print news organizations that had developed professional structures of news gathering toward the end of the twentieth century started to shun the inhibitions around market centricism and openly declare themselves as commercial entities.

India presents an important case to examine the cultures of private news media and how they aggressively introduced commercial models of news production, while simultaneously articulating and normalizing economic reforms in the newly liberalizing nations of the global South. But the Indian case does more than that: it reveals how the private news media advocated for economic reforms by imagining and constructing a "new reader" as an aspirational subject of the globalizing economy. News outlets cast their aspirational discourses in the language of liberty—of sexual freedom, urban lifestyle choices, and a celebration of youth cultures. The distinct urban modernity of the aspirational imagining of "new India" in a global world, I argue, is deeply gendered. It has implications for the public visibility of gender issues and for gender constructions more broadly.

How did the "liberal discourse" around women's rights to lifestyle, fashion, and sexual freedom become entangled with economic reforms? To critique changes inside the newsrooms that fashioned this entanglement and the culture wars these provoke beyond the newsroom, I delve into the transition of the *Times of India*. The *TOI* is the largest circulated English daily in India and owns regional language newspapers with large readerships in various subnational states of India. To more specifically unpack the nexus between economic liberalization, urban modernity, and gender, I hone in on "Page 3 journalism," a new form of celebrity and lifestyle journalism established by *TOI*. My analysis is based on ethnographic fieldwork carried out at prominent newspapers including the *TOI* (and *Prajavani, Vijaya Karnataka, the New Indian Express, Deccan Herald, the Hindu, Kannada Prabha, Ee Sanje*) between 2008 and 2010, and again between 2012 and 2015, as well as ongoing research in Bangalore, the southern Indian city that became the outsourcing hub for the global high-tech industry in the 1990s and as a result, a poster child for economic reforms in India. During the first phase of fieldwork inside *TOI*'s Bangalore newsroom, the metro desk covering city news had eight reporters (seven women and one man); the crime bureau had two men; education was covered by two women; the political bureau had one woman and three men; and the business desk had two men and two women. Aside from interacting with them, I interviewed four women and nine men who were senior editorial executives (resident editor, deputy resident editor, senior assistant editors, news editors, brand executives, and advertising executives).

I first briefly summarize the state of journalism in India in the years of economic reforms, to contextualize the newsroom dynamics that shaped *TOI*'s "Page 3 journalism." After discussing Page 3 journalism's role in articulating economic reforms with a gendered discourse around pleasure and choice, I conclude by emphasizing the importance of going beyond the more established lens of examining the allocation of roles to women and men journalists inside the newsrooms or textual analysis of news representations. I urge a critical analysis of new conceptions of news and audiences in the liberalizing economies of the south and their contradictory implications for gender constructions.

Journalism in post liberalization India

The Indian news media's transition to greater commercialization in the last three decades follows broader economic and political shifts triggered by a host of developments. In the early 1990s, the state protected national economy was supplanted by market-centric policies designed to boost consumption, encourage private enterprise, relax the state licensing regime, and enable closer integration with the global economy. Economic liberalization policies introduced in 1991 by the state institutionalized trade and industry deregulation trends already underway in India in the 1980s. The new policy promoted the private sector as the torchbearer of India's emergence as a global economic power and the educated middle class as the drivers of growth and innovation. A range of factors converged on the rationale of market centrism. The pro-reforms ideology that pivoted around the imaginary of the consumption friendly "new middle class" mounted an attack on the post-colonial model of state developmentalism. This was partly in response to rural and provincial accumulation that had accelerated in the 1980s (Chari, 2004). Enormous expansion of state subsidies for the rural sector led to a "ruralization of politics" and the growth of regional elite. Both of these outcomes posed a challenge in various ways to Indian federalism as well as the urban elite. A more urgent reason was the balance of payment crisis of 1989: a massive decline in the foreign exchange reserves paved the way for the International Monetary Fund to directly intervene in India's economic policies. Together, the balance of payment crisis, the perceived threat of ruralization of politics, private sector anxieties about state overspending, and disenchantment with state developmentalism provided the domestic context for economic liberalization policies to gain prominence under the influence of multilateral agencies. The liberalization discourse challenged *dirigiste* development (strong state directive control over the key sectors of the economy and public policy, as opposed to a merely regulatory role) and paved the way for the "big business community" to operate in "highly profitable areas hitherto reserved for the public sector" and benefit from substantial tax-incentives and subsidies (Maiorano, 2016, p. 211). This marked the exhaustion of secular, national development, a vision once supported by Nehru himself, as well as of Cold War geopolitics and global circuits of development ideology (Chari, 2004, pp. 35–44).[2]

In a climate of economic reforms, the news media system transitioned from its state-controlled model in the broadcasting sector and limited private enterprise in print media into a highly competitive private media field riding on the growth of middle-class consumer markets, advertisement industry, and increasing literacy of (potential) readers. The changes marked a shift from the earlier forms of the nationalist press (newspapers as a key means for the struggle for independence from the British Empire) and the developmentalist press (media as a legitimizing tool for the postcolonial state's control over economy and development).[3] Major news organizations responded to "open commercialisation" (Jeffrey, 2000, p. 58) by restructuring their newsrooms with a reforms-friendly news discourse (Ninan, 2010; Rao, 2010).

Despite various modulations, at its core the pro-reform discourse framed the postcolonial state as obstructive, corrupt, and inefficient, in contrast to an efficient and globally prepared private sector. News portrayals of a liberalizing India elided how key policy initiatives of the postcolonial state were instrumental in promoting industry growth and in using state subsidized higher education to produce educated workers. The news media celebrated the private sector, especially the home-grown Information Technology industries, as having succeeded without state support. Indeed, the common refrain was that the high-tech sector succeeded "despite" the presumably obstructive state.

Scholars regard the shift in the news industry and news representations of development in post-reform India as a "neoliberal nexus" between the corporate elite, political elite, and media industries; they criticize "news media as an active and eager participant in the abuse of power" (Muralidharan, 2010, p. 10). Elites' hold over the news media is without doubt a sobering reality of post-reform India. But the multilingual composition of the news field—the existence of newspapers in different regional languages and their multifarious cultural practices of news— has continued to produce diverse perspectives that complicate the easy alliance between market and state interests (Udupa, 2015).

Set against a conflictual appropriation of the reforms discourse shaped largely by the news media's bilingual dynamics,[4] a new understanding of news and news audiences gained ground among India's major commercial newspapers. Emblematic of the trend, the *Times of India* announced the changed strategy in bold and unyielding terms: news as a shared discourse of unfolding events no longer needed the cloak of a "public good." It was a commercial product designed to appease the consumers, plain and simple. Although the paper's history dated back to the colonial times, *TOI* underwent a major transformation in the late 1980s when two businessmen, brothers Samir Jain and Vineet Jain, inherited the paper as part of the family media conglomerate Bennett Coleman and Co. The brothers quickly decided to give the paper a new identity they felt to be in sync with the changing times. The decision to openly define news as a consumer product—"just like toothpaste"—created a stir in the journalistic community for its brazen disavowal of news as public articulation of societal concerns and a reflexive space central to democratic processes. However, the *TOI* model of bottom-line journalism provoked less moral panic in the later years; by the turn of the millennium, the paper's "deromanticized" vision of news as a commercial enterprise stabilized as a norm of Indian journalism.

The *TOI*'s market-led agenda hinges on a distinct discourse about news and news audiences that pivots around the figure of a "new reader" in "new India" who is imagined as urban, mobile, flexible, economically ascendant, culturally modern, and overwhelmingly young. Furthermore, goes the narrative, the new reader is frustrated with corrupt politics and ready to assume civic responsibility to change and repair the city (and the country). Although shaped by the paper's bottom-line emphasis and the pressure to seek advertising revenue in urban news markets, the imagining of a new reader resulted from a complex mix of cultural and political influences. Journalists on the newsfloor shared the middle-class disgruntlement about the postcolonial state and corrupt politics. Other sources of influence emerged from the competing news companies that tried to win "monetizable" readers with varied market and cultural strategies. Yet another source of influence and inspiration was the business successes of home grown high-tech companies that stood as the signposts for private enterprise and drivers of India's economic power.

Gender provides a compelling lens to unravel the complexity of this transition, in terms of the efforts to target women readers as consumers as well as newsroom restructuring that led to feminization of a section of journalistic work, illustrated by the editorial team for "Page 3 journalism." Relatedly, the paper has fashioned a liberal discourse around youth cultures and sexualized bodies; this has become one key element in its advocacy for economic deregulation and the framing of the state as inept and inefficient. The significance of this transition could be assessed in relation to the changing counters of gender politics in and of the Indian news media.

News and gender

Gender issues and news media have had a tenuous relation in post-independence India. As early as in the 1970s, sustained attention to the portrayal of women in media and participation of women in media production became a key concern for feminist scholarship. Both the 1975 UN First World Conference on Women held in Mexico City, with its declaration of the 1975–1985 period as the UN Decade for Women, and the 1981 UNESCO report "Unequal Opportunities: The Case of Women and the Media" (Gallagher, 1981) encouraged greater institutionalization of feminist studies in India. Feminist scholars and activists in India have since given critical scrutiny to the pervasive gender stereotypes in media representations, and the failure to "reflect a woman's way of thinking, experiencing and feeling" (Rao, 2001, p. 45). Similarly, gender discrimination inside the newsrooms and professional journalism has drawn strong criticism. Led largely by professional women journalists turned commentators, critical reports have highlighted the discriminatory practices against women within news organizations, including severe underrepresentation of women journalists at the higher levels of newsroom decision making, a gendered division of labor that relegates "soft assignments" to women and assaults against women journalists (Khabar Lahariya, 2015). This focus on gender relations inside the news organizations, occupational hazards of journalistic work, and news representations of women has led to admirable scholarship and popular visibility to gender concerns. Yet, this increasing attention is not an unmistakable sign of a progressive feminist tide around gender-based freedom and justice. The visibility of feminist concerns and women as subjects in the news media is ridden with contradictions.

Maitrayee Chaudhuri (2014) captures the tensions by observing that in contemporary media and popular culture, gender is "hypervisible." She plots the hypervisibility of gender across three overlapping contexts: the influence of three decades of institutionalized feminism; the imperatives of neoliberal economic policies; and the scale of the media and communication industry in the making of popular and public culture (2014, p. 146). Journalists' discussions of the mass gang rape that shook New Delhi and the rest of India in December 2012 is illustrative. The "hypervisibility" of gender was evident in the scale of news media coverage and social media attention the incident provoked, which raised serious questions about women's safety and violence against women in contemporary India. In an important volume on the role of media in framing and mobilizing popular urban protest against the gang rape, Schneider and Titzmann contend that discourses around gender, mobility, space, politics, and the media offer a "serious critique of the existing system" (2015, p. 14). On the flip side, the very media attention to gender in this grave, tragic incident fed the global outcry around "India as a rape capital." The uproar on social media brought the gender question perilously close to colonial stereotyping of India as an incorrigible zone of danger for women.

A similar contradiction in the visibility of gender in news media is evident in the new-found openness about female sexuality. Advertising agencies and consumer market research companies are at the forefront of a public culture that has shunned the colonial (Victorian) mores of taming female sexuality. Female sexuality is in abundance in public cultures of contemporary India—from cinema to advertisements and online cartoons to stand-up comedy. Female protagonists in popular advertisements, for instance, are rarely tied to the nineteenth-century Indian middle-class values that articulated Victorian prudism with a reinvented image of a traditional Hindu woman to idealize domesticated, sexually sanitized women (Sinh, 2014). Women in contemporary advertisements boldly claim their sexuality in portrayals of a free expression of sexual desire. They are seen gazing at and "devouring" men for sexual pleasure. Female protagonists of expressive sexuality are not limited to advertisement billboards. An emergent social media culture of female blogging, "chick flicks," amateur music videos, and digital ventures of seasoned women filmmakers testify to growing assertions of female desire in public space. Digital projects such as *Agents of Ishq* by documentary filmmaker Paromita Vohra and online music videos of millennial rapper Sofia Ashraf are riveting illustrations of this trend.[5]

While empowering as bottom up media production, "hypervisibility" of female sexuality is also continuously incorporated into global consumer cultures. Perusing consumer market research studies in post-reform India, Chaudhuri shows how market research firms have been able to appropriate "relatively new ideas of the metro-sexual and recognition of female sexuality" (2014, p. 149). Such uses of sexuality and gender, she contends, are "at once reflecting new mores and actively shaping them" (2014, p. 150). Some scholars criticize the trends as blatant commercialization of sexual identities. Gugler argues that capitalist accumulation in post liberalization India "seeks to turn alternative sexual identities and LGBT communities as potential consumers for the advertisement and pornographic industries" (2015, p. 143). Without denying the role of the "industrial scale of regular monitoring, research and analysis" that goes behind capitalist appropriation of sexual difference and sexuality, Chaudhury argues that the phenomenon is more complex. She treats the growing visibility of female sexuality in popular media cultures as a nexus between neoliberal fashioning of the self as enterprise and postfeminist discourse of desire as self-realization:

> The contemporary Indian media and popular culture appear to promote . . . recurring gendered ideological motifs . . . namely an ideology of self-realization. This . . . is done at two levels: self as enterprise which one can build up; and a cult of self-expression. If the first finds its way in stories of women bosses, the latter is in the growing visibility of sexuality in the media and popular culture.
>
> *(2014, p. 151)*

I use Chaudury's important argument on the nexus between neoliberal self-as-enterprise and postfeminist assertion of sexuality to examine below how the newsrooms of the *TOI* and other commercial newspapers became an important site where such new ideas and combinations were worked out. How did the TOI newsroom restructure its norms and narratives to forge a peculiar combination of sexuality, individual freedom, market enterprise, and female liberation? What new form of journalism was behind this phenomenon, and how did the journalists make meanings and routines out of it?

Page 3 journalism in a high-tech city

"They all come from a set template," Mira Raj reveals, using the deadpan tone of an exhausted journalist. Raj is a leading editorial member at the *Bangalore Times* (BT), a supplement distributed with the "main issue" of the *TOI's* Bangalore edition. Described as a lifestyle supplement, BT features stories of celebrities from sports, cinema, advertising, fashion, high-tech industry, and occasionally formal politics, together with a heady mix of gossip, leisure write ups and lifestyle advice. Racy images of fashion models accompany the text's vibrant fonts and stylish headlines. Targeting middle-class and upper middle-class readers, the supplement presents itself as mirroring the desires and aspirations of a lively, young, urban Indian.

BT's swanky newsroom in *TOI's* main building has a dampened air of routine newswork, which is nowhere close to the go-get-it sort of youth energy or the lively spirit of flaunting pleasure the supplement seeks to portray on its pages. Raj almost indifferently described to me during my ethnographic study of the news-room BT's set formula and its entertainment and lifestyle orientation. The "set look" for the front page requires two big pictures, short interviews and the buzz around Hollywood and Bollywood. "We also carry stories that affect the young people, work-life balance and other such stories for the IT crowd [information technology workers in Bangalore]. Yes, it is very clearly for the young readers."

Around Raj's enclosed cubicle are rows of open workstations for the editorial team. Most team members are in their early 20s. Many are young women. BT's women reporters look more stylish than their peers on the "main desk," which supplies stories on politics, business, civic issues, sports, and education for the "main issue." BT reporters flaunt high heels, body-hugging shirts, finely manicured nails, and colorful handbags. The difference is perhaps merely cosmetic: they look as serious and worried about deadlines as any of their peers on the "main desk." I hear a reporter clamping the phone down with frustration after a canceled appointment, and frantically seeking her colleagues' support to find a replacement. The next second, I see a young man journalist walking into Raj's cubicle to get her approval for a page layout. A regulated pace of work and template driven schedules go behind the daily manufacture of casual leisure as news. A seasoned woman reporter says that BT reporters are guided to "concentrate on entertainment, nightlife, techie lifestyles, safety for women and such issues." The news they produce is known as "Page 3." That "women's safety" issues are part of the lifestyle page's priorities indicates a new bundling of topics and concerns in BT's appeal for young readers. The yoking together of lifestyle, leisure, celebrity gossip, and women's rights reveals the unique character of "Page 3" that figures high on the *TOI's* new agenda.

During the early years of transition to a "market model" of news, with Page 3 as one of its elements, *TOI* used Bangalore's success story as the outsourcing hub for the global high-tech industry as a key trope to develop a new style and approach. Bangalore became a unique laboratory to experiment with the market model of news. Management was clear that *TOI* news style should be "engaging and not preachy" and "ready to give a distinct identity to the new Bangalorean." On the one hand, the *TOI's* expansion in Bangalore depended on the city's newly configured status as a global technology hub. Many high-tech migrants had come around the country to secure well-paying new economy jobs, thereby forming a significant group of consumers. About 70 percent of *TOI's* Bangalore readers in 2010 were domestic migrants with relatively high disposable income. *TOI's* market model of news depended on liberalized economy's new class groups and the claims to public discourse that came with economic growth among these segments. On the other hand, the paper articulated new discourses around citizen-consumer and aspiring new Indians in its struggles to dominate the news market and define a new audience, in the midst of heightened commercial competition in the news field. I have defined this dialectic of a neoliberalized habitus on *TOI's* news floors and the production of a similar habitus in *TOI* audiences as "mediated desire." Following Bourdieu (1977), "mediated desire" could be located as a part of the ongoing struggle for dominance and difference within the news field and among the class groups in the city.

Mediated desire is the discourse and practices of desire-as-aspiration that extends beyond the realm of commodity consumption into new imaginations of urban revival, civic activism, cultural ascent, social mobility, body and self; it results from a range of mediations that go beyond mere market manipulation (Udupa, 2015). Mediated desire reveals how the seemingly unrelated ideas of consumption, civic activism, beautified bodies, corporate leadership, and responsibilized citizenry were merged into a dominant sensibility of legitimate aspiration of the new reader. It is within this formulation of "mediated desire" that Page 3 journalism as a distinctly sexualized and assertive gender discourse made its way into the news discourse.

Three interrelated elements constitute the logic of Page 3 journalism: notions of positivity, celebrities, and free will. In a curious expression, journalists on the *TOI* floor defined them in terms of "quotients": positivity quotient, celebrity quotient, and freewill quotient. The mandate, he described, is to check if the news stories have adequate quotient of the three parameters, alone or in combination. In its new post-reforms avatar, the *TOI* decided that news stories should not just paint a dismal picture of life and society. It must actively push for the "positive" side of things. Journalists and management alike translated this guideline as cheerful and colorful portrayals of business success, philanthropy, and female bodies. The *TOI* introduced many stylistic changes to realize this, such as bold and colorful images on most of the pages in the main issue, and more prominently on the pages of Page 3 supplements. A senior editor spelled out the positivity mantra:

In fact, we believe in actively promoting positivity. That is the mandate our management has given us. We should promote the positivity quotient and don't be negative all the time. Look at the positive aspect. Whenever someone does a good job, we never fail to appreciate it. It can be anybody, [even] some rare person from the government or bureaucracy. There are few[er] examples available in the government. But in society at large, there are hundreds of such people—do-gooders, good Samaritans.

Positivity, journalists were told, should have an aesthetic appeal even if it didn't involve substantive social contribution. Indeed, regardless of the senior editor's high sounding talk about good Samaritans, Page 3 journalism's distinct "positivity" comes from the colorful portrayals of "celebrities" whose affluent lifestyles are often the only criterion for what the supplement features. A BT journalist listed "sports, corporate world, art, music, cinema" as domains where celebrities are spotted. "A celebrity is anybody who has made an achievement and interests the readers," she stated, in what seemed like an awkward tautology. Politicians rarely make the list. BT journalists said they trained themselves well to spot the celebrities and compose stories out of them. A young woman journalist in her mid-20s stated:

> We do larger-than-life stories. That is how heroes are created. On page one, there has to be some celebrity quotient in the pictures we publish.

Party goers who are known only in Bangalore are "local socialites," she said; they do not carry as much "weight" as socialites with a nation-wide appeal, such as Vijay Mallya (a multimillionaire businessman now residing in the UK to escape legal actions in India for charges of business malpractices). BT journalists claimed that, with regular "exposure" on their pages, they have turned many aspiring socialites, movie actors, and fashion models not known in the "party circles" into celebrities and public figures. "*Bangalore Times* created stars," Sunita claimed, with a hint of pride.

The market model of news impacts celebrity journalism directly by allowing aspiring stars to pay the *TOI's* in-house public relations team, Medianet, in exchange for featured space in BT and Page 3 supplements in other cities. Of course, some stars are too big to be charged. Bangalore-based fashion designer Prasad Bidapa, for instance, does not pay, a BT journalist told me: "He knows he will appear anyway. But if a model stands next to him and wants to be published, he may have to pay." Medianet plays a go-between by allocating featured space for fixed sums of money, but small players like photographers also make opportunities (and cash) by promising flattering portrayals of stars-in-the-making. Such side transactions sometimes go unnoticed by the management. All these practices have cemented the idea that celebrities are an indispensable feature of Page 3 journalism. "You are catering to the young audience. What do the young read? Fashion, food . . . So, celebrities get built up!," a BT journalist reasoned.

Stories about celebrities are composed with pull-out quotes and textual flourish, but more important is the multichromatic visual appeal of the accompanying images. Scantily clad female fashion models and cinema stars are seen to be particularly "bold" for the Indian middle-class sensibilities.

At the confluence of positivity and celebrity news—of visual splendor and racy texts—stands the value of free will and enterprise. *TOI* journalists covering business said "good Samaritans" positively contributed to society because their sheer grit and will made them successful. Implying that they were successful not because of inherited property or patronage, they linked good work by good Samaritans to a spirit of enterprise. In such representations, collective responsibility for development is superseded by stories of individual success stories. Thus, for *TOI* management, individual freedom and enterprise stands at the heart of a conscious strategy of news for a young India. This approach combines the notion of responsibilized citizens with the imagination of new young Indians ready to assert their individuality against the regressive traditional mores. This has also brought gender into greater prominence. The ready availability of bold images of scantily clad women, along with texts that call on women to unapologetically assert sexuality, appeals to a "liberal" position for which free expression of sexuality is key. Middle-class women's safety and lifestyle choices are likewise framed in the language of rights and modernity. On several occasions, the paper thus staunchly opposed attempts by the Hindu right-wing groups and other conservative forces to clamp down on public expressions of sexuality and lifestyle choices of women, including their choice to consume alcohol in the pubs.

In a highly publicized controversy in 2012, a group of Hindu nationalist supporters barged into a pub in a coastal city near Bangalore, to target female revelers consuming alcohol with their male friends. Local television channels taped and showed the young male attackers dragging the girls out of the pub, and physically thrashing them. The attack appeared to showcase middle-class anxieties about the moral degradation of urban youth. As a man journalist at *Vijaya Karnataka* (a Kannada language newspaper owned by the *TOI* group) paraphrased the attackers' point of view, the anxiety was "evidenced" by the free expressions of pleasure and desire by "party-going girls wearing skimpy outfits." The attack got an ambiguous response in what I have defined as the *bhasha* media (a section of English language news media and largely regional language news media) owing to the cultural sensibility of "*madivanthike*" [restraint and hesitation] towards open expressions of female sexuality and pleasure (Udupa, 2015). However, the *TOI* made its position clear. Framing the attack as "moral policing" and "Talibanization," the paper's front pages condemned the attack and vociferously advocate for women's rights to drink, dine, and dance. "It is about curbing the liberty of individuals," a senior *TOI* reporter said with a twinge of indignation. "These women were not doing anything wrong, they were not indulging in any indecent act. But they were bashed up! Papers should take a stand on those who don't tolerate this."

A senior editorial member (a man) explained the rationale behind the coverage as the *TOI* "worldview." This worldview celebrated individual freedom and choice, and the free youth spirit that is at once a driver of cultural modernity and economic progress:

Let me tell you our basic premise of our thinking. This is something I tell new entrants to our paper. The *Times of India* is a liberal paper. It believes in the citizens' freedom of choice. We don't appreciate somebody imposing views on something, on somebody. A few years ago, a certain girl's [only] college in Bangalore had put some norms [sic] that banned tight jeans for girls. Now, who is to decide no tight jeans? . . . Tight jeans are a very amorphous, very unclear concept. Who is to decide? When it comes to jeans or all these, please don't impose. Youngsters wear whatever they want so long as they conform to norms of decency.

Editorial members did not entirely agree about norms of decency. A small number of middle aged men journalists told me that pub visits by young girls and alcohol consumption in general were not as culturally appropriate as the urban liberal position of the *TOI* suggested. But the *TOI* "worldview" was non-negotiable. One senior editor clarified the TOI tone: "It is to appeal to the youngsters who are believed to be free thinking, with a free will, who are libertarian. We have the template. We follow it." He explained that this template is binding, hinting that his own conviction about moral policing was laced with resigned pragmatism as a paid employee of a paper that gave little room for journalists' discretion. A senior reporter was more direct about the binding authority of the top management: "Journalists could have different views. If the same journalist comes and works in the *Times*, within one week he will change, he will fall in line. He *has* to fall in line."

Coverage for incidents of "moral policing," journalists believed, is one of the key elements of the *TOI* "worldview." Sometimes, journalists confronted the dilemma of giving publicity to the otherwise unknown groups of vandalizers targeting women, but the editorial team stood by the *TOI* "worldview" to take a liberal position and actively condemn moral policing instead of ignoring it as inconsequential acts of disparate and negligible groups. "The idea is to expose these elements," explained a senior editorial member. "Some people disagree with our approach and say we are giving publicity to Hindutva [right-wing Hindu nationalist] forces. But it is like arguing we give publicity to Taliban by writing about their ill practices! We have to remove that mindset. If we should do that, we need to attend to all small little things. Otherwise it will pervade more [sic]!"

On *TOI* news floors, moral policing was understood not only as an attack on women's rights, but more seriously as a symptom of insidious and corrupt politics. A senior editorial member asserted:

> Moral policing, be it by religious fundamentalists or by self-styled organizations claiming to be sociocultural but are really political or by people in power, . . . is frowned upon by *Times of India*. We are quite open about it. . . . We make no bones about our position.

In the *TOI* formulation, women's rights to stylistic choices thereby blends easily with the neoliberal rhetoric against corrupt politics, and relatedly, a celebration of individual freedom and enterprise. On the one hand, the "main issue" of the paper publicizes gender by offering wide critical coverage for gender regressive vandalism. The Page 3 supplement, on the other hand, continues to defy the parameters set by the moral police by celebrating precisely what the latter condemned. These editorial moves place the gender question at the nexus of market-friendly reforms and urban modernity. Expressions of female sexuality and free lifestyle choices go hand in hand with the celebration of individual enterprise, personal wealth, and free will, together constituting the aspirational ethos of "mediated desire." The peculiar entanglement of gender rights with "mediated desire" hinges on a particular understanding of female freedom as unhindered expression of sexuality and lifestyle choices among the middle classes, who also constitute the largest segment of the paper's monetizable audiences.

The *TOI's* staunch position against the masculinist politics of right wing nationalist groups and simultaneous espousal of market discourse creates a puzzling mix of values that evades an easy normative critique. The narrative of fiercely independent women ready to assert their claims over the public space by dressing and dining at free will may be empowering, at least for a section of urban women who find it easy to combine fashion, pubbing, partying, and pleasure with gender-based claims over participation and parity with men. It creates the conditions of positive media reception for voices that challenge the conservative forces. The paper itself has assumed a voice of direct advocacy in many cases. Yet, the limits of *TOI's* gender-based advocacy are evident in the middle-class consumption framework, without which neither the expressive freedom around sexuality nor women's safety issues make sense as news in the template offered to journalists.

Gender, reforms, and urban modernity

TOI's Page 3 journalism is symptomatic of a mediated shift of discourse in the new India from "the virginal pedestal of ideal modern middle class femininity" (Parameswaran, 2009, p. 90) to a confident, assertive, aspirational sexuality, and individual freedom of expression.[6] Page 3 journalism reveals the way gender-sensitive rights conceived as free individual expression became the language of urban modernity articulating a pro-reform discourse. As news organizations came under the influence of economic liberalization—both as beneficiaries of an expanding consumer market and actors in a competitive news market—what ensued was a pressure to redefine the audiences to be in tune with the changing times. In this context, a market-mediated assertive sexuality entered the newsrooms as a prerequisite for urban modernity.

The ways in which assertions of female sexuality and lifestyle choices are bound up with ideas of free will, enterprise, and urban modernity on the *TOI* newsfloor, suggest a complex intermingling of values. Page 3 journalism has objectified female bodies and sexualities in an expanding market for advertising, popular entertainment, and consumer products, setting even higher price tags for expressions of femininity and experience of pleasure. In the same vein, however, the constructed ethos of a "liberal" paper has helped to create conditions of defiance against conservative gender constructions of domesticated sexuality and denial of public visibility to feminist voices. The paradox of Page 3 journalism as both an empowering space of assertive sexuality and an objectifying market machinery reflects the dilemma of modernity more generally in postcolonial societies such as India.

The news media's significant role in configuring a nexus between gender, urban modernity, and economic reforms illustrated by this newsroom ethnography emphasizes the need to examine gender and journalism beyond the conventional lens of gender relations in news production or news representations of women's issues. It calls for a critical scrutiny of the contradictory logics of news that make gender a legitimizing trope for economic reforms within newly liberalizing economies of the global South, while also energizing the demands for cultural expressions as a means for gender-based justice.

Notes

1 In 2017, global daily print circulation was close to 750 million (World Association of Newspapers, 2017).
2 Chari notes that the "populism of agrarian subsidies extended its contradictions into the reform process" (2004, p. 44). Despite the subsidies, agriculture suffered in the post reforms decades, leading to a very high number of farmers' suicides (Raina, 2016).
3 The history of the Indian news media is more tangled than a simple periodization in terms of the "nationalist" and "developmentalist" press. Some publishers were business-minded even during the colonial years of nationalist agitation and most definitely through the post-independence years of selective capitalism. However, the key ideological and structural frameworks that underpinned journalism in the colonial and post-independence years reveal the predominance of nationalist sentiments during the peak of the liberation struggle (roughly between the middle and later decades of the nineteenth century and 1947) and later, the presumed role as an instrument of development for the postcolonial state until the early 1980s. Following independence, the press was inscribed into the national, secular developmental vision of the newly independent Indian nation, most famously termed as "Nehruvianism," privileging state-led development and planning.
4 Although the news field is multilingual at the national scale, each subnational region in India is dominated by news media in the region's official language and English. Hence, the specific dynamics of newswork is largely defined by the tensions between regional language news and English language media.
5 Such initiatives sit uneasily with growing vigilante action and abusive cultures of the right-wing Hindu nationalist groups. Furthermore, social media-enabled activism exemplified by the #MeToo movement has ignited a new generation of feminists to mobilize action against sexual harassment. This has occurred in an atmosphere of "hypervisibility" to a distinct urban sensibility of desiring and assertive women demanding safety, justice, and parity.
6 The culture wars and clashes between TOI-style journalism and "bhasha" media complicate the easy diffusion of Page 3 journalism and its gender constructions. However, precisely because of the expansion of TOI-style journalism and related tropes of assertive sexuality in popular entertainment, and all the deflections and reactionary backlash that have emerged in response, gender has become the key target for the reform-friendly liberal discourse as well as for conservative right-wing forces.

References

Bourdieu, P. (1977). *Outline of a theory of practice* (R. Nice, trans.). New York, NY: Cambridge University Press.

Chari, S. (2004). *Fraternal capital: Peasant-workers, self-made men and globalization in provincial India*. Delhi, India: Permanent Black.

Chaudhury, M. (2014). Gender, media and popular culture in global India. In L. Fernandes (Ed.), *Routledge handbook of gender in South Asia* (pp. 145–159). London: Routledge.

Gallagher, M. (1981). *Unequal opportunities: The case of women and the media*. Paris: Unesco Press.

Gugler, T. K. (2015). New media, neosexual activism and diversifying sex worlds in post-liberlization India. In N-C. Schneider & F-M. Titzmann (Eds.), *Studying youth, media and gender in post liberalization India* (pp. 143–166). Berlin: Frank&Timme.

Hassan, K. (2016). Why did a military dictator liberalize the electronic media in Pakistan? In S. Udupa & S. D. McDowell (Eds.), *Media as politics in South Asia* (pp. 77–94). London: Routledge.

Jeffrey, R. (2000). *India's newspaper revolution: Capitalism, politics and the Indian language press, 1977–1999*. New Delhi: Oxford University Press.

Lahariya, K. (2015). Going beyond harssment: Women journalists in Uttar Pradesh. *Economic and Political Weekly, 50*(39), 2349–8846. ISSN (Online).

Maiorano, D. (2016). The politics of economic reforms in India. In K. A. Jacobsen (Ed.), *Routledge handbook of contemporary India* (pp. 203–215). London and New York, NY: Routledge.

Muralidharan, S. (2010). Media: Stenographer to power. *Economic and Political Weekly, 45*(49), 10–14.

Parameswaran, R. (2009). Moral dilemmas of an immoral nation: Gender, sexuality and journalism in page 3. *Image of the Journalist in Popular Culture, 1*, 70–104.

Rahman, A. (2016). Print and electronic media. In A. Riaz & M. S. Rahman (Eds.), *Routledge handbook on contemporary Bangladesh* (pp. 325–339). New York, NY: Routledge.

Raina, R. S. (2016). Agriculture and the development burden. In K. A. Jacobsen (Ed.), *Routledge handbook of contemporary India* (pp. 99–117). London and New York, NY: Routledge.

Rao, L. (2001). Facets of media and gender studies in India. *Feminist Media Studies, 1*(1), 45–48.

Rao, U. (2010). *News as culture: Journalistic practices and the remaking of Indian leadership traditions*. Oxford: Berghahn Books.

Schneider, N-C., & Titzmann, F-M. (2015). *Studying youth, media and gender in post liberalization India*. Berlin: Frank&Timme.

Sinha, M. (2014). Gendered nationalism: From women to gender and back again? In L. Fernandes (Ed.), *Routledge handbook on gender in South Asia* (pp. 13–27). London: Routledge.

Thomas, P. N. (2010). *Political economy of communications in India: The good, the bad and the ugly*. New Delhi: Sage Publications.

Udupa, S. (2015). *Making news in global India: Media, publics, politics*. Cambridge: Cambridge University Press.

Udupa, S. (2017). Gaali cultures: The politics of abusive exchange on social media. *New Media and Society, 8*(2), 187–206.

World Association of Newspapers. (2017). *World press trends 2017: Facts and figures*. Retrieved January 5, 2018, from www.wptdatabase.org/world-press-trends-2017-facts-and-figures

PART III

Engendering news audiences and activism

14

REFUGEES AND ISLAM

Representing race, rights, and cohabitation

Beverly M. Weber

In a 2016 article published in *The Guardian*, German journalist Konstantin Richter, who had previously published several pro-refugee pieces, lamented the failure
of Germany's *Willkommenskultur*—the culture of welcoming refugees with open
arms. Drawing on his personal experience of hosting refugees in his home in order
to comment on the nation's experience of opening the borders to refugees, the
journalist noted that some of his guests did not thank him and wife for their hospitality. Germans, Richter argued, had been overly flattered that they were viewed
internationally as welcoming; but now, "the spirit of the *Willkommenskultur*—taking
in people randomly, exuberantly, without getting to know them and establishing a
meaningful relationship—doesn't feel right any more" (Richter, 2016).

Richter's article exemplifies the proliferation of news media texts (and political speech) that describe individuals and the nation as disappointed in the results
of broadly welcoming refugees into Germany over the last years, disappointment
in the "welcome culture." Expectations of refugees' gratitude and likeability had
permeated both news media and political speech. When granting refugee rights no
longer "feels good," then the limits of rights themselves have been reached, and calls
to close the borders are often deemed legitimate.

The end of good feelings seemed particularly dominant in the public imagination in Cologne after New Year's Eve 2015, when over 1000 crimes in or near
the Cologne train station were reported. Over half of them involved sexualized
violence in some form. These numbers have been widely reported, as has the fact
that the majority of the suspects in these crimes, when they could be identified,
were "North African." Very rarely reported was that very few of the 36 convictions
for crimes that night were for sexualized violence; the vast majority were for petty
theft. The lack of attention to *what* crimes had been convicted, and the overwhelming attention to *who* had committed crimes, repeated a public narrative in which

white German women were seen, once again, as the vulnerable victims of sexualized violence at the hands of men of color.

To unpack such stories, one must consider the complex histories of gendered racialization that inflect them. In particular, I argue in this chapter, the representations of refugees are deeply circumscribed by the limits of conceptualizations of cohabitation. "Disappointment" is enabled by an imagination of refugee migrants as always belonging to a community elsewhere. Expectations of gratitude and of the "good refugee" as response to the host culture's hospitality are easily transformed into a relationship of exclusion. I use the term cohabitation here following Judith Butler, in turn following Hannah Arendt and Emmanuel Levinas. Butler suggests that we consider unchosen cohabitation as a "precondition of political life," given the need for

> institutions and policies that actively preserve and affirm the nonchosen character of openended and plural cohabitation. Not only do we live with those we never chose and with whom we may feel no immediate sense of social belonging, but we are also obligated to preserve those lives and the open-ended plurality that is the global population.
>
> *(Butler, 2012, p. 144)*

These remarks foreground complex questions: What defines cohabitation after the admission of refugees and the securing of basic physical needs? What forms of cohabitation could challenge ongoing racism and Islamophobia in Europe? How do we ensure that we imagine cohabitation as a "living with" rather than a relationship of "hosting" or "welcoming"? And, particularly relevant to this collection: How do the ways that we write about refugees impact the possibilities for imagining recent immigrants as part of the communities in which they now live, as participants in creating new futures for these communities?

As a cultural studies scholar, I often draw on news media as a primary source for considering how racism is produced, circulated, and challenged in contemporary Germany. I consider the role of power in representation, how the production and circulation of meaning (and, therefore, knowledge) both produce and are impacted by dynamics of power. Specifically, this chapter addresses how power dynamics are replicated through imagination of who can and can't be seen as cohabitants of Europe. The conceptual questions both journalists and researchers pose to inform their writing, the words they choose, the topics they emphasize, the tone they employ—all of these have an impact on what worlds the reader imagines as possible. These questions matter greatly to journalistic representation of refugees in news, as well as to academic representation in research. Journalism and academic research intersect here in their power to produce knowledge, and the ethical imperatives that derive from that power. Indeed, a primary difficulty in contemporary German news coverage of refugees is the inability to consider refugee participation in the local and national communities. Butler recently told an interviewer for the German weekly *Die Zeit* (Butler & Hark, 2017) that the idea of hospitality requires a consideration of the "we" of any country and the question of cohabitation, of the implications of a radical plurality. Instead of trying to adapt migrant to German culture as it is, she called on Germans to go beyond hospitality in order to consider Germany as a multi-national, multi-racial country that serves as home to many kinds of religions.

The role of the German news media in contributing to, challenging, and inter-rupting racialized understandings of cohabitation is complex. Many of the themes I discuss in this chapter have been extensively covered in long, complex reports, commentaries, and interviews that carefully and critically engage the intersections between racism, Islamophobia, sexuality, and gender. If cohabitation serves to mark the limits of hospitality, gestures to cohabitation are not wholly absent from the German news media either. At various moments, stories have sought to imagine a "miteinander, nicht nebeneinander, leben"—living with one another, not next to one another ("Araber im Allgäu," 2016; "Willkommen in Deutschland," 2015). How to think about shared communities that include refugees as active participants in the community and civic society became particularly difficult in stories reporting on gender and sexualized violence. Here, I consider how these issues emerge regard-ing the representation of gender and Islam vis-à-vis refugees; representation of the rights of GLBTQI persons as refugees and their experience of violence; and the understanding of Europe that is sometimes raised as an antidote to anti-refugee sentiment, particularly on the radical right.

Gender, Islam, race, and refugees

News media representations of refugees remain embedded in an ongoing associa-tion of Islam with gender violence (Shooman, 2014; Weber, 2013; Yıldız, 2009). Certainly, not all refugees are Muslim, but a complex slippage leads to a near-equation in the public imagination of contemporary refugees with Islam. German news media for decades linked Islam to an inevitable violence against women. Because Islam and gender justice were seen as incompatible, women of Muslim heritage rarely gained press attention unless they seemed to reject a role for Islam in German public society. This tendency changed slowly in the 2000s as more jour-nalists of Muslim heritage gained a voice in mainstream newspapers. For example, in the early 1990s, when Germany's headscarf debates first began, nearly all news media representations of Muslim women wearing headscarves portrayed Muslim women as victims of a religious violence that was inherently linked to sexualized and familial violence, a violence that belonged to a space elsewhere. Yet, the head-scarf debates themselves became a long and transformative intervention into the public sphere[1] that ultimately enabled a diversified set of voices to emerge, includ-ing Muslim women who viewed themselves as participating in German democracy (Weber, 2013, pp. 77–112, 2015).[2]

Nevertheless, these old tropes were again mobilized in the service of racialized anti-immigrant sentiment (Boulila & Carri, 2017; Weber, 2016b), as the news cov-erage of the sexualized violence in Cologne on New Year's Eve 2015 demonstrates.

Two images in the German press demonstrate how this violence played into racialized fears of the Muslim Other, and reattached those fears to contemporary refugees. The most widely circulated image, from the cover image of the magazine *Focus*, showed black handprints on the body of a nude blonde woman with light skin. Despite widespread criticism in social media and in other print media, the *Focus* editor defended the cover image by saying that "we have represented what unfortunately happened" (Álvarez, 2016).[3] A second image appeared in the *Süddeutsche Zeitung* of January 9–10, 2016 to promote the special section on the Cologne violence. In this cartoon-like illustration a black hand reaches up between the legs of a white woman's body. The *Süddeutsche Zeitung* posted a brief apology on Facebook, but the image remained online.

The stark messages presented in both the photograph-like *Focus* image and the *Süddeutsche Zeitung* illustration rely on a particularly pointed gendered discourse of racial difference that has generally become taboo, and rarely emerges in such explicit ways. This moment was striking, however, as these tropes of the radical right moved into centrist discourses, although not without great controversy and tremendous criticism. At times, the violence of Cologne was seen as an example of Islamist terror (Boulila & Carri, 2017), although some journalists emphasized that violence against women is not a Muslim import, and that we must think of the complex intersections of racism and sexism (Beitzer, 2016).

In the parliamentary debate that occurred to discuss the violence of New Year's Eve, representatives across the political spectrum highlighted the importance of police protection of public safety (for women) but were completely silent about the history of racism inherent in public surveillance and police action in Germany (Weber, 2016a). Greens politician Katrin Göring, for example, was proud that provinces governed by coalitions including the Greens had additional police available on New Year's Eve. One Center-right CSU representative declared: "Germany is a state of right and security. This is also the reason why Germany is viewed so positively in the world." Another Center-right CDU representative called for a renewed focus on police work. Furthermore, long rejected reforms to rape law suddenly received tremendous attention and support, as much sexualized violence, particularly groping, reported in Cologne was difficult to prosecute under German law at the time, which required demonstration of physical resistance on the part of the victim (Boulila & Carri, 2017; Weber, 2016a). Further, the lower house of the German parliament passed a law declaring Tunisia, Morocco, and Algeria "safe countries of origin." This declaration became a *de facto* if not *de jure* prohibition of asylum claims from those countries. The upper house struck down this law the following year (further see Weber, 2016a).

My point here is not to downplay the importance of avenues of prosecution for all forms of sexualized violence, but rather to highlight what this suggests about considering recent immigrants to Germany as part of German local and national communities. When the response to sexualized violence is immediately linked to questions of police presence, countries of origin, and calls for increased surveillance, the violence is rendered a problem that derives from *outside* of Europe, an imported violence. This obscures the reality of ongoing gender violence in Europe today, and the ways in which European culture might contribute to such violence.

The violence in Cologne has also sparked intense debates about the intersections of feminism and anti-racist activism. In mainstream news media, a particularly pointed example took place in the pages of the centrist weekly newspaper *Die Zeit*. The liberal feminist magazine *EMMA* published a 2017 dossier on "thought prohibitions and psycho-terror" that suggested that anti-racist feminists, who had called for a recognition of Islamophobia in responses to Cologne, were simply distracting from the sexism of Muslim immigrants (a frequent position taken by *EMMA* and its founder, Alice Schwarzer). Butler and Sabine Hark jointly wrote a response published in the centrist weekly *Die Zeit* pointing out the need for a politics that was both anti-racist and feminist, that would work towards cohabitation across difference without dismissing such difference, and that would not appropriate racist and Islamophobic discourses (Butler & Hark, 2017). Schwarzer (2017) responded, also in *Die Zeit*, by claiming that the violence of Cologne was a form of "jihadism from below," referring to the perpetrators as "Muslim refugees and illegals." Schwarzer, besides frequently mischaracterizing Butler's work and Butler and Hark's article, simply dismisses refugees as those from a sexist, Muslim elsewhere. The dehumanizing term "illegals" renders their distance from German society a defining characteristic of their existence.

The news coverage of two murders of women students, Maria L. and Carolin G.,[4] further demonstrates the difficulty of imagining refugees as part of the here and now in complex ways. These cases provide a particularly interesting contrast, because as two rape-murder cases in and near the city of Freiburg, they initially were linked in the public imagination, if not in the police investigations themselves. Carolin G. was kidnapped, raped, and murdered in November 2016 while jogging near Freiburg. The arrested suspect is a Romanian national, a truck driver also suspected in a similar murder in Austria. Maria L. was raped and left to drown in a river in Freiburg in October 2016. A refugee who was initially thought to be an "unaccompanied minor" from Afghanistan, who has admitted to being nearly 20, but who is thought by many to be 22, has given a full confession and is being tried for the murder at the time of this writing.

The differing tone and extent of the coverage of the murderers is notable. While both have received extensive coverage, it is the murder at the hands of a refugee that has been designated a "trauma for Freiburg" ("Prozess im Fall Maria L.: Freiburg hofft," 2017), and sparked national debate about important social questions. Although both investigations led to the arrest of suspects, both of whom have confessed to the murders, the investigation into Carolin G.'s murder was deemed a victory for forensics (Crolly, 2017), while the investigation of Maria L.'s death was said to demonstrate the problems created by limited access to EU databases as well as problems with the asylum process (*Die Welt*, 2016; Bewarder, 2016b). A particularly obvious example appeared in the center-right daily newspaper *Die Welt*, which highlighted how Bavaria's Minister of Finance, Regional Development and Home Affairs, connected the events of Cologne with the murder of Maria L.:

> For the Minister of Finance and Heimat Markus Söder (CSU), these are symptoms of a development that requires a rapid response. 'When citizens no longer dare to visit neighbourhoods, then the state has lost his authority,' he said to *Die Welt*. The CSU politician called upon the CDU and his own party to show a clear position: 'Now, it is about protection of the homeland;' this is an existential point for the party. 'The State must act significantly more decisively than in the past. We lost control over our borders in the last year. Now we are beginning to lose control over streets and plazas.'
>
> *(Issig, 2016)*

In such representations, the violence of Cologne and the murder of Maria L. are inextricably linked, and simultaneously detached from the murder of Carolin G. The coverage of the murder of Maria L., in other words, drew on and referred to the larger public fear of refugees as promoters of violence. Coverage of Carolin G. emphasized aspects that suggested overall European progress and safety. This association of Cologne with the murder of Maria L. suggests a conception of violence against women as primarily a problem from outside of Europe, perpetrated by non-Europeans. For example, a story in the *Süddeutsche Zeitung* suggests that the murder will "be part of the history of refugee politics, like the sexual attacks on New Year's Eve at the Cologne train station," and demonstrates the failure of European refugee politics as well as a failure of authorities to accurately use European wide crime data (Bewarder, 2016a, 2016b; Kelnberger & Szymanski, 2016; Lohse & Soldt, 2016). These stories presented gender violence perpetrated by a refugee as an extra-European problem that can be resolved by tightening borders, increasing police presence, reducing privacy protections, and deporting refugees. In contrast, gender violence perpetrated within Europe by Europeans is depicted as a unique problem, a singular instance, that is solved in a "moment of glory" and "spectacular success" for forensic science (Crolly, 2017). These issues are not about what journalists personally believe, but rather, what ideas are often reinforced in the way that a story is covered. With Carolin G., the news coverage did not raise the specter of "larger social problems," as it did with Maria L. Indeed, the tendency to think about violence against women as inherent to cultures outside of Europe, but unusual or exceptional in European cultures, occurs even in stories that attempt to engage carefully and sympathetically with the history of a perpetrator. One story, for example, seeks to consider Hussein K.'s psychological history, and whether there was a failure to care for him when he arrived in Germany (Soldt, 2016). Yet even here, disturbance is the theme: "this doesn't fit in our Freiburg."

Some important alternatives exist, however. For example, an online-only story at the website of the weekly news magazine *Der Spiegel* criticized the absence of a discussion of gender violence and its pervasiveness in Europe (Ruf, 2016). The sensationalist tabloid *Bild* published a brief story poignantly describing a meeting of refugees to mourn Maria L., who had been an active volunteer in local refugee organizations ("Mord an Studentin in Freiburg," 2016). These two stories noted the ways in which the death, as well as the family's life and politics had been appropriated for right-wing discourses of anti-refugee sentiment—Maria L. volunteered with a refugee group, and her father was known for advocating pro-refugee policies. The *Bild* article included an inset box that contextualized the murder in the larger issues of sexualized violence and murder; it noted that most perpetrators are German, many refugee groups have rates of criminality actually lower than those of German citizens, and that people of immigrant heritage are no more likely to commit crimes than those who are not. The *Spiegel online* reporter interviewed refugees and German residents in Freiburg who criticized the national, local, and online discussions of Maria L's death. In both cases, the journalists embedded refugees in the context in Freiburg, and sexualized violence in Europe.

The 2017 case of Yasmina T. further demonstrates these issues. Raped and murdered in Düsseldorf by a plumber working in her building, her story barely made a ripple in national press. Local coverage, which was more extensive, sometimes identified her as a Moroccan German student killed by a German man, a father of three who confessed to the murder ("Tat in Düsseldorf," 2017). In the few stories that appeared in national newspapers, Yasmina T. was not given a name, nor was she identified as of Moroccan heritage. Instead, these stories focused on the fact that the autopsy had not noticed that she had been raped and strangled (*Die Welt*, 2017; *sueddeutsche.de*, 2017); the fact that her death resulted from murder only came to light when DNA found at the scene proved a match to a man who had been accused but not prosecuted in two prior sexual crimes.

Here, then, a murder similar to the Freiburg murders perpetrated by a German man against a woman of North African heritage provoked no questions of national problems, policy, or even interest. Instead, Yasmina T.'s case almost disappeared from the national stage altogether. The few national stories depersonalized her and emphasized the forensic issues. Nobody responded to her case or to Carolin G.'s, to demand a larger discussion about sexualized violence committed by European men. In contrast, Maria L.'s murder was mobilized for anti-refugee and Islamophobic sentiment. These differences in media coverage rely on an understanding of refugees as always already outside the national community. Only this "outsideness" of the perpetrator makes the case of Maria L. relevant to national debates.

Representing GLBTQI refugees

Just as with questions of gender violence, discussions of violence against GLBTQI people often become moments that challenge the otherwise increasingly nuanced representation of Islam and Muslims. Returning to the debate between Schwarzer and Butler discussed above, Schwarzer had mischaracterized Butler's rejection of the 2010 Christopher Street Day (CSD) award for Civil Courage in Berlin by connecting it to what Schwarzer regards as the inherent homophobia of Muslim refugees: According to Schwarzer, Butler rejected the prize because the CSD "dared to thematise the homophobia in the Arab and Turkish community" (Schwarzer, 2017). However, Butler had turned down the award after meeting with several representatives of activist groups serving GLBTQI people of color in Berlin. Those representatives discussed how white gay groups in Berlin excluded them from participation, while people of color and Muslims were stigmatized as the source of homophobia in Berlin. One of the organizations Butler mentioned, SUSPECT, a group of queer and trans migrants of color as well as allies, characterizes their standpoint as the outcome of a long history of gay white politics targeting rather than creating alliances with people of color: SUSPECT suggests that Butler's rejection of the prize serves as a critique of "the tendency of white gay politics to replace a politics of solidarity, coalitions and radical transformation with one of criminalization, militarization and border enforcement" (SUSPECT, 2010).

Schwarzer's mischaracterization of Butler's writings set up a binary in which there is no space for specifically addressing GLBTQI people of color or anti-racist activists as part of the German community. She repeats the trope that has many affinities with the perspective on the West and feminism as the civilized saviors of Muslim women. As Fatima El-Tayeb summarizes:

> Within this binary discursive formation, the Western LGBT community has the role of civiliser, while queer Muslims have nothing to offer, as they, like all Muslims, are products of a culture that is fundamentally inferior to the secular West. This dichotomy puts all nonwhite, non-Western queers in a similar predicament: communities of colour appear as by default homophobic and heterosexual, the queer community as by default white, reflecting a global discourse of progress and human rights in which the white West invariably takes the lead, maybe not always progressively enough, but certainly always more so than anyone else.
>
> *(El-Tayeb, 2011, p. 120)*

This binary has the additional effect of representing queer Muslims and queers of color as inevitably from elsewhere, producing a "spatiotemporal regime of knowledge management" that suggests an inevitable incompatibility with the time and place in which they live (El-Tayeb, 2013, p. 308). Indeed, such binaries cover up the existence of queer refugees, other than as victims of violence at the hands of other refugees. As Jin Haritaworn et al. note in discussing gay imperialism, the mud that certain white gay and lesbian groups "sling onto Muslim communities lands on queer Muslims themselves" (Haritaworn, Tamsila, & Erdem, 2008, p. 83).

Mainstream news media have certainly been critical of the most egregious violations of GLBTQI rights, including those that rely on a binary of a queer-friendly Europe and a homophobic Muslim world. For example, journalists provoked an outcry against the Federal Office of Migration and Refugees (BAMF) for asking invasive questions of asylum seekers. In July 2017, the *Die Zeit* revealed some questions asked of a Pakistani refugee: "How often did you have sexual intercourse with your boyfriend? How did you experience sex?" (Kastner, 2017); many other outlets picked up the story and framed it with headlines suggesting a critical stance vis-à-vis the BAMF.[5]

More frequently, however, stories describe violence against GLBTQI people in asylum homes, often linking this violence to criminality among refugees, which is alleged to be higher than that of the overall population. Many such stories suggest that refugees arrive in Germany only to find that they are subject to the same homophobic violence that they experienced before leaving for Germany. Indeed, the experiences of homophobic violence in the context of refugee homes must be addressed. However, the framing of such violence has varying implications for and imagination of cohabitation.[6] For example, a story published in the center-left Berlin daily *Der Tagesspiegel* suggests that violence within asylum homes leads to rising fears of refugees in Germany, proposing that the truth that is "felt" is even worse than one might imagine from the statistics on criminality. The report describes this "felt truth" as:

> The impressions that many citizens have when they see refugees that deal drugs, that are aggressive, that sexually harass them or come on to them, when they see that refugees steal or assault. A feeling of latent threat by refugees emerges. A dangerous mood, because suddenly even respectable [unbescholtene] people come under suspicion.
>
> *(Bachner, 2017)*

In addressing violence specifically targeting "homosexuals," the report suggests that refugees are both "perpetrators and victims." In this framing, refugees, including queer refugees, remain both excluded from the society in which they live and denied agency as actors against oppression. They are either perpetrators or victims. Indeed, they become part of a formation perceived to create a sense of existential threat among the German population.

An alternative way of depicting violence against GLBTQI people in refugee spaces is provided by a conservative national daily: The *Die Welt* journalist here seeks instead to locate homophobic violence by refugees against refugees in Germany's larger homophobic contexts. The reporter, having interviewed customers in a gay bar, points out that homophobic sentiment arises in a variety of contexts, including the radical right political movement Pegida (Rohrmeier, 2015). The reporter mentioned Lara Liqueur a bisexual drag queen, DJ and programmer who once ran for mayor of Dresden: "During the aggressive campaign of [Pegida candidate Tatjana] Festerling, Lara Liqueur no longer took the public tram. 'I was afraid.' Not of verbal attacks—of physical ones. The mood in Dresden can heat up quickly." But three gay Muslim refugees live under their real names, freely move around, and apparently did not notice problems, telling the reporter, "We've never heard of homophobia here" (Rohrmeier, 2015).

Rohrmeier here implicitly problematizes a triumphant narrative of arrival in queer-friendly Germany, suggesting that although gay refugees find themselves under reduced threat and able to be gay more openly, they are moving in a society in which homophobia has reemerged quite explicitly: particularly in the right wing political group Pegida, which is pro-traditional family, yet also has gay members who appropriate violence against GLBTQI refugees for their own anti-Islam agenda. Rohrmeier quotes an activist: "Now the conservatives are suddenly completely concerned about homosexuals." This piece comes from a perspective that considers refugee experience *in Germany*. If only briefly, it points to a complex landscape of homophobia and queer friendliness, and simultaneously depicting refugees as participants in the here and now of Germany.

Sarah Levy also considered refugees carefully as part of contemporary German communities, in a story highlighting refugee voices that originally appeared in the Hamburg edition of the centrist news weekly *Die Zeit*, with excerpts later distributed in *Die Zeit online*. For example, a gay refugee referred to as Zain relates the experiences of silence and societal exclusion for gay men in Syria. "I experienced for the first time in Hamburg, what it means to be free. I found myself. Now I can begin my life" (Levy, 2016). Zain decouples Islam from homophobia (a move similar to one made by many Muslim women in the previous decades who sought to distinguish Islam from "tradition" as the source of violence against women), arguing instead that homophobia results not from religion, but from "conviction, culture and tradition." For Zain, marching in the upcoming Christopher Street Day Parade will be the first time "I openly show myself as a gay man." Levy's story, like many others that allow refugees to tell their own story, notably recognizes Zain as a man who is embedded in a local community: working as a translator, organizing other queer refugees who need help with finding their way in a new place. Without denying the complex experiences of GLBTQI refugees, who have faced significant discrimination in their countries of origin as well as within refugee communities in Germany, Zain's story is told from a perspective that considers him as somebody living in Germany. In particular, marching in the CSD parade with other gay refugees is not only a moment of public action, but also a participation in both local (Hamburg) and national (as CSD is celebrated in cities throughout Germany) queer politics and visibility as well.

Although much journalism replicates perspectives that exclude refugees from German communities, some stories allow refugee voices to point to active community participation. Yet even these stories put a fairly heavy emphasis on narratives of happy arrival, while ignoring the significant barriers facing queer refugees in Germany. Again, surveillance and increased police presence rarely serve the interests of GLBTQI people of color (SUSPECT, 2010). Indeed, the UN has repeatedly noted the problems with police profiling in Germany (Committee for the Elimination of Racial Discrimination, 2015). The government has refused to address this problem, claiming instead that racial profiling is not illegal in Europe so long as the police also consider unnamed "other factors" in choosing whom to stop ("Rassismus in Deutschland," 2015). Haritaworn has examined how white gay organizations in Germany since the 1990s have particularly targeted immigrant populations as the source of homophobia, mobilizing calls for increased military and police surveillance that allow the police in particular to "reinvent themselves as protector, patron, and sponsor of minorities at the very moment that their targeting of racialised populations and areas is reaching new levels" (Haritaworn, 2010, p. 83).

The new right, refugees, sexism, and homophobia

The emergence of new radical right groups and parties, and their starkly anti-refugee positions, generate a complex set of considerations for interrogating news media representations, including journalistic representations. German journalists have carefully and persistently criticized the racism, sexism, and homophobia of right wing groups such as Pegida, and even of the recently formed right party, the Alternative for Germany (AFD). However, often such critical coverage of Pegida and the AfD relies on a false hope of a tradition of European values that must simply be restored. In Pegida and AFD coverage, a desire to look back to "alternative" European values to those of the right often limits the potential for understanding refugees as part of the here and now of German society. Stories critical of Pegida, for example, often emphasize a European tradition of humanism, the Enlightenment, or even Christianity that provides an alternative set of values in support of human rights; women's rights and GLBTQI rights are often considered as already achieved. Framing a critique of racism and anti-refugee sentiment in terms of recovery of the "proper" European values has some problematic ramifications for how refugees are understood in contemporary Germany.

A large body of scholarship within critical race studies and postcolonial studies has examined the simultaneous emergence of colonialism, notions of race, and conceptions of the liberal democratic subject, as well as their mutual constitution, and the ways in which these legacies contribute to the ongoing racialization of the human (Lowe, 2015; Piesche, 2005; Spivak, 2003; Weheliye, 2014; Wynter, 2003). In other words, ideas of universal human rights as well as universal human possibility have most often excluded large groups of people from supposedly "universal" definitions. As Lisa Lowe writes:

> [T]he uses of universalizing concepts of reason, civilization, and freedom effect colonial divisions of humanity, affirming liberty for modern man while subordinating the variously colonised and dispossessed peoples whose material labor and resources were the conditions of possibility for that liberty. . . . We see the longevity of the colonial divisions of humanity in our contemporary moment, in which the human life of citizens protected by the state is bound to the denigration of populations cast in violation of human life, set outside of human society.
>
> *(Lowe, 2015, p. 7)*

A simplistic return to the "correct" European values belies how the very idea of Europe and the tradition of Enlightenment also produced modern understandings of race that in turn created modern racisms, and also excluded women from universal rights. Immanuel Kant, for example, developed notions of "universal" education and progress that saw only white Europeans as capable of attaining such progress (Eze, 1995; Piesche, 2005). Instead, an ethical cohabitation requires an idea of Europe that must be constantly renegotiated and an understanding that new immigrants will contribute to this project, rather than imagining European values as a gift that might be granted to others in the name of welcome.

For example, during an interview, historian Heinrich August Winkler discusses Pegida as an anti-Western, anti-Enlightenment group that espouses the same values that have "led Germany into the catastrophe" of the past (Gloger & Poscher, 2015). Winkler urges recognition that Europe is held together by "Western values: human rights, the ideas of the just state, and the division of powers. As long as these values are not valid worldwide, this project remains incomplete" (Gloger & Poscher, 2015).

In the leftist Berlin daily *taz, die tageszeitung*, columnist, film and cultural critic Georg Seeßlen uses similar words but contextualizes them differently when he calls for a negotiation of democratic civil society against Pegida:

> Democratic civil society is the self-organization of people, who do not merely defensively turn against the right, but rather take up the project of Enlightenment, humanism and democratization that has been betrayed by normative democratic states, the neoliberal organization of market and the media.
>
> *(Seeßlen, 2017)*

Seeßlen's approach to claiming a project of civil democracy does not articulate it as a reclaiming of Europe, but rather, as a project in process. He thereby opens the possibility for new negotiations of what Europe can or should be, and the incorporation of the new residents of Europe into those negotiations.

Journalist Peter Unfried offers up another approach that explicitly criticizes the notions of European community that do not think about the history of European violence. Responding to the Charlie Hebdo attacks in the pages of *taz, die tageszeitung*, Unfried speaks of a "justified anger." The need to show this anger understandably leads, in Unfried's view, to the show of solidarity embodied in the phrase "I am Charlie." But the very "we" created by the notion of "I am Charlie" must be rethought here:

> But under the surface it is neither about religion nor about the suspension of the freedom of the press. If anybody can construct a 'we,' then it is those of us who are already within this we. They are those that are outside or are afraid of it. It is, therefore, about a global suspension of this inside and outside . . . the problem is, that Western values don't yield this.
>
> *(Unfried, 2015)*

Unfried implies a critique of the history of European values, rather than imagining a set of already existing, and already achieved, European values that can be called upon in the interest of protecting rights.

Conclusion: representations that open up possibilities for cohabitation

This somewhat schematic sketch of contemporary issues surrounding racism, sexism, and homophobia in contemporary representations of refugees in the German news media leads to a few points necessary in order to open up, or to leave open, conceptualization of refugees as part of the time and place in which they live—as community members, as makers of European futures, as potential allies against violence. First, locating the origins of sexist and homophobic violence solely or primarily in the country of origin obscures a complex picture; sexist and homophobic violence exist throughout the world. We ought to be able to create representations of experiences of homophobia and misogyny that validate refugee experience, recognize the existence of queer refugees, *and* recognize that activists against homophobic and sexist violence also exist in refugee communities. By the same token, those who write about refugees should be wary of easy binaries of the civilized West and the backwards other. Many refugees, with good reason, apply for asylum based on homophobic and gender-based discrimination in their previous country of residence. This does not legitimate a representational politics that excludes people from these countries from participation in contemporary German society, and ignores the work and activism of Muslim women and GLBTQI people and women and GLBTQI people of color. Furthermore, refugees arrive into a complex context in which certain rights may be protected, but homophobia, transphobia, sexism, racism, and Islamophobia continue to exist; where homosexuality in many ways has only recently been decriminalized; and where rape law until very recently required "active physical resistance" on the part of women. Ending gender violence, violence against GLBTQI people, and all forms of discrimination requires complex alliances and strategies to change cultures throughout European communities, not only among refugees. Representations that may allow the reader to think of those recent arrivals to a community as co-creators of the future will seek out input from and representations of those groups that are made up of feminists of color and GLBTQI people of color and their allies. Such representations may imagine and participate in the work toward a Europe-in-the-making, a Europe that struggles against racialized, sexualized, and gender violence as a shared project of cohabitation.

Notes

1 I use "public sphere" here in a Habermasian sense frequently used in communication and media studies, as an ideal space in which public opinion to influence the state can be formed through citizen participation in public debate, and in which news media play a key role (Habermas, 1974).
2 The more complex representations of Muslim Germans of immigrant heritage often took place in more conservative news outlets—one cannot easily line up discussions around Islamophobia along a left-right spectrum.
3 All translations into English from sources cited in German are my own.
4 Although the full names of these women are known, I follow the German press convention of using the last initial.

5 From 2006 to 2011 interview guidelines in the conservative state of Baden Württemberg notoriously asked Muslim applicants for residence permits questions about the acceptance of homosexuality. This practice was ultimately banned by the Federal Administrative Court.

6 Stories addressing these issues among refugees focus heavily on gay men, to a much lesser extent on lesbians. Discussions of other forms of non-normative sexualities or gender identities are virtually absent.

Bibliography

Álvarez, S. (2016, January 10). Wir bilden ab, was leider passiert ist. *Der Tagesspiegel*. Retrieved from www.tagesspiegel.de/medien/focus-chef-verteidigt-umstrittenes-cover-wir-bilden-ab-was-leider-passiert-ist/12810242.html

Araber im Allgäu. (2016, March 23). *ZDF*. Retrieved from www.zdf.de/uri/p12_beitrag_41380728

Bachner, F. (2017, May 3). Viele Straftaten bleiben wohl verborgen. *Der Tagesspiegel Online*. Retrieved from www.tagesspiegel.de/berlin/fluechtlinge-in-berlin-viele-straftaten-bleiben-wohl-verborgen/19745850.html

Bewarder, M. (2016a, December 4). Und die Vertreter der Willkommenskultur schweigen. *Die Welt*. Retrieved from www.welt.de/politik/deutschland/article159975211/Und-die-Vertreter-der-Willkommenskultur-schweigen.html

Bewarder, M. (2016b, December 15). Freiburger Mordfall Maria L.: Fatale Systemlücke im Fall Hussein K. *Die Welt*, sec. Deutschland. Retrieved from www.welt.de/politik/deutschland/article160335828/Europas-fatale-Systemluecke-im-Fall-Hussein-K.html

Boulila, S. C., & Carri, C. (2017, August). On Cologne: Gender, migration and unacknowledged racisms in Germany. *European Journal of Women's Studies, 24*(3), 286–293. doi:10.1177/1350506817712447

Butler, J. (2012). Precarious life, vulnerability, and the ethics of cohabitation. *The Journal of Speculative Philosophy, 26*(2), 134–151. doi:10.5325/jspecphil.26.2.0134

Butler, J., & Hark, S. (2017, August 3). Gender-studies: Die Verleumdung. *Die Zeit*, sec. Kultur. Retrieved from www.zeit.de/2017/32/gender-studies-feminismus-emma-beissreflex

Committee for the Elimination of Racial Discrimination. (2015). *International convention on the elimination of all forms of racial discrimination: Concluding observations on the combined nineteenth to twenty-second periodic reports of Germany*. CERD /C/ DEU /CO / 19–22. United Nations. Retrieved from https://documents-dds-ny.un.org/doc/UNDOC/GEN/G15/139/15/PDF/G1513915.pdf?OpenElement

Crolly, H. (2017, June 4). Mord an Carolin G.: Spur 4334 Und Eine Sternstunde Der Kriminalistik. *Die Welt*. Retrieved from www.welt.de/vermischtes/article165231684/Spur-4334-und-eine-Sternstunde-der-Kriminalistik.html

Die Welt. (2016, December 16). Mord an Maria L.: Daten von Hussein K. Waren in EU-System Gespeichert. Retrieved from www.welt.de/politik/deutschland/article160342160/Daten-von-Hussein-K-waren-in-EU-System-gespeichert.html

Die Welt. (2017, July 17). Mord blieb fast unentdeckt: Klempner tötet junge Düsseldorferin nach Arbeitseinsatz. Retrieved from www.welt.de/vermischtes/article166742369/Klempner-toetet-junge-Duesseldorferin-nach-Arbeitseinsatz.html

El-Tayeb, F. (2011). *European others: Queering ethnicity in postnational Europe*. Minneapolis, MN: University of Minnesota Press.

El-Tayeb, F. (2013). Time travelers and queer heterotopias: Narratives from the Muslim underground. *The Germanic Review: Literature, Culture, Theory, 88*(3), 305–319. doi:10.1080/00168890.2013.820637

Eze, E. C. (1995). The color of reason: The idea of "race" in Kant's anthropology. *The Bucknell Review, 38*(2), 200.

Gloger, K., & Poscher, U. (2015, January 29). Die Zeit des Kuschelns ist vorbei. *Stern.* Retrieved from www-lexisnexis-com

Habermas, J. (1974). The public sphere: An encyclopedia article (1964). *New German Critique, 3*, 49–55.

Haritaworn, J. (2010). Queer injuries: The racial politics of "homophobic hate crime" in Germany. *Social Justice, 37*(1 (119)), 69–89.

Haritaworn, J., Tamsila, T., & Erdem, E. (2008). Gay imperialism: Gender and sexuality discourse in the "War on Terror." In A. Kuntsman & E. Miyake (Eds.), *Out of place: Interrogating silences in queerness/raciality* (pp. 71–95). Ann Arbor, MI: University of Michigan Press.

Issig, P. (2016, December 15). Söder über sexuelle Gewalt "Unsere Frauen und Töchter bekommen Angst." *Die Welt,* sec. Deutschland. Retrieved from www.welt.de/politik/deutschland/article160313627/Unsere-Frauen-und-Toechter-bekommen-Angst.html

Kastner, B. (2017, July 10). Peinliche Fragen an homosexuelle Asylbewerber. *sueddeutsche. de,* sec. politik. Retrieved from www.sueddeutsche.de/politik/vorwurf-der-diskriminierung-peinliche-fragen-an-homosexuelle-asylbewerber-1.3580316

Kelnberger, J., & Szymanski, M. (2016). Mord in Freiburg: "Die Daten waren allen europäischen Sicherheitsbehörden zugänglich." *sueddeutsche.de,* 2016, sec. politik. Retrieved from www.sueddeutsche.de/politik/freiburg-symbol-des-versagens-1.3296615

Lohse, E., & Soldt, R. (2016, December 14). Identität von Flüchtlingen: Durch alle Raster gefallen. *FAZ.NET,* sec. Gesellschaft. Retrieved from www.faz.net/1.4574596

Levy, S. (2016, August 4). Homosexuelle Flüchtlinge: Endlich nicht mehr schweigen. *Die Zeit,* sec. Hamburg. Retrieved from www.zeit.de/hamburg/stadtleben/2016-08/homosexuelle-fluechtlinge-hamburg-homosexualitaet-syrien-christopher-street-day/komplettansicht

Lowe, L. (2015). *The intimacies of four continents.* Durham, NC: Duke University Press Books.

Mord an Studentin in Freiburg—Flüchtlinge trauern um Maria. (2016, December 9). *bild. de.* Retrieved from www.bild.de/news/inland/mord/fall-maria-fluechtlinge-trauern-49243030.bild.html

Piesche, P. (2005). Der ›Fortschritt‹ der Aufklärung—Kants ›Race‹ und die Zentrierung des weißen Subjekts. In M. M. Eggers, S. Arndt, G. Kilomba, & P. Piesche (Eds.), *Mythen, Masken und Subjekte: kritische Weissseinsforschung in Deutschland* (pp. 14–17). Münster: Unrast.

Prozess im Fall Maria L.: Freiburg hofft, Trauma zu überwinden. (2017, September 5). *stern. de.* Retrieved from www.stern.de/7606910.html

Rassismus in Deutschland vor dem Ausschuss der Vereinten Nationen. Antwort der Bundesregierung auf die Kleine Anfrage der Abgeordneten Sevim Dağdelen, Wolfgang Gehrcke, Jan Korte, weiterer Abgeordneter und der Fraktion DIE LINKE.—Drucksache 18/5199. (2015, July 2). *Deutscher Bundestag.* Retrieved from http://dip21.bundestag.de/dip21/btd/18/054/1805435.pdf

Richter, K. (2016, April 1). Germany's refugee crisis has left it as bitterly divided as Donald Trump's America. *The Guardian,* sec. Opinion. Retrieved from www.theguardian.com/commentisfree/2016/apr/01/germany-refugee-crisis-invited-into-my-home-welcoming-spirit-divided

Rohrmeier, S. (2015, October 18). Dresden: Schwule Flüchtlinge von Moslems Drangsaliert. *DIE WELT.* Retrieved from www.welt.de/politik/deutschland/article147722602/Schwule-Fluechtlinge-von-Moslems-gepeinigt.html

Ruf, C. (2016, December 6). Getötete Studentin in Freiburg: Das Ringen um Besonnenheit. *Spiegel Online,* sec. Panorama. Retrieved from www.spiegel.de/panorama/gesellschaft/freiburg-nach-mord-an-studentin-wie-die-stadt-auf-rechte-hetze-reagiert-a-1124684.html

Schwarzer, A. (2017, August 11). Gender-studies: Der Rufmord. *Die Zeit*, sec. Kultur. Retrieved from www.zeit.de/2017/33/gender-studies-judith-butler-emma-rassismus/komplettansicht

Seeßlen, G. (2017, August 16). Das Rechte Gegen Rechts; Schlagloch von Georg Seeßlen. Zauberwort Und Hoffnungsschimmer: Die Demokratische Zivilgesellschaft. *taz, die tageszeitung*, sec. Meinung und Diskussion.

Shooman, Y. (2014). *". . . weil ihre Kultur so ist": Narrative des antimuslimischen Rassismus*. Bielefeld: Transcript.

Soldt, R. (2016, December 11). *Freiburger Mordfall Maria L.: Das alles passt nicht zu unserem*. Freiburg. FAZ.NET, sec. Gesellschaft. Retrieved from www.faz.net/1.4568422

Spivak, G. C. (2003). Righting wrongs. In N. Owen (Ed.), *Human rights, human wrongs: The Oxford amnesty lectures, 2001* (pp. 164–227). Oxford: Oxford University Press.

sueddeutsche.de. (2017, July 18). Sexualmord beinahe übersehen—Klempner gesteht. sec. *panorama*. Retrieved from www.sueddeutsche.de/panorama/duesseldorf-sexualmord-beinahe-uebersehen-klempner-gesteht-1.3592808

SUSPECT. (2010, June 20). Judith Butler turns down civil courage award from Berlin pride: "I Must Distance Myself from This Racist Complicity." *MR Online*. Retrieved from https://mronline.org/2010/06/20/judith-butler-turns-down-civil-courage-award-from-berlin-pride-i-must-distance-myself-from-this-racist-complicity/

Tat in Düsseldorf: Familienvater gesteht Sexualmord an 25-Jähriger. (2017, July 17). *RP Online*. Retrieved from www.rp-online.de/nrw/staedte/duesseldorf/mordfall-in-dues seldorf-flingern-35-jaehriger-toetete-nach-vergewaltigung-aid-1.6954102

Unfried, P. (2015, January 12). Agenten Des Paranoiawachstums; Nach dem Mordan-schlag auf die Redaktion der Satirezeitschrift "Charlie Hebdo" in Paris: Helfen "West-liche Werte"? DIE EINE FRAGE. *Taz, Die Tageszeitung*. Retrieved from www.taz.de/!5024262

von H. Beitzer, A. (2016, January 6). Sexuelle Gewalt: Über Köln sprechen—Ohne Ras-sismus. *sueddeutsche.de*, sec. Panorama. Retrieved from www.sueddeutsche.de/panorama/uebergriffe-in-koeln-ueber-sexuelle-gewalt-sprechen-ohne-rassismus-1.2806434

Weber, B. (2013). *Violence and gender in the "New" Europe*. New York, NY: Palgrave Macmillan.

Weber, B. (2015). Islam, feminism, and agency in Germany today. In H. Ahmed-Ghosh (Ed.), *Contesting feminisms: Gender and Islam in Asia* (pp. 251–269). Albany, NY: Suny Press.

Weber, B. (2016a). The German refugee "Crisis" after Cologne: The race of refugee rights. *English Language Notes, 54*(2), 77–92.

Weber, B. (2016b). "We Must Talk about Cologne": Race, gender, and reconfigurations of "Europe." *German Politics and Society, 34*(4), 68–86. doi:10.3167/gps.2016.340405

Weheliye, A. G. (2014). *Habeas Viscus: Racializing assemblages, biopolitics, and black feminist theo-ries of the human*. Durham, NC: Duke University Press.

Willkommen in Deutschland. Ein Dorf und seine Flüchtlinge. (2015, March 10). *ZDF*. Retrieved from www.zdf.de/uri/p12_beitrag_37324194

Wynter, S. (2003). Unsettling the coloniality of being/power/truth/freedom: Towards the human, after man, its overrepresentation—An argument. *CR: The New Centennial Review, 3*(3), 257–337. doi:10.1353/ncr.2004.0015

Yıldız, Y. (2009). Turkish girls, Allah's daughters, and the contemporary German subject: Itinerary of a figure. *German Life and Letters, 62*(4), 465–481.

15

BLACK LIVES MATTER AND THE RISE OF WOMANIST NEWS NARRATIVES

Allissa V. Richardson

As a frontline demonstrator in August 2014 during what came to be known as the Ferguson protests, Brittany Ferrell recalled the unimaginable sting in her lungs and nose as she gasped for air. "I felt like I didn't know if I would make it home that night," she said in a February 2017 interview. She added, "There was the police that were shooting rubber and wooden bullets at protestors. There were gunshots. There were dogs. There was fire . . . and it was like we knew it and we still went out, night after night after night."

Ferrell also protested by day. With her bullhorn in hand, she appears in one documentary film, teetering precariously in the rear flatbed of a pickup truck. An unnamed man helps her catch her balance. The image creates a new visual rhetoric for black protest. Whereas the photographic grammar of the twentieth-century Civil Rights Movement relied heavily upon black women, wearing dresses and white gloves, behind charismatic male leaders (Gillespie & Clinton, 1998; Hickey, 2013), the Black Lives Matter Movement has placed women at the forefront, with men literally supporting them. This is no accident. The women leaders of BLM interviewed for this study described being intentional—and, at times, shrewd—about managing their core messages, their affiliations with particular organizations within the broad Movement, and the legacies that they create with every Tweet. They are keenly aware of the relative obscurity of their forebearers as black women activists. Hence, they launch and lead their own groups. This study focused on four black women founders of three leading organizations that comprised the early Black Lives Matter Movement of 2014: Brittany Ferrell, Alicia Garza, Brittany Packnett, and Marissa Johnson. I also included Ieshia Evans—a high-profile, anti-police brutality activist who preferred to identify as an "independent protestor," rather than align with an organization within the Movement.

Having contacted all five via Twitter to request hour-long semi-structured interviews, I interviewed one person, on-camera, after she hosted a Black Lives

Matter rally at a US mid-Atlantic university. Four participants consented to recorded Skype or FaceTime interviews. I integrated two established philosophies for my interview map: phenomenology and the functional approach to narrative analysis (Bruner, 1991). Phenomenology focuses on the lived experiences of the study's subjects by evaluating a subject's: (1) intentionality, (2) intuition, (3) empathy, and (4) intersubjectivity (Husserl, 1970). Here this meant focusing on (1) the black woman activist's stated purpose for producing protest journalism; (2) whether or not she intuits her bearing witness as an act of protest; (3) how she views her body in relation to the world (for example, whether she sees herself in the body of a dead black woman who has been gunned down by police); and (4) how she believes her reportage impacts the broader Black Lives Matter Movement. Phenomenology allowed me to identify common threads in how this cohort of black feminist activists *see* themselves and *situate* themselves as protest journalists who have political agency and unprecedented media visibility.

I coded my interviews using Jerome Bruner's functional approach to narrative analysis. Bruner proposed that people chiefly use narratives to construct their realities and make meanings of events. For instance, although the initial claim that Michael Brown had his hands up and screamed, "Don't shoot!" just before a white police officer killed him, proved to be untrue (Capeheart, 2015; Lee, 2015), that narrative arguably compelled people to join the protest in Ferguson in 2014. Online photo memes of African American NFL football players (NBC Staff, 2014), college students (*Clutch* Staff, 2014), Congresspersons (Larson, 2014), and even media personalities (Marsh, 2015)—all with their hands up in the air— went viral. An eponymous organization, Hands Up United, sprang up (see www. handsupunited.org). Some narratives continued to stick, even if they were not true, because people needed to shape chaotic events into a coherent story that made it easier to process. For this reason, "[The] domain that must be widely (though roughly) shared for a culture to operate with requisite effectiveness is the domain of social beliefs and procedures—what we think people are like and how they must get on with each other" (Bruner, 1991, p. 21). Part of probing a black feminist activist's lived experience, then, involved examining her perceived status in the world, within the Movement, and within the context of her relationship to others, such as black male activists and white feminists. I looked for these themes when I analyzed the data. I listened to how they made sense of police brutality and other acts of anti-black racism for themselves (and for others) by telling stories online too.

I used MaxQDA, to code 73 segments within the five interviews. The top five narrative themes include: (1) distrust of legacy media, with 13 coded segments; (2) private and state-sponsored intimidation, with 13 coded segments; (3) sexist news portrayals of black feminist activists, with nine coded segments; (4) the push for inclusion of black queer activists, with eight coded segments; and (5) paying homage to black social movements past, with five coded segments. After briefly describing the five women, I highlight key portions of the interviews to show these themes.

Meet the participants

Both Alicia Garza and Marissa Johnson wished to be identified primarily as Black Lives Matter activists who are affiliated with an official chapter. Garza is one of the three co-founders for the organization. Her love letter to black people after George Zimmerman's acquittal in the Trayvon Martin murder trial in July 2013 contained the original #BlackLivesMatter hashtag. When her friend, Patrisse Cullors, shared her letter to Twitter it went viral. Some said the Movement was born then. Other activists believe the Movement did not take off until August 2014, in Ferguson, Missouri. Based in Oakland, California, Garza is an award-winning community organizer who specialized in workplace equality in the Bay Area prior to establishing Black Lives Matter. She self-identifies as a member of the LGBTQIA community and emphasizes the inclusion of queer leaders in the Movement.

Marissa Johnson, a member of the Black Lives Matter Seattle chapter, gained notoriety in 2015 when she interrupted Presidential hopeful Sen. Bernie Sanders (I-Vt.) at his Seattle campaign rally. Her assumption of his podium dominated the news headlines for several weeks. Prior to this act of protest, Johnson organized "die-ins" at Seattle businesses to oppose the shooting deaths of unarmed black men by police. One such event shut down Seattle's downtown mall on Black Friday 2014. Johnson self-identifies as "an evangelical Christian, a former theology student, and a biracial, queer woman."

Two participants told me that the Movement did not begin until the Ferguson, Missouri, uprisings in August 2014, in the wake of Michael Brown's death. In the months that followed those protests, they called themselves the "Day 1's," to differentiate themselves from what they regard as late-coming opportunists who capitalized on legacy media appearances but did not have actual boots on the ground in the early campaigns. They were the early fact-checkers of the Movement, churning out data and eyewitness news from the front lines that served often as a corrective to legacy media reports. Brittany Ferrell is a Day 1. Ferrell is a native of St. Louis, Missouri. She is a co-founder of the now-defunct organization, Millennial Activists United. When she began protesting in the days after Brown's death, she went on Twitter to find like-minded demonstrators in her age group, since she said the earliest activists were mothers of friends of Michael Brown's mother, Lesley McSpadden. She met Alexis Templeton, whom she married at the zenith of the protests, and Ashley Yates. (Both Yates and Templeton declined to be interviewed for this study.) The three women pushed to have Officer Darren Wilson prosecuted for Brown's murder. Alas, the local legislature failed to indict Wilson in November 2014. Ferrell self-identifies as "a mother, a nurse, and Alexis's wife."

Brittany Packnett is also a Day 1. A native of St. Louis, Missouri Packnett co-founded We the Protestors in 2014. The group launched a reform campaign in August 2015, called Campaign Zero, which is a 10-point plan to reduce police violence in America (see www.joincampaignzero.org). Along with DeRay Mckesson, Johnetta Elzie, and Samuel Sinyangwe, Packnett created the policy-oriented organization after the four met on the front lines in Ferguson. Packnett was an appointee to President Barack Obama's 21st Century Policing Task Force. She self-identifies as "a Christian, a daughter, a sister, a community activist, and the girlfriend of civil rights photographer Reggie Cunningham."[1]

Ieshia Evans was the subject of some viral photographs of the Alton Sterling protests in August 2016. Evans, wearing a dress, was pictured in a peaceful standoff with Baton Rouge police wearing riot gear.[2] Since becoming a media sensation, Evans has conducted international interviews about her assumed affiliation with the Black Lives Matter Movement. She bristles when one suggests that she is part of the organization; no one from the group, she says, ever reached out to her after she was profiled in the press. She emphasized in our interview that she went down to Baton Rouge from her native New York in the summer of 2016 on her own. Evans eventually was arrested and charged with obstructing a highway. After being released from jail, she said she planned to return to New York and live a quiet life. When someone created a fake Twitter account in her name, however, she decided to bear witness on the platform with her own verified account. Evans self-identifies as a mother and a black woman.

Distrust of legacy media

All five participants told me that they distrust traditional media outlets. This was the most popular code in the corpus. Each woman shared that she used social media outlets, such as Twitter, to spread her own news when she was on the front lines of protest. Brittany Packnett, of We the Protestors, explained that Twitter became invaluable, for example, when police officers tear-gassed peaceful protestors in August 2014. She explained that she saw a CNN report that claimed the predominately black residents of Ferguson were looting a local McDonald's. She said her Twitter feed was full of protestors discussing the antidotes to teargas. Milk was a remedy, Packnett said, so protestors rushed into a local McDonald's restaurant to ask its managers for milk. Packnett used Twitter to correct this important omission in the news. She said:

> That is the instantaneous correction that you're allowed to have. Twitter also gave us immediate access to CNN . . . [and] on the ground people would go up to cameras and say, 'People are tweeting me right now, calling me right now and saying that you're reporting incorrectly, so we will stand here in front of your cameras until you decide to tell the truth.'

Brittany Ferrell, the founder of Millennial Activists United, said that Twitter was the reason she got involved in the Movement. She found like-minded black feminist activists online, then began organizing demonstrations in her hometown of Ferguson in August 2014. She believes that part of the reason her organization is now-defunct is negative media portrayals of the Movement. She said:

> They've done a very good job in portraying BLM [Black Lives Matter] over-all as a hate group. And I don't expect anything else because when I think

about the media and I think about who they serve, they serve the majority and the majority is not looking to do away with white supremacy. They benefit from it.

Asked to elaborate on her belief that legacy media have misrepresented the Black Lives Matter Movement, Ferrell explained:

Blackness is oftentimes very, very misunderstood. When you're black and you're angry or you're black and you're fighting for something, people don't really receive that very well. It's almost like if we're too angry we just become violent. People don't believe that we're worth what we're fighting for.

Ferrell added that she believed the framing of Black Lives Matter and its protestors in the news as lawless rebels without a cause was intentional. She explained:

I do think that they framed us in a way so that people would look at this movement and not understand it, or to think that it's violent or to think that we are not making progress when in fact that we are . . . mainstream media is not for the people. They're not trying to get us free.

I asked Ferrell what she thought about the framing of the Women's March in Washington, DC, which was organized to highlight women's rights and, in part, to denounce President Donald Trump's growing catalog of misogynistic behaviors. In an infamous "hot mic" moment, President Trump bragged to an entertainment reporter that a man of his stature simply can "grab them [women] by the pussy" without anyone ever complaining.[3] Women's March participants defiantly (and ironically) donned pink hats, stylized to resemble vaginas, to many of the nation-wide protests. Although two of the Women's March organizers are women of color, the demonstration was regarded popularly as a white feminists' march (Gebreyes, 2017). Ferrell's voice rises in anger as she dissects the media framing of Women's March:

I feel like a lot of white women went out and they were like, 'Oh, this march is *peaceful.*' And really putting the emphasis on *peaceful.* . . . Our demonstrations were also peaceful, but when you see a sea of white women with pink vagina hats on their heads, white women are not going to be met with the same type of aggression from police officers as a community of traumatized torn black people who continue over and over and over again to be traumatized. To be told that we don't matter. To be in communities where we don't have food, we don't have jobs, we don't have nothing! White women had the audacity to emphasize how safe their protests were! . . . Of course they were. They're protecting you! No one's protecting us. So [the news media] frame this narrative about how *this* is peaceful, and *this* is not. And it's like no, *this* is valued in society and *we* are not!

Ferrell seemed very near tears but recomposed herself. She concluded quietly that black feminist activists should embrace and create independent media outlets, such as blogs, podcasts, and web video series, to reframe their organizational missions and leaders. In fact, all of the women said that they encourage the next generation of black feminist activists not to place as much emphasis on courting traditional press. In 2017, for example, Packnett, launched *Pod Save the People*, a weekly podcast dedicated to Movement politics.[4] Packnett co-anchors the show with the fellow founders of We the Protestors/Campaign Zero, Deray McKesson and Samuel Sinyangwe. Similarly, Black Lives Matter's Marissa Johnson said that she co-founded *Safety Pin Box* after her disillusionment with televised news.[5] Her media literacy company's website states that its mission is to educate "white people who want to be allies in the fight for Black liberation." *Safety Pin Box* has a weekly email newsletter and a dedicated Twitter feed. Both outlets host in-depth discussions about white privilege, and how whites can use that privilege to end racial equality.

Overall, the participants shared a common desire to see the news frame the Movement favorably. Whereas I thought I might see a higher priority on black feminist labor being highlighted in the news, the women I interviewed saw "the work itself"—not the activists or even the riots—as the news lede. This is not to say that these women do not want to be recognized for their efforts. Rather, they believe an accurate portrayal of the Black Lives Matter Movement makes room for their contributions to be celebrated, rather than condemned.

Private and state-sponsored intimidation

Brittany Ferrell recalled being out running errands when an unmarked car drove up near her, and a white man with a camera leaned out of the passenger side window and started snapping photos of her. She explained: "There's not a day that goes by that I don't think about who's listening, who's watching. I've become inured to feeling like safety is an illusion." Ferrell said that the cameraman became a fixture in the days leading up to her March 2017 sentencing date. She explained that a woman drove through a crowd of Black Lives Matter protestors who had blocked off I-70 in St. Louis to commemorate the one-year anniversary of Michael Brown's death in August 2015. "[She] used her vehicle to try and run protestors over," Ferrell said. "I allegedly struck her driver's side door with my size 6 shoe and now I'm facing a felony. It's definitely political retaliation towards the Movement. It's definitely an effort for them to make an example out of me." Ferrell remarked that she becomes all the more bitter about her felony charge when she considers that the same prosecutor who failed to indict Officer Darren Wilson for killing Michael Brown was, at the time of the interview, trying to convict her of a felony for allegedly kicking a vehicle. Ferrell eventually got a suspended sentence and probation as part of a plea deal in March 2017.

Marissa Johnson said she brought white allies with her when she interrupted Senator Sanders at the podium. These friends formed a human barricade between her and the audience. It proved essential, she said: an audience member bit one of her white allies when he could not get to Johnson himself. Her friends could not protect her from the aftermath of the rally, however: "I've gotten thousands of death threats. I still do, a year-and-a-half later. Every time something would happen in the [2016 Presidential] election again, I'd get new death threats."

I asked how people find her. She explained "through Twitter, through my phone." She sighed, adding:

> People call me, people found my phone number, yeah. Through my phone, through emails, through Twitter, through Facebook. . . . I finally went through [Facebook] and cleaned it out like eight months after it [the rally] happened and it literally was just thousands and thousands and thousands of messages. I still get tons of those messages every day.

Johnson sees her experiences as par for the course. She said: "The tactics that we chose—if you're really aware of the legacy of people who take that road—then you understand that everything up to death is on the table." Johnson took a long pause to think about her answer to the question of whether she believes her protest was worth it. Nodded slowly, she said: "I'm really happy about what we were able to contribute to history and trying to advance the people's agenda forward. That being said, had I known what it would cost me personally, I don't know that I would've."

Sexist news portrayals of black feminist activists

"It's sexism. It's misogynoir. It's ageism," Marissa Johnson said, pounding her fist into her hand for emphasis in describing how she regards the media portrayal of her 2015 stand against Sen. Sanders. She said that she was angered by early coverage of her and fellow protestor, Mara Willaford. She explained:

> [It was] like we're just little girls and we just got mad, and we just yelled and other things happened to happen out of it. White supremacy in that moment could never conceive that we had intentionally crafted this plan, executed it effectively, and done things that people would have told us that we could not have done.

Johnson said she noticed this narrative—of the unintended girl protesters gone viral—continued for about a week until she reluctantly agreed to an MSNBC interview. In the segment, she revealed the planning that went into the interruption and confirmed her affiliation with Black Lives Matter's Seattle chapter. ". . . [A] week out, then folks are able to start saying, 'Oh actually, I see why they did what they did and actually here are already some outcomes of this' and then two weeks out, 'What they did was spot on. Here's why what they did was genius.'" As frustrated as Johnson was about the eventual news coverage she received, she acknowledged that sexism actually helped her achieve the interruption in the first place. "I had a white man who was with me," she recounted, laughing. She added, "His job was to help me get in." She said she held hands with him and no one noticed them initially. Senator Sanders's event organizers were focused on someone else, Johnson explained:

> What was interesting was that I also had a black man who was there and when the organizers of the Bernie [Sanders] rally saw him and saw me, they knew we were going to something, but they assumed he was going to be the one to do it because he was a man. He went over to a different corner and they put all the security over where he was and so when time came and they introduced Bernie, the white man who was with me helped me separate the barriers. I ran, and ducked and dived up the stairs.

Johnson shook her head as her laughter trailed off. She said she is torn when she thinks about the approach, as it highlighted how heavily surveilled black men are when they are innocent and how invisible black women are until they behave "badly." Her eyes began to well with tears.

Echoing Johnson's sentiments, Ferrell said sexism led her to launch Millennial Activists United in 2014 with two fellow black feminist activists. As the uprisings gained steam in her hometown, Ferrell began to notice that people began looking for a charismatic male leader: "They romanticized the early civil rights movement." They were, she said, looking for their Malcolm X or their Martin Luther King.

Ferrell added that many of her Twitter followers and local friends self-identified as black feminist women. Critics of her growing base implied ". . . [I]f you are not male then you are not worth listening to. You are not worth leading." Ferrell said mainstream news media outlets even began to anoint certain men as the official leaders of the Ferguson uprisings, on the backs of black women's labor. The men would often do nothing to acknowledge the steadfast women organizers publicly, she said, which caused rifts among various organizations vying to "headline" the Black Lives Matter movement.

"I just knew I had to control my own story," Ferrell explained. Ferrell said she accepted nearly all mainstream media interviews that came her way. She developed a network of journalists she trusted. She felt she needed to go on record, she explained. This is how she came to be one of the few women referenced in the documentary, *Ferguson: Duty to Fight, Duty to Win*. In the film, a male protestor supports her by the waist as she is chanting, bullhorn in hand, in the back of a pickup truck. I asked her about this developing black protest iconography—of the men now standing behind the women—which subverts all traditional imagery for black women demonstrators in movements past. She nodded slowly, recalling times when she had to stand her ground when doing this work "because people like to undermine you. They like to condescend you. They like to tell you where your place is. I've had my fair share of having to push back on people that have been coming to me with some sexist or patriarchal point of view or standpoint."

Near the end of the interview, Ferrell, who is a licensed nurse and was almost about to start her 12-hour shift, explained the difficulty of undoing white supremacy, sexism, and patriarchy:

> It's been a struggle for myself and other women in this movement because a lot of times you can be labeled as divisive when calling out sexism, but it's our duty to do that. It's our duty to do that because all that's going to happen if we don't is people are going to recreate structures that are going to continue to marginalize people—women, queer people, trans folks—so we have to confront those issues head on, at the same time we confront white supremacy and racism.

Only one of my participants said that black feminists should de-emphasize their womanhood in the Movement. Ieshia Evans, now known internationally for facing off with Baton Rouge, Louisiana police, said that today's demonstrators should primarily focus on racial inequality. "I've actually had people who have tried to divide and conquer the situation and try to get me to sway my opinions in more of a feminist direction," she said. "I shut that down automatically. Before anyone has ever discriminated against me for having a vagina they discriminated against me because of the color of my skin. My people first and then my sex."

Evans further reasoned that being a woman did not protect her from being handled roughly by police. When Evans was arrested amid her demonstration, the police neither "Mirandized" her, nor told her what charges she faced. The police "met me with war gear" while "I was in a sundress," she said. She did not feel like a lady then, she said with a wry laugh.

The push for inclusion of black queer activists

Participants vigorously debated the role of queer black women in the Black Lives Matter Movement. Three of the five interviewees identify openly as members of the LGBTQIA community. Alicia Garza, co-founder of the Black Lives Matter Movement, explained:

> As a black woman who is queer, I think one of the things that just feels important for us to understand, I think, historically, is that it's always been true: that black women and women of color have been kind of the very foundation of what it's meant to get free, and then we're pushed aside or kind of erased.

Garza is married to a woman, Malachi Larrabee-Garza, who prefers the pronoun "he" as a modifier. As Alicia and her husband have given extensive, first-person interviews about what it is like to be a queer activist of color, she preferred to discuss the inclusion of these marginalized groups in more general terms.[6]

When asked pointedly whether she believes Black Lives Matter is more progressive about gender and sexuality than past black social movements, Garza briefly paused for a moment. We were on a university campus, where she would speak to a small group of student leaders on the importance of self-care. Many of the workshop participants milled outside the room where we interviewed her, waiting to hear her answer:

> It's certainly not perfect, but one of the things that we can continue to do is craft our organizations, our culture, our demonstrations, our movement in way that not only makes visible the leadership and the work of women of color and queer women and trans women and poor women, but that we also name what those contributions *are*. That we be very specific about what it is that we contribute.

Garza shared that she was very frustrated when other groups began to co-opt the Black Lives Matter slogan. "What do you feel when you hear All Lives Matter?" I asked her. "Nope!" she said while shaking her head. She explained "[What] feels really important is making visible folks who feel invisible." She said focusing on anti-Blackness, specifically, opens the door for a greater discussion still about *which* black lives matter. She referenced the cultural silence about violence against black people who identify openly as gay, bisexual or transsexual. "This is a moment where we can shift that, and I think what we're seeing is that we're watching old ways of being go away and new ways of being come in," Garza said.

The general, political consensus is that groups who are working under the broad umbrella of Black Lives Matter should prioritize unarmed black men, she explained further. She wanted Black Lives Matter to be a different kind of modern ally, she said. At the same time, she mentioned that some storied organizations that are fighting systemic, anti-black racism alongside her group adhere staunchly to "respectability politics." Leaders of these historic groups are worried that members of the LGBTQIA community will muddle the messages and priorities of the cause to end police brutality, she said. They are unable, however, to marginalize LGBT-QIA leaders in ways that they used in the past, since social media enables anyone to grab the proverbial bullhorn. While Garza declined to name the legacy black organizations that engage in gatekeeping, she said simply "It's important for us to fight for our space without fighting each other."

Since Garza's October 2015 interview, many of the groups that were birthed in Ferguson under the broad Black Lives Matter campaign either have rebranded, merged, or dissolved. Ferrell's organization, Millennial Activists United (MAU), dissolved. Ferrell and two other black feminist lesbians activists launched MAU amid the Ferguson uprisings in August 2014. They found each other on Twitter.

Ferrell said that when she began looking for ways to get involved in her hometown of Ferguson, many of the early organizers either were older black women—like the friends of Mike Brown's mother, Leslie McSpadden—or men who had a lot of "chauvinist energy," she said. There were not many black women "twenty-somethings" on the front lines, she said, let alone any queer black women her age. She went on Twitter to search for them, she said. She had a feeling that they were there, watching the news as events escalated in her hometown, yet too afraid to come forward. After exchanging private messages with Ashley Yates and Alexis Templeton, the trio agreed to form a new organization that would involve women like them. "It was created out of a need for young activism organizers who wanted to do something, but didn't feel like they had a place to do something," Ferrell said.

Ferrell explained that young black women often must do "double duty" when they want to engage in activism if they are also mothers. For younger women with small children and a limited support system, childcare can be costly. This leads women who may have had bigger visions to settle for support positions within a movement, instead of major strategic ones, she said. "We had a lot of young people, a lot of queer people, and a lot of women who were doing so much work that was not being recognized. Their work was not being taken seriously, but it was the work that we felt like a lot of men got the credit for."

When black queer women did deign to take on leadership positions in the early Ferguson protests of 2014, Ferrell said they did not feel safe. In private messages and threads on Twitter, black queer women activists discussed the unique threats that three layers of marginalization often elicited. "We wanted to create a space for young people regardless of your identity and regardless to your gender, your sexuality, if you are ready to do this work for black lives this is your space. So we wanted to open that up so people could feel safe coming in with their whole selves, not to feel like they have to fit in anybody's box—and to collectively organize power."

Part of MAU's strategy was to allow its members to operate without much publicity or fanfare. While Templeton and Yates took turns fielding press inquiries from *The New York Times* and NPR (Corley, 2014), Ferrell said many other women offered first aid to those hurt by police during frontline protests. (In fact, Ferrell said the experience explains her decision to pursue a nursing career.) MAU women cooked food for protestors, helped write lengthy proposals for local police reform and, in Ferrell's case, even fell in love. She and Templeton became engaged in December 2014, one month after the city of St. Louis decided not to indict Officer Wilson on any charges for the killing of Brown. Both of them were very depressed by the decision, she recalled, but found hope in each other. "We were forged in the fire," Ferrell said. She explained how their roles as romantic public figures create "its own set of traumas":

> It's a lot that we talk about that we have weathered through . . . but I can definitely say that because of this experience, it's a love that has never really felt like any other love that I've ever experienced. Knowing that somebody is so committed to something in the same way that you are and that they are on this journey—to make sure that they're whole and they're healthy in the same way that you are—it's something very powerful about the type of love that Alexis and I have grown into during this movement.

Paying homage to black social movements past

Although I never asked participants to think of a black feminist activist forebearer that they admire, four of the five women referenced unsung heroines from the Civil Rights Movement of the 1950s and 1960s. Marissa Johnson recounted that when she interrupted Sanders, she was wearing a shirt that said, "Fight like Fannie Lou Hamer." "And it was really funny because I had that shirt on and yet people were like, 'Why did she do that? We don't understand!' and I'm like . . . all she [Hamer] did was go after Democrats! I think in that way, she's someone I would be connected to."

A couple of months and nearly 2000 miles away, Ferrell identified similarly with Hamer's story. Hamer registered thousands of black Mississippians in her home state to vote. She even challenged the Democratic party to hear their concerns by demanding a delegation at its National Convention in 1964 (Lee, 2000). Ferrell said: "I didn't even learn about Fannie Lou Hamer until I was in undergrad. It was like she put in work for the [Civil Rights] Movement and yet no one knew about her, but we knew about all the men!"

Both Johnson and Ferrell said that Hamer's obscurity in history is something they considered actively when strategizing their own interactions with legacy media outlets. Johnson leveraged television's reach. Ferrell said she decided to find journalist allies within the ranks of print and online media. Ferrell added that in wooing modern press, she made sartorial choices that criticized previous generations of activists for omitting women. One of her favorite protest shirts, because it challenges what modern black leadership should look like, is a black hoodie that reads, "Not your respectable negro," she said.[7]

Brittany Packnett suggested that today's Movement may look like more than one "thing," after all. Of all the participants, she is the most visible activist who is still working on the front lines, with a weekly podcast and a Twitter following of 138,000 people. She said she drew inspiration from "late 60s and 70s folks" like "Kwame Ture, Gil Scott-Heron, Maya Angelou and Audre Lorde." According to Packnett, these are "people who took the foundations of the midcentury Civil Rights Movement and built something intentionally radical on top of it."

She scoffed when asked what she thought of people who criticized her current group, *Campaign Zero*, for operating under the Black Lives Matter banner when it is not affiliated with an official chapter. She and her friend and fellow protestor, Deray McKesson, enjoyed presidential appointments and late-night television show appearances while many unknown activists continued to toil in obscurity, two of the activists in the corpus (who wished to remain nameless) complained. Packnett frowned and said that legacy media are to blame largely for lumping all the organizations together. Still, she emphasized the value in coalition-building, like activists did in past generations. "There were lots of organizations who had lots of different tactics, aims and leaders and constituents, but they were oriented towards the same goal. A goal of racial equity and freedom. Goals of economic empowerment, goals of the American Dream. . . . So in the same way that SNCC, SCLC and NAACP and CORE and the [Black] Panthers all had different tactics, they were all a part of broader movement."

Conclusion

"I'm just a regular degular girl from New York," Ieshia Evans said, emphasizing her home state in her pronounced Brooklyn accent.[8] She said she had no idea that she would become a global icon from one photograph. After conducting interviews with publications in Europe, Africa, the Caribbean, and the United States, Evans shared that she planned to go dark for a while. "You won't see me too much in a little bit," she said. "I am in my learning phases right now. I was asleep for so long . . . but I am 'woke' now." Evans declined to say what her activism will look like in the future.

Marissa Johnson said that many activists leave the public eye with little fanfare because: "It's very dangerous and it's hard to maintain. There's not proper structures in place. It's not very sustainable to do that kind of work really effectively long term because it's super traumatic." Johnson said she considers herself an "elderstateswoman" of the Black Lives Matter Movement, simply because today's news cycles move so quickly. The Movement needs fresh faces to continue to grow, she said. It also needs black women activists who will document their contributions. To these ends, all participants are creating original media or taking legacy media interviews on their own terms, at the time of this publication. Evans appeared on an MTV news program in 2017 to criticize Pepsi's controversial commercial, where model Kendall Jenner (who is white) handed a white police officer a soda to quell a protest.[9] Pepsi pulled the advertisement when Black Twitter lampooned it.

Ferrell was one of the principal characters of the 2017 film, *Whose Streets. Rolling Stone* magazine called it the "Doc of the Year" and "a chronicle of activism as a triumph" (Fear, 2017). Garza completed a book chapter that offered a "herstory" of the Movement (2014). Johnson is the owner of *Safety Pin Box*, which offers "ally training" for white people.[10] Lastly, Packnett hosts a weekly podcast, *Pod Save the People*. The show grew from a call-in program to a live show in Washington, DC's Lincoln Theater in February 2018.

All these examples illustrate a new generation of black feminist activists who are as media savvy as they are passionate about their causes. This small cadre of women led one of the most sustained, meaningful black social movements in the new millennium. Using little more than smartphones and social media, they harnessed incredible organizing power that bucked respectability politics and highlighted the contributions of black women activists. Some of the women, like Ferrell and Evans, never had organized a movement before. Others, such as Garza, Johnson and Packnett already were working in organizing spaces when the political "stars" aligned. For all the participants, their experiences on the front lines revealed how fraught activism can be for black women. There are added layers of personal danger. There is sexism that stings. There is white silence—even from fellow feminists—that infuriates. Still the work passes on to generations anew, like Ferrell's daughter, who is nine.

"I am passing her my baton," Ferrell said smiling, before ending our Skype session. Then, she checked her reflection in her rearview mirror and fastened her hospital ID badge to her medical scrubs. She had work to do.

Notes

1 Cunningham is a fellow native of St. Louis who photographed the Ferguson protests extensively. See: www.bepureblack.com/untitled-gallery.
2 See: http://time.com/4403440/baton-rouge-protest-photo-ieshia-evans/.
3 See: www.nytimes.com/2016/10/08/us/donald-trump-tape-transcript.html/
4 See: https://crooked.com/podcast-series/pod-save-the-people/.
5 See: www.safetypinbox.com.
6 See: Alicia Garza + Malachi Garza on Being Partners in Love & Activism: www.you tube.com/watch?v=DOb85JOTw0s.
7 See: Faces from the New Civil Rights Movement: http://afropunk.com/2015/02/ bhm-faces-from-the-new-civil-rights-movement-alexis-templeton-and-brittany-fer rell-of-millennial-activists-united/.
8 See Urban Dictionary entry for regular degular: www.urbandictionary.com/define. php?term=Regular%20Degular.
9 See: www.youtube.com/watch?v=yyziH2eORvQ.
10 See: www.safetypinbox.com.

References

Bruner, J. (1991). The narrative construction of reality. *Critical Inquiry*, *18*(1), 1–21.
Capehart, J. (2015). "Hands up, don't shoot" was built on a lie. *Washington Post*. Retrieved from http://wapo.st/2d4DOjv
Clutch Magazine Staff. (2014). Photo: Howard University students stand in solidarity with #Ferguson. *Clutch Magazine*. Retrieved from www.clutchmagonline.com/2014/08/ photo-howard-university-students-stand-solidarity-ferguson/
Corley, C. (2014). With Ferguson protests, 20-somethings become first-time activists. *NPR*. Retrieved from https://n.pr/2FI38cy
Fear, D. (2017). "Whose streets?" review: Portrait of Ferguson may be the doc of the year. *Rolling Stone*. Retrieved from https://rol.st/2FDFqOF
Garza, A. (2014). A herstory of the #BlackLivesMatter movement. In J. Hobson (Ed.), *Are all the women still white?* (pp. 23–28). Albany, NY: Suny Press.
Gebreyes, R. (2017). Women's March organizers address intersectionality as the movement grows. *The Huffington Post*. Retrieved from https://bit.ly/2IeMiHN
Gillespie, M., & Clinton, C. (Eds.). (1998). *Taking off the white gloves: Southern women and women historians* (Vol. 1). Columbia, MO: University of Missouri Press.
Hickey, G. (2013). The respectability trap: Gender conventions in 20th century movements for social change. *Journal of Interdisciplinary Feminist Thought*, *7*(1), 2.
Husserl, E. (1970). *The crisis of European sciences and transcendental phenomenology: An introduction to phenomenological philosophy*. Evanston, IL: Northwestern University Press.
Larson, L. (2014). Four members of congress do "Hands Up" gesture on house floor. *New York Daily News*. Retrieved from http://nydn.us/11OBRBt
Lee, C. K. (2000). *For freedom's sake: The life of Fannie Lou Hamer* (Vol. 122). Champaign, IL: University of Illinois Press.

Lee, M. Y. H. (2015). "Hands up, don't shoot" did not happen in Ferguson. *The Washington Post*. Retrieved from http://wapo.st/1P6ubQS

Marsh, K. (2015). "Hands up, don't shoot" never happened, but networks keep using it. *NewsBusters*. Retrieved from http://bit.ly/2dA4pKB

NBC Staff. (2014). Rams players enter field in "Hands up, don't shoot" pose. *NBCNews.com*. Retrieved from http://nbcnews.to/1vyhzbe

16

BE CUTE, PLAY WITH DOLLS, AND STICK TO TEA PARTIES

Journalism, girls, and power

Cynthia Carter

The title of this chapter is taken from comments made in 2016 by Hilde Lysiak, then a 9-year-old publisher of an online and print community newspaper. Elaborating on this point, she declared, "I didn't start publishing Pennsylvania's *Orange Street News* so that people would think I'm cute. I want to get the truth to people, even if it makes grownups mad." To illustrate this point, Lysiak recalls finding out about a robbery on her street, so she began knocking on doors to see if anyone had heard or seen anything. In response to adults who thought it inappropriate and risky for a young girl to be chasing a story in this way, Lysiak retorted,

> I could see them saying a boy should go and play with racing cars instead of how they told me to play with dolls. Or maybe they wouldn't have said much at all. The thing is, I like playing with dolls, and having tea parties. I also think racing cars are really cool! Grownups shouldn't assume that a kid—boy or girl—should be doing just one thing or another. Kids can do exceptional things and still be kids!

Feminist journalism research has produced a rigorous evidence base, constructed over decades, establishing that men and men's interests and actions tend to be highly valued in society and more widely and prominently covered by journalists than those of women (Ross, Boyle, Carter, & Ging, 2018; Ross & Carter, 2011). Additionally, scholars have deconstructed and challenged hierarchical, binaristic gendered norms that articulate the masculine with the public sphere of deliberative debate on serious issues such as politics, economics, and war and the feminine with the private sphere of sexuality, reproduction, domesticity, and emotions. Similarly, researchers investigating children's gendered relationships to news have routinely found that they have a good understanding of which news topics are associated with and reported on by men (war, economics, politics, sports) and those linked to and covered by women (home, family, fashion, and beauty) (Carter, Messenger Davies, Allan, & Mendes, 2009; Lemish, 1998, 2013; Lemish & Alony, 2014; Davies, 2004). How do children learn about the gendering of news? What is girls' connection to the public sphere? Under what circumstances and where are their voices found (or not) within it? How might asking these and related questions open up the conceptualization of girls and girlhood in more fluid ways that challenge hegemonic masculine assumptions about journalism and the news?

Girls (and boys) are always already shaped by both the private and public. Yet, very little research to date has tried to map the complex relationships between journalism, girls, and power. Girlhood studies academics Kim and Ringrose urge researchers to challenge "engrained constructions of youth, particularly girls, as lacking in political agency" (2018, pp. 47–48). A central step is to identify girls who have already seized online and offline opportunities to occupy the public sphere, developing critical voices that contest gender binaries and insisting on their right to be there and be heard (Bobkowski & Belmas, 2017). There is a need for sustained examination of media and girlhood that directly engages with issues related to girls as citizens—as news audiences and producers of news, political comment, and intervention. What forms does girls' participation in the public sphere as journalists, political bloggers, or social media commentators already take? To what extent do they challenge taken for granted assumptions about girls' public agency?

Despite evidence that girls are engaging in the public sphere now more than ever, scholars have rarely addressed these issues, with the notable exception of the growing field of research around girls' feminist social media activism (Keller, 2015, 2016; Sowards & Reegar, 2006). Feminist journalism research might specifically ask how and why are girls reimagining feminism in online spaces? How might girls' contributions to public debates be used to think rethink girlhood, in general, as well as girls' relationships to journalism and power?

Thinking about how such insights might revitalize feminist research on journalism and gender and analytically tease out these points, I briefly discuss theories of childhood and of gender. I then offer case studies of two young girls who have established themselves as producers of news and opinion: Hilde Lysiak, who founded at age 7 a community newspaper *Orange Street News*; and Maelo Manning, who launched her UK-based political blog, LIBDEMCHILD when she was 10. Examples of such activities are growing in number around the world. I only have enough space here to briefly mention an additional three, below.

Jana Tamimi is a 12-year-old Palestinian who has been reporting (in English and Arabic) on the Israeli-Palestinian conflict. She began covering events at age 7, after two members of her family were killed. Using her mobile phone, she regularly makes video reports on the West Bank and distributes them through her Facebook page, which currently has approximately 270,000 followers worldwide (Wikipedia, 2018). She considers herself "a journalist covering the Third Intifada because I am living the Intifada" (Smith, 2016). Reporters around the world have interviewed Tamimi. Whilst most have praised her stories, she has also been criticized by some of being used as a pawn in a propaganda war.

In India, Chandi is former editor of the print newspaper *Balaknama* or *Voice of Children*, entirely run by street children with an average age of 14. Their stories highlight issues affecting the over 18 million children who, like themselves, live and work on the streets. The newspaper, which now has a regular readership in the thousands, also champions the acknowledgment and extension of the rights of street children to a proper home, food, education, and protection from violence. Chandi regularly featured stories of specific importance to girls, such as sexual abuse, pregnancy, and child marriage (Ruiz-Grossman, 2016; Sharma, n.d.; Venkatraman, 2016).

In 2008, aged 15, US teenager Julie Zeilinger managed to get an interview (her first as an aspiring journalist) with feminist Gloria Steinem (Crump, 2010). In 2009, she set up the feminist blog *F-bomb*, describing it as the "first online platform and community for teen feminists [...] providing socially conscious youth with the personal and professional tool of a media platform" and an "accessible entry to a broader social justice dialogue" (Zeilinger, 2018). In Zeilinger's view, mainstream feminist websites and blogs failed to address issues of particular importance to girls in an Internet age, such as body image and sexism in the media from a teen perspective. Teen feminists from 200 countries around the world have submitted posts. In 2014, *F-bomb* partnered with the Women's Media Centre, an organization founded by Gloria Steinem, Jane Fonda, and Robin Morgan, to create the *WMC F-bomb*, an "intersectional teen feminist media platform created by and for socially conscious youth" (Women's Media Center, 2018). Zeilinger is currently an Editor at MTV News and regularly writes for a range of news outlets, including CNN, *Huffington Post*, and *Forbes*.

Theories of childhood, theories of gender

Sociologist Chris Jenks (1992) suggests that adults have typically defined childhood in relation to adulthood: they treat childhood as existing at a certain time and in a particular space that requires adult guidance and protection from harm. Childhood ends when children have matured sufficiently and come to accept society's norms and values as constructed and policed by adults.

Following on from this, two main schools of thought have shaped how researchers have approached the relationships between fictional and factual media and children. The first regards childhood as marked by a series of psychological and physical developments or "stages" (Piaget, 1969). According to Lemish (2007), this theory is rooted in the belief that each stage in a child's life represents a unique period of development. Everyone is "typified by its own special behavioural and cognitive characteristics" (2007, p. 38). All humans pass through broadly similar stages of development from childhood to adulthood in roughly the same chronological order. Typically, gender, ethnicity, and class are not seen to fundamentally influence passage through the life stages, although they may speed up or slow down certain cognitive developments.

How adults think children should act at different stages contributes to how adults treat, care for and perceive a responsibility to keep children safe from emotional and physical harm. Overall, embedded in this conceptual framework is a presumption that childhood is a period of innocence and vulnerability. Much of the media and journalism research to date has tended to start from this theoretical base. Children's lack of worldly experience, according to this theory, leaves them susceptible to corruption (by "bad" adults and harmful media), so adults ("good" ones) and child-friendly media have the responsibility to protect them. This also means that exposure to bad things happening in the world, particularly news about violence and sexuality, must be carefully handled to protect children's emotional wellbeing (van der Molen, 2004).

A second school of thought, the position I adopt, regards "childhood" as a social construction and thus arbitrary and ever-changing (Jenks, 1992, 2004). It rejects the definition of childhood primarily in terms of cognitive and physical (brain) developments. Instead, it stresses the importance of the social, economic, cultural, and political context in which children are situated. For "social constructionists," development theorists' ahistorical and universalistic ideas about childhood are problematic because they do not account for differences amongst children that might be attributable to gender, class, ethnicity, disability, sexuality, and other forms of identity.

Historian Phillippe Ariès (1962) epitomizes the historical, contextual conceptual agenda of this second school of thought. His views have been highly influential in the development of the field of the "sociology of childhood." Researching Western historical records and art dating back to medieval times, Ariès found that childhood did not exist in the way we understand it today (1962, p. 125). The idea that childhood might last until age 18, for example, is a "recent" social construction that only began to take shape from the nineteenth century. In medieval society, he claims, "as soon as the child could live without constant solicitude of his mother, his nanny or his cradle-rocker, he belonged to adult society" (1962, p. 125). The modern-day conception of the child as vulnerable and in need of protection from harm, he argues, comes out of a sincere wish to safeguard, but it also helps to secure the interests of adults and their power over children.

These are key points to bear in mind when considering how the news media typically represent children—as naïve, easily influenced, and defenseless (Carter & Messenger Davies, 2005).

Nevertheless, attending to the conceptual assumptions shaping this type of thinking, and the ideologies underpinning them, allows for a deeper understanding of how they developed and influence policy related to children's welfare, education, and exposure to media. Moreover, cultural beliefs around childhood innocence construct a set of age-related, developmentally led, expectations. Children, especially younger ones, ought to be engaged in childish play (entertainment, fun) and not with concerns of the grownup world (news, civic engagement) (Lysiak, 2016; Pompeo, 2015). Adult perceptions about childhood are accordingly central to understanding children's relationships to journalism, and especially the extent to which they think children ought to be interested in the news as audiences or as nascent journalists.

Western conceptions of childhood have also been shaped by gendered assumptions about boys' and girls' "natural" inclinations, interests, behavior, and thus common-sense ideas about which media they will find interesting. Girls' media tastes are routinely associated with popular forms having to do with relationships, beauty, fashion, and pop music, as found, for example, in girls' magazines, soap operas, and reality TV (Blue & Kearney, 2018). Boys' tastes are also closely aligned with popular media, but they are presumed to gravitate primarily toward rock music, sport, and gaming (Cann, 2018; Wannamaker, 2011). A recent Pew Research Centre survey (Anderson & Jiang, 2018) of 743 US teenagers found that boys and girls share an interest in social media; but their use is structured along gender, ethnic, and class lines. Taken as a group, more girls than boys are near constantly online (50% to 39%), whilst Hispanic teens are more likely than whites to use the internet continuously (54% to 41%). Girls use social networking sites such as Snapchat more than boys (42% to 29%). Boys are more likely to say YouTube is their most used platform (39% to 25%).

Turning to factual media, boys are generally regarded as more interested than girls, and also more engaged than girls, with news topics that are normatively linked to men's interests and actions. Feminist scholars have reasoned that gender norms shape cultural expectations about what are the appropriate interests, behaviors, and activities for girls and for boys respectively, however much these norms are now questioned and challenged. Accordingly, presumptions about the "natural" media interests of girls and of boys as essentially or, at the very least, routinely different, have shaped not only media production, but also scholarship examining the media lives of boys and girls (Blue & Kearney, 2018; Cann, 2018; Gotz, Lemish, Aidman, & Moon, 2005; Senft, 2008; Wannamaker, 2011).

As already noted, girls' interactions with news and politics has seldom been the focus of feminist enquiry (Lemish & Alony, 2014). Part of the reason for this comes down to a longstanding research interest in girls' ideological and material connections to the private sphere, i.e., the focus on femininity, domesticity, and emotion that shapes entertainment-based media genres aimed at girls and women (Kearney, 2011; Mazzarella & Pecora, 1999; McRobbie, 2000). Where citizenship is discussed, scholars have tended to focus on the role of media in the formation of feminine identities and consumer empowerment (Banet-Weiser, 2007). Historically, entertainment media genres have provided discursive spaces where girls have been widely represented, directly addressed as an audience and offered opportunities to have their voices heard on topics such as popular music, fashion, makeup, and boys (Gill, 2007; McRobbie, 2008; University of Birmingham, 1978). Yet, failure to sufficiently explore girls' relationship to news and the public sphere risks naturalizing gender binaries and reinforcing the positioning of girls in the private sphere of emotions and domesticity, with its attendant focus on individual experience and the personal.

Girls, journalism, and power

Considering girls' historical relationships to journalism and the news provides a context for understanding current ones. According to Shelley (2009), by the nineteenth century British periodicals aimed at middle-class girls and women urged them to consider career opportunities then emerging in journalism:

> The female journalist was frequently upheld as a positive role model in journals aimed at young educated middle-class girls who may have been contemplating a writing or journalistic career. Persuasive periodical accounts of women journalists emphasised both the rigors and attractions of the profession, often casting the female journalist as a heroic New Woman figure adaptable to modern and challenging work environments.

Nevertheless, Chambers, Steiner, and Fleming (2004) have argued that in the US and UK, "women journalists present a paradox." By the nineteenth century it became increasingly common for women to pursue journalism careers. Nonetheless, they were also routinely marked as "other," as "different" from their male colleagues. So, by the late twentieth century,

> In print news, official rhetoric proclaims that a journalist's gender is irrelevant. However, while maleness is rendered neutral and male journalists are treated largely as professionals, women journalists are signified as gendered: their work is routinely defined and judged by their femininity.
>
> *(2004, p. 1)*

Historically "real," professional (masculine, objective, public) journalism has been regarded as including certain topics such as politics, economics, war, law, and business. Conversely, "human interest" topics like public health, sex, divorce, domestic violence, and poverty (often at the center of women's advocacy forms of journalism) and news focusing on domesticity, family, fashion, and beauty (feminine, subjective, private) have been widely dismissed as "special interest" and peripheral to "real" journalism. Yet, as Chambers et al. (2004) have noted, even when girls and women do "real journalism," their gender discursively positions them as "feminine" and therefore as "other" within what remains, to this day, a profession in which masculine ways of knowing and doing journalism are central in defining what counts as journalism.

Lysiak nicely illustrates this last point. She ends her *Guardian* (2016) opinion piece stating: "Yes, I'm a nine-year-old girl. But I'm a reporter, first. I report the news." She knows that for many people, being a child and a girl would automatically disqualify her from being taken seriously, of being capable of doing "real journalism." This point is echoed by historical studies on the tension women journalists felt, from the earliest days of newspapers, between their identities as journalists and as women: "They wanted to be recognized, respected and rewarded as journalists, but their sense of membership in a female sorority was perceived to undermine professionalism" (Steiner, 1998, p. 155).

Recent critical research on young people and news has tended to focus on news consumption habits. Their supposed declining interest in news is widely regarded as a concern, since citizens have a responsibility to be well informed in order to make reasoned political decisions (Clark & Marchi, 2018). Regarding gender, several significant findings stand out. First, until the teen years, girls' and boys' recollection of the news is broadly similar (Gunter, Furman, & Griffiths, 2000) as is their level of news consumption (Carter et al., 2009; Smith & Wilson, 2002). Why is it, then, that older children's news interests appear to stratify along gendered lines? What is occurring within society that might diminish girls' interest in the news? Research does not support the conclusion that girls are less interested in news than boys (Clark & Marchi, 2018; Lemish & Alony, 2014). If girls are so uninterested, why are young women earning journalism degrees in many countries around the world, often outnumbering their male peers (Boateng, 2017; Reid, 2015; Joseph, 2015; York, 2017)? Why, then, do "authoritative news" and "real" journalism remain so closely aligned with the masculine public sphere, privileging boys' and men's voices and views? (Jia et al., 2016).

In the next section, I consider two girls taking advantage of opportunities afforded new online spaces to participate in the public sphere. I do so to explore the extent to which such spaces might provide meaningful opportunities to challenge the gendered, generational binaries that have shaped traditional news and journalism, thus affording girls the chance to develop a presence, a voice, in democratic deliberation. Such opportunities are not boundless, so I will also assess the discursive limits to their public participation.

Hilde Lysiak

Hilde Lysiak publishes the *Orange Street News*, a full color, four-page hyperlocal newspaper available in print (monthly) and online form, from her hometown of Selinsgrove, Pennsylvania (Pompeo, 2015). She launched it in 2014, when she was 7. Mailed subscriptions for the print edition cost $10 a year. Her father, a former *New York Daily News* journalist, helped her put together a Facebook page, website and YouTube channel for the newspaper. By 2016 the website had over 18,000 page views, driven, in part, by her reporting about both drug problems in the local middle school (Jackman, 2016) and a range of serious local crime incidents. In 2016 she also came to national and international media attention, with interviews with the *Washington Post, National Geographic, Columbia Journalism* Review, and the *Guardian*, amongst others.

The *Orange Street News* story that raised the paper's profile and boosted her own status as a serious young journalist centered on what she thought to be a case of vandalism in the neighborhood. Having gone to the police station to find out more, she overheard the police chief saying he had to leave to respond to what she later described as an "important situation." Lysiak discovered that it was a possible murder that had taken place close to her home. She went to the crime scene to gather information, which she then dictated to her father, who posted on the *OSN* website under the headline "Exclusive: Murder on Ninth Street." She later shot a video of the crime scene which she uploaded to the *OSN* website and YouTube channel. Local reaction was mixed. To the many adults who criticized her and her family because they believed a 9-year-old girl should not be doing this sort of thing, Lysiak (2016) responded:

My parents and I have also been warned that covering this story meant my reporting was no longer 'cute.' I don't think people should be able to decide for me who I should be and what I should be doing. I never began my newspaper so that people would think I was cute. I started *The Orange Street News* to give people the information they need to know.

(Guardian, *April 6*)

Lysiak realizes that adults assumed any news stories reported by a child would and should be "cute" (funny, silly, naïve) and never even remotely resemble anything that might be construed as "real" journalism. Adults are supposed to do "serious" and children do "cute." Moreover, assumptions shaping responses to Lysiak's journalism are gendered—cute is a word more closely associated with girls than boys when talking about actions (as opposed to "being cute" or good looking).

Arguably, what Lysiak does and says should make a difference in terms of providing a role model for young girls (and boys). Nonetheless, it is likely she is seen to be exceptional. Public responses to her activities as a young journalist fall within a narrow range, from those who think she ought to be playing with dolls and hosting pretend tea parties, to disbelief that what she is doing is in any way "proper" journalism. Some are patronizing of her efforts, suggesting that it is really her father who is behind the *Orange Street News*; others grudgingly admit that she has some passion, talent, and perseverance—all necessary to succeed in journalism. At the same time, a stubbornly binary and ultimately gendered view of what constitutes "real" journalism remains. Against this, Lysiak is judged either to be doing what is necessary to fulfill the gendered expectations of doing serious reporting or not— much of which is down to both her age and gender.

Joe Pompeo (2015), for example, former senior media editor at Politico, evaluates Lysiak in both age and gender terms in his *Columbia Journalism Review* article headlined "Is this 8-year-old's newspaper better than yours?" (unlikely, is the sub-text; after all she's only 8!). Pompeo paints an amusing picture of Lysiak as a "freckly blonde 8-year-old" on her bike chasing a story about recent tornado damage in her hometown. He encourages readers to see her as taking her role as journalist and publisher seriously and trying to do a good job, but also to think that she is just a cute little girl not producing "real journalism." Pompeo does, however, concede that since reporting appears to be "low on the list of desirable careers" it is "refreshing to see someone so young so interested in journalism." Whilst she is "far from being a pro" her paper "provides a service in a town without a dedicated local news outlet." Townspeople who want to follow local happenings basically have no choice but to read something put together by an 8-year-old girl. In the end, Pompeo questions Lysiak's achievements, implying that age, gender, hair color, and freckles combine to undermine her authority as a journalist. He concludes:

For locals, it may seem more novelty than pillar of the Fourth Estate. But if Hilde were to stick with it, *The Orange Street News* could evolve into something more meaningful.

Part of the issue with Lysiak's age and gender is also linked to Pompeo's skepticism about hyperlocal newspapers, which he regards as less than proper journalism because they focus on community (rarely important) news. Although *OSN* covers real news stories about murder, burglary, fires, tornadoes, and so on, Pompeo regards its human-interest focus on a small town and use of a personal mode of address as reinforcing a traditional gender binary in journalism practice between hard and soft news, event-oriented stories versus features, "real" (men's) versus "women's" journalism. He implies anything resembling good reporting in *OSN* is a reflection of the skills, knowledge, and expertise of Lysiak's father, who ensures certain standards of genuine journalism are adhered to. As such, the discursive boundaries are re-set and (re)produce binaries across age, gender, urban/rural, objective/subjective as to reify and (re)produce news as either serious/objective/masculine or trivial/subjective/feminine. *OSN* isn't that much different than other hyperlocals, which are also coded as "feminine." What marks *OSN* out as different is that it is written and published by a young girl. Pompeo concludes, "its 8-year-old worldview notwithstanding," the main difference between *OSN* and adult-run community newspapers is that Lysiak's stories are "usually shorter than what you'd expect to see in a professional neighborhood newspaper, but they do the trick."

Maelo Manning

In 2010, when she was 10 years old, Maelo Manning launched her UK-based political blog "LIBDEMCHILD."[1] As the child of two Liberal Democrat party members, Manning often attended party meetings, workshops, and conferences, becoming politically knowledgeable early on. From the start, she realized young people had few opportunities to have their opinions heard at such party events. Consequently, she decided that by creating a blog she would construct a platform not only for herself, but also for other politically aware and active children and young people. On her blog's "About Me" link, she currently identifies herself as "a liberal democrat and feminist of mixed race (half Asian and half Caucasian)" who is studying Politics, Philosophy and Law at Kings College London. She regards the blog as "especially necessary in an age where Brexit, a move largely voted against by young people, and the election of Trump, an open misogynist and sexual abuser, defines western politics." I interviewed Manning (2017) for this chapter to find out more about the challenges she faced as a politically active girl and how the blog allowed her to engage, as a young, mixed race feminist in the public realm of political discourse.

When she launched the blog she received a lot of support from adults and children in the Liberal Democrat political party. That said, she recalls it was still difficult for children to develop a public voice. Girls, in particular, did not feel entirely welcome. Social media was then in its early days and political issues not as widely addressed as now. Almost a decade after she started the blog, many more spaces for girls exist to address a wide range of issues and to more broadly participate in political dialogue. Moreover, as Sowards and Renegar (2006) suggest, online spaces afford opportunities for girls to contribute to rethinking and rebuilding collective forms of feminism for a new technological, social, and political era.

In Manning's view, social media are facilitating the growth of a generation of "politically vocal girls" and girls' and women's use of social media has increased their political standing. Nevertheless, she contends, boys often have a much easier time because the public sphere is still more closely tied to the lives of boys and men than girls and women: "I see this every day with men dismissing feminism, people making subtly racist comments which most people don't challenge and with adults making fun of politics on social media." Moreover, "class and race definitely play a part in how seriously people are taken in politics." As a mixed race woman, she says, "I am still met with shock when I tell people of my political involvement and opinions. My mother, who is Indian, is often not taken seriously when she presents her political opinions even though she is highly educated."

Despite advances girls have made in terms of being heard, in her view, discrimination on the linked basis of age and gender continues to prevent young girls from being taken seriously, "as young people are viewed as ignorant and women have always been prevented from full involvement in politics." This point supports my central argument that adults tend to view children and young people as deficient cognitively, socially, culturally, and politically. As such, their contributions to public deliberation are typically regarded as naïve and ill-informed and routinely ignored. As Manning submits, "young girls are the demographic that face the greatest challenge in politics even if barriers are being removed."

Although many social, political, economic, and technological changes over the past decade have benefitted some girls and women, many wonder about their right to inhabit and have voice in the public sphere, as journalists, political commentators or, indeed, as politicians. Manning notes how male-dominated Parliament, particularly Prime Minister's Question Time,[2] is "off-putting to young girls. It seems like a male-dominated shouting match rather than an ordered political debate." This weekly scheduled, macho style of political exchange, frequently coupled with patronizing comments about women MPs, creates an inhospitable atmosphere for women. The chaotic sexism of Westminster makes it seem "impossible for young girls to even begin to think about being involved in politics." This despite the fact that the current Prime Minister is a woman, whom Manning regards as embodying "anti-feminist ideals." Manning concludes:

> The fact that only a 1/3 of Parliament is female is very discouraging and is something that has always horrified me as it makes political involvement for women seem like an impossibility even if girls manage to overcome the confusion of understanding political jargon and debate.

Despite this apparent pessimism, Manning continues to encourage girls to get involved in public debate. Notwithstanding many challenges to her right to a voice of her own by those who would dismiss her as a naïve young girl, the experience of starting and continuously contributing to her blog has been positive. Public acknowledgment from the news media and political websites has been "the most empowering experience of my life."

Public exposure for her views and comments has left Manning hopeful for a better future. "Even if my voice is just a drop in the ocean it is a start." She is not alone, remarking that "I am only one of many of hundreds of young girls trying to improve politics and make it more accessible for other girls." What has, however, marked her out as different from many of her contemporaries is that she has "been able to offer a consistent perspective of a young girl to the political debate and this is so important in order for politics to be representative, as it is supposed to be in the UK." Acknowledged for her contributions to public discourse, she recommends blogging to other girls:

> The representation of young girls of different classes, races, religions and abilities is essential for a truly holistic view of young girls wants/needs in politics and this can only be achieved through more and more girls becoming involved in politics.

Manning's views on how public/political discourse links to journalism, news, and current affairs are insightful. Historically, journalism has not served girls and women particularly well; as a result, they have been prevented from having an impact upon the political processes that govern and shape their lives. As Clark and Marchi argue, when girls and women are underrepresented in online discussions of news and politics, "the views that are *held* by the public are not the views that are *heard* by the public, resulting in skewed public debates" (2018, p. 188). Manning (2017) agrees, contending that "when girls engage with the news, and are, in turn, taken more seriously by newsmakers, they inevitably become more socially aware and are able to better their own position." One clear example of this is the reemergence of feminist critique facilitated by social media (Kellar, 2015, 2016; Kim & Ringrose, 2018; Sowards & Renegar, 2006). "I see so many young girls now referring to themselves as feminist," Manning notes,

> The emergence of a new generation of feminists due to engagement with politics online has bolstered the impact that girls directly have on politics and our own ability to improve our circumstances.

One problem of becoming more public and expressing one's views as girls and women is the online backlash. Manning gets many hateful comments regarding the views she expresses on the blog. But "none of them have really impacted upon my confidence to post online because I know that is just something that accompanies an online presence, particularly one with a feminist perspective." Much of the criticism has come from people who assumed no young girl could write so knowledgeably—that she must be simply parroting what her parents told her to say. She found this accusation "very hurtful and off-putting." Often such remarks appeared to imply that young people either hold no political views of their own and are therefore vulnerable to manipulation by adults, including parents, or are not sufficiently knowledgeable to warrant public spaces to express their political ignorance. Perhaps, she suggests, this is why many young people find becoming politically involved so difficult.

Manning has also received insults about her weight and eyebrows. Someone suggested that expressing feminist ideas made her seem 40 years old. In addition to such sexist (and ageist) slurs, she has also encountered racist abuse. For example, she was sent a photo of a KKK member holding a noose as a threat when she tweeted about racism in the US. Manning says that many abusive comments were a direct retaliation against her speaking out.

> But I have really gotten used to this hatred and I would rather face it then stay silent on issues that I really care about. This retaliation against young people and women speaking out online is so prevalent and I witness it every day against other girls. The assumption that women have no place in politics definitely manifests itself online especially amongst internet trolls who believe they can remain anonymous.

Nonetheless, Manning remains optimistic about the potential of social media to help transform young people's lives as they create possibilities for public participation. For her, what is particularly impressive is how social media facilitated feminism's reemergence and revitalization as well as young people's political activism. Her December 31, 2014 blog entry "2014 Was the Year of the Young Person," listed young people's important contributions to political discussion over the year (Manning, 2014). The highlights included 16 and 17-year-olds' voting in the referendum on Scottish independence; participation in raising public awareness around police racism and brutality after the police killing of 18-year-old Mike Brown in Ferguson, Missouri; protests over the high cost of tuition fees in the UK; and, young people talking about transgender issues after the suicide of 17-year-old Leelah Alcorn, whose parents refused to allow her to transition. Manning believes that girls' increased interest in online political activities have "ushered in a whole new generation of politically aware young women who are able to interact with politics and shape the political debate."

Conclusion

The contemporary reemergence and rethinking of more critical, collective forms of feminism offers important opportunities to re-examine how the gendering of news and journalism have generally privileged the voices and views of boys and men. This has personal, social, and political consequences for young girls as citizens.

I have advocated here for feminist research on critical, politically engaged reconceptualizations of girls and girlhood. The goal, in my view, is to challenge hegemonic norms and assumptions about what constitutes "real" news and journalism and who is authorized to do it. Girls and boys are always already shaped by both the private and public. So to assign a gender to one or the other sphere, or to particular forms of news content and news practices, is problematic, particularly at a time of widespread acknowledgment of transgender fluidity. A key task of such research would be to identify and analyze where girls are already making a range of civic contributions and developing critical voices that challenge gender binaries. The efforts of Hilde Lysiak and Maelo Manning offer just two examples, which I hope might encourage further research exploring the extent to which they challenge taken-for-granted assumptions about girls' public agency. Documenting such activities would help to expand feminist knowledge and the gendering of journalism. At the same time, it would contribute to the critical task of attending to wider societal issues around journalism, social justice, gender fairness, and equality.

Notes

1 The blog was renamed when Manning turned 18. It is now called "Liberal Girl Aged 18."
2 Prime Minister's Question Time is televised to the public on the Parliamentary Channel and online, when the UK Parliament is in session. This is the only opportunity to which citizens have access where Members of Parliament put questions directly to the Prime Minister.

References

Anderson, M., & Jiang, J. (2018, May 31). *Teens, social media & technology 2018*. Pew Research Centre, Internet & Technology. Retrieved from www.pewinternet.org/2018/05/31/teens-social-media-technology-2018/

Ariés, P. (1962). *Centuries of childhood*. New York, NY: Vintage.

Banet-Weiser, S. (2007). *Kids rule! Nickelodeon and consumer citizenship*. Durham, NC: Duke University Press.

Blue, M. G., & Kearney, M. C. (Eds). (2018). *Mediated girlhoods: New explorations of girls' media culture* (Vol. 2). New York, NY: Peter Lang.

Boateng, K. J. A. (2017, June). Reversal of gender disparity in journalism education—Study of Ghana institute of journalism. *Observatario*, 118–135. Retrieved from www.research gate.net/publication/318662298_Reversal_of_Gender_Disparity_in_Journalism_Edu cation-_Study_of_Ghana_Institute_of_Journalism

Bobkowski, P. S., & Belmas, G. I. (2017). Mixed message media: Girls' voices and civic engagement in student journalism. *Girlhood Studies, 10*(1), 89–106.

Cann, V. (2018). *Girls like this, boys like that: The reproduction of gender in contemporary youth cultures*. London: IB Taurus.

Carter, C., & Messenger Davies, M. (2005). "A fresh peach is easier to bruise": children, young people and the news. In S. Allan (Ed.), *Journalism: Critical issues* (pp. 224–238). Maidenhead and New York, NY: Open University Press.

Carter, C., Messenger Davies, M., Allan, S., & Mendes, K. (2009). *What do children want from the BBC? Children's content and participatory environments in an age of citizen media*. Retrieved from www.bbc.co.uk/blogs/knowledgeexchange/cardifftwo.pdf

Chambers, D., Steiner, L., & Fleming, C. (2004). *Women and journalism*. London: Routledge.

Clark, L. S., & Marchi, R. (2018). *Young people and the future of news*. Cambridge: Cambridge University Press.

Crump, S. (2010, May 2). Julie Zeilinger, creator of thefbomb.org, examines teen feminist issues. *Cleveland.com*. Retrieved from www.cleveland.com/arts/index.ssf/2010/05/julie_zeilinger_creator_of_the.html

Gill, R. (2007). *Gender and the media*. Cambridge: Polity Press.

Gotz, M., Lemish, D., Aidman, A., & Moon, H. (Eds.). (2005). *Media and the make-believe worlds of children: When Harry Potter meets Pokemon in Disneyland*. Mahwah, NJ: Lawrence Erlbaum.

Gunter, B., Furnham, A., & Griffiths, S. (2000). Children's memory for news: A comparison of three presentation media. *Media Psychology, 2*, 93–118. doi:10.1207/S153278 5XMP0202_1

Jackman, T. (2016). 9-year-old reporter breaks crime news, posts videos, fires back at critics. *Washington Post*. Retrieved from www.washingtonpost.com/news/true-crime/wp/2016/04/05/9-year-old-reporter-breaks-crime-news-posts-videos-fires-back-at-critics/?noredirect=on&utm_term=.d2b7358b95f0

Jenks, C. (1992). *The sociology of childhood*. Aldershot: Ashgate.

Jenks, C. (2004). Constructing childhood sociologically. In M. J. Kehily (Ed.), *An introduction to childhood studies* (pp. 77–95). Maidenhead: Open University Press.

Jia, S., Lansdall-Welfare, T., Sudhahar, S., Carter, C., & Cristianini, N. (2016). Women are seen more than heard in online newspapers. *Plos One*. PONE-D-15-28076R2.

Joseph, A. (2015). Media and gender in India: Part of the IFJ media and gender in Asia-Pacific research project. *IFJ*. Retrieved from www.ifj.org/uploads/media/INDIA.pdf

Kearney, M. C. (Ed.). (2011). *Mediated girlhoods: New explorations of girls' media culture*. New York, NY: Peter Lang.

Keller, J. (2015). *Girls' feminist blogging in a postfeminist age*. New York, NY: Routledge.

Keller, J. (2016). Making activism accessible: Exploring girls' blogs as sites of contemporary feminist activism. In C. Mitchell & C. Rentschler (Eds.), *The politics of place: Contemporary paradigms for research in girlhood studies* (pp. 261–278). New York, NY: Berghahan Books.

Kim, C., & Ringrose, J. (2018). "Stumbling upon feminism": Teenage girls forays into digital and school-based feminisms. *Girlhood Studies, 11*(2), 46–62.

Lemish, D. (1998). What is news? A cross-cultural examination of kindergartners' understanding of news. *Communication: European Journal of Communication Research, 23*, 491–504.

Lemish, D. (2007). *Children and television: A global perspective*. Oxford: Wiley-Blackwell.

Lemish, D. (2013). Boys are . . . girls are . . . how children's media and merchandising construct gender. In C. Carter, L. Steiner, & L. McLaughlin (Eds.), *Routledge companion to media and gender* (pp. 179–189). New York, NY: Routledge.

Lemish, D., & Alony, R. P. (2014). The gendered nature of news consumption by children and youth. *Participations, 11*(1). Retrieved from www.participations.org/Volume%2011/Issue%201/10.pdf

Lysiak, H. K. (2016, April 6). Yes, I'm a nine-year-old girl: But I'm still a serious reporter. *The Guardian*. Retrieved from www.theguardian.com/commentisfree/2016/apr/06/nine-year-old-reporter-orange-street-news-truth

Manning, M. (2014). 2014 was the year of the young person. *Blog Entry*. Retrieved from http://libdemchild.blogspot.com/search?q=transgender

Manning, M. (2017, October 10). Personal email interview.

Mazzarella, S. R., & Pecora, N. O. (Eds.). (1999). *Growing up girls: Popular culture and the construction of identity*. New York, NY: Peter Lang.

McRobbie, A. (2000). *Feminism and youth culture* (2nd ed.). London: Routledge.

McRobbie, A. (2008). *The aftermath of feminism: Gender, culture and social change*. Thousand Oaks, CA: Sage Publications.

Messenger Davies, M. (2004). Innocent victims, active citizens. *Mediactive, 3*, 55–66.

Piaget, J. (1969). *The origins of intelligence in the child*. New York, NY: International University Press.

Pompeo, J. (2015, September–October). Is this 8-year-old's newspaper better than yours? *Columbia Journalism Review*. Retrieved from www.cjr.org/the_profile/orange_street_news.php

Reid, A. (2015, January 23). Women outnumber men on UK journalism degrees. *Journalism.co.uk*. Retrieved from www.journalism.co.uk/news/women-outnumber-men-on-uk-journalism-degrees/s2/a563890/

Ross, K., Boyle, K., Carter, C., & Ging, D. (2018). Women, men and news: "It's life, Jim, but not as we know it" *Journalism Studies, 19*(6), 824–845.

Ross, K., & Carter, C. (2011). Women and news: A long and winding road. *Media, Culture & Society, 33*(8), 1148–1165.

Ruiz-Grossman, S. (2016, April 27). Street teens in India launch their own newspaper. *HuffPost*. Edition UK. Retrieved from www.huffingtonpost.co.uk/entry/balak nama-street-children-newspaper-india_us_571f8bf2e4b0b49df6a90bb5?guccounter=1

Senft, T. M. (2008). *Camgirls: Celebrity & community in the age of social networks*. New York, NY: Peter Lang.

Sharma, M. (n.d.). Balaknama: Making headlines that matter. *Hindustan Times*. Retrieved from www.hindustantimes.com/static/making-headlines-that-matter/

Shelley, L. (2009). Female journalists and journalism in Fin-de-siècle magazine stories. *Nineteenth Century Gender Studies, 5*(2). Retrieved from www.ncgsjournal.com/issue52/shelley.htm

Smith, R. (2016, April 26). Meet Janna Jihad, the 10-year-old journalist reporting on deadly conflict in the West Bank. *News.com.au*. Retrieved from www.news.com.au/technology/online/social/meet-janna-jihad-the-10yearold-journalist-reporting-on-deadly-conflicts-in-the-west-bank/news-story/b8d2e662e6d396c9ee12fcc8a9fff62c

Smith, S. L., & Wilson, B. J. (2002). Children's comprehension of and fear reactions to television news. *Media Psychology, 4*(1), 1–26.

Sowards, S. K., & Renegar, V. R. (2006). Reconceptualizing rhetorical activism in feminist contexts. *Howard Journal of Communications, 17*(1), 57–74.

Steiner, L. (1998). Newsroom accounts of power at work. In C. Carter, G. Branston, & S. Allan (Eds.), *News, gender and power* (pp. 145–159). London: Routledge.

University of Birmingham, Centre for Contemporary Cultural Studies (1978). *Women take issue: Aspects of women's subordination*. London: Hutchinson (for the Centre for Contemporary Cultural Studies).

van der Molen, J. W. (2004, June). Violence and suffering in television news: Toward a broader conception of harmful television content for children. *Paediatrics, 112*(6), 1771–1775.

Venkatraman, S. (2016, April 14). Meet the street children making their own newspaper in India. *The Guardian*. Retrieved from www.theguardian.com/global-development-profes sionals-network/2016/apr/14/street-children-journalist-balaknama-newspaper-delhi-india

Wannamaker, A. (Ed.). (2011). *Mediated boyhoods: Boys, teens, and young men in popular culture*. New York, NY: Peter Lang.

Wikipedia. (2018). *Janna Jihad*. Retrieved from https://en.wikipedia.org/wiki/Janna_Jihad

Women's Media Center. (2018). *WMC FBomb*. Retrieved from www.womensmediacenter.com/fbomb/

York, C. (2017, September 18). Women dominate journalism schools, but newsrooms are still a different story. *Poynter*. Retrieved from www.poynter.org/news/women-dominate-journalism-schools-newsrooms-are-still-different-story

Zeilinger, J. (2018). *The FBomb*. Retrieved from http://juliezeilinger.com/thefbomb/

17

MEDIATED, GENDERED ACTIVISM IN THE "POST-ARAB SPRING" ERA

Lessons from Tunisia's "Jasmine Revolution"

Sahar Khamis

Seven years after the so-called Arab Spring uprisings erupted, a wide array of outcomes unfolded in the six countries that witnessed these waves of revolt. Likewise, different outcomes unfolded for Arab women, who were instrumental in instigating and supporting these movements. This chapter sheds light on the various courses that Arab women's activisms and resistances have taken in "post-Arab Spring" countries. I ask: How did the conditions of these countries and their various paths to political reform influence the political, social, and legal conditions of women, as well as the level, form, and intensity of their activism and resistance efforts, both online and offline? How did Arab women engage in the three simultaneous, parallel struggles, and what tools did they use? I include the voices of some Arab women journalists, activists, and professionals who participated in these movements in different capacities. I focus on Tunisia, whose path to democratic transition and women's activism was the smoothest: Tunisia's "Jasmine Revolution"[1] yields various lessons for both the political realm of democratic transition and the social realm of gender activism.

Arab women's shifting roles and realities in a transforming region

In 2011 the "Arab Awakening" movements began to sweep across Tunisia, Egypt, Libya, Syria, Bahrain, and Yemen. This historical moment, which signified the resistance, resilience, and struggle of Arab peoples against dictatorship, oppression, and corruption, was often hailed as ushering a new future for Arab people (El Nawawy & Khamis, 2013; Jumet, 2017).

The Arab Spring began when a young fruit and vegetable vendor from a small Tunisian town set himself on fire, in objection to a sad combination of economic distress, repression, and humiliation (Mili, 2018). A few days after the Tunisian revolution, Egyptians were inspired to break their own shackles and end President

Hosni Mubarak's three decades of dictatorial rule. Many Egyptians felt that if a small country like Tunisia could demonstrate such heroism, why not a country with Egypt's political and demographic heft (Khamis & Vaughn, 2013). The driving force behind the Tunisian and Egyptian revolutions, and then the rest of the "Arab Spring" uprisings, were primarily young people. They were mostly upper-middle class, urban, educated, and technologically savvy, since the challenges of influencing nations and addressing global issues is more likely to inspire creative solutions from young citizens with access to digital communication tools (Bennett, 2008). And cyberactivism, "the act of using the Internet to advance a political cause that is difficult to advance offline" (Howard, 2011, p. 145), was crucial to the "Arab Spring," when young people relied on internet-enabled communication platforms, such as Facebook, Twitter, YouTube, and blogs (Khamis & Vaughn, 2013).

Also important to the "Arab Spring" movements was women's heroism across the six countries. Many women, even in some of the more traditional, conservative countries, like Libya and Yemen, took to the streets, protesting, marching, chanting, and calling for ending decades of oppression by authoritarian regimes. Here they were not playing stereotypical roles for women, such as nurturing or supporting men in their struggle for freedom. Rather, they were at the front lines of resistance, risking their own lives and safety, and exposing themselves to arrest and assault (Alamm, 2012; Al-Malki, Kaufer, Ishizaki, & Dreher, 2012; Khamis, 2016). Youth activism and women's activism during the "Arab Spring" uprisings were two sides of the same coin, since most women activists were under the age of 40, and many of them, like most people their age, relied heavily on social media tools to amplify their messages of dissent and protest. The reliance of Arab women activists on social media tools to achieve political and social gains exemplifies "cyberfeminism," i.e., "the innovative ways women are using digital technologies to reengineer their lives," to raise awareness about women's issues, and overcome the challenges confronting them (Daniels, 2009, p. 103). Through this phenomenon, feminist activists deploy new media tools in order to shake and challenge political and social power structures by participating in the "remaking of power" (Mili, 2015, 2018) in their respective countries.

Sadly, many Arab women activists paid high prices for their courage and bravery: imprisonment, exile, harassment, rape, and even death. For example, in September 2017 a 60-year-old Syrian human rights activist who was investigating torture inside Assad's prisons, and her daughter, a journalist with the Syrian opposition network Orient News, were brutally stabbed to death in their apartment in Istanbul, Turkey. Syrian-American journalist Laila Alhusini explained why she was devastated by the news:

> These were two brave, outspoken women, who were fighting for the basic human rights of their own people who suffered the worst humanitarian crisis in modern times. They flee from their home country out of concern for their own safety, but, even in exile, they were not safe! Unfortunately, they are not

the first, and I'm afraid they will not be the last, women activists and journalists to pay such high price for their courage and bravery!

(Personal interview, September 2017)

On a positive note, Arab women's heroism drew local, regional, and international attention, appreciation, and recognition. For the first time an Arab woman won the Nobel Peace Prize—Yemeni activist and journalist, Tawakkul Karman, who was known as "the mother of Yemen's revolution," due to her active role in organizing peaceful, pro-democracy protests in Yemen, one of the more traditional, conservative Arab countries. Arab women have been constantly engaging in three interconnected and intertwined struggles, namely: the political struggle against tyranny, dictatorship and autocracy; the social struggle against misogyny, patriarchy, and stagnant traditions; and the legal struggle against laws that deny them their basic rights. These struggles took varying forms, directions, and levels of intensity over different phases, extending before, during, and after the "Arab Spring" uprisings (Khamis & Mili, 2018). The early stages of Arab feminism were mostly characterized by a top-down, state-imposed form of elitist, or even token, feminism that was oftentimes envisioned and led by the ruler in power and/or the first lady. In contrast, the contemporary form of bottom-up, grassroots feminism involves a wide array of Arab women (Charrad & Zarrugh, 2014; Khamis & Mili, 2018; Labidi, 2014; Mili, 2015, 2018).

The path to democratization and reform in most of the so-called Arab Spring countries was not as smooth or straightforward as hoped for: it brought widely varying, but mostly undesirable, outcomes. The same for the path to gender equity and reform. In most cases, the level of political freedom allowed in each country, or lack thereof, had a strong and clear correlation to, on one hand, the level of women's activism and, on the other hand, the success of women's gender equity movements, politically, socially, and legally, or lack thereof. Often, setbacks to reform and democratization in the Arab region inevitably resulted in dire consequences simultaneously for women's movements and activism (Khalil, 2014). For example, Egypt shifted from a glorious moment of historical solidarity in 2011 to deep division, polarization, and fragmentation in 2013, when its first democratically elected president, Mohamed Morsi, was deposed in what has variously been described as a military coup, a popular uprising, and a popularly backed coup (Jumet, 2017). This resulted in setbacks not just politically, but also socially, in terms of women's ability to participate fully and equally in Egypt's socio-political transformation. Egyptian activist and academic Amal Bakry sadly explains that the reversal in Egypt's attempt to secure democratization resulted in a significant backlash in women's activism. A politically active group such as "No Military Trials for Civilians," in which women assumed positions of leadership and visibility, both online and offline, is not visible or active to the same degree. She added that many activists are now in a state of despair, hopelessness, and fatigue, due to fears of torture, violations of human rights, and a general atmosphere of repression and apprehension, which deters many of them from continuing their struggle with the same degree of vigor and resilience. According to Bakry:

> Many activists, both men and women, have abandoned politics altogether, while some have fled the country and live in exile. There is, of course, a small number of 'activism survivors' who are still speaking out and resisting, but their numbers are dwindling and their activities are also shrinking, due to the current political climate in the country, sadly enough!
>
> *(Personal interview, September, 2017)*

Likewise, Egyptian-American academic Nahed Eltantawy says Egypt's current atmosphere of confined and restricted freedoms affects not just political groups fighting for citizens' rights, but also social groups fighting against all forms of discrimination and violence, including violence and harassment against women. She finds that the performance, visibility, and activity level of many of these groups, especially those that were created and led by women, have dropped, due to the stifling of freedoms and Egypt's suffocating political environment. She echoes Bakry's point regarding the feelings of young activists, both male and female, of loss of hope, despair, and discouragement:

> Even when some of these young activists use their social media platforms today, it is mostly to lament the current state of affairs, to express their disappointments and frustrations, and to vent their emotions, rather than to call for action or to inspire change through proactive steps and meaningful organization, as they used to do during the good old 'golden' days of the 2011 revolution.
>
> *(Personal interview, September, 2017)*

Notably, Bahrain, a small oil-rich Gulf country, where the popular uprising against the regime failed, but women's rights enjoyed a more favorable outcome, represents an interesting anomaly. Shedding light on this paradox, Bahraini journalist and activist Nada Alwadi explained:

> Although the governmental crackdown on the popular uprising in Bahrain in 2011 generally resulted in an overall atmosphere of fear, intimidation, and apprehension, and forced a number of Bahraini activists and journalists, including myself, to flee the country and to live in exile, out of fear for their safety and the safety of their families, there was one small breakthrough in favor of women which came about rather unexpectedly. In the aftermath of this governmental crackdown, which resulted in excluding, arresting, or exiling many of the conservative Shiite opposition leaders, some of whom were religious clerics who wanted to adopt a conservative Shiite family law, a relative improvement came about in the push for women's rights, through some pro-government women activists, who captured this unique opportunity to pass less conservative, and more women-friendly, family laws, which are in line with international human rights laws and conventions.
>
> *(Personal interview, August, 2017)*

Alwadi added that some of the few conservative Shiite clerics who didn't get arrested or exiled decided to boycott the political process and the elections. This allowed women's voices to be more loudly heard, both offline and online, in the process of legislating new family laws that were more women-sensitive and less restrictive or oppressive. Yet, she also acknowledged that such breakthroughs remain limited, partial, and far from ideal, mainly because champions of such laws include pro-government women, who mostly represent a top-down form of state feminism that doesn't represent, or speak for, the majority of Bahraini women. These limited reforms are also being used by the authoritarian Bahraini regime, according to Alwadi, as a tool to improve its image and to boost its credibility and popularity, both domestically and internationally. Therefore, one should regard such limited gains with a degree of "cautionary optimism," as Alwadi puts it, since they are necessary, but certainly not sufficient. They do not reflect an overall change in the dominant Bahraini mindset or the prevailing public opinion regarding women's rights and gender equality. Overall, however, they do represent a good step in the right direction.

This hasn't been seen in other post-Arab Spring countries, except for Tunisia. Politically, Tunisia provides a successful model of peaceful coexistence, successful coalition-building, and effective, bloodless rotation of power (Calamur, 2015). Thanks to its small size, minimum foreign intervention in its internal affairs, and its high literacy rate of over 90 percent (unlike most Arab countries, which suffer from high illiteracy rates), as well as the dedication, hard work, and coordination of its civil society actors (four of its civil society organizations won the 2015 Nobel Peace Prize), Tunisia is a model to be emulated by fellow Arab Spring countries. Socially, "Tunisian exceptionalism" extends beyond the political sphere into the social sphere of securing gender equity and protecting women's rights, given the success of Tunisian women's activism, both online and offline, as discussed below.

Tunisia's success story: breaking new ground in gender equity and women's rights

Tunisia, the only country so far that survived its tumultuous waves and unsettling outcomes, has been a pioneer in women's rights since its birth as a modern state in 1956 (Khamis, 2017). However, its feminist movement traces back to before its independence from France, with the emergence of a Tunisian reform movement focusing upon women's rights by the early twentieth century. The reformers called for modern education for all children, changes to laws and traditions judged prejudicial to women, unveiling, and, eventually, the vote (Charrad, 2001). This first phase of feminism in Tunisia attracted the support of middle-class, urban men and women who were tied to the nationalist movement.

The second stage of Tunisia's feminism was intertwined with postcolonial nation-building, after gaining its independence from France in 1956. Under the vision of its modern founder, President Bourquiba, who ruled Tunisia from 1956 to 1987, Tunisia leaped forward on the road to secure women's rights and gender equality ahead of its Arab neighbors. One of Bourquiba's most significant achieve-ments was introducing the Code of Personal Status (CPS), which was consid-ered the most revolutionary law in the Arab world at that time (Charrad, 2001; Labidi, 2014; Mili, 2013, 2015). This phase of feminism brought excellent gains for Tunisian women, such as the right to free education and making girls' education compulsory until 16 years of age, which remarkably boosted literacy rates in the country, in general, and among women and girls, in particular, and raising the age of marriage to 17 years for girls and 18 years for boys (later changed to 20 years for boys). Since then, Tunisian women have also seen rights to free education, equal pay for equal work (Charrad & Zarrugh, 2014; Mili, 2015, 2018).

The main problem with this early phase of feminism, however, was that it was a "top-down" form of "state feminism." Officially imposed by the top political lead-ership, it didn't always trickle down sufficiently to alter existing cultural predisposi-tions, social attitudes, and traditional mindsets, among the broader base of both men and women (Moghadam, 2003; Nazir, 2005).

Not until the third, current phase of feminism, which accompanied the "Arab Spring" movements, did we start to see the emergence of across the board, grassroots activists who started to embrace elements of both modern and traditional Tunisian identity, as well as merging both secular and religious views, and advancing political and social causes simultaneously through a myriad of online and offline tools. Amel Mili, a Tunisian-American academic and a former judge in Tunisia, remarks:

> It is through this third phase that genuine progress in gender equity and women's rights can truly be achieved, because it represents a more inclu-sive, diverse, comprehensive, and balanced approach to gender equity and gender activism, which attracts women across the board and speaks to their needs and demands. Most importantly, it allows them to speak 'for' and 'about' themselves in their own voice.
>
> *(Personal interview, September, 2017)*

When Ben Ali came to power in 1987, he tried to boost his popularity by main-taining many of the gender gains secured under his predecessor Bourquiba, and to add new ones, such as offering state financial support to divorced women and their children, as well as granting Tunisian citizenship to the children of Tunisian women who married foreigners (Mili, 2018). He also allowed a relatively wider margin of freedom, at least initially, regarding forming grassroots civil society organizations. Taking advantage of this (temporary) democratic opening, Tunisian women activ-ists formed the NGO *Tunisian Association of Democratic Women* (TADW). The crea-tion of this organization and similar organizations is important because it marks a shift in gender politics from a top-down approach, where progress is driven by state actors, to a bottom-up approach, where gender activists take matters in their own hands and drive the evolution of gender standards. Hence progress no longer depends on the goodwill of powerful state actors, but rather on the dedication of the main stakeholders, i.e., Tunisian women themselves (Mili, 2013, 2015, 2018).

The eruption of Tunisia's "Jasmine Revolution" in 2011 showed that Tunisia's struggles for gender equality are closely intertwined with struggles for democratic governance (Mili, 2018). Many young women activists, who deployed all their online and offline tools and resources in order for their voices to be heard, captured this golden moment to ensure that their parallel struggle to uphold democracy and liberation from dictatorship, and to secure gender equity and liberation from patriarchy, misogyny, and social repression are widely recognized (El Nawawy & Khamis, 2013; Khamis & Mili, 2018).

One of the most prominent figures in this regard is the young, yet very brave and outspoken, Tunisian blogger, Lina Ben Mhenni, whose blog "A Tunisian Girl," published in Arabic, English, and French, went viral and reached a vast national and international audience. Mhenni drew wide admiration from those who shared her liberal stand and desire for freedom, as well as equally widespread criticism, or even attacks, from those who didn't agree (El Nawawy & Khamis, 2013). Born to activist parents (her father was a political prisoner, and her mother was part of the student union movement), she inherited courage and boldness. She was one of the few Internet activists and bloggers who used their real names, rather than using a pseudonym to protect her identity in order to avoid regime retaliation and dangerous consequences. This was a double-edged sword for her. On one hand, it earned her international visibility and recognition: she won the Deutsche Welle International Blog Award and El Mundo International Journalism Prize and was nominated for the Nobel Peace Prize in 2011 (Walker, 2011). On the other hand, however, her blog, as well as her Facebook page and her Twitter account, were frequently censored under the Ben Ali regime, because she was offering uncensored accounts of what was going on inside her country to both a local and an international audience (Walker, 2011).

Mhenni was also equally daring in both her political and social views, opening fire on political systems of repression, such as Ben Ali's dictatorship and the corruption of his regime and police forces, as well as social systems of repression, as exemplified in stagnant traditions and discrimination against women (El Nawawy & Khamis, 2013). She was determined to continue activism after the deposing of Ben Ali, which she described as only the beginning, rather than the end, of the revolution. Notably, the prominent Egyptian activist and blogger, Nawara Negm, was similarly a young woman at the time of the uprisings, with two prominent, politically active parents, who were imprisoned several times due to their activism, and a very large following on her blog and other social media platforms, in addition to her on-the-ground activism. Like Mhenni, Negm broke political and social taboos, tackling issues such as violations of human rights, police brutality, and governmental corruption, as well as sexual harassment on the streets of Cairo. By doing so, she and other young bloggers created a spillover from the realm of "cyberactivism" (Howard, 2011) to the realm of mainstream media, which was compelled to cover these sensitive issues, for the first time (El Nawawy & Khamis, 2013). However, unlike Mhenni, Nawara, has unfortunately stopped her activism, both online and offline, mainly due to the current political atmosphere in Egypt, which became highly repressive, polarized, and fragmented. This underscores the close connection between a country's margin of political freedom and its margin of mediated social activism. In launching these two parallel political and social struggles, Tunisian feminist activists and bloggers, as well as other young bloggers in other parts of the Arab world, exemplified the growing phenomenon of "cyberfeminism," with its multiple manifestations and implications (Daniels, 2009).

With the fall of Tunisia's dictator, Ben Ali, who ruled from 1987 to 2011, and after conducting free and fair elections, Tunisia's moderate Islamist party *Ennahda* (which means "the renaissance") came to power. Its well-organized structure and leadership enabled it to attract a wide base of popular support, and thus to win the elections, despite decades of repression under successive regimes (Mili, 2018). Some people tried to redefine the principle of gender equality under *Ennahda* party as "gender complementarity." This principle appears benign on the surface. But in reality and in practice, it denies women equal opportunities, as it largely confines their roles to the traditional, private domain of marriage and motherhood (Charrad & Zarrugh, 2014). This led to wide resistance and opposition from many segments of society, cutting across ideological, generational, and even gender, differences. Large numbers of protestors, including men, joined public demonstrations against this new provision and held signs declaring their support for gender "equality," not "complementarity" (Khamis, 2017; Mili, 2018). These acts of resistance became visible and these voices of protest were amplified and went viral with the help of some Tunisian women's organizations.

These tensions signified a rhetorical tug of war, which led some activists and bloggers, who continued their struggle against all forms of repression and injustice after the "Jasmine Revolution," to speak up against what they saw as "the double discourse" of *Ennahda* Islamist party, which talks about women's rights, on one hand, while trying to take actions which could potentially curb these rights, on the other hand. Mhenni said:

> I personally think they (*Ennahda*) have a double discourse. For example, when their leaders are speaking to the media they have one discourse—but on social media, in videos of their members' behavior, for example, they say that women should stay at home as a solution for employment.
>
> *(Walker, 2011)*

Out of fear of losing hard-earned gender gains under *Ennahda* party, groups of Tunisian women started working very hard to ensure the "constitutionalization of gender equity" (Mili, 2015, 2018). Having been excluded from a committee working to draft the 2014 constitution, and not being invited to the national constitutional assembly to give feedback on the draft constitution, some women activists created a fictitious/virtual national assembly where they worked for months to draft a Tunisian constitution and conveyed it to the National Assembly (Mili, 2015). This shows Tunisian women's resourcefulness and determination to ensure agency and a voice in the legal domain, even when they are officially excluded from the decision-making process.

The constitution ultimately included many important gender equity provisions. It became the nucleus for a new law passed in 2017 combatting violence against women and emphasizing gender equality. Hailed as a landmark in shielding women from violence, this law widens the definition of "violence" by including sexual, physical, emotional, economic, and political violence. This constitutes an unprecedented, comprehensive level of acknowledgment of violence. It also criminalizes all forms of "discrimination" based on gender in all spheres (Khamis, 2017). This law, the first in the Arab world, moved the notion of violence out of the private, domestic sphere and into the public sphere. Tunisia's legal breakthrough also ushers a new era of gender gains for the Arab region as a whole. For example, one of the provisions eradicates the controversial article that Tunisian feminists often called the "Law of Shame" because it provided rapists with a legal loophole to escape from punishment, if they marry their victims—including when the victim was a minor. The new law raised the age of consensual sex to 16 years, and criminalized any sexual contact with a minor (Feki, 2017; Khamis, 2017). Emulating Tunisia's successful model, Jordan and Lebanon have also abolished the infamous "Law of Shame." Just as Tunisia's "Jasmine Revolution" snowballed to five other Arab countries, its legal reform and gender equity revolution is now creating a ripple effect in the rest of the region, thanks to the amplification of these voices of change and calls for reform through many mediated platforms, such as Facebook pages, YouTube videos, and blogs.

On the social front, the Tunisian Association of Democratic Women (TADW) established the first counseling center for victims of domestic violence in March 1993, and spoke out against all forms of violence perpetrated on women, including political violence directed at dissidents and political candidates, as well as economic violence in the job market and the workplace. This group created a Facebook page in both French and Arabic, in order to reach interested communities and supporters on social media (Mili, 2013, 2015). This group organized a virtual/fictitious tribunal for victims of violence: Feminists from the MENA (Middle East and North Africa) region came to take part in the tribunal, as did women who were victims of all types of violence. They told their stories to the public, openly and frankly (Mili, 2015). This innovative approach helped to increase the salience and visibility of the sensitive issue of violence against women by breaking the silence around this taboo issue, which has been traditionally hidden. Moreover, it involved a spillover from the realm of citizen journalism to the realm of mainstream media, which covered this unprecedented event.

A shocking campaign to combat and expose physical and sexual violence against women in Tunisia was launched online in 2016, under the telling name "WARRI," which means "show" in Arabic. The aim was to spread awareness about gender-based violence, which at least half of Tunisian women suffer in some form at some point in their lives (Albawaba, 2016). Its visual imagery was highly controversial, especially among conservative groups in Tunisia, since a lot of the women were posing semi-naked, in order to show the bruises, injuries, and bleeding wounds in different parts of their bodies. Nevertheless, the website received more than 11,000 likes as soon as it was created, and the numbers kept growing, as more and more people started to support this daring campaign, which was started by an equally daring male Tunisian photographer known for championing gender-based causes (Albawaba, 2016). When Facebook took down one of the semi-nude photos of one of the injured victims, the campaign objected by boldly posing a question: "Which is more dangerous, nudity or violence?!" With its slogan "violence is more serious than nudity," the website answered its own question.

Learned lessons and future forecasts

The revisiting of Arab women's multiple roles, activisms, and resistances across different Arab countries before, during, and after the "Arab Spring" uprisings, offer several lessons about what works and what doesn't regarding the fight for gender equity and women's rights (Khalil, 2014).

First and foremost, women's rights must be recognized, protected, and safeguarded as an inextricable part of the wider context of human rights. Whenever human rights are violated, due to autocracy, dictatorship, and corruption, women are likely to be hurt, usually more than men, due to gender inequity, misogyny, and patriarchal power structures that disfavor women, and that are still well-entrenched in many places, especially in developing countries (Nazir, 2005; Moghadam, 2003).

Second, the realities and challenges faced by Arab women are part and parcel of the socio-political realities and challenges of their respective countries, which have their own unique power dynamics, paths to democratization and reform, and recipes for modernization and transformation. Therefore, as the varied outcomes following the "Arab Spring" uprisings teach us, there is no such thing as a standard "one size fits all" path to democratization, in general, and to addressing the political, social, and legal challenges facing women. Women's movements are deeply embedded in their respective countries' political and social contexts. As Taylor (1999) points out, "the relation between gender activism and social activism is bidirectional, in the sense that gender agendas affect the course of social movements, and that social movements affect the social definition of gender relations."

Third, in orchestrating their efforts in their fight for their rights, Tunisian women relied upon innovating and developing a unique combination of communication and journalistic tools, both online and offline, which included new forms of protest, such as signing petitions, organizing sit-ins and gatherings in public spaces, and utilizing social media platforms, such as Facebook, Twitter, YouTube, and blogs, in addition to creating virtual/fictitious assemblies and tribunals. Through mixing these modes of expression together, Tunisian women succeeded in securing a loud "voice" and a strong "agency" for themselves in their struggle to achieve gender equity, including their success to codify "gender parity" laws within the Tunisian constitution, and to protect women's rights in the various political, social, and legal spheres (Khalil, 2014; Labidi, 2014; Mili, 2015). In doing so, they not only demonstrated their resilience, determination, and perseverance, rather, they also illustrated their creativity, talent, and innovativeness. Most importantly, they set a clear example showing the intertwined relationship between political activism, social activism, and legal activism, which are all encompassed under the broader umbrella of gender-equity activism (Taylor, 1999). A comprehensive, holistic, community-based, bottom-up, grassroots, participatory approach was required to achieve both a positive political transformation and a successful social transition, as Tunisia suggests. Women's various acts of activism and resistance do not just cross-cut different tools of communication and modes of expression; rather, they also cross-cut the boundaries between the private and the public, the social and the political, the traditional and the modern, the religious and the secular, as well as the online and the offline (Radsch & Khamis, 2013).

Fourth, solidarity-creation and coalition-building between groups representing different ideological forces and political orientations were important, as evident in the awarding of the Nobel Peace Prize in 2015 jointly to the Quartet of Tunisian organizations. These four had different orientations, but worked together, across their differences, to ensure a peaceful and smooth democratic transition in Tunisia. Indicating their hope that this will happen in other Arab countries (but has not yet done so), the Nobel Prize Selection Committee said the success of the Quartet's efforts "shows that Islamist and secular political movements can work together to achieve significant results in the country's best interests" (Calamur, 2015). This has special significance for the growth and success of women's movements in the Arab world, since the tug of war between different forces, especially those representing Islamization, on one end of the spectrum, and secularization, at the other end, is most likely to continue, and to even increase, over the coming years. Unless these different forces become able to reconcile, no real gains can be achieved, in terms of either transitioning to democracy or advancing women's rights (Khamis & Mili, 2018).

One good example—one that needs to be emulated in other Arab countries—of bridging the gap between traditionalism and modernization, and between religiosity and secularization, is a group of women activists. Known as "*Hrayer Tunis*" or "Tunisia's Free Women," they brilliantly balanced Tunisia's traditional and modern identities in an effort to combat religious extremism, by referring to indigenous Tunisian symbols and cultural icons, rather than Western lifestyle. For example, in pushing back against strict, *Salafi* (traditional) religious influence, which culminated in the emergence of the *Niqab* (the full-face veil), which is alien to Tunisian society and which renders women totally invisible, the group showed images of women wearing beautiful colorful, yet modest, traditional Tunisian clothes (Mili, 2015). This enabled the group to cleverly reclaim the narrative of authenticity and originality from those who interpreted it within strict and alien religious references; it showed that virtues such as modesty and decency have always been part of Tunisia's positive cultural heritage, and that close-mindedness and rigidity shouldn't replace diversity and inclusion in the quest for a genuine cultural identity. In amplifying their message, they used an innovative combination of posters, graffiti, billboards, as well as social media sites.

Finally, allowing Arab women to have a voice in the process of nation-building in their own countries and to narrate their own stories in their own words, is always important. They must speak in their own voice about what they perceive to be their greatest victories, most pressing challenges, and most significant hopes. Only by hearing Arab women's voices as they are expressed and amplified through both mainstream media and social media platforms, can we begin to understand their complex, multidimensional lived realities and multifaceted roles, identities, hopes, and challenges, which are as evolving, dynamic, and in flux as their own volatile region (Radsch & Khamis, 2013).

In the future, new waves of gender-related reform and activism will probably sweep more quickly, effectively, and smoothly, through the countries that did not suffer from the turbulent conditions or devastating effects brought by the Arab Spring movements. This is mainly because the Arab Spring countries that have been suffering from urgent political and economic challenges have typically relegated gender-related reform to a lower level of priority, at least for the time being (Khamis, 2017). In many of these countries, the stifling of freedoms, internal divisions, and political fragmentation, let alone sectarian violence and civil war, resulted in major setbacks in women's engagement and activism, both offline and online. The degree to which these new waves of gender-related reform and gender equity movements will be adopted in the Arab region, and the pace of their adoption, as well as the next countries most likely to adopt them are all uncertain. One certainty is, however, that Arab women's activism will continue simultaneously in the political, social, and legal spheres to overcome tyranny, dictatorship, patriarchy, misogyny, repressive cultural practices, and oppressive laws.

Some Arab countries, as did Jordan and Lebanon, for example, will likely try to follow Tunisia's lead in trying to secure women's equal rights and full citizenship. In emulating Tunisia, however, these countries should remember that securing those political, social, and legal gains required a combination of a good educational system, high literacy rates, successful political transition, peaceful rotation of power, effective grassroots coalition-building, and persistent, organized efforts on the part of a wide array of women's groups. These important lessons from Tunisia's "Jasmine Revolution" need to be passed on to other Arab countries. Many Arab countries are at the crossroads of transition, and the road ahead remains largely uncharted, so whether and when they follow that model and take that journey remains to be seen. But again, one thing is certain: The winds of change for Arab women have already started blowing, and they will not stop.

Note

1 Tunisia's revolution was called the "Jasmine Revolution," given the "peacefulness" of the young protesters who ignited and orchestrated it. This also partly explains why the uprisings in the region were called the "Arab Spring."

References

Alamm, W. (2012, March 5). *Reflections on women in the Arab Spring: Women's voices from around the world*. Middle East Program: Woodrow Wilson International Center for Scholars. Retrieved from www.wilsoncenter.org/sites/default/files/International%20Women%27s%20Day%202012_4.pdf

Albawaba. (2016, December 21). *Check out this striking campaign combatting violence against women in Tunisia*. Retrieved from www.albawaba.com/loop/check-out-striking-campaign-combatting-violence-against-women-tunisia-917554

Al-Malki, A., Kaufer, D., Ishizaki, S., & Dreher, K. (2012). *Arab women in Arab news: Old stereotypes and new media*. Doha: Bloomsbury Qatar Foundation Publishing.

Bennett, W. L. (2008). Changing citizenship in the digital age. In W. L. Bennett (Ed.), *Civic life online: Learning how digital media can engage youth* (pp. 1–24). Cambridge, MA: MIT Press.

Calamur, K. (2015, October 9). A prize for the Jasmine Revolution. *The Atlantic*. Retrieved from www.theatlantic.com/international/archive/2015/10/nobel-peace-prize-tunisia-quartet/409849/

Charrad, M. M. (2001). *States and women's rights: The making of postcolonial Tunisia, Algeria, and Morocco*. Berkeley, CA: University of California Press.

Charrad, M. M., & Zarrugh, A. (2014). Equal or complementary? Women in the new Tunisian constitution after the Arab spring. *The Journal of North African Studies, 19*(2), 230–243.

Daniels, J. (2009). Rethinking cyberfeminism(s): Race, gender and embodiment. *Women's Studies Quarterly, 37*(1–2), 101–124.

El-Nawawy, M., & Khamis, S. (2013). *Egyptian revolution 2.0: Political blogging, civic engagement, and citizen journalism*. New York, NY: Palgrave Macmillan.

Feki, S. (2017, August 22). A new tune on women's rights in the Arab world. *The New York Times*. Retrieved from www.nytimes.com/2017/08/22/opinion/womens-rights-rape-laws-arab-world.html?mcubz=0

Howard, P. N. (2011). *The digital origins of dictatorship and democracy: Information technology and political Islam*. New York, NY: Oxford University Press.

Jumet, K. D. (2017). *Contesting the repressive state: Why ordinary Egyptians protested during the Arab spring*. London: Oxford University Press.

Khalil, A. (2014). Gender paradoxes of the Arab Spring. *The Journal of North African Studies, 19*(2), 131–136.

Khamis, S. (2016). Five questions about Arab women's activism five years after the Arab Spring. *CyberOrient, 10*(1). Retrieved from www.cyberorient.net/article.do?articleId=9772

Khamis, S. (2017, September 12). *A new Tunisian law tackles violence against women*. A Policy Analysis Report Published by the Arab Center in Washington, DC. Retrieved from http://arabcenterdc.org/policy_analyses/a-new-tunisian-law-tackles-violence-against-women/

Khamis, S., & Mili, A. (2018). Introductory themes. In S. Khamis & A. Mili (Eds.), *Arab women's activism and socio-political transformation: Unfinished gendered revolutions*. New York, NY: Palgrave Macmillan.

Khamis, S., & Vaughn, K. (2013). From "safety valves" to "mobilization tools": How new media revolutionized the Tunisian and Egyptian political landscapes. *Journal of African Media Studies, 5*(1), 69–86.

Labidi, L. (2014). *Electoral practice of Tunisian women in the context of a democratic transition*. Washington, DC: The Wilson Center.

Mili, A. (2013). Gender standards vs democratic standards: Revisiting the paradox. *International Journal of Women Studies, 14*(2), 3–11.

Mili, A. (2015). Political-social movements: Community based: Tunisia. In S. Joseph (Ed.), *Encyclopedia of women & Islamic cultures*. http://dx.doi.org/10.1163/1872-5309_ewic_COM_002018

Mili, A. (2018). Citizenship and gender equality in the cradle of the Arab Spring. In S. Khamis & A. Mili (Eds.), *Arab women's activism and socio-political transformation: Unfinished gendered revolutions*. New York, NY: Palgrave Macmillan.

Moghadam, V. M. (2003). *Gender and social change in the Middle East*. Boulder, CO: Lynne Rienner Publishers.

Nazir, S. C. (2005). *Women's rights in the Middle East and North Africa.* New York, NY: Freedom House.

Radsch, C., & Khamis, S. (2013). In their own voice: Technologically mediated empowerment and transformation among young Arab women. *Feminist Media Studies, 13*(5), 881–890.

Taylor, V. (1999, February). Gender and social movements: Gender processes in women's self-help movements. *Gender and Society,* Special Issue: Part 2, *13*(1), 8–33.

Walker, T. (2011, October 8). Tunisia: "This is the start of a global wave of protests." *Green Left Weekly.* Retrieved from www.greenleft.org.au/content/tunisia-%C3%A2%C2%80%C2%98-start-global-wave-protests%C3%A2%C2%80%C2%99

18

THE (IN)VISIBILITY OF ARAB WOMEN IN POLITICAL JOURNALISM

Noha Mellor

While the expansion of the Arab news and media industries over the past two decades has provided unprecedented opportunities for women to access and succeed in the media field, journalists are still not expected to question the political order. The rise of satellite television and transnational Arab media since the mid-1990s has allowed Arab women journalists to capitalize on the new opportunities for work, not only as producers and anchors, but also as field reporters. Arab women journalists have also pursued career opportunities outside their native countries in the Middle East/North Africa (MENA) region: Many satellite channels are based in Dubai; and other Western-subsidized Arabic services (including *BBC Arabic*, *Russia Today*, *France 24* and *Deutsche Welle*) are in the UK, France, Germany, Russia, and the USA.

Because of the high demand for new journalists, some Arab news outlets have even hired people with only a few years of experience. Many women have taken advantage of such openings as a means of establishing themselves in journalism, particularly in jobs as presenters, while a few of them have managed to get jobs as field reporters. Many women, however, have not managed to fend off the newsroom's discrimination against them. Indeed, I argue, that only larger societal changes in each Arab country will bring an end to discrimination. Arab women are often expected to serve as positive role models and representatives of their country, reflecting a modern image of the nation, instead of challenging the government and championing the social reforms so acutely needed. Additionally, Arab women journalists are generally expected to support rather than challenge the patriarchal order in times of political turbulence, in order to preserve the perceived social stability provided by adhering to the status quo. Those few who defy the status quo may risk putting their future career prospects in jeopardy or be forced to abandon the high status political beat, which is largely dominated by men journalists.

This chapter discusses some of these challenges faced by Arab women journalists. Recent turmoil and repercussions against political reforms in many Arab countries have exacerbated the challenges. I argue that emerging political challenges have silenced many women media professionals, discouraging them from expressing political opposition to the ruling regimes. The political turmoil in the region has only intensified the challenge facing women journalists trying to get their voices heard and sustain their presence in public spheres, which remain largely dominated by men. Although women media professionals, some of whom are also political activists and bloggers, joined their male counterparts in street protests across the region during the "Arab Spring," societal and political restrictions forced women to withdraw from the public spaces once the old regimes were overthrown. This, I argue, is reminiscent of past events such as the Algerian women's struggle alongside Algerian men against the French occupation until independence in 1962 when women were forced to abandon political activities, and expected to wear the veil and return to domestic duties (Kutschera, 1996). Women's unrewarded sacrifices in recent years demonstrate that Arab political and media spheres have been structured by a deep-rooted patriarchal order. In this chapter, I begin by discussing some of the current challenges facing Arab women journalists. In the second half, I provide several examples of such challenges in Egypt, demonstrating a collision of political culture and journalism that combines to preserve the patriarchal status quo of journalistic practice in Egypt.

Gender in the newsroom

With the proliferation of satellite television targeting Arabic-speaking audiences across the world, political news has gained more prominence (Mellor, 2011, p. 90). Soft news, which focuses on, for instance, everyday issues such as gender equality or problems in the education and healthcare systems in Arab countries, has not been prioritized by news institutions. Given a widespread assumption that political news requires broad knowledge about history, foreign affairs, and diplomacy, opportunities for job promotions are usually restricted to those working on the political beat. Journalists who work with political news are thus regarded as more knowledgeable and have a higher professional status than their colleagues reporting on social or cultural affairs. Women journalists who work in political news often tend to present themselves as tough and fearless, particularly when they are in front of the camera, in order to legitimize their position as a political reporter. This attitude in television reporting is adopted in order to add to their image as professional journalists, distinct from other women in entertainment genres who are not directly exposed to violent images of war and conflict or political struggle (Mellor, 2012). For some of those women who work as field reporters in conflict-stricken parts in the region, being women can give them access to certain places or to talking to sources who might be uncomfortable talking to male journalists (Palmer & Melki, 2018).

In Qatar, where the international network al-Jazeera is based, national Qatari newsrooms, including the al-Jazeera network, tend to hire women journalists from

Arab and Asian countries. However, the Qatari government does not allow these women to cover local corruption cases or pursue investigative journalism and in-depth reporting in some political cases (Kirat, 2016). Generally, in the Gulf region, women managed to enter the journalistic field only a few decades ago, and Gulf news institutions' policies tend to provide more training and promotion opportunities for men rather than women journalists which reflects the under-appreciation of women's work in the journalism field (Kirat, 2004). In Saudi Arabia, the Saudization nationalization scheme, or the policy implemented by the Saudi Ministry of Labour requiring Saudi companies to fill up their workforce with Saudi nationals, has not been applied to the broadcasting sector where non-Saudi women presenters still outnumber Saudi women presenters particularly in state television (Al-Nasser, 2012).

Saudi Arabia has some, although relatively few, prominent Saudi women journalists. But many Saudi women work outside of Saudi Arabia, often due to the harsh criticism they faced inside the kingdom for working in newsrooms where the majority of journalists are male. The highly outspoken Nadine al-Budair, for example, criticized Muslim clerics in 2016 after three Muslim Belgians committed suicide bombings in Brussels; al-Budair called such clerics "hypocrites" for continually saying that the terrorists behind such attacks did not represent Islam, without directly condemning the terror act and explaining in detail how those terrorists deviated from the teachings of Islam (Memri, 2016). In fact, in 2009 al-Budair triggered a notoriously hot debate with her satirical article, "Me and My Four Husbands." In this article, published in the Egyptian privately owned newspaper, *Al-Masri al-Youm*, she asked if she, as a Muslim woman, could have four husbands in the same way that a Muslim man is allowed to have up to four wives (Memri, 2010).

Indeed, before changing the culture within newsrooms, wider structural changes are needed in Arab societies. A range of factors such as gender discrimination, sexual harassment and lack of enabling legal and social environment discourages Arab women from entering journalism. Those who manage to enter it may find themselves confined to specific, lower status, roles (Melki & Mallat, 2016). The so-called Arab Spring helped shake up power structures, not only regarding governance and political structures, but also within newsrooms, where women journalists demanded equal opportunities in the political beat as field reporters and despite suffering anti-women verbal and physical abuse in public places. The recent turmoil in the region has undoubtedly pushed political news back to the top of the news outlets' agenda. Arab women's participation in the 2011-uprisings that swept across the region raised hopes that their long-due rights would finally be granted and that they would play a future role in the shaping of their new governments (*The Guardian*, 2011), but this did not happen.

Women facing two battles

Women's participation in the early uprisings across the Arab region since 2011 represented a new face of Arab women as activists and agents of change, in contrast to the stereotypical media image of Arab women as passive and submissive (Al-Malki et al., 2012). Women took to the street in Egypt, Tunisia, Libya, Bahrain, Syria, and Yemen, to protest against the status quo and demand political reforms. One example is the Bahraini activist and blogger Zainab al-Khawaja, who later went on hunger strike following the arrests of her father, husband, and brother-in-law (*Guardian*, 2016). When the late former President of Yemen, Abdallah Saleh, criticized allowing men and women to congregate in public spaces and organizations, including media institutions, claiming that this gender-mixing was un-Islamic, Yemini women joined men in the street to protest against Saleh's rule (*Care International*, 2013). In Egypt, some of the many young women who felt empowered by the 2011 uprising have released their testimonies of the protests (see, for instance, el-Tounsi, 2011).

Following the uprisings, women's gains in terms of equal civil rights remained uncertain. According to the World Economic Forum's *Global Gender Gap* report (2012), women's political participation in the Middle East declined slightly in 2012 compared to 2011, and their involvement in Arab parliaments remains at a low 14 percent (*Care International*, 2013, p. 7). Violence against women has escalated to an alarming level, and sexual harassment, in particular, has become the main reason for keeping women away from street protests (*Care International*, 2013, pp. 7–8).

Many women journalists aided in the uprisings and provided relevant news coverage. Libyan women journalists, for example, helped establish opposition newspapers during the unrest in 2011. But later their employment situation worsened in the wake of the civil war and the armed conflict among rival factions. Women journalists in Tunisia continue to experience workplace harassment; their responsibilities have been largely confined to covering local news and so they have not managed to become editors (*Deutsche Welle*, 2015). Citing the dangers of a field as an excuse to send male reporters, editors have also prevented Egyptian women journalists from covering events in the field. "There were times when I was deterred from covering field events and was told that male reporters would be required because they were more capable of facing risks," said one woman during a Deutsche Welle symposium in 2015 discussing the problems facing women journalists in the Middle East (cited in *Deutsche Welle*, 2015).

Women correspondents in conflict-stricken areas such as the Palestinian territories and Iraq have often found a new mission in their reportage. The 2003 war in Iraq, for instance, helped to open up the journalism work to women given that many television and radio stations launched after the fall of Saddam and these offered new opportunities for those eager to work as journalists. That said, conflict in Iraq subsequently worsened the security situation and intensified sectarianism; this has had a heavy impact on the working conditions of Iraqi women journalists. Several have since faced threats of violence and assaults by both political and religious factions (al-Rawi, 2010). A recent survey showed that nearly 79 percent of sampled women journalists in Iraq said that they were subject to sexual harassment while at work (Al-Hattab, 2013). In fact, the Iraqi Women's Journalists Forum (IWJF) held a conference in Baghdad in 2015, in part, to discuss sexual harassment, and then commissioned a study of the implications of this on women journalists. The conference attendees concluded that the prevalent social rules of separating girls and boys from an early age has had negative impacts on both women and men, resulting in a sexist culture and gender segregation in the newsroom. The deteriorating security situation in Iraq, moreover, has exacerbated sexual harassment against women (ICSSI Baghdad, 2015). The IWJF suggested a number of measures to protect women, such as changing school curricula to raise awareness of the problem, and introducing legislation that would harden the legal penalty for crimes involving violence against women.

Using sexual violence to expel women from public spaces

In Egypt, sexual harassment has reportedly reached an epidemic level: almost all Egyptian women between the age of 10 and 35 having been subjected to various forms of sexual harassment at some point (el Deeb, 2013). Politically motivated sexual assaults of women activists, bloggers, and journalists began well before the 2011 uprising. In 2005, in a notorious incident known as Black Wednesday, state-hired thugs and security forces sexually assaulted many of the more than 500 women taking part in the mass demonstrations organized by *Kefaya* [Enough] movement against President Mubarak's regime. Both government supporters and critics say part of the reason the response to this incident was so large is that the security services have long used women as pawns to control individual men. In Arab societies, a family's honor is often directly linked to a woman's perceived purity. The 2005 incident prompted a massive protest spearheaded by a number of women activists and journalists in a campaign called "the street is ours" in collaboration with the Egyptian Center for Women's Rights and the new Women's Research Center (Sika, 2014).

In 2011 the organization *Reporters Without Borders* warned female journalists not to travel to Cairo to cover the unrest following instances of grievous sexual assaults on several foreign women journalists. For example, French journalist Caroline Sinz was brutally assaulted by a mob in Tahrir Square. CBS News chief foreign affairs correspondent, Lara Logan, was sexually assaulted by a crowd that altogether had between 200 and 300 men (Sherwood, 2011). People posting reactions to Logan's rape via social media supported taking action against such violence targeting women reporters. News blogs were particularly articulate in challenging patriarchal authority and interpretations of rape such as those which blamed rape victims for not being sufficiently cautious (Harp, Loke, & Bachmann, 2014). The incident was not the first assault against an American journalist: Mona Eltahawy, an Egyptian-American journalist who formerly worked for Reuters, also experienced sexual assault. Eltahawy was detained for 12 hours in November 2011 by Cairo security forces and was physically assaulted while in detention. Eltahawy had previously been lauded by US media for her coverage of the uprising and for writing about the Egyptian blogger, Aliaa Elmahdy, who posted naked images of herself in October 2011. Elmahdy intended her blog posts as a dramatic protest against the marginalization of women, sexual harassment and violence against women, and increasing restrictions on women's freedom of speech (Abid, 2017, p. 159).

In March 2011, soon after Mubarak bowed to the mounting protests against him and stepped down, women protestors including bloggers and activists began to suffer from increasing sexual assaults, particularly in Cairo. This violence represents the result of the repeated collision between protestors, including women, and security forces. The assaults pushed women, as the perpetrators intended, back to the sidelines. Exacerbating the indignity was the subjection of many women protestors to so-called virginity tests, which are permitted by the Supreme Council of the Armed Forces (SCAF) (Abid, 2017, p. 159). Some women activists were violently dispersed from Tahrir Square by the military police. Other women were arrested at the Square and detained in military prisons, where they were sexually assaulted under the guise of virginity tests. For instance, a young Egyptian activist, Samira Ibrahim was arrested there, tortured and forced into receiving a virginity test. Ibrahim was the only woman who brought a case in front of Egyptian courts. Her case brought a mixed reaction from Egyptians. Many blamed her for initiating the case and some even blamed women protestors congregating in Tahrir Square in the first place. In any case, a military court exonerated the military doctor who actually conducted the virginity tests on the protestors.

In December 2011, women protesting outside the Egyptian Cabinet offices were targeted by the armed forces. Again, many women were subjected to sexual violence, triggering a massive mass demonstration by women under the slogan "the women of Egypt are a red line" (FIDH, 2014, p. 14). Following another protest in 2014, an Islamic cleric, Sheikh Sami Abdel Qawi, attributed harassment to women's dress code strongly implying that "Westernised" clothing style was to blame for such attacks on women and promoting victim-blaming discourse (Langohr, 2014). In Jordan, too, the state-controlled discourses circulated by and through Jordanian news media's coverage of women's virginity legitimized patriarchal control of women's bodies in the name of protecting women's virginity. The humiliation triggered strong public protest, especially on social media.

In this respect, both the state and family patriarchs enforce their control to inspect and protect women's virginity (Mahadeen, 2015). Maintaining virginity remains one means of controlling women's sexuality in cultures where non-virgin unmarried women are often regarded as source of family dishonor. As many crimes of violence against women go uninvestigated, the state essentially sends the message giving perpetrators of sexual violence a kind of immunity from prosecution and calling the public sphere unsafe for women. This encourages women to minimize their presence in public spaces and implies that "men are responsible for protecting their women from other men" (Ahmad-Zaki & Abd AlHamid, 2014).

As the Egyptian journalist Habiba Mohsen (2012) says, asking why a woman went out in public is the first reaction when women are trying to bring cases of sexual assault to court: "Blaming it all on the woman for being present at a demonstration, blaming the 'weaker link of the chain,' seems to be a satisfying solution for some sectors of Egyptian society." With the rising number of women participating in public protests since the 2011 revolution in Egypt, the rate of sexual violence against women has increased rapidly. Such violence against women can be read as an attempt to expel them from public spaces and to re-inscribe pre-revolutionary limits (Ahmad-Zaki & Abd AlHamid, 2014), and targeted violence against women could contribute to maintaining the gendered status quo by pushing women away from participating in political activities whether as street demonstrator or as a political reporter. Sexual violence against women remains unchallenged. Assaults on women protestors usually end up intimidating their male relatives, including fathers and brothers, who are urged to stay silent in the name of protecting family honor.

For women journalists, staying in public spaces and being exposed to such a risk of assault is a form of activism. Rawya Rageh, an Egyptian broadcast journalist, explained that in societies where women must fight for control over their own bodies, they must fight to reassert their right in the public space. So, she said, "being a woman journalist is almost a form of activism" (Yakupitiyage, 2016). Thus, although women joined men in the public squares in Egypt demanding political freedoms and the end of autocracy, "unlike men, women face two battles: the first for political change and the second to obtain a real change of their societal status to become fully equal to their male counterparts" (Heideman & Youssef, 2012, p. 14). The following section mentions Egyptian women who are in the broadcast news industry in order to demonstrate the ongoing struggle of journalists who face that twofold battle inside the field: for professional recognition inside the newsrooms largely dominated by men; and to maintain their presence in the political beat.

Driving women away from the political beat: the case of Egyptian news media

Women journalists' response to street protests in 2011 took different shapes and they assumed various roles. Some women wanted to emulate the Western role of the journalist as a watchdog. Another group of journalists has emerged that has sought to assume a new role for journalists as activists, such as women journalists like Mona Shazly, Reem Maged, Liliane Daoud, and Dina Abdel Rahman. Bouthaina Kamel, a veteran journalist and activist, for another example, defied the regime then in power by standing in the 2012-presidential elections as an alternative to those representing the military or Islamist institutions (she did not receive enough signatures to make the ballot). Nevertheless, many women journalists were forced to abandon the political beat or leave Egypt altogether.

Hala Sarhan's case represents the challenges facing women journalists when, against the odds, they find themselves covering the political beat for their news organization. Sarhan's career began with hosting light talk shows and ended with serious political programs after the toppling of Mubarak. Throughout her successful career, Sarhan was marked by her daring style and choice of topics—such as prostitution in Egypt. Not surprisingly, the state and its media accused her of attempting to tarnish Egypt's reputation by discussing such sensitive issues. Sarhan remained outside Egypt between 2008 and 2011 after she claimed that Mubarak's government conspired against her to stop her show, "They came after me because they couldn't put pressure on me. They couldn't use me and I wouldn't be part of their gang. I didn't serve their regime," she said (quoted in Hope, 2011). Sarhan returned to Egyptian television in 2011 with a political show called *Nassbook* (People's Book), a name that was meant to parody *Facebook*, and that depended on live interaction with viewers via social media sites such as *Facebook* and *Twitter*. The show was taken off air, however, following Sarhan's discussion of the potential complicity of the military in the physical assault and killing of 2011 protesters. She left journalism altogether following the 2013 coup when the Egyptian army chief, Abdel Fattah el-Sisi, led a coalition to remove the former President Mohamed Morsi in 2013. Shortly after, el-Sisi suspended the Egyptian constitution. His government curtailed dissent amongst journalists, activists, and NGOs.

Other Egyptian women have risen to journalistic fame since Mubarak's fall. Reem Maged is an example of an outspoken activist woman willing to criticize Mubarak's regime, and later, the Supreme Council of the Armed Forces (SCAF) and President Morsi's government. This critical stance caused her political show to be taken off air for two years (2011–2013); when she returned with a show about women's issues, it did not last long. Maged was interrogated by security forces after she interviewed a socialist activist who discussed torture inside military prisons. She was also called up for an investigation during Morsi's rule, because she apparently insulted the judiciary system (*Ahram Online*, 2015). Her program *Gamea Moanas Salem* ("Feminine Plural") was broadcast on the privately owned satellite channel *ONTV*, with the aim of discussing sensitive social issues pertaining to women, but it was suspended after only two episodes—no explanation was given. Commenting on the possible reasons behind that decision, Maged declared, "I do not understand the logic of banning, I see it as arrogance and guardianship. What makes it painful to me is that I willingly haven't been working for two years [. . .] During these two years, I insisted on not working for a non-Egyptian channel [. . .] for emotional rather than professional reasons" (quoted in *Ahram Online*, 2015). Interviewed on a handful of occasions, Maged told one interviewer that senior *ONTV* officials had informed her about the emerging political pressures to suspend her show. To this she replied, "We should not accept any authority that acts like a guardian on the Egyptian people, telling them what they should watch, and what they should not watch," (quoted in Dawoud, 2015).

Dina Abdel Rahman also faced unfair dismissal. She was suspended from the private channel *Dream TV* and later from another private channel *Capital Broadcasting Center (CBC)*, owned by the Egyptian businessman, Mohammad al-Amin, for expressing pro-revolutionary views. Abdel Rahman was sacked from *Dream TV* following her televised interview with a retired air force major, when she challenged him to provide evidence of his accusation that two presidential candidates would implement an American agenda. The retired military leader also criticized Abdel Rahman for airing one journalist's criticism of Supreme Council of the Armed Forces regarding the attack on young activists, and thus turning the people against the army. He suggested that Abdel Rahman select only "respectable" journalists as guests. She sarcastically replied by asking him to provide her a list of such respectable figures. The show was suddenly disrupted following that conversation, and Abdel Rahman's sacking was publicly announced (El Gundy, 2011).

The British-Lebanese journalist Liliane Daoud similarly criticized the Supreme Council of the Armed Forces. She joined the Egyptian *ONTV* channel in 2011, and hosted a political show, *The Full Picture*, but left the channel and was forced out of Egypt in 2016. Daoud was accused of criticizing the military in her show; consequently, when *ONTV* was sold to another businessman who was supportive of the military, Daoud's contract was not renewed (Ensor, 2016). TV presenter Mona al-Shazly also had to abandon political talk shows, choosing instead to host a light family show on the *CBC* satellite channel (Adly, 2014). Al-Shazly was famous for her interview with the secret administrator of "We are all Khaled Said" Facebook group, which mobilized protesters for the January 25 uprising. The interview was broadcast live on February 7, 2011, one day before Mubarak stepped down. She also displayed photographs of protestors killed during the early days of the revolution (al-Hady, 2011). Al-Shazly also challenged Hisham Qandil, the prime minister during the period that the Brotherhood movement was in power in 2012–2013, when the activists were calling for the government's dismissal regarding their dissatisfaction with the economic and security policies (*Ahram Online*, 2013a).

Finally, one of the most controversial figures in Egypt since 2011 has been Bothaina Kamel, the first woman to run in Egypt's presidential elections in 2012, having already been well-known for her political activism during Mubarak's rule. Kamel's broadcasting career began in 1992 with a radio program called *Itirafat Layliyya* ("Nightly Confessions"); it soon became very popular. However, it was banned in 1998, after the criticism from the Religion Programs Committee. The reason given was that the show aired listeners' phone calls in which they shared intimate personal stories, touching on taboo issues such as sexual abuse and premarital sex. Kamel was accused of tarnishing Egypt's reputation abroad by hosting a religiously inappropriate show, which prompted Kamel to announce that Islamic fundamentalism had also penetrated state institutions. Kamel then moved to the Saudi-owned satellite channel *Orbit* to broadcast a similar program called *Argouk Ifhamny* ("Please Understand Me") between 2000 and 2011. During that period, she also became involved in a few political activist campaigns, including the *Kefaya* [Enough] movement against Mubarak's plan to pass on Egypt's rule to his son. Kamel also co-founded *Egyptian Women for Change* in 2010 to promote political and social transformation; as would be expected, she joined the protests against Mubarak in 2011. Following the ousting of Mubarak, Kamel returned to state television but she soon accused her editors of marginalizing her, following her open criticism of the military and the Muslim Brotherhood. Kamel was recommended for the "International Women of Courage Award," but declined it, because it was sponsored by the US Department of State. Accepting the award, she said, meant accepting the state that supplied the Egyptian military with weapons used against Egyptian revolutionaries (Antoun, 2012). Kamel was suspended and questioned during Morsi's rule for being critical on air of the Brotherhood; in fact, she described some state media as being mouth-pieces for the Brotherhood while reading news bulletins on state television (Sha-hine, 2012). She said that everyone should tell the truth, even at the cost of one's life, indicating that those opposing the Brotherhood tended to risk theirs (Shahine, 2012). Kamel alleged she was accosted in 2013 by men whom she described as Muslim Brotherhood supporters; they smashed her car and physically attacked her (*Ahram Online*, 2013b).

These women demonstrate the collision of political culture and journalism in a society where the current conception of masculinity preserves the patriarchal status quo (whether by the military or Islamic movements), while assigning a secondary role to women. The political sphere then appears as a field naturally dominated by (strong) male leaders. Women who seek to challenge top leadership positions or hold those leaders to account may just end up being marginalized to soft news and social issues, if not exiled from journalism altogether. The political environ-ment constrains women's opportunities in political journalism, in particular, and in the political sphere, in general. Strong male leaders embody the image of patriotic manhood (usually confined to military men), while women are assigned the role as nurturing supporters and motherhood, serving as symbols of a patriarchal national-ist ideology, and of gender segregation.

Thus, the battle for women Arab journalists is not just about fairer representa-tion in editors' positions or as reporters and anchors; the real battle is against mascu-line nationalist politics. Numerous women have actively participated in challenging a long dormant public sphere debates and views. Their challenge now is resisting the constraining political environment that has pushed many women away from taking their rightful place in political journalism.

Conclusion

Since the 1950s and 1960s, when many Arab states gained independence, calls have been issued for the remodeling of an Arab identity distinct from Western values and ideologies. Arab women have played a central role in the cultural pro-duction of the nation in the Arab states; nevertheless, later the states were irked by educated women's demands for citizenship rights equal to those enjoyed by men. Such demands particularly irked Islamic institutions such as the Committee for the Promotion of Virtue and the Prevention of Vice in Saudi Arabia. More recently these institutions accepted women's participation in public life, as long as such participation reconciles with the teachings of Islam, which includes enforcing sex segregation in public places. States and institutions then aimed at distinguish-ing the struggle of Arab women from Western feminist values by preserving the existing gender relations and the patriarchal order within Arab societies (al-Ali, 2000). On the other hand, reconciling Islamic and religious values with universal rights was not an easy task for Islamist groups. For instance, during its short-lived rule in Egypt, the Muslim Brotherhood issued a statement in 2013 denouncing the proceedings of the UN Commission on the Status of Women aiming to end violence against women. The Brotherhood denounced the UN declaration as a step that would "lead to complete disintegration of [Muslim] society, and would certainly be the final step in the intellectual and cultural invasion of Muslim countries" (cited in Fecteau, 2017, p. 81).

Although massive protests that erupted in many Arab countries since 2011 have brought global attention to the demands of Arab populations for their political rights, protests have not generally brought real change to the marginalization of Arab women. Arab women actively participated in street protests, although they were expected to withdraw from the political sphere once old regimes had been overthrown. Women's participation, as the Egyptian feminist Nawal El Saadawi once wrote, "was not needed except in military or economic crises, in war or when their men or the state needed them to work outside their home. Women are brought up to sacrifice their lives for others, to be rewarded later in Paradise after their death" (El Saadawi, 2006, p. 47). The MENA region remains a largely masculine and conservative affair aimed at maintaining the patriarchal order under the guise of embracing tradition and nation-building.

On a positive note, if women journalists and activists struggle to get heard in traditional media, their voices have become louder and clearer than ever before on social media (see e.g. Radsch & Khamis, 2013; al-Rawi, 2014). These voices will continue to challenge present conception of women's and minorities' rights in the future. Social media activism, particularly that initiated and maintained by women in the Middle East, has had an impact on legitimating and reinforcing women's rights to speak and be heard in public and in attracting, albeit sometimes temporarily, world attention to women's dilemmas in the Middle East.

References

Abid, F. (2017). Arab feminists' sexual revolution and social activism after the 2011 Arab Spring: Aicha Ech-Channa's À Hautes Voix as a case study. In J. Lobah & H. Tayebi (Eds.), *Trajectories of change in post-2011: Challenges and prospects* (pp. 158–173). Rabat: Hanns Seidel Foundation Morocco.

Adly, A. (2014, February 14). Mona al-Shazly leaves political shows. *Elaph*. Retrieved from http://elaph.com/Web/Entertainment/2014/2/877221.html#sthash.IikxfH2T.dpuf

Ahmad-Zaki, H., & Abd AlHamid, D. (2014, July 9). Women as fair game in the public sphere: A critical introduction for understanding sexual violence and methods of resistance. Jadaliyya. Retrieved from www.jadaliyya.com/Details/30930/Women-As-Fair-Game-in-the-Public-Sphere-A-Critical-Introduction-for-Understanding-Sexual-Violence-and-Methods-of-Resistance

Ahram Online (2013a, February 14). Egypt government won't resign, says PM Qandil. *Arham Online*. Retrieved from http://english.ahram.org.eg/NewsContent/1/64/64792/Egypt/Politics-/Egypt-government-wont-resign,-says-PM-Qandil.aspx

Ahram Online (2013b, October 6). Ex-presidential hopeful Bothaina Kamel attacked by "Morsi supporters." *Ahram Online*. Retrieved from http://english.ahram.org.eg/News Content/1/64/83353/Egypt/Politics-/Expresidential-hopeful-Bothaina-Kamel-attacked-by-.aspx

Ahram Online (2015, May 15). Egyptian presenter Reem Maged's new TV show suspended. Retrieved from http://english.ahram.org.eg/NewsContent/1/64/130340/Egypt/Poli tics-/Egyptian-presenter-Reem-Mageds-new-TV-show-suspend.aspx

Al-Ali, N. (2000). *Secularism, gender and the state in the Middle East: The Egyptian women's movement.* Cambridge: Cambridge University Press.

Al-Hady, O. (2011, February 12). The martyrs of the 25th of January revolution. *Al-Masry Al-Youm.* Retrieved from http://today.almasryalyoum.com/article2.aspx?ArticleID=287 608&IssueID=2044

Al-Hattab, J. (2013, March). 79% of female journalists in Iraq face sexual harassment. *Al-Arabiya.* Retrieved from https://bit.ly/2Hbckwf

Al-Malki, A., Kaufer, D., Ishizaki, S., & Dreher, K. (2012). *Arab women in Arab news: Old stereotypes and new media.* London: Bloomsbury Academic.

Al-Nasser, A. R. (2012, January 25). Saudi women broadcasters are not welcome in state television. *Al-Riyadh*, Issue 15920. Retrieved from http://www.alriyadh.com/704180#

Al-Rawi, A. K. (2010). Iraqi women journalists' challenges and predicaments. *Journal of Arab & Muslim Media Research, 3*(3), 223–236.

Al-Rawi, A. K. (2014). Framing the online women's movements in the Arab world. *Information, Communication & Society, 17*(9), 1147–1161.

Antoun, N. (2012, April 5). Profile: Bothaina Kamel. *Ahram Online.* Retrieved from http://english.ahram.org.eg/NewsContent/36/122/38566/Presidential-elections-/Presiden tial-elections-news/Profile-Bothaina-Kamel.aspx

Care International. (2013). *Arab Spring or Arab Autumn? Women's political participation in the uprisings and beyond: Implications for international donor policy.* Policy Report. London: Care International.

Dawoud, K. (2015, May 22). Reem Maged versus the government. *Atlantic Council.* Retrieved from www.atlanticcouncil.org/component/content/article?id=24393:reemmaged-versus-the-government

Deutsche Welle. (2015, June 15). After the Arab Spring: Harassment and discrimination are the main challenges for women journalists. *Deutsche Welle Arabic.*

El Deeb, B. (2013). Study on ways and methods to eliminate sexual harassment in Egypt. *UN Women.* Retrieved from http://harassmap.org/en/wp-content/uploads/2014/02/287_Summaryreport_eng_low-1.pdf

El Gundy, Z. (2011, July 25). Famous Egyptian TV host sacked after challenging ex-army officer on air. *Ahram Online.* Retrieved from http://english.ahram.org.eg/NewsPrint/17266.aspx

El Saadawi, N. (2006). Creativity, dissidence and women. *Quaderns de la Mediterrània.* Retrieved from www.iemed.org/publicacions/quaderns/7/045_ElSaadawi.pdf

El Tounsi, A. (2011). *Amani: A girl from Tahrir.* Cairo: Shabab Books (in Arabic).

Ensor, J. (2016, June 28). Egypt expels former BBC journalist Liliane Daoud. *Daily Telegraph.* Retrieved from www.telegraph.co.uk/news/2016/06/28/egypt-expels-former-bbc-journalist-liliane-daoud/

Fecteau, A. (2017). The Arab Spring and women's rights activism on Facebook. In L. Touaf, S. Boutkhil, & C. Nasri (Eds.), *North African women after the Arab Spring: In the eye of the storm* (pp. 77–96). Basingstoke: Palgrave Macmillan.

FIDH, Nazra for Feminist Studies, New Women Foundation, and The Uprising of Women in the Arab World. (2014). *Egypt: Keeping women out: Sexual violence against women in the public sphere.* Retrieved from www.fidh.org/IMG/pdf/egypt_women_final_english.pdf

The Guardian (2011, April 22). Women have emerged as key players in the Arab Spring. *The Guardian.* Retrieved from www.theguardian.com/world/2011/apr/22/women-arab-spring

The Guardian. (2016, March 14). Bahrain detains activist Zainab al-Khawaja and her one-year-old son. *The Guardian.* Retrieved from www.theguardian.com/world/2016/mar/14/bahrain-detains-activist-zainab-al-khawaja-and-one-year-old-son

Harp, D., Loke, J., & Bachmann, I. (2014). Spaces for feminist (re)articulations: The blogosphere and the sexual attack on journalist Lara Logan. *Feminist Media Studies, 14*(1), 5–21.

Heideman, K., & Youssef, M. (Eds.). (2012). *Reflections on women in the Arab Spring: Women's voices from around the world.* Washington, DC: Woodrow Wilson International Center for Scholars.

Hope, B. (2011, August 24). Egypt's "Oprah" returns to television. *The National.* Retrieved from www.thenational.ae/news/world/middle-east/egypts-oprah-returns-to-television

ICSSI Baghdad. (2015, October 5). The Iraqi women journalists forum breaks the silence about sexual harassment of girls and women in Iraq. Retrieved from www.iraqicivilsociety.org/archives/4720

Kirat, M. (2004). A profile of women journalists in the United Arab Emirates. *The Journal of International Communication, 10*(1), 54–78.

Kirat, M. (2016). A profile of journalists in Qatar: Traits, attitudes and values. *The Journal of International Communication, 22*(2), 171–187.

Kutschera, C. (1996, April). Algeria's fighting women. *The Middle East,* pp. 40–41.

Langohr, V. (2014, July 7). *New president, old pattern of sexual violence in Egypt.* Middle East Research and Information Project. Retrieved from www.merip.org/mero/mero070714

Mahadeen, E. (2015). Media, state, and patriarchy. *Feminist Media Studies, 15*(5), 763–778.

Melki, J. P., & Mallat, S. E. (2016). Block her entry, keep her down and push her out. *Journalism Studies, 17*(1), 57–79.

Mellor, N. (2011). *Arab journalists in transnational media.* New York, NY: Hampton Press.

Mellor, N. (2012). Hearts of steel. *Feminist Media Studies, 12*(2), 180–194.

MEMRI. (2010, January 27). *Saudi journalist: Why is polygamy only for men?* Special dispatch, no. 2773. Retrieved from www.memri.org/reports/saudi-journalist-why-is-polygamy-only-men

MEMRI. (2016, April 2). Saudi TV host Nadine Al-Budair takes to task apologists who claim terrorists have nothing to do with Islam and the Muslims: They emerged from our schools and universities clip, no. 5436. Retrieved from www.memri.org/tv/saudi-tv-host-nadine-al-budair-takes-task-apologists-who-claim-terrorists-have-nothing-do-islam/transcript

Mohsen, H. (2012, March 16). What made her go there? Samir Ibrahim and Egypt's virginity test trial. *Al-Jazeera.* Retrieved from www.aljazeera.com/indepth/opinion/2012/03/2012316133129201850.html

Palmer, L., & Melki, J. (2018). Shape shifting in the conflict zone. *Journalism Studies, 19*(1), 126–142.

Radsch, C. C., & Khamis, S. (2013). In their own voice: Technologically mediated empowerment and transformation among young Arab women. *Feminist Media Studies, 13*(5), 881–890.

Shahine, G. (2012, December 20–26). The media power game. *Ahram Weekly,* Issue 1127. Retrieved from http://weekly.ahram.org.eg/News/598.aspx

Sherwood, H. (2011, November 25). Egypt protests: Plea to keep women reporters out of Cairo withdrawn. *The Guardian*. Retrieved from www.theguardian.com/world/2011/nov/25/egypt-protests-reporters-women-safety

Sika, N. (2014). An Egyptian spring for Arab women? In M. Olimat (Ed.), *Arab Spring and Arab women: Challenges & opportunities*. New York, NY: Routledge.

World Economic Forum (2012). *Global gender gap report*. Geneva: World Economic Forum. Retrieved from http://www3.weforum.org/docs/WEF_GenderGap_Report_2012.pdf

Yakupitiyage, T. (2016, April 28). Violence against women journalists threatens media freedom. *IPS News*. Retrieved from www.ipsnews.net/2016/04/violence-against-women-journalists-threatens-media-freedom/

19

OBSTACLES TO CHINESE WOMEN JOURNALISTS' CAREER ADVANCEMENT

Haiyan Wang

In the past 20 years, the number and proportion of women journalists in China has substantially increased (BBC Chinese, 2018). In 1995, a national survey showed that women accounted for 33 percent of the total number of Chinese journalists (Chen et al., 1998), but data after 2000 shows a considerable increase. Women made up 37.1 percent of the total in the 2001 Shanghai survey (Jia, 2001), 40.9 percent in the 2003 national survey (Zheng & Chen, 2004), 43.8 percent in the 2005 Guang-zhou survey (Lin, 2010), 43.2 percent in the 2013 Shanghai survey (SJA, 2014), and 45.9 percent in the most recent national statistics released by a central regulatory body, the General Administration of Press and Publication (GAPP, 2016). However, women tend to be employed in roles with lower pay and less power: The pro-portion of women at executive and management levels is typically low; men also have better chances than women do to become investigative reporters and editorial writers, groups who are viewed as more "powerful" than other types of journalists (IWMF, 2011; Svensson & Wang, 2014; Wang, 2016a). That is, women's employ-ment in Chinese journalism presents a contradictory picture: mass participation on one hand and skewedness towards low positions on the other hand. It suggests that the increase in women's employment in journalism has not solved the profes-sion's gender-based inequality. Against this background, this chapter sketches out the major obstacles constraining and limiting women journalists' careers in China. With the rise of the Chinese economy and "soft power," China has become an important world player, attracting global attention not only because of its increasing influence in political and economic arenas, but also because it is a crucial part of global civil society and humanitarian projects such as feminism. Because Chinese women face situations that are both similar and different from their counterparts in other parts of the world, their experience may shed light on gender equality issues in the journalism profession more broadly.

Literatures on the professional obstacles facing women journalists

Examining women journalists' experience in different contexts and at different points in time, scholars agree that gender matters in the journalism profession—in a negative way for women, creating many obstacles to women's career progression. Among the dimensions illustrating the working of the "gender problem" for women journalists is the difficulty of balancing work and family. In the UK, many women journalists said work-family tensions limited their career opportunities: "[T]he near impossibility of successfully combining family and career still seems an insurmountable problem. . . . Even women who don't have children identify the difficulties and believe that making workplaces more friendly towards working mothers would be a positive way forward" (Ross, 2001, p. 533).

Scholars representing many countries have thoroughly documented that the newsroom is itself deeply gendered (de Bruin, 2000; Lavie & Lehman-Wilzig, 2005; Melin-Higgins, 2004; Ross, Boyle, Carter, & Ging, 2016). This manifests in newsroom hierarchies, routines, daily production practices, and conventions, as well as in the process of journalists' socialization into the newsrooms. In particular, assumptions about gender-appropriateness have been central in defining the profession. While professionalism tends to be associated with rationality, objectivity, decisiveness, and thus is seen to be more aligned with men's characteristics, femininity has long been associated with emotional and irrational qualities that contradict the requirements of professionalism.

Nevertheless, gender does not work in isolation: it works within certain historical, material and cultural/social conditions. As Steiner (2012) argues, gender is not the only factor limiting the choices of women journalists. It comes together with other interdependent but also intersecting problems, such as age, race, class, that therefore require a more holistic approach to understanding women journalists' career opportunities. In Korea, Kim (2006) argues the mixture of patriarchal structure with capitalism forms the basis for the marginalization of women in journalism. She thoroughly documents the exclusionary mechanisms on multiple levels—organizational, extra-organizational, and personal. At the organizational level, the newsroom is typically characterized by strong masculine bonds and a general distrust of women. At the extra-organizational level, sources regard women journalists as less competent given traditional views that women belong in the private domain, not the public fields and the profession's heavy reliance on informal and sometimes ethically compromised or immoral interactions with sources. Regarding the former, Kim (2006) argues that the traditional Korean view is that women should remain in the private area because of their inability to understand the complicated public field. As an example of the latter, Kim (2006) mentions how Korean journalists often enjoy meeting up with news sources at bars where there are prostitutes; and they accept and give bribes. Kim contends that such behaviors can work to exclude journalists who refuse to participate in this unethical behavior. At the personal level, women journalists' pursuit of career advancement is typically constrained by their domestic roles in housework, pregnancy, and childcare that are assigned to them by society, their families, and even themselves.

While acknowledging the pervasiveness of gender-based inequalities in the Hong Kong journalistic workforce, Tsui and Lee (2012) found that some women were indeed able to defy structural constraints to develop relatively successful journalism careers. They attributed this to different conditions formed by the interaction of gender and various other forces, including position within a news organization, the news organization's position in the news market, the journalist's social class, socio-economic status, and kind of family support.

Regarding professional obstacles to women journalists in China, scholars like-wise usually emphasize structural reasons. Cao (2012) argues that with the increased commercialization and conglomeration of media industries in China, women jour-nalists are increasingly becoming "knowledge workers" (*zhishi laogong*) whose labor is devalued and exploited, given flexible employment, low wages, and precarious working conditions. I have similarly argued that the commercialization of Chinese media has rendered women journalists as "naked swimmers"—meaning first that, borrowing a phrase popular in the 1980s, journalists are swimming in the sea of the market economy without any protective clothing, since the state, the market, NGOs, and trade unions are all hostile to women, or at least they are not women-friendly (Wang, 2016b). Women journalists are also "naked swimmers" in the sense that they are exposed to sexist jokes, pornography, and even direct sexual harass-ment in their workplaces but again powerless to fight it. More than half of women journalists Jia (2001) surveyed claimed they suffered discrimination in some way; most of them had significant difficulties when they tried to attain executive-level responsibilities. The disadvantaged position of women journalists is even evident in journalism prizes. Men—as judges and winners—dominate the Fan Changjiang News Prize and Taofen News Prize, the top two prizes for Chinese journalists and editors (Huang, 2011). Overall, the complicated and multi-leveled obstacles to women journalists' career success are well-documented.

Method

I interviewed 43 Chinese journalists between 2010 and 2016. Recruited through snowballing the men and women journalists worked for print media in Beijing, Shanghai, Guangzhou, Shenzhen, Xi'an, Chengdu, Wuhan, and Changsha. These eight metropolitan cities are home to major national and regional media organi-zations; and the journalistic cohorts are relatively large in terms of number and willing to share stories with outsiders. Most of them are in their 30s, with a few slightly over 40 years old; otherwise, they represent a range of seniority and industry experience. They were asked about career choices and opportunities, organizational culture, newsroom culture, relationship with work colleagues, work-family balance, and so on. Some of the interviewees also actively maintain personal blogs. Their entries cover a wide range of topics such as news, politics, travels, family, friends, and work. With their consent, I accessed their weblogs and used the information in their writings as supplementary data. In addition, relevant media reports and publicly available documents, such as comments on popular BBS forums, were consulted to help understand the general situation of Chinese women journalists.[1] Analysis of the interviews and journalists' written documents, as well as triangulating relevant public documents, shows how Chinese women journalists' attempts at career advancement are constrained by four kinds of obstacles. Below I explain, in turn, the institutional obstacles, organizational obstacles, cultural obstacles, and self-disciplinary obstacles.

Institutional obstacles

Chinese women journalists are constrained, first, by state-level institutions, which work against women's career progression, especially by limiting women's agency and weakening their power to protect their employment rights. These institutional obstacles are often invisible, but they manifest themselves in the paradoxical ways that state policies are developed and implemented. Many countries have introduced policies to facilitate women's rights; besides state policies, non-governmental organizations (NGOs) such as women's associations and trade unions also pursue gender justice. Many Chinese policymakers would argue that China has women's rights legislation as well as pro-women NGOs. For example, a 1992 law protects women's political, economic, and employment rights (*Zhongguo Funu Quanyi Baozhang Fa*); a 1995 labor law (*Zhonghua Renmin Gongheguo Laodong Fa*) likewise addressed women's employment. Although their terms are not designed specifically to regulate media and journalism jobs, the general rules of "equal employment opportunities and equal wages" (*tonggong tongchou*) for both sexes are explicit. Meanwhile, both the national labor organizations such as the All-China Federation of Trade Unions (*Quanguo Zonggong hui*), and national women's organizations such as the All-China Women's Federation (*Quanguo fulian*), have thousands of local branches. Specifically, the All-China Journalists' Association (*Zhongguo Jixie*) and the Women Journalists' Association (*Nu jixie*) likewise have local branches. But, in a one-party authoritarian state like China, where civil society organizations cannot operate without official supervision, the above-mentioned state-engineered and state-run associations are essentially different from autonomous NGOs, as defined by the mainstream standard (Spires, 2012). Since their launch, they have been little more than party-state organs tasked with making Chinese women into statist subjects and laborers. In addition, as the country marches on toward a market economy, these organizations, widely regarded as "baggage" inherited from the old socialist system, have been marginalized. Meanwhile, bottom-up feminist and labor movements are suppressed because of the authoritarian state's general intolerance of the development of civil society (Li & Li, 2017). Therefore, women journalists have no protected employment rights. In principle, every journalist formally employed in the Chinese media industry is a member of both the journalists' association (*jixie*) and the trade union (*gonghui*); women journalists automatically become members of the women journalists' association (*nujixie*) and women's federation (*fulian*). These organizations also have local branches in each "state unit" (*guojia danwei*, meaning organizations that are run by the state—which every newspaper is). But many men and women told me they did not even realize that they belonged to any of these associations. A male Guangzhou journalist in his mid-30s described the trade union as seldom making its presence felt in journalists' working lives:

> Trade Union? . . . To be honest, I never know what their real function is. Only when I get my salary notice each month, can I feel its existence, because it reminds me I've contributed 2 Yuan to the 'Trade Union'. And then at the end of the year, I will be given some domestic stuff, usually rice and cooking oil. We are told that these are 'festival gifts' from the Trade Union, wishing us a happy new year. Hahaha. . . . That's all.
>
> *(p. 16)*

So, his first reaction to my question was surprise, as if it were completely strange. It took a while for him to recall his connection with the trade union. Moreover, that connection has nothing to do with protecting his workplace rights. When journalists have trouble getting paid or having a contract renewed, they certainly do not seek help from the trade union. Moreover, since all local trade union personnel are appointed and financed by the news organization, its function is not to fight for workers' rights but to ease tensions between the news organization and its employees. It has reduced itself to a source of small gifts and largely evokes the past socialist age with nostalgia. "Nothing more than that," the interviewee emphasized.

For the journalists' association and women's federation, the situation is highly similar: none regard journalists' or women's workplace rights as their top priority. Ironically, some have even drifted away from their original purpose and are now discriminatory and hostile to women. Fincher's (2014) study of urban Chinese women's struggles over property rights found that the Women's Federation has been crucial in promoting the media discourse of "leftover women," reinforcing gender stereotypes. It stokes fears among unmarried women in their late 20s, encouraging them to give up their property rights. A woman Guangzhou journalist said the women's federation in her news organization pivoted on the Qi'pao, a traditional Chinese women's silk dress, once routinely worn by upper-class women, and tailored to tightly fit the figure:

> On International Women's Day this year, our unit launched a 'Qi'pao show.' The Women's Federation said, in order to show the 'elegance' and 'beauty' of 'traditional' 'oriental' [original emphasis] women, all women staff should please wear Qi'pao to work on that day. . . . Some women colleagues thought it silly. They didn't wear it. Some thought it novel. Good fun, right? Besides, they would select the 20 most 'beautiful babies' and 20 most 'charming ladies' on that day.

Although Chinese women now wear the Qi'pao only on special occasions, according to my interviewee, women journalists were persuaded to wear the Qi'pao for the purpose of a "show" whose aims were explicitly to demonstrate the "elegance and beauty of traditional oriental women." It is about the display of women's bodies. This show's audience is unstated but is easy to guess—mostly male colleagues. Ironically, it was the *Women's Federation that* asked women journalists to organize this show on *Women's Day*, supposedly to honor gender equality.

The show aroused heated discussion among a group of liberal-minded Guangzhou journalists. A journalist who identified herself as a feminist activist said she was outraged. She said she and some of her colleagues opposed "objectifying women" and "exploiting women's bodies for men's pleasure"; they "never thought such an utterly entirely ridiculous proposal would come out of the Women Federation, the women's own organization." As this case demonstrates, the official associations are not only weak, but likely to become an apparatus for reinforcing gender inequality in the workplace. My interviewees mentioned several complicated reasons for these women's associations and trade unions being weak and even dysfunctional. Partly, however, it turns on the market-centric logic of China's media organizations: party propaganda and profit are their overriding aims. News organizations are unlikely to support labor/women's/journalists' associations because they do not generate revenue. Meanwhile, as a matter of state policy, these associations cannot seek independence from the news organizations. Therefore, their influence has gradually diminished. They have become a kind of fading "socialist" decoration, still hanging on the wall.

Organizational obstacles

The organizational obstacles to women's careers in journalism mainly come in the form of job contracts and salary systems. China has two types of employment relationships between journalists and news organizations. The market system involves journalists signing an annual contract with their employing media organization. The "quota" system, in contrast, guarantees journalists lifetime employment and even socio-political status as governmental officials (*guojia ganbu*). Along with the deepening of media marketization reforms, yearly contracts have gradually replaced lifelong employment, so fewer and fewer journalists get the more desirable type of contract. Not surprisingly, because they entered the profession in the post-1992 era, none of my interviewees, regardless of gender, had quota contract.

Meanwhile, journalists are no longer proud "state cadres" (*guojia ganbu*). Instead, they are "news laborers" (*xinwen mingong*). One consequence is that journalists must work very hard in order to earn a decent salary, and more importantly, to keep their jobs. Journalists on commercial contracts earn both fixed salary and a monthly bonus. Their fixed salary is relatively low, usually 20 percent of their total income. The so-called bonus is dependent on the quality and quantity of their work. In addition, the total annual bonus a journalist earns must reach the minimum set by the news organization, because it is directly related to the possibility of signing a job contract for the next year. In this way, the yearly commercial contract creates intensifying job pressure. Many journalists I studied quoted a catchphrase to describe the pressure of their job: "females are used as males, males are used as mules," referring to a hard-working animal that often works like a slave under the whips and scolds of its owner. The "mule" metaphor both describes how hard they must work and simultaneously registers their complaints against bad conditions. This is related to the second consequence of "news labor"; journalists are deprived of the free health-care, free children's education, and affordable housing services which were available in the pre-reform era.

At first glance, this kind of job pressure is gender-neutral. But for women jour-nalists who are at the same time expected to bear children and fulfill their family roles, the pressure and fear are doubled. Many women journalists marry late, usually in their 30s, and have children after they are 35 years old. As with their Western counterparts, whether to have children is a difficult decision for women (Ross, 2001). But, the negative impact of motherhood on their careers is much more direct and immediate. "From the moment you get pregnant, you are dumped to the lowest level of the hierarchy," a woman journalist in Guangzhou said. The commer-cialized contract distributes money mainly on the basis of work quality and quan-tity; women's special needs during pregnancy and maternity are barely considered. Therefore, the salary for women journalists who take pregnancy or maternity leave immediately reduces to next to zero. This journalist recalled her experience during her took two months of maternity leave:

> My unit only paid me the fixed salary. Well, no work, no bonus. That's the rule. . . . But then my housing insurance, security and health insurance are all deducted from it. In the end I only had 82 Yuan coming to my account each month. It's not even enough to buy a pack of milk powder for my child. I was so sad. So in the third month, I stopped breastfeeding and went back to work. I can't afford to take leave any longer.

That is, the salary system affects childbearing women to the extent that even mini-mal food supplies are threatened. It dramatizes the inherent contradiction between being a professional and a mother. The "no work, no bonus" system is designed to encourage uninterrupted work. Although, by national law, women employees can take three to four months' maternity leave and men employees can take 3 to 15 days paternity leave, such working conditions mean journalists cannot really enjoy their leave. More importantly, because the bonus is tied up with contract renewal, the journalist who earns a small bonus risks being demoted or fired. This pushes some childbearing women journalists to the limit of their physical capacity. A Chengdu journalist said she worked nearly until the birth of her child; 15 days after giving birth, she was already back in the newsroom.

Many women journalists agonize over returning to their old jobs so soon after giving birth. They shift to less-privileged positions in their news organization, such as copy-editing and administration, or simply find another job in a different indus-try and start over. In this way, motherhood has forced many women journalists out of their profession. For example, a former current affairs reporter for a local

Chengdu press group changed to working as an administrative officer in its human resource department. Her newspaper, like many others in China, has adopted a performance evaluation system in which each journalist's basic salary is determined annually. She was demoted after she returned from maternity leave and was unable, despite several attempts, to resume her original rank. As a result, she decided to leave journalism and find another job. With quavering speech, she emphasized show her promotion was stopped because she was "short of one thing":

> I was just short . . . I was just short of that one thing . . . just short of one thing . . . then I would be promoted. . . . I cried. Our executive saw me and said, oh, you cried, why, blah blah. They do not understand us at all. I was demoted from the first tier because I had a child. I was helpless. Then there was an opportunity, but I couldn't get promotion this time. My colleagues, they all said . . . 'you should complain.' They said, 'you should be promoted, you can.' But how difficult it is to be promoted, you know? So I said, I can't stand this eighteen-story hell. I think, at that time I was cornered, feeling very sad.

Fighting a merciless enemy, then, she left journalism. In fact, for many women journalists, giving birth is the major factor that interrupts and even terminates their journalism career. As another interviewee in Shenzhen said: "The time a woman decides to have a child is the time she decides to leave her career." While some women journalists publicly complain about the women-unfriendly contract and salary systems and dismiss them as "unfair" and "unethical" to women, many do not realize its exploitative nature and take it for granted. A man who is department head in Guangzhou said:

> I think if a woman wants to have children, she should not have any ambition in her career. Bearing a child takes her at least a year. And when she comes back to work, she needs another year to readapt. It's biophysically deter-mined. They are naturally slower (in climbing the career ladder). So . . . they need not complain.

Here, he tries to naturalize women's relative disadvantage in the newsroom by referring to biology. To him, women are slow in climbing the career ladder because of the category they are born into, not because of any socio-cultural factors. His use of terms such as "determined" and "naturally" imply that this condition is undeni-able and should be taken for granted. So, women should accept this condition and live with it. Later, he made clear that his lack of sympathy for women's difficulties in career advancement is related to the market-centric contract and salary system:

> To be honest, I don't want to have women reporters in my department. They are troublesome, getting married someday, having children and taking mater-nity leave, and then you have to do their jobs yourself. Otherwise, your bonus

will be affected. Your performance will receive a low evaluation. You can't keep your position any more.

The department head's bonus depends on the average bonus of the staffers he supervises; his performance evaluation is linked to the overall performance of the reporters in his department. The work of each reporter is decisive to his own career. Under this pressure, he tends to refuse to let women journalists, especially those of childbearing age, enter his department. Women are "troublesome." In his eyes—and this attitude to women journalists is typical of media organization management—they make more trouble than contributions to the department.

Cultural obstacles

The sexism prevalent in Chinese newsroom culture also contributes to gender inequality. Scholars have documented sexist culture in newsrooms around the world, including Australia (North, 2007), Africa (Opoku-Mensah, 2004), the Caribbean (de Bruin, 2004), Korea (Kim, 2006), the UK (Ross et al., 2018), the US (Weaver, 1992), and so on. With China, scholars seem also to accept the dominant view that workplace sexism is natural. But, the sexist newsroom culture that women journalists face is not natural or insignificant, and complaints are not mere over-reaction.

Many women discussed being judged by their appearance, sometimes from the moment they begin their careers. When recruiting new staff, many news organizations require women applicants to be "good-looking" and meet the standards of height, weight, breast size, and so on. An interviewee in Chengdu explained that, of course, job ads do not mention physical appearance:

> But my colleagues in the human resources department clearly told me this. They have a standard in mind. They want males. If they don't get males, alternatively they want girls, young girls with pretty faces and slim figures.

This woman described the different ways of evaluating men and women applying for journalism jobs. Men confront no obvious "appearance" requirement. A "pretty face" and "slim figure" are clearly preferred for women. Although they may describe this phenomenon in neutral tones, refraining from expressing any emotions, women often regard it as humiliating, as insulting their intellectual ability. But women often are powerless to fight back, if they want the job. Meanwhile, those women who successfully entered journalism are also likely to confront appearance-based discrimination. According to a woman journalist who has stayed with the profession for 11 years:

> In men's eyes, there are only two types of women, either 'mei nu' (young, beautiful women) or 'da ma' (middle-aged ladies). Their looks, talk and attitudes are all very offensive. Sometimes when hanging out together after work, they will say, 'oh, there are no "mei nu," how boring!' They just talk like this. They don't care what you think.

As a woman in her late 30s with a child, she was often categorized as the "da ma" type by her male colleagues. The men are often unconscious of the harm this does to her and other women colleagues, and of how this discourse limited what she could do and say. Her male colleagues, she told me, talk regularly and openly about women's appearance in the office and judge their female colleagues' clothing, hairstyles, makeup, and even bodies. Pornographic images, usually of naked or half-naked women, appear on their computer screens. Women journalists are even invited to view and comment on these images. However, as far as the men are concerned, this behavior is often not meant to be offensive to women but to give themselves some "fun" in their heavily burdened jobs. A man told me what he and other men do after work, instead of going home:

> We (colleagues) get together, eat, drink, review our stories over the past day or (week), and discuss what reports we will do next. One day after the meeting, a colleague said, 'Let's play a game. Suppose we are now going home, and we are allowed to take a woman from here to spend a night with. Who would you choose?' Then we vote, in the presence of these women colleagues. . . . We often play this kind of game. Just for fun.

As this example suggests, men appeared not to recognize their sexist attitudes. If they are conscious of it, they tend to see a sexist but natural and acceptable newsroom culture to which subordinate women journalists must accommodate themselves. Sexual objectification of women becomes a normalized, quotidian newsroom practice. These practices enable men to display their prestige and power. The subordination of women constitutes a major source of male domination in the newsroom. Some women interviewed for this study said that they left journalism because of the difficulty of accepting this sexist newsroom culture. A Shenzhen women explained why she had recently quit journalism altogether:

> When they made sexist jokes to me, I often returned a cold face. I didn't want to react in the way they expected, like . . . laughing, returning another joke. . . . But gradually I noticed the consequences. They saw me as a boring and uninteresting person, well . . . because I am not playful. I felt I was isolated. It was getting very hard. So I quit.
>
> (p. 122)

Moreover, rather than being sympathetic, men blame women for not utilizing their "female" advantages properly. Responding to a question about whether the sexist newsroom culture causes difficulties for women's careers, one man said that it is "nobody's fault but women's":

> Women have natural advantages. They should utilize them. . . . They should make the boss feel it is pleasant to have them around. That way, they will have good chances in their careers even though they can't make good journalists.

Some feminist women journalists respond to the sexist newsroom culture confronting it. Others choose to ignore it or avoid it. But inevitably, some will choose to conform to it, to keep their job. Shen Bing, a 37-year-old TV anchor who allegedly was mistress to a former high-ranking Politburo Standing Committee member, admitted in her autobiography that Chinese women journalists often use sex to advance their careers (Shen, 2014). Although Shen's stories cannot be proven, they nevertheless provide a glimpse of the extremes to which desperate and powerless women journalists will go when subjected to this sexist culture. A post-#MeToo survey done by a former journalist found that more than 80 percent of Chinese women journalists have experienced varying degrees of sexual harassment in the workplace. But less than 4 percent of them reported the encounter to their company or the police; the majority chose to remain silent (Lai, 2018).

Self-disciplinary obstacles

Besides the external obstacles at the institutional, organizational, and cultural level, an internal obstacle involves women's agency or self-discipline. In the Foucauldian sense, discipline is a type of power or technique for exercising power in modern society. Discipline has replaced older forms of punishment based on repression or violence, to assure the ordering of human groups. It imposes a sense of regulation and a code of conduct on the part of individuals and stops them from behaving in undesirable ways. In the case of Chinese women journalists, I contend, such disciplinary power can arise not only from external institutions or apparatus, but also from women's internal sense of self. They tend to impose regulations or codes of conduct on themselves, consciously or subconsciously, in order to better fit in to the society. Specifically, this is reflected in women journalists' conformity to social stereotypes and expectations about how women should behave, and their resulting adjustments to their behaviors and decisions.

Women journalists in China face stereotypes both about their social role as a woman; and their professional role as a woman journalist. In China journalism is often deemed to be unsuitable for women. Jobs such as teachers, civil servants, or corporate secretaries are normally deemed much more suitable. Many women journalists, especially those working as investigative reporters, told me that their families often think journalism is not appropriate for women. A woman in Beijing explained on her personal blog why she is not sure how long she will continue as a journalist:

> My brother often asks me to give up being a reporter and prepare for the Civil Service Exam. Dad says it is a dangerous job, and makes him worried. Mum says (it is) not decent, running around outdoors every day. Mum taught me to stay in the kitchen and cook since (I was) nine years old in order for me to be a good housewife in the future. She told me that 'Man is a tree, woman is a vine'. But I have not had the life that Mum wants me to live.

Accordingly, women journalists often consciously or subconsciously internalize the stereotypes and accept these as "correct" ways of being a woman. An interviewee from Xi'an said she is very "bothered" by how people she knows often attach such labels as "strong," "brave," and "staunch" to journalistic work, and how she is thought to be "lacking female characteristics" because she works as a journalist. She said with self-pity:

> This job influenced me a lot. I was always a literary and artistic young woman, with long hair and colorful skirts. . . . But after becoming a journalist, I am often exposed to the dark side of the society, such as violence, death, and even rape. To be immersed in this environment for a long time, even the most feminine woman will become wild, aggressive, and rough. We make men terrified to be close to us.

Such self-pity is often one reason that women journalists eventually leave the profession. It causes an internal conflict that women cannot resolve. In a media conference I attended, an award-winning journalist came to the stage for a speech. After describing her passion for journalism, the woman tearfully ended her speech:

> I have to say sorry to my husband, I am not a good wife. I have to say sorry to my son, I am not a good mum. And I have to say sorry to my parents and parents-in-law, I am not a good daughter or daughter-in-law. . . . Because of my work as a journalist, I haven't fulfilled my duties to them. I am sorry.

Social expectations always prioritize Chinese women's role as a good wife or mother over an aggressive professional pursuing a career. One of the triggering factors underlying the occurrence of domestic violence is often that a woman cannot meet her family role expectations as wife, mother or daughter-in-law. Lin Lixian, an anchorwoman at a television station in Fujian Province, was stabbed to death by her father-in law. He was said to have hoped she would bear another grandson for the family, which Lin refused.[2] Hong Mei, a television reporter in the Inner Mongolia Autonomous Region, was beaten to death by her husband because she often left the family home for work appointments.[3] Although these are isolated and extreme cases, they reflect part of the reality facing women in China. No wonder many women journalists experience major tensions between being a woman and being a journalist. One journalist, who is a (single) mother of a 7-year-old child, said:

> I often feel guilty about my family, especially my daughter. She often asks me 'Mum, why you are not like other mums and often go out rather than staying at home?' I told her, 'This is Mum's job. Mum loves this job, and everybody needs a job to prove his/her competence. Besides, we need money to live.' My daughter then said, 'But I feel we have less time together since you became a journalist.' I had to tell her 'Mum will not be a reporter long, just wait for a couple of years.' She replied 'But I will not want to live with

you after I grow up.' Her words made me feel sad and sorrowful when I went for another business trips.

(p. 126)

This journalist left her newspaper job soon after I interviewed her. Another single mother felt pity for her child and blamed herself for having no other choice. She said she often had to bring her son with her when she went to gather news and interview people:

> Once I went to a remote village to gather news and I brought my child with me. We took a long-distance bus to go there. There was no highway, only bumpy and muddy village roads. I couldn't imagine how my little boy could make the trip, but he did. When we arrived there, I had to work. I left him on the village playground and let him play with the rural children. From time to time I came back to check on him, but only to see him all covered in mud because his mother had no time to look after him. When my friends heard of it, they all said, 'We have never seen a mother like this.' It was a crime. It made me feel very bad.

Such widely felt family-work tensions also explain why many women journalists remain single or are divorced. But being single or divorced is also hard for Chinese women. Even though the women themselves think that it is acceptable to be unmarried, people in their social network pity them. Family, relatives, friends, and colleagues care greatly about their unmarried status and urge them to date and find a husband. In the beginning, the journalist may find being forced into dating activities annoying; gradually they internalize the social expectation that a woman should be married and become anxious that they have not found a husband. A well-known investigative journalist who is still single at the age of 46 told me that she did not choose to remain single. It just happened that she never met someone who suited her. If she had a choice, she said, she would definitely choose being a beloved wife over being a famous journalist.

Conclusion

At the institutional level, state policies and institutions do not necessarily promote the development of women's agency or protect women's equal rights to work. At the organizational level, women-unfriendly contracts and the modern salary system tend to block women journalists' chances to advance, especially when they reach the age and life-stage of child-raising and family responsibilities. At the cultural level, women journalists are subject to deep sexism in the newsroom. At individual self-disciplinary level, women journalists are caught up in the dilemma of meeting social and stereotypical expectations while attempting to pursue a successful career. The tension has often led them to conform to the former and retreat from the latter. Taken together, the career opportunities of women journalists in

China are limited by a complicated set of factors that are both structural and cultural, both external and internal.

China has a long way to go to change this situation. As a Communist regime established on the basis of Marx and Engels's visions of an egalitarian society, China is supposed to be inherently gender-equal. Feminism has been enshrined as a state project ever since the infancy of the Communist Party in the 1920s. Mao's legendary dictum that "women hold up half the sky" has been part of political and popular imagination about gender relations since the 1950s. But a patriarchal state can hide behind the grand discourse of egalitarianism to deny that gender inequality is a social problem and avoid addressing the problem. Of course, it is unfair to say that the "state feminism" project has achieved nothing. It has indeed helped women to gain marriage autonomy, political rights, social welfare, and employment opportunities. These achievements, however, arrived on the condition of subordinating feminist concerns to various political and economic goals of the state. This has cultivated a political mindset that women's issues are always secondary to the nation's socio-political and economic development. "Women hold up half the sky" became a political myth rather than a reality in women's everyday experience of life and work. This situation is unlikely to change fundamentally in the short term.

In the last decade, the rapid development of ICTs and the digitization of the media industry has brought signs that women are beginning to overtake men as the majority of China's journalism workforce. More women are able to take senior and executive positions in newsrooms. This has given rise to the hope that technology may help change gender relations in journalism. These developments are worth paying attention to, but we must avoid technological optimism. Recent increases in the number and power of women journalists is occurring alongside the general decline in the salaries and social status of journalism jobs. More women than men in the newsrooms is likely to be the result of more men than women having opportunities to pursue better paid and higher social status jobs outside journalism. This will inevitably invite worries about whether journalism will become another "pink ghetto." Other outcomes are, however, possible and more positive and these deserve future research.

Notes

1 Parts of this analysis were published in: Wang, H. (2016a). "Naked Swimmers": Chinese women journalists' experience of media commercialization. *Media, Culture & Society*, *38*(4), 489–505.
2 The news was reported by Sohu News. Retrieved October 10, 2015, from www.sohu. com/a/35027719_114735
3 The news was reported by youth.cn. Retrieved from http://news.youth.cn/jsxw/201704/ t20170407_9434998_1.htm

References

BBC. (2018, March 8). Women journalists in the field of political news (zhengzhi xinwen chang zhong de nujizhe: zhujue or zhuangshiwu?). *BBC Chinese*. Retrieved from www. bbc.com/zhongwen/simp/chinese-news-43322502

Cao, J. (2012). Female knowledge labor and employment policy in printed press industry in China. *Communication and Society (Chuanbo yu shehui xuekan)*, *20*, 11–40 [in Chinese].

Chen, C., Zhu, J. H., & Wu, W. (1998). The Chinese journalist. In Weaver D. (Ed.), *The global journalist: News people around the world* (pp. 9–30). Cresskill, NJ: Hampton Press.

de Bruin, M. (2000). Gender, organizational and professional in journalism. *Journalism*, *1*(2), 217–238.

de Bruin, M. (2004). Organizational, professional, and gender identities—Overlapping, coinciding and contradicting realities in Caribbean media practices. In M. de Bruin & K. Ross (Eds.), *Gender and newsroom cultures: Identities at work* (pp. 1–16). Cresskill, NJ: Hampton Press.

Fincher, L. H. (2014). *Leftover women: The resurgence of gender inequality in China*. London: Zed Books.

GAPP (General Administration of Press and Publication). (2016). *Analysis and report of the press industry in 2015*. Beijing: GAPP [in Chinese].

Huang, S. (2011). *News prizes as social control* (Unpublished Ph.D dissertation), City University of Hong Kong, Hong Kong.

IWMF (International Women's Media Foundation). (2011). *Global report on the status of women in the news media*. Retrieved from http://iwmf.org/pdfs/IWMF-Global-Report.pdf

Jia, Y. F. (2001). The survey report of women journalists in Shanghai. *Shanghai Journalism Review*, *11*, 16–21 [in Chinese].

Kim, K. H. (2006). Obstacles to the success of female journalists in Korea. *Media, Culture & Society*, *28*(1), 123–141.

Lai, C. (2018, March 7). Over 80% of female journalists in China have experienced workplace sexual harassment, poll by journalist shows. *Hong Kong Free Press*. Retrieved from www.hongkongfp.com/2018/03/07/80-female-journalists-china-experienced-workplace-sexual-harassment-poll-journalist-shows/

Lavie, A., & Lehman-Wilzig, S. (2005). The method is the message: Explaining inconsistent findings in gender and news production research. *Journalism*, *6*(1), 66–89.

Li, J., & Li, X. (2017). Media as a core political resource: The young feminist movements in China. *Chinese Journal of Communication*, *10*(1), 54–71.

Lin, F. (2010). Research report: A survey report on Chinese journalists in China. *The China Quarterly*, *202*, 421–434.

Melin-Higgins, M. (2004). Coping with journalism: Gendered newsroom culture In M. de Bruin & K. Ross (Eds.), *Gender and newsroom cultures: Identities at work* (pp. 197–222). Cresskill, NJ: Hampton Press.

North, L. (2007). Just a little bit of cheeky ribaldry? *Feminist Media Studies*, *7*(1), 81–96.

Opoku-Mensah, A. (2004). Hanging in there: Women, gender, and newsroom cultures in Africa. In M. de Bruin & K. Ross (Eds.), *Gender and newsroom cultures: Identities at work* (pp. 107–120). Cresskill, NJ: Hampton Press.

Ross, K. (2001). Women at work: Journalism as en-gendered practice. *Journalism Studies*, *2*(4), 531–544.

Ross, K., Boyle, K., Carter, C., & Ging, G. (2018). Women, men and news. *Journalism Studies*, *19*(6), 824–845. doi:10.1080/1461670X.2016.1222884

Shen, B. (2014). *Shen Bing's own account: My story with Zhou Yongkang*. Hong Kong: Biaodi Press [in Chinese].

SJA (Shanghai Journalists Association). (2014). Survey and report of women journalists in Shanghai in 2013. *Shanghai Journalism Review*, *3*, 35–42 [in Chinese].

Spires, A. J. (2012). Contingent symbiosis and civil society in an authoritarian state: Understanding the survival of China's grassroots NGOs. *American Journal of Sociology*, *117*(1), 1–45.

Steiner, L. (2012). Failed theories: Explaining gender difference in journalism. *The Review of Communication*, *12*(3), 201–223.

Svensson, M., & Wang, H. (2014). Gendering investigative journalism: Norms and practices inside and outside the newsroom. In M. Svensson, E. Sather, & Z. Zhang (Eds.), *Chinese investigative journalists' dreams: Autonomy* (pp. 91–110). Lanham, MD: Lexington Books.

Tsui, C., & Lee, F. (2012). Trajectories of women journalists' careers in Hong Kong. *Journalism Studies, 13*(2), 370–385.

Wang, H. (2016a). The gendered myth of women investigative journalists: From the perspective of construction of social stereotypes. *Journalism Bimonthly (Xinwen daxue), 4*, 19–24 [in Chinese].

Wang, H. (2016b). "Naked swimmers": Chinese women journalists' experience of media commercialization. *Media, Culture & Society, 38*(4), 489–505.

Weaver, C. (1992, September 23–27). A secret no more. *Washington Journalism Review.*

Zheng, B., & Chen, X. (2004). Journalists' views on paid journalism: A survey on Chinese journalists' professional ethics. *Shanghai Journalism Review, 5*, 20–22 [in Chinese].

PART IV

Politics and identities
in the news

PART IV

Politics and identities
in the news

20

FEMINISM AND GENDER IN THE POST-TRUTH PUBLIC SPHERE

Catharine Lumby

In *Kill All Normies: Online Culture Ware from 4Chan and Tumblr to Trump and the Alt-Right*, Irish journalist Angela Nagle (2017) analyzes the revival of the "culture wars" between the left and right of politics that emerged during the 1990s in US culture and politics. She argues that the new culture wars are now being waged on the Internet—on online and social media—and that they include misogynistic attacks on feminists, as well as racial abuse.

Nagle's argument is that on online and social media:

> As old media dies, gatekeepers of cultural sensibilities and etiquette have been overthrown, notions of popular taste maintained by a small creative class are now perpetually outsourced by viral online content from obscure sources, and culture industry consumers have been replaced by constantly online, instant content producers.
>
> *(Nagle, 2017, p. 3)*

Nagle is fascinated by the way that both the right and left of politics are fragmenting in an online world and how, increasingly, the conventional political debates emerge in either irony-cloaked satire or vitriolic personal attacks. Sometimes the former can mask the latter. Those who fail to understand this cultural turn, whatever their politics, she argues, are doomed to marginalization, or to be dismissed as "normies."

For example, Andrew Bolt is a right-wing columnist for the Australia-based *The Herald Sun*, a newspaper that is part of the News Corporation, a global company with media arms in the UK and the US. Bolt is notorious among intellectuals and progressive thinkers in Australia for his conservative views. Whether writing on climate change, Indigenous rights or feminism, anger is one of Andrew Bolt's signature emotions, and one that has served him well in the traditional media. Yet, as

Bolt found out in 2013, Twitter is not a compliant platform for lecturing people. What's more, writing a blog read mainly by his fans is very different from engaging with the Twittersphere. During the run-up to the 2013 Australian Federal election, he, or perhaps his newspaper, sent a tweet inviting people to question him on anything regarding the forthcoming election. The idea was clearly an invitation to approach Bolt so he could offer his opinions on the election and on politics in general.

The swift Twitter response from Bolt's opponents mocked his "ask me anything" status as a guru on politics. Questions included: "Is it true that winter is coming?" and "Do you know the way to Scarborough Fair?" During his online chat and in a subsequent post Bolt reacted to being mocked with anger. In response to the question: "What would you do if I sang out of tune?" he wrote:

> It's bizarre that the Left has spent 24 hours hyperventilating on Twitter and thinking up questions to hurl at the great Satan of conservatism, and this is one of the best they could come up with. Understand now why you are losing the intellectual debate, guys?
>
> *(Olding, 2013)*

The Bolt Twitter storm in Australia illustrates a trope now common in political debate: the contest between self-righteous anger and satire. For Bolt critics, his indignant hectoring simply proved their point. For Bolt supporters, the ripostes proved that lefties were part of a deluded cabal who had no capacity to engage in serious political debate. This impasse, common in social media, represents a clash of discursive frames.

Here, I explore the question of whether social media offer an authentic opportunity for feminist activists to respond to sexist speech and behavior and especially to explore which speaking and listening modes are most effective. Given the fragmentation of the social media public sphere, I cannot empirically quantify the effectiveness of particular ways of speaking and listening. I can, however, analyze case studies that demonstrate de facto instances of successful campaigns. The question I pursue here is what are the affordances of online and social media platforms and networks for progressive discussions of gender and political activism? I will focus on the way mainstream media brought to light sexual harassment and assault cases that then, in a dialogic manner, caught fire on social media.

Drawing on the rapidly emerging literature on the "post-truth" public sphere and the rise of extremist online anti-feminist discourse (Jane, 2017, p. 2), I examine different models for understanding the contemporary media sphere, including the "counter-public sphere." I relate contemporary developments to earlier critiques of the Habermasian model for understanding "rational" public discourse.

As Nancy Fraser frames it, the Habermasian public sphere:

> designates a theater in modern societies in which political participation is enacted through the medium of talk. It is the space in which citizens

deliberate about their common affairs, hence, an institutionalized arena of discursive interaction.

(Fraser, 1993, p. 2)

Jurgen Habermas's widely critiqued model of the public sphere relies on a very particular construction of what constitutes the theater in which "citizens" meet to discourse, and, of who belongs in that theater. Put simply, as exemplified by the Greek agora, only certain people were eligible to engage in discourse: in Western historical terms, until recently, the podium for speaking was reserved for Anglo propertied men. Over the course of the twentieth and the twenty-first century, the gradual diversification of media in terms of platforms, genres, and outlets, however, has radically increased both the diversity of voices and equally the ways of speaking about personal, political, and social life. The impulse at the heart of liberal democracies has also, albeit slowly at times, eroded the barriers of class, race, culture, gender, and privilege.

The post social media public sphere

In *Gotcha: Life in a Tabloid World* (Lumby, 1999), I confidently espoused the virtues of an increasingly democratized public sphere. I wrote that book at the dawn of an era in which average people were beginning to access the Internet and well before the arrival of social media. In essence, I argued that the breaking down of the barriers between the public and private spheres benefited women and others whose issues had been marginalized and seen as a personal matter. *Gotcha* ended with a note of caution—one that rings in my ears:

> The media is the foundation of our public conversation today, and, like democracy itself, it can sometimes seem like a Tower of Babel. But it also offers moments of unexpected convergence, media events which draw us together as a local, national or global community to think about differences and our claims to identity. Negotiating these differences doesn't require us to reach agreement, but it does entail a recognition that there are always other ways of speaking and looking around.
>
> *(Lumby, 1999, p. 249)*

I continue to be confounded by the question of how we conjure with the Moebius strip that threads together the strands of the virtual media world and the reality of democracy and identity politics. I am, of course, far from alone in this. In *Popular Reality* (1996) John Hartley was one of the first media scholars to sketch what he called the postmodern public sphere. Hartley argued, as he has in much of his subsequent work, that the image has triumphed over rational discourse and the hierarchies that have structured a male-dominated and elitist public sphere. He argues that the image-saturated culture initiated by television in the mid-1950s, accelerated by the rise of our fascination with celebrity, has essentially overwritten a public sphere that was originally, in the Western world, dominated by a concept of debate fashioned on the Greek agora. That is, by a system of governance that sidelined the views of "ordinary" people who had little say in public life. Hartley memorably wrote that this new public sphere was both "intensely personal (inside people's homes and heads)" and "extensively abstract (pervading the planet)" (1996, 157). Hartley's work builds on the critiques of Habermas's discussion of the public sphere, which are most comprehensively captured in a seminal collection, *The Phantom Public Sphere* (Robbins, 1993). In his introduction, Bruce Robbins explains the argumentative "blockage" that *The Phantom Public Sphere* tries to find a way through:

> Leftists of the 1990s do not know how to argue for the democracy we want without mobilizing an image of the public so hazy, idealized, and distant from the actual people, places and institutions around us that can as easily serve purposes that are anything but democratic.
>
> *(Robbins, 1993, p. xii)*

Robbins and his contributors explore a third way of unpacking the relationship between the putative public and private divide. Citing a 1991 piece by Jacques Derrida, Robbins paraphrases the question they pose:

> How then to open the avenue of great debates, accessible to the majority, while yet enriching the multiplicity and the quality of public discourses, of evaluating agencies, of 'scenes' or places of visibility?
>
> *(Robbins, 1993, p. xii)*

After these critiques appeared, the media sphere changed in previously unimaginable ways: the rise of media users as routine producers and distributors, the emergence of growing social media platforms and the evidence of a public global appetite for information and images produced by amateurs as opposed to professionally trained journalists. A particularly relevant feature of this new fragmented sphere is the ability of different communities not only to disseminate their own ideological material, but equally to speak back to other groups and individuals.

The term "fake news" has become a meme with the election of Donald Trump in 2016. In fact, the term has been around for much longer. While it wasn't dubbed so, the nineteenth-century Yellow or Penny Press could be said to carry fake news: news that was delivered with heavy doses of sex, violence, and sensationalism with little regard for the truth (Lumby, 1999). More recently, discussions about the rise of satirical political US TV comedy used the term, as documented in a collection *The Stewart/Colbert Effect: Essays on the Real Aspects of Fake News* (Amarasingam, 2011) which uses the term fake news as a shorthand for comedy shows hosted by savvy left-leaning comedians such as Jon Stewart and Stephen Colbert. Armarnath Amarasingam's preface cites a 2007 Pew Center survey saying that Stewart landed in fourth place, tied with Brian Williams, Tom Brokaw, Dan Rather, and Anderson Cooper, as the journalists America most admired: "For a purveyor of fake news, Stewart has become one of the most trusted newsmen in the country" (2011, p. 3).

The term "fake news" and its antecedent "alternative facts" has proliferated since Donald Trump's inauguration—arguably a familiar pattern when it comes to the right appropriating terms that originate on the left of politics which are then recycled by conservatives to dismiss progressive values. Claire Wardle of *First Draft News* (2017) identifies seven types of fake news

1 satire or parody ("no intention to cause harm but has potential to fool")
2 false connection ("when headlines, visuals of captions don't support the content")
3 misleading content ("misleading use of information to frame an issue or an individual")
4 false content ("when genuine content is shared with false contextual information")
5 imposter content ("when genuine sources are impersonated" with false, made-up sources)
6 manipulated content ("when genuine information or imagery is manipulated to deceive," as with a "doctored" photo)
7 fabricated content ("new content is 100% false, designed to deceive and do harm")

The term "fake news" is relevant to this chapter precisely because it captures a fault line in public sphere discourse in an era when the lines between mainstream public sphere discourse, news media and social and online discourse have fractured irreversibly. The reality of a media landscape where sources of information are so diverse is that we are all risk living in our own information bubble and so are prone to dismissing other sources of information as "fake news." Not unlike the phrase "political correctness," "fake news" can mean what anyone wants it to mean. It's a term that can be used to discredit information we don't like without really unpacking the veracity of the sources.

To cite the US President Donald Trump's Counselor to the President, Kellyanne Conway, who responded to claims made by the White House that Trump's inauguration crowd was the largest in history (contradicting objective evidence), the statements were not lies but were instead "alternative facts."

One of the questions undergirding my thinking is the extent to which all opinions are potentially rendered morally and factually equivalent on the Internet. Answering this larger and more abstract question is, of course, well outside the scope of this chapter. I pose this question rather as background to my more specific research question: to what extent do social media platforms act as a progressive force in feminist activism?

Feminism and digital activism

A leading Australian scholar investigating the affordances of feminist online activism suggests that activism can descend into "non-engagement or talking past one another." Emma Jane writes:

> The heated exchanges between feminists and men's rights activists- as well as the tit-for tat- 'digilantism'- are to demonstrate [in this article] the way

> online debates can involve a series of escalating hostilities in which antago-
> nists appear to increasingly mirror each other.
>
> *(Jane, 2016, p. 2)*

Here Jane tackles what has become known as "manspreading"—the practice of some men in a public place to sit with their legs widely spread and taking up more room than others. Jane focuses on the online campaigns against the practice, which involved exposing men who refused to move aside: posting photographs, memes, and a series of related posts satirizing their behavior. Offline behavior was also posted—for example, women sitting in the laps of men who refused to move (Jane, 2016). Jane inter-rogates Chantal Mouffe's (2005) well-known theory of "agonistic pluralism," which posits that conflict is a necessary and essential part of democratic debate, indeed that rifting is essential to democracy. Following Mouffe, Jane looks at the effectiveness of various strategies to make women's invisibility in some public spaces visible.

Jane notes that humor, satire, and sarcasm are frequent features of the memes and comment threads that follow social media posts. But, importantly she considers whether feminist digilantism may alienate and divide—or be itself invisible—to a broader public. Is it, in essence a mirror of the trolling that feminist activists sometimes endure? Is it a form of activism that only resounds in an echo chamber? In her words:

> Does escalating, mimetic antagonism result in the hardening of opposing views instead of (or at least alongside of) a productive outcome? Or is the exchange *itself* the only outcome required?
>
> *(Jane, 2016, p. 9)*

Her questions go to the heart of understanding political activism in an era of frag-mented identity politics and a fractured media and public sphere. It is a complex question and one that Jane intentionally leaves open.

Concerns about how we manage and enable democratic discussion have a long history. Scholars Coleman and Blumler (2009) describe a model they term "direct representation," which would use online media to engender dialogues that impart information and foster mutuality between citizens and their representatives. They envisage a "civic commons" that would "gather the public together, not as specta-tors, followers or atomized egos, but as a *demos* capable of self-articulation" (Cole-man & Blumler, 2009, p. 197). Joshua Cohen, a key political theorist in the field of deliberative democracy, has warned that adopting a cyber-utopianism is not only misplaced but dangerous (Cohen, 2009). The concept of participatory democracy (Chadwick & May, 2003) has been generative for media studies theorists seeking to understand the ecologies of online communities and the limits and potential of their agency (Burgess & Green, 2009; Benkler, 2006; Flew, 2009). This litera-ture is extremely resonant for the questions this chapter pursues in examining the potential for media users to identify precedents in existing models of participa-tory democracy and in considering how we might conceive of digital citizenship, including digital activism, in the online and social media world.

The instructive case of Harvey Weinstein

In October 2017, *The New Yorker* broke a major investigative story that exposed the claims of a series of women, many of them high-profile professionals in the entertainment industries, accused independent film producer Harvey Weinstein of sexually harassing and assaulting them. The allegations are continuing to flow at the time of writing this chapter. The allegations were all the more shocking to those outside Hollywood because Weinstein was widely regarded as a liberal who championed the careers of women and progressive political causes and used his power to fundraise for the Democratic party (Farrow, 2017). In his detailed *New Yorker* article, for which he interviewed 13 women, Farrow gives the evidence that the producer, whose movies have earned more than 300 Oscar nominations, was "also trailed by rumors of sexual assault and harassment" for more than two decades (Farrow, 2017, p. 42).

Farrow explains why reporters had failed to pursue these persistent rumors:

> [P]revious attempts by many publications, including *The New Yorker*, to investigate and publish the story over the years fell short of the demands of journalistic evidence. Too few people were willing to speak, much less let a reporter to use their names, and Weinstein and his associates used non-disclosure agreements, payoffs, and legal threats to suppress their accounts.
>
> *(Farrow, 2017, p. 42)*

The traditional mainstream media, according to Farrow, faced two problems in reporting on the rumors that had dogged Weinstein. First was the risk of incurring a lawsuit from an extremely powerful and wealthy man. The more important problem was getting people to go on the record. Reputable mainstream media outlets are, quite rightly, very reluctant to base their stories on anonymous sources. The issue for women who are the survivors of sexual harassment or assault is that they have often been forced to tell their stories in single file: to the courts, to counselors and to the media. They feel isolated and are often uncertain if other women will come forward to add credence to their story.

The game changing role of social media, revealed through the #MeToo movement was that social media gave women a rapidly evolving collective voice. Women and some men, in other words, were able to tell their story in a forum where the information was made public and others felt inspired to add similar stories, knowing that the weight of numbers would make it unlikely they would be sued or harassed.

Digging deeper into how the social media landscape has been involved in responding to sexual harassment through #MeToo and related memes reveals a deeper truth about power and gender. In describing how Weinstein got away with his abuse of power for so long, US journalist Rebecca Traister recounts her own stories of abuse and looks at the high-profile men across the West, who include Roger Ailes, Bill Cosby, Bill O'Reilly, and Donald Trump—who have all been recently exposed for the alleged assault and harassment of women. Making a very important point about the way a "public conversation" has changed the capacity of women (and many men) to speak out and to feel supported. She posits:

> [O]ur consciousness has been raised. And while repercussions have been mixed—Cosby is set to go to trial again in April; Ailes and O'Reilly lost powerful jobs but walked away with millions; Donald Trump was elected president—it is in part the fact that we have had a public conversation that has helped those for whom telling their stories seemed impossible for so long suddenly feel that speaking out might be within their reach.
>
> *(Traister, 2017)*

Since Harvey Weinstein was denounced, on as yet unproven charges, by numerous women, the floodgates on the persistent and hidden issue of sexual harassment have opened across the Western world. A range of powerful men has been forced to, or has voluntarily stepped aside from their roles and the list continues to grow. There was also a new kind of news cycle—the recycling of material found on the internet, which feeds, unchecked and unverified, into the mainstream media and back again on an endless loop (Price, 2013, p. 135). There is no question—even a brief Google trawl will confirm—that #MeToo has been a game changer in the way that public awareness of sexual harassment and assault has grown because of the interaction between social media and traditional media stories. As I note above, no empirical proof of how much awareness has changed is yet available. What we do know is that many organizations globally are now prepared to stand against predators. And #MeToo has been a very prominent part of that shift. On March 21, 2018, a Google search on the hashtag showed that over 27 million people had accessed or read material in relation to material published using the hashtag.

Destroying the joint

On August 31, 2012 the well-known Australian writer and media commentator Jane Caro noticed a growing trend on Twitter about a conservative Australian radio commentator Alan Jones. Jones had earlier denounced women political leaders by asserting on his show that women were "destroying the joint." Caro joined the Twitter storm he unleashed by tweeting: "Got time on my hands tonight, so I thought I'd come up with new ways to destroy the joint, being a woman and all. Ideas welcome" (Caro 2013, p. 1). Her feminist friends, many of them Australian journalists, activists, and educators with whom she had an informal network, responded quickly:

> What followed was extraordinary, entirely spontaneous and hilarious. Women and men took up the challenge in droves. Jill Tomlinson (clearly more savvy about Twitter than I am) added the now famous hashtag, Jenna Price created a Facebook page, Yvette Vignando whipped up some t-shirts, wristbands and other collateral, and a tweet became a phenomenon. By the end of the first

weekend, #destroythejoint was trending worldwide and I was being interviewed by the BBC World Service!

(Caro, 2013, p. 6)

The Australian-based Destroy the Joint hashtag garnered media attention. Among
other results, Alan Jones was called to account by his advertisers, many of whom
stopped promoting their brands on his show. The high-profile Australian feminist
journalist and academic Jenna Price set up a Facebook page that garnered 20,000
followers and a reach of 300,000 and a broader network (Friends of Fans) of 3 million people within six weeks. Price writes: "Advertisers pay to get that kind of
influence. On social media it is free" (2013, p. 141). She notes that the mainstream
media was extremely skeptical of the capacity of the Destroy the Joint team to put
a dent in the power of a high-profile shock jock like Jones—a man who regularly
brought Australian politicians to their knees. But it did.

A month later, long after the first advertisers withdrew their sponsorship
because of social media pressure (and emails, texts and phone calls are definitely part of social media), long after a furious Mr Jones railed against car
manufacturer Mercedes for backing away from him at the speed of an SLK,
Tim Burrowes of media news site *Mumbrella* [a high profile Australian site]
admitted he'd underestimated the impact of the campaign: 'Reputationally,
definitely it will have a long-term effect. The commercial impact may not be
that great but people will remember what went on.'

(Price, 2013, p. 143)

In subsequent years, the Twitter and Facebook arms of Destroy the Joint have
remained highly active and ready to campaign and call out sexism on a daily basis.
That tweet Jane Caro sent out on a Friday night over a glass of wine has grown
into a movement, which, as Price notes, put feminism back on the front page of
Australian newspapers and at the head of bulletins on radio and television. Price
has been campaigning for women's rights for decades. She started and edited a page
in *The Sydney Morning Herald* in the 1980s called "Agenda" that took "women's
issues" seriously. [Full disclosure, I was a journalist writing for that page in 1989
and Price was my editor.] Price describes how she started out promoting her views
on equality.

It's 1979. My record is clean and I plan to keep it that way. A good Jewish girl
doesn't want too much trouble.

My boyfriend is driving the getaway car, a brown Morris 1100. He is
dressed in tan cords and his shoes have pink laces. I'm in what I remember as
overalls. The spray cans are in the back.

We're in Sydney's central business district. Time and time again over two
hours, he pulls up and I hop out. He keeps the engine running.

Equality is a myth. Women are better.

> Huge red letters, dripping. The aerosol technique left a lot to be desired yet the politics were heartfelt.
>
> *(Price, 2013, p. 128)*

With this anecdote Price draws the link between early forms of second wave activism and social media activism: from placards and billboard defacement to tweets and posts. She makes a convincing case that social media has enabled spirited feminists to challenge misogyny and sexism and to respond rapidly and nimbly to men in power who abuse that power or simply leave women's human rights unaccounted for in their decision making. As Price points out, social media activism can be directly linked to real world outcomes and actions.

Destroy the Joint is a positive case study in successful social media activism. Yet, the online and social media activism did not come without a cost, as Price also details. The Facebook page she set up, and that a small army of sympathizers moderated, was hacked; and the University she works at received death threats for employing her, which ended up in a police investigation. Most chillingly, she received a voice message from a man who said he was going to find her daughters and rape them.

Her response to this familiar hate speech remains optimistic:

> I rang the boy in the tan cords and pink shoelaces to tell him about the voice message. He was, as ever, calm, and ready to drive the getaway car.
>
> Now it's misogynists who won't get away anymore. We are on to you. Everyone is on to you. Even, finally, the commercial media.
>
> *(Price, 2013, p. 147)*

Price's response—which mirrors that of many women who have been subject to threats of rape and violence for using social media to call out sexism online—relies on courage, experience, and the support of those around her (Jane, 2016). It still leaves a question, however: to what extent do online and social media campaigns fuel antagonistic responses and to what extent they are furthering agonist democracy?

#MeToo

Uma Thurman, the actress who appeared in two of Harvey Weinstein's best-known films, *Pulp Fiction* and *Kill Bill*, posted on Twitter, after multiple other actresses and employees had already spoken out. She wrote this:

> H A P P Y T H A N K S G I V I N G I am grateful today, to be alive, for all those I love, and for all those who have the courage to stand up for others. I said I was angry recently, and I have a few reasons, #MeToo, in case you couldn't tell by the look on my face. I feel it's important to take your time, be fair, be exact, so . . . Happy Thanksgiving Everyone!
>
> *(Except you Harvey, and all your wicked conspirators—I'm glad it's going slowly—you don't deserve a bullet) -stay tuned*
>
> *Uma Thurman (@ithurman)*

The use of the hashtag MeToo to encourage survivors of sexual assault and harassment to speak out was developed in response to a tweet by actress Alyssa Milano. She posted on October 15, 2017:

> Me too. Suggested by a friend: 'If all the women who have been sexually harassed or assaulted wrote Me too as a status, we might give people a sense of the magnitude of the problem.'
>
> *(@Alyssa—Milano)*

Within one day the post received more than 38,000 comments, 13,000 retweets and 27,000 likes. It turns out that activist Tarana Burke had already used the "me too" phrase in 2007, with a particular focus on women of color who had experienced sexual assault. Burke had founded the Me Too campaign, with its motto "Empowerment through empathy" as a grassroots movement to aid sexual assault survivors in underprivileged communities "where rape crisis centers and sexual assault workers weren't going" (Hill, 2017).

"It wasn't built to be a viral campaign or a hashtag that is here today and forgotten tomorrow," Burke told *Ebony*. . . . "It was a catchphrase to be used from survivor to survivor to let folks know that they were not alone and that a movement for radical healing was happening and possible" (Hill, 2017).

Burke observed: "The power of 'me too' has always been in the fact that it can be a conversation starter or the whole conversation, but it was us talking to us." Her comment arguably goes to the heart of the power of social media to change the broader conversation on issues that previously have been prosecuted in isolation from the stories of the people who live with their impact on a daily basis. Advocacy groups speaking out on the issue of sexual assault and harassment are not new. Yet, the women who tell their stories have traditionally told them individually: to counselors, to human rights bodies, and to the court. From a legal perspective, #MeToo resembles an enormous class action (albeit one fraught with multiple challenges given general legal protocols and principles).

What the response from black women reveals, however, is that "collective" feminist conversations are never collective. Fault lines always quickly open, as feminist history has taught us (Hooks, 1989). Identity politics necessarily fracture the exhilaration that comes with the establishment of any political or social movement. Several high-profile black women tweeted their understandable indignation that Burke initially went unrecognized for her leadership on sexual assault. Hill wrote of their complaints:

> If it weren't for actress Rose McGowan's rape allegation against Weinstein, the conversation around sexual assault may have never made its way to social media. But the problem is, Black women were quickly isolated from the dialogue before we could familiarize ourselves with it. We weren't excluded for lack of relation to conversation around sexual assault and misogyny's impact on our livelihoods. Black women regularly experience sexual assault as well and are often coerced into silence.
>
> *(Hill, 2017)*

Michael Warner, who has written authoritatively about the "counter public sphere," offers this critique of Habermas's account of the public sphere, in which the private and public neatly separate:

> As the subjects of publicity—its 'hearers,' 'speakers,' 'viewers' and 'doers'—we have a different relation to ourselves, a different affect, from that which we have in other contexts. No matter what particularities of culture, race, gender, or class we bring to bear on public discourse, the moment of apprehending something as public is one in which we imagine—if imperfectly-indifference to those particularities, to ourselves.
>
> *(Warner, 1993, p. 234)*

Another scholar who has likewise sought to understand the limitations of social media to bring issues of social justice to the public sphere and to unite people who share similar concerns is political theorist William Connolly. In *The Ethos of Pluralization*, Connelly argues that the ghost at the heart of liberal democracy is the insistence on a drive toward consensus. Indeed, he suggests that this drive—the drive toward collectivism on issues—is responsible for social disharmony. He writes:

> The stronger the drive to the unified nation, the integrated community, and/ or the normal individual, the more powerful becomes the drive to convert differences into modes of otherness. . . . The biggest impetus to fragmentation, violence, and anarchy today does not emerge from political engagement with the paradox of difference. It emerges from doctrines and movements which suppress it.
>
> *(Connolly, 1995, p. xxi)*

Connolly offers one of the most powerful statements I've come across in trying to unpack the question of how we conjure, on one hand, with the importance of acknowledging difference and the importance of collective action. Moreover, Connolly's analysis resonates in relation to social media, reminding us that the rifts and fractures now visible online are nothing new. What makes it different is the visibility of how we manage difference and how we work to ensure that difference does not enable those in power to assert their power over others. Social media, in other words, is openly social communication where the rifts and differences in our politics and culture are made visible rather than curated by professional journalists and other public figures.

The social media coalface

Nina Funnell is a high-profile Australian commentator and investigative reporter who works to prevent sexual assault and harassment. She is working in an era when social media is both integral to her investigative journalism—and is equally a problem for her when it comes to dealing with trolling. Interviewed for this chapter, she responded:

> In many ways, social media has been a democratising force in that it has freed up how women's stories can be told and who they can be told by. When women have experienced immense powerlessness, being in control of how one tells one's story and where is often a crucial step in reclaiming a sense of power back over the experience. Indeed, the ability to use social media- to self-publish one's thoughts, reflections and experiences—can also be liberating. It enables women to control how they present their stories to the world, without having to pass through the filter of a journalist.

She congratulated feminists for being very vocal in criticizing trolling—often using social media to do so: "In many ways, this trolling only proves the point: that we haven't achieved equality and that there is still a long way to go." There is indeed a long way to go on many fronts when it comes to respect for difference and respect for women's rights in the workplace. What needs research is the extent to which the new post-public sphere differs from the Fourth estate model. This was a place where gatekeepers decided whose voices and views were acceptable or palatable for the general public. But in the era of social and online media whether there is a "public sphere" or who the "general public" are is less clear.

To recap, the questions posed in this chapter remain simply that—questions. Hopefully, productive and generative questions. Social media and gender studies are emergent and volatile fields of investigation. It is simply impossible to empirically gauge the extent to which a given hashtag has changed the attitudes and behaviors of men in power who seek to use that power over women. Quality of engagement is just as important, if not more important, than quantity when it comes to social media reach and effect. We are still in the early days of testing the waters of online feminist activism. But research in the field is growing, as is the expertise of younger activists in using social media to promote feminist causes.

We must look beyond the utopianism that characterized much of the early writings on the globalization of the Internet and social media. As Nagle writes:

> The online culture wars of recent years have become ugly beyond anything we could have possibly imagined. . . . Now, one is almost more inclined to hope that the online world can contain rather than further enable the festering undergrowth of dehumanizing reactionary online politics now edging closer to the mainstream but unthinkable in the public arena just a few short years ago.
>
> *(2017, p. 120)*

Nagle is largely pessimistic about how online and social media is affecting attitudes to women and other groups who are marginalized. However, she also offers a challenge to feminists: how do we speak back to hate speech? What are the most effective tools in digital activism for mobilizing real world action and for supporting each other when it comes to inevitable digital antagonism? It's a challenge worth confronting.

Acknowledgments

I would like to thank my colleague Dr Theresa Senft for thoughtful comments on this article.

References

Amarasingam, A. (2011). *The Stewart/Colbert effect: Essays on the real impacts of fake news.* Jefferson, NC: McFarland.

Benkler, Y. (2006). *The wealth of networks: How social production transformed markets and freedom.* New Haven: Yale University Press.

Burgess, J., & Green, J. (2009). *YouTube: Online video and participatory culture.* Cambridge: Polity Press.

Caro, J. (2013). *Women destroy the joint* (J. Caro, Ed., pp. 1–6). Brisbane: University of Queensland Press.

Chadwick, A., & May, C. (2003). Interactions between states and citizens in the age of the internet: "e-governance" in the United States, Britain and the European Union. *Governance: An International Journal of Policy, Administration and Institutions, 16*(2), 271–300.

Cohen, J. (2009, February 28). *Reflections on information technology and democracy.* Paper presented at The Public Good: The Impact of Information Technology on Society. Mountain View, CA. Retrieved January 27, 2013, from http://bostonreview.net/BRwebonly/cohen3.php

Coleman, S., & Blumler, J. G. (2009). *Realising democracy online: A civic commons in cyberspace.* London: Institute for Public Policy Research.

Connolly, W. (1995). *The ethos of pluralization.* Minneapolis: University of Minnesota Press.

Farrow, R. (2017, October 23). Abuses of power. *The New Yorker*, pp. 42–49.

Flew, T. (2009). Democracy, participation and convergent media: Case studies in contemporary online news journalism in Australia. *Communication, Politics & Culture, 42*(2), 87–109.

Fraser, N. (1993). Rethinking the public sphere. In B. Robbins (Ed.), *The phantom public sphere* (pp. 1–32). Minneapolis: University of Minnesota Press.

Hill, Z. (2017). A black woman created the me too campaign against sexual assault 10 years ago. *Ebony.* Retrieved November 23, from www.ebony.com/news-views/black-woman-me-too-movement-tarana-burke-alyssa-milano#ixzz4zgIxTL5P

Jane, E. (2016). "Dude . . . stop the spread": Antagonism, agonism and #manspreading on social media. *International Journal of Cultural Studies*, Sage Publications, 1–16.

Jane, E. (2017, April–June). Feminist diligante responses to a slut-shaming on Facebook. *Social Media and Society*, 1–10.

Hartley, J. (1996). *Popular reality.* New York, NY and London: Arnold.

Hooks, B. (1989). *Talking feminism, thinking black.* Boston, MA: Thinking Press.

Lumby, C. (1999). *Gotcha: Life in a tabloid world.* Sydney: Allen and Unwin.

Mouffe, C. (2005). *On the political.* London: Routledge.

Nagle, A. (2017). *Kill all normies: Online culture wars from 4Chan and Tumblr to Trump and the alt-right.* London: Zero Books.

Olding, R. (2013). Andrew Bolt #askbolt unleashes a twitter storm. Retrieved October 10, 2017, from www.smh.com.au/digital-life/digital-life-news/andrew-bolt-askbolt-hashtag-unleashes-a-twitter-storm-20130820-2s8fh.html

Price, J. (2013). The writing on the walls. In J. Caro (Ed.), *Women destroy the joint* (pp. 128–148). Brisbane: University of Queensland Press.

Robbins, B. (1993). *The phantom public sphere* (B. Robbins, Ed.). Minneapolis: University of Minnesota Press.

Traister, R. Why the Harvey Weinstein allegations didn't come out until now. *The Cut*. Retrieved November 15, 2017, from www.thecut.com/2017/10/why-the-weinstein-sexual-harassment-allegations-came-out-now.html

Wardle, C. (2017, February 16). Fake news: It's complicated. Retrieved from https://firstdraft news.org/fake-news-complicated/

Warner, M. (1993). The mass public and the mass subject. In B. Robbins (Ed.), *The phantom public sphere* (pp. 234–256). Minneapolis: University of Minnesota Press.

21

WOMEN AND WAR PHOTOGRAPHY

En/gendering alternative histories

Stuart Allan

"In the perfect light of a crystal-clear morning, I stood outside a putty-colored cement hospital near Ajdabiya, a small city in Libya's northern coast, more than five hundred miles east of Tripoli," photojournalist Lynsey Addario (2015) would later recall about a particular day in March 2011. Standing amongst a small group of journalists looking at a car hit during an air strike, she observed hospital staff performing the grim task of gathering and bagging human remains scattered in the debris. "I picked up my camera to shoot what I had shot so many times before, then put it back down, stepping aside to let the other photographers have their turn," she remembered. "I couldn't do it that day" (2015, p. 1).

The civil uprisings widely heralded as signs of an "Arab Spring" were gathering momentum across the region. Addario, by then more than ten years into her career, was in Libya on assignment for *The New York Times* with fellow photographer Tyler Hicks, and reporters Stephen Farrell and Anthony Shahid. Doing her best to keep a heavy sense of foreboding in check, she traveled with them by car toward the center of Ajdabiya in search of the encroaching battle's frontline. Suddenly finding themselves under artillery fire, they returned to the hospital to reconsider how best to proceed. She watched in alarm as other journalists scrambled into cars to leave, but said nothing to her colleagues. "I didn't want to be the cowardly photographer or the terrified girl who prevented the men from doing their work," she later wrote (2015, p. 10). Setting off once again with their driver, Mohamed Shaglouf, they had not traveled far before they approached a military checkpoint where they were forced to stop, surrounded by government soldiers loyal to Muammar Qaddafi. "In one fluid movement," she recalled, "the doors flew open and Tyler, Steve, and Anthony were ripped from the car." As "gunshots shattered the air" around the checkpoint now under rebel attack, Addario broke free from a soldier pulling at her cameras and ran for it. Several terrifying moments later, however, all four journalists were caught and ordered "face-down into the dirt" at gunpoint, their driver already dead. "I waited for the crack of the gun," she wrote, "for the end of my life" (2015, p. 14). Instead soldiers bound her wrists and ankles, then carried her to a pickup truck, where she was stunned by a punch to the face. In what became a horrifying ordeal over six days, the four endured physical and psychological abuse, including sexual violence toward Addario, before finally being turned over to the Libyan authorities, who released them shortly thereafter (2015, pp. 281–302).

Reflecting on this traumatic experience in her memoirs, *It's What I Do: A Photographer's Life of Love and War*, Addario describes asking herself questions that "still haunt me: Why do you do this work? Why do you risk your life for a photograph?" (2015, p. 15). In considering these questions, this chapter will make apparent how such self-reflexivity about personal motivations has helped to lend shape to war photographers' evolving embodiment of their craft since the mid-nineteenth century. Answers have varied considerably from individual to individual in differing contexts, of course, making any attempt at broad generalization impossible to sustain, yet nevertheless prove revealing of normative values of practice undergoing redefinition in harrowing situations. This chapter, in striving to reverse accustomed emphases placed on men photographers in historical treatments, pinpoints how women have negotiated such tensions in fulfilling reportorial priorities. The social contingencies of gender relations (unevenly imbricated with those of class, ethnicity, and sexuality, amongst others), and their relevance to the photographic representation of conflict, will be shown to warrant much closer attention than they have typically benefited from to date. "Histories of women's work are often merely mainstream reinterpretations of a male tradition," Williams (1994) has noted, when what is required is "a different approach to the nature and importance of war photography" (1994, pp. 13–14). To the extent familiar premises have converged into guiding frameworks, then, this chapter will seek to reappraise understandings of women's commitments to photography in wartime, not least the articulation of alternative ways of seeing through the camera's lens.

In the analysis to follow, this chapter identifies pertinent developments occurring from the last decade of the nineteenth century through to the 1960s, the crucial period during which prevailing conceptions of war photography as a masculine pursuit were forged. Drawing upon diverse historiographies as well as primary source materials, it explores how and why the status of women war photographers evolved while, at the same time, examining the implications for deconstructing commonplace instantiations of gender difference. In so doing, it renders problematic certain tacit, taken-for-granted presumptions concerning war photography and its lived repertoires of visual form and practice. Research into gender and war, Gallagher (1998) observed two decades ago, recognizes "how attention to gender makes us re-envision what we know about war, as well as how war illuminates and recasts the workings of gender" (1998, p. 2). Despite being interdisciplinary by necessity, related investigations seldom delve into photography's importance in this regard—even though "the troubled nature of vision for women in a belligerent culture" is "one of the crucial elements that has traditionally marked the gendered division of war experience" (1998, pp. 2–3; see also Brothers, 1997; Butler, 2009;

Oldfield, 2016; Zarzycka, 2017). Over recent years, the scope and volume of apposite scholarship has steadily increased, yet it remains the case that historical studies of war photography need to be read against the grain in order to bring to the fore questions of gender and power. Such an ambition animates this chapter's mode of enquiry.

Refocusing the "women's angle"

The en/gendered significance of war photography invites a countervailing heuristic. Although women's formative contributions to shaping certain technical innovations associated with photography's emergence and gradual consolidation garner scholarly interest today, historical accounts make little mention of their involvement in pertinent forms of conflict documentation during the nineteenth century (see also Hodgson, 1974; Jay, 1982). "War, a man's game, seemed destined at the start to be recorded by men alone," Lewinski (1978) contended in his classic history, *The Camera at War* (1978, p. 26). Much depends on how "war photography" is being defined, but exceptions to this view are difficult to identify prior to the close of the nineteenth century. "More women than we yet know of were busy taking portrait likenesses," Rosenblum (2010) writes, "but before 1890 they were hardly ever to be seen in field or forest, or on battlegrounds where men with cameras (and guns) were testing the new medium as a way to authenticate reality and promote ideological positions" (2010, p. 52). She notes that while women "might follow soldier-husbands to distant wars (in the Crimea or on American Civil War battlegrounds, for example) or join them on wide-ranging expeditions to foreign continents," her research has uncovered scant evidence of camera usage in such situations during this period.[1] To the extent it is possible to generalize, women photographers working in the late nineteenth century typically occupied an elevated class position, which afforded them the social capital to mitigate against gender discrimination to some degree. On this basis, they were much more likely to have "internalized distinct aspects of middle class cultural and social values of the period," Gover (1988) argues, "and projected this ideology into their photography." The woman with a camera, she continues, "usually maintained a refined and genteel stance"; that is, "her photography enhanced rather than denied her role in shoring up family autonomy," in part by attempting "to express pictorially the essence of the domestic and feminine" (1988, pp. 104–105; see also Callister, 2008; Steiner, 2016).

Exceptions help to illuminate the contours of conventions. During the Spanish-American War of 1898, which saw the US intervene in the Cuban War of Independence, Anna Northend Benjamin distinguished herself as a correspondent for *Leslie's Illustrated Weekly*, reporting on the US army's preparations for the conflict in Florida before managing to overcome numerous obstacles to gain passage to Cuba (not least a government ban on women reporters in the warzone). "Prior to the Cuban conflict," Roth (1997) writes, "female reporters were expected to report from the 'women's angle,' emphasizing stories concerning their own gender, chance meetings, health problems, and care of the wounded in hospitals."

Benjamin's dispatches, "devoid of the usual sentimental renderings of the military camp life," effectively "deglamorized the conflict" (1997, p. 27; see also Brown, 1969). Occasional mention is made in historical accounts of Benjamin carrying a camera with her, although few details of her photographic practice seem to exist beyond passing references in her actual reportage. By way of example, her September 1898 article, "Santiago After the Surrender," includes 14 photographs without attribution, though she does mention her camera work. "We stood on the deck in a row and levelled our cameras at the old castle," she remarks at one point, and at another: "We walked inside and pointed to our cameras. He nodded his head, so we set them up and took some photographs of an opposite shrine" (Benjamin, 1898, pp. 21, 26). The images in question document the presence of Spanish officers and soldiers, an artillery gun, "a box of Mauser bullets," a barricade, a "Cuban hut near the trenches," and a military hospital, amongst other features, thereby bringing to the article a sense of visual instantaneity to underwrite its journalistic authority. Curiously, this apparent ambiguity in Benjamin's "we" may be revealing as well, possibly suggesting a certain apprehension about laying claim to be a practitioner of pictorial journalism, the fledgling figure of the photo-correspondent eluding precise resolution.

Closer to the home front, war photography of a different order is highlighted in a *New York Times* article, headlined "Happy Spaniards," published in July 1898. It describes "a most novel and interesting picture" transpiring outside a prison, situated on Seavey's Island in the Piscataqua River in Kittery, Maine. Spanish prisoners of war "had swarmed to the water's edge to wash their bowls, plates and spoons" following their afternoon meal, an "animated scene" prompting notice by those passing on leisure boats.

> Many ladies in the boats had provided themselves with kodaks, and hundreds of pictures were taken of the prisoners that will prove valuable souvenirs of the American-Spanish war as time goes by. The Spaniards enjoyed having their pictures taken, and many of them gathered in groups and posed in picturesque attitudes and waited their turns for the camera.
>
> A colored prisoner, black as Erebus, waded out into the water up to his knees, and, striking his bowl and plate together to attract attention, placed his hands by his side, rolled the whites of his eyes heavenward, and stood expectant. Scores of kodaks snapped, and the colored sailor triumphantly rejoined his comrades on the shore.
>
> (The New York Times, *July 21, 1898*)

Regrettably typical of the day is the article's inferentially prejudicial projection of the "colored prisoner," but its recognition that these women's snapshot "souvenirs" held the potential to capture an intimate authenticity of lasting significance to war photography is noteworthy. It rightly anticipates the casual everydayness of such imagery would provide future viewers with a telling insight into this otherwise normalized, hidden in plain sight dimension of the conflict (see also Allan,

2011). Moreover, it points to the apparent success of the Kodak company's campaign, underway since 1893, to promote amateur photography as a leisure activity inclusive of women. The "Kodak Girl" featuring in advertisements of the day, West (2000) argues, reinforced associations of femininity with limited mechanical competence. "Measured against the man she can never become," the Kodak Girl "can never achieve the status of professional photographer, her position forever remains that of a novice, dependent on technological simplicity" (2000, p. 53; see also Kotchemidov, 2005).

Evidently undaunted by gender stereotypes prevailing in the 1890s, Frances Benjamin Johnston was a passionate advocate of professional photography for women, which on occasion took her into the realm of war-related imagery.[2] Having established a highly successful portrait studio in Washington, DC, she supplemented her income by undertaking documentary assignments for George Grantham Bain, founder of Bain News Service (arguably the first news-photography agency in the United States), and similar syndicates (Carlebach, 1997; Daniel & Smock, 1974; Davidov, 1998; Meister, 2010). A self-declared "lady photographer," one renowned for her attention to aesthetic form and detail, Johnston drew upon her extensive personal connections with prominent Washington figures to facilitate her more journalistic efforts. In 1899, for example, she was able to call on the support of future US president Theodore Roosevelt to approach Admiral George Dewey (the "Hero of Manila Bay"), who welcomed her aboard the battleship *USS Olympia* in August of that year to photograph its triumphal tour of European seaports. Given that Dewey's conduct of the war was encountering growing criticism in some quarters of the press at the time, his willingness to co-operate was all the more understandable. Johnston, in turn, was well-accustomed to the demands of creating officially appropriate imagery, her entrepreneurial experience in portraiture having encompassed five presidential administrations by then. The 150 photographs she produced on *Olympia* served to help domesticate American imperialism, Wexler's (2000) analysis contends, in part by constructing images of war as peace:

> It is obvious in Johnston's photographs that the officers and the crew of the *Olympia* were acting their part in some such fiction. They are too fresh-faced, too gallant, and quite too clean to be believed. [. . .] Because Johnston was a 'lady,' looking at her pictures aboard the battleship *Olympia* implied not only that she looked and saw what she 'oughtn't' have seen; she might also have looked and *not* seen what she *ought* to have seen. Johnston alone, as a 'lady photographer,' could deliver the blindness with which 'the innocent eye' engaged the colonial dream.
>
> *(Wexler, 2000, pp. 34, 49)*

By rendering white, middle-class women photographers' "domestic visions" of the time consistent with shipboard life, Wexler maintains, Johnston's "innocent eye" images sought to avert attention in proscribed ways, effectively denying by omission the structural consequences of colonial violence in a manner culturally acceptable for reading publics.[3] "That which is logically the furthest thing from the ideal of domestic peace—imperial aggression—is represented in Johnston's photography as a peace that keeps the peace," she adds (2000, pp. 33, 35). At the same time, this assignment's commercial success was remarkable. Bain reportedly sold one of Johnston's images of Dewey to *Leslie's Illustrated Weekly* for $100, then a record sum for a news photograph (Carlebach, 1997, p. 69).

Eyewitness photo-reportage

At the outbreak of the First World War in 1914, pictorial newspapers and magazines were driving intense market-demand for news photographs, spurred on by improvements in half-tone printing processes and promising experiments in photo-telegraphy, amongst other factors. Still, despite "growing recognition for the status of the topical photograph as a news medium, a contribution to propaganda, a popular souvenir, a work of art in exhibition, and as an item for inclusion in a national archive," Carmichael (1989) observes, "there was little for its taker, the photographer" (1989, pp. 146, 148). In contrast with the public appreciation afforded war correspondents, war artists or filmmakers, she continues, the photographer's "role remained that of a craftsman providing a service rather than an individual achievement" (1989, p. 148). Moreover, to the extent this inchoate identity was being acknowledged, it was typically in overtly androcentric terms. That is, only men were deemed up to the challenge of being official photographers, Tylee (1997) points out, British women being prevented "from ever glimpsing even the corner of a real battlefield" (1997, p. 66). In other national contexts, one of the very few women to be accredited as an official war correspondent was Alice Schalek, who secured recognition from the Austro-Hungarian *Kriegspressequartier* (War Press Office) to report primarily from the Italian front from 1915 to 1917. Her eyewitness reports and photographs, many of the latter published in the illustrated German magazine *Berliner Illustrirte Zeitung*, proved remarkably popular with readers. In the eyes of some critics, however, Schalek's reportage romanticized the conflict with undue subjectivity; others were alarmed by her ever-sharper criticisms of its conduct. She lost her accreditation in September 1917 for reasons that remain unclear, although her dismissal followed complaints brought before the *Reichsrat* by conservative politicians alleging her work represented "the sorry effort of feminine lust for sensationalism and overheated curiosity" (cited in Seul, 2016, p. 230).[4]

For women civilian photographers denied official accreditation, further possibilities emerged, including being commissioned by the armed forces for particular assignments. One of the most noteworthy examples of the latter in the UK was Christina Broom, who, prior to the war, benefited from a successful commercial relationship with the elite Household Division, regarded as the public face of the British Army. A decade's experience negotiating military protocols to produce portraits, as well as coverage of ceremonial events, and the like, enabled her to cope with gender and class prejudices to a considerable degree. Broom's photographs of the Division mobilizing for war "amid the patriotic fervour then sweeping the country," Roberts (2015a) writes, "capture a grim urgency as men gather their equipment and assemble for departure" to France (2015a, p. 93). This professional assignment amounted to a "personal farewell" of sorts; six months later, "virtually all the soldiers photographed by Broom in August 1914 were dead, maimed or imprisoned" (2015a, p. 94). Even Broom's coverage of wounded soldiers returning from combat maintained what Chanin (2016) aptly calls her "pictorial and patriotic forethought," which informed her commitment to documenting "the swiftly-changing impact of the war" in a positive light (2016, p. 248; see also Sparham, 2015). Given the potential publicity value of this type of photography for shaping public opinion, the importance of tracing shifting, uneven vicissitudes of visual form and practice beyond a simplified amateur-professional dichotomy assumes even greater significance. Indeed, as a form of "war photography" in its own right, it exemplified how the medium could be pressed into the service of the state's declared agenda to bolster public support for military intervention.

Further opportunities for civilian contributions arose as women engaged in volunteer work—particularly as nurses, ambulance drivers or mechanics—in often treacherous conditions, some of whom resolved to make a photographic record of what they were witnessing in everyday lives far from home. A keen amateur photographer, Florence Farmborough traveled from England to serve as a surgical hospital nurse with the Russian Red Cross on the border of Galicia, near the Eastern Front. "Tending the wounded, and doing whatever was possible to ease the suffering of the dying, this was to be her daily task, often for extended periods," Jolliffe (1979) notes, but Farmborough also made the most of opportunities to take photographs of colleagues and patients, as well as soldiers and "the ravages of the battlefield." In Jolliffe's estimation, "[n]othing could express more vividly the nature of being at war, with its horrors, its contrasts, and its paradoxes, then the story Miss Farmborough tells through these photographs" (1979, p. 7). Elsie Corbett, daughter of an English MP, used her camera when serving with the Red Cross in Serbia to capture scenes of devastation in the wake of military action. In Belgium, Elsie Knocker (a trained nurse) and 18-year-old Mairi Chisholm—the "Madonnas of Pervyse"—operated a frontline casualty post in the ruined village behind the trenches of the Western Front. In addition to diaries, they kept personal photo-albums of images shot with portable hand cameras, creating impromptu documentation of the horrific distress around them while coping with bombardment and sniper fire (a particularly severe gas attack forced them to withdraw back to England in 1918). Much of the imagery features one or both of them, such as Knocker peering through a shell hole, as well as others showing another woman volunteer standing atop a demolished tank in "No Man's Land," the decaying corpse of a German soldier, a shell burst at Pervyse, ruined buildings in Dixmude, Flanders, or visiting staff officers in informal poses, amongst others (Cowing, 2009; Higonnet, 2010; Oldfield, 2016; Williams, 1986).

Readily apparent to many observers at the time was the significance of these alternative visions of warfare for the historical record, and thereby collective memory across generations. In October 1918 the Women's Work Subcommittee of

London's National War Museum commissioned the established portrait-taker Olive Edis to travel to the Western Front, making her Britain's first woman to be accredited as a war photographer. The military resisted letting her travel across the Channel, but she was finally granted permission following the Armistice of November 11, 1918, arriving in France on March 2, 1919. In the aftermath of hostilities, logistical issues proved formidable for Edis, her assignment being to document women's diverse contributions to the British Army's support services. She recalls in her diary entry for March 11, 1919 an encounter with Lieutenant Colonel A.N. Lee, who explained his reasons for challenging her involvement, and also his satisfaction with the work of the official photographers, all of whom were men. "I explained that the Imperial War Museum thought that a woman photographer, living among the girls in their [Women's Auxiliary Army Corps] camps, was likely to achieve more intimate pictures, more descriptive of their every day lives, than a man press photographer," she wrote. "I felt very pleased that a woman should get that chance" (Edis, 1919). While many of the women photographed were posed, Edis sought to effect an informal documentary style, which Philo-Gill (2017) contends was in contrast with the typically more overt propaganda orientation of her male counterparts.

Breaking boundaries

The first woman war photographer killed in the field is widely considered to be Gerda Taro (real name Gerta Pohorylle, born in Stuttgart in 1910), who was accidently crushed by a reversing Republican tank on July 25, 1937, the last day of the Battle of Brunete during the Spanish Civil War. Evidently in the moment of collision, she was perched on the running board of a military vehicle transporting wounded soldiers to Madrid. Admired by Loyalist soldiers at the front lines, some of whom affectionately called her "La Pequeña Rubia" ("the little redhead"), Taro had only recently succeeded in securing a byline in captions. Most of her work up until then had appeared under the singular name "Capa," referring to her companion Robert Capa, the highly celebrated war photographer of the day. Capa was renowned for images such as "The Falling Soldier," which ostensibly captured— in the words of *Life* (1937a) magazine—the instant a Republican militiaman "is dropped by a bullet through the head," creating a sensation around the world.

Unbeknownst to the public, "Robert Capa" was an invention Taro (then still known as Pohorylle) created with her Hungarian lover, André Friedmann, the year before. Having chosen the name because it sounded less "foreign" in a xenophobic climate, they attributed it to an eminent yet strangely elusive American photographer whose work Pohorylle claimed to represent—a ruse that decidedly improved the prospects of two Jewish refugees intent on garnering commissioning editors' attention in Paris. Sharing Rolleiflex and Leica cameras between them, the couple's signature of "Capa" lent their collaborative efforts a strong public profile, one which at Pohorylle's insistence evolved to become a "Capa and Taro" stamp by the time of her death. *Life* (1937b) acknowledged Taro's passing with a two-page spread,

"The Camera Overseas: The Spanish War Kills its First Woman Photographer," in which she is described as a "pretty little woman," one "who was not afraid of gore," and whose "pictures were some of the best out of Spain in the last year" (1937b, pp. 62–63). Despite widespread sorrow at the news of her death—the funeral cortege was observed by several thousand mourners as it made its way through the streets of Paris—Taro was virtually forgotten soon afterwards. She suffered from what Maspero (2008) calls "the most cruel fate" of being lost in Capa's shadow, credited at most with a "passing role in the biography of a famous person" until the 1990s, when she finally "emerged from oblivion" thanks to renewed scholarly interest in the Spanish Civil War (2008, pp. 7–8).[5] Growing awareness of Taro's war photography was further enhanced upon the recovery in Mexico City of three battered suitcases, considered lost since 1939, containing 126 rolls of film with some 4500 negatives shot during the conflict by Capa, Taro and David "Chim" Seymour. In 2007, the first major exhibition of Taro's work was organized by the International Center of Photography in New York, which—in the words of a newspaper reviewer at the time—signaled the "dramatic rediscovery" of a figure "all but airbrushed out of history" (Diu, 2007; see also Lee, 2007).

By the outset of the Second World War, women photographers were making serious inroads into photojournalism, many of whom—like Taro before them—regarded it as an extension of their activist commitments. "There was a day when the male news photographer sniffed scornfully when told that it was possible that the woman with the camera would match wits—and plate for plate, picture for picture—with the man firmly entrenched in the profession," A.J. Ezickson (1938) wrote in his book, *Get that Picture!: The Story of the News Cameraman*. "Humph! Woman? Impossible! That job was too risky, too dangerous," he continued, explaining why such views were increasingly being shown to be misguided. "Women photographers are edging in, overcoming all objections, belieing the popular illusion as to their frailty, lack of nimbleness in covering a spot news assignment, inability to handle weighty equipment" (1938, p. 151). The volume contains one reference to women's contributions to war photography, namely Taro—"the girl who laughed at bullets and shells"—respected for "her stout courage," before turning its attention to Margaret Bourke-White and her remarkable success as an industrial news photographer, including two assignments to a pre-war Soviet Union (1938, pp. 147, 155). Commentators at the time were certainly aware of the growing salience of women's contributions to the prevailing stylistic features of photo-essays for news magazines, such as *Berliner Illustrierte Zeitung* and *Münchner Illustrierte Presse* in Germany, *Life* and *Look* in the US, *Vu* and *Paris-Match* in France, or *Weekly Illustrated* and *Picture Post* in Britain, amongst others. Photojournalists and weekly mass-circulation picture magazines were becoming interdependent by the outbreak of hostilities, Williams (1986) argues, with women photo-reporters considered to be best positioned covering humanistic, non-controversial domestic stories perceived—by news editors who were almost always men—to be of particular interest to women readers supporting the war effort. In the case of *Picture Post*, she adds, its underlying philosophy was a "muscular optimism intended to stress the fortitude and inventiveness of the British under stress"; the ensuing "double-bind" being that "it asked women to photograph women as men wanted them to be" (1986, pp. 122, 141).

Life magazine, in contrast, promoted the work of Margaret Bourke-White, the first woman photographer on its staff, within a much wider sphere of reportage. "A pioneer in feminist territory, she was not a feminist," a biographer would later point out. "Like many women who broke barriers, she fought not for her gender but for herself and ended up a role model because she won" (Goldberg, 2006, p. 165). One of Bourke-White's male colleagues recalled she may have been regarded by some as "imperious, calculating, and insensitive," but in addition to possessing "the unerring instinct of a journalist," she consistently demonstrated "the mastery of the medium and the eye of an artist" as well as "the daring, cunning, and intuition to be where news was happening" (Callahan, 1998, p. 97). Already a household name in the US by the late 1930s, she enjoyed celebrated status as a "girl photographer" in the public imagination. On assignment for *Life* in Moscow in 1941, Bourke-White was the only foreign photographer to witness first-hand the German aerial bombardment of the city, effectively scooping rival publications. The following year she became the first woman accredited as a war correspondent by the US Army Air Forces, which led to her reporting from North Africa in January 1943 (having survived a German torpedo attack on the troopship en route). The March 1 edition of the magazine featured the lead story, "LIFE'S BOURKE-WHITE GOES BOMBING: First woman to accompany US Air Force on combat mission photographs attack on Tunis," which related how she persuaded a commander to allow her to record an airport's destruction from a B-17 four miles above.[6] "Indestructible Maggie" reported from the Italian front later the same year, central Europe during the last major German offensive campaign in 1944, and returned to Germany in the final months of the war as cities in ruin surrendered, including Weimar where US troops liberated the Buchenwald concentration camp on its outskirts. "Using the camera was almost a relief," Bourke-White (1963) recalled in her memoir, *Portrait of Myself*. "It interposed a slight barrier between myself and the horror in front of me. Buchenwald was more than the mind could grasp" (1963, p. 259). Such harrowing circumstances entailed adopting a "self-imposed stupor" in order to cope. "I have to work with a veil over my mind," she wrote. "In photographing the murder camps, the protective veil was so tightly drawn that I hardly knew what I had taken until I saw prints of my own photographs" (1963, p. 259; see also Bourke-White, 1946; Goldberg, 1986; Zelizer, 2001).

Just as Bourke-White endeavored to be "the eye of the time" for *Life*, it was the avowed determination of Lee Miller—*Vogue* magazine's sole war correspondent—to document the genocidal atrocities of Buchenwald as well, and shortly thereafter the Dachau concentration camp, with unflinching intensity. "*Vogue's* printing of Lee's material represented an achievement in fashion publishing which has never been repeated," her son Antony Penrose (1991) later wrote. "The grim skeletal corpses of Buchenwald are separated by a few thicknesses of paper from delightful recipes to be prepared by beautiful women dressed in sumptuous gowns"

(1991, p. 205).[7] The moral injunction for readers confronted with such distressing imagery to "BELIEVE IT" (the header taken from Miller's cable to her *Vogue* editor, which added "I implore you to believe this is true") similarly informed the eye-witness reportage of her fellow US photographers Thérèse Bonney, Georgette M. "Dickey" Chapelle, and Toni Frissell, amongst others, across a diverse range of contexts. Each of them, in different ways, sought to "bring the war home" for sometimes skeptical readers, notwithstanding the military's official terms of accreditation prohibiting women from entering combat zones (see Blanch, 1943; Frissell, 1979; Gallagher, 1998). In Chapelle's case, seeking permission to go ashore on Iwo Jima earlier that year, she found herself being told "The front is no place for a woman" by an Admiral. "I know that sir," she is said to have replied. "It's no place for a man either, but no man reporter can tell the mothers, daughters, wives, and sisters the story of men dying like a woman reporter" (cited in Haines, 2006).

The personal resources necessary to negotiate gendered inequalities were considerable for women photographers—recurrently patronized as "girls" amongst the men—compelled to endure discrimination ostensibly justified as "a natural state of affairs" grounded in gender essentialism (Oldfield, 2016). Many of them expressed deep frustration when their demands for equal treatment with their male contemporaries were resisted, trivialized or ignored (McCusker, 2006; Steiner, 2016; Tucker, 1975). Few appear to have subscribed to beliefs they possessed an innately female vision or exceptionally empathetic approach to their work, although some readily acknowledged a sense of duty to portray the experiences of other women involved in the conflict (Penrose, 2005; Stigneev, 2006; Williams, 1994). The figure of the "combat photographer" had been undergoing an ever-deeper process of "masculinization" over the war years, Vettel-Becker (2005) contends, with the constant struggle to stay out of harm's way providing men with "a chance to reassert virility through those traditional markers of masculinity signified by the warrior male" (2005, p. 34). The ensuing images frequently displayed a performative valorization predicated on personal daring, risk, and sacrifice, that is, a "material inscription of the photographer's body in action" and, as such, "indisputable evidence that manhood has been achieved" through the corporeal quest for visual "truth" (2005, pp. 37–39, 41). The projection of this heroic masculinity almost inevitably entailed reaffirming a patriarchal politics of othering, one where it seemed "common sensical" to deny women access to the proving grounds of the battlefield for their own safety.

This pursuit of the visual "truth" of warfare set into motion ideologically domesticated framings on the home front in the US, where the self-censorship tacitly prescribed by popular allegiance to the patriotic war effort was seldom called into question (Sorel, 2000). Still, amongst those prepared to wield her camera as a political tool to challenge and provoke was Dorothea Lange (publicly renowned for her "Migrant Mother" FSA photograph), who accepted a government commission to record the plight of law-abiding Japanese-Americans undergoing "evacuation" and "relocation" in the aftermath of the Pearl Harbor attack (over two-thirds of the 110,000 involved were US citizens, many others having lived in the country for decades). In self-fashioning a conception of photographic advocacy, Lange's reportage bore witness to their forcible imprisonment behind barbed wire fences in internment camps, revealing with plaintive immediacy how the callous mistreatment they suffered under government exclusion orders amounted to institutionally racist persecution. Very few of these images were published, however. The vast majority were seized and impounded by military censors—convinced they were "too critical" to be seen—for the duration of the war (Friedewald, 2014; Gordon, 2017). "Lange's photographs capture not only the oppression of a people but also their struggle to retain their dignity," Berger (2017) maintains, pointing out these "images of incarcerated Japanese-Americans are notable for their compassion and empathy, capturing the self-possession, complexity and struggles of Americans victimized by stereotypes and viewed by many as criminals" (see also Davidov, 1998; Fisher, 1987).

Elsewhere in the US during the war, signs were emerging that the insidious barrier of racism imposed upon the prospects of ethnic minority photographers was slowly beginning to ease, albeit unevenly due to similarly entrenched prejudices amongst many white journalists and editors. Relatively few black news photographers were able to find steady employment, for example, with women typically encountering gendered double standards with regard to their perceived suitability for a profession regarded as a white man's exclusive domain. Positive exceptions, while infrequent, have come to light, including those volunteering for national service who were previously making their living taking portraits of soldiers and their families (proficiency with cameras was particularly important, African Americans being denied entry to military photo-training courses). Within the Women's Army Corps, Elizabeth "Tex" Williams's sheer perseverance saw her become an official photographer, covering air and land combat training maneuvers, amongst other events, in a series of postings across the country. Matters improved in the aftermath of the conflict, with African American women, including Emma Alice Downs and Grendel A. Howard, benefitting from military programs designed to broaden photographic skills beyond portraiture (Rosenblum, 2010, p. 182). In the main, though, few records of these contributions exist, making pertinent details difficult to recover today. "As male-oriented a field as photography is, nonetheless quite a number of professional women have mastered its techniques," Moutoussamy-Ashe (1986) observes, "yet the few who have been mentioned historically have been white" (1986, p. xvi; see also Willis, 2002).

"What's a woman doing here?"

In the years following the Second World War, photojournalists and commentators alike increasingly recognized the importance of enlarging war photography beyond the immediate realm of the battlefield to render visible the wretched misery of those caught up in violent conflict and its aftermath—often most poignantly the women and children affected. To the extent this shift of emphases signaled an alternative orientation, it tended to be viewed by commissioning editors as one most capably achieved by women photographers, a documentary ambition more closely aligned with the empathetic priorities of human interest coverage than ostensibly dispassionate, impartial reportage. Tensions over photojournalism's macho culture, tacitly complicit in a normalization of militarization, would persist for some time, with only gradual, grudging improvement. Nevertheless, editors sourcing for photo agencies, NGOs, charities, and the like, were at least becoming less dismissive of women on the basis of sexist presumptions about physical and emotional weakness, latent pacifism, technical ineptitude or subjective "artsy-ness" at the expense of "objectivity."

With the rise of television news following the Korean conflict hastening the decline of photo-magazines such as *Picture Post* in the UK (its doors closing in 1957), speculation mounted regarding *Life*'s continued viability across what was a rapidly changing visual ecology at the outset of the Vietnam War (Moeller, 1989; Williams, 1994). By the mid-1960s, "female reporters" were, as Elizabeth Becker (2017) put it, intent on "rewriting the rules so that the phrase 'woman war correspondent' would never again be an oxymoron," a commitment that "seemed almost natural, since the women's movement was helping us imagine we could have the same opportunities as men" (Becker, 2017; Mander, 2010). However, with little prospect of employment with a news organization, only two women war photographers found their own way there in the early years of the conflict. One was Catherine Leroy from France, aged 21 in 1966, who would produce extraordinarily compelling photo-reportage. "I bought a one-way ticket to Saigon, and flew off with $150 and a Leica," she later remembered. "I wanted to be a war photographer, but I had never heard a shot fired in anger" (cited in Clifton, 2006). The year before, the aforementioned Dickey Chapelle, on operations with US Marines near Chu Lai, became the first American woman photographer killed in action. Her experiences reporting from numerous war zones for over two decades had been vividly detailed in her autobiography, *What's a Woman Doing Here? A Reporter's Report on Herself*, which appeared in print shortly after her arrival in Vietnam (Chapelle, 1962). Evidently the title had not been agreed with Chapelle, her preference being *With My Eyes Wide Open*. The publisher's choice apparently "set her teeth on edge. Why couldn't it be a book about a reporter, instead of a *woman reporter*?" (Haines, 2006; see also Ostroff, 1992).

As the Vietnam War became increasingly divisive in the US, noteworthy images lending expression to sharply polarized viewpoints grew in prominence, including beyond photojournalism narrowly defined. Precisely what constituted "war photography" proved progressively open to dispute, not least amongst commentators alert to how this "living-room war" (Arlen, 1966) was impacting upon popular support. "Boy with a straw hat waiting to march in a pro-war parade, N.Y.C., 1967" is the full title of a somewhat disconcerting photograph taken by Diane Arbus on a street crowded with protestors demonstrating against US military intervention. The young man in question wears a straw hat and suit with bow tie, his jacket lapels displaying badges that read "God Bless America: Support Our Boys in Vietnam" and "Bomb Hanoi," an American flag by his side. Evaluative appraisals often dwell on his eyes, interpreting the intensity of his stare into the camera's lens in different ways; for some it is a steadfast look of defiance, for others it relays vulnerable uncertainty, while for still others—such as Susan Sontag (1973)—he is yet another "freak" in the "moral theater of Arbus's straight-on, contemplative portraits." In any case, its lasting significance may be explained, in part, as a telling instance of youthful identification subtly unsettling expectations, and as such a transgression of more familiar tropes of patriotism and loyalty taking shape across the visual continuum of the Vietnam war's photo-reportage.[8]

To close, this chapter's recasting of accustomed relations of in/visibility for women war photographers amounts to an alternative mode of inquiry, one underwritten by a heuristic commitment to discerning the lived contingencies of their varied, purposeful accomplishments over the historical period under scrutiny. In elucidating the case for a more expansive—and thereby inclusive—conception of war photography's evolving normative boundaries, it has proven necessary to de-center traditional emphases on the first-hand relaying of violent combat imagery as its defining characteristic. Such histories have recurrently revolved around great (male) names in a visual canon reaffirmed through repetition, attributing prodigious moments of transformation to fearless heroism (exemplified in Robert Capa's well-known maxim, "If your pictures aren't good enough, you're not close enough"), sudden strokes of brilliance mastering technological innovation or re-inflecting the conventions of aesthetic form under unforgiving constraints. Just as what counts as "photography" has undergone dramatic change across gendered relations of mediation on both sides of the camera, so too have corresponding formulations of "war" (see also Allbeson & Oldfield, 2016; Callister, 2008; Hayes, 2005; Parry, 2018). To pry open restrictive purviews to identify women's achievements largely overlooked in the past, the easy appeal of this celebrated mythology of war photography must be disrupted by critical, contrary understandings of its fissured gaps, inconsistencies, exclusions, and re-alignments. Much work remains to be done, however. "To make present the work of women who have remained invisible in the writings of history is, in itself, only an opening on further questions," Fisher (1987) aptly points out. "Such research invites reflection on their prior absence as a meaningful silence within the historical discourse that informs our own times" (1987, p. 3). By carefully disentangling how these hierarchical norms of othering are inscribed and legitimated in practice, this chapter has shown that new conditions of possibility emerge to inspire future investigations as well as social action.

Acknowledgments

I am grateful to my co-editors of this volume, Cynthia Carter and Linda Steiner, as well as Tom Allbeson, for very helpful comments on the first draft of this chapter.

Notes

1 The one exception Rosenblum (2010) acknowledges being Julia Margaret Cameron's portraits of maidservants and plantation workers in Ceylon (now Sri Lanka) from 1875 until her death four years later (2010, pp. 52–53; see also Friedewald, 2014; Herbert, 2014).

2 "It is no longer an unusual or uncommon thing to see a camera in the hands of a woman," the *New York Times* observed in 1893. "Photography has opened to the sex a wide field of pleasure and profit, and they have not been slow to avail themselves of the opportunity" (*New York Times*, 1893, p. 18). A *Washington Times* article published two years later identified Johnston as "the only lady in the business of photography in the city, and in her skillful hands it has become an art that rivals the geniuses of the old world." She is described as "a lady of slight build and gentle manners," whose photographs "are like fine engravings" (*Washington Times*, 1895, p. 9). In 1897, Johnston's article "What a Woman Can Do with a Camera," published in the *Ladies Home Journal*, encouraged readers to recognize: "Photography as a profession should appeal particularly to women, and in it there are great opportunities for a good-paying business—but only under very well defined conditions." The personal qualities necessary for success, she added, included "good common sense, unlimited patience to carry her through endless failures, equally unlimited tact, good taste, a quick eye, a talent for detail, and a genius for hard work." She also "needs training, experience, some capital, and a field to exploit" (Johnston, 1897).

3 Opportunities to depict the ethnic diversity of the Olympia's crew, were overlooked. According to Wexler (2000), "except for 'Three Chinese Cooks,' Johnston absented men of color from the visual record" (2000, p. 31).

4 "On my way, there is more than enough harvest for my camera," Schalek writes in a *Neue Freie Presse* article published on 14 April 1916. "Where else than in this unique Gorizia can still be found a church whose appearance differs every day? This morning, the tower got hit under fire; now it looks even more interesting than the world famous tower of Pisa" (cited in Seul, 2016, p. 233). At the same time, several of Schalek's writings challenged official rationales for the war as she became increasingly disillusioned. Also worth noting here is her published response to criticisms regarding the reliability of a woman war correspondents' perspective: "I think it is not un-womanly, indeed it is the right of women, to trace the inner metamorphoses in the psyche of their brothers, fathers, husbands, and sons" in relation to the war's impact on them. "The reporting of male war reporters usually excludes this aspect of the war," she continued. "I myself, however, wish to bring to the attention of newspaper readers the fact that our own army as well as that of the enemy, consists of human beings" (cited in Seul, 2016, p. 239; see also Callister, 2008).

5 Rogoyska (2013) summarizes several of the factors involved, stating Taro's "early death, the overshadowing of the Spanish Civil War by the Second World War, and her connection with communism all contributed to her obscurity." As the decades passed, "she was relegated to a mere historical footnote: 'Capa's girlfriend'" (2013, p. 7). For further re-assessments of Taro's significance, see also Aronson & Budhos, 2017; Maspero, 2008; Schaber, 2009.

6 Evidently the commander in question, General James H. Doolittle, was almost demoted for granting Bourke-White permission. "While the military loved the dramatic press coverage [the photographs garnered], it did not like anyone, especially a woman, who evaded the public relations office regulations or broke rules in other ways" (Colman, 2002, p. 35).

7 The British Ministry of Information (MoI) recognized the importance of such publications—*Vogue* on both sides of the Atlantic, as well as *Good Housekeeping*, *Harper's Bazaar*, *Cosmopolitan*, *Seventeen*, and so forth—for influencing public perceptions of the conflict and its impact on daily life. "Women's magazines had a special place in government thinking during the war because, with men in the forces, women carried the whole responsibility of family life," then *Vogue* editor Audrey Withers explained, "and the way to catch women's attention was through the pages of magazines which, in total, were read by almost every woman in the country." She recalled "a group of editors were frequently invited to briefings by ministries that wanted to get across information and advice," adding "they sought advice from us too" (cited in Roberts, 2015b, p. 19; see also Hilditch, 2017; Schröder, 2015).

8 Arbus's work continues to prove controversial today. "Are her portraits," a *New York Times* obituary written by staff photographer James Estrin (2018) asked, "empathetic acknowledgments of a shared humanity, or are they exploitative depictions that seize upon their

subjects' oddities to shock her audience?" At the same time, the very recency of this obituary, published 46 years after Arbus died in July 1971, underscores a further important dimension for this chapter's purposes. On the occasion of International Women's Day in March 2018, the *Times* announced its project "Overlooked" dedicated to featuring the lives of accomplished women not accorded a place on its obituary pages in the past. "Looking back at the obituary archives can provide a stark lesson in how society valued various achievements and achievers," *Times* editors Jessica Bennett and Amisha Padnani remarked. "Since 1851, *The New York Times* has published thousands of obituaries. The vast majority chronicled the lives of men, mostly white ones" (*New York Times*, 2018).

References

Addario, L. (2015). *It's what I do: A photographer's life of love and war.* New York, NY: Penguin.

Allan, S. (2011). Amateur photography in wartime: Early histories. In K. Andén-Papadopoulos & M. Pantti (Eds.). *Amateur images and global news* (pp. 41–60). Chicago, IL: University of Chicago Press.

Allbeson, T., & Oldfield, P. (2016). War, photography, business: New critical histories. *Journal of War & Culture Studies, 9*(2), 94–114.

Arlen, M. J. (1966, October 15). Living-room war. *The New Yorker.*

Aronson, M., & Budhos, M. (2017). *Eyes of the world: Robert Capa, Gerda Taro, and the invention of modern photojournalism.* New York, NY: Henry Holt and Co.

Becker, E. (2017, November 17). The women who covered Vietnam. *The New York Times.*

Benjamin, A. N. (1898, September 3). Santiago after the surrender. *The Outlook,* pp. 21–28. Retrieved from www.unz.com/print/Outlook-1898sep03-00021/

Berger, M. (2017, February 8). Rarely seen photos of Japanese internment. *The New York Times.*

Blanch, L. (1943, July 1). History in the taking. *Vogue.* Retrieved from www.marshallfounda tion.org/library/digital-archive/history-in-the-taking/

Bourke-White, M. (1946). *Dear fatherland rest quietly.* New York, NY: Simon and Schuster.

Bourke-White, M. (1963). *Portrait of myself.* New York, NY: Simon and Schuster.

Brown, C. B. (1969). A woman's odyssey: The war correspondence of Anna Benjamin. *Journalism Quarterly, 46*(3), 522–530.

Brothers, C. (1997). *War and photography: A cultural history.* London: Routledge.

Butler, J. (2009). *Frames of war.* London: Verso.

Callahan, S. (1998, September–October). The last days of a legend. *American Photo,* 33–34, 95, 97.

Callister, S. (2008). Being there: War, women and lantern slides. *Rethinking History, 12*(3), 317–337.

Carlebach, M. L. (1997). *American photojournalism comes of age.* Washington, DC: Smithsonian Institution Press.

Carmichael, J. (1989). *First World War photographers.* London: Routledge.

Chanin, E. (2016). Gallery review. *Modernism, 23*(1), 243–248.

Chapelle, D. (1962). *What's a woman doing here? A reporter's report on herself.* New York, NY: William Morrow and Company.

Clifton, T. (2006, July 21). Obituary: Catherine Leroy. *The Guardian.*

Colman, P. (2002). *Where the action was: Women war correspondents in World War II.* New York, NY: Crown.

Cowing, E. (2009, December 6). Madonnas of the Western Front. *The Scotsman.*

Daniel, P., & Smock, R. (1974). *A talent for detail: The photographs of Miss Frances Benjamin Johnston 1889–1910.* New York, NY: Harmony.

Davidov, J. F. (1998). *Women's camera work: Self/body/other in American visual culture.* Durham, NC: Duke University Press.

Diu, N. L. (2007, December 9). Gerda Taro: The blonde of Brunete. *The Telegraph*.

Edis, O. (1919). Diary entry for 11 March 1919. *Olive Edis: Through the lens of Britain's first female war photographer*. Retrieved from https://oliveedisproject.wordpress.com/2016/03/11/11th-march-1919/

Estrin, J. (2018). Diane Arbus. *The New York Times*. Overlooked interactive feature. Retrieved from www.nytimes.com/interactive/2018/obituaries/overlooked-diane-arbus.html

Ezickson, A. J. (1938). *Get that picture! The story of the news cameraman*. New York, NY: National Library Press.

Fisher, A. (1987). *Let us now praise famous women: Women photographers for the US government 1935–1944*. London: Pandora.

Friedewald, B. (2014). *Women photographers: From Julia Margaret Cameron to Cindy Sherman*. London: Prestel.

Frissell, T. (1979). Toni Frissell. In M. K. Mitchell (Ed.), *Recollections: Ten women of photography* (pp. 102–119). New York, NY: Viking Press.

Gallagher, J. (1998). *The World Wars through the female gaze*. Carbondale: Southern Illinois University Press.

Goldberg, V. (1986). *Margaret Bourke-White: A biography*. London: Heinemann.

Goldberg, V. (2006). Margaret Bourke-White: A distinctly modern woman. In C. McCusker (Ed.), *Breaking the frame: Pioneering women in photojournalism* (pp. 165–167). San Diego: Museum of Photographic Arts.

Gordon, L. (2017). Dorothea Lange's censored photographs of the Japanese American internment. *Asia-Pacific Journal, 15*(3), 1–15.

Gover, C. J. (1988). *The positive image: Women photographers in turn of the century America*. Albany, NY: State University of New York Press.

Haines, D. (2006, Summer). One helluva woman. *Combat Magazine, 4*(3). Retrieved from www.combat.ws/S3/BAKISSUE/CMBT04N3/DICKEY.HTM

Hayes, P. (2005). Introduction: Visual genders. *Gender & History, 17*(3), 519–537.

Herbert, E. (2014, February 20). Julia Margaret Cameron in Ceylon: Idylls of freshwater vs. Idylls of Rathoongodde. *Berfrois*. Retrieved from www.berfrois.com/2014/02/eugenia-herbert-julia-margaret-cameron-in-ceylon/

Higonnet, M. R. (2010). X-Ray vision: Women photograph war. *Miranda, 2*. Retrieved from https://journals.openedition.org/miranda/1085

Hilditch, L. (2017). *Lee Miller, photography, surrealism and the Second World War*. Cambridge: Cambridge Scholars Publishing.

Hodgson, P. (1974). *Early war photographs*. London: Book Club Associates.

Jay, B. (1982, March 20). Women in photography: 1840–1900. *British Journal of Photography, 129*.

Johnston, F. B. (1897, September). What a woman can do with a camera. *Ladies Home Journal, 14*, 6–7. Retrieved from www.cliohistory.org/exhibits/johnston/whatawomancando/

Jolliffe, J. (Ed.). (1979). *Russian album, 1908–1918: Florence Farmborough*. London: Michael Russell Publishing.

Kotchemidov, C. (2005). Why we say "cheese": Producing the smile in snapshot photography. *Critical Studies in Media Communication, 22*(1), 2–25.

Lee, F. R. (2007, September 22). A wartime photographer in her own light. *The New York Times*, p. B7.

Lewinski, J. (1978). *The camera at war: War photography from 1848 to the present day*. London: W & J Mackay.

Life. (1937a, July 12). Death in Spain: The Civil War has taken 500,000 lives in one year. *Life*, p. 19.

Life. (1937b, August 16). The camera overseas: The Spanish war kills its first woman photographer. *Life*, pp. 62–63.

Mander, M. S. (2010). *Pen and sword: American war correspondents, 1898–1975*. Urbana, IL: University of Illinois Press.

Maspero, F. (2008). *Out of the shadows: A life of Gerda Taro*. London: Souvenir Press.

McCusker, C. (Ed.). (2006). *Breaking the frame: Pioneering women in photojournalism*. San Diego: Museum of Photographic Arts.

Meister, S. H. (2010). Crossing the line: Frances Benjamin Johnston and Gertrude Käsebier as professionals and artists. In C. Butler & A. Schwartz (Eds.), *Modern women: Women artists at the museum of modern art* (pp. 125–139). New York, NY: Museum of Modern Art.

Moeller, S. D. (1989). *Shooting war: Photography and the American experience of combat*. New York, NY: Basic Books.

Moutoussamy-Ashe, J. (1986). *Viewfinders: Black women photographers*. New York, NY: Dodd, Mead & Company.

New York Times (1893, October 1). Women who press the button: Photography as art to which they are likely to excel. *The New York Times*, p. 18.

New York Times (2018, March 8). *The New York Times* introduces *Overlooked*. *The New York Times*.

Oldfield, P. J. (2016). *Calling the shots: Women's photographic engagement with war in hemispheric America, 1910–1990* (Unpublished PhD thesis), Durham University. Retrieved from http://etheses.dur.ac.uk/11786/

Ostroff, R. (1992). *Fire in the wind: The life of Dickey Chapelle*. Annapolis: Bluejacket Books.

Parry, K. (2018). Private pictures and public secrets: Responding to transgressive soldier-produced imagery in United Kingdom news. *Journalism Studies, 19*(8), 1098–1115.

Penrose, A. (1991). Lee Miller: The ubiquitous image. In H. Roberts (Ed.), *Lee Miller: A woman's war* (pp. 6–13). London: Thames and Hudson.

Penrose, A. (Ed.). (2005). *Lee Miller's war*. London: Thames and Hudson.

Philo-Gill, S. (2017). *The women's army auxiliary corps in France, 1917–1921*. Barnsley: Pen & Sword.

Roberts, H. (2015a). Ceremony and soldiering: Mrs Albert Broom's photography of the armed forces in Britain 1904–1939. In A. Sparham (Ed.), *Soldiers and suffragettes: The photography of Christina Broom* (pp. 87–98). London: Philip Wilson Publishers.

Roberts, H. (2015b). Lee Miller: A woman's war. In H. Roberts (Ed.), *Lee Miller: A woman's war* (pp. 16–23). London: Thames and Hudson.

Rogoyska, J. (2013). *Gerda Taro: Inventing Robert Capa*. London: Jonathan Cape.

Rosenblum, N. (2010). *A history of women photographers* (3rd ed.). New York, NY: Abbville.

Roth, M. P. (1997). *Historical dictionary of war journalism*. Westport, CT: Greenwood Press.

Schaber, I. (2009). The eye of solidarity: The photographer Gerda Taro and her work during the Spanish Civil War, 1936–37. In I. Schaber, R. Whelan, & K. Lubben (Eds.), *Gerda Taro*. New York, NY: ICP, Steidl.

Schröder, K. A. (Ed.). (2015). *Lee Miller*. Ostfildern: Hatje Cantz Verlag.

Seul, S. (2016). A female war correspondent on the Italian front, 1915–17: The Austrian travel journalist and photographer Alice Schalek. *Journal of Modern Italian Studies, 21*(2), 220–251.

Sontag, S. (1973, November 15). Freak show. *The New York Review of Books*, pp. 13–19. Retrieved from www.nybooks.com/articles/1973/11/15/freak-show/

Sorel, N. C. (2000). *The women who wrote the war*. New York, NY: Perennial.

Sparham, A. (Ed.). (2015). *Soldiers and suffragettes: The photography of Christina Broom*. London: Philip Wilson.

Steiner, L. (2016). Bodies at war: The dangers facing women war photographers. In B. von der Lippe & R. Ottosen (Eds.), *Gendering war & peace reporting* (pp. 33–47). Göteborg: Nordicom.

Stigneev, V. (2006). Out of Russia: World War II photographs by Olga Lander. In C. McCusker (Ed.), *Breaking the frame: Pioneering women in photojournalism* (pp. 53–56). San Diego: Museum of Photographic Arts.

Tucker, A. (1975). *The woman's eye.* New York, NY: Alfred A Knopf.

Tylee, C. M. (1997). The spectacle of war: Photographs of the Russian front by Florence Farmborough. *Women: A Cultural Review, 8*(1), 65–80.

Vettel-Becker, P. (2005). *Shooting from the hip: Photography, masculinity and postwar America.* Minneapolis: University of Minnesota Press.

Washington Times (1895, April 21). Washington women with brains and business. *The Washington Times*, p. 9. Retrieved from https://chroniclingamerica.loc.gov/lccn/sn870 62244/1895-04-21/ed-1/seq-9.pdf

West, N. M. (2000). *Kodak and the lens of nostalgia.* Charlottesville: University Press of Virginia.

Wexler, L. (2000). *Tender violence: Domestic visions in an age of US imperialism.* Chapel Hill, NC: University of North Carolina Press.

Williams, V. (1986). *The other observers: Women photographers in Britain 1900 to the present.* London: Virago.

Williams, V. (1994). *Warworks: Women, photography and the iconography of war.* London: Virago.

Willis, D. (2002). *Reflections in black: A history of black photographers, 1840 to the present.* New York, NY: WW Norton & Company.

Zarzycka, M. (2017). *Gendered tropes in war photography: Mothers, mourners, soldiers.* London: Routledge.

Zelizer, B. (Ed.). (2001). *Visual culture and the holocaust.* London: Athlone Press.

22

THE GENDERED RACIALIZATION OF PUERTO RICANS IN TV NEWS COVERAGE OF HURRICANE MARIA

Isabel Molina-Guzmán

On September 20, 2017 Category 5 Hurricane Maria made catastrophic landfall on the US Commonwealth of Puerto Rico. At the time of writing, in May 2018, the death toll attributed to Maria stood at more than 4000.[1] Prior to the hurricane many US journalists and a large slice of the US public were unaware of the island's colonial status, a status that has defined the Caribbean island since the United States took ownership of it in the Spanish-American War of 1898. Ironically, 2017 also marked the centennial of the Jones-Shafroth Act of 1917, which granted Puerto Ricans born on the island US citizenship, subject to federal laws, but not the right to vote in federal elections. The Jones Act further cemented the island's colonial status by declaring US military rights over the island's coasts and coastal waters, which prevented Puerto Rico's closest geographical neighbors from providing hurricane assistance. So limited was public knowledge about Puerto Rico that in the wake of the devastation caused by the hurricane *The New York Times* reported that only 54 percent of US survey respondents knew Puerto Ricans were US citizens, much less knew of its complicated colonial status (Dropp & Nyhan, 2017).

In this chapter, I present a qualitative, intersectional feminist analysis of US television and online English-language news coverage of Hurricane Maria to explore some of the ways in which gender, news, power, and Puerto Rican identity are embedded across the reporting of this event. While I do not focus specifically on journalistic representations of Puerto Rican women, I examine the role of gender, race, and ethnicity in informing the news visuals, journalistic language, and editing. Documenting the racialized stereotypes of femininity and masculinity framing the news coverage helps explain how Western news values and ideologies shape and are shaped by public discourses about Puerto Ricans. To do so, I build on postcolonial feminist communication scholarship (Hegde, 2016; Kumar & Parmeswaran, 2018; Stam & Shohat, 2012; Shome, 2016) and Latina feminist communication scholarship (Baez, 2018; Beltran, 2009; Cepeda, 2010; Molina-Guzmán,

2010; Valdivia, 2010; Vargas, 2009). Specifically, the chapter responds to the call for communication frameworks that "recognize the affective charge of enduring symbolic structures (e.g., nation, culture, home) and the strategic ideological (often jingoistic) goals that drive the deployment of essentialized discourses of alterity" (Kumar & Parmeswaran, 2018, p. 348). I identify the dominant symbolic structures found within Hurricane Maria news coverage in order to analyze the ideological messages regarding Puerto Rican identity.

I first briefly discuss the interdisciplinary approach for analyzing journalistic discourse about Puerto Ricans, and then review the journalistic underrepresentation of US Latina/o communities, and the ways in which such invisibility contributes to stereotypic gendered and racialized news discourses of Latina/o and Puerto Rican difference. I document the journalistic practices that produce a narrative of the island and its residents, both men and women, as feminized and powerless and simultaneously racialized as ethnic Others and non-normative US citizens. The analysis illustrates the gendered racialization of the Puerto Rican nation that contributes to the symbolic colonization of Latinas/os and reifies contemporary US nativist and economic nationalist discourses. I conclude by reflecting on the cultural and political consequences of a journalistic narrative that leaves unquestioned the unequal power structures of the United States.

A critical feminist Latina studies approach to news discourse

Latina/Latino Studies is concerned with the people, culture, and experiences of communities living in the United States who, either because of ethnic ancestry or immigration, hail from more than 26 different Latin American and Spanish Caribbean nations (Aparicio, 2003; Oboler 1995, 2007; Rodriguez, 2000).[2] In particular, this academic field is concerned with studying how the colonial and postcolonial relationship between the United States, these countries, and US Latina/o communities shapes migration to the US and public policy and law surrounding these communities. Additionally, by paying particular attention to the specificity of ethnic groups within the pan-ethnic umbrella, Latina/o Studies focuses on Latina/o communities' experiences of gender, sexual, ethnic, and racial discrimination in the US. Working within this tradition, feminist Latina media scholars foreground the intersectional role of Latina womanhood, gender, sexuality, ethnicity, and race in media discourses, representations, and production practices.[3] Latina feminist approaches emphasize theorizing how women and gender function in English- and Spanish-language media to disrupt or reinforce dominant ideological structures.

I follow Stuart Hall et al.'s (1978; see also Hall et al., 2000) critical methodological approach to the study of media representations of difference, which calls for the examination of media texts as an institution of civil society and informal structure of power. More specifically, journalism studies scholars analyze how routine news media practices are shaped by gendered and racially biased conceptualizations of objectivity or what the editors of *News, Gender and Power* termed a "hierarchy of

credulity" (Carter et al., 1998, p. 5). Thus, news discourses and the journalistic practices that shape them are often informed by socially available and widely circulated
social construction of gender, ethnicity, race, and nation (Bird, 1992), and in turn
play a critical role in the reproduction of social and political power and inequality
specifically around issues of race, ethnicity, and gender (van Dijk, 1991; Zelizer &
Allan, 2010).

To map out the journalistic practices and discourses at play in the Hurricane
Maria coverage, I selected a sample of 36 TV and digital stories from September 22
to October 30, 2017 broadcast or published on CNN.com.[4] According to the
Nielsen ratings, CNN is the third most watched news network, and the first in
online news viewership measured by the number of news story downloads.[5] CNN
also has broad international presence. I focus on the period after the hurricane's
landfall to eliminate weather-centered stories and instead emphasize coverage of
the effects of the storm. Duplicate stories and news updates of the same story package were eliminated resulting in 36 distinct items for in-depth analysis.

Latinas/os, Puerto Ricans and the legacy
of journalistic invisibility

Although Latinas/Latinos currently are the largest ethnic-racial minority group in
the United States at 18 percent of the population, English-language national and
local print and television news have historically under-covered Latina/Latino communities, lives, and issues (Contreras, 2017; Molina-Guzmán, 2010; Santa Ana, 2012;
Subervi, Torres, & Montalvo, 2005; Subervi, 2015; Sui & Paul, 2017; Vargas, 2000).[6]
A study by Pew Research Center (2009b) found that only 2.9 percent of news stories from various media outlets contained substantial references to Latinas/os; those
stories were mostly focused on the confirmation of Supreme Court justice Sonya
Sotomayor, the Mexican drug war, the H1N1 flu outbreak originating in Mexico,
and US immigration policy. A study of the main television news networks from
2008 to 2014 confirmed a similarly stark pattern of invisibility with only 0.78 percent stories dealing with Latina/o issues and 0.41 percent focused exclusively on
Latinas/os (Subervi, 2015). This news pattern has remained unchanged since the
National Association of Hispanic Journalist began tracking TV news coverage of
Latinas/os in 1995. The 2015 study confirmed: "Latinos and Latino issues continue to be for the most part absent in the general market news media, and when
included, they are usually presented in the context of crises in crime, poverty, and
immigration" (2015, p. 7). A more recent 2017 study of local news confirmed the
continued underrepresentation and stereotypic news coverage of Latinas/os (Sui &
Paul, 2017). Consequently, Latina/o communities rarely appear in the news. When
they are covered, the stories tend to be negative in tone, focused on undocumented
immigration, crime, poverty, or other forms of crisis.

Additionally, news about Latinas/os is rarely told by journalists who have personal experiences or are educated about the groups themselves. The journalists
who cover Latina/o news are rarely Latina/o themselves nor do they specialize in

writing about ethnic and racial minority communities. In other words, most news-rooms lack journalists informed or versed on the issues or perspectives of ethnic and racial minority communities (Contreras, 2017). Latina/o news anchors and report-ers remain scarce with Latina/o TV reporters appearing in 17 percent of all stories and in only 15 percent of the 1 percent of stories about Latinas/os or Latina/o issues (Subervi, 2015). In sum, US Latina/o journalistic voices and Latina/o issues remain marginalized, indeed nearly invisible, within the US journalistic imaginary.

In the context of journalistic invisibility, the most visible ethnic group is of Mexican descent. As previously discussed, much of the US English-news coverage has focused on Mexico and undocumented migration through the US-Mexican border. The journalistic emphasis on undocumented Mexican immigration and anti-immigration discourses emphasizing criminality, poverty, and cultural differ-ence has symbolically colonized or flattened Latina/o ethnic diversity (Chavez, 2008; Molina-Guzmán, 2010; Santa Ana 2012). Symbolic colonization in the news involves a process of semiotic association, a storytelling mechanism in which news media practices reinforce heteronormative whiteness through homogenizing dif-ferences within Latinidad to reproduce dominant US norms, values, beliefs, and public understandings about US Latinas/Latinos.

The overrepresentation of Mexico and Mexicans in US news reinforces the public perception that equates Latinas/os with US Mexicans in general, and undoc-umented Mexicans specifically. Within coverage of Latina/o news most other Latina/o ethnic groups are rarely visible and thus further marginalized within the US imaginary about Latinidad. US Mexicans make up the largest Latina/o demo-graphic at 63.3 percent of the population (Flores, 2017). According to the most recent US Census, 65.5 percent of Latinas/os are actually US born citizens and Central Americans make up the fastest growing demographic of undocumented immigrants. Asian immigrants are the fastest growing population overall. Although Puerto Ricans are the second largest Latina/o demographic, Puerto Rican com-munities are rarely covered in the news.

Key differences in news coverage of Latina/o communities. Until the 1980s, news media discourses about Cubans and Cuban migration revolved around notions of Cuban exceptionalism and US Cold War foreign policy: news, films, and televi-sion programs constructed Cuban exiles as either self-sacrificing women and chil-dren or white, educated, politically conservative men committed to US capitalism and democracy (De los Angeles Torres, 1999, 2003, 2009; DeSipio & Henson, 1997; Molina-Guzmán, 2005). Beginning in the 1980s coverage of Cuban migra-tion became more negative as news stories focused on the illegal immigration of poor, black Cuban male refugees who are often depicted as criminal and deviant (Molina-Guzmán, 2010). In contrast, US Mexican and Puerto Rican migrants have been mostly represented through negative news coverage, especially during periods of economic downturn; this trend continues (Chavez, 2008; Grosfoguel, 2003; Loza, 2016; Santa Ana, 2012).

In particular, the scant US news coverage about Puerto Ricans, at least in the twentieth century, overwhelmingly depicted Puerto Rican migrants as unclean, uneducated, poor, and racially not white. News coverage of Puerto Rican men focused on urban criminality, especially during the 1970s and the height of the Independence Movement on the island (Rodriguez, 1997). Puerto Rican women were initially depicted as ideal domesticated labor in the 1960s during the Operation Bootstrap migration that brought thousands to work as maids and in garment and electronics factories. The news coverage of Puerto Rican women shifted in the 1970s and 1980s towards news coverage of them as urban welfare recipients (Ramos-Zayas, 2003; Rodriguez, 1997). The news discourses about Puerto Ricans in the 1980s and 1990s cohered with cultural representations of Puerto Ricans in theater, film, and television that likewise depicted them as working-class, uneducated laborers, criminals, or maids (Negron-Muntañer, 2014). Thus, when Hurricane Maria made landfall on the island, news coverage of Puerto Ricans was defined by general invisibility and stereotypic representations of the community as poor, uneducated, and not-white.

Analyzing power, gender, and ethnicity in the Hurricane Maria news

Powerlessness through the feminized gendering of Puerto Ricans. In the early days of the coverage, dramatic images of natural devastation dominated the narrative. Visuals of destroyed homes and streets and emergency evacuations, especially those featuring women, children, and the elderly, dominated the news coverage. As is typical of television news relying on emotionally impactful visuals, the early coverage focused on the destruction and dramatic images of rescues. Within these stories, interviews of men—who were always depicted as heterosexual—centered on the men's economic anxiety about their inability to provide food or a safe home for their wives and children (Weir & Clarke, 2017). The women and children in these stories are shown. They were seen but not heard or interviewed; when seen, the news images depicted them as alone and often needing economic, physical, or emotional assistance (Krupa & Criss, October 19, 2017). For example, the companion digital story to its TV report leads with "Jose Diaz hadn't seen his wife, Lydia Pabon, cry in years" (Gillespie, Sanchez, & Morris, 2017). And, forty seconds into the 128-second report, Pabon is depicted crying on-screen as the journalist narrates "Lydia and Jose are desperate and disheartened." Over images of the destroyed home, the news narration reports that when the hurricane began to hit their home they prepared to die together. Filmed walking side-by-side through the rubble of Lydia's home, a home inherited from her parents, the news story focuses on her emotional state and the remains of her home—providing a human interest angle to the destruction.

The Pabon story illustrates the feminized discourse of the heteronormative family and Puerto Rican identity in the journalistic narrative. While it differs significantly from negative news stories about Puerto Rican urban poverty, male criminality, and female sexuality, it coheres with findings of more positive news coverage about Latinas/os focused on domestic life and heteronormative family structures (Molina-Guzmán, 2010; Vargas, 2000). In doing, the journalistic narrative contributes to the feminine gendering of Puerto Ricans on the island as emotional and family-oriented—two characteristics stereotypically associated with women and Latinas/os (Molina-Guzmán, 2010). The gendering of women in the news narrative is in itself not remarkable: Tuchman (1978) documented the patriarchal nature of US news organizations and newswork. Rakow and Kranich (1991) affirmed the masculine narrative construction of US news narratives in terms of sourcing practices and news genres. What is analytically interesting is the intersection of the patriarchal and masculine nature of newswork and narrative on one axis, and the Western ideological values informing the journalistic storytelling about non-white communities on the other axis. At the center of both axes is a journalistic narrative that centers US, white, middle-class heterosexuality norms and those who differ from the norm as Other, different, exotic.

Consequently, the news coverage of Hurricane Maria follows the pattern identified by Vargas (2000) where the selection of news sources and the selection and framing of news stories about Latinas/os are shaped by two interconnected sociological processes: racialization and gendering. The scant scholarship on Latinas/os in English-language news documents, that when not focused on immigration and criminality, the coverage emphasize instead stories dealing with Latina/o domestic, cultural, and religious life. Soft-news stories about the Latina/o community avoid coverage of more serious news about Latina/o economic or political issues. Because Western patriarchal logics privilege the power and authority of political and economic agents who are most often white men, the implicit journalistic association of Latinas/Latinos as a cultural rather than an economic or political group feminizes and racializes them as powerless.

Journalistic gendering in this context is defined as the use of language and visuals that foreground binary feminine or masculine characteristics to frame public understanding about a particular news event, issue or figure. Although I recognize gender and sexuality as fluid categories of identity and analysis, at this historical juncture the majority of national US journalistic texts reinforce fixed, binary categories of gender identity. Indeed, while the 2017 Associated Press Stylebook recommends that journalists avoid binary gender references, it does not recommend the use of gender-neutral pronouns other than the use of "they, their, or them" in reference to transgender sources.[7] Thus, analyzing the gendering of Puerto Ricans in the Hurricane Maria coverage is to think about more than binary female or male bodies per se but rather to analyze the semiotics of "women as sign" in the story, and to further study the interconnection between "woman as sign" and "Latinas/os as sign" (Rakow & Kranich, 1991).

The journalistic language and visuals surrounding Hurricane Maria femininely gendered the Puerto Rican community as powerless to assist itself, dependent on the US government, and irrationally governed by the domain of heterosexual family life. Similar to the findings of other studies of English-language news coverage of Latinas/os, when the news is not negative in tone; positive journalistic narratives, such as the nomination of Puerto Rican Sotomayor or undocumented youth activists, tend to reinforce feminized and racialized notions of cultural difference, deficit, and dependence (Vargas, 2000). Even when the stories are not negative in tone, the gendered ethnic difference of Latinas/os is constructed as a barrier to assimilation into the patriarchal norms of middle-class whiteness. Like white female cisgender identity (white girlhood or white womanhood), both Latina and Latino identity is framed as a deficit that must be disciplined to overcome inequality and move beyond governmental dependence.

In the news coverage of Puerto Ricans and Hurricane Maria, therefore, gendering and racialization intersect to produce a journalistic narrative of Othering. I have conceptualized this process as symbolic colonization (Molina-Guzmán, 2010). Symbolic colonization assumes the values assigned to and associated with Latinas/os in national TV news reflecting preexisting hierarchical gender, ethnic, and racial relationships that privilege normative white Western masculinity at the top and marginalize difference from the norm (Molina-Guzmán, 2010). Such news imbues white heteronormative cis-men with more political power and economic value than white heteronormative cis-women, who hold more political power and economic value than brown heteronormative cis-women and so on. In other words, regardless of the ethnic-specific Latina/o community, the storytelling techniques remain unchanged. Puerto Ricans in the coverage of Hurricane Maria are embedded in the same journalistic narrative of cultural deficit and dependence, of gendered ethnic and racial difference, of Otherness from the Western norm of white heteropatriarchy.

Symbolic colonization and gendered ethnic difference. Gendering in the Hurricane Maria coverage contributes to the racialized construction of Latina/o people as inherently Other, foreign, a type of ideological devaluation with political, economic, and cultural consequences (Holland, 2012). The mainstream news media, as a part of US civil society, functions as a hegemonic force; it socially constructs an objective representation of reality that is nevertheless inflected with a heteronormative, patriarchal, and ethnocentric view of the world. Postcolonial scholar Edward Said (1978) argued Western narratives engaged in the paradox of hyper-masculinity and hyper-femininity to construct the Middle East as inherently different, exotic, and Other. In other words, the feminized discourse of Arabic domesticity and the family, with its implication of non-normative sexual fertility, contributed to the racialized Othering of Islam and the Middle East. A similar type of gendered ethnic difference is embedded in journalists' narratives of Maria.

The scholarship on the role of ethnicity and race in news coverage of natural disasters, particularly hurricanes, documents a similar discursive use of gendered narratives and visuals to produce difference (Ben-Porath & Shaker, 2010; Giroux, 2006; Lacy & Haspel, 2011). For example, regarding Hurricane Katrina news coverage, Lacy and Haspel conclude:

> (D)ominant US news media produced a diffuse mythic narrative, transforming New Orleans into a primitive swamp that unleashed primordial and sinful creatures in the form of dangerous black brutes who looted, raped, murdered, and took over the city. The narrative implied that large militaristic

forces, harnessed by white paternalistic heroes, were necessary to rescue New Orleans' women, children, and elderly from the black beasts.

(2011, p. 21)

The Katrina news images and stories situated black women, children, and the elderly as victims of hyper-masculine, hyper-sexual, and criminal black men rather than the victims of government inaction and lack of preparedness. The paradox of black victimhood and black criminality in the news footage gendered and racialized New Orleans as different from white heterosexual norms (Lacy & Haspel, 2011).

Apocalyptic language and visuals were also used in news coverage of Maria thus contributing to the production of gendered Puerto Rican difference. Perhaps laying bare the ethnocentric ideologies of US journalism, the use of apocalyptic language was not used to report on the devastating impact of Hurricane Harvey, which resulted in the flooding of large portions of Houston equal to the financial damage caused by Katrina. Indeed, a Google search of "Hurricane Harvey apocalyptic" resulted in one British news story, one news story about Hurricane Maria, and three stories about biblical references to the end of the world.[8] Yet, journalistic headlines and reporting reproduced the language of apocalypse in the Maria coverage: "Hurricane Maria: Puerto Rico officials describe 'apocalyptic condition'" (Chavez, September 24, 2017), "Puerto Rico, a month later is 'post-apocalyptic'" (Santiago, October 21, 2017), and "'This is like in war': A scramble to care for Puerto Rico's sick and injured" (Ferré-Sadurní, Robles, & Alvarez, September 26, 2017). No matter the news lead or headlines, the language, photographs, and footage about the hurricane's devastating damage dominated the frame. For instance, this special report about the damage explained "(I)t looks like a bomb went off. Once lush green hillsides are now brown and broken by the power of Maria's wind" (Weir, September 25, 2017). A dominant set of images circulate in the Maria coverage—garbage-strewn and mud-covered streets, destroyed and roofless homes made of wood and metal, people waiting in long lines, drinking or bathing in unsanitized water.

The survivors of Maria were constructed as grief-stricken victims desperately dependent on US federal assistance. Reinforcing the feminized discourses of victimhood and cultural deficit and dependence is the prevalent journalistic use of footage featuring women, children, and the elderly living in hospitals, shelters or destroyed homes. Indeed, 20 of CNN's 36 TV and digital stories depicted images of women, children, and the elderly. With a few significant exceptions, the men and women in the TV news coverage are rarely interviewed on camera; when they are, their voices are often dubbed over and translated by reporters for the convenience of English-dominant audiences.

Additionally, the news coverage's emphasis on footage of the Puerto Rican countryside, where only pockets of the island population live and where homes are mostly constructed of wood and metal, contributed to a journalistic narrative of the island as economically under-developed and its people as culturally deficient and dependent. What dominated was human interest news about the lack of safe infrastructure; destruction of homes that would be considered below US construction standards; the vulnerable of women, children, the sick, and the elderly; and, the island's dependence on the US federal government for assistance. All this reinforced a familiar narrative of Latina/o cultural deficit and dependence.

Interestingly, journalists appeared to reference Katrina for making sense of Maria. Reports often included questions about criminality or lack thereof. For example, one reporter explicitly asked the mayor of Aguas Buenas about looting:

> Bill Weir: How would you describe people's desperation? Are you seeing looting? Are you seeing anger?
>
> (Weir translating Javier Garcia): There has been looting. There have been robberies. And when it comes to the feelings of the people of this town we are saddened because we are still looking for people.
>
> *(Weir, September 24)*

Mayor Javier Garcia responds in a matter of fact tone. For Garcia, the level of criminal activity is not his main concern but rather the need to find survivors and provide assistance to his community. The story's visuals reveal the town's devastation. And the interview affirms the pathos of grief. In stark contrast to the TV coverage of Katrina, Garcia's calm demeanor and matter-of-fact response about the heart-wrenching search for the missing undercut the more sensationalistic reporting of crime. In a follow-up digital story "Puerto Rico mayor delivers food and water and find desperation" (Weir & Clarke, October 17, 2017), the focus is on Garcia's sense of the devastation almost a month after Maria's landfall and his individual response to the lack of federal assistance. The story never mentioned looting and crime.

Even stories about Puerto Ricans taking action in the absence of US federal assistance were undercut by a frame depicting the island as economically underdeveloped. Stories about the lack of clean drinking water juxtapose the voice-over narration against footage of Puerto Ricans funneling water from river streams and potentially toxic sources to collect it in plastic drums and containers. The implication of the coverage is that Puerto Rico is descending back to its pre-modern era, such as this report: "He said living in the storm's aftermath is like traveling back in time" (Lavandera, October 14, 2017). The cameraperson films a delivery of river water in plastic containers to the home of on-air source Nelson Vasquez, who explains in fluent English, "Our great-grandmothers, they used to carry cans of water on their hip from the lake to wash clothes." The visuals and journalistic language work against each other. Puerto Rico is returning to its "primitive past." But, images of the delivery of water in a truck to an intact cement home powered by an electrical generator contradicts the story's frame. Other stories about the lack of electricity, fuel, or water depict Puerto Ricans collecting water, bathing, or cleaning in streams, rivers, and clean-water sites. News viewers are reminded of Puerto Rico's foreignness even though Puerto Ricans are US citizens.

The gendered colonial Othering of Puerto Ricans. These news stories carry such emotional weight in part because of the historical dearth of coverage about Puerto

Rico in the US news and the lack of public awareness about Puerto Rico's colonial relationship to the United States. Prior to the hurricane, Puerto Rico's infrastructure had been in decades of decline due to the colonial political and economic structure of the island. The rise of US agri-business and the economic decline of sugar plantations decimated the majority of the island's agriculture in the early 1900s. Additionally, the combination of colonial-era legislation mandating that Puerto Rican imports and agricultural exports flow through coasts along the US mainland, and the creation of tax-incentives for US corporations with factories on the island but limiting financial tax benefits to the island's economy, have left Puerto Rico with few self-sustaining industries other than tourism. Furthermore, Puerto Rico's government, which has historically been run by politicians from the same established political families, have mismanaged the island's pension system and the US federal subsidies provided to the island in exchange for tax breaks. Finally, the past decade has seen the flight of working-age or college-educated Puerto Ricans from the island to the mainland further depleting its state income base. In 2017 more Puerto Ricans lived in the US mainland than resided on the island. Meanwhile, in the last 50 years Puerto Rico's government accrued more than $70 million in debt eventually resulting in the US Congressional take-over of its finances. Before Hurricane Maria, Puerto Rico's residents faced higher rates of unemployment and poverty than US states; a failing water, power, and transportation infrastructure; rolling power black-outs and clean water allocations; and, inflationary-level food, medical, and energy prices. This context is pivotal to understanding why the damage caused by Maria became more crippling and difficult to recover from than the damage experienced in Texas and Florida.

Journalists' failure to provide context and, in television news, their preference for images over text reified the construction of Puerto Ricans as gendered ethnic Others, unable to care for themselves and dependent on the US federal government. Visuals of women, children, the sick, and the elderly in the Maria news coverage circulates a narrative of a Puerto Rican people dependent on the US federal government. Others are depicted as living in hazardous conditions while waiting to be rescued (Valencia, October 20, 2017). Digital and TV news coverage about the lack of clean water, food, power, gasoline, currency, as well as images of complete structural devastation reinforce a sense of Puerto Rico as economically undeveloped, culturally foreign, and not of the United States.

In the Katrina coverage, TV journalists initially focused on black men as villains and eventually shifted to the failure of the federal response, and the life-saving work of heroes, many of them white local officials and civil volunteers. Federal government officials attempted to absolve themselves of responsibility for the failed response to Katrina by blaming the unforeseen nature of weather (Lacy & Haspel, 2011). Similarly, in the absence of federal assistance, the news highlighted the work of mostly white nurses, veterans, and volunteers who traveled to Puerto Rico to provide assistance. In contrast to Katrina, President Trump and other federal officials attempted to absolve themselves of the humanitarian crisis by engaging in a nationalistic discourse grounded in racist and sexist rhetoric. Trumps' rhetoric and factually incorrect tweets about the island (showing he did not know the island was part of the United States), drove the news coverage about the federal response. Instead of empathy with the Puerto Rican people, Trump tweeted about the need for the island's government to pay down its debt and called for the people of Puerto Rico to take responsibility for the post-hurricane recovery effort. Trump's rhetoric calls forth popular conservative messages about limiting the US welfare state, in particular programs that benefit ethnic and racial minority populations, who are allegedly taking advantage of the federal largesse. Implicit in the conservative rhetoric are stereotypic assumptions about communities of color as poor, uneducated, and lazy (Collins, 2005).

Except in this instance, the victim talked back to patriarchal power. Almost one month after Maria's landfall on the island, local Puerto Rican officials, especially San Juan mayor Carmen Yulín Cruz, openly criticized the federal response in general and Trump's personal rhetoric in particular. Cruz labeled Trump as racist (Cooper, September 30, 2017). Wearing a black t-shirt with the slogan "Help us/We are Dying" Cruz, who spent more than a decade living in Pittsburgh, PA and who speaks fluent English, provided a compelling camera-ready voice of Puerto Rican opposition and resistance. Cruz's dual role as victim and voice of Puerto Rican resistance was highlighted in the banner text to the above story, "Crisis in Puerto Rico. Trump attacks San Juan mayor as she begs for help." Given the racist and misogynistic tone embedded in nationalist rhetoric, it is particularly telling that the banner frames Trump as the aggressor: he attacks Cruz, who "begs for help" on behalf of the Puerto Rican people. Highlighting the Othering discourse of the journalistic narrative and Trump rhetoric, Anderson Cooper shares with Cruz how it personally hurts him to talk to Puerto Ricans who repeatedly remind him that "We are Americans. We are Americans." Implied in the plea to be recognized as "Americans" is the belief that they are not perceived as belonging to the United States.

Interestingly Cruz was the Puerto Rican official source who most openly criticized Trump and the federal response (Ryan, October 20, 2017). Indeed, she came to embody Puerto Rico's threat to US racial order when she observed on camera that Puerto Ricans, who lean towards Democratic, will leave the island in droves and in doing so influence the electoral system on the mainland. Her observation alongside news coverage of the massive re-settlement of Puerto Ricans from the island to the mainland reinforces their ethnic and racial Otherness and threat to the white, hetero-patriarchal political hegemony. Yet, while Cruz's visibility provides an oppositional voice and body, Trump's racializing call for Puerto Ricans to help themselves implied Puerto Ricans were being lazy in their refusal to do so.

Conclusion: postcolonial reflections on gender, power, and the news

The symbolic colonization of Puerto Ricans in the news coverage produces a visual and textual flattening of ethnic and national specificity that contributes to the colonial Othering of the island and its people. Specifically, TV news coverage of Puerto Ricans affected by Hurricane Maria reinforce a gendered racialized construction of Latinas/os as non-normative and non-citizens, feminized as vulnerable and politically powerless, a liminal status critical ethnic studies scholar Lisa Cacho (2012) defines as "social death." As Henry Giroux observed of Hurricane Katrina:

> The bodies of the Katrina victims laid bare the racial and class fault lines that mark an increasingly damaged and withering democracy and revealed the emergence of a new kind of politics, on in which entire populations are now considered disposable, an unnecessary burden on state coffers, and consigned to fend for themselves.
>
> *(2006, p. 174)*

Similarly, even when Puerto Ricans inserted themselves as political agents in news narratives, such as government official's demanding federal assistance, the overall news narrative undercut the legal, economic, and political voices of Latina/o activists and political figures. The ways in which these stories are told have social and political consequences.

Research on news images of Hurricane Katrina documents that people's ethnic and racial identity in news images increased the salience of racial and ethnic identity to audiences' understanding of the story: White audiences were more likely to attribute the cause of problems related to Katrina to the ethnic and racial identity of those affected rather than the government (Ben-Porthat & Shaker, 2010). It did not have the same effect on minority news audiences. Thus, journalistic images of visually identifiable ethnic and racial minorities during Hurricane Katrina primed some white audiences to blame the victims and hold the federal government less accountable for the aftermath (2010, p. 477). Because editors often select news photographs and video footage for their ability to grab attention and evoke emotional responses, audiences are more likely to recall pictures than words (Ben-Porthat & Shaker, 2010; Dixon & William, 2016). Likewise, the cultural privileging of the visual as a lens or mirror of the "real" in the West often means that news audiences read them as more objective or credible (Morgan & Signorielli, 2012).

Within the context of the United States and its continuing involvement in regional imperialism and globalization, general-market news production is a significant hegemonic mechanism for how the nation imagines itself. As a hegemonic text embedded in ethnocentric, masculine ideologies, and professional practices, the journalistic narrative produced about Hurricane Maria is grounded in Western assumptions of economic development and decision-making as the norm against which the failures of gendered ethnic, and racial Others is evaluated. Trump's rhetoric of toxic masculinity, a white masculine discourse in which women and ethnic and racial minorities are inherently inferior and expected to be subservient, further highlights the inherent power and authority of white patriarchal colonial logics. Writing of the Middle East, Edward Said concluded that "the Orient is at the bottom something either to be feared (the Yellow peril, the Mongol hordes, the brown dominions) or to be controlled (by pacification, research and development, outright occupation whenever possible)" (1978, p. 301). The unincorporated US territory of Puerto Rico and its people appear so foreign to the US nation that the journalistic narrative and Trump's rhetoric ignore them as a member of the nation. Maintaining US structures of gender and racial power requires the cultural and political devaluation of women, ethnic, and racial minorities. The gendering of Puerto Rican and Latina/o difference through symbolic colonization in the Hurricane Maria news coverage is but one example of how power is maintained through the institutions of civil society.

Notes

1 www.nytimes.com/2018/05/29/us/puerto-rico-deaths-hurricane.html.
2 In using the term "U.S. Latinas/os," I am invoking the pan-ethnic term used by activists, journalists, and scholars to signal Latina/Latino and Latin American identity in the United States. Beginning with the 2010 US Census, this became an official pan-ethnic category alongside Hispanic. The label gained scholarly attention when sociologist and community organizer Felix Padilla (1985) employed it in his ethnography of the ethnic and racial discrimination faced by Chicago's Mexican and Puerto Rican communities and the coalitional response of community organizers to address inequities in education, housing, and social services. Latinidad refers to the cultural signifiers of people who self-identify or are identified by the English and Spanish-language media as belonging to the pan-ethnic group Latina/Latino.
3 See the work of Valdivia for a full literature review of Latino media and feminist approaches.
4 Morten Kristensen (Institute of Communications Research, graduate research assistant) collected the TV and digital coverage from the CNN.com website.
5 http://tvbythenumbers.zap2it.com/cable-news/cnn-leads-all-competitors-in-digital-video-for-third-straight-month/ retrieved June 14, 2018.
    https://deadline.com/2017/12/fox-news-highest-ratings-cable-news-2017-1202230070/
6 Recognizing the significant role of Spanish-language news networks, for the sake of brevity, US English language news will be referred to as US news for the remainder of the chapter.
7 www.apstylebook.com
8 www.google.com/search?client=safari&rls=en&ei=OOgnW93VGIu2sAX35pfgBA&q= hurricane+harvey+apocalyptic&oq=Hurricane+Harvey+and+the+apoc&gs_l=psy-ab. 1.1.0i22i30k1l2.53394.57185.0.64609.21.17.3.0.0.0.118.1422.14j2.16.0....0...1.1.64.psy-ab.. 2.19.1494...0j0i67k1j0i13i30k1j0i13i10i30k1j0i22i10i30k1j0i8i13i30k1.0.YqtcrRYVvF8

References

Aparicio, F. R. (2003). Jennifer as Selena: Rethinking Latinidad through popular culture and media. *Latino Studies*, *1*, 90–105.

Báez, J. (2018). *In search of belonging: Latinas, media, and citizenship*. Urbana, IL: University of Illinois Press.

Beltran, M. (2009). *Latina/o Stars in U.S. eyes: The making and meaning of film and TV stardom*. Urbana, IL: University of Illinois Press.

Ben-Porath, E. N., & Shaker, L. K. (2010). News images, race, and attribution in the wake of hurricane Katrina. *Journal of Communication*, *60*, 466–490.

Bird, E. (1992). *For enquiring minds: A cultural study of supermarket tabloids.* Nashville, TN: University of Tennessee Press.

Cacho, L. M. (2012). *Social death: Racialized rightlessness and the criminalization of the unprotected.* New York, NY: New York University Press.

Carter, C., Branston, G., & Allan, S. (Eds). (1998). *News, gender, and power.* London: Routledge.

Cepeda, M. E. (2010). *Musical imagination: U.S-Colombian identity and the Latin music boom.* New York, NY: New York University Press.

Chavez, L. (2008). *The Latino threat: Constructing immigrants, citizens, and the nation.* Stanford, CA: Stanford University Press.

Chavez, N. (2017, September 24). Hurricane Maria: Puerto Rico officials describe "apocalyptic" conditions. Retrieved from https://www.cnn.com/2017/09/24/americas/hurricane-maria-puerto-rico-aftermath/index.html

Collins, P. H. (2005). *Black sexual politics: African Americans, gender, and the new racism.* New York, NY: Routledge.

Contreras, R. (2017). The X factor: The struggle to get Latinos in US news stories amid a Latinx push and a changing journalism landscape. *Social Dynamics, 29*(3), 177–185.

Cooper, A. (2017, September 30). *San Juan mayor on Trump: No time for this.* Retrieved from https://www.cnn.com/videos/us/2017/09/30/san-juan-mayor-carmen-yuln-cruz-anderson-cooper-sot-nr.cnn

de los Angeles Torres, M. (1999). *In the land of mirrors: The politics of Cuban exiles in the United States.* Ann Arbor, MI: University of Michigan Press.

de los Angeles Torres, M. (2003). *The lost apple: Operation Pedro Pan, Cuban children in the U.S., and the promise of a better future.* Boston, MA: Beacon Press.

DeSipio, L., & Henson, J. R. (1997). Cuban Americans, Latinos, and the print media: Shaping ethnic identities. *Press/Politics, 2*(3), 52–70.

Dijk, T. A. van. (1991). *Racism and the press.* London: Routledge.

Dixon, T., & William, C. (2016). The changing misrepresentation of race and crime on network and cable news. *Journal of Communication, 6*(1), 24–39.

Dropp, K., & Nyhan, B. (2017, September 26). Nearly half of Americans don't know Puerto Ricans are fellow citizens. *The New York Times.* Retrieved from www.nytimes.com/2017/09/26/upshot/nearly-half-of-americans-dont-know-people-in-puerto-ricoans-are-fellow-citizens.html

Flores, A. (2017, September 18). How the U.S. Hispanic population is changing. Retrieved from www.pewresearch.org/fact-tank/2017/09/18/how-the-u-s-hispanic-population-is-changing/

Gillespie, P., Sanchez, B., & Morris, J. (2017, October 3). US war veteran's home destroyed in Puerto Rico. Retrieved from www.cnn.com/2017/10/03/americas/puerto-rico-war-veteran-ponce/index.html

Giroux, H. (2006). Reading hurricane Katrina: Race, class, and the biopolitics of disposability. *College Literatures, 33*(3), 171–196.

Grosfoguel, R. (2003). *Colonial subjects: Puerto Ricans in a global perspective.* Berkeley, CA: University of California Press.

Hall, S. M., Critcher, C., Jefferson, T., Clarke, J., & Roberts, B. (Eds.) (1978). *Policing the crisis: Mugging, the state, and law and order.* New York, NY: Holmes and Meier.

Hall, S. M., Schehr, L., & Lawrence, R. (Eds.) (2000). *Representation: Cultural representations and signifying practices.* London: Sage Publications.

Hegde, R. (2016). *Mediating migration.* London: Polity Press.

Holland, S. (2012). *The erotic life of racism.* Durham, NC: Duke University Press.

Krupa, M., & Criss, D. (2017, October 19). Puerto Rico's misery, four weeks after Maria, seems like it may never end. Retrieved from www.cnn.com/2017/10/18/us/puerto-rico-numbers-by-the-numbers-four-weeks-trnd/index.html

Kumar, S., & Parameswaran, R. (2018). Charting an itinerary for postcolonial communication and media studies. *Journal of Communication, 68*(2), 347–358.

Lacy, M., & Haspel, K. (2011). Apocalypse: The media's framing of black looters, shooters, and brutes in hurricane Katrina's aftermath. In M. Lacy & K. Ono (Eds.), *Critical rhetorics of race*. New York, NY: New York University Press.

Lavandear, E. (2017, October 14). Daily struggle to survive in Puerto Rico. Retrieved from https://www.cnn.com/videos/us/2017/10/14/puerto-rico-daily-struggle-lavandera-pkg-nr.cnn

Loza, M. (2016). *Defiant Braceros: How migrant workers fought for racial, sexual, and political freedom*. Chapel Hill, NC: University of Chapel Hill Press.

Luis Ferré-Sadurní, L., Robles, F., & Alvarez, L. (2017). "This is like in war": A scramble to care for Puerto Rico's sick and injured. *The New York Times*, 26 Sept.

Molina-Guzmán, I. (2005). Gendering Latinidad in the Elián news discourse about Cuban women. *Latino Studies, 3*, 179–204.

Molina-Guzmán, I. (2010). *Dangerous curves: Latina bodies in the media*. New York, NY: New York University Press.

Morgan, M. J. S., & Signorielli, N. (Eds.). (2012). *Living with television now: Advances in cultivation theory & research*. New York, NY: Peter Lang.

Negron-Muntañer, F. (2014). *The Latino media gap: The state of Latinos in US media*. Report. Retrieved from https://fusiondotnet.files.wordpress.com/2015/02/latino_media_gap_report.pdf

Oboler, S. (1995). *Ethnic labels, Latino lives: Identity and the politics of (re)presentation in the United States*. Minneapolis, MN: University of Minnesota Press.

Oboler, S. (2007). Citizenship and belonging: The construction of US Latino identity today. *Revista Iberoamericana*.

Padilla, F. M. (1985). *Latino ethnic consciousness: The case of Mexican Americans and Puerto Ricans in Chicago*. Notre Dame, IN: University of Notre Dame Press.

Pew Research Center (2009a). Hispanic in the news: Events drive the narrative. Retrieved October 16, 2017, from www.journalism.org/2009/12/07/hispanics-news/

Pew Research Center (2009b). Sotomayor spin wars dominate the narrative. Retrieved October 16, 2017, from www.journalism.org/2009/06/01/pej-news-coverage-index-may-25-31-2009/

Rakow, L., & Kranich, K. (1991). Woman as sign in television news. *Journal of Communication, 41*(1), 8–23.

Ramos-Zayas, A. (2003). *National performances: The politics of class, race, and space in Puerto Rican Chicago*. Chicago, IL: University of Chicago Press.

Rodriguez, C. (Ed.). (1997). *Latin looks: Images of Latinas and Latinos in the U.S. media*. Boulder, CO: Westview Press.

Rodriguez, C. E. (2000). *Changing race: Latinos, the census, and the history of ethnicity in the United States*. New York, NY: New York University Press.

Ryan, J. (2017, October 20). San Juan mayor: Trump gets 10 out of 100 for hurricane response. Retrieved from https://www.cnn.com/2017/10/20/politics/san-juans-says-trump-scored-a-10-of-100-cnntv/index.html

Said, E. (1978). *Orientalism*. New York, NY: Pantheon.

Santa Ana, O. (2012). *Juan in a hundred: The representation of Latinos on network news*. Austin, TX: University of Texas Press.

Santiago, L. (2017, October 21). *Puerto Rico a month later is "post-apocalyptic."* Retrieved from https://www.cnn.com/videos/us/2017/10/20/santiago-puerto-rico-hurricane-maria-dnt-clean-lead.cnn

Shome, R. (2016). When postcolonial studies meets media studies. *Critical Studies in Media Communication, 33*(3), 245–263.

Stam, R., & Shohat, E. (2012). *Race in translation: Culture wars around the postcolonial Atlantic.* New York, NY: New York University Press.

Subervi, F. (2015). *Latinos in TV network news 2008–2014: Still mostly invisible and problematic.* Communication Workers of America and the Newspaper Guild. Retrieved from https://www.mediadiversityforum.lsu.edu/latinos-in-tv-network-news-2008-14.pdf

Subervi, F., Torres, J., & Montalvo, D. (2005). *The portrayal of Latinos & Latino issues on network television news, 2004 with a retrospect to 1995: Quantitative & qualitative analysis of the coverage.* Austin, TX: National Association of Hispanic Journalists.

Sui, M., & Paul, N. (2017). Latino Portrayals in local news media: Underrepresentation, negative stereotypes, and institutional predictors of coverage. *Journal of Intercultural Communication Research, 46*(3), 273–294.

Tuchman, G. (1978). *Making news: A study in the construction of reality.* London: Free Press.

Valdivia, A. (2010). *Latino/as in the media.* London: Polity Press.

Valencia, N. (2017). *Residents losing hope in Puerto Rico.* Retrieved from https://www.cnn.com/videos/world/2017/10/08/puerto-rico-arecibo-hurricane-maria-valencia.cnn

Vargas, L. (2000). Genderizing Latino news: An analysis of a local newspaper's coverage of Latino current affairs. *Critical Studies in Media Communication, 17*(3), 261–293.

Vargas, L. (2009). *Latina teens, migration, and popular culture.* Bern, SW: Peter Lang International Academic.

Weir, B. (2017). Weir in Puerto Rico: Looks like bomb went off. Retrieved from https://www.cnn.com/videos/us/2017/09/25/puerto-rico-devastation-bill-weir-lkl-wolf.cnn

Weir, B., & Clarke, R. (2017, October 16). Mudslide hits Puerto Rico neighborhood that Trump visited. Retrieved from www.cnn.com/2017/10/16/us/puerto-rico-guaynabo-bridge-destroyed/index.html

Zelizer, B., & Allan, S. (Eds.). (2010). *Keywords in news and journalism studies.* Berkshire: Open University Press, McGraw Hill Education.

23

WHEN WOMEN RUN FOR OFFICE

Press coverage of Hillary Clinton during the 2016 presidential campaign

Erika Falk

Although the first woman to run for president in the United States was Victoria Woodhull in 1872, the history of US women who could be considered serious candidates by modern standards (i.e., women with significant national political experience seeking major party nominations) began in 1964 when Senator Margaret Chase Smith sought the Republican nomination for president. Smith was followed in 1972 by congressional representatives Shirley Chisholm and Patsy Mink; Representative Pat Schroeder in 1988; Reagan Administration Secretary of Transportation and Bush Administration Secretary of Labor, Elizabeth Dole in 2000; Senator and Ambassador Carol Mosely Braun in 2004; and Representative Michele Bachmann in 2012. So, it is unclear why in 2016 a *Philadelphia Inquirer* editorial appeared calling Hillary Clinton "the first serious female candidate for U.S. president" (Rubin, 2016, p. A18). In truth Clinton was just the latest in a long series of serious women presidential candidates. Such reporting is not anomalous. Using the *first woman* or *novelty frame* to perpetually describe women candidates is just one of many interesting patterns of press coverage that have persisted over time.

Here I examine newspaper coverage of the 2016 presidential race between Democratic candidate Hillary Clinton and Republican candidate Donald Trump to determine the degree to which historical patterns of gendered press coverage (noting gender, framing women as firsts, disparate coverage of appearance, and unequal amounts of coverage) were present in the 2016 race. Despite the spread of egalitarian ideals and significant increases in women's rights since women first started running for electoral office, the disparity in press coverage between men and women candidates for president has seen little change. I argue that the persistence of gendered patterns of press coverage affect perceptions of women candidates and reflect how unconscious stereotypes and traditional sex roles remain entrenched in contemporary American society.

Coverage of gender

Studies have consistently found that newspaper coverage of political campaigns is more likely to mention the gender of a woman than a man candidate. Examining print coverage of races occurring in 2000 for state gubernatorial elections and the US Senate, Banwart, Bystrom, and Robertson (2003) found that although articles focused on the men candidates did not mention their gender, about 12 percent of articles focused on the women candidates did. Similar results were reported by Bystrom, Banwart, Kaid, and Robertson (2004), Bystrom, Robertson, and Banwart (2001), Robertson, Conley, Szymczynska, and Thompson (2002), and Major and Coleman (2008).

At the presidential level, Miller, Peake, and Boulton's (2010) study of newspaper coverage of the 2008 Democratic primaries found Clinton's gender mentioned nine times more than Obama's. Moreover, "references to Clinton's gender were significantly correlated with the questioning of her electability" (p. 178). They argued that "such articles implicitly cued readers to think that a woman may not be electable to the highest office in the United States because of the fact of her gender" (p. 178). Miller and Peake (2013) similarly found a disparity in gender marking in the top-circulating newspapers during the general election of 2008. Press reports mentioned Republican vice-presidential candidate Sarah Palin's gender six times more often than Democratic vice-presidential candidate Joe Biden's. These results are consistent with Falk's (2010) study of nine women candidates for president.

Studies have also found that reporters are more likely to mention a woman candidate's gender the more prestigious the position she pursues. Meeks (2012) analyzed eight US newspapers that covered women running for US Senator, Governor, Vice President, or President between 1999 and 2008:

> As candidates ran for higher levels of office, the gap for gender labels . . . grew . . . and the disparity was particularly prominent when they ran for the White House. In particular, Sarah Palin received almost 40% more gender labeling coverage than her male competitors for the White House.
>
> *(Meeks, 2012, p. 185)*

Data from the 2016 presidential campaign between Democratic Party candidate Hillary Clinton and Republican Party candidate Donald Trump were consistent with these findings. I searched in the Lexis/Nexis database of US newspapers from April, 2015 (when Clinton declared her candidacy) through November 7, 2016 (the day before the election) for the phrases "man candidate" or "male candidate" in the same sentence as "Trump." I likewise searched for "woman candidate" or "female candidate" in the same sentence as "Clinton." To avoid erroneously pulling references to other members of the Clinton or Trump families and to avoid erroneously pulling up other uses of the word "trump" as in "trump card," I used the Lexis/Nexis Index function that classifies stories about major personalities. Thus, I searched only those stories previously coded as being about one of the candidates. This and all subsequent searches were done using these search parameters unless otherwise specified.

Clinton's gender was marked regularly and explicitly in newspaper stories and far more frequently than Trump's was. The electronic search yielded 188 cases, 151 instances of "female candidate" and 37 instances of "woman candidate." The same database contained just 47 references in articles about Trump. "Man candidate" was used 25 times and "male candidate" 22 times. Even by this crude measure, Clinton's gender was marked four times as often as Trump's.

A qualitative analysis of these data shows an even more striking disparity. The computerized search described above included references that were not about the candidates as in, "A male candidate would have called out Trump's lie with authority" ("Trump's Furious Descent," 2016, p. 24), which fits the search criteria but does not describe Trump. The electronic search also included cases where the gender references were oblique, as in, "It is still very difficult for male candidates to feel comfortable going against and attacking women, with the exception of Donald Trump" (Sulek, 2015, para 13); this implies Trump is male without saying so directly. A more thorough analysis found that in *only one* of the computer-counted cases of male/man candidate was Trump's gender directly marked, while almost half (89 of 188) of the total computer-selected instances about Clinton's gender noted her gender clearly and directly. The following examples are emblematic of how gender was marked for Clinton:

- "She's not your typical woman candidate" (Page, 2016, p. 1A);
- "Hillary Clinton became the first female candidate to clinch the presidential nomination of a major political party" (Sheehy, 2016, p. 8); and
- "The two female candidates, Hillary Clinton and Carly Fiorina . . ." (Friedman, 2016a, p. 15).

In January 2017 (i.e., after the election), I did a Google search of "male candidate" or "man candidate," "Trump," and "president." This search yielded about 47 total results, but none of these websites actually described Trump as a "man candidate" or a "male candidate." The equivalent search for Clinton yielded about 36,500 results. When I more closely examined the results on the first page of the Google search, all the references were to Clinton's sex. The first two links were emblematic of the ones that followed. "Hillary Clinton became the first female presidential candidate nominated by a major party, namely the Democratic Party" ("List of Female," 2017, para. 3), and "The survey also asks specifically about satisfaction with Hillary Clinton as the first female presidential nominee" ("A Woman President," 2016, para. 2). These results suggest journalists and writers describe women candidates by their gender with regularity while almost never doing so for men.

News values are what scholars use to describe how the media determine what is news. Because news outlets are more likely to cover what is new and unusual over the common, mentioning the gender of women candidates may simply reflect news norms because women candidates are less common in public life than men.

However, such practices may have social implications. For example, noting the gender of women may imply that the gender of political candidates is relevant and cue stereotypes in readers. In fact, studies show that marking gender in news coverage has important consequences. For example, Dayhoff (1983) exposed subjects to mock newspaper articles about candidates for political office that either used gender neutral (e.g., "journalist") or gender marked (e.g., "lady journalist") language. Although Dayhoff's dated language would be unlikely to occur today (e.g., "gal" for "person"), the results were revealing. Subjects who read the gendered coverage of women running for a traditionally masculine office (Sheriff) evaluated women candidates more negatively than those in the neutral language condition. Lake Research Partners' study in 2010 yielded similar results. Half the subjects (all of which were likely voters) were shown a story in which the woman candidate was attacked in gendered terms (e.g., "ice queen" & "Stupid Girl"). The control group heard attacks but not gendered attacks (e.g., "tax and spend liberal" & "She refused to answer questions"). Lake Research Partners (2010) found that although voters began by supporting the hypothetical woman candidate, "sexist language damages her lead significantly more than standard attacks. The effect is pronounced with every demographic group" (p. 5). Miller and Peake (2013) analyzed newspaper content and collected national survey data during the 2008 general election campaign in which Sarah Palin was the Republican Party vice-presidential nominee. They found that "press mentions of Palin's gender dampened favorability toward her and assessments of her readiness to be president" (p. 497). Thus, a persistent pattern of marking or highlighting the gender of women candidates may reduce their favorability.

First woman or novelty frame

Reporters may also cue readers about the importance of gender for women candidates in the political sphere by framing women as firsts. Many women in addition to the most prominent ones listed in the introduction have mounted substantial presidential campaigns. These women have garnered substantive press coverage (e.g., Victoria Woodhull in 1872 and Belva Lockwood in 1884), gotten on the ballot in all 50 states (e.g., Lenora Fulani in 1988), and received Federal Primary Matching Funds (e.g., Sonya Johnson in 1984). Despite this long history of women running for the presidency, researchers have documented that women presidential candidates are often described as firsts even when they are not (known as the *first woman frame* or the *novelty frame*) (Falk, 2010; Heith, 2001; Heldman, Carroll, & Olson, 2005).

As the following examples demonstrate, the press has clung to, even though it must increasingly qualify, the *first* frame when describing women presidential candidates (emphasis added in all examples). Notwithstanding that Chase Smith's presidential run had at least two women predecessors, the *Bangor Daily News* incorrectly stated in 1963 that "Even in defeat she [Chase Smith] could take solace in that great accomplishment alone and also always be proud and happy that she had the distinction of having been the **first woman** in the country to bid for that office" (Arnold, 1963, p. 10). In 1972, the *Seattle Times* had to modify the frame with a reference to Chisholm's race to describe her as a first. "Representative Shirley Chisholm today became the **first black woman** to begin a serious bid for the presidency of the United States" ("Shirley Chisholm Declares," 1972, p. 2). This type of description fits a larger pattern in which reporters must increasingly qualify the *first* frame to maintain it, as can be seen even more clearly in 1988 when *The New York Times* described Pat Schroeder this way, "the **first woman** to seek to seek the Presidency since 1972" (Gailey, 1987, p. 33). This is a puzzling construction, considering the author here admits Schroeder was not setting any precedents. The next time a woman ran for president, *The New York Times* again qualified her candidacy by adding the word *really*, presumably because the women candidates that preceded Elizabeth Dole, were serious but not *really* serious. "It now seems likely that the **first woman** to become a really serious candidate for president of the United States will be Elizabeth Dole" (Collins, 1999, p. A24). Despite the fact that many women had run before Dole, she was portrayed as the first woman candidate in 15 percent of articles (Heith, 2001). "Almost half of the in-depth stories employed the "first woman" frame in writing about Elizabeth Dole" (Heldman et al., 2005, p. 325). Since nothing was novel about Clinton's campaign in 2008, to maintain the novelty frame, reporters had to speculate about how she might be a first (even though at the time she was not). This sentence from *The New York Times* is illustrative: "If successful, Mrs. Clinton, 59 would be the **first female** nominee of a major American political party . . ." (Healy & Zeleny, 2007, p. 1).

A search of the phrase "first woman" or "first female" within the same sentence as "Clinton" in the Lexis/Nexis database of US newspapers during the 2016 campaign yielded over 1,300 cases. A qualitative examination of just those in which Clinton was described as a first in the headline showed the majority qualified the description to make it true by referencing Clinton's actual nomination as in, "Clinton officially nominee: **First woman** to represent major party in US history" (Lucey, 2016, p. A1). Many examples of headlines, however, used less precise and arguably incorrect language in describing Clinton as a first. "Clinton steps into history as 1st woman White House nominee" (Pace & Lucey 2016, p. A1) and "Hillary Clinton makes history as **first female** presidential nominee" (Casteel, 2016, p. 4).

A Google search similarly indicated that Clinton was widely described (often incorrectly) as a first. A search for "Clinton and 'first woman' or 'first female' presidential candidate" yielded about 233,000 results. As above, some of these references qualified the claim to make it technically correct, while others were simply inaccurate. The first three links (from Wikipedia, *Mother Jones*, and *The Atlantic*) reflected many of the results that followed. "In 2016, Hillary Clinton became the **first female** presidential candidate nominated by a major party, namely the Democrats" ("List of Female," 2017, para. 3), "The moment Hillary Clinton became the **first female** presidential nominee in history" (West, 2016, headline), and "Hillary Clinton has become the **first-ever woman** nominated by a major party for the United States presidency" (Green, 2016, para 1). Clearly, 144 years after the first woman ran for president, describing women as a *first* remains a dominant construction.

The effects of the novelty frame are less clear. Describing women candidates as firsts may heighten gender role incongruence and thus may reinforce the notion that women are unnatural or "deviant" (Meeks, 2012, p. 178) in the public sphere. Heldman et al. (2005) argued precisely this in noting that during Elizabeth's Dole's 2000 run for the presidency, the frequent use of the first "first woman" frame "reinforced the idea that Dole was an anomaly rather than a serious contender for the presidency" (p. 325). Others have advanced the idea that the novelty construction could suggest that the candidate possesses a pioneering spirit and is attempting to overcome past discrimination; Meeks (2012) proposed that such framing could suggest an "historic quality to a woman's candidacy, describing her as a transformative figure" (p. 179). However, the articles that resulted from this search were not generally written in the context of describing or highlighting historical discrimination and proscriptions on women in the public sphere. Rather, in most of the newspaper stories that described Clinton as a first in the headline, the body of the article contained fairly typical political content (i.e., described the regular proceedings of the convention or provided political analysis). Thus, the use of the word "first" functioned to highlight how unusual Clinton was in the political sphere rather than focusing on her pioneering spirit or ability to break through extant prejudice.

Although further research is needed about the effect of such constructions on broad audiences, there is some evidence of positive effects on young women. Caughell (2016) found that describing a female state house representative running for governor as potentially "the first female governor" (p. 737) in the state's history increased women's perception of the candidate's favorability and was associated with greater intention to vote for her. She concluded that highlighting the historic nature of a woman candidate's campaign "may be disadvantageous in some instances, such as when candidates are trying to appeal to less educated or conservative voters," but that "such tactics may favorably sway other voters" (p. 740). Campbell and Wolbrecht (2006) also suggested potentially positive effects among select young women. They found that "when the press makes women politicians more visible by highlighting how unusual female politicians are, young girls find future political activity more attractive and possible" (p. 245).

Appearance

Analyses of how often journalists offer physical descriptions of men and women candidates for president not surprisingly find that women's appearance is more likely to be described than men's (Falk, 2010, 2012; Heldman et al., 2005; Valenzuela & Correa, 2009). For example, Miller, Peake, and Boulton (2010) found that newspaper articles during the 2008 Democratic primary mentioning Hillary Clinton were significantly more likely to report on her clothing and appearance than were those about Barack Obama. During the 2008 general election, newspaper articles mentioned Republican vice-presidential candidate Sarah Palin's appearance four times more often than when covering Democratic vice-presidential candidate Joe Biden (Miller & Peake, 2013). Other studies found evidence of disparities in the frequency of newspapers' mentions of women's and men's appearance in lower-tier races (Bystrom et al., 2004; Robertson et al., 2002).

I searched the Lexis/Nexis database of US newspapers for either "Clinton wore" or "Trump wore," finding 25 descriptions of Clinton's clothing and just six of Trump's. The data set was small enough that I could read each article to see if the reference was about the candidate's attire. The following were typical of the descriptions of Clinton's attire:

- "Hillary Clinton wore a white pantsuit when she made history" ("Women in White," 2016, p. 1D);
- "Gone is the big strand of costume pearls Mrs. Clinton wore at the second debate" (Friedman, 2016b, p. 5); and
- "Hillary Clinton wore pantsuits from the American label Ralph Lauren" (Safronova, 2016, p. 6).

Although Clinton's attire was mentioned more than four times as often as Trump's, the descriptive nature of the two candidates' outfits were similar, as these examples demonstrate: "Mr. Trump wore his usual dark suit with a white shirt and a red tie" (Gelles, 2016, p. 1) and "Trump wore a blazer, white dress shoes and a white ball cap" (Hohmann, 2015, p. A4). It is worth noting that in data drawn from Lexis/Nexis, these references were more likely to appear in fashion and celebrity pages than in hard news.

In January 2017, I conducted a Google search for "'Donald Trump wore' and election 2016" that yielded about 33,900 hits. The same search for Hillary Clinton yielded about 43,500. Thus, Clinton's attire had 28 percent more references than Trump's. Moreover, a qualitative look suggests these electronic search results depressed the actual differences in the frequency of reporting about appearance. In fact, most of the results from the electronic search about Trump were references to what *women* in Trump's life (daughter Ivanka or wife Melania) wore while campaigning with him or on his behalf. Reflecting the broader pattern, the headlines of the first four links in the Trump search focused on what women wore:

- "Melania Trump Celebrates Husband Donald Trump's Victory in $4,000 White Jumpsuit" (Walano, 2016);
- "Clinton wears the color purple for concession" (Irby, 2016);
- "Future First Lady Melania Trump Wore a $3,990 Jumpsuit on Election Night" (Tuck, 2016); and
- "In a political upset, Melania Trump wears white to her husband's victory rally" (Tschorn & Harper, 2016).

Other references further down on the search page did refer to Trump. Although a few stories referred to Trump's tie color, most of these references were not to his clothing but to his campaign paraphernalia (e.g., his "Make America Great Again" campaign hat). By contrast, the headlines on the search results from the first page for Clinton generally did focus on what she wore:

- "On Election Day, the Hillary Clinton White Suit Effect" (Friedman, 2016c);
- "Trump and Clinton's surprising debate attire" (Fears, 2016); and
- "Hillary Clinton Votes Wearing Ralph Lauren Pantsuit" (Feitelberg & Chabbott, 2016).

Some interesting nuances emerged in these online articles. For example, despite the headline, "This is why Hillary Clinton wore a $12,000 Armani jacket," Whitten's (2016) article argued that journalists tended to focus unfairly on the clothing of women while overlooking men in this regard. The author observed that the cost of Clinton's jacket was widely written about, while "Republican candidate Donald Trump has often been spotted in Brioni suits, which can cost a whopping $7,000 each, if not more," but this did not make news the way the cost of Clinton's clothing did (para. 9).

Despite the feminist context in which some of the references to Clinton's attire appeared, experiments on the effects of covering attire have shown that calling attention to women's appearance reduces perceptions of their competence (Heflick, Goldenberg, Cooper, & Puvia, 2011). Name It. Change It. exposed more than 1000 likely voters to one of four conditions that included a profile and news stories about a man and a woman running for office. The profiles included a neutral, positive, or negative description of the candidates' attire, or no descriptions at all. All three conditions that included information about the woman candidates' appearance were associated with less favorability toward that candidate. Moreover, women who were described physically were considered less effective and qualified. The study found no similar effects for men, though the authors noted that "in reality, men are not covered in a similar way on appearance" (Name It. Change It., 2010, p. 7). Heflick and Goldenberg's (2009) study of Republican vice-presidential candidate Sarah Palin found that when subjects were asked to focus on her appearance, those subjects reported lower perceptions of competence than subjects simply asked to focus on the person. Moreover, those focusing on appearance expressed "reduced intentions to vote for the McCain–Palin ticket" (p. 600). Similar effects were found when subjects were exposed to a Facebook thread that either included references to a woman candidate's attractiveness or did not. Compared to control group ratings, subjects in the appearance condition rated the candidate as less competent and serious (Funk & Coker, 2016).

Although my findings do not represent a comprehensive measure of how often the 2016 candidates' appearances were described, they offer a clear picture of disparity between coverage of the man and the woman candidate and therefore are consistent with longstanding documentation of how women's bodies and appearance are subject to greater attention than men's. These results thus may support feminist observations that Western culture treats women as objects of the male gaze. These findings are also important given research that suggests drawing attention to women candidates' clothing and appearance is likely to be associated with lower ratings of the candidate.

Amount of coverage

Studies show that women presidential candidates in the United States get less press coverage than do men. When I compared the coverage of nine women who ran for president between 1872 and 2008 to the coverage of the most equivalent men running the same races as judged by vote count or polling, I found that the press wrote more and longer stories about men compared with women. When these nine races were aggregated, approximately twice as many stories appeared about men and the articles were 12 percent longer (2010, 2012).

These over-time findings are consistent with studies focusing only on more recent campaigns. Heldman et al.'s (2005) study of press coverage of the Republican nomination for president in 1999 found that, although public opinion polls showed Elizabeth Dole running ahead of John McCain throughout the period of the analysis, Dole was covered less frequently than McCain. Not only was McCain mentioned more frequently in news stories, but he got substantive coverage in twice as many articles as did Dole. The newspapers also featured him near the top of an article with greater frequency and were more likely to run stories about him than her on the front page. Similarly, the Pew Research Center (2008) found that Obama received more press coverage than Clinton in 11 of 17 weeks of the Democratic primary; Clinton got more coverage in four of those weeks. During June 2008 a Pew survey showed that 54 percent of respondents named Obama as the candidate they had heard most about, while 27 percent named Clinton (Pew Research Center, 2008, p. 3).

Reporters in other counties are also more likely to cover political men than women. Sampert and Trimble (2003) examined English language newspaper headlines about Canada's 2003 federal election between the New Democratic Party (NDP), led by a woman, and the opposition Conservative Party, led by a man. Although the Conservative Party held fewer seats when the parliament was dissolved, news outlets published more stories about the man and his party than they did about the woman and her party. Schonker-Schreck (2004) compared press coverage of candidates running in the Labor and Likud party primaries in Israel in 1996. She found that the press wrote five times as many stories about the men candidates as about the women candidates. Finally, in a study of English language news coverage of sitting heads of state (not candidates) from ten countries across the globe, Norris (1997) found that women leaders were covered in slightly fewer stories than men (an average of 3.8 compared with 4.4 stories daily).

In the 2016 presidential campaign, US newspapers in the Lexis/Nexis database ran over 15,500 stories that headlined with Trump and just over 6,000 headlined with Clinton. Thus, without saying anything about the valence of the coverage, for everyone story that headlined with Clinton, 2.5 were headlined with Trump, a pattern consistent with past elections in which the volume of news coverage tilts in favor of men over women.

Depressed coverage of women may perpetuate the sluggish entrance of women into the political sphere. Studies indicate a role modeling effect for exposure to political women; awareness of political women inspires greater political interest and involvement among other women (e.g., Atkeson, 2003; Campbell & Wolbrecht, 2006). Thus, the diminished coverage of women compared with men suggests that reporters' unconscious bias may unwittingly perpetuate extant stereotypes and under-representation of women by failing to fully reflect the presence of women in the political sphere.

Discussion

Long-standing and multi-study evidence documents that men and women who run for president are treated differently. Reporters are more likely to describe women as being gendered and more likely to describe their appearance than when writing about men candidates. Reporters are overall less likely to cover women than men who are running for president. A smaller but growing body of research suggests how such disparities may affect the public. The extant evidence indicates that when voters read about a woman candidate's gender and appearance it will reduce her favorability, and less press exposure for women candidates for president may make them less visible both as contenders for office and as role models for other women.

Given the dramatic changes in women's roles in society over the last century, why would disparities in the media coverage of men and women candidates persist? One answer may be that stereotypes remain a more prominent component of contemporary knowledge structures than one might expect. In fact, research shows that despite women's gradual move from the private into the public sphere, many people continue to associate women with traits related to domestic roles and men with traits linked to political roles. Sandra Bem (1987) conducted the seminal study documenting this phenomenon in the modern era. She found that subjects asked to choose traits that were desirable in men mentioned ones traditionally related to leadership and politics (e.g., leader, aggressive, ambitious, forceful). The list of attributes described as desirable in women meanwhile included traits more associated with the domestic sphere (compassionate, childlike, yielding, soft-spoken).

Prentice and Carranza's 2002 review of 15 years of literature since Bem found that the stereotypes Bem had documented persisted. They concluded that "the intensified prescriptions and proscriptions for women reflect traditional emphases on interpersonal sensitivity, niceness, modesty, and sociability, whereas the intensified prescriptions and proscriptions for men reflected traditional emphasis on strength, drive, assertiveness, and self-reliance" (Prentice & Carranza, 2002, p. 275).

In addition to identifying the ways in which trait stereotypes affect modern thinking, feminist theory has long argued that men in Western culture are conceptualized as subjects and actors while women are objects and "others" (Beauvoir, 1952). One outcome of objectifying women—treating them as bodies valued predominantly for their use to others—is that "in Western cultures, women's, but not men's, physical appearance is a primary basis of their worth" (Heflick et al., 2011, p. 572). Schema theory can help explain why latent trait stereotypes combined with the objectification of women and emphasis on women's appearance could result in unequal press coverage. Schema theory says that ideas are represented in memory as nodes (or units) with relations among the concepts as pathways or connections between nodes. Thus, whenever part of the memory network is used or activated the associative pathways are also triggered, making related concepts easier to retrieve. Knowledge schemas refer to related words and ideas stored in memory and connected through networks, with access to certain ideas activated and facilitated by others related to them. Cappella and Jamieson (1997) explain:

> Initial learning and later retrieval are related to the activation of information stored in memory. This activation in turn depends on the external cues semantically related to stored information. . . . The more frequently concepts and their associations are activated, the more well learned [they become] and easier it is to retrieve them later.
>
> *(p. 115)*

Characteristics related to stereotypes are more quickly retrieved than non-related characteristics (e.g., Banaji & Curtis, 1996; Kunda & Spencer, 2003). This process explains why schemas about gender may lead to stereotypical coverage even without a person's conscious intent. "Gender roles are automatically activated by gender-related cues in virtually all situations, [and] the high accessibility of expectations based on gender likely maintains their impact" (Eagly & Karau, 2002, p. 575). Thus, reporters, like all others, should find ideas informed by stereotypes easily accessible and this in turn should affect the news gathering and writing process (Major & Coleman, 2008).

For example, since US women are more likely than men to be judged by and associated with their appearance, appearance will be more accessible and easily recalled when the idea of a *woman* is activated. Thus, it follows that reporters are more likely to assume a physical description to be relevant, important, or salient when covering women candidates. Similarly, if society associates men with concepts related to the public sphere and subjectivity (action, leading, politics), when reporters write about men candidates they may be more likely to think of politically pertinent material such as policy positions that may yield more overall news coverage.

This theory can also explain other patterns of gendered reporting. If society associates women with domestic and family responsibility one would expect, as Heldman (2007) found, that "women face more questions about their family responsibilities on the campaign trail than men and that voters are concerned that female candidates will neglect their families if they gain public office" (p. 27). Moreover, a *first woman* frame might appear regularly in reports about women candidates because it seems consonant with our unconscious associations of women with domesticity, if not with actual history. In other words, existing cognitive schemata

358 Erika Falk

about men and women are likely to affect how journalists collect, select, and write the news.

In fact, press secretaries of women members of Congress believe the news media regularly frames and covers women politicians qua women. Specifically, press secretaries of women politicians believe that those women are "viewed by the media as a woman representative, rather than as a representative who happens to be a woman" (Niven & Zilber, 2001, p. 160). In contrast, the press secretaries of men, although finding many problems with press coverage, did not identify stereotyping as a problem. Conceptualizing press bias in the context of how ideas in memory are built, stored, and activated through cognitive schemas helps explain why the press continues to mark gender in women, frame them as novelties in the political sphere, write less about them, and describe what they wear. Moreover, quick or dramatic changes to these trends are unlikely. Only when society begins to see women politicians as actors (i.e., not objects and mothers) will the stereotypes influencing reporters and their readership be diminished.

On November 5, 2015, late-night comedian Jimmy Kimmel interviewed young elementary school boys about their thoughts on women in leadership positions. Though intended for comedic effect, the interview left little doubt that traditional sex roles remained firmly embedded in modern thought and culture. One boy said, "I think women are not presidents." The second agreed, justifying the sentiment, "They are too girly. . . . They make girl rules . . . like free makeup in the world." At this, the first elaborated, "They will probably decorate the White House. . . . They might even paint it pink." When asked if women can do anything men can do, the boys responded, "No." One child explained, "They are too weak" (Jimmy Kimmel Live, 2015). The interview showed children born after 2000 still articulating a view of women clearly informed by, if not wholly built on, cognitive structures based in traditional sex roles and stereotypes. Press depictions of women candidates for heads of state remain remarkably influenced by nineteenth-century ideas of womanhood. Despite successive waves of feminism and remarkable change in the participation of women in the public sphere over the last 100 years, the data from the 2016 US presidential campaign suggest that unconscious thoughts and cognitive structures based in traditional sex roles and sex stereotypes remain a part of the collective thinking.

References

Arnold, L. (1963, November 16). Maine's political whirl: Vote boost for Republicans seen behind V-P move by Mrs. Smith. *Bangor Daily News*, p. 10.
Atkeson, L. R. (2003). Not all cues are created equal: The conditional impact of female candidates on political engagement. *The Journal of Politics*, 65(4), 1040–1061.
Banaji, M., & Hardin, C. D. (1996). Automatic stereotyping. *Psychological Science*, 7(3), 135–141.
Banwart, M. C., Bystrom, D. G., & Robertson, T. (2003). From the primary to the general election: A comparative analysis of candidate media coverage in mixed-gender 2000 races for governor and U.S. senate. *American Behavioral Scientist*, 46(5), 658–676.

Beauvoir, S. (1952). *The second sex: The classic manifesto of the liberated woman*. New York, NY: Random House.

Bem, S. (1987). Probing the promise of androgyny. In M. R. Walsh (Ed.), *The psychology of women* (pp. 206–225). New Haven, CT: Yale University.

Bystrom, D. G., Banwart, M. C., Kaid, L. L., & Robertson, T. A. (2004). *Gender and candidate communication*. New York, NY: Routledge.

Bystrom, D. G., Robertson, T. A., & Banwart, M. C. (2001). Framing the fight: An analysis of media coverage of female and male candidates in primary races for governor and U.S. senate in 2000. *American Behavioral Scientist, 44*(12), 1999–2013.

Campbell, D., & Wolbrecht, C. (2006). See Jane Run: Women politicians as role models for adolescents. *The Journal of Politics, 68*(2), 233–247.

Cappella, J., & Jamieson, K. H. (1997). *Spiral of cynicism: The press and the public good*. Oxford: Oxford University Press.

Casteel, C. (2016, July 26). Hillary Clinton makes history as first female presidential nominee. *The Daily Oklahoman*, p. 4.

Caughell, L. (2016). When playing the woman card is playing Trump: Assessing the efficacy of framing campaigns as historic. *PS: Political Science & Politics, 49*(4), 736–742.

Collins, G. (1999, February 10). Mrs. Dole takes a leap into the gender gap. *The New York Times*, p. A24.

Dayhoff, S. (1983). Sexist language and person perception: Evaluation of candidates from newspaper articles. *Sex Roles, 9*(4), 527–539.

Eagly, A. H., & Karau, S. J. (2002). Role congruity theory of prejudice toward female leaders. *Psychological Review, 109*(3), 573–598.

Falk, E. (2010). *Women for president: Media bias in nine campaigns* (2nd ed.). Champaign, IL: University of Illinois Press.

Falk, E. (2012). Unnatural, incompetent, and unviable: Press portrayals of women candidates for president. *Michigan State Law Review, 5*, 1671–1684.

Fears, D. (2016, September 26). Trump and Clinton's surprising debate attire. *The New York Post*. Retrieved from http://nypost.com/2016/09/26/trump-and-clintons-surprising-debate-attire/

Feitelberg, R., & Chabbott, S. (2016, November 8). Hillary Clinton votes wearing Ralph Lauren Pantsuit. *Women's Wear Daily*. Retrieved from http://wwd.com/fashion-news/fashion-scoops/hillary-clinton-election-day-pantsuit-ralph-lauren-10701266/

Friedman, V. (2016a, January 8). Rubio's boots are made for gawking. *The New York Times*, p. 15.

Friedman, V. (2016b, January 21). It's not about her clothes. *The New York Times*, p. 5.

Friedman, V. (2016c, November 7). On election day, the Hillary Clinton white suit effect. *The New York Times*. Retrieved from www.nytimes.com/2016/11/07/fashion/hillary-clinton-suffragists-white-clothing.html?_r=0

Funk, M., & Coke, C. R. (2016). She's hot, for a politician: The impact of objectifying commentary on perceived credibility of female candidates. *Communication Studies, 67*(4), 455–473.

Gailey, P. (1987, June 6). Schroeder considers running for president. *The New York Times*, p. 33.

Gelles, D. (2016, October 16). He believes in climate change and in Trump. *The New York Times*, p. 1.

Green, E. (2016, July 26). "We are preparing to shatter the highest glass ceiling in our country": The women who cheered Hillary Clinton into her official nomination showed why this moment in American history is so important—and fragile. *The Atlantic*. Retrieved from www.theatlantic.com/politics/archive/2016/07/hillary-clinton-first-female-presidential-nominee/493163/

Healy, P., & Zeleny, J. (2007, January 21). Clinton enters '08 field, fueling race for money. *The New York Times*, p. 1.

Heflick, N., & Goldenberg, J. (2009). Objectifying Sarah Palin: Evidence that objectification causes women to be perceived as less competent and less fully human. *Journal of Experimental Social Psychology*, *45*(3), 598–560.

Heflick, N., Goldenberg, J., Cooper, D., & Puvia, E. (2011). From women to objects: Appearance focus, target gender, and perceptions of warmth, morality and competence. *Journal of Experimental Social Psychology*, *47*, 572–581.

Heith, D. (2001). Footwear, lipstick, and an orthodox sabbath: Media coverage of nontraditional candidates. *White House Studies*, *1*(3), 335–347.

Heldman, C. (2007). Cultural barriers to a female president in the United States. In L. C. Han & C. Heldman (Eds.), *Rethinking madam president: Are we ready for a woman in the white house?* (pp. 17–42). Boulder, CO: Lynne Rienner.

Heldman, C., Carroll, S. J., & Olson, S. (2005). She brought only a skirt: Print media coverage of Elizabeth Dole's bid for the Republican presidential nomination. *Political Communication*, *22*(3), 315–335.

Hohmann, J. (2015, July 24). Trump goes to the border, says Hispanics "Love" him. *The Washington Post*, p. A4.

Irby, K. (2016, November 9). Clinton wears the color purple for concession. *McClatchy*. Retrieved from www.mcclatchydc.com/news/politics-government/election/article 113652699.html

Jimmy Kimmel Live. (2015, November 5). *Hillary Clinton, Bob Odenkirk and David Cross*. Television Series Episode. Hollywood, CA: ABC.

Kunda, Z., & Spencer, S. (2003). When do stereotypes come to mind and when do they color judgment? A goal-based theoretical framework for stereotype activation and application. *Psychological Bulletin*, *129*(4), 522–544.

Lake Research Partners. (2010). Simulation of the impact of sexism in campaigns. *Name it: Change it*. Washington, DC. Retrieved from www.lakeresearch.com/news/NameIt ChangeIt/NameItChangeIt.pres.pdf

List of female United States presidential and vice-presidential candidates. (2017). *Wikipedia*. Retrieved from https://en.wikipedia.org/wiki/List_of_female_United_States_presidential_and_vice-presidential_candidates

Lucey, H. (2016, July 27). Democratic national convention; Clinton officially nominee; First woman to represent major party in US history. *Charleston Gazette-Mail*, p. A1.

Major, L. H., & Coleman, R. (2008). The intersection of race and gender in election coverage: What happens when the candidates don't fit the stereotypes? *The Howard Journal of Communication*, *19*(4), 315–333.

Meeks, L. (2012). Is she "man enough"? Women candidates, executive political offices, and news coverage. *Journal of Communication*, *62*, 175–193.

Miller, M., & Peake, J. J. (2013). Press effects, public opinion, and gender: Coverage of Sarah Palin's vice-presidential campaign. *The International Journal of Press/Politics*, *18*(4), 482–507.

Miller, M., Peake, J. J., & Boulton, B. A. (2010). Testing the *Saturday Night Live* hypothesis: Fairness and bias in newspaper coverage of Hillary Clinton's presidential campaign. *Politics & Gender*, *6*, 169–198.

Name It: Change It. (2010). *Examination of the effect of media coverage of women candidates' appearance*. Washington, DC. Retrieved from www.nameitchangeit.org/page/-/Name-It-Change-It-Appearance-Research.pdf

Niven, D., & Zilber, J. (2001). How does she have time for kids and congress? Views on gender and media coverage from house offices. *Women & Politics, 23,* 147–165.

Norris, P. (1997). Women leaders worldwide: A splash of color in the photo op. In P. Norris (Ed.), *Women, media, and politics* (pp. 149–165). Oxford: Oxford University Press.

Pace, J., & Lucey, C. (2016, July 27). Clinton steps into history as 1st woman White House nominee. *St. Louis Post-Dispatch,* p. A1.

Page, S. (2016, June 6). Why are you yelling: Women still face a political double standard; Clinton at cusp of history, but obstacles remain on landscape. *USA Today,* p. 1A.

Pew Research Center. (2008). *Many say coverage biased in favor of Obama.* Washington, DC. Retrieved from www.people-press.org/2008/06/05/many-say-coverage-is-biased-in-favor-of-obama/

Prentice, D., & Carranza, E. (2002). What women and men should be, shouldn't be, are allowed to be, and don't have to be: The content of prescriptive gender stereotypes. *Psychology of Women Quarterly, 25,* 269–281.

Robertson, T., Conley, A., Szymczynska, K., & Thompson, A. (2002). Gender and the media: An investigation of gender, media, and politics in the 2000 election. *The New Jersey Journal of Communication, 10*(1), 104–117.

Rubin, T. (2016, July 15). Worldview: Time for a woman to Lead U.N. *The Philadelphia Inquirer,* p. A18.

Safronova, V. (2016, October 7). The Trump suit, mystery solved. *The New York Times,* p. 6.

Sampert, S., & Trimble, L. (2003). "Wham, bam, no thank you ma'am": Gender and the frame game in national newspaper coverage of the election 2000. In M. Trembley & L. Trimble (Eds.), *Women and electoral politics in Canada* (pp. 211–226). Oxford: Oxford University Press.

Schonker-Schreck, D. (2004). Political marketing and the media: Women in the 1996 Israeli elections—A case study. *Israeli Affairs, 10*(3), 159–177.

Sheehy, K. (2016, June 8). One giant leap for womankind! *The New York Post,* p. 8.

Shirley Chisholm declares her candidacy for president. (1972, January 25). *Seattle Times,* p. 2.

Sulek, J. P. (2015, September 14). Republican debate: How will Carly Fiorina handle Donald Trump? *Whittier Daily News,* n.p.

Trump's furious descent: Rage takes over the GOP's presidential candidate. (2016, October 10). *New York Daily News,* p. 24.

Tschorn, A., & Harper, M. (2016, November 9). In a political upset, Melania Trump wears white to husband's victory rally. *Los Angeles Times.* Retrieved from www.latimes.com/fashion/la-ig-election-night-style-20161108-story.html

Tuck, L. (2016, November 9). Future first lady Melania Trump wore a $3,990 jumpsuit on election night. *Yahoo Style.* Retrieved from www.yahoo.com/style/melania-trump-wore-a-3990-jumpsuit-on-election-night-082244871.html

Valenzuela, S., & Correa, T. (2009). Press coverage and public opinion on women candidates: The case of Chile's Michelle Bachelet. *The International Communication Gazette, 71*(3), 203–223.

Walano, R. (2016, November 9). Melania Trump celebrates husband Donald Trump's victory in $4,000 white jumpsuit. *US Magazine.* Retrieved from www.usmagazine.com/stylish/news/melania-trump-wears-white-jumpsuit-on-election-night-photos-w449484

West, J. (2016, July 26). The moment Hillary Clinton became the first female presidential nominee in history. *Mother Jones.* Retrieved from www.motherjones.com/politics/2016/07/hillary-clinton-nominated-official-democrat-president-dnc

Whitten, S. (2016, July 9). This is why Hillary Clinton wore a $12,000 Armani jacket. *CNBC*. Retrieved from www.cnbc.com/2016/06/09/this-is-why-hillary-clinton-wore-a-12000-armani-jacket.html

A woman president. (2016). *Center for women and politics*. Rutgers, NJ. Retrieved from http:// presidentialgenderwatch.org/polls/a-woman-president

Women in white: Did Hillary and Melania borrow a page from Jackie Kennedy's style book? (2016, August 2). *Palm Beach Post*, p. 1D.

24

CONCEPTUALIZING MASCULINITY AND FEMININITY IN THE BRITISH PRESS

Paul Baker and Helen Baker

This chapter examines what is popularly meant by the term *masculinity*, what representational patterns the word occurs in, and what this can tell us about societal understandings around its past, present, and future. In order to achieve these aims, we have taken into account all of the uses of the word *masculinity* in a very large body of text, namely every article that mentions the term in a selection of British national newspapers published throughout a decade in the early twenty-first century.

We focus on press language because newspapers are a powerful (Fairclough, 1995) form of mass media that are socially constitutive "through shaping understandings, influencing audience attitudes and beliefs (particularly through their reinforcement), and transforming the consciousness of those who read and consume it" (Richardson, 2007, p. 29). They are thus a good "site" for making sense of popular discourses in societies. As Brescoll and LaFrance (2004) have shown, readers tend to accept newspaper explanations about sex differences as scientifically valid, as opposed to reflecting the political perspective of a newspaper. The press offers representations of social phenomena, and as Gerbner, Cross, Morgan, and Signorielli (1986) work on "cultivation theory" indicated, media have long-term effects on audiences that compound over time due to the repetition of images and concepts. It is this aspect of repetition that we are especially interested in, because repeated use of language helps to construct and solidify particular understandings of masculinity as "received wisdom."

We will demonstrate how journalists afford masculinity with a privileged status in relationship to femininity. This is not a matter just of the frequency with which it is mentioned, but the ways in which it is referred to, particularly in terms of how journalists think it can be achieved and its impact on societies. While newspapers do not necessarily paint masculinity as necessarily good or positive, we also show that they do imbue it with a notion of power, which implies that it requires consideration and attention.

After outlining relevant literature on journalism, gender, and the corpus linguistics approach, we describe how we collected our two corpora of newspaper articles and outline our techniques of analysis. We then describe our findings and discuss the implications of our research. We end by offering some caveats relating to the level of generalizability we can make.

Gender research in the press and corpus linguistics

A wide range of qualitative and quantitative methods of analysis has been used to study journalists' ability to both reflect and influence perceptions about gender. Researchers have considered content (e.g., topic), language (e.g., those which look at features like evaluation or grammatical agency) or more multimodal approaches (which consider the interaction between written text and images).

Many studies have highlighted how newspapers advantage men and masculinity in various ways. For example, studying British coverage of the 2000 Wimbledon tennis championships, Vincent (2004) found that the athletic achievements of female players tended to be under-valued in favor of trivialized or sexualized representations, whereas the (mostly male) journalists tended to display reverence for male players' athleticism. Examining articles about men and dieting, Gough (2007) found gender difference was constructed through a filter of hegemonic masculinity: Dieting was framed as woman-centred, and cooking seen as traditionally feminine and for other people's pleasure. Men's cooking was presented as a more solitary, selfish activity, with men's food seen as "fuel" and male knowledge about food viewed as lacking, with the exception of celebrity male chefs. Gannon, Glover, and Abel (2004) also found articles about male experience of infertility, drawing on hegemonic masculinity through the use of stereotypically masculine analogies with warfare and mechanics (e.g., healthy sperm being described as possessing a "turbo charge" or equating the act of impregnation with a military campaign). Analysis of reporting on a 37-year-old UK man who, only days after being released from prison, shot three people, including his ex-girlfriend, found that journalists utilized conservative, traditional models of masculinity as a way of explaining his crimes, rather than engaging in objective reporting (Ellis, Sloan, & Wykes, 2012).

The above studies adopted methods of discourse analysis or content analysis, identifying representations by carrying out a close reading. This approach is viable for a relatively small number of articles. The present study examines references to the term masculinity in the British press across a very wide range of articles (over 5 million words), so we supplement the discourse analysis approach by using techniques from corpus linguistics (McEnery & Hardie, 2012)—a form of language analysis that uses computational techniques to identify frequent and salient linguistic patterns. Once identified, these patterns must be qualitatively interrogated by human analysts, who employ close reading and categorization of concordance data, as well as considering social context in order to explain their findings.

In examining the word *masculinity* in this way, we also decided to consider what it is not. Therefore, we concurrently carried out a matched analysis of the word *femininity*, building a second corpus of articles using the same source and time frame. While our primary focus is masculinity, it can be useful to consider the concept in relation to representations of femininity, particularly in terms of which representations are commonly shared between the two and which are more frequently characterized by one or the other. Our study builds on a small but growing body of research that uses corpus linguistics techniques to examine aspects of language and gender. For example, Pearce (2008) used the British National Corpus (containing 100 million words of general British English, mainly from the 1990s) to examine language patterns in which the word forms MAN and WOMAN most frequently occurred. He looked at verb collocates (verbs which tended to co-occur frequently near or next to MAN and WOMAN), categorizing those which positioned MAN/WOMAN as the grammatical subject or object. MAN collocated as the agent or "doer" of verbs like *chase, climb, jump, leap, march, haul, race,* and *stomp,* indicating male propensity for physical action, but MAN was also the object of verbs like *accuse, arrest, convict, hang,* and *jail,* which positioned men as more likely to be viewed as criminals. WOMAN was the agent of verbs that implied emotional intemperance: *berate, nag,* and *wail,* while being the object of verbs that positioned women as sexual conquests: *bed, date, ravish, sexualize,* and *shag.*

Taylor (2013) used corpora of British broadsheets to examine the terms *boy, girl,* and related words. She demonstrated that *girl* shared many of the same collocates with the word *woman,* whereas this was not the case for *man* and *boy.* Her analysis thus indicates that *girl* and *woman* are more likely to be perceived as synonymous identities. Baker and Levon (2015, 2016) examined collocates in the British press of terms relating to six different types of racial and class-based masculinity, such as *black man* and *working-class man,* finding that different sets of collocates were positioned in relation to one another within a broader ideological field of gender and power.

The study reported on here expands on previous work by also focusing on representations within newspapers. However, unlike the research described above, which examined concrete concepts like *man* and *girl,* we consider representations relating to the more abstract concepts of *masculinity* and *femininity,* which tend to be strongly (although not always) seen as a collective set of gendered qualities relating to men and women respectively.

A corpus analysis is often approached from a theory-neutral perspective, first allowing for linguistic patterns to emerge that then can be interpreted and explained through the incorporation, combination, or creation of new or existing theories. For this research we found that Connell's (1995) theory of hegemonic masculinity was useful in terms of helping to explain the patterns we found. Put briefly, the theory conceptualizes masculinity as hierarchical, multiple, and variable, relating to dominance and gendered power relations that are sustained through a series of cultural dynamics, encompassing large numbers of people in society. Important aspects of the theory involve the concept of hegemonic masculinity itself (as a powerful, somewhat idealized, and non-normative state of masculinity); the subordination (or dominance) of some forms of masculinity (such as gay masculinity) over others; the marginalization (or social exclusion) of other forms (such as black masculinity); and the concept of complicity, which involves the majority of people having a vested interest in maintaining the gender relations hierarchy, due to the smaller amounts of power awarded to those who exist at lower rungs. To some extent all men benefit from the patriarchal dividend, and women can also be complicit in helping to prop up the system.

Method

The articles were collected from nine daily national British newspapers and their Sunday equivalents: *The Daily Telegraph, The Guardian, The Independent, The Times, The Sun, The Mirror, The Daily Mail, The Daily Star*, and *The Express* from January 1, 2007 to December 31, 2016.

The masculinity corpus contained 5,627,655 words. The femininity corpus contained 4,244,634 words. There were 5871 occurrences of the word *masculinity* and 4347 of *femininity*, suggesting that to an extent the British press places more focus on the former concept. Our analysis involves a survey of collocates of the words *masculinity* and *femininity*. In order to obtain a wide-ranging picture and comparison of the most common ways that these concepts are represented, we focus on three collocational relationships or patterns that were found to be productive in terms of giving access to representations. To ensure broad coverage, each pattern involved a different part of speech, and was thus based around the most frequent adjective, verb and noun patterns respectively.

These patterns are:

1   Adjective + *masculinity/femininity*

This sequence involves cases where the target word comes directly after an adjective (e.g., *toxic masculinity*). These adjective modifications directly reveal how masculinity or femininity is characterized.

2   Verb + Possessive Pronoun + *masculinity/femininity*

This pattern indicates processes around masculinity and femininity (e.g., *use her femininity*), answering the question regarding what actions people carry out with their masculinity or femininity.

3   Noun + *of* + masculinity/femininity

The most frequent collocate of both *masculinity* and *femininity* is the word *of*, most often occurring one place directly to the left of these words. In almost all cases, *of masculinity/femininity* occurs after a noun (although there are a handful of verb cases like *think of masculinity*). The noun pattern can indicate genitive structures that show masculinity or femininity as possessing a particular quality or state, e.g., *crisis of masculinity* indicates that masculinity is represented as in or undergoing a crisis. However, this grammatical pattern can also indicate nominalized verb processes where the agent is obscured (e.g., the term *celebration of masculinity* could be reworded as *[unnamed subject] celebrated masculinity*).

For each of these patterns we identified the corresponding adjectives, verbs, and nouns and then placed these words into categories or themes. This categorization was a bottom-up process; it developed as the analysis progressed. Often, concordances of the collocational patterns had to be examined in order to make accurate categorizations. We counted the number of cases in each category and compared the frequencies of the different categories for masculinity and femininity to ascertain typical and atypical representations. However, as the overall frequencies of *masculinity* and *femininity* are different, we have also represented the frequencies as percentages in order to make cross-comparisons easier. For example, adjectives relating to the concept "Modern" occur before masculinity in 164 cases. As there are 5871 cases of masculinity in the corpus in total (164 / 5871) ⋆ 100 gives 2.79 percent of cases where the word *masculinity* occurs after a "Modern" type of adjective. The equivalent percentage for femininity is 1.82 percent.

Our analysis below focuses on the most frequent categories for each pattern. We have taken all categories where the combined frequency of words in the categories equals at least 10 for either *masculinity* or *femininity*. This resulted in 17 categories for the adjective pattern, 5 categories for the verb pattern and 15 for the noun pattern. These collocational patterns were explored via concordance analysis, which examined all the instances of the patterns within the contexts in which they occurred, to garner a sense of what the collocational patterns were used to achieve. Examples from articles are given in the analysis below in order to illustrate some of the most typical patterns.

Analysis

Adjective + masculinity/femininity

Table 24.1 shows the immediate left hand adjectival collocates of the terms *masculinity* and *femininity*. Numbers in brackets after each word indicate their frequency, while raw and percentage frequencies are given for the groups of words that have similar meanings and have been placed into categories.

Table 24.1 shows that both masculinity and femininity are likely to often be represented in terms of adjectives that attempt to position them in terms of a traditional-modern distinction (the first two rows of the table). This dominant construction suggests that both expressions of gender are seen as having (recently) changed, with the traditional forms of masculinity and femininity represented as problematic and threatened:

> Men's Rights Activists have called for a boycott of Mad Max: Fury Road, describing it as 'feminist propaganda' and bemoaning liberal Hollywood's attempt to undermine **traditional masculinity**.
>
> *(The Independent, May 14, 2015)*

TABLE 24.1 Adjective collocates of *masculinity* and *femininity*

Category	ADJECTIVES of masculinity	Total	ADJECTIVES of femininity	Total
Modern	modern (127), contemporary (33), fresh (3), alternative (1)	164 2.79%	modern (39), new (21), contemporary (17), different (1), fresh (1)	79 1.82%
Old fashioned	traditional (40), raw (21), unreconstructed (18), conventional (9), old fashioned (9), old-school (9), macho (7), primal (6), typical (6), essential (4), primitive (4), classical (3), laddish (3), classic (2), outdated (1), stereotypical (1)	142 2.42%	traditional (29), conventional (12), old fashioned (8), timeless (6), old-school (5), retro (5), Victorian (4), classic (3), archetypal (3), 1950s (2), outdated (2), retrograde (2), stereotypical (2), early (1)	84 1.93%
Weak or threatened	fragile (26), anxious (22), threatened (18), damaged (10), flawed (10), lost (7), diminished (6), beleaguered (5), confused (4), overwrought (4), thwarted (4), tortured (4), troubling (4), doomed (3), bruised (2), sterile (2), troubled (2), warped (2), weak (2), wounded (2), vulnerable (1)	140 2.38%	fragile (3), restrictive (3), fractured (2), rejected (2), broken (1), lost (1)	12 0.27%
Extreme	hyper (76), extreme (26), overt (10), unbridled (8), uber (5), exaggerated (3), cartoonish (2), ultra (2), inherent (1), theatrical (1), ultimate (1)	135 2.30%	hyper (16), exaggerated (12), overt (5), ultra (5), enhanced (3), heightened (3), idealized (3), flamboyant (3), cartoon (2), burgeoning (2), extreme (2), intense (2), obvious (2), unapologetic (2), brazen (2), dramatic (1), sheer (1), ultimate (1)	67 1.54%
Nationality	American (56), British (31), Australian (11), English (10), French (4), Scottish (4), Japanese (3), Italian (2), Western (2), Irish (1)	124 2.11%	French (15), Gallic (3), Italian (3), English (2), Western (2), American (1)	26 0.60%
Bad	toxic (116), dark (2), evil (2), narrow (1), pathetic (1), sinister (1)	123 2.09%	dangerous (9)	9 0.02%
Powerful	rugged (35), hegemonic (25), red-blooded (7), alpha (6), muscular (6), stoic (4), confident (4), imposing (3), robust (3), tough (3), masterful (2), strong (2), strutting (1), big (1), powerful (1), pumped (1), showy (1), stony (1), sweating (1), thrilling (1), toned (1)	108 1.84%	strong (5), tough (4), fierce (3), powerful (3), bold (1), confident (1), empowering (1), fearless (1)	19 0.44%

Category	Descriptors	n	%	Descriptors	n	%
Aggressive	aggressive (13), brooding (11), violent (8), rampant (6), inarticulate (5), brutal (4), rough (4), uncompromising (4), gruff (3), hard (3), smoldering (3), beery (3), beer-slurping (1), threatening (1), pugnacious (1), rampaging (1), shouty (1), brutish (1)	85	1.45%	aggressive (3)	3	0.07%
Ethnicity	black (50), white (12)	62	1.06%	black (6), white (1)	7	0.16%
Good	positive (9), heroic (7), successful (5), healthy (3), great (2), ideal (2), attractive (1)	29	0.49%	ideal (4), cool (2), fabulous (2), good (1), intelligent (1), perfect (1)	11	0.25%
Soft	tender (3), fluid (2)	5	0.09%	soft (12), delicate (6), frothy (5), passive (4), sweet (4), demure (3), gentle (3), dainty (2), chocolate-box (2), fun (1)	42	0.97%
Authentic	true (8), real (6), authentic (4), natural (2), pure (2), serious (3)	25	0.43%	natural (7), pure (7), true (7), inherent (4), real (4), easy (2)	31	0.71%
Sexualized		0	0%	elegant (5), flirty (4), exquisite (3), romantic (3), sexy (3), chic (2), dreamy (2), glamorous (2), pretty (2), breathy (2), sexual (1), voluptuous (1)	30	0.69%
Age	teenage (3), aging (2)	5	0.09%	youthful (14), girlish (2), girly (1)	17	0.39%
Not real	false (2)	2	0.03%	fake (6), supposed (3), fantasy (2), plastic (2), faux (2)	15	0.34%
Sexuality	heterosexual (11), gay (4), straight (4)	19	0.32%		0	

It could be that female audiences are reacting to an era in which **traditional masculinity** has left a sinking economy, the possibility of environmental catastrophe and violent conflicts in the Middle East and beyond, by yearning for a softer and nurturing hero.

(The Observer, June 28, 2009)

Some of the words in the traditional category suggest an understanding of these older forms of masculinity as less advanced than the modern ones, e.g., *primal* and *primitive*, while others imply negative evaluations like *outdated*, *retrograde*, and *stereotypical*. Not all of these adjectives are negative though—for example *classic*, *classical*, *old-school*, and *timeless* suggest a framing of "older" forms of gender as having value and being worth preserving, although a closer look at concordance lines indicates that about half the cases of such words also involve negative evaluations, e.g., *classical masculinity* is described as objectifying others while *old-school masculinity* is called redundant and brutal.

However, the newer forms of masculinity are represented more positively:

For me, David represents a notion of **modern masculinity**: strong, fit, healthy, but also sensitive and considerate.

(The Times, December 15, 2007).

Many of the other categories of representation in Table 24.1 are linked more strongly to masculinity, compared to femininity—especially the constructions of masculinity as weak/threatened, bad, extreme, powerful, and aggressive. Masculinity is thus viewed as a force to be reckoned with, but also something that is potentially problematic and dangerous. After *modern*, the most frequent adjectival collocate of *masculinity* is *toxic*, which metaphorically constructs masculinity as poisonous, and appears to be a (even more) critical evaluation of the older, traditional form of masculinity.

Toxic masculinity finds expression in fascism, sexism, white supremacy, Islamophobia, xenophobia, jingoism, capitalism, homophobia, rape culture and patriarchy, in the glamourisation of military culture

(The Independent, July 27, 2016).

Masculinity is often ascribed adjectives that liken it to a powerful human body in action: *pumped*, *rugged*, *muscular*, *strutting*, *strong*, *sweating*, *toned* or as carrying emotional states that also suggest resilience, power or violence: *stoic*, *confident*, *brooding*, *uncompromising*, *threatening*, *pugnacious*. The hegemonic aspect of masculinity is made explicit through adjectives like *hegemonic*, *alpha*, *masterful*, *strong*, and *powerful*, yet there is also a side of masculinity which is represented as uncouth or stupid: *inarticulate*, *brutal*, *beery*, *beer-slurping*, *rampaging*, *shouty*—resulting in a personification which brings to mind a football hooligan or Viking invader.

Masculinity is also personified by use of adjectives that describe it as under threat in some way: *bruised*, *weak*, *wounded*, *tortured*, *damaged*, *fragile*. Not only is masculinity seen as capable of carrying out violence or forms of domination on others, but it is also implied to be subjected to violence, resulting in damage to itself.

Many of these cases involve criticisms of men who demonstrate what is viewed as traditional, problematic, and toxic masculinity:

> Homophobia on a show about cars, the most classic white elephant of pathetic **threatened masculinity**, is so fucking tragic.
>
> (The Guardian, *December 27, 2016*).

> Responding to those who have ridiculed the brand for accommodating **fragile masculinity**, he says: 'Haters are going to hate.'
>
> (The Independent, *August 30, 2016*)

> #MasculinitySoFragile started as a way to lampoon **toxic masculinity**. This is the idea that men must constantly prove their masculinity via aggression, violence, or sexual domination. In particular, **fragile masculinity** describes an attitude in which masculinity is rigid and strong, yet at the same time so porous as to be threatened by femininity.
>
> (Independent on Sunday, *September 27, 2015*).

Masculinity is also more often classified according to different types of sexuality, ethnicity, and nationality. For example, we are more likely to find terms like *heterosexual masculinity*, *black masculinity* or *British masculinity* as opposed to these "types" of femininity. Notably, there were no cases that referred to *gay* or *straight* (or related words) *femininity*, and 98 references collectively to *British*, *American* or *Australian masculinity*, but no equivalent cases for *femininity*. This suggests a more sophisticated and detailed focus on masculinity (or masculinities for that matter), especially from a Western perspective, with greater acknowledgment of its intersectionality with other identity traits:

> Ali embodied everything about **black masculinity** and potency that white America feared.
>
> (The Guardian, *June 5, 2016*).

> Choreographed by ex-Riverdance principal Breandan de Gallai, Linger explores **gay masculinity** through photography, film, music, and movement.
>
> (The Times, *August 13, 2016*).

> Is the grown-up geek the new face of middle-aged **British masculinity**?
>
> (The Times, *March 21, 2016*)

Table 24.1 also makes apparent that femininity is much more likely to be defined by adjectives such as *delicate*, *sweet*, *demure*, *gentle*, and *dainty*, which emphasize its softness or passivity. Furthermore, femininity is frequently modified by adjectives framing it in a sexualized setting. These instances appear almost exclusively, however, in descriptions of women's fashion. For example:

> What you want is a cute bra-and-pants set that adds **flirty femininity** (a sprinkling of dandelion embroidery in your cleavage, perhaps).
>
> (The Sunday Times, *August 17, 2014*)

Femininity then is presented as an external aspect or superficial entity, which, in the form of clothing, can lend women heightened sex appeal.

Table 24.1 also indicates differences in the ways that masculinity and femininity are deemed to be real. Although a number of adjective—*true, pure, real,* and *natural*—attach to both masculinity and femininity in order to emphasize their authenticity, femininity is far more frequently judged to not be genuine. Phrases such as *faux femininity* and *fake femininity* appear in contexts that criticize women for exhibiting a false femininity in order to manipulate other people or in which women themselves cheerfully admit to such schemes:

> The two characters make no secret of their hatred of the former Prime Minister who is criticised for her '**fake femininity**', 'her counterfeit voice' and her 'philistinism.'
>
> (Mail on Sunday, *December 14, 2014*)

> Heels supply entry-level vampishness, are the object by which constructed, **faux-femininity** is bestowed. My own attitude is that of the playful homovestite—a woman who gets a kick out of hamming up her femininity—content to be an object of the male gaze so long as I get to feel in control of matters, and give just as good as I get.
>
> (The Guardian, *October 28, 2008*)

This notion of women "using" their femininity in order to promote their own interests is expanded upon in the next section.

Verb + possessive pronoun + masculinity/femininity

Table 24.2 shows the verb collocates that occur before a possessive pronoun, then the word *masculinity* or *femininity*.

Table 24.2 has only five categories, although we see an even greater separation between those which apply to masculinity and those linked to femininity. *Masculinity* appears in three patterns Assert, Question, and Lose, with the latter only occurring four times. The most common pattern is Assert (76 cases), involving verbs like *prove, express,* and *demonstrate*. These verbs appear in contexts that imply that masculinity is something that requires authentication, via specific actions, often involving bravery:

TABLE 24.2 Verb collocates of possessive pronoun + *masculinity/femininity*

Category	*his/their/my/our masculinity*	*Frequency*	*her/their/my/our femininity*	*Frequency*
Assert	prove (36), assert (21), express (7), demonstrate (7), proving (5)	76 1.29%	show (7), declare (4)	11 0.25%
Question	question (8), challenged (5)	13 0.22%		0 0%
Lose	lost (4)	4 0.07%	lost (14), losing (6), diminishes (26), lose (3)	49 1.12%
Use		0 0%	using (11), use (14), used (10)	35 0.81%
Accept		0 0%	accept (18), embrace (6)	24 0.55%

> As well as being wonderfully surreal—at one point to **prove his masculinity** a villain rides a shark, strapped with dynamite, into a live volcano
>
> *(The Sun, June 28, 2013)*

Other actions that involve asserting one's masculinity include sliding across the ice on your belly, being a CIA agent, having your chest waxed, and being aggressive in bed.

Related to the category of asserting one's masculinity are the categories Lose and Question. If masculinity needs to be proven, then this also implies that someone has questioned its existence. In the first example below, masculinity is linked to heterosexuality (and sexual performance), whereas in the second example, a quote from a man with testicular cancer indicates how masculinity is linked specifically to the male body.

> And he told a reporter who dared **question his masculinity**: 'Come to my house and see if I'm gay. And bring your sister.'
>
> *(Independent on Sunday, November 18, 2012)*

> The doctors say it's only a testicle but you start to **question your masculinity**
>
> *(Daily Mirror, August 20, 2013)*.

Masculinity is not necessarily challenged by other men. In the following example, a man is described as having his masculinity (implicitly) "challenged" by his wife's powerful job.

> Viewers were kept in suspense at the end of series one over whether she would get back together with her husband, Philip Christensen (Mikael

Birkkjaer), who told her his affair with another woman was because her premiership had **challenged his masculinity**.

(Independent on Sunday, *December 30, 2012*)

Another article characterized the politician Sarah Palin as telling her male opponents to "man up" as a way of challenging their masculinity. Cases like these could be argued as a form of complicity, with Palin "buying in" to the hegemonic masculinity social order for personal gain. Palin herself is represented as a mixture of traditional femininity: "high heels, skirts about the knee, figure-hugging two pieces and hairstyles straight from the pages of the latest magazines," but also implied to have incorporated many values associated with traditional masculinity, "bold in [her] willingness to step out and be heard . . . indisputably a leader" (*Daily Telegraph*, October 30, 2010). It is this mixture of gendered roles that makes her newsworthy, precisely because it is unusual. Palin is thus implied to embody a combination of powerful aspects from two genders, being referred to as a "mama grizzly," who are described as "staunchly conservative women 'with common sense,' who, like the large brown bear native to North America, 'just kind of know when there's something wrong.'" The brown bear is physically impressive and dangerous, but it is also imbued with intuition (a typically feminine trait). This combination is thus potentially constructed as more powerful than femininity in itself (for women), inasmuch the same way as the "modern" forms of masculinity (being sensitive and caring as well as strong and tough), ascribed to men like David Beckham, are also viewed positively.

However, masculinity also involves personal tastes (or a lack of them). One article implied that liking nice socks or smells makes someone question their masculinity, while a perceived lack of the qualities outlined in Table 24.1 can also raise questions. For example, a man who experiences fear during a trip to the dentist has his masculinity questioned. Masculinity is thus characterized as a state that must be regularly demonstrated, amid fears that it can be compromised in myriad ways. There is a sense of anxiety about masculinity then—and a kind of circular reasoning—masculinity itself is performed by proving your masculinity.

The most dominant category for femininity is that of Lose (49 cases), which includes verbs such as *diminishes* and *lost*. These terms appear in texts, which, to an even greater extent than that of masculinity, link femininity to the female body, particularly to hair and breasts. Women who lose these body parts, usually as a result of illness, are described as evaluating the impact upon their femininity. The words of a female politician who suffers from alopecia and those of a woman who underwent an elective double mastectomy act as illustrations:

It felt just like grief, as though I was experiencing a great loss—and I was. In my mind, I was **losing my femininity** and I began to panic.

(The Sun, *June 6, 2013*)

I do not feel any less of a woman. I feel empowered that I made a strong choice that in no way **diminishes my femininity**.

(The Observer, *December 29, 2013*)

Assert is another category shared by both masculinity and femininity, but the instances associated with the latter are less frequent. The verbs *show* and *declare* attach to femininity in articles that suggest that a woman's femininity is revealed by the types of clothing, such as dresses and skirts, which are traditionally associated with the female gender. Again, femininity is presented as something that can be obtained simply by the adornment of a piece of cloth.

In Italy, a woman knows she can be glamorous and sexy; here the women feel almost guilty to **show their femininity** but it's part of the job of a woman to look impeccable. It is complete madness a woman has to look like a man to be equal.

(The Sunday Telegraph, *August 17, 2014*)

The research found women who wear skirts are rated more positively. They are regarded as more confident and more likely to earn a higher salary. In other words, women who are no longer afraid to **show their femininity** are finally coming out on top.

(Daily Mail, *September 22, 2011*)

These texts also suggest that some women consciously eschew femininity. The Accept category, which is unique to femininity, highlights similar texts with the verb *embrace*: "I think it's sad when women feel the need to dress like men—female politicians are the worst culprits. I think you can **embrace your femininity** and still be taken seriously" (The Times, June 17, 2009). However, there is a hint that femininity is imposed upon reluctant girls as they reach maturity. A professional model notes that she "had to learn to **embrace my femininity**" whereas in her childhood "you could just be you" (The Sunday Times, September 16, 2012). The verb *accept* operates in a similar, albeit more positive, way, but an intimation remains that it is not unusual for femininity to be strategically rejected by women.

Another category that is present for femininity but not masculinity is Use. In these articles, women describe, or are described as, exploiting their femininity in order to persuade other people to follow their agendas. Many of these texts again associate the use of femininity with the styling or modification of the female body in order to increase its sexual appeal:

Luisa, who has had a boob job and is planning to have liposuction in October, said: 'I **use my femininity**. I'm quite aware of the way I look and that people find me attractive.'

(The Sun, *July 21, 2013*)

However, others present femininity as something more nuanced, which can convey power or, conversely, symbolize softer characteristics:

> If I want to **use my femininity** to get something from a man, I'll wear very high heels. Not to arouse him sexually. But I'm so tall—I'm 6ft 2in in heels—that it works a treat.
>
> *(The Sunday Times, March 22, 2009)*

> The handbag was Mrs Thatcher's symbol of femininity, and although she was undoubtedly a powerful and charismatic woman, she didn't hesitate to **use her femininity** to get her way, much as my more traditional mother did.
>
> *(The Independent, April 10, 2013)*

Noun + of + masculinity/femininity

Table 24.3 shows cases of nouns followed by the word *of*, then *masculinity* or *femininity*. The nouns were placed into 16 categories, although only 7 of them occurred at least 1 percent of the time with either masculinity or femininity.

For both *masculinity* and *femininity*, the most commonly found categories are Definition, Type, and Symbol, although there are rather large differences here with these categories found to be more frequently applied to masculinity. These categories, along with the less frequent category Study, tend to involve attempts to make sense of masculinity and femininity, for example:

> There is something of the dandy in her collections, where slightly 'off' details—trousers cut to swing around the ankles, shrunken and cinched-in tailoring, opulent embroidery juxtaposed with sporty pieces—are designed to make you look and think a bit harder—about **notions of masculinity** and what men want to wear.
>
> *(The Independent, January 12, 2016)*

> 'Smoking for young lads is often a **symbol of masculinity** and toughness,' says McNally, 'but you just need to show them the robust evidence linking smoking to impotence. You can literally see their image of smoking change before your very eyes.'
>
> *(The Guardian, November 27, 2017)*

> Simon Beaufoy's script is a moving **exploration of masculinity**.
>
> *(Daily Telegraph, October 15, 2016)*

The higher frequency of references to Types of masculinity confirms the earlier analysis on adjective patterns, which found a wider set of references to masculinity relating to nationality, sexuality, and ethnicity.

TABLE 24.3 Noun collocates with of + *masculinity*/*femininity*

	NOUNS *of masculinity*	5871	NOUNS *of femininity*	4347
Definition	notions (72), sense (49), ideas (45), idea (29), view (26), nature (25), vision (20), model (18), models (18), definition (15), images (15), concepts (14), image (14), portrait (14), themes (14), concept (13), notion (12), conception (9), perceptions (9), views (9), definitions (9), portrayal (9), constructions (7), deconstruction (6), depiction (6), representation (6), conceptions (5), picture (5), construct (4), understanding (2), identity (1)	482 8.21%	notions (46), vision (34), sense (32), idea (22), view (19), ideas (18), images (13), image (12), construction (10), notion (10), perceptions (8), views (7), definition (6), model (4), concept (3)	244 5.25%
Type	version (42), kind (26), aspects (14), forms (12), side (12), versions (11), stereotypes (10), archetypes (10), brand (9), sort (9), archetype (6), figures (6), kinds (5), levels (5), specimen (5), part (4), stereotype (4), type (4), examples (3), style (2)	198 3.38%	version (34), brand (14), kind (9), aspects (8), side (7), stereotypes (7), versions (6), forms (4), type (4), level (3), part (3), style (1)	100 2.15%
Symbol	symbol (21), sign (17), badge (13), codes (15), trappings (9), mark (7), symbols (5), tropes (5), face (3), language (1)	184 3.13%	symbol (24), trappings (14), symbols (6), sign (5), signifiers (5), signs (5), face (3), signifier (3)	65 1.40%
Crisis	crisis (121), fragility (6), pressures (6), failure (2), challenging (1), costs (1)	137 2.33%	crisis (4)	4 0.09%
Ideal	ideal (21), bastion (13), standard (12), ideals (11), epitome (9), essence (5), embodiment (4)	75 1.28%	ideals (16), epitome (8), essence (5), best (1)	30 0.65%
Study	examination (24), exploration (24), study (7), discussion (5), discussions (5), thought (5), questions (3)	73 1.2%		0 0%
Display	expression (9), display (9), assertion (6), test (6), displays (5), show (5), air (4), performance (3)	47 0.80%	performance (7), expression (4)	11 0.24%
State	state (9), subject (8), issue (5), issues (5), role (4),	31 0.53%	issues (6)	6 0.13%

(Continued)

TABLE 24.3 (Continued)

	NOUNS of masculinity	5871	NOUNS of femininity	4347
Lack	lack (10), loss (5), death (3)	18 0.31%	lack (15)	15 0.32%
Parody	parody (9), caricatures (5), caricature (4)	18 0.31%	caricature (6), parody (6)	12 0.26%
Cult	cult (13), culture (10)	13 0.22%		0 0%
Culture	culture (10)	10 0.17%		0 0%
Myth	myth (5), myths (5)	10 0.17%		0 0%
Celebration	celebration (4)	4 0.07%	celebration (23)	23 0.49%
Amount	all (3), bit (1), most (1), much (1)	6 0.10%	touch (25), hint (12), dose (7), all (4), one (3), just (2)	53 1.14%

> McQueen's collection took the theme of different **types of masculinity**, from classic Hollywood leading men to mods and skinheads to football hooligans and shadowy villains.
>
> <div align="right">(The Guardian, <i>January 16, 2006</i>)</div>

The greater reference to Types of masculinity also echoes the finding about masculinity being divided into old and new forms:

> In recent days, the actions of one cricketer and the words of another have provided excellent examples of two competing **versions of masculinity**.
>
> <div align="right">(The Times, <i>November 26, 2013</i>)</div>

This article goes on to describe a cricketer who quits a series of matches because of a stress-related condition, while a second cricketer is critical of his decision, describing it as poor and weak. The article makes a distinction between two kinds of strength—the strength to acknowledge having problems and the strength of soldiering on regardless. The article concludes by claiming that most men today are more like the first cricketer than the second.

These categories indicate that, compared to femininity, masculinity is subjected to a greater amount of examination, categorization, and attempts to make sense of it. It is thus represented as an object of study. As seen with its earlier characterization, masculinity receives much attention because it is viewed as being in crisis, problematic, and capable of causing harm.

Other categories in Table 24.3 confirm earlier findings—such as the Display category, which echoes the verb patterns relating to asserting masculinity.

> An epic, natural-ice-lined, bone-busting **test of masculinity** and bravado, the Cresta Run delivers more than 125kph all taken in from a prone, head-first perspective.
>
> <div align="right">(The Independent, <i>December 8, 2014</i>)</div>

> Orlich claims she was excluded from golf outings, and recounts **displays of 'masculinity'** including a push-up contest on the trading floor.
>
> <div align="right">(The Guardian, <i>September 16, 2010</i>)</div>

Other collocates in this pattern indicate the hegemonic status of masculinity—in particular *badge of masculinity* metaphorically frames masculinity as an award that can be worn (and also demonstrated as having being earned, inasmuch the same way as a war medal).

> The comic said Gordon Ramsay and Jamie Oliver used foul language as a 'badge of masculinity.'
>
> <div align="right">(The Sun, <i>November 18, 2008</i>)</div>

Words relating to the category of Ideal are also more frequently applied to masculinity, again suggesting its hegemonic nature—it is a state that tends to be talked about more in its purest, best form. However, analysis of concordance data reveals that these ideals of masculinity are most usually cited in order to critique them as unattainable or not worth attaining:

> Perry, famous for dressing up as a young girl, suggested that the rugged **ideal of masculinity** espoused by Grylls, famous for sleeping inside a dead animal, has no practical application in modern life.
>
> *(Sunday Telegraph, May 1, 2016)*

> Many men who have used violence subscribe to **ideals of masculinity** that promote being tough controlling women and celebrate male heterosexual performance.
>
> *(The Independent, September 20, 2013)*

The category Amount also supports earlier conclusions regarding the perceived "softness" of femininity. Just as femininity is framed as being delicate and light, it is described as being applied in an almost imperceptible way, almost like a dab of perfume. For instance, "the bow adds a **hint of femininity**" (*The Daily Telegraph*, September 24, 2014) and "she brought a **touch of femininity** to the world of tennis" (*Daily Mail*, June 29, 2015). The Celebration category is also relatively more frequent in the context of femininity. Again, this ties in with previous findings as it often appears in articles, which discuss women's fashion. A female designer, for example, characterizes her latest collection as "a **celebration of femininity**" and her interviewer goes on to describe its incorporation of wasp-waists, corsetry, and exaggerated curves (*The Independent*, October 3, 2012). In a smaller number of instances, it is men who are explicitly named as celebrating femininity, albeit in a reluctant and inadequate manner:

> So that is how I've always thought of 8 March, if I've thought of it at all: a rather retrograde **celebration of femininity**, a chance for men to show the women in their lives that they care on this one day, if not on all the rest.
>
> *(The Independent, March 6, 2015)*

It is thus deemed important that men recognize femininity, but there is also an assumption that this level of recognition will be wanting.

Conclusion

This chapter shows how the British national press privileges masculinity over femininity in a range of different ways. The greater amount of reference to masculinity, its association with power and strength, the more detailed categorization system around it, the implication that it can be difficult to achieve so must be "proven," but that once demonstrated it can be worn as a badge, all indicate its hegemonic status. Even the larger amount of words that relate to its study and analysis, indicate its ability to generate attention.

At the same time, these newspapers problematize masculinity to a much greater extent than femininity, which is, of course, one of the reasons for its study. The wider range of "types" of masculinity, and the more conflicting representations (new/old, weak/strong, good/bad) indicate different perspectives and reappraisals, which are viewed as socially important. The journalistic framing of masculinity as powerful implies that it has more scope to cause social change in society, and to impose control on people, sometimes through violence. Taken together, the newspaper articles analyzed here represent masculinity as an important problem that requires study so that it can be understood and then recast in more progressive ways. Yet, the fact that masculinity is recognized as hegemonic creates a paradox. Once members of a society can recognize and engage in sustained critique of unequal power structures, then the hegemonic system can be threatened and replaced with something else. Our analysis of news articles suggests that this critique is already well underway. However, we should remember that the corpus comes only from British newspapers, and thus demonstrates the cumulation of social changes in the UK, thus incorporating advances towards gender and racial equality, rights of gay, lesbian, bisexual and trans people, and increased acknowledgment of intersectionality.

Additionally, we should note that the majority of references to masculinity and femininity (95%) occurred in the broadsheet or "quality" newspapers as opposed to tabloid or "popular" papers, and two-thirds of the references occurred in liberal newspapers as opposed to conservative ones. So the focus on these concepts is much more likely for journalists writing for a more liberal, educated audience. Thus, not all newspaper readers across the UK are exposed to the same representations about masculinity and femininity or the same number of mentions. The people who are perhaps most open to the view of masculinity as requiring an overhaul are already more likely to agree with this perspective. Working class or conservative newspaper readers are not likely to learn about masculinity and femininity as abstract concepts with the stereotypes and debates around them clearly set out, but instead are perhaps more likely to pick up more traditional messages implicitly and through other forms of language (e.g., privileging of male identity through techniques like male firstness (Freebody & Baker, 1987, p. 98) or incorporated around phrases like "be a man" or "he's a real man"). More research is needed to more closely interrogate the ways in which tabloids challenge or confirm notions of masculinity and femininity, while not referring to those terms explicitly.

Our second finding is a repeated but relatively subtle suggestion that the newer forms of masculinity and femininity involve some sort of combination in order to create a more balanced, well-rounded identity that encompasses the best of both. Modern-day celebrities like David Beckham and Sarah Palin are seen to embody this combination of qualities in the articles we analyzed. The articles collectively suggest a future for gender relations then, one that consists of *both/and* rather than *either/or*. Despite this, the celebration of the new combined forms still acknowledge and reify the existing stereotypes—there is something called masculinity, which is tough and conquering, and it is to be combined with something called femininity, which is gentle and nurturing. The analysis suggests cracks in the hegemonic order have already appeared. But we only examined representations, and representations often depict what should be, rather than what is. Yet the representations suggest change is afoot; potentially encouraging changes for those who advocate gender equality, both reflecting and paving the way for future generations to express their gender in a wider set of ways.

References

Baker, P., & Levon, E. (2015). Picking the right cherries? A comparison of corpus-based and qualitative analyses of news articles about masculinity. *Discourse and Communication, 9*(2), 221–336.

Baker, P., & Levon, E. (2016). "That's what I call a man": Representations of racialized and classed masculinities in the UK print media. *Gender and Language, 10*(1), 106–139.

Brescoll, V., & LaFrance, M. (2004). The correlates and consequences of newspaper reports based on sex differences. *Psychological Science, 15*(8), 515–520.

Connell, R. W. (1995). *Masculinities*. Oxford: Polity Press.

Ellis, A., Sloan, J., & Wykes, M. (2012). "Moatifs" of masculinity: The stories told about "men" in British newspaper coverage of the Raoul Moat case. *Crime Media Culture, 9*(1), 3–21.

Fairclough, N. (1995). *Media discourse*. London: Arnold.

Freebody, P., & Baker, C. (1987). The construction and operation of gender in children's first school books. In A. Pauwels (Ed.), *Women, language and society in Australia and New Zealand* (pp. 80–107). Sydney: Australian Professional Publications.

Gannon, K., Glover, L., & Abel, P. (2004). Masculinity, infertility, stigma and media reports. *Social Science & Medicine, 59*, 1169–1175.

Gerbner, G., Cross, L., Morgan, M., & Signorielli, N. (1986). Living with television: The dynamics of the cultivation process. In J. Bryant & D. Zillman (Eds.), *Perspectives on media effects* (pp. 17–40). Hillsdale, NJ: Lawrence Erlbaum.

Gough, B. (2007). "Real men don't diet": An analysis of contemporary newspaper representations of men, food and health. *Social Science & Medicine, 64*, 326–337.

McEnery, T., & Hardie, A. (2012). *Corpus linguistics: Method, theory, practice*. Cambridge: Cambridge University Press.

Pearce, M. (2008). Investigating the collocational behaviour of MAN and WOMAN in the BNC using sketch engine. *Corpora, 3*(1), 1–29.

Richardson, J. (2007). *Analysing newspapers: An approach from critical discourse analysis*. Hampshire: Palgrave Macmillan.

Taylor, C. (2013). Searching for similarity using corpus-assisted discourse studies. *Corpora, 8*(1), 81–113.

Vincent, J. (2004). Game, sex, and match: The construction of gender in British newspaper coverage of the 2000 Wimbledon championships. *Sociology of Sport Journal, 21*, 435–456.

INDEX